★ ★ ★ ★ ★ ★

I0096123

ECONOMIC

REPORT

OF THE

PRESIDENT

TRANSMITTED TO CONGRESS | MARCH 2024

TOGETHER WITH THE ANNUAL REPORT
OF THE COUNCIL OF ECONOMIC ADVISERS

★ ★ ★ ★ ★ ★

Contents

---

*For a detailed table of contents of the Council's *Report*, see page 11.

★ ★ ★ ★ ★ ★

Economic Report
of the
President

Economic Report of the President

March 21, 2024

To the Congress of the United States:

When I was elected President, a pandemic was raging and our economy was reeling, and trickle-down economics had undermined our nation's growth long-term. I was determined to rebuild from the middle out and bottom up, not the top down, because when the middle class does well, we all do well. We can give everyone a fair shot and leave no one behind. Our plan has brought transformational progress.

In the near term, my Administration moved quickly to help hard-working families and businesses make it through the pandemic, with a historic rescue plan that vaccinated the nation, delivered immediate economic relief to people in need, and sent funding to states and cities to keep essential services going. We worked with the private sector and labor unions to ease bottlenecks and shortages in our supply chains, getting goods flowing again and making our economy more resilient for the future. Today, America is in the midst of the strongest recovery of any advanced economy in the world.

Along the way, we've achieved one of the most successful legislative records in generations, bringing new opportunities to communities of all sizes nationwide. We're tackling years of underinvestment in public infrastructure, clean energy, and advanced manufacturing, making sure the future is made in America by American workers. We're making the biggest investment in American infrastructure in generations, including over $400 billion for 46,000 projects in 4,500 communities to date. These projects are rebuilding the nation's roads, bridges, railroads, ports, airports, public transit, water systems, high-speed internet, and more, in every part of the country. We're also making the most significant investment in fighting climate change in history—advancing breakthroughs in clean technology, boosting energy independence, lowering electricity costs for hardworking families, and revitalizing fence-line communities smothered by a legacy of pollution. At the same time, we're working with the private sector to strengthen America's semiconductor and advanced manufacturing industries as well, empowering workers and small businesses to share in the benefits.

Already, my Investing in America agenda has attracted $650 billion in private investment from companies that are building factories here in America. We've ignited a manufacturing boom, a semiconductor boom, a battery boom, an electric-vehicle boom, and more. My agenda is creating hundreds of thousands of good-paying jobs, so folks never have to leave their hometowns to find work they can raise a family on. Today, America once again has the strongest economy in the world. A record 15 million jobs have been created on my watch, giving 15 million more Americans the dignity and peace of mind that comes with a steady paycheck. The unemployment rate has been below 4 percent for the longest stretch in over 50 years, and we've seen the lowest unemployment rate for Black Americans on record. Economic growth is strong. Wages are rising faster than prices. Inflation is down by two-thirds. We have more to do, but folks are starting to feel the results. Real income and household wealth are higher now than they were before the pandemic, and consumer sentiment has surged more in recent months than any time in decades. Americans have filed a record 16 million new business applications since I took office, and each one of them is an act of hope.

Importantly, we're paying for many of these historic investments by making our tax system fairer. We've cut the deficit by $1 trillion since I took office, one of the biggest reductions in history, and I've signed legislation to cut it by $1 trillion more over the next 10 years, in part by raising the corporate minimum tax to 15 percent and making the wealthy and big corporations start paying their fair share.

It's clear that we're making tremendous progress for the American people, but we have more to do to finish the job. My Administration is going to keep fighting to lower costs for hardworking families, on everything from prescription drugs, to housing, childcare, and student loans. Folks in Washington have tried to reduce prescription drug costs for decades; our historic Inflation Reduction Act is getting it done. It for example caps the cost of insulin for seniors at $35 a month, down from as much as $400; and starting next year, no senior on Medicare will pay more than $2,000 a year in total out-of-pocket drug costs, even for expensive medications that can cost many times more. It also protects and expands the Affordable Care Act; as a result, more Americans have health insurance today than ever.

We're also making real gains in expanding access to housing: More families own homes today than did before the pandemic, rents are easing, and a record of around 1.7 million housing units are under construction nationwide. We'll keep working to lower housing costs and boost supply, by expanding rental assistance; speeding builders' access to federal financing to build more affordable homes; and reducing mortgage payments for first-time homebuyers. Meanwhile, we're standing up for workers and consumers, and cracking down on unfair hidden "junk fees" that companies like airlines, banks, and insurers slip onto people's bills.

At the same time, we're working to get every child in America the strong start they need to thrive. The American Rescue Plan expanded the

Child Tax Credit, cutting child poverty nearly in half in 2021. We'll keep fighting to restore it, and to guarantee the vast majority of American families access to high-quality childcare for no more than $10 a day. Our rescue plan also made the biggest investment in public education in American history; today, we're pushing to further boost funding to schools in need, to expand tutoring and afterschool programs, and to ease teacher shortages. I'm keeping my promise to ease the crushing burden of student debt as well. Despite legal challenges, we've canceled $138 billion in student loans for nearly 3.9 million Americans, including more than 750,000 teachers, nurses, firefighters, social workers, and other public servants. Such widespread debt cancellation is freeing people to finally consider buying a home, having a child, or starting the small business they always dreamed of. In all, our agenda is making the promise of America real for many millions more Americans than ever before.

The story of America is one of progress and resilience, of always moving forward and never giving up. It is a story unique among nations – we are the only country that has emerged from every crisis stronger than we went in. That is what's happening across America today. There is still work to do, but I've never been more optimistic about our future. We are the United States of America, and there is nothing beyond our capacity when we do it together.

Joseph R. Biden Jr.

(1)

★ ★ ★ ★ ★ ★

The Annual Report
of the
Council of Economic Advisers

★ ★ ★ ★ ★ ★

Letter of Transmittal

Council of Economic Advisers
Washington, March 21, 2024

Mr. President:

The Council of Economic Advisers herewith submits its 2024 *Annual Report* in accordance with the Employment Act of 1946, as amended by the Full Employment and Balanced Growth Act of 1978.

Sincerely yours,

Jared Bernstein
Chair

Heather Boushey
Member

C. Kirabo Jackson
Member

★ ★ ★ ★ ★ ★

Contents

Appendixes

Figures

Tables

Boxes

★ ★ ★ ★ ★ ★

The Benefits of Full Employment

This chapter is dedicated to Dr. William Spriggs and his lifelong efforts to promote economic justice for all. It is hoped that the chapter reflects his view: "Full employment should mean full employment for all; not some." (Spriggs 2015)

This chapter discusses the economic effects of tight labor markets—loosely speaking, when jobs are plentiful relative to searchers—on working families and the macroeconomy. This topic is of great consequence for working Americans, and thus also for the worker-centered policies of the Biden-Harris Administration. The chapter draws attention to three economic periods characterized by tight labor markets: the late 1990s, the late 2010s, and the most recent period, starting in the wake of the COVID-19 pandemic.

The chapter first describes the concept of "full employment," and then considers an economic framework rooted in firm market power, known as monopsony power (Manning 2003). An immediate consequence of this framework is the critical role of tight labor markets in improving workers' bargaining position for higher wages and better jobs. The monopsony framework also helps to lay the foundation for understanding the deep and important benefits of full employment, particularly for groups often left behind when labor markets are slack.

This chapter's central findings also highlight the benefits of full employment for labor market outcomes—such as unemployment, labor force participation, wages, and other measures—across demographic groups that are often economically vulnerable. In particular, the CEA finds that demographic groups (e.g., as determined by education, race, and sex) with higher average unemployment rates relative to other groups see larger declines in unemployment rates during expansions. Relatedly, groups with lower average labor force participation see relatively larger increases in their participation rates during expansions than do those with higher participation rates. The implication of these results is that strong labor markets lead to a convergence in critical labor market outcomes across groups, a finding echoed by Cajner and others (2017) and Aaronson and others (2019). The converse is also true: economic downturns and slack labor markets are particularly harmful for relatively less advantaged groups.

This chapter also highlights several striking findings related to tight labor markets and traditionally disadvantaged demographic groups. First, racial gaps in labor market outcomes shrink in tight labor markets. In the most recent periods of full employment—just before the COVID-19 pandemic and in the last two years—the unemployment and employment gaps between Black and white men each fell to the lowest level on record. Second, economically vulnerable groups (e.g., the relatively less educated) are more likely to switch jobs when the unemployment rate is low, enabling them to climb the job ladder when jobs are plentiful. Third, workers who face a work-limiting disability are more likely to obtain jobs in particularly strong labor markets. Fourth, wages and earnings tend to be flat during periods of weak or stagnant labor markets but grow when the economy experiences a tight job market, such as in the late 1990s, the late 2010s, and the post-COVID years. Fifth, wages and annual earnings converge during tight labor markets, as previously demonstrated with unemployment and participation rate convergence; the effect appears in a remarkable narrowing of the ratio of wages between the 90th and 10th percentiles and 90th and 50th percentiles since 2015.

Because of the depth of these benefits, the chapter next considers which policy choices can help attain and maintain a full-employment labor market, highlighting two crucial pillars of effective macroeconomic stabilization policy that can work toward this goal: (1) data-driven monetary policy and (2) temporary fiscal policy. Both can be used to ameliorate negative shocks to economic growth and output gaps. The chapter also considers a potential cost of full employment: higher inflation than would otherwise occur. Here, the CEA's analysis finds little evidence to suggest that persistently tight labor markets are necessarily costly in inflationary terms; indeed, the period before COVID-19 featured historically low unemployment with quiescent inflation. Many previous episodes of full employment did not clearly correlate with high inflation (though some early ones did, recent periods did not). And though strong labor demand played a role in the excess inflation of 2021–22, much of it was clearly due to nondemand, non–labor market factors, including the pandemic and its impact on supply chains.

The chapter concludes with a review of the period since June 2022, when total personal consumption expenditures price inflation peaked at 7.1 percent. From the perspective of the Phillips curve model, decreasing inflation comes at the cost of increasing unemployment, a decrease in inflation expectations, or favorable supply shocks. Since June 2022, the U.S. economy has experienced a substantial degree of disinflation, with relatively little sacrifice in the form of labor market deterioration. This suggests that recent inflation has largely been driven by factors other than the low unemployment rate. The most likely explanation, since longer-term inflation expectations remained anchored, is a resolution of supply disruptions—both in production and labor supply—caused by COVID-19 and the recovery from it. This explanation is supported by a recent CEA analysis showing that supply-side variables, both alone and interacting with demand, explain most of the disinflation over the past few years (CEA 2023a).

It is, of course, always possible that further disinflation will require more declines in economic activity than have occurred thus far. But the disinflation that has occurred to date has very clearly not been accompanied by a sacrificing of the tight labor market conditions that deliver critical benefits to American households.

What Is Full Employment, and Why Does It Matter?

Full employment is neither a new concept nor the sole purview of economists. Societal discussions of full employment predate economics as a discipline.[1] In simple terms, full employment describes an economy in which workers able and willing to work can obtain the jobs and hours they want. Modern economics has generally defined full employment by citing the theoretical concept of the lowest unemployment rate consistent with stable inflation, which is referred to as u^* ("u-star"), the natural rate of unemployment, or the nonaccelerating inflationary rate of unemployment (termed NAIRU).[2] (See box 1-1.)

Regardless of the specific model or definition, if unemployment is at u^*, the labor force is at full capacity, such that the number of workers needed (labor demand) roughly matches the number willing to work at the wages offered (labor supply). The value of u^* is necessarily above zero, as, even at full employment, so-called frictional unemployment exists, in which some job seekers (i.e., the unemployed) are between jobs while others may have wage demands that employers are unwilling to pay.

A separate and economically important way of conceptualizing u^* is to note that when unemployment is at its natural rate, additional demand for workers is more likely to generate inflation than boost real incomes. This conception of u^* returns to the trade-off embodied in the Phillips curve, as discussed above—specifically, the negative relationship between

---

[1] See, for example, the British *Historical Register* (1731, 187): "The more distinct the Employment is, the better, for many Inconveniencies have attended one Manufacture interfering with another; besides, there will be an Intercourse of Trade created by one Part of the Kingdom supplying the other with their distinct Manufactures; this will give full Employment to the whole Kingdom, and a universal Cheerfulness to every Body: For the Poor are never happier, nor their Minds easier, than when they have full Employment; and when they are employed, Riches are diffused over the Nation."

[2] This definition replaces employment with unemployment, primarily because individuals have many reasons for choosing to forgo work and attend school, retire, take care of family, etc. Full employment is a case in which demand is sufficient to provide employment to those who want to work. Of course, the unemployment rate itself may not be the only, or most inclusive, measure of labor market tightness, as addressed in box 1-1. Further, the government could enact many policies to boost incentives for individuals to join the labor force (some of which are highlighted in box 1-4 below), which might change the equilibrium rate of employment, although not necessarily the natural rate of unemployment.

Box 1-1. Alternative Measures of Labor Market Tightness

One working definition of full employment is the unemployment rate that is consistent with stable inflation. But the unemployment rate has notable downsides as a yardstick of labor market slack when set against the definition: it ignores workers who are out of the labor force, workers who are underemployed, and job openings that are unfilled—among other potential downsides.

While this chapter relies on the unemployment rate and the Congressional Budget Office's estimate of the natural rate of unemployment, this box considers four common alternative measures of labor market slack: (1) the ratio of vacancies to unemployment (V/U); (2) U-6, a broader measure of unemployment that incorporates some nonparticipants and some part-time workers; (3) the prime-age employment-to-population ratio; and (4) the quits rate.

A number of features make the ratio of vacancies to unemployment, V/U, appealing. First, in a large class of models of unemployment (Pissarides 2000), the degree of tightness in the labor market is measured via this ratio. Second, as a counterpart to the supply of workers who want jobs, V/U directly accounts for vacancies, a measure of the unmet demand for workers (Elsby, Michaels, and Ratner 2015). When there are more job openings than unemployed, the labor market is considered tight, since firms will have more difficulty recruiting and workers will have an easier time finding a job. V/U is strongly correlated with the unemployment rate, and researchers have found that it has a lower forecast error than the unemployment gap when predicting core personal consumption expenditures and wage inflation (Barnichon and Shapiro 2022). (Of course, there are critiques of vacancies as a measure of unmet labor demand, as well. For example, Davis, Faberman, and Haltiwanger 2013 show that recruiting intensity by firms is itself cyclical.) Further, Benigno and Eggertsson (2023) suggest that the unemployment-inflation relationship becomes nonlinear after V/U goes above 1, leading to accelerating prices when the labor market gets tight.

Both U-6 and the prime-age employment-to-population ratio are measures that expand the definition of job searchers beyond the unemployed. Focusing only on the unemployed assumes that those who are outside the labor force have a negligible job finding rate. However, when disaggregating into more granular groups, individuals who are out of the labor force but want a job are just as likely to transition to employment as the long-term unemployed. And even some nonparticipants who say they do not want a job transition to employment (Kudlyak 2017). Therefore, the unemployment rate could understate the true available labor supply (Hornstein, Kudlyak, and Lange 2014).

Figure 1-i. Measures of Labor Market Tightness

Z-score

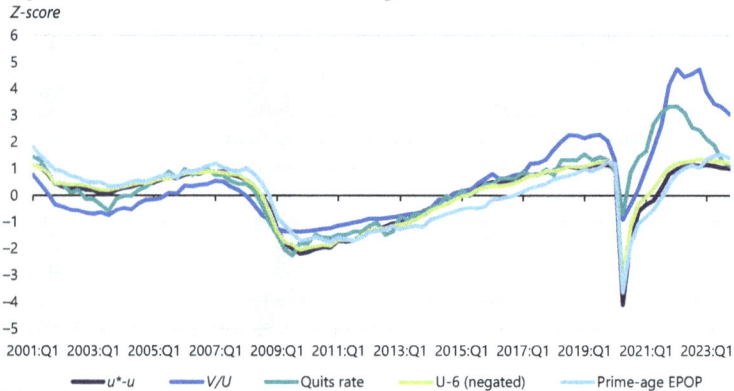

Legend: u*–u | V/U | Quits rate | U-6 (negated) | Prime-age EPOP

Council of Economic Advisers

Sources: Bureau of Labor Statistics; Congressional Budget Office (CBO); CEA calculations.
Note: EPOP = employment-to-population ratio. u = unemployment rate. u^* = CBO's natural rate of unemployment. U-6 rate includes marginally attached individuals and those working part time for economic reasons. V/U = job openings divided by unemployment. Z-scores were calculated using the sample mean and standard deviations of each measure from 2001 to 2019. Gray bars indicate recessions.
2024 Economic Report of the President

U-6 starts with the standard unemployment rate as a base, but it also includes so-called marginally attached individuals and workers who are part time for economic reasons. Individuals are considered marginally attached if they would accept a job if offered one and have looked for work in the last year but not in the last four weeks. Workers are considered part time for economic reasons if they report working less than 35 hours per week due to slack work, unfavorable business conditions, an inability to find full-time work, seasonal declines in demand, or other economic reasons.

The prime-age employment-to-population ratio (PAEPOP) further includes all nonparticipants as potential job searchers. Focusing on those who are prime age (i.e., 25–54) excludes the effects of population aging and abstracts from school-going and retirement years. Researchers find that, compared with unemployment, the PAEPOP is equally predictive of core personal consumption expenditures inflation and is potentially a better predictor of real wage growth (Furman and Powell 2021).

One additional measure of labor market tightness is the quits rate, which counts the number of employed individuals who have voluntarily left their job (excluding retirements and transfers) in a month as a percentage of employment. The quits rate is a good indicator of the strength of a labor market, as an elevated number of employed individuals voluntarily leave their jobs if they believe they can find a better job (Gittleman 2022; Yellen 2014; CEA 2022). Researchers also find that the quits rate and job-to-job switching behavior is a better predictor of wage growth and inflation than the unemployment rate (Karahan et al. 2017; Moscarini and Postel-Vinay 2017; Furman and Powell 2021). Faccini and Melosi (2023) found that elevated quits were directly linked to increases in the inflation rate in 2021.

Figure 1-i plots all four alternative measures, along with the unemployment gap, after normalizing each measure by its mean from 2001 to 2019 (inverting when necessary) and dividing by its standard deviation to make them comparable. All five measures track each other relatively well during the period before the COVID-19 pandemic, although the V/U ratio did indicate a slightly tighter labor market before COVID-19.

Both during and after the pandemic, both V/U and the quits rate diverge from the movements in the other three series. The two measures have suggested a notably tighter labor market since 2021 than the unemployment rate itself. The evolution of the two variables is precisely why policymakers have become focused on movements in the Beveridge curve and wage pressures in the labor market.

unemployment and inflation that has been at the center of macroeconomic models for decades.[3]

Estimates of the Natural Rate of Unemployment

Although the historical record confirms a negative correlation between unemployment and inflation in general (Crump et al. 2019), a number of both theoretical and empirical problems render u^* impractical for policy purposes. First, u^* is unobservable, meaning it must be estimated, which can only be done in the context of a particular model, and typically with wide margins of error (see chapter 1 of the 2016 *Economic Report of the President,* CEA 2016a). Figures 1-1 and 1-2 offer two perspectives on the issue. Figure 1-1 compares current estimates of the natural rate from multiple organizations—the Congressional Budget Office's (CBO's) reports, various Federal Reserve System estimates, the CEA's analyses, and those of professional forecasters. Clearly, estimates of u^* vary considerably over time and across estimators; the range of estimates spanned nearly 2 percentage points at its maximum at the height of the global financial crisis and exceeded 2 percentage points in the post-COVID period. However, even in the relatively calm period before COVID-19, the estimates varied by nearly a full percentage point.

---

[3] For example, a very simple reduced-form Phillips curve implies a u^* derived from this regression: $\pi_t - \pi^* = \alpha + \beta u_t + \epsilon_t$, where π_t is inflation and u_t is the unemployment rate. Setting $\pi_t = \pi^*$ (typically 2 percent) defines u_t^* as $-\alpha/\beta$.

Figure 1-1. Estimates of the Natural Rate of Unemployment

Percent

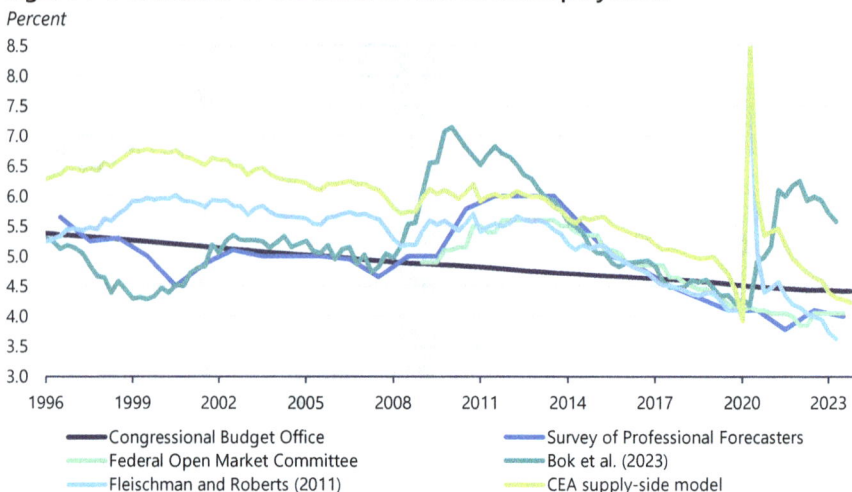

Council of Economic Advisers

Sources: Congressional Budget Office; Federal Reserve Bank of Philadelphia; Federal Reserve Board of Governors; Federal Reserve Bank of San Francisco; Bok et al. (2023); Fleischman and Roberts (2011); CEA calculations.
Note: Gray bars indicate recessions.
2024 Economic Report of the President

Second, the particular model underlying an estimate of the natural rate of unemployment is crucial. For example, some estimates are considered "long-run" estimates, which can be thought of as the unemployment rate toward which the economy would tend in the absence of shocks. Short-run shocks, such as those that impede matching workers and jobs in the labor market or that temporarily raise unemployment (or inflation), can raise the short-run natural rate, as they likely did after the global financial crisis and COVID-19. In figure 1-1, the natural rates presented reflect a combination of concepts. The CBO's estimate is akin to a long-run rate, while the Survey of Professional Forecasters' estimate is likely a combination of concepts across the different analysts who respond to the survey.[4] Bok and others (2023) present a number of measures, including one based on a Phillips curve concept of the stable inflation rate of unemployment, making it akin to a short-run approach.

Related to the distinction between the time horizon and model underlying any estimate of u^*, figure 1-2 offers another perspective on the difficulty of precisely estimating the value. The figure presents several vintages of CBO forecasts of the natural rate starting in the mid-1990s. As is apparent, the estimates are subject to large revisions over time. This is partly because the CBO has itself changed the definition of the natural rate over time,

---

[4] For a detailed discussion of the differences, see Bok et al. (2023).

Figure 1-2. The CBO's Estimates of the Natural Rate of Unemployment, 1996–2033

CBO 10-year projections (percent)

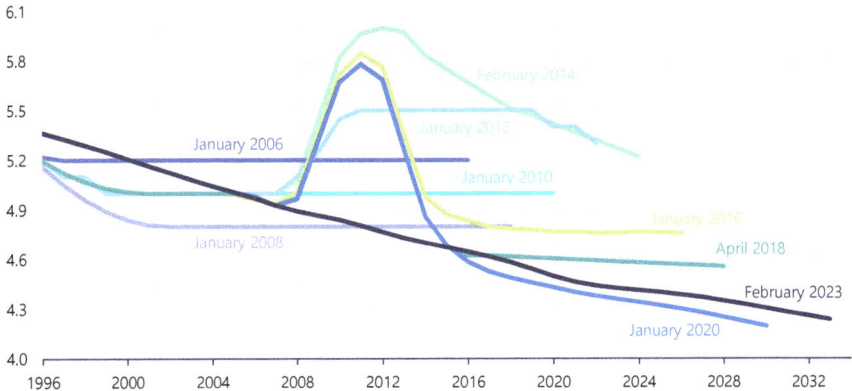

Council of Economic Advisers

Sources: Congressional Budget Office (CBO); CEA calculations.
Note: The natural unemployment rates shown are annual averages of quarterly projections by the Congressional Budget Office. Gray bars indicate recessions.
2024 Economic Report of the President

settling recently on a long-term concept, whereas previously the agency distinguished short- and long-run rates.

Regardless of the reason, any entity's estimate of u^* in a given year may change dramatically if unemployment surprisingly falls below the estimated u^* for a sustained period, as it did in the pre-COVID era of low unemployment. The CBO's estimate of u^* for 2019, for example, fell when it updated its estimates from 2016 to 2018 and then again in 2020. Finally, as figures 1-1 and 1-2 show, u^* is not a constant. Its movements are generated by changes in the macroeconomy, workers' demographics, and fiscal and monetary policy changes. For example, the CBO's estimate of u^* was revised up at the onset of the global financial crisis (as were many other estimates); but as unemployment decreased in the latter stages of the recovery from the crisis, the CBO's estimate of u^* repeatedly moved down. There is good reason that the economist James Galbraith quipped, in a critique of u^*, "It's not only invisible; it moves" (Galbraith 2001).

Another key limitation of using u^* as a policy goal is that it embeds variation in labor market outcomes across groups. This variation in structural labor market outcomes may be undesirable for society. As the CEA explores in some detail, there is considerable structural variation in unemployment levels (and other labor market indicators) between demographic groups in the labor market. Black male workers, for example, historically (starting in 1976, when the data became available) have unemployment rates averaging 7 percentage points above the rate white men face. The differences cannot be explained in full by other observable characteristics (e.g., differences in education), suggesting that discrimination may be a factor in the persistent differential. Therefore, were policymakers simply to aim for historical estimates of u^*, which have been consistent with large racial gaps, they risk embedding permanent disadvantages in groups that have long been left behind.

For all its shortcomings, the CEA still views u^* as a useful concept, as long as analysts understand that it cannot accurately be pinned down to a specific rate, especially in real time, and that it leaves out critical dynamics at play in the U.S. economy and labor market. Today, most economists would agree that 5 percent is above u^*, at least over a long enough period to allow acute short-run shocks to be worn away, and 3 percent is likely below it. Indeed, before the pandemic, the jobless rate was in the range of 3.5 to 4 percent and did not create inflationary pressures. During the current recovery, rates in this range have been maintained while inflation has fallen. In other words, recent history shows that unemployment rates between 3.5 and 4 percent can be consistent with sustainable inflation in the long run and allow the U.S. economy to enjoy the benefits of full employment.

The recent postpandemic period of tight labor markets and elevated inflation raises two questions: (1) Has u^* increased structurally, so that the pursuit of maintaining tight labor markets engenders greater overheating and inflationary risks than in prior cycles? Or (2) is pandemic economics a special case, and thus, outside its unusual effects, can the U.S. labor market still flourish with low unemployment not necessarily accompanied by high inflation?

To explain the importance of engaging in this section's u^* target practice, the next section gives a brief theoretical framework to delineate the interaction of labor markets at full employment and the empirical findings that the CEA presents in this chapter.

A Monopsonistic Labor Market

A brief summary of a basic labor market model helps ground an understanding of imperfect labor markets, in which employers wield some degree of wage-setting power, and which economists typically call monopsony power. In contrast, the textbook version of a perfect labor market envisions identical firms that are unable to set wages below the market level, lest they lose all workers to other employers, a case in which employers face a perfectly elastic labor supply curve. One implication of the perfect competition model is that wage discrimination and worker exploitation do not persist because competing firms can attract workers with better working conditions and pay. Discriminating firms with poorer labor standards must either improve or go out of business.

In reality, with monopsony power, firms are able to use their relative strength in the hiring market to set wages to some degree. (For a summary of the empirical literature, see Ashenfelter et al. 2022.) Whereas a pure monopsony would feature only one employer in a given market, the real world is of course more complicated and closer to a model that features both monopsony and competition (Manning 2003, 2021; Yeh, Macaluso, and Hershbein 2022; CEA 2016b, 2022).

There are many plausible mechanisms that can lead to monopsonistic competition—for example, search frictions that delay job matching, employer concentration, job heterogeneity, and institutional or legal constraints like noncompete agreements (Burdett and Mortensen 1998; Manning 2021; CEA 2016b; Card et al. 2018; Berger, Herkenhoff, and Mongey 2022; U.S. Department of the Treasury 2022). The most commonly proposed source of monopsony power is the presence of search frictions, which impede the process whereby workers match with suitable employers. A canonical search model of monopsony power follows Burdett and Mortensen (1998), in which firms post wages to attract workers. A critical implication of the model is that the labor supply curve faced by the firms is upward sloping: higher wages reduce attrition, improve the ability to hire, and increase employment. This model is in stark contrast to the perfectly competitive model, in which firms are wage takers and face perfectly elastic labor supply curves.

Crucial for the analysis here is that the degree of labor market power a firm can wield is intimately related to the relative prevalence of available jobs and workers. In a tight labor market, monopsony power is reduced because workers' outside options improve as the likelihood of finding an alternative or better job rises. The ability of workers to switch to new jobs, or to quit and quickly find new jobs, allows them to raise their threat point with firms in wage negotiations. Relatedly, firms face elevated attrition rates and more difficulty recruiting workers. The improved bargaining position of workers helps to raise labor's share of income, as discussed in box 1-2.

One important implication of an economic setting in which employers wield market power when competing for employees is that screening or discriminating against workers based on gender, race, disabilities, or other characteristics—for example, by changing hiring practices or weeding out résumés based on workers' characteristics—becomes a less economically feasible option when the job market is very tight. To do so risks failing to meet demand for the product or service that the employer sells, thereby reducing potential profitability and falling behind (nondiscriminatory) competitors. Informally, employer discrimination in tight labor markets risks "leaving money on the table." Thus, the economic framework of monopsonistic competition suggests that—and CEA research documents extensively—tighter labor markets are salutary for addressing persistent racial, gender, and other labor market gaps between advantaged and less advantaged groups.

Box 1-2. Workers' Bargaining Power and Full Employment

One consequence of tight labor markets, where jobs are plentiful relative to searchers, is that workers' bargaining power improves. The reasoning is intuitive: workers' bargaining power is in part derived from the range of options available in the labor market. In strong labor markets, it is relatively easy to find jobs, and the job offers available are more likely to include elevated wages or expanded opportunities. (See the evidence given below on wages and occupational upgrading.) For a more detailed discussion, see Stansbury and Summers (2020).

Another way that workers can exert bargaining power is through unionization and union activity. Figure 1-ii shows that the share of union members that engage in a work stoppage (y axis) increases when the gap between the unemployment rate and the CBO's natural rate decreases (x axis). The figure is striking in light of the surge in union activity in recent years. In the two years before the COVID-19 pandemic, about 450,000 workers engaged in work stoppages per year, highlighted by the educator strikes in 2018–19 (BLS 2024). The strike activity in these years was higher than had been registered since the mid-1980s. And in 2023, there was once again a notable wave of strikes, the most prominent of which occurred among workers who belong to the United Auto Workers union at the Big 3 auto plants. Of course, work stoppages are only one example of union activity, which is easy to measure and thus lends itself to this analysis; other examples of union activity by workers include filing for

Figure 1-ii. Share of Union Workers Involved in Work Stoppages, 1949–2022

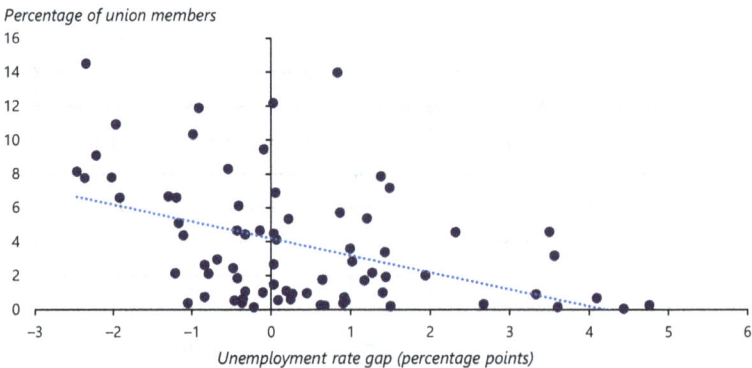

Percentage of union members

Unemployment rate gap (percentage points)

Council of Economic Advisers

Sources: Bureau of Labor Statistics; Congressional Budget Office (CBO); Freeman (1998); Department of the Treasury (2023); CEA calculations.
Note: Dotted line is the line of best fit for the graphed series. The unemployment rate gap indicates the gap between the unemployment rate and the CBO's estimate of the natural rate of unemployment.
2024 Economic Report of the President

Figure 1-iii. Change in the Labor Share and the Unemployment Rate Gap, 1948–2023

Four-quarter log change in labor's share of income

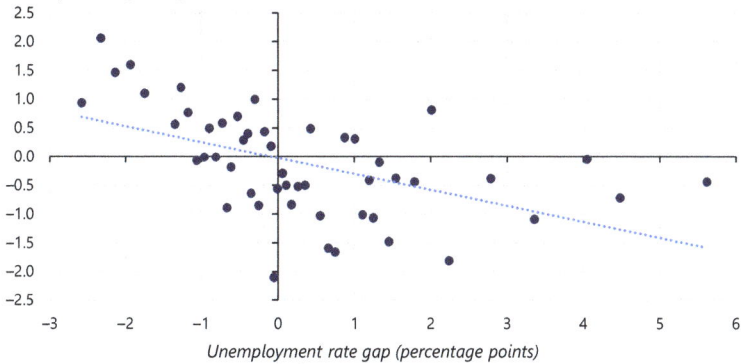

Unemployment rate gap (percentage points)

Council of Economic Advisers

Sources: Bureau of Labor Statistics; Congressional Budget Office (CBO); CEA calculations.
Note: Dotted line is the line of best fit for the graphed series. The unemployment rate gap indicates the gap between the unemployment rate and the CBO's estimate of the natural rate of unemployment. Labor's share is for the nonfinancial corporate business sector.
2024 Economic Report of the President

union elections and negotiating for fair contracts, which have important effects on the working conditions of those covered by union contracts.

The result of forces that raise bargaining power is that a larger slice of the economic pie goes to workers (both union and nonunion) as the economy achieves full employment. One measure of the size of the slice is what economists call labor's share of income, or, roughly speaking, the share of total income that accrues to workers in the form of compensation. Figure 1-iii shows that a higher labor's share (y axis) is associated with lower unemployment rate gaps (x axis).

Although the theoretical models provide a qualitative framework for defining full employment, the CEA's analysis shows that full employment is clearly associated with labor market conditions that are tight enough to provide workers with meaningful bargaining power. Such power is evident in the empirical results presented in the next section on the benefits of full employment.

Evidence on the Benefits of Full Employment

This section provides a set of stylized facts on the benefits that strong labor markets and full employment provide to workers, especially those who belong to groups that are typically less attached to the labor market and are less well compensated than other groups.

Long-Run Trends in Labor Market Outcomes

Long-run trends in unemployment and employment rates, disaggregated by race and ethnic groups, paint a striking picture of the beneficial effect of strong labor markets on these outcomes—a note highlighted by Spriggs (2017). In this chapter, CEA researchers extend the methodology used by Cajner and others (2017), who estimate gaps in the unemployment rate and employment-to-population ratios across selected demographic groups that are unexplained after controlling for age, geographic region, marital status, and education.[5] Figure 1-3 plots the unexplained portion of the unemployment rate for Black men minus white men and Black women minus white women using a common decomposition method.[6] Panel B of the figure shows Hispanic men minus white men and Hispanic women minus white women.[7]

There are several notable features of the differences in unemployment rates across groups that cannot be explained by observable characteristics. First, even after accounting for differences in explanatory variables, the unemployment rates of Black men and women are considerably higher than those of white men and women. However, the unexplained gaps have been shrinking since the early 1980s. Second, weak labor markets are particularly detrimental for economically vulnerable groups; during the global financial crisis, the unexplained gap in unemployment rates between Black and white men rose by about 2 percentage points, while the gap between Black and white women increased by 1.5 percentage points. Further, the unexplained unemployment rate gaps were persistently higher for the less advantaged groups after the recession: it took nearly 10 years for the Black male

---

[5] This work follows Cajner et al. (2017) in estimating Oaxaca-Blinder decompositions for each year of data starting in 1976 and reporting the unexplained portion of the difference in labor market outcomes (i.e., the portion not due to differences in the means of the explanatory variables). While age and gender are obvious choices for exogenous factors that are important in shaping employment and unemployment, Cajner et al. discuss the merits of controlling for variables that are outcomes of choices, such as education. For example, if certain groups face structural barriers to education, then controlling for education may understate the differences in labor market outcomes due to discrimination faced by the group.

[6] This chapter follows Cajner et al. (2017), who focus on the absolute difference in labor market outcomes across groups rather than the ratios of labor market outcomes.

[7] It is important to note that the demographic groups shown here are not meant to be exhaustive of the groups that are economically vulnerable; indeed, within the relatively coarse groups presented, there is substantial heterogeneity in labor market outcomes and general socioeconomic well-being.

Figure 1-3. Racial Gaps in the Unemployment Rate

A. Black versus white

Percentage points of labor force

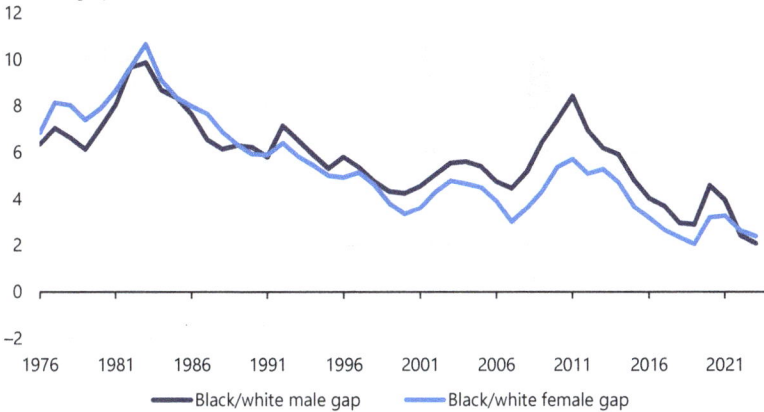

Black/white male gap — Black/white female gap

B. Hispanic versus white

Percentage points of labor force

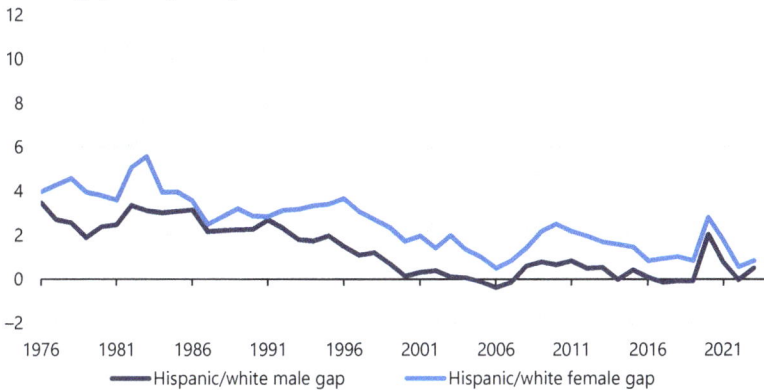

Hispanic/white male gap — Hispanic/white female gap

Council of Economic Advisers
Sources: Current Population Survey; CEA calculations.
Note: White and Black populations are non-Hispanic. Estimated using methodology from Cajner et al. (2017).
Gray bars indicate recessions.
2024 Economic Report of the President

unemployment rate to recover relative to the white male unemployment rate. Nonetheless, it did recover, and when the labor market approached perhaps the tightest periods covered by the CEA data, in 2018–19 and 2022–23, the unemployment rate for Black men was as close to that for white men as has been on record.

Figure 1-4 presents unexplained gaps in employment-population ratios using the same controls and comparing the same demographic groups as shown in figure 1-3. Employment-population ratios are determined by the unemployment rate and labor force participation, which together help summarize labor market outcomes across groups. While the cyclicality of

Figure 1-4. Racial Gaps in the Employment-Population Ratio

A. Black versus white
Percentage points of population

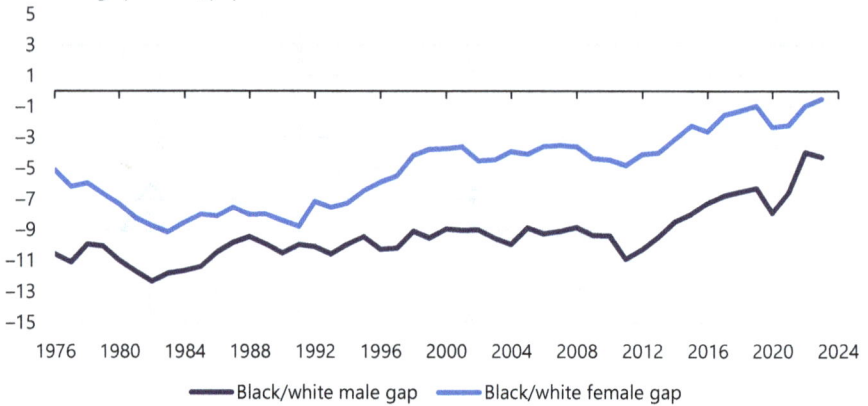

Black/white male gap ▬▬▬ Black/white female gap

B. Hispanic versus white
Percentage points of population

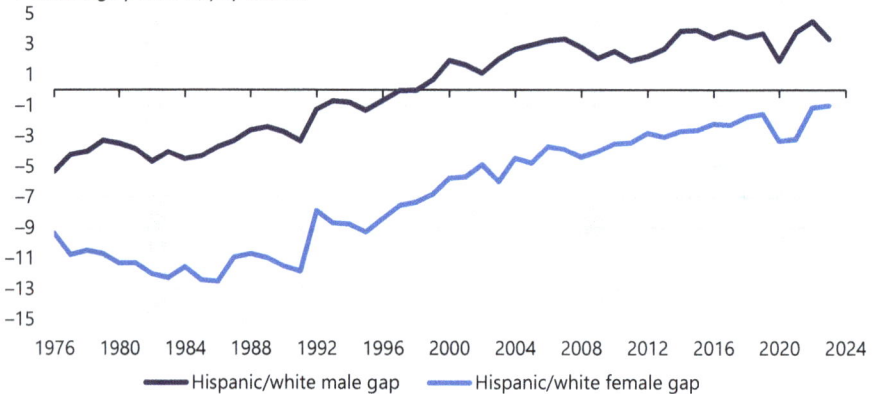

Hispanic/white male gap ▬▬▬ Hispanic/white female gap

Council of Economic Advisers
Sources: Current Population Survey; CEA calculations.
Note: White and Black populations are non-Hispanic. Estimated using methodology from Cajner et al. (2017). Gray bars indicate recessions.
2024 Economic Report of the President

employment-population ratios is less pronounced, in part due to long-running trend changes in labor force participation, the figures show that strong labor markets are critical in closing the gaps in labor market outcomes between groups. For example, the gap between Black and white women narrowed substantially in the full employment labor market of the late 1990s. After the 2000 recession occurred, and the labor market remained weak until well into recovery from the global financial crisis, there was a lack of relative improvement for both Black men and women relative to white men and women. When the labor market reached full employment in 2015–19, the gap closed substantially, and it continued to do so after the COVID-19 pandemic.

Because the analysis controls for characteristics that partially determine labor market outcomes, such as age, their interpretation hinges on the source of the unexplained gaps shown in figure 1-4. One determinant is clearly racial prejudice, which has long been a determinant of labor market and other economic outcomes (Charles and Guryan 2008; Lang and Lehmann 2012). Why would tight labor markets reduce racial discrimination in employment?[8] First, it does so because workers can more easily find alternative and better jobs, and they can leave for better opportunities when they experience discrimination. Second, tight labor markets increase the cost of discriminatory behavior, making it less economically feasible. If the subset of employers that discriminates by race can find, despite their prejudices, the workers they need to maximize profitability, it is relatively costless to do so, especially since they may not suffer the legal or reputational harm from engaging in discriminatory behavior. But if the labor market is tight enough that discrimination is costly and leads to lost profits, employers may be less likely to discriminate and more likely to remove hiring barriers that exclude qualified workers. This dynamic is at least part of the reason why strong labor markets are salutary for narrowing racial gaps in the labor market.

A Rising Tide Lifts Some Boats More Than Others: Cyclical Variation Across Groups

The CEA's analysis shows that in the United States, economically vulnerable demographic groups—those that, on average, experience worse labor market outcomes—are the same groups that benefit most from full employment. This examination starts by following a methodology similar to that developed by Wolfers (2019) to estimate the relationship between lower aggregate unemployment rates and the labor market outcomes of a broad swath of demographic groups.

First, the CEA splits the prime-age population into 16 groups defined by four race/ethnicity categories (Black non-Hispanic, white non-Hispanic, other non-Hispanic groups, and Hispanic), sex, and two education groups (a high school degree or less, and some college or more). Second, the CEA calculates the cyclical responsiveness of unemployment for each group across all business cycles after 1976, when granular microdata became available. Cyclical responsiveness is defined as the average increase (or decrease) in

---

[8] While employment discrimination against protected classes is illegal, racial gaps in the labor market persist. Strong antidiscrimination enforcement by agencies such as the Equal Employment Opportunity Commission and Department of Labor's Office of Federal Contract Compliance Programs are important for creating the long-term structural changes in employment practices that will prevent such discrimination.

Figure 1-5. The Cyclicality of Unemployment versus Average Unemployment

Change in unemployent rate over expansions and recessions (percentage points)

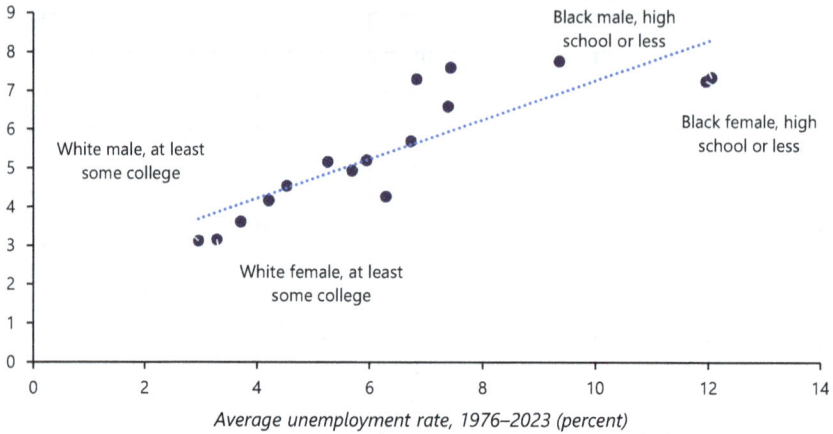

Average unemployment rate, 1976–2023 (percent)

Council of Economic Advisers

Sources: Current Population Survey; CEA calculations.
Note: Dotted line is the line of best fit for the graphed series. Sample restricted to prime age (25-54) individuals. White and Black populations are non-Hispanic.
2024 Economic Report of the President

the unemployment rate from the peak (trough) of a business cycle to the respective trough (peak), with dates defined by the business cycle minimum and maximum of the aggregate unemployment rate gap. Third, the CEA calculated the average unemployment rate for each group over the whole period, 1976–2023.

Figure 1-5 shows the average group-specific unemployment rate on the x axis and average cyclical responsiveness of the unemployment rate on the y axis, along with the regression line relating the two.

This picture shows a remarkably strong relationship—and not a mechanical one or one that need occur—between the group-average unemployment rate (higher x-axis value) and the degree to which the group's unemployment rate changes over the business cycle. For example, the top-right point of figure 1-5 gives the cyclical sensitivity for prime-age Black non-Hispanic men with an education of high school or less. The group's average unemployment rate is a staggering 12 percent, and this rate changes by about 7 percentage points over the average business cycle. Further, the regression line shows that if a group has a 1-percentage-point higher average unemployment rate, its unemployment rate is expected to change by about 0.5 percentage point more over the business cycle.

Figure 1-6 replaces the unemployment rate with the labor force participation rate (LFPR), which also shows clearly that less advantaged groups

Figure 1-6. The Cyclicality of the LFPR versus Average LFPR

Change in LFPR over expansions and recessions (percentage points)

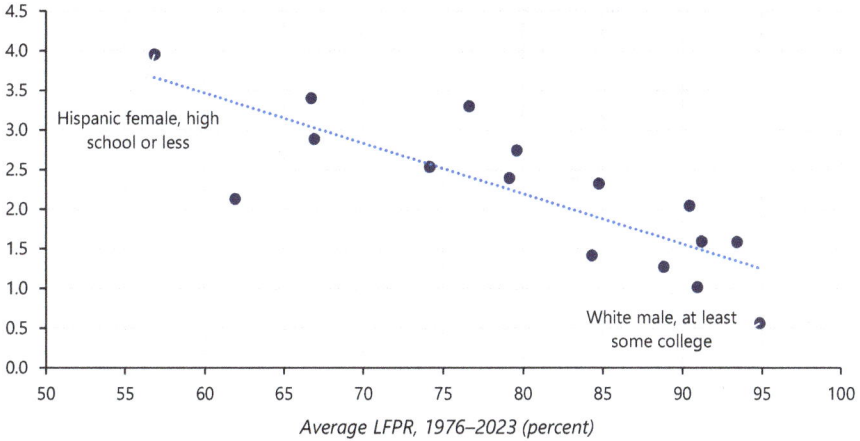

Council of Economic Advisers

Sources: Current Population Survey; CEA calculations.
Note: LFPR = labor force participation rate. Dotted line is the line of best fit for the graphed series. Sample restricted to prime age (25–54) individuals. White and Black populations are non-Hispanic.
2024 Economic Report of the President

benefit more from strong labor markets.[9] The groups with a relatively low average LFPR (moving to the left on the x axis in the figure) experience relatively larger increases in the LFPR over the business cycle than other groups.

In addition to unemployment rates falling, and LFPR rising, workers from less advantaged groups have more success climbing the job ladder than they otherwise would in a weaker job market. The ability to change jobs, find better matches, and bargain for higher wages and benefits are all crucial features of an economy that provides long-lasting opportunities for workers (Topel and Ward 1992; Bjelland et al. 2011; Haltiwanger et al. 2018; Bosler and Petrosky-Nadeau 2016). Figure 1-7 shows that the ability of economically vulnerable groups to reap the benefits of moving up the job ladder is greater when the economy is at full employment than when it is not. The analysis focuses on differences between demographic groups in job-to-job switching rates—that is, the rate at which a worker takes a job at

---

[9] There are likely two reasons why the relationship is not as precise for the LFPR. First, there are persistent long-term trends in the LFPR that are not controlled for and that may make it difficult to infer the cycle from the trend (CEA 2014; Aaronson et al. 2014). Second, the cyclicality of the LFPR is typically more muted than for the unemployment rate and likely has more complicated lag structures (Cajner, Coglianese, and Montes 2021).

Figure 1-7. The Cyclicality of Job-to-Job Rate Gaps, by Race and Education

A. By Race (Black—white)
Job-to-job rate gap (percentage points)

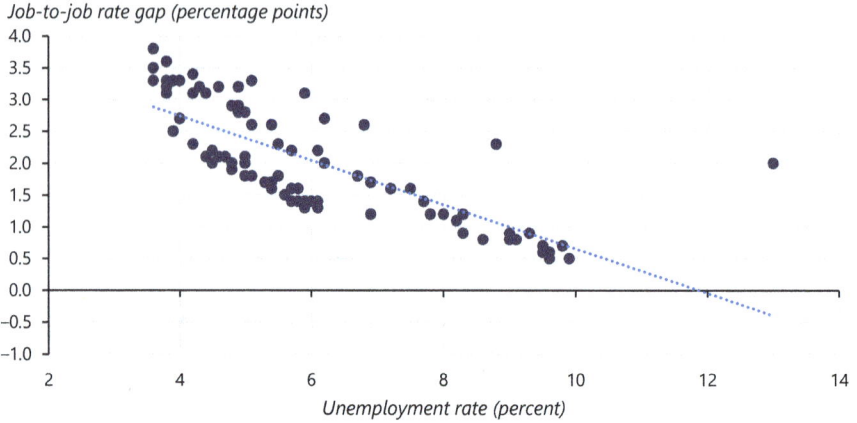

Unemployment rate (percent)

B. By Education (High School—Some College or More)
Job-to-job rate gap (percentage points)

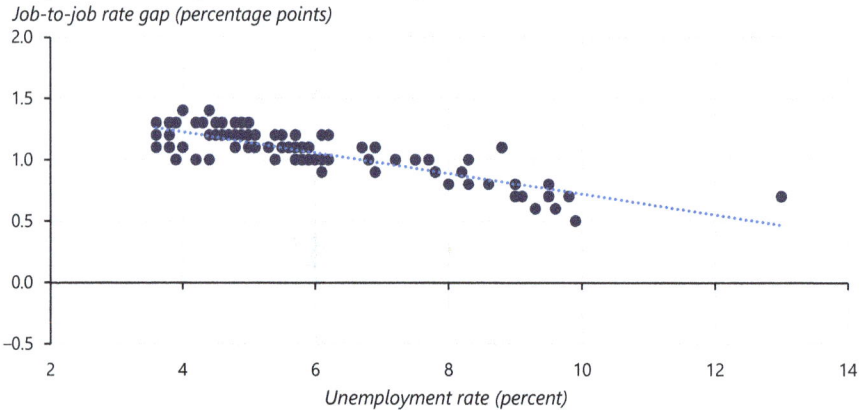

Unemployment rate (percent)

Council of Economic Advisers
Sources: Census Bureau; CEA calculations.
Note: Dotted line is the line of best fit for the graphed series. White and Black populations are non-Hispanic.
2024 Economic Report of the President

a different employer in a quarter—as produced by the Census's Longitudinal Employer-Household Data.[10]

Panel A of figure 1-7 represents the difference in job-to-job transition rates of Black workers relative to white workers. For example, from 2000:Q3 through 2022:Q3, the average job-to-job switching rate for Black workers was 6.8 percent and was 4.7 percent for white workers, an average

---

[10] The Census measure analyzed by the CEA is defined as, roughly, the number of workers whose job is with one employer in quarter t and another employer in $t + 1$. Workers are included if they spend one quarter or less unemployed between jobs at different employers. That number of job-to-job switches is divided by the average number of jobs in both quarters t and $t + 1$. For additional information, see Census (2023).

Figure 1-8. Monthly Transition Rate of the Disabled from Nonparticipation to Employment

Percent

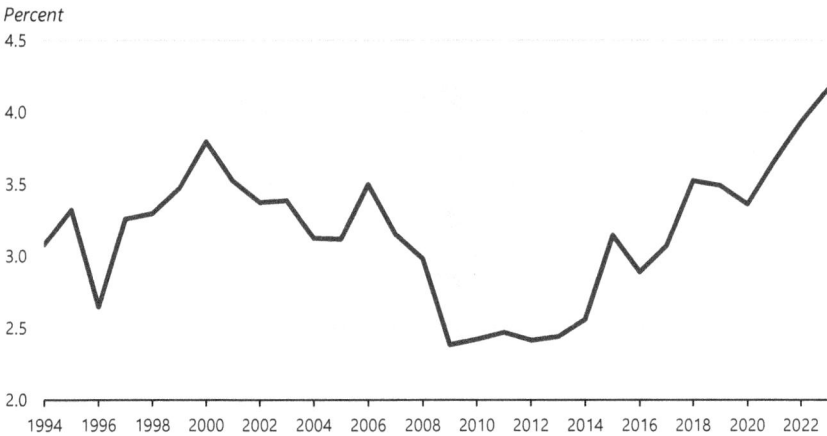

Council of Economic Advisers

Sources: Current Population Survey; CEA calculations.
Note: Graph shows the annual average share of prime age (25–54) individuals with self-reported disabilities who report not being in the labor force in month *t* and employed in month *t*+1. Gray bars indicate recessions.
2024 Economic Report of the President

gap of 2.1 percentage points. However, when the unemployment rate was below 4 percent in 2019, that gap increased to 3.4 percentage points. Meanwhile, when the unemployment rate was above 9 percent in 2010, the gap shrank to 0.7 percentage point. This cyclical pattern manifests in the downward-sloping regression line in panel A of figure 1-7.

Panel B of figure 1-7 echoes these findings for education groups, showing the difference in the job-to-job switching rate of those with only a high school degree relative to those with a college degree or more. The regression line is again downward sloping, indicating that strong labor markets benefit the job ladder prospects of the less educated relative to the more educated. Box 1-3 sheds additional light on the importance of cyclical upgrading for average wages, and box 1-1 above further discusses a related measure—the quits rate—as an alternative measure of labor market tightness.

Another important example of the kinds of workers who benefit directly from full employment are those with work-limiting disabilities. Figure 1-8 gives the rate at which prime-age workers who report a work-limiting disability move from nonparticipation to employment, calculated from longitudinally matched Current Population Survey data; the rate rises substantially when unemployment falls. Once such workers find jobs, they accumulate experience and can switch to better jobs. This dynamic process can lead to long-lasting benefits for these workers and their families, as well as for the overall productive capacity of the economy (Yellen 2016).

Box 1-3. Occupational Upgrading

Tight labor markets tend to boost average wage levels, and the CEA's analysis presented in this chapter shows that workers take advantage of strong labor markets to switch jobs. This box shows that these two dynamics are related: during tight labor markets, workers climb the occupational job ladder and move into jobs associated with higher pay.

To evaluate occupational advancement, the CEA uses an occupational index that takes the median wage in 2018 and 2019 according to detailed occupation and follows the share of the workforce in each occupation both backward and forward in time. To measure the occupational wage level in 2018 and 2019, the CEA takes the median of the hourly wage in the Current Population Survey Outgoing Rotation Group by occupation (using IPUMS's harmonized 2010 definitions). More formally, the index is calculated from parameters b_0 and b_1 in this ordinary-least-squares regression: $W_{it} = b_0 + b_1 t + BX_{it} + e_{it}$, where the sample uses individual-level Current Population Survey data and includes each individual in the labor force at time t in harmonized occupation i; W_{it} is the median wage of occupation i as of 2018–19, while X_{it} is a vector of demographic controls.

In panel A of figure 1-iv, the index is estimated with controls for sex, age, and birth cohort. It shows that while occupational advancement is indeed cyclical, it has shown steady progress over the last four decades. The index shown in panel B further controls for education. An important interpretative distinction between education and the other controls is that education is likely sensitive to economic conditions: Educational attainment may in part be countercyclical if individuals choose to enroll in educational programs when the labor market is weak.

Over the last 40 years, average educational attainment has risen in the United States. In fact, the flatness of the line in panel B of figure 1-iv relative to the clear upward slope of the line in panel A suggests that education has been a key driver of occupational advancement since 1980: As workers have become increasingly likely to graduate from high school and earn a college degree, they have been able to move into higher-paying occupations.

In addition, the results suggest that the recessions of the early 1980s, and also in 2001 and 2008, represented a significant occupational decline among American workers that did not immediately recover (again, holding education constant). In contrast, during the tight labor markets of the late 1990s and from 2014 to 2019, occupational advancement began to accelerate again, then accelerated further during the COVID-19 pandemic. Over the roughly 10 years starting in 2014, workers made up for the earlier 30 years of losses in occupational advancement. By 2023, workers were on average in higher-paying jobs than at any point since 1980, even when controlling for education. This result suggests that

Figure 1-iv. Occupational Advancement Index

A. Age–Sex Controls
Index: 2018–19 = 100

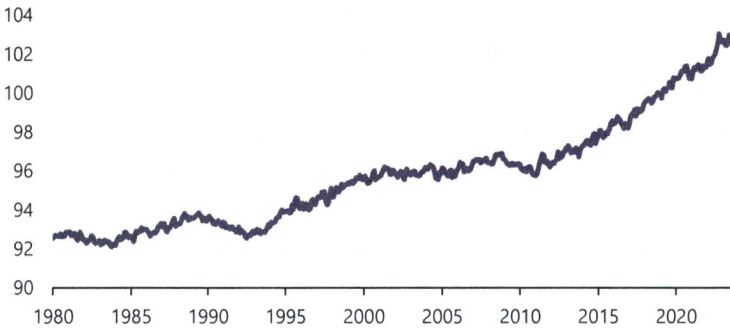

B. Age–Sex–Education Controls
Index: 2018–19 = 100

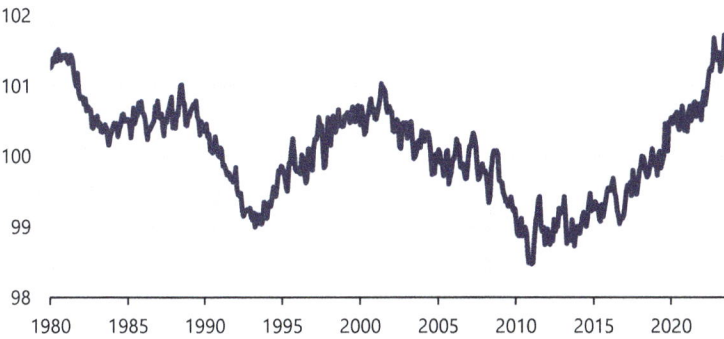

Council of Economic Advisers
Sources: Current Population Survey; CEA calculations.
Note: Both series include cohort controls. Gray bars indicate recessions.
2024 Economic Report of the President

strong labor markets act through channels other than education and can help workers catch up on the occupational ladder when prior recessions have pushed them down.

Figure 1-9. Median Real Wages, by Race and Ethnicity

2022 dollars

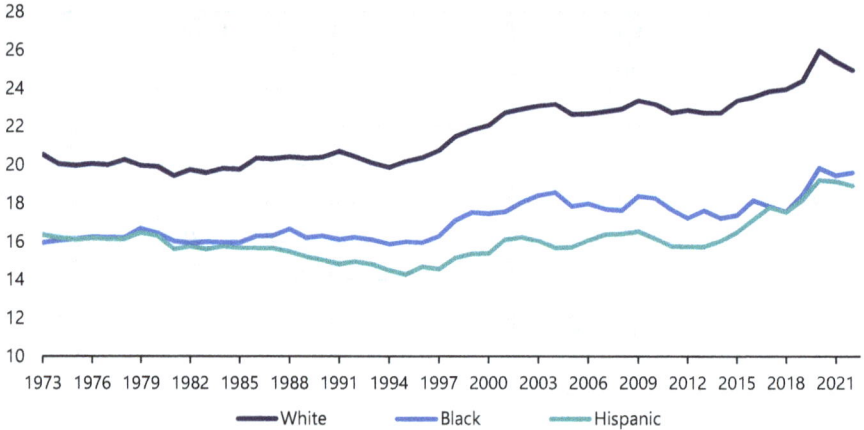

Council of Economic Advisers

Sources: Bureau of Labor Statistics; Economic Policy Institute's State of Working America Data Library.
Note: White and Black populations are non-Hispanic. Gray bars indicate recessions.
2024 Economic Report of the President

Full Employment's Effect on Wages and Household Incomes

The strong bargaining power afforded by tight labor markets raises not only employment rates but also wages and incomes for less advantaged groups. Figure 1-9 shows the median real wages of white non-Hispanic, Black non-Hispanic, and Hispanic workers since 1973. In the figure, real wages are stagnant over long stretches, aside from the periods of sustained growth during the tight labor markets in the late 1990s, late 2010s, and the immediate period following the COVID-19 pandemic.[11] Indeed, in the 23 years from 1973 up to 1996, when the CBO estimates the labor market began the prolonged period of full employment in the late 1990s, the unemployment rate was only below the natural rate in about 27 percent of quarters; in those years, white and Black median wages were roughly flat, whereas Hispanic wages fell by about 10 percent. From 1996 through the end of the data in 2023, the unemployment rate was below the natural rate in 47 percent of quarters, and wage growth performed better, rising 22, 23, and 29 percent at the median for, respectively, white, Black, and Hispanic workers.

---

[11] The composition of the workforce is known to have important implications for the dynamics of wages, especially during business cycles when the lowest-paid workers typically lose jobs sooner than more highly paid workers. This introduces an upward cyclical bias that can make the decline in wages during recessions less pronounced than it otherwise might be (Solon, Barsky, and Parker 1994; Daly and Hobijn 2017). This composition effect had a large impact on the wage data shown in figures 1-9 and 1-10, especially during the COVID recession, and is one reason why wages appeared to rise sharply at the onset of that downturn (CEA 2021).

Figure 1-10. Hourly Wage Compression, Pre- and Post-COVID

Index: 2015:Q1 = 100

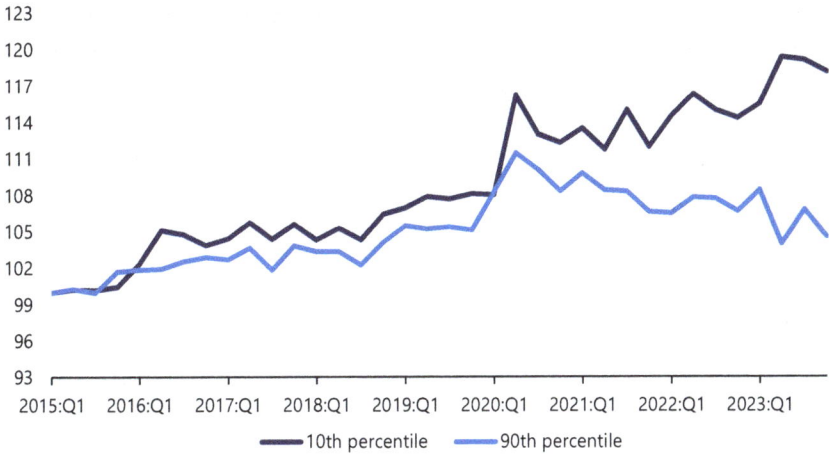

Council of Economic Advisers
Sources: Current Population Survey; CEA calculations.
Note: Estimated using methodology from Autor, Dube, and McGrew (2023). Gray bars indicate recessions.
2024 Economic Report of the President

Figure 1-10 also shows that real wages converged during the recent tight labor markets, especially at the low end of the income distribution. In figure 1-10, the CEA replicates the recent work of Autor, Dube, and McGrew (2023), who estimate wage convergence in the periods before and after COVID-19, adjusting for demographic differences due to age, labor market experience, race and ethnicity, region, and nativity.[12] Demographic controls were especially important during the peak of the COVID-induced recession due to the enormous shifts that occurred in the workforce.

Figure 1-10 shows the remarkable compression of wages in the labor market both before and after the pandemic, which were both periods of full employment. The 10th-percentile wage grew about 3 percentage points more than that of the 90th percentile in the pre-COVID period, from 2015:Q1 to 2019:Q4; in the period after COVID, starting at the business cycle trough in 2020:Q2 and going through 2023:Q4, real wages grew by about 7 percentage points more at the bottom of the distribution than at the top. While there are surely factors other than the strong labor market driving the post-COVID wage compression—for example, the shift to remote work likely has held down wage growth among higher-wage workers (Barrero et al. 2022)—the

---

[12] Autor, Dube, and McGrew (2023) implement a Dinardo-Fortin-Lemieux (1996) reweighting procedure, which allows for the comparison of wages at different points of the distribution under the assumption that the distribution of individual characteristics is fixed at a base year—in this case, immediately before the pandemic.

Table 1-1. Wage Compression in the Pre- and Post-COVID Labor Markets

Percent change in ratio over period

Ratio	2015:Q1–2019:Q4	2020:Q2–2023:Q4
90th percentile / 10th percentile	–3	–8
90th percentile / 50th percentile	–3	–2
50th percentile / 10th percentile	0	–5

Council of Economic Advisers

Sources: Current Population Survey; CEA calculations.

Note: This table shows the ratio of wages at the indicated percentiles. Estimated using methodology from Autor, Dube, and McGrew (2023).

2024 Economic Report of the President

Table 1-2. Predicted Changes in Real Household Incomes over Selected Business Cycles

Type of Household	Percentile	1992–2000 Expansion		2006–09 Recession		2009–19 Expansion	
		Predicted Percent Change in Real Income	Percent of Actual Change in Real Income	Predicted Percent Change in Real Income	Percent of Actual Change in Real Income	Predicted Percent Change in Real Income	Percent of Actual Change in Real Income
All	10th	7	52	-11	63	12	43
	25th	4	27	-6	47	7	28
Black	10th	7	41	-12	64	13	29
	25th	6	14	-10	146	11	45
Single mothers	10th	8	44	-13	53	14	-145
	25th	6	14	-9	135	10	65

Council of Economic Advisers

Sources: Current Population Survey; Congressional Budget Office; CEA calculations.

Note: Estimated using methodology from Bernstein and Bentele (2019).

2024 Economic Report of the President

compression of wages occurred alongside the strongest stretch in the U.S. labor market since the mid-1960s.

Table 1-1 records the changes in standard wage inequality ratios over the two periods. The data reinforce the remarkable compression of wages, especially between the top and bottom earners, as measured by the 90/10 wage ratio.

Following the methodology of Bernstein and Bentele (2019), figure 1-11 shows the effect on real annual earnings (equal to annual hours worked times hourly wages) of a 1-point increase in the aggregate unemployment rate relative to the CBO's at five quantiles of the earnings distribution for the overall population, Black households, and households headed by single mothers.[13] The relationship between labor market slack and incomes is larger for low and middle earners than for high earners across all groups; further, incomes respond more for low-income Black households, and those headed by single mothers.

---

[13] In particular, figure 1-11 plots the coefficients from group-specific regressions of the log real annual earnings from the Annual Social and Economic Supplements to CPS data on the CBO unemployment rate gap.

Figure 1-11. Effects of a Looser Labor Market on Household Income

Change in annual earnings (percent)

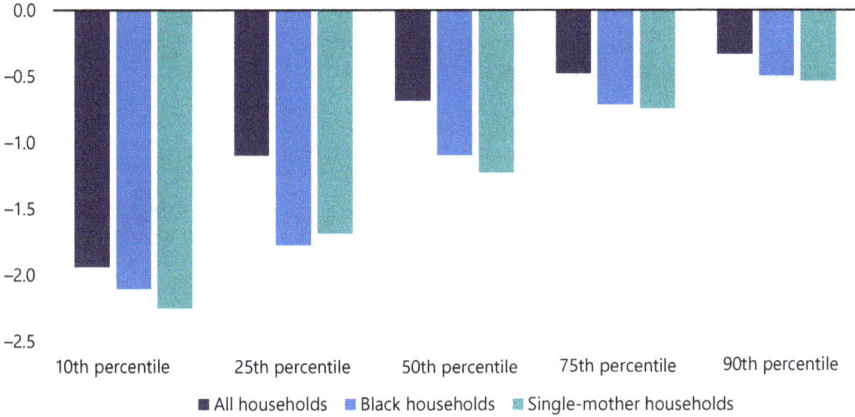

Council of Economic Advisers
Sources: Current Population Survey (CPS); Congressional Budget Office (CBO); CEA calculations.
Note: Estimated using methodology from Bernstein and Bentele (2019) with data from the 1977–2023 CPS Annual Social and Economic Supplements. Each bar shows the expected change in household income associated with a 1-percentage-point increase in the CBO's estimate of the unemployment rate gap.
2024 Economic Report of the President

The lighter blue bars in figure 1-11 show the coefficients for Black households, which are larger in magnitude at each point of the distribution than those of the overall population (navy bars); however, the biggest difference for Black households relative to the population is at the 25th percentile. The same gradient is apparent among households headed by a single mother, a group typically faced with lower wages and that is less attached to the labor market than many other groups (Miller and Tedeschi 2019).

What do the coefficients mean in terms of real wage and income growth? Table 1-2 shows, in the first column for each period, the predicted percent change in real income based on the CEA's simple model for various groups during periods when the labor market tightened and slackened. The second column of each period reports the predicted income change (from the first column) as a share of the actual income changes experienced by the relevant group. The results show that a large share of income gains and losses are associated with aggregate labor market performance, reinforcing the view that a strong economy is crucial to the well-being of economically vulnerable groups.

Getting to and Staying at Full Employment

As the section above shows, the benefits of a persistently tight labor market, especially for groups that are often left behind in periods of slack, are deep and economically meaningful. But while recent U.S. economic history has

Figure 1-12. The Congressional Budget Office's Estimate of the Unemployment Rate Gap

Percentage points

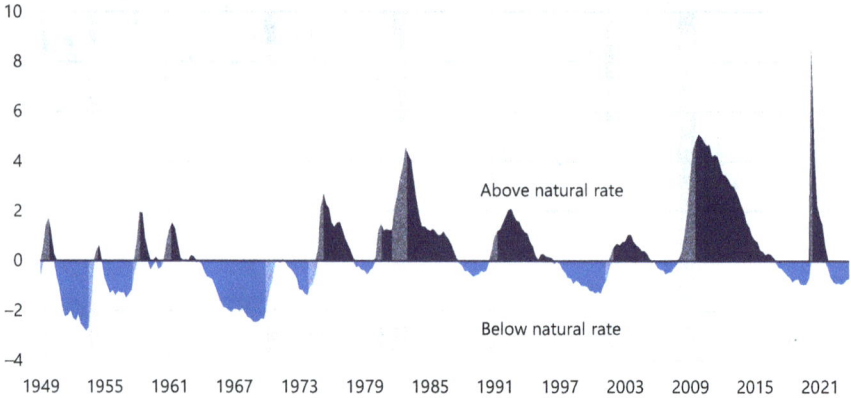

Council of Economic Advisers
Sources: Bureau of Labor Statistics; Congressional Budget Office; CEA calculations.
Note: Gray bars indicate recessions.
2024 Economic Report of the President

featured several periods at or near full employment, the longer sweep of post–World War II history is less encouraging. Figure 1-12 shows the quarters when $u > u^*$ in dark blue and quarters when $u < u^*$ in light blue, using the CBO's measure of u^*. The figure shows that over the first half of postwar history, from 1949 to 1981, the U.S. labor market spent 64 percent of quarters with the unemployment rate below the natural rate; however, over the second half of the period, starting in 1982, the United States achieved full employment in 38 percent of quarters. Moreover, in the first half, when the unemployment rate was below the CBO's natural rate, the gap between the unemployment rate and CBO's natural rate averaged –1.2 percentage points; in the second half, it averaged only –0.6 percentage point when it was below the natural rate.

Aside from missing out on the benefits laid out in this chapter, another cost of not being at full employment is what economists call hysteresis, meaning lasting or structural damage to the economy's supply side, which lowers its potential growth rate (Yellen 2016). The economy's growth rate is broadly a function of the growth in the workforce's size and the growth in the productivity of this workforce (CEA 2023b). If, for example, potential workers stay out of the workforce due to weak labor demand, they risk sacrificing the productivity-enhancing experience and skills associated with steady workforce attachment. One influential analysis by Reifschneider, Wascher, and Wilcox (2013) frames the problem as the "endogeneity of supply with respect to demand," meaning that labor supply is influenced by labor demand. One channel through which this operates is when weak labor demand reduces potential labor supply if workers who experience long-term unemployment spells lose skills and, therefore, become persistently less employable. Another channel through which this operates is that less employment requires less capital investment, which can, in turn, reduce the supply of productive capital in the economy.

In the context of this chapter, the implication is that extended periods of unemployment exceeding u^* can generate persistently damaging hysteresis. While there is not much evidence for the notion that extended periods of tight labor markets can lead to reverse hysteresis (i.e., improvements in the economy's potential growth rate), the dynamic is certainly plausible (Yellen 2016). If, as this chapter has shown, full employment pulls workers into the labor market who might otherwise be left behind, the positive effects of reverse hysteresis might be realized. Full employment could also have positive effects on other supply-side fundamentals, such as productivity.

The benefits of full employment raise the question of which policy choices help lead to it and what trade-offs the choices involve. The inflation/unemployment trade-off embedded in the Phillips curve framework has long dominated the policy discussion and, as Baker and Bernstein (2013) show, was one reason for the long periods of slack shown in figure 1-12. In recent years, however, more economists have recognized the measurement challenges in u^* (see the uncertainty embedded in figure 1-1), leading policymakers, including those with the Federal Reserve, to become more "data driven" and rely less over time on point estimates of u^* (Staiger, Stock, and Watson 1997; Powell 2018).

More specifically, a data-driven argument surfaced that, because analysts could not identify u^* reliably enough to steer fiscal and monetary policy, and the price Phillips curve was viewed as relatively flat, economic policymakers could allow labor markets to tighten with a low risk of substantial inflationary consequences (Powell 2018). Findings like those shown above regarding the equalizing benefits of tight labor markets, including pulling in new workers from the sidelines (which also dampens inflationary pressures), further strengthened the argument (Bernstein and Bentele 2019; Cajner, Coglianese, and Montes 2021).

The full employment experiences of the late 1990s and the period before the pandemic showed the logic of the position through data on critical variables, such as jobs, the LFPR, wages, racial gaps in the labor market, and more. During those periods, both unemployment and inflation remained relatively low, representing a favorable trade-off on behalf of economically vulnerable groups without salient inflationary risks. And indeed, as figure 1-2 shows, during the tight labor market before the pandemic, estimates of the natural rate continued to be revised down over time, rewarding the Federal Reserve's data-dependent approach.

Table 1-3. Inflation and Labor Market Outcomes Since Total PCE Peak

Outcome	June 2022 (percent)	December 2023 (percent)	Change (percentage points)
Total PCE, yearly	7.1	2.6	−4.5
Total PCE, three-month annualized	7.4	0.5	−6.9
Core PCE, yearly	5.2	2.9	−2.3
Core PCE, three-month annualized	5.1	1.5	−3.6
Unemployment rate	3.6	3.7	0.1
Black unemployment rate	5.8	5.2	−0.6
LFPR	62.2	62.5	0.3
Black LFPR	62.2	63.4	1.2
Nonfarm payrolls[a]	152,348	157,347	3.3

Council of Economic Advisers
Sources: Bureau of Labor Statistics; Bureau of Economic Analysis; CEA calculations.
Note: PCE = Personal Consumption Expenditures Price Index; LFPR = labor force participation rate. Unemployment rates and LFPRs are adjusted for the 2023 population control revisions.
[a] Nonfarm payrolls are in thousands and nonfarm payroll change is in percent.
2024 Economic Report of the President

The past several years have challenged this pattern. When the pandemic began and the economy shut down, the unemployment rate soared to almost 15 percent and inflation turned negative. Then, as the economy reopened, lifted by historically strong fiscal and monetary support, unemployment fell sharply while inflation rose to a 40-year high in the summer of 2022. Such movements are associated with a steep price Phillips curve, rather than a flat one. As stated previously in this chapter, the period raises two questions: (1) Has u^* increased structurally, so that the pursuit of maintaining tight labor markets engenders greater overheating and inflationary risks than in prior cycles? Or (2) is pandemic economics a special case, and thus, outside its unusual effects, can the U.S. labor market still flourish with low unemployment not necessarily accompanied by high inflation?

The CEA pursued the same question in the 2023 *Economic Report of the President*, wherein, based on the evidence available, the researchers concluded that "the combination and interaction of numerous factors exacerbated the elevated inflation. Although it is difficult to determine the relative importance of each factor, the pandemic, and responses to it, had substantial effects on both the supply and demand sides of the economy. Specific factors of note include pandemic-induced supply disruptions, shifts in consumer demand, the accumulation of excess savings, and stimulative fiscal and monetary support throughout 2020 and 2021" (CEA 2023b, 52).

Given the developments over the year since the previous assessment, the CEA has found more evidence that supply factors played a key role in both inflation's rise and its subsequent decline. Consider that if full employment were the main cause of the increase in inflation, the subsequent disinflation the economy has experienced should have brought about a substantial slackening of the labor market. However, the low magnitude of the

Figure 1-13. Core PCE Price Inflation and Unemployment Rate Gap

Percent (core PCE), percentage points (unemployment rate gap)

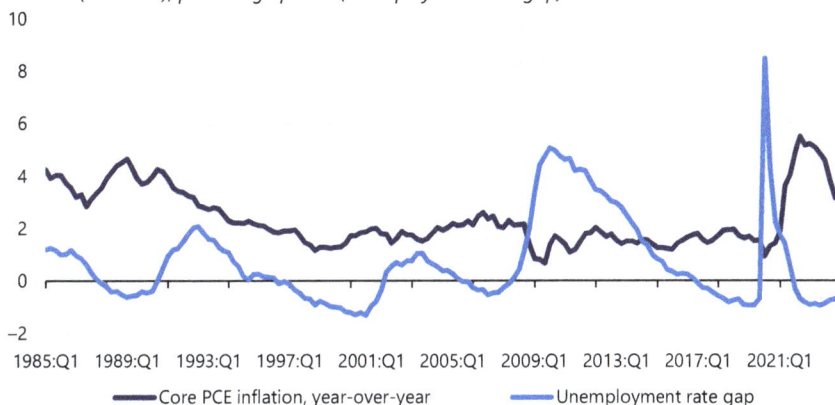

Council of Economic Advisers
Sources: Bureau of Labor Statistics; Bureau of Economic Analysis; Congressional Budget Office (CBO); CEA calculations.
Note: PCE = Personal Consumption Expenditures. Core PCE inflation is year-over-year percentage change. The unemployment rate gap indicates the gap between the unemployment rate and the CBO's estimate of the natural rate of unemployment. Gray bars indicate recessions.
2024 Economic Report of the President

so-called sacrifice ratio—the amount of increased unemployment or reduced economic activity required to lower inflation—during the recent disinflation since the peak in June 2022 suggests otherwise. Table 1-3 shows the decline in personal consumption expenditures inflation—total and core, which excludes volatile food and energy prices—along with the changes in various labor market variables (also see figure 1-13). Over the period covered, which includes the most recent data available at publication time, the disinflation has required little sacrifice in terms of labor market slack or job loss.

This phenomenon is mirrored in the evolution of job openings and unemployment, which have been analyzed via the Beveridge curve, as shown in figure 1-14, with the job openings rate on the y axis and the unemployment rate on the x axis. The Beveridge curve has become a common tool for analyzing shifts in the unemployment rate, allowing analysts to parse changes in unemployment vis-à-vis job openings to determine if changes in unemployment are more of a structural or cyclical nature (Daly et al. 2011; Elsby, Michaels, and Ratner 2015; Barlevy et al. 2023). An outward shift in the curve (i.e., a rise in unemployment for a given level of job openings) indicates a likely deterioration in the ability of workers to find available jobs, one of the factors economists use to infer u^*.

Figure 1-14 shows three distinct periods, the first after the global financial crisis up to the COVID-19 pandemic, the second in the pandemic-induced recession and recovery through June 2022 (the peak of personal

Figure 1-14. The Beveridge Curve, Pre- and Post-COVID

Job openings rate (percent)

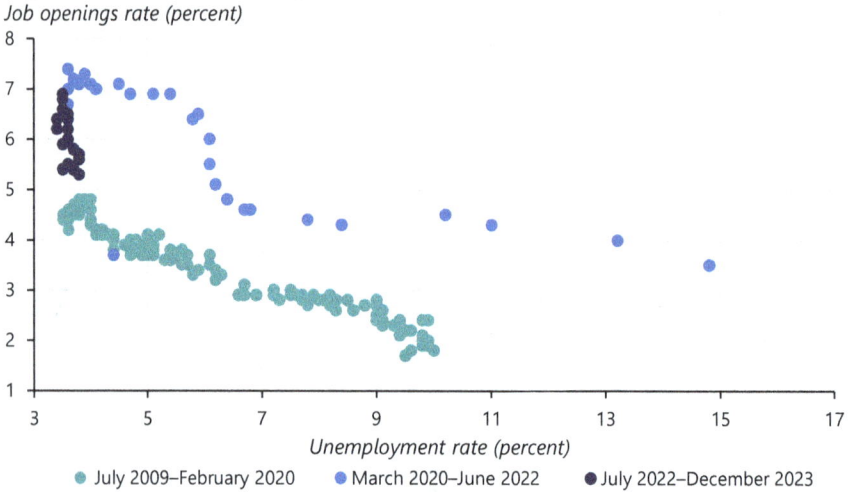

Unemployment rate (percent)

● July 2009–February 2020   ● March 2020–June 2022   ● July 2022–December 2023

Council of Economic Advisers
Sources: Bureau of Labor Statistics; CEA calculations.
2024 Economic Report of the President

consumption expenditures inflation), and the third from July 2022 to December 2023, coinciding with the start of the period of disinflation covered in table 1-3. Since June 2022, the job opening rate has fallen sharply, by over 20 percent, while the unemployment rate has only edged up; this is in sharp contrast to the typically close negative relationship between vacancies and unemployment (Elsby, Michaels, and Ratner 2015; Figura and Waller 2022; Blanchard, Domash, and Summers 2022).

One interpretation of the recent decline in vacancies without a commensurate increase in unemployment is an improvement in what the economics literature describes as the efficiency of the matching process between workers and available jobs, or "matching efficiency." This interpretation would imply a period of deteriorated matching efficiency—the blue locus of points during the recovery from COVID through June 2022—potentially resulting from a rise in labor market churn, including a large increase in worker quits, caused by disruptions resulting from COVID (Barlevy et al. 2023). Thus, one possibility is that the recent improvement in matching efficiency, which reduced job openings for a roughly constant unemployment rate, may reflect post-COVID renormalization. Another potential explanation, one put forth by Figura and Waller (2022), is that, in theory, the Beveridge curve ought to be especially steep at high openings and low unemployment rates. The reason is that as the number of vacancies rises relative to the number unemployed—that is, moving to the upper left of the Beveridge curve diagram—it becomes increasingly hard to fill open jobs; thus, firms

Figure 1-15. Phillips Curve, Pre- and Post-COVID, MSA-Level Data

Year-over-year change in core CPI (percent)

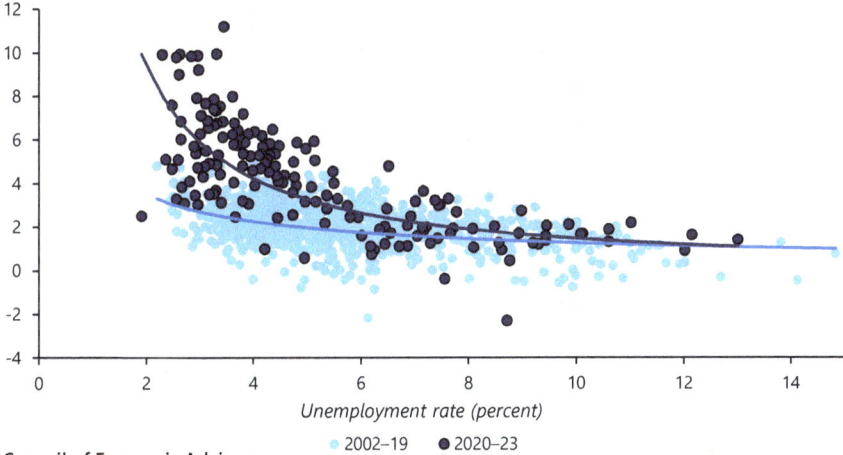

Unemployment rate (percent)

● 2002–19   ● 2020–23

Council of Economic Advisers

Sources: Bureau of Labor Statistics; CEA calculations.
Note: MSA = Metropolitan Statistical Area. CPI = Consumer Price Index. Core CPI includes all items less food and energy. Data are semiannual and not seasonally adjusted. Fitted lines are predictions from log-log specification regressions. The lighter blue fitted line is estimated over the pre-COVID period, and the dark navy line is estimated starting in 2020.
2024 Economic Report of the President

must post increasingly more vacancies to fill each open position, thereby reducing unemployment only a small amount for all the additional vacancies. Consequently, Figura's and Waller's view was that the job openings rate could fall without a large increase in job losses or unemployment as the economy slid down a steep Beveridge curve.

Ultimately, the underlying reasons why job openings have come down substantially with little sacrifice in terms of higher unemployment may not be known for many years. This limits analysts' ability to answer the crucial question: Will matching efficiency continue to improve, *or* has the labor market reached a flatter portion of the Beveridge curve and will any further reduction in openings require an increase in unemployment? In other words, it remains to be seen whether the labor market can benefit from further normalization, putting reduced pressure on wages and prices, without a substantial deterioration of job and income prospects for Americans.

While these economic conditions have supported low-sacrifice-ratio dynamics thus far, the current inflationary episode is not over. The key question for staying at full employment then becomes: Can inflation continue to decline without a large rise in unemployment? Figure 1-15 offers some perspective, showing the price Phillips curve both before COVID and since the pandemic, with year-over-year core Consumer Price Index inflation on the y axis and the unemployment rate on the x axis for an available set of

21 metropolitan statistical areas (or, roughly speaking, major cities).[14] The Phillips curve steepened considerably during the COVID era, as can be seen by comparing the light blue pre-COVID line with the dark blue line. (See also Barlevy et al. 2023.) The recent disinflation with little unemployment sacrifice has likely been due in part to a movement back down the steeper Phillips curve.

Because the normalization of inflation is a work in progress, analysts cannot, at this time, conclude which sacrifice ratio the American economy will ultimately face, though the evidence thus far supports a relatively low one. Either way, the fact remains that, based on the benefits of full employment labor markets and costs of slack, especially to economically vulnerable groups, fiscal and monetary policymakers should use expansionary macroeconomic policy to achieve and stay at full employment in periods of slack, while maintaining a data-driven view in terms of reacting to inflationary pressures. Regarding fiscal policy, an appropriately timed and targeted fiscal stimulus is a crucial pillar of economic policy to close the output gap in periods of recession or in response to negative shocks to growth. As demonstrated here, the other pillar is data-driven monetary policy that takes into account both the numerous benefits attending a tight labor market and the uncertainty surrounding u^* in the context of fulfilling the Federal Reserve's dual mandate of full employment and stable prices. However, while macroeconomic stabilization policy can help achieve full employment for some groups, other groups will undoubtedly be left behind where these policy remedies are ill suited to address structural disadvantages. Box 1-4 considers potential policy levers.

Conclusion

Analysts of the United States economy have learned many critical macroeconomic lessons in recent decades. One such lesson is that the difficulty of estimating the lowest unemployment rate consistent with stable inflation makes it challenging for policymakers to bring about periods of full employment. These lessons have, however, reinforced the importance of policymakers following a data-driven approach to evaluating the supply and demand forces that shape the tightness of the labor market. Further, while analysts cannot reliably identify u^*, the evidence does suggest that (1) unemployment below 4 percent helps facilitate the many benefits of full employment, and (2) outside large supply/demand shocks of the type that occurred during the COVID-19 pandemic, low unemployment can be consistent with low and stable inflation.

---

[14] McLeay and Tenreyro (2019) and Hazell et al. (2022) show that regional variation in inflation and unemployment can identify dynamics that national data fail to pick up.

Box 1-4. Policies Targeting Structural Labor Market Slack

This chapter focuses largely on cyclical labor market slack and urges the use of fiscal and monetary policies to attain and maintain full employment in the labor market. But disaggregated labor market data focusing on economically vulnerable populations reveal that many people suffer not just from cyclical unemployment but also from structural unemployment. A simple way to understand this distinction is to note that for workers facing structural barriers, even at full employment, their unemployment rate will be elevated.

As the CEA's analysis has shown, full employment helps less advantaged groups in both absolute terms (e.g., reduced unemployment and elevated real earnings) and relative terms (stronger gains compared with others). However, other policies are needed to help some workers overcome structural barriers that are somewhat invariant to labor market cycles.

Affordable childcare. While the tight labor market in the current cycle has facilitated historic workforce gains by women, including those with children, the absence of affordable childcare is a structural barrier that suppresses the ability of those with childcare responsibilities to fully participate in strong labor markets. The link between affordable childcare, which is demonstrably underprovided in America (U.S. Department of the Treasury 2021), and employment has been well researched; this work is summarized in chapter 4 of the 2023 *Economic Report of the President* (CEA 2023b, 132). This literature review finds the availability of affordable care has "large, positive effects on maternal employment. . . . Several studies of programs in other countries—specifically Canada, Germany, and Norway—also confirm the responsiveness of mothers' employment to [childcare] expansions." Mothers most affected by the enhanced availability of care tend to be "relatively disadvantaged (i.e., single mothers and those with lower levels of education)." Finally, the research finds that "policies that expand access to [care] can boost [working mothers'] productivity in the workplace by allowing them to get additional education or job training and increasing the likelihood they will work full time." The Biden-Harris Administration's commitment to affordable childcare takes seriously the distributional and macroeconomic consequences of affordable childcare. A recent CEA analysis shows that the American Rescue Plan's historic investment in the childcare industry succeeded in slowing cost growth for families, stabilizing employment and increasing wages for childcare workers, and increasing maternal labor force participation (CEA 2023c).

Antidiscrimination. As discussed in the text of this chapter, full employment makes it more expensive for employers to racially discriminate; but history has clearly shown that tight labor markets are far from

The Benefits of Full Employment | 55

sufficient in preventing discrimination (Kline, Rose, and Walters 2022). For example, even in periods when the overall unemployment rate is below 4 percent, the unemployment rate for Black workers averaged 6.1 percent. Some argue that because highly educated groups have lower unemployment, the differential is due to Black workers' lower levels of education, on average. But figure 1-3 shows that even after controlling for education, Black workers face higher unemployment rates than white workers.

The research evidence shows that at certain periods in U.S. history, antidiscrimination policies have helped to partially overcome structural barriers. In the 1960s, legislation was passed targeting gender and racial labor market discrimination. Various studies show that these new laws first exposed and then helped ameliorate extensive workplace discrimination, which partially blocked the cyclical benefits of full employment for discriminated groups (Tomaskovic-Devey et al. 2006; Kurtulus 2016; Sanchez Cumming 2021). (The Equal Pay Act of 1963 prohibited unequal pay based on gender for equal work, and the 1964 Civil Rights Act—Title VII—prohibited workplace discrimination by race, gender, and other protected classes, and the Age Discrimination in Employment Act of 1967 prohibited employment discrimination against older workers. Notably, enforcement mechanisms were initially limited—e.g., employers accused of discriminatory practices could be investigated but not sued; Sanchez Cumming 2021. Later, in 1990, the Americans with Disabilities Act was passed, which extended the protections of Civil Rights Act of 1964 to those with disabilities.)

It is, however, well documented that the track record of the programs implementing these policies is uneven, and evidence shows that their effectiveness waned beginning in the 1980s, in part due to a lack of funding and commitment to their cause by government sponsors and agencies. Sanchez Cumming (2021, 7) points out that the Reagan Administration actively tried to repeal an Executive Order enforcing equity in workplace practices by government contractors. Though the administration failed in the repeal effort, Sanchez Cumming writes that "there was a decline in the number of sanctions issued for noncompliance, fewer firms were required to adopt affirmative action plans, and compliance reviews rarely found that women workers or workers of color were unfairly underrepresented in contractors' workforces." Even as antidiscrimination laws and U.S. institutions advocating for labor market equity led to important progress toward fairer and more equitable labor market outcomes, employment discrimination today continues to be a pervasive feature of the U.S. economy. Insufficient funding and vulnerability to political whims often prevent a robust enforcement effort from further ameliorating discrimination in the labor market. Indeed, the relative lack of progress has led some racial justice advocates to call for more ambitious and direct programs to counter the effects of structural, systemic racism, most notably guaranteed jobs programs. Paul, Darity, and Hamilton (2018, 5), for example, argue on behalf of a "federal job guarantee [that] would provide a job, at non-poverty wages, for all citizens above the age of 18 that sought one."

Affordable housing in robust economic areas. Chapter 4 of this Report documents the lack of affordable housing in America, which, in the context of full employment, serves to amplify the spatial mismatch between where low-income households can afford to live and places with robust labor demand. As an Urban Institute (2019) analysis puts it, "This spatial mismatch between regional employment clusters and potential worker populations limits access to jobs." Important research by Ganong and Shoag (2017) documents how the problem has worsened over time as affordable housing in places with strong labor demand has become increasingly scarce. Their work documents a sharp decline in "income convergence" across places and ties it both to housing costs and, as emphasized in chapter 4 of this Report, restrictions on land use.

Other structural barriers. While childcare, housing, and discrimination are among the most salient structural barriers to full employment, other frictions also exist. Increased industrial concentration, whereby powerful firms dominate single industries, can suppress job creation and quality through anticompetitive effects, thereby reducing structural demand even during strong cycles. Because unemployment and education levels are negatively correlated, individuals without access to higher education face structural barriers to labor market opportunities. There are also structural disincentives to elevated labor supply in the tax code, including the "marriage tax penalty" (i.e., filing jointly means incurring a larger tax bill than filing separately) and the phasing out of schedules for government benefits that raise the marginal tax rate of an extra hour of work.

Finally, two recent developments are worth noting. First, the significant rise in working from home has the potential to reduce a structural barrier to work for caretakers and others (e.g., those with long commutes). Some recent evidence from Hansen and others (2023) suggests that more than 10 percent of jobs may allow for the option, though it is too soon to tell whether the trend will persist.

Second, an important recent analysis by Hobijn and Şahin (2021) of labor market flow data finds that it can take longer to return to full employment after a labor market shock when the shock causes people to leave the labor force. That is, the research finds that when workers leave the labor force, it can lengthen the amount of time it takes to return to full capacity in the labor market. This finding argues for policies, such as those more common in European economies, that keep people connected to work during a downturn, versus the emphasis in the United States on unemployment insurance for those separated from work due to layoffs. In fact, the United States has a policy known as short-time compensation (informally called "work sharing"), administered by the unemployment insurance system, which can be used to help keep people at work during periods of weak demand by reducing their hours and using the system's funds to partially make up the lost earnings. Of course, it is possible that an economic shock could lead to structural changes such that a fulsome recovery would be facilitated by workers moving to different jobs in different sectors, so each downturn could require its own analysis regarding the policy choice to encourage work sharing. To the extent that work sharing can lessen the time it takes the job market to return to full employment, its use is consistent with reaping the benefits documented in this chapter.

In addition, the CEA's research finds that tight labor markets provide benefits across a large swath of the population. Groups with higher average unemployment rates see larger declines in unemployment during full employment labor markets than groups with relatively low unemployment rates. Groups with less attachment to the labor force on average also see a relatively larger increase in participation rates when the unemployment rate falls. Relatedly, racial gaps in labor market outcomes narrow in tight labor markets. In the most recent period of full employment just before COVID-19 and in the last year, the gaps between Black and white men in unemployment and employment have fallen to the lowest rates on record. Economically vulnerable groups—for example, the comparatively less educated—are more able to switch jobs when the unemployment rate is low and climb the job ladder when jobs are plentiful. Workers who face a work-limiting disability are also brought in from the sidelines and obtain jobs more often in particularly strong labor markets. As this chapter has shown, these labor market benefits translate into higher wages and income, particularly for workers who are more likely to be left behind in slack labor markets.

While wages and earnings tend to be flat in periods of weak or stagnant labor markets, they grow when the economy experiences a tight period, as in the late 1990s, late 2010s, and after the COVD-19 pandemic. There is also a wage convergence across groups and percentiles, just as there is in unemployment and employment rates. Indeed, there has been a remarkable decline in wage inequality since 2015, a time that has featured two periods of full employment.

Given the importance of full employment for racial equity, inequality, workers' empowerment, and the Biden-Harris Administration's fundamental goal of ensuring that workers have the bargaining power they need to claim their fair share of the growing economy, it is clear that maintaining tight labor markets must be an integral policy goal of American administrations. Many economists have recognized that labor markets do not necessarily settle into full employment and have reevaluated the importance of policies that actively promote full employment conditions. And every time this has occurred, the benefits of full employment have blossomed. Economists and policymakers must therefore use the policy tools at their disposal to get to and stay at full employment.

☆ ☆ ☆ ☆ ☆ ☆

Chapter 2

The Year in Review and the Years Ahead

At the start of 2023, many macroeconomic forecasters expected the United States' economy to dip into a recession later that year (figure 2-1). They also predicted that 2023 would be characterized by an anemic growth rate. The economy was instead surprisingly resilient, as measured by indicators including real gross domestic product (GDP), the unemployment rate, real personal consumption expenditures, real disposable personal income, and real private nonresidential investment (figure 2-2). This resilience was especially notable for coinciding with slowing inflation.

Trends—including fiscal drag, rising interest rates, and mounting geopolitical risks—had been perceived as major economic headwinds, informing these pessimistic forecasts. Additional fundamentals—such as a low saving rate and lackluster consumer sentiment—risked exacerbating reduced

Figure 2-1. Recession Probability Indicators, 2008–23

Percent probability or index: June 2022 = 100

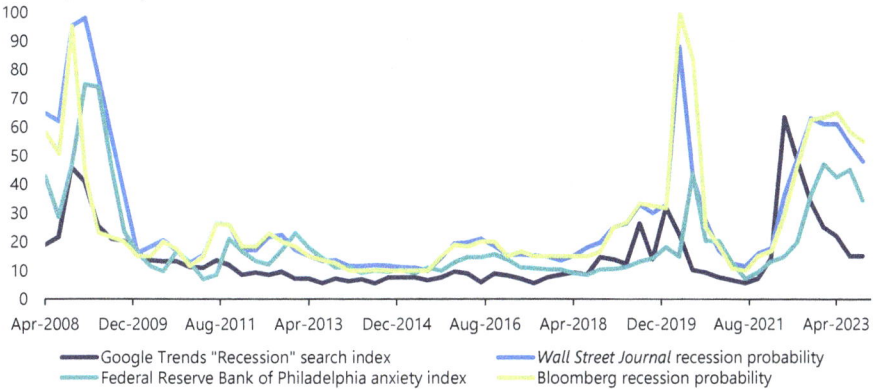

Council of Economic Advisers

Sources: Federal Reserve Bank of Philadelphia; *Wall Street Journal*; Google; Bloomberg; CEA calculations.
Note: Gray bars indicate recessions. Google Trends data are indexed relative to their peak month, June 2022, and are data from January 1, 2004, to December 31, 2023, downloaded on January 11, 2024. Data from the Federal Reserve Bank of Philadelphia indicate Q2 of the given year. Anxiety index represents the probability of a decline in real GDP for the subsequent quarter.
2024 Economic Report of the President

61

Figure 2-2. Selected U.S. Economic Measures, 2019–23

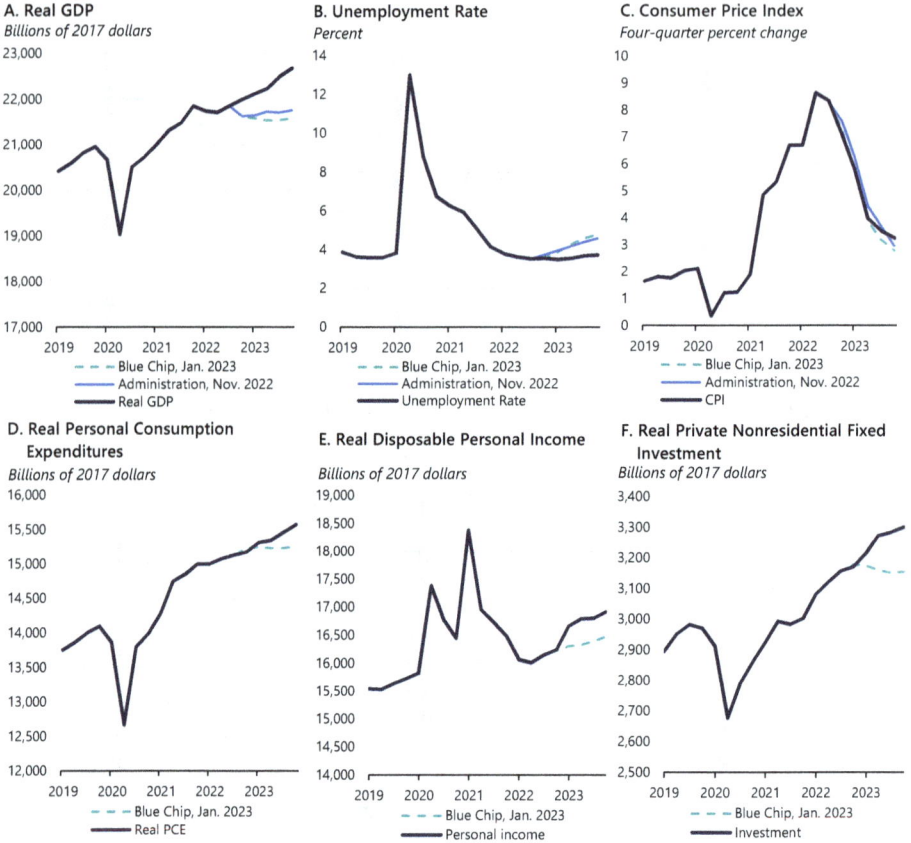

A. Real GDP
Billions of 2017 dollars

- – – Blue Chip, Jan. 2023
- —— Administration, Nov. 2022
- —— Real GDP

B. Unemployment Rate
Percent

- – – Blue Chip, Jan. 2023
- —— Administration, Nov. 2022
- —— Unemployment Rate

C. Consumer Price Index
Four-quarter percent change

- – – Blue Chip, Jan. 2023
- —— Administration, Nov. 2022
- —— CPI

D. Real Personal Consumption Expenditures
Billions of 2017 dollars

- – – Blue Chip, Jan. 2023
- —— Real PCE

E. Real Disposable Personal Income
Billions of 2017 dollars

- – – Blue Chip, Jan. 2023
- —— Personal income

F. Real Private Nonresidential Fixed Investment
Billions of 2017 dollars

- – – Blue Chip, Jan. 2023
- —— Investment

Council of Economic Advisers

Sources: Blue Chip Economic Indicators; Bureau of Economic Analysis; Bureau of Labor Statistics; CEA calculations.
Note: CPI = Consumer Price Index. All values are seasonally adjusted. Years indicate Q1 of the corresponding year. Administration forecast was finalized in November 2022 but published in the 2023 *Economic Report of the President* and the Fiscal Year 2024 Budget. Gray bars indicate recessions.
2024 Economic Report of the President

aggregate demand, rising unemployment, and cutbacks in consumer spending.[1] Meanwhile, the spring 2023 banking crisis raised concerns about diminished credit availability and, in tandem with rising interest rates and fading fiscal support, reinforced worries of a coming recession—the so-called hard-landing scenario. A yield curve inversion in late 2022 and early

---

[1] A saving rate below the desired long-run rate may force consumers to curb spending if incomes do not rise. The effects of net worth—otherwise neglected in this argument—are reviewed in box 2-1 later in this chapter.

2023 was consistent with these forecasts, signaling that financial markets may have also been anticipating a recession.[2]

The U.S. economy not only defied these 2023 forecasts but it even progressed at a significant pace.[3] In retrospect, the economy's marked slowdown in 2022 appears to have reflected temporary supply constraints after the strong rebound in 2021, rather than an impending recession. The level of real GDP in 2023 even exceeded some forecasts from before the COVID-19 pandemic—including those of the Congressional Budget Office (CBO)—and was boosted in part by strong continued consumer spending and a revival in manufacturing structures investment (CBO n.d.). State and local purchases also grew at a robust pace of 4.5 percent in 2023.[4] Meanwhile, sound household balance sheets in recent years and a strong labor market have allowed U.S. consumers to increase their spending at a pace closely resembling the average pace in prior expansions.[5] In 2023, the unemployment rate edged up slightly from near-record lows, but remained below 4 percent for the entire year. Labor force participation rates also increased from 2022 to 2023, both in the aggregate and for men, women, and across most age and racial groups.

Meanwhile, progress in lowering inflation was substantial. From 2022 to 2023, headline Consumer Price Index (CPI) inflation decreased by 2 percentage points and core CPI inflation, which excludes the more volatile categories of energy and food, decreased by 3 percentage points. Declining inflation during a period of accelerating real activity reinforces the hypothesis that the resolution of supply issues—both supply chains and labor supply—has played an important role in reshaping the economy away from the perceived trends that influenced 2023 forecasts. These developments in

---

[2] The yield curve is said to be "inverted" when shorter-term interest rates (e.g., the federal funds rate) exceed longer-term rates (e.g., the 10-year Treasury rate). While these inversions are infrequent, they often precede recessions.

[3] See table 2-1 later in this chapter.

[4] Unless otherwise stated, the yearly growth rate is calculated on a Q4/Q4 basis.

[5] See box 2-1 later in this chapter.

2023—a resilient labor market and strong activity coupled with declining inflation—are consistent with a "soft landing" scenario.

But challenges remain. Elevated real interest rates compared with earlier during the pandemic—against the backdrop of a labor market that appears to have rebalanced—could reduce investment in rate-sensitive sectors. In addition, the impact of geopolitical conflicts on markets and supply chains remains uncertain. To the extent that consumer attitudes respond to price levels rather than, or in addition to, inflation, consumer sentiment could remain weaker than economic data would predict, since prices are unlikely to broadly decline outright. However, recent real wage gains could potentially help support both confidence and consumer spending.

This chapter begins with a review of the economy in 2023. It first examines the acceleration in real GDP and its sources, and then surveys major labor market developments, highlighting their consistency with the "soft landing" scenario. Next, the chapter describes recent progress in disinflation. It then describes developments in financial markets, exploring both potential upside and downside risks. Finally, the chapter reviews the forecast underpinning the President's Fiscal Year 2025 Budget and summarizes the near-term and long-term outlooks.

The Year in Review: The Continuing Recovery

This section describes the continued postpandemic recovery in 2023 and the easing of supply chain bottlenecks, explores the state of demand and supply rebalancing in the labor market, and provides updates on the progress of disinflation over the past year.

Output in 2023: A Return to Normal Growth

Real GDP accelerated to a pace of 3.1 percent over the four quarters of 2023, somewhat above the average growth of about 2.4 percent in the expansion period before the COVID-19 pandemic, and higher than the anemic 0.7 percent pace in 2022:Q4. Table 2-1 disaggregates real GDP growth into its major components.

Table 2-1. Real GDP Growth and Its Components, 2023:Q4

Component	Q4/Q4 Growth (percent)	Contribution to Q4/Q4 GDP Growth (percentage points)	Contribution to Q4/Q4 GDP Growth, Average from 2010 to 2019 (percentage points)
	(1)	(2)	(3)
Total	3.1	3.1	2.4
Consumer spending	2.6	1.8	1.6
Goods	3.5	0.8	0.8
Durables	6.1	0.5	0.4
Motor vehicles and parts	4.1	0.1	0.1
Nondurables	2.2	0.3	0.3
Services	2.2	1.0	0.8
Investment	1.8	0.3	0.9
Business fixed investment	3.1	0.5	0.9
Nonresidential investment	4.1	0.6	0.7
Structures	14.8	0.4	0.1
Equipment	−0.1	0.0	0.4
Intellectual property	2.6	0.1	0.3
Residential investment	−0.1	0.0	0.1
Change in private inventories	-	−0.2	0.1
Net exports	-	0.3	−0.1
Exports	2.1	0.2	0.4
Imports	−0.2	0.0	−0.6
Government	4.3	0.7	0.0
Federal	4.0	0.3	0.0
Defense	3.3	0.1	0.0
Nondefense	4.7	0.1	0.0
State and local	4.5	0.5	0.0

Council of Economic Advisers
Sources: Bureau of Economic Analysis; CEA calculations.
Note: GDP = gross domestic product. Column 2 lists the contribution of each component to the annual rate of growth of real GDP. These may not precisely sum to totals because of approximations to the formulas used in the National Income and Product Accounts. Column 3 lists the average GDP growth and contribution for the time period listed.
2024 Economic Report of the President

Consumer spending. Resilience in consumer spending (personal consumption expenditures, or PCE) largely accounts for the increase in real GDP growth over the past year. Spending growth increased across all major subcategories of consumption. Goods PCE, which has run ahead of its prepandemic trend since the third quarter of 2020, grew 3.5 percent in 2023 after declining in 2022. And while both durable and nondurable consumption grew, the former (including notable growth in motor vehicles) is responsible for the lion's share of the growth in goods consumption. Real services PCE also grew in 2023, at a rate similar to its growth in 2022. Figure 2-3 illustrates how the shares of services and goods consumption as a portion

Figure 2-3. Goods' and Services' Shares of Personal Consumption

Services as a share of nominal consumption   *Goods as a share of nominal consumption*

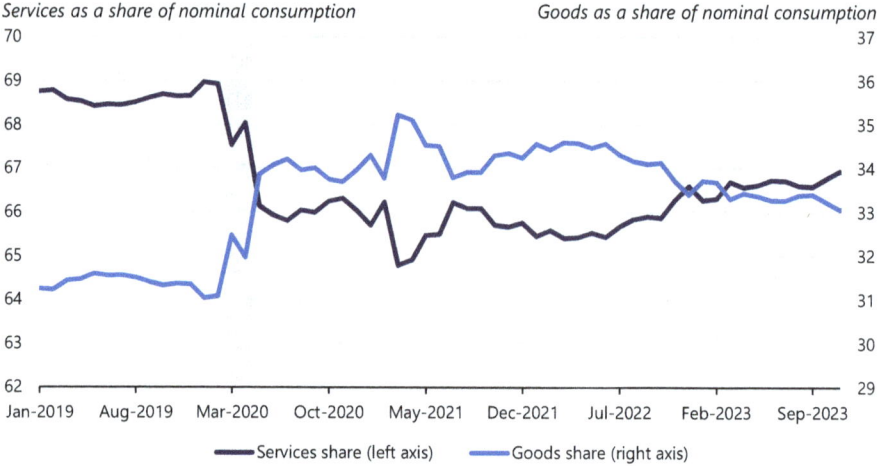

Services share (left axis)   Goods share (right axis)

Council of Economic Advisers
Sources: Bureau of Economic Analysis; CEA calculations.
Note: Gray bars indicate recessions.
2024 Economic Report of the President

Figure 2-4. Share of U.S. Employees Working from Home

Percent

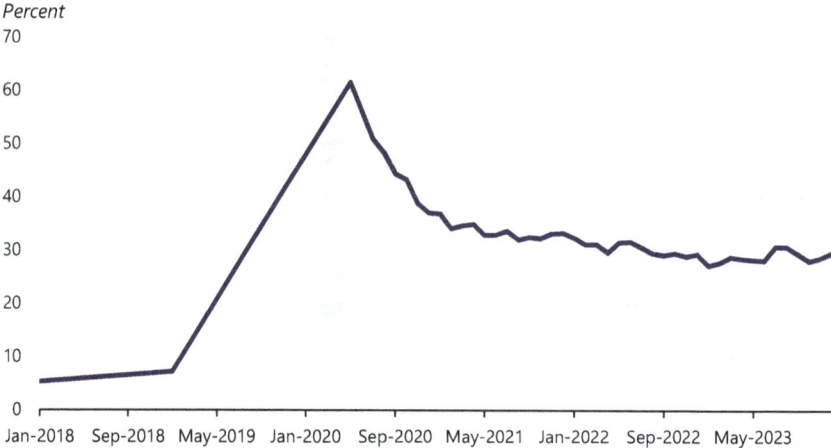

Council of Economic Advisers
Source: Barrero, Bloom, and Davis (2023).
Note: Gray bars indicate recessions.
2024 Economic Report of the President.

of total consumption have been sluggishly reverting to their prepandemic trends. Future years' data will indicate whether a structural, long-lasting shift in consumer preferences is under way.

One factor that may help explain such a pattern is the sustained increase in remote work since 2020 (figure 2-4). People working from home

Figure 2-5. Real Private Fixed Investment in Manufacturing Structures, 1959–2023

Contribution to year-on-year real GDP growth (percentage points)

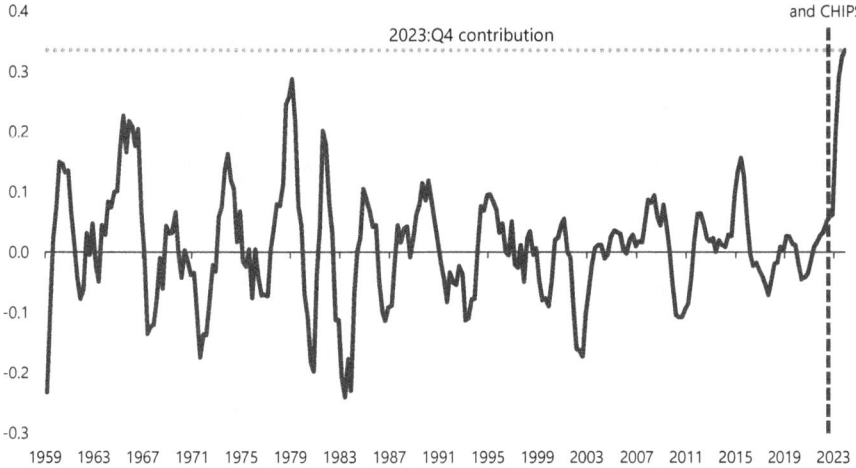

Council of Economic Advisers

Sources: Bureau of Economic Analysis; CEA calculations.
Note: IRA = Inflation Reduction Act; CHIPS = Creating Helpful Incentives to Produce Semiconductors—or the CHIPS and Science Act.
Gray bars indicate recessions.
2024 Economic Report of the President

may tend to spend more on goods (e.g., groceries and home improvement) than on services (including restaurants and transportation).

Investment. Real private fixed investment increased 3.1 percent during the four quarters of 2023, a growth rate slower than the norm for the period before the COVID-19 pandemic. Residential investment continued to be a drag on GDP, as high mortgage rates and the short supply of single-family homes weighed on the housing market (see chapter 4 of this *Report*).

In contrast, investment in nonresidential structures boomed last year, increasing 14.8 percent, the fastest clip seen since 2014. A combination of factors likely drove this outcome. First, the shift to goods consumption during the pandemic caused businesses to both rethink their supply chains and consider expanding domestic production capacity. Meanwhile, the Inflation Reduction Act (IRA) and the CHIPS and Science Act have strongly incentivized domestic investment in clean energy manufacturing (White House 2022, n.d.). Figure 2-5 demonstrates that the surge in nonresidential investment is concentrated in manufacturing structures; manufacturing structures' contribution to GDP growth last year neared the highest level on record. Investment in other nonresidential structures, especially in offices and commercial structures (figure 2-6), has yet to recover to norms from before the pandemic, and changes to working arrangements may yet prove long-lasting, rebalancing the market more permanently (see figure 2-4). And while investment in equipment and intellectual property decelerated in

Figure 2-6. Real Private Investment: Structures

Year-on-year percent change

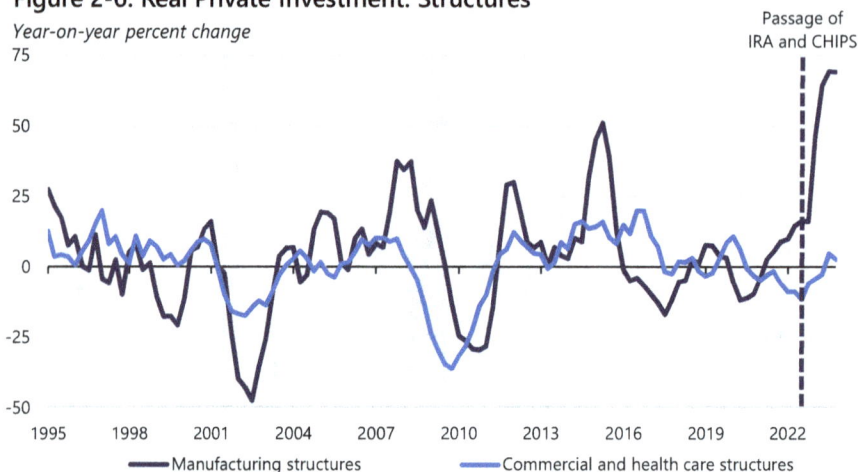

Council of Economic Advisers

Source: Bureau of Economic Analysis.
Note: IRA = Inflation Reduction Act; CHIPS = Creating Helpful Incentives to Produce Semiconductors—or the CHIPS and Science Act. All values are chained. Gray bars indicate recessions.
2024 Economic Report of the President

2023, this slowdown may be attributable to firms redirecting their resources toward manufacturing structures. Investment in equipment and intangibles is likely to pick up over subsequent years, as newly built manufacturing facilities require the installation of new equipment.

Finally, inventory investment continued to suppress GDP growth in 2023. In the pandemic's immediate aftermath, inventory investment's contribution to GDP growth climbed to highs not seen since the Korean War, as firms scrambled to adapt to the shift of consumption from services to goods. However, some sectors suffered from a bullwhip effect as consumption patterns rebalanced toward services in 2022. With inventory-sales ratios above desired levels, pressures mounted to bring business inventories back in line with demand. This phenomenon has been particularly acute in the merchant wholesale trade sector, in which the inventory-sales ratio currently sits at 1.43 months' supply, a historically high figure that is well above the 2019 average of 1.37 (figure 2-7). The rebalancing of inventories with sales still appeared to be in progress last year.

Imports and exports. As the world economy abruptly closed in 2020, the pandemic-induced recession injected turbulence into the contribution of net exports to real GDP growth. However, large swings in this category appear to be behind us, similar to the normalization of inventory investment. In 2023, net exports contributed 0.3 percentage point to GDP growth on a four-quarter basis; the large positive contributions in the first and last quarters were only partially offset by contributions moving closer to the normal prepandemic rate of expansion in the middle of the year (see chapter 5).

Figure 2-7. Ratio of Real Inventories to Sales: Merchant Wholesale Trade, 2013–23

Months' supply

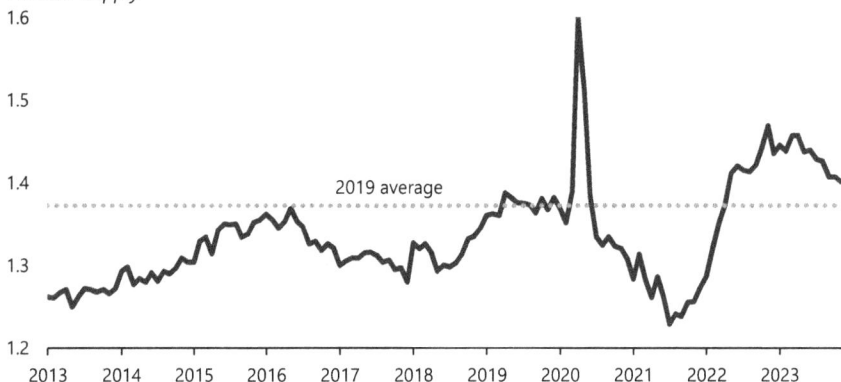

Council of Economic Advisers
Sources: Bureau of Economic Analysis; CEA calculations.
Note: Data are seasonally adjusted. Gray bars indicate recessions.
2024 Economic Report of the President

Government spending. The Federal Government's real purchases in 2023 (expenditures and gross investment) contributed a quarter percentage point more to GDP growth than they had in 2022. Defense and nondefense expenditures each contributed about equally to GDP growth. Real State and local government purchases accelerated in 2023, as these governments took advantage of strong budget positions to increase employment (figure 2-8). The Fiscal Impact Measure (FIM) index—which captures the overall effects of Federal, State, and local fiscal policy on GDP growth—suggests that the large fiscal drag, which had suppressed growth in recent years due primarily to the roll-off of pandemic emergency aid, was no longer a drag on GDP growth by the end of 2023 (figure 2-8).[6]

Private domestic final purchases. Private domestic final purchases (PDFP) are a measure of GDP that includes only consumption and fixed investment, removing more volatile components like inventory investment, government purchases, and net exports. PDFP accelerated from a pace of about 0.8 percent during the four quarters of 2022 to 2.7 percent in 2023. Most of this boost in PDFP is due to consumer expenditures and nonresidential investment, whereas residential investment—among the sectors that is most sensitive to higher interest rates—was a slight drag on growth. PDFP growth can better summarize economic momentum and better predict future GDP growth than GDP itself (CEA 2015), and this relationship may be even more salient in today's economic climate. The contributions to GDP from

---

[6] The FIM measures the contributions of overall fiscal legislation to GDP growth. It considers Federal, State, and local purchases, including taxes and transfers (Asdourian et al. 2024).

Figure 2-8. Fiscal Impulse by Source

Percentage-point contributions to quarterly SAAR of real GDP growth

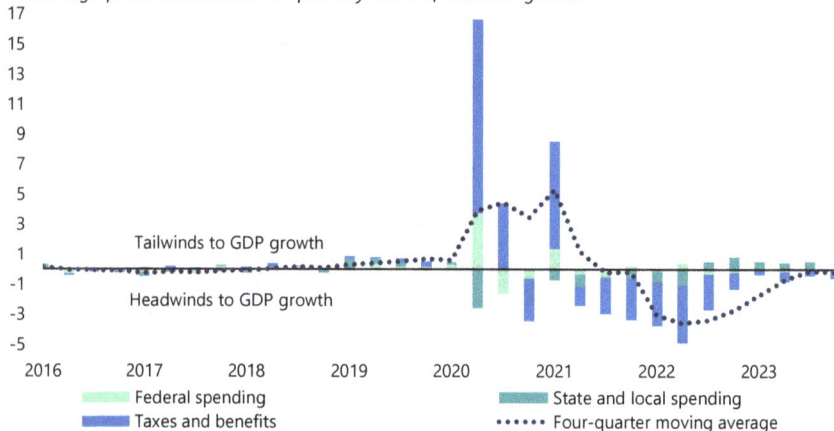

Tailwinds to GDP growth

Headwinds to GDP growth

Federal spending
Taxes and benefits
State and local spending
•••••• Four-quarter moving average

Council of Economic Advisers

Source: Brookings Institution.
Note: GDP = gross domestic product; SAAR = seasonally adjusted annual rate. Fiscal policy includes Federal, State, and local programs. Gray bars indicate recessions.
2024 Economic Report of the President

those measures excluded from PDFP, such as inventory investment and net exports, have proven especially volatile due to pandemic-induced shocks and supply chain disruptions (figure 2-9). As a result, those components of GDP growth have become noisier and provide a less meaningful signal about the economy's underlying momentum.

The Gradual Rebalancing of Demand and Supply in the Labor Market

The labor market gradually eased over the course of 2023. The unemployment rate averaged 3.6 percent for the year, close to the annual lows observed just before the pandemic, and payroll employment grew 255,000 per month on average, well above the break-even pace needed to absorb labor force growth while also maintaining the unemployment rate.[7] The average quarterly job growth pace slowed down a bit more at the end of the year to a three-month pace of about 227,000 jobs per month, still a robust pace but significantly lower than the average monthly pace of 377,000 jobs created in 2022 (figure 2-10). This slowdown was expected; employment in most sectors is now higher than it was in February 2020—the date of the last prepandemic labor report—and in some sectors was even above the level implied by extrapolating from prepandemic trends. In fact, employment

---

[7] The CEA estimates the break-even pace to be between 80,000 and 100,000 jobs a month, depending on immigration and the rate of the trend in labor force participation, among other factors. Consistent with the robust and persistent pace of job growth, the unemployment rate in 2023 was the lowest on record since 1969.

Figure 2-9. Real GDP Compared with Lagged Real GDP and PDFP

A. Real GDP and Lagged Real GDP, 1995 to 2019

Percent change, annualized rate

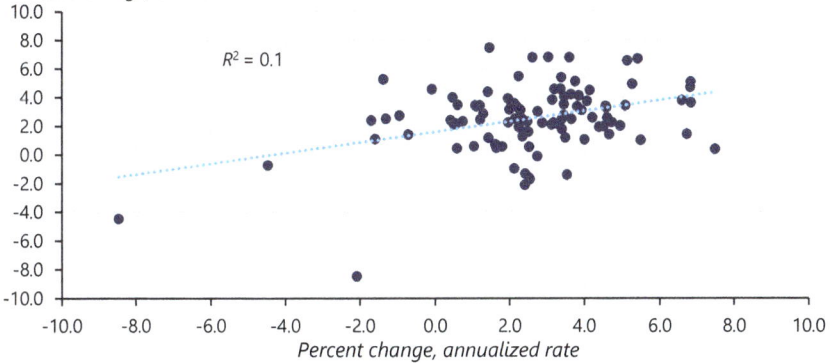

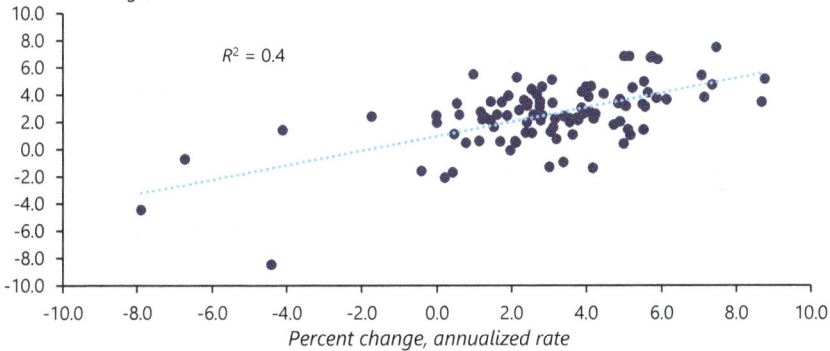

$R^2 = 0.1$

Percent change, annualized rate

B. Real GDP and Lagged Real PDFP, 1995 to 2019

Percent change, annualized rate

$R^2 = 0.4$

Percent change, annualized rate

Council of Economic Advisers

Sources: Bureau of Economic Analysis; CEA calculations.
Note: GDP = gross domestic product; PDFP = private domestic final purchases. Data are quarterly. Real GDP is on the y axis. In panel A, one-quarter lagged real GDP is on the x axis. In panel B, one-quarter lagged real PDFP is on the x axis.

growth in 2023 can be mostly attributed to a handful of sectors in which the rebalancing of the labor market is still in progress. As of December 2023, the level of employment in the leisure and hospitality, education and health services, and government sectors remain below February 2020 levels; however, payroll gains in these sectors in 2023 were above their respective 2019 averages.

Several additional indicators suggest that the labor market has slowed and that the gradual rebalancing between labor supply and labor demand may be nearly complete. After peaking in 2022, both the hires rate and the

Figure 2-10. Monthly Change in Nonfarm Employment

Thousands

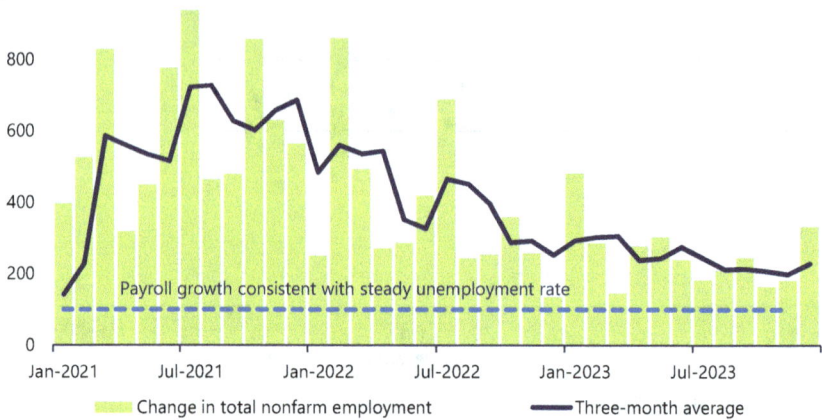

Payroll growth consistent with steady unemployment rate

Change in total nonfarm employment ▬ Three-month average

Council of Economic Advisers
Sources: Bureau of Labor Statistics; CEA calculations.
2024 Economic Report of the President

quits rate have declined to 2019 levels (figure 2-11).[8] The quits rate is an especially meaningful gauge of wage pressures and the scarcity of workers; its decline suggests that workers are less confident than they were during the pandemic recovery that higher-paying jobs await them elsewhere (Moscarini and Postel-Vinay 2017).

The salary gap between those staying in one job and otherwise comparable workers who switch jobs decreased in 2023 after having increased significantly during the pandemic-induced recession and its associated recovery (Federal Reserve Bank of Atlanta 2024). This metric is consistent with the narrative suggested by the quits rate, that the labor market has slowed, though the job openings rate remains well above 2019 levels (figure 2-11, panel B).

There are nevertheless reasons to doubt the job openings rate's ability to measure tightness, and the same can be said for measures that incorporate job openings, such as the gap between available jobs and available workers or the number of job openings per unemployed worker. As a comparison of the two panels of figure 2-11 demonstrate, the job openings rate may be

---

[8] While the Job Openings and Labor Turnover Survey's (JOLTS; BLS 2024) quits rate reached an all-time high of 3 percent in the spring of 2022, the survey dates only to the early 2000s. To offer some comparison with earlier job markets, particularly the robust labor markets of the 1970s, the closest historical analog is the discontinued Manufacturing Labor Turnover Survey (MLTS), which was conducted through the early 1980s, though it covered only the manufacturing sector. The comparison suggests that the labor market in the manufacturing sector was as tight in 2022 as it had been in the 1970s: Per JOLTS, the quits rate in the manufacturing sector reached 2.7 percent in March 2022, similar to its peak of 2.8 percent in 1973 per the MLTS.

Figure 2-11. Quits, Hires, and Job Openings Rates

A. Quits and Hires Rates

Percent

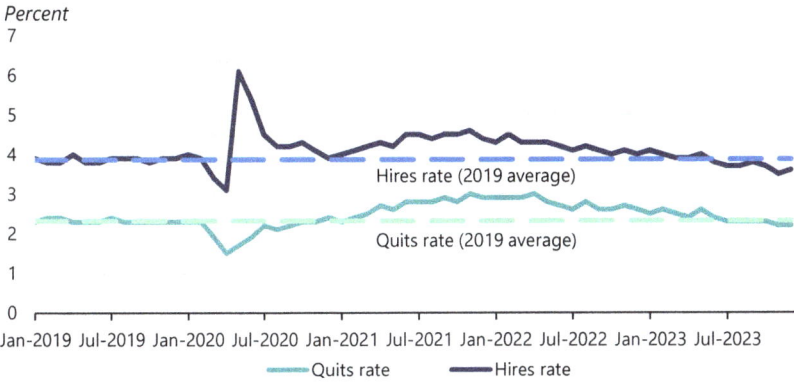

Hires rate (2019 average)

Quits rate (2019 average)

Jan-2019 Jul-2019 Jan-2020 Jul-2020 Jan-2021 Jul-2021 Jan-2022 Jul-2022 Jan-2023 Jul-2023

— Quits rate   — Hires rate

B. Quits and Job Openings Rates

Percent

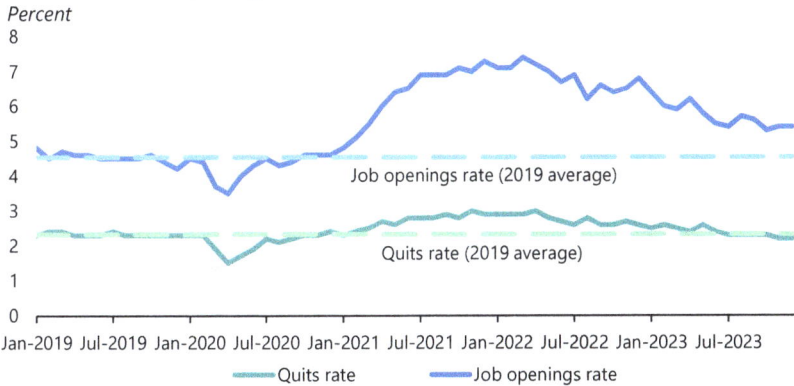

Job openings rate (2019 average)

Quits rate (2019 average)

Jan-2019 Jul-2019 Jan-2020 Jul-2020 Jan-2021 Jul-2021 Jan-2022 Jul-2022 Jan-2023 Jul-2023

— Quits rate   — Job openings rate

Council of Economic Advisers

Sources: Bureau of Labor Statistics (Job Openings and Labor Turnover Survey); CEA calculations.
Note: The quits rate is defined as the number of quits as a percentage of employment. The hires rate is defined as hires as a percentage of employment. The job openings rate is defined as job openings as a percentage of employment and job openings. Data are seasonally adjusted. Gray bars indicate recessions.
2024 Economic Report of the President

generally more sensitive to business cycles than either the hires or the quits rate—and that relationship has been especially strong since the pandemic. For example, job openings may be nonlinear with regard to tightness; firms may be more likely to post external vacancies for different jobs when they are starved for labor than when labor markets are more normal. As a consequence, elevated levels of job openings may (as shown in figure 2-12) exaggerate the true state of market tightness. If job openings soon catch up with quits and hires, they may fall quite rapidly in the near future. As shown in figure 2-13, panel B, the adjustment of job openings with the implied common cyclical component from quits and hires or by alternative methods (Mongey and Horwich 2023; Elsby et al. 2015; Cheremukhin and Restrepo-Echavarria 2024) suggests that market tightness is back to normal

Figure 2-12. Measures of Labor Market Tightness

A. Jobs versus Available Workers

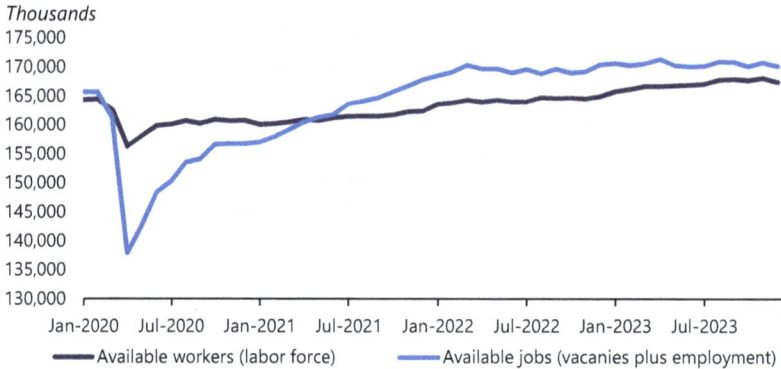

Thousands

Legend: ━━ Available workers (labor force)　　━━ Available jobs (vacanies plus employment)

B. Job Openings per Unemployed Person

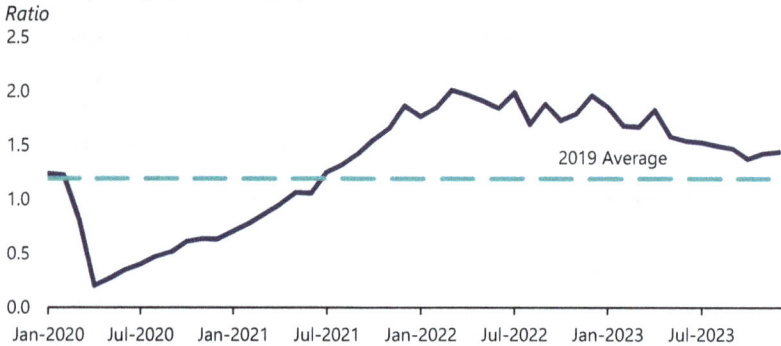

Ratio

2019 Average

Council of Economic Advisers

Sources: Bureau of Labor Statistics (Job Openings and Labor Turnover Survey); CEA calculations.
Note: Unemployed persons are over age 16 years. Gray bars indicate recessions.
2024 Economic Report of the President

prepandemic levels and that the current position of the labor market is back on the prepandemic Beveridge curve (the relationship between job openings and the unemployment rate). These adjustments imply that standard Beveridge curve calculations shown in figure 2-13, panel A, may overstate the further progress to come in the labor market's rebalancing (as implied, e.g., by Figura and Waller 2022).

Meanwhile, both layoffs and the number of job losers who were laid off have been essentially flat in 2023 (figure 2-14). These indicators tend to rise rapidly at the onset of recessions, and their relative quiet supports the view that the U.S. economy is returning to more normal, sustainable conditions while avoiding a recession. Initial claims for unemployment insurance, another often-cited leading indicator of recessions, remained flat in 2023.

Finally, the labor supply appears to have firmed up: the labor force participation rate of prime-age civilians—those between the age of 25 and

Figure 2-13. Beveridge Curves

A. Standard Beveridge Curve

Job openings rate

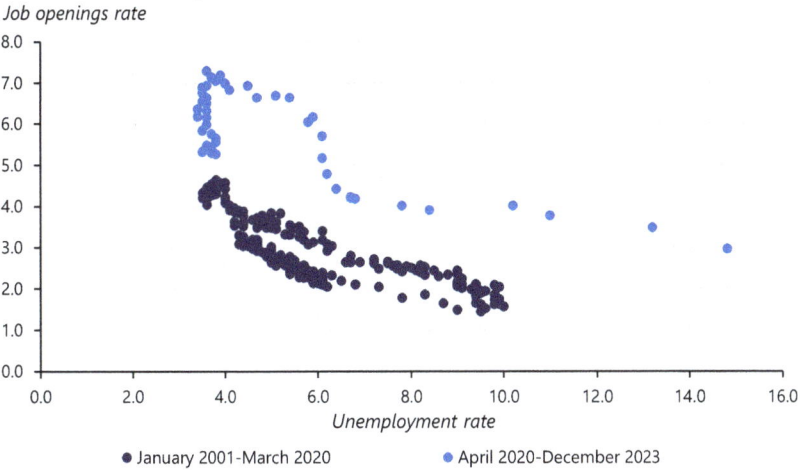

● January 2001-March 2020   ● April 2020-December 2023

B. Beveridge Curve with Adjusted Vacancies

Job openings rate

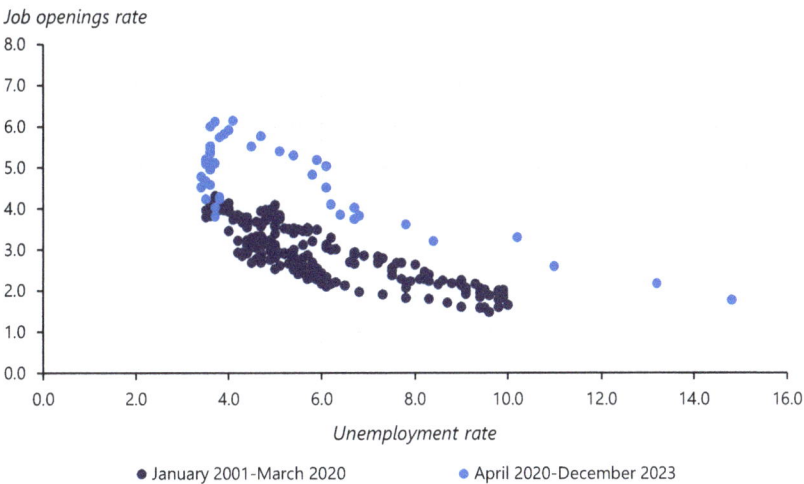

● January 2001-March 2020   ● April 2020-December 2023

Council of Economic Advisers
Sources: Bureau of Labor Statistics (Job Openings and Labor Turnover Survey); CEA calculations.
Note: The job openings rate is defined as job openings as a percentage of employment and job openings. In panel B, the modified Beveridge curve using vacancy rates is adjusted to reflect long-term labor market relationships. Data are monthly and seasonally adjusted.
2024 Economic Report of the President

54 years—is close to a 20-year high, and the participation rate for prime-age women exceeded its all-time high this year (figure 2-15). Employers' allowances of more flexible work schedules during and since the COVID-19 pandemic—including the rise in work-from-home arrangements—may also have contributed to record labor force participation among prime-age

Figure 2-14. Measures of Employment Separation

A. Layoffs and Discharges

Thousands

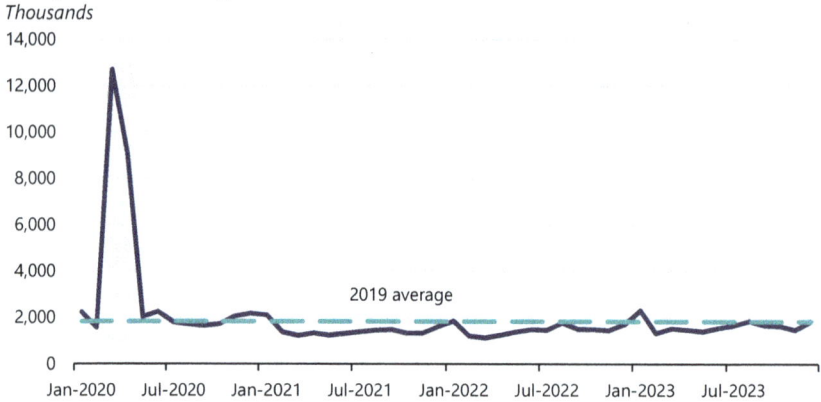

B. Job Losers on Permanent Layoffs

Thousands

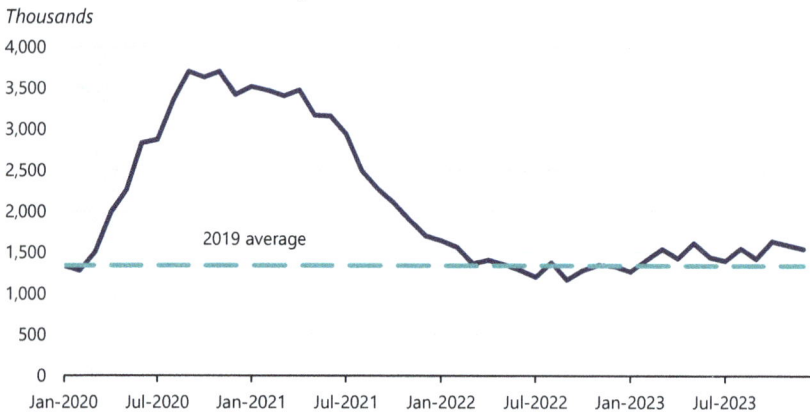

Council of Economic Advisers
Sources: Bureau of Labor Statistics (Job Openings and Labor Turnover Survey); Current Population Survey; CEA calculations.
Note: Gray bars indicate recessions.
2024 Economic Report of the President

women.[9] It is likely that increasing access to affordable childcare, a key policy goal of the Biden-Harris Administration, would be associated with further improvements in the labor supply (CEA 2023a).[10]

These positive developments in labor force participation rates are especially remarkable given the backdrop of a downward, long-run trend in the labor force as a result of the aging U.S. population. Labor force

---

[9] Survey evidence suggests that, on average, women place a higher value on flexible work arrangements relative to men. See Aksoy et al. (2022) and Mas and Pallais (2017).

[10] Research by Francine Blau and her colleagues suggests that a meaningful portion of the growing gap in the labor force participation rate of prime-age women between the United States and other advanced nations can be explained by weak U.S. family policies (Blau and Kahn 2013).

Figure 2-15. Women's Prime Age (25–54) Labor Force Participation

Percentage of population

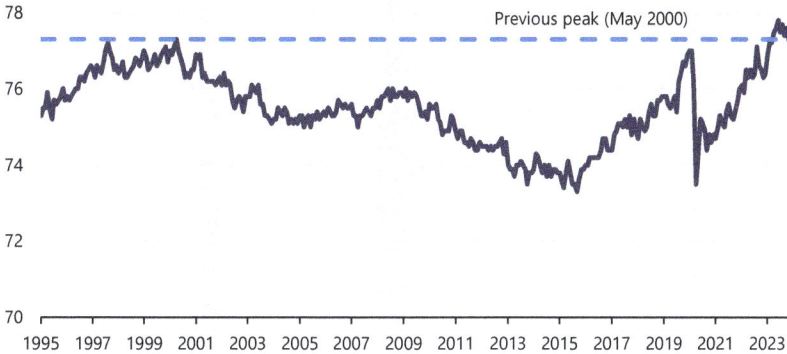

Previous peak (May 2000)

Council of Economic Advisers
Source: Bureau of Labor Statistics.
Note: All values are seasonally adjusted. Data are monthly. Gray bars indicate recessions.
2024 Economic Report of the President

Figure 2-16. Factors Affecting the Size of the Labor Force, February 2020–October 2023

Thousands of workers

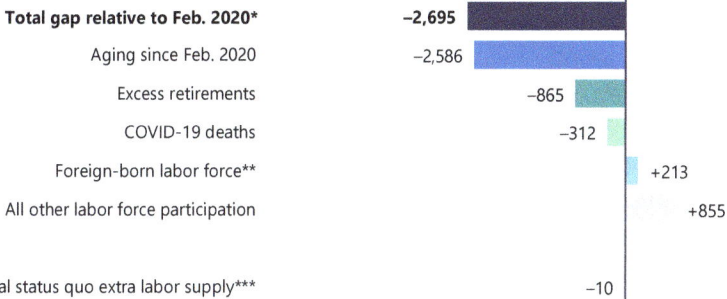

Total gap relative to Feb. 2020*	−2,695
Aging since Feb. 2020	−2,586
Excess retirements	−865
COVID-19 deaths	−312
Foreign-born labor force**	+213
All other labor force participation	+855
Potential status quo extra labor supply***	−10

Council of Economic Advisers
Sources: Current Population Survey; CEA calculations.
Note: * = Adjusted for annual population controls. ** = Relative to 2012–18 trend. *** = Sum of factors less aging, immigration, and COVID-19 deaths.
2024 Economic Report of the President

participation for civilians age 65 years and above has steeply declined in the postpandemic economy. While increased retirements have been expected due to population aging, they have substantially exceeded expectations since the onset of the pandemic. According to the CEA's calculations, excess retirements subtracted almost 900,000 workers from the labor market in 2023 (figure 2-16).

Figure 2-17. Business Sector Productivity and Trend

Percent, annual rate

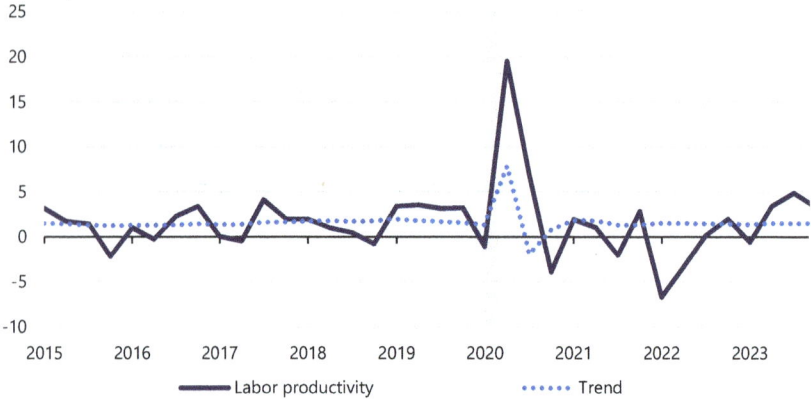

Council of Economic Advisers

Sources: Bureau of Labor Statistics; Federal Reserve Board; CEA calculations.
Note: The trend is estimated with a modified version of the FRB/US supply-side component, which adds demographic controls. Gray bars indicate recessions.
2024 Economic Report of the President

The slowdown in labor markets and the acceleration of real GDP imply that labor productivity (figure 2-17) rebounded in 2023 after a decline in 2022.[11] Productivity has displayed its typical cyclicality in recent years, and now closely approximates its prepandemic trend, a result of businesses catching up to desired hiring levels. Despite this, the future path of productivity is uncertain. One potential upside risk to productivity growth is artificial intelligence; whether developments in artificial intelligence will ignite a similar acceleration in productivity as the information technology revolution induced in the late 1990s remains to be seen (see chapter 7).

All the available metrics of nominal wage inflation—such as the Employment Cost Index, average hourly earnings, unit labor costs, and the Atlanta Fed's wage tracker—show that nominal wage growth has moderated over the last year (Federal Reserve Bank of Atlanta 2024). A strong labor market has nevertheless fostered progress on real labor compensation. Compensation growth, as measured by the Employment Cost Index—which includes both benefits and salaries and which controls for compositional effects—has been outpacing inflation since 2022:Q4 (figure 2-18), implying that workers' purchasing power has improved over the last year. Moreover, real average hourly earnings—an alternative, more timely measure of wages and salaries, albeit one more susceptible to compositional effects—have more than caught up with inflation and are now above prepandemic levels, especially for the 80 percent of the workforce in production and nonsupervisory occupations. Moderate wage growth above the inflation rate is an

---

[11] Labor productivity is measured as output per hour in the business sector.

Figure 2-18. Private Sector Compensation Growth and Inflation
Year-on-year percent change

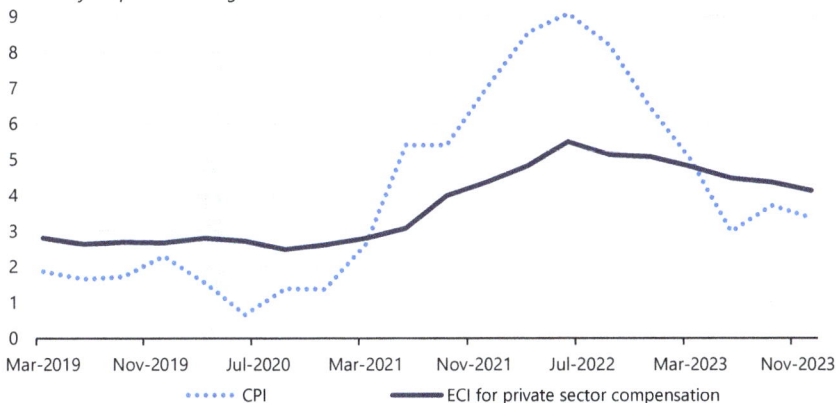

Council of Economic Advisers
Sources: Bureau of Labor Statistics; CEA calculations.
Note: CPI = Consumer Price Index; ECI = Employment Cost Index. Gray bars indicate recessions.
2024 Economic Report of the President

important factor in providing continued support for aggregate consumer spending as excess savings are gradually depleted. Of particular importance for overall purchasing power, the pace of wage growth among the lowest quartile of the wage distribution exceeded inflation in 2023.[12]

Inflation in 2023

After peaking in the summer of 2022, inflation trended downward through the end of 2023. Disinflation in the food, energy, and goods sectors is largely responsible for this reversal (figure 2-19). Inflation in the services sector—which is largely influenced by wages, the most important cost in services production—has been retreating more slowly, in step with the gradual moderation of wage inflation.

Housing inflation appears to have played an outsized role in keeping inflation above target in 2023. Rental contracts are renewed only infrequently, and are therefore slower to adjust to rental price pressures (which include building maintenance and labor costs, utilities, and general costs of living). However, data on newly signed contracts, such as the Zillow rent index and the Bureau of Labor Statistics' New Tenant Rent Index, all showed a decline in the last two quarters of 2023, suggesting that housing inflation should lessen over the coming quarters (figure 2-20).

Outside forecasters expected that core inflation would recede more quickly in 2023, an expectation consistent with their forecasts of weak real

---

[12] Consumers in the lowest quartile of the wage distribution tend to have a higher marginal propensity to consume.

Figure 2-19. Contributions to Headline CPI Inflation

Percentage-point contribution to 12-month change

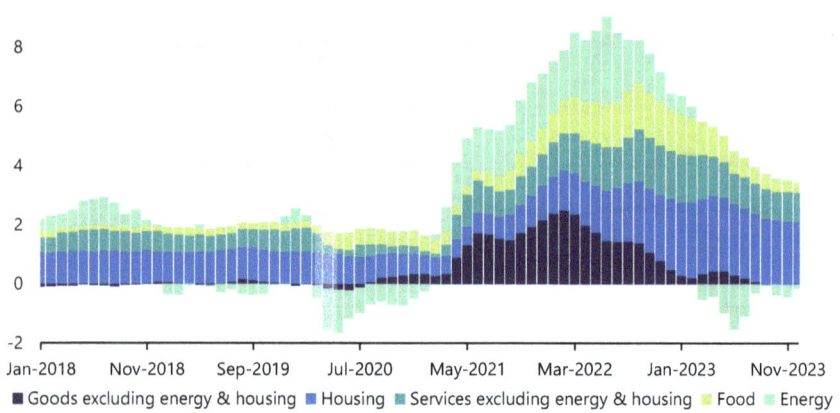

Council of Economic Advisers
Sources: Bureau of Labor Statistics; CEA calculations.
Note: CPI = Consumer Price Index. Gray bars indicate recessions.
2024 Economic Report of the President

Figure 2-20. Selected Measures of Rent Growth

Four-quarter percentage change

Council of Economic Advisers
Sources: Bureau of Labor Statistics; Federal Reserve Bank of Cleveland; Zillow.
Note: CPI = Consumer Price Index. BLS = Bureau of Labor Statistics. Data are quarterly. Gray bars indicate recessions.
2024 Economic Report of the President

economic activity and a high unemployment rate (see figure 2-2, panel B).[13] But in contrast to these expectations—and to the economies of the 1970s and 1980s—progress on reestablishing price stability for the U.S. consumer has

---

[13] Some commentators were skeptical that any progress in the fight against inflation would happen without sharp increases in the unemployment rate. On this point, also see chapter 1 of this *Report*.

Figure 2-21. Contributions to GDP Growth, per the Federal Reserve's Financial Conditions Impulse on Growth (FCI-G)

Percentage points

Council of Economic Advisers

Sources: Federal Reserve Board; CEA calculations.
Note: BBB = Better Business Bureau. Data are from FCI-G (baseline), and inverted such that the figure is read as a fiscal impact measure.
2024 Economic Report of the President

thus far been achieved without substantial increases to unemployment rates or a slowdown in growth. Several causes can be ascribed to the decline in inflation, the most prominent of which are tighter monetary policy, progress in the resolution of supply bottlenecks, and lower import prices.

The tightening of monetary policy restrains aggregate demand by inducing higher interest rates, which typically cool the housing market and demand for durable goods, both of which are sensitive to interest rates. Higher interest rates may also cause a decline in the stock market, further reducing consumption through a wealth effect. According to the Federal Reserve Board's Financial Conditions Index Impulse on Growth (FCI-G)—a measure that captures the overall effects of financial markets on real GDP growth—monetary policy and its effects on financial markets created a headwind to economic growth in the middle months of 2022.[14] However, according to the FCI-G, neither housing prices nor the stock market curbed GDP growth in 2023 (see figure 2-21 and box 2-1).

A second factor contributing to disinflation—one that accords more closely with the acceleration in real GDP—is progress in the resolution of supply bottlenecks. While supply bottlenecks are difficult to measure precisely—a likely reason why some forecasters had downplayed the role of their resolution in reducing inflation and instead forecasted weak real

---

[14] The FCI-G measures how financial conditions, including asset prices, house prices, and interest rates—all of which are also affected by monetary policy—have the potential to affect the real economy (Ajello et al. 2023).

Box 2-1. Strong Balance Sheets Supported Household Consumption in 2023

At the outset of 2023, forecasters anticipated that high mortgage rates, a historically low saving rate, and lackluster consumer sentiment would exert a notable deceleration in consumer spending. Moreover, lower-income households' excess savings—presumed to have fueled consumption early in the recovery from the COVID-19 pandemic—were thought to be depleted by the end of 2022. Many observers have therefore been surprised by consumer resilience in the face of such strong headwinds (figure 2-i).

Figure 2-i. The Saving Rate
Percentage of disposable income

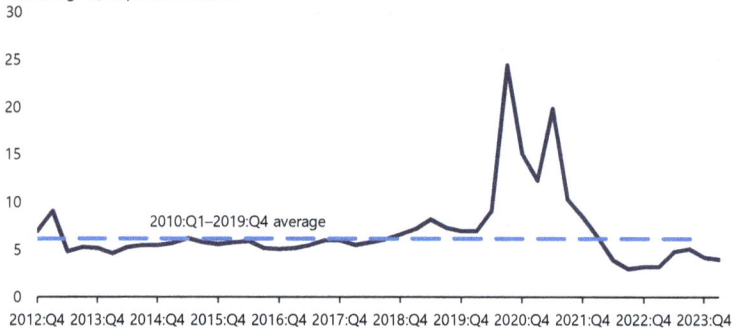

2010:Q1–2019:Q4 average

Council of Economic Advisers
Source: Bureau of Economic Analysis.
Note: Data are seasonally adjusted. Gray bars indicate recessions.
2024 Economic Report of the President

Several factors likely contributed to last year's acceleration in consumption, including low unemployment, strong job growth, and rising real wages. But an especially important factor was the resilience of household balance sheets. Household liquid assets, defined as the real value held in currency and deposits—including money market funds shares—stayed above its prepandemic trend in 2023. Net worth relative to income—which includes all liquid, financial, and housing household assets—also ended the year higher than its level before the pandemic (figure 2-ii). In particular, housing wealth held up well in 2023. Despite high mortgage rates, undersupply in the housing market has so far supported house prices. Traditionally, housing wealth supports middle-class homeowners' consumption. These consumers are able either to extract resources from their homes in the form of home equity lines—a channel likely dampened by the recent rise in interest rates—or to lower their saving rate, capitalizing on the perceived high present discounted value of their homes. Finally, high interest rates did not substantially dent the

Figure 2-ii. Wealth-to-Income Ratio versus Consumption Rate

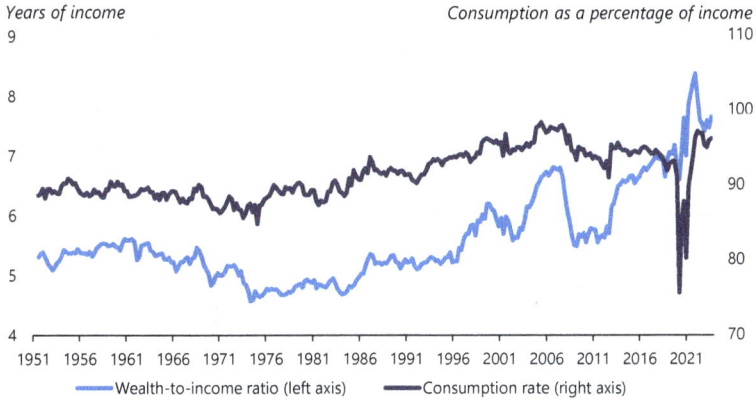

Years of income

Consumption as a percentage of income

—— Wealth-to-income ratio (left axis)   —— Consumption rate (right axis)

Council of Economic Advisers

Sources: Bureau of Economic Analysis; Federal Reserve Board; CEA calculations.
Note: The 2023:Q4 value is estimated by the CEA. Gray bars indicate recessions.
2024 Economic Report of the President

stock market's performance in 2023, which appears to be relevant in gauging the support of consumption from wealthy consumers.

economic activity—the few available measures suggest substantial progress. For instance, the share of manufacturing plants reporting insufficient labor has decreased significantly from its peak in 2022, a pattern that likely reflects the improvement in the labor supply, especially among prime-age workers, as documented above.[15] Meanwhile, the Institute for Supply Management's supplier delivery index and the New York Federal Reserve Bank's Global Supply Chain Pressure Index (GSCPI) each indicate a decline in supply chain pressures over the past year (figure 2-22).[16]

Core import prices—another cost driver, and a third potential explanation for the recent decline in inflation—have also receded. Import prices are themselves driven by many different factors, including foreign demand, foreign inflation, global supply chain pressures, and the relative strength of the dollar. Over the course of 2023, nonpetroleum import prices fell 1.6 percent, which put downward pressure on the cost of many inputs for domestic production.

---

[15] These data are from the Quarterly Survey of Plant Capacity (U.S. Census Bureau n.d.).

[16] The Institute for Supply Management's index gauges changes in supplier delivery times. A measure below 50 implies that deliveries are moving faster, and that supply chain pressures are easing. The GSCPI summarizes several supply chain indicators, including an index of supplier deliveries.

Figure 2-22. Indicators of Supply Chain Pressure

Standard deviation points

Index: 50+ equals slower

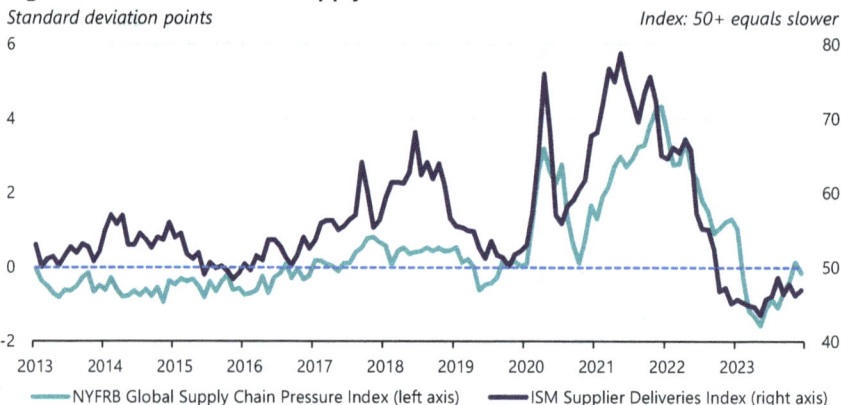

Council of Economic Advisers

Sources: Federal Reserve Bank of New York (NYFRB); Institute for Supply Management (ISM).
Note: A value above 50 for the Supplier Deliveries Index indicates slower deliveries. The NYFRB Global Supply Chain Pressure Index is normalized such that zero indicates the series average value with positive/negative showing how many standard deviations above/below the average the point is. The data are not seasonally adjusted. Gray bars indicate recessions.
2024 Economic Report of the President

The factors that contributed in 2023 to the diminishing effects of inflation can also be evaluated within the framework of the Phillips curve. Augmented with proxies for supply shocks and the interaction of demand and supply bottlenecks, the Phillips curve succinctly captures inflation's rise in the COVID-19 pandemic years leading into 2023, as well as its subsequent decline, during which there was no labor market or aggregate demand deterioration (CEA 2023b). Consider a Phillips curve that includes (1) relative import prices as a cost-push factor, (2) the New York Federal Reserve Bank's GSCPI as a measure of supply chain pressures, and (3) an interaction term between the GSCPI with slack (proxied by the CBO's unemployment gap measure)—all of which are meant to capture the demand-induced bottlenecks at a time of supply chain disruptions.[17] Inflation expectations are proxied by the Survey of Professional Forecasters' long-run PCE inflation expectations. Figure 2-23 shows that the model ascribes the majority of the increase in inflation from 2018 to 2022 to supply chain disruptions and most of the subsequent decline to the unsnarling of supply chains and the resolution of demand bottlenecks. Notably, the role of slack, in isolation, is minimal in explaining the recent evolution of inflation.

Long-term inflation expectations had been steady for decades when inflation began to rise in 2021, and these expectations remained low even as inflation started its climb. Figure 2-24 plots two of the most commonly tracked measures of inflation expectations: the median expected annual price percent change over the next 12 months, and the median expected

---

[17] The Phillips curve used in these calculations builds from Yellen (2015).

Figure 2-23. Change in Core PCE Inflation

Percentage points, annual averages of quarterly annualized rate

	2018–22	2022–23*
Expectations	+0.4	-0.1
Import prices	-0.1	-0.4
Slack	-0.0	+0.0
Slack–supply chain interaction	+0.9	-0.6
Supply chains	+1.6	-0.5
Residual	+0.3	+0.2
Total	**+3.0**	**-1.4**

Council of Economic Advisers
Sources: Yellen (2015); Bureau of Economic Analysis; Congressional Budget Office;
Bureau of Labor Statistics; CEA calculations.
Note: * = First three quarters of 2023 only. PCE = Personal Consumer Expenditures price index.
2024 Economic Report of the President

Figure 2-24. Actual and Expected Inflation, 2012–23

12-month percent change

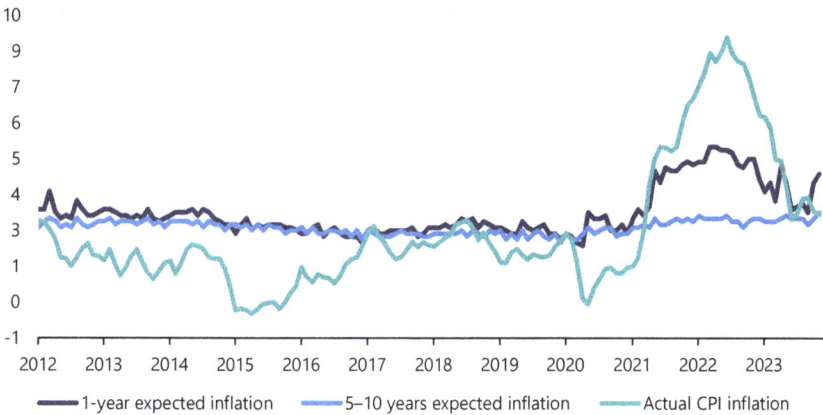

Council of Economic Advisers
Sources: University of Michigan; Bureau of Economic Analysis; CEA calculations.
Note: CPI = Consumer Price Index. Data are monthly. Gray bars indicate recessions.
2024 Economic Report of the President

average annual price percent change over the next 5 to 10 years, from the University of Michigan's monthly survey of households. Both measures peaked during 2022 and declined through the end of 2023. Long-term inflation expectations in particular were reassuringly stable, indicating that although households expected elevated inflation in the short run, they did not expect inflationary conditions to last (box 2-2).

Box 2-2. Consumer Attitudes and Economic Data

Consumer perceptions about the economy, as measured by surveys, can be useful indicators of how the general public experiences macroeconomic developments. Two of the most prominent monthly indices measuring consumer attitudes are "Consumer Confidence," published by the Conference Board, and "Consumer Sentiment," published by the University of Michigan. As figure 2-iii illustrates, these two measures broadly co-move over time. Both plunged when the pandemic hit, and both remain below their respective prepandemic levels.

Figure 2-iii. Indicators of Consumer Attitudes

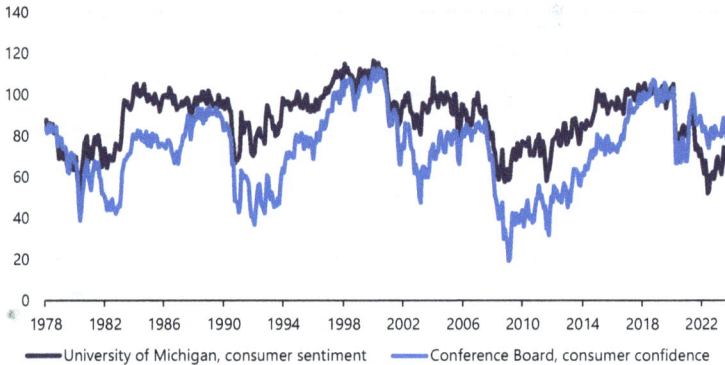

Index: 2019 = 100

Council of Economic Advisers
Sources: University of Michigan; Conference Board; CEA calculations.
Note: Gray bars indicate recessions.
2024 Economic Report of the President

Historically, consumer attitudes have closely tracked a handful of key economic aggregates, especially the unemployment rate, income growth, inflation, the stock market's performance, and housing prices. An ordinary-least-squares regression, estimated from 1978 through mid-2022 and controlling for both population demographics and the spread of COVID-19, suggests that changes in these five measures explained most of the variation in consumer sentiment, even during the extraordinary depths of the pandemic (figure 2-iv). However, since mid-2022—around the time headline inflation peaked on a 12-month basis—a large gap has opened between actual and predicted sentiment.

This gap—already a historic anomaly—is particularly notable since sentiment has often been a leading indicator of economic health; it may either be signaling future weakness unanticipated by other measures, or that the pandemic shifted the relationship between the economy and consumer sentiment. (For example, the Conference Board includes both consumer confidence and consumer sentiment in its composite

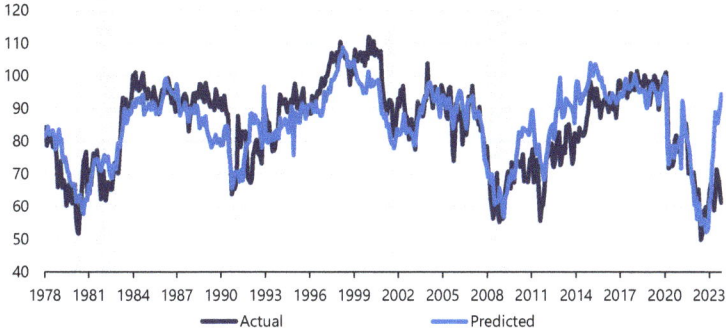

Figure 2-iv. University of Michigan Sentiment, Actual and Predicted

Index: 1966:Q1 = 100

Council of Economic Advisers

Sources: University of Michigan; Bureau of Labor Statistics; Bureau of Economic Analysis; CEA calculations.
Note: Predicted ordinary least squares of University of Michigan microdata are estimates from January 1978 to June 2022 using year-over-year percent change in the Standard & Poor's 500; real disposable personal income per household (split into wage and nonwage); housing prices; Personal Consumption Expenditures price indexes for food, energy, core goods, and core services; and the year-over-year differences in the unemployment rate and log total COVID-19 cases. Estimates also include fixed effects by sex, age, education, birth cohort, Census region, month in survey sample, and calendar month. Data are as of November 2023. Gray bars indicate recessions.
2024 Economic Report of the President

index of leading indicators for the United States; see Conference Board 2024.) This chapter already discusses the possible near-term upside and downside risks to the economy. On the possibility that sui generis factors have altered the link between sentiment and the economy, several hypotheses require further attention.

Price changes (inflation) versus price levels. Consumer attitudes may be sensitive to both high price changes (inflation) and high price levels—products whose prices remain higher than consumers expect, even after prices stop rising. This hypothesis implies that simple models that only include inflation could mechanically overstate the improvement in sentiment attributable to disinflation. That is, after a period of high inflation, consumers may have a lingering distaste for the resulting high level of prices that an inflation-only model would struggle to capture.

A straightforward, though hardly dispositive, test of the price level hypothesis is to allow explicit terms for changes in inflation to enter the regression model asymmetrically, such that declines in inflation affect sentiment differently than rises in inflation. (Simply adding price levels to a regression presents a statistical challenge, because price levels are almost always nonstationary and thus can lead to spurious regression results. The change in the price level, inflation, is already included in the base model.) If this hypothesis were true, one would expect disinflation to affect sentiment positively to a lesser extent than rising inflation affects sentiment negatively, since falling but still-positive inflation implies that the price level remains high. Augmenting the simple regression model with these terms, the CEA finds exactly that: for energy, food, and core

Figure 2-v. University of Michigan Sentiment: Actual, Predicted, and Augmented

Index: 1966:Q1 = 100

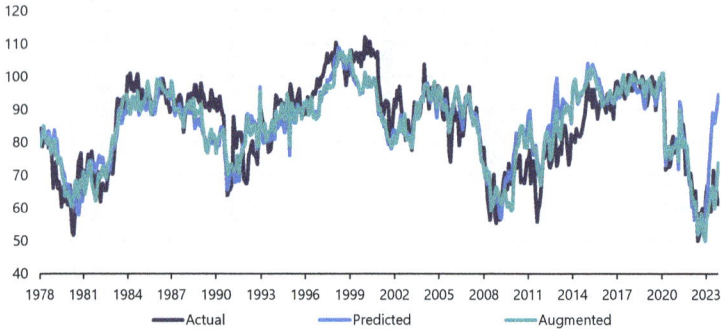

Council of Economic Advisers

Sources: University of Michigan; Bureau of Labor Statistics; Bureau of Economic Analysis; CEA calculations.
Note: Predicted ordinary least squares of University of Michigan microdata are estimates from January 1978 to June 2022 using year-over-year percent change in the Standard & Poor's 500; real disposable personal income per household (split into wage and nonwage); housing prices; Personal Consumption Expenditures price indexes for food, energy, core goods, and core services; and the year-over-year differences in the unemployment rate and log total COVID-19 cases. Estimates also include fixed effects by sex, age, education, birth cohort, Census region, month in survey sample, and calendar month. Augmented model includes change in inflation and an asymmetry term. Data are as of November 2023. Gray bars indicate recessions.
2024 Economic Report of the President

goods, a decline in inflation has less of an initial effect on sentiment than does a rise in inflation of the same magnitude. As figure 2-v shows, the augmented model's in-sample predictions are not substantially different from those of the baseline model, but its out-of-sample predictions for the period since June 2022 are far superior, suggesting that price levels matter for sentiment.

Broader, COVID-19-related shifts. An analysis by the Federal Reserve Bank of Chicago (Herbstman and Brave 2023) finds that relationships between economic variables and sentiment broadly pivoted during the pandemic. This shift was especially true of labor market variables; growth in earnings and employment affected sentiment less positively during the pandemic than before. (Note that one key difference between the Consumer Sentiment and Consumer Confidence estimates is their sensitivity to labor market conditions; see Hirsch 2012. The Conference Board's Consumer Confidence index explicitly incorporates labor market experiences and expectations into its composite, whereas the University of Michigan's Consumer Sentiment index does not use specific labor market questions in its measure.)

One plausible hypothesis is that the pandemic experience, including the government's fiscal responses to the virus's impact on American life, affected sentiment in ways not fully captured by conventional economic metrics. The government provided unusually strong fiscal support to families in 2020 and 2021, when the pandemic's effects were felt the most, and the rise and fall in unemployment during the pandemic was overwhelmingly and unprecedentedly driven by temporarily furloughed workers, many of whom reclaimed their positions when lockdowns ended. Either mechanism might explain why pandemic-era rises in the unemployment rate had less of a negative effect on sentiment than would be expected from prior cycles.

Other factors. Observers have suggested various other candidates to explain the gap between economic indicators and consumer sentiment. For instance, heightened political partisanship, and the evolving tendency for consumers to base their survey responses on political rather than economic factors, may be being factored into the indices at a rate not previously seen (Hartman 2022). Meanwhile, social media has become a far more common source of news, for younger Americans especially, and has been shown to disproportionately elevate negative and often false information—making a gap between reliable indicators and sentiment more plausible (e.g., O'Kane 2023). The shortage of affordable housing, the subject of chapter 4 of this Report, is another potential factor generating negative sentiment, particularly among younger families for which homeownership is often out of reach. And as certain pandemic-era supports have expired, real disposable income has fallen for families who had been beneficiaries of those transfers—a final potential factor behind the large residual.

Financial Markets in 2023

Markets had an eventful 2023, highlighted by at least three consequential developments. First, risk-free interest rates—especially those with long horizons, such as the benchmark 10-year Treasury note—climbed to levels not seen since leading up to the global financial crisis, before reversing most of the increase toward the end of the year. Even with little net change over the year, long-maturity, risk-free rates remained high relative to the past 10 years, a trend that has resulted in higher borrowing costs for businesses, consumers, and the government. Second, and relatedly, the high-profile failure of a few banks affected lenders' willingness to extend credit and exerted upward pressure on the cost of borrowing relative to the risk-free rate of interest, further tightening credit conditions. However, most of these effects were short-lived, due in part to a rapid and effective policy response. Third, the component in interest rates that nets out inflation effects—the real rate of interest—rose markedly in 2023. The real policy rate remained high, though much of the increase in long-maturity real rates reversed toward the end of the year, and rates across maturities remained high relative to the post–financial crisis period. Understanding the drivers of real rate movements is important for assessing the durability of recent economic trends.

Figure 2-25. Selected Nominal U.S. Interest Rates

Percent

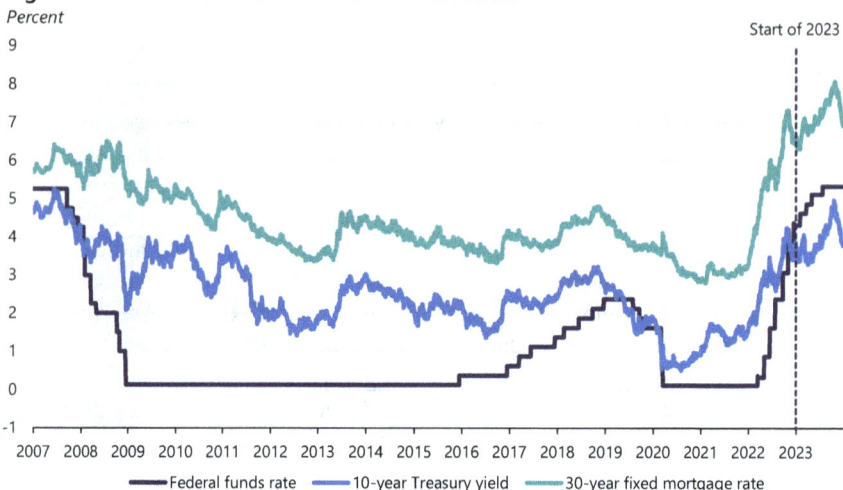

Council of Economic Advisers

Sources: Federal Reserve Board; Bloomberg.
Note: The 30-year fixed mortgage rate is the average U.S. 30-year fixed mortgage products rate from Bankrate.com via Bloomberg.
Federal funds rate corresponds to the midpoint of the federal funds target rate range. Gray bars indicate recessions.
2024 Economic Report of the President

The Rise in Long-Term Rates

Key interest rates—including the federal funds rate, the 10-year Treasury rate, and the 30-year fixed mortgage rate—all rose during most of 2023. After peaking in October, long-maturity rates declined, reversing much of the earlier rise; but the policy rate remained at its highest level since 2001 (figure 2-25). Long-maturity yields were atypically low in the sustained period of zero-rate monetary policy from the end of 2008 through the end of 2015, and then again from 2020 to 2022. The 10-year yield was below 2.2 percent when policy tightening began in March 2022; since then, the overnight policy rate has risen over 5 percentage points, and long-maturity Treasury yields have risen as high as 5 percent on an intraday basis—the largest policy rate increase and the largest 10-year Treasury yield increase per tightening cycle since the 1980s. By the end of the year, the 10-year Treasury yield had fallen below 4 percent, while the overnight federal funds target rate remained above 5 percent, with a cumulative 1-percentage-point increase during 2023.

As a benchmark for riskier rates, long-maturity Treasury yields are the basis for rates that are important for businesses and consumers, such as corporate bond yields and the 30-year fixed mortgage rate. The national average 30-year fixed rate for conforming mortgage loans rose more than the 10-year

Figure 2-26. Outstanding Loan Amounts Relative to GDP

Percent

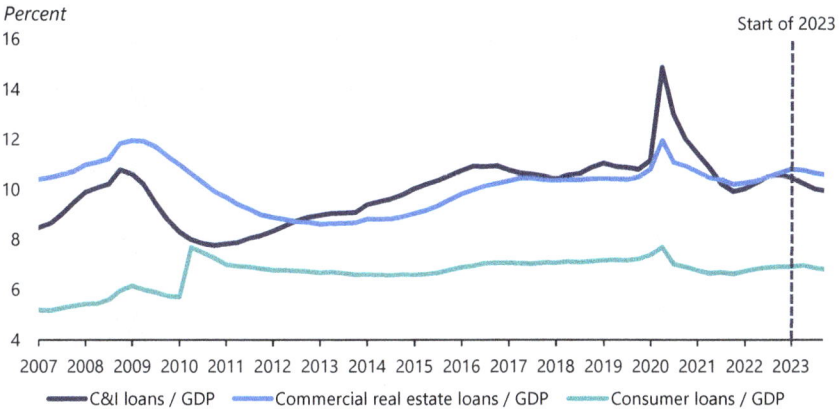

Council of Economic Advisers

Source: Federal Reserve Board; Bureau of Economic Analysis; CEA calculations.
Note: C&I = commercial and industrial; GDP = gross domestic product. Loan amounts are for all commercial banks from the Federal Reserve's H.8 release. Gray bars indicate recessions.
2024 Economic Report of the President

Treasury yield,[18] as illustrated by the teal line in figure 2-25, peaking above 8 percent, before falling to about 7 percent at the end of 2023. Meanwhile, the quantity of outstanding commercial loans declined relative to the rate of GDP growth (figure 2-26). While banks tightened standards for loans to businesses and households early in 2023, the decline in borrowing was also partly driven by lower demand in a higher-rate environment (figure 2-27).

The effect of a higher-rate environment on asset prices can have large implications for the broader economy. A sharp rise in rates produces steep unrealized (or "mark-to-market") losses for fixed-rate security holders. From March 16, 2022—when the Federal Reserve began to hike its policy rate—until March 8, 2023, the 10-year Treasury yield rose nearly 2 percentage points. As higher rates on newly issued securities drove down the price of extant securities with lower fixed rates, the holders of securities with lower fixed rates, including banks, experienced large mark-to-market losses, as illustrated in figure 2-28. For example, consider a bank with 10-year Treasury holdings originally worth $50 billion, purchased in March 2022, when the 10-year rate was 2 percent. By March 2023, the value of the bank's Treasury securities would have fallen by about $8 billion. These dynamics tipped various banks, including Silicon Valley Bank and Signature Bank, into insolvency.

One of the main channels through which banking stress reaches the real economy is constrained credit. Credit conditions initially tightened and

---

[18] Conforming mortgage loans are insurable by the Federal housing agencies. In order to "conform," a loan must meet the quality terms and conditions (e.g., a minimum credit score for a borrower and a maximum amount borrowed) set forth by the U.S. Federal Housing Finance Authority.

Figure 2-27. Credit Conditions for Business Loans

Net percentage of domestic banks

Start of 2023

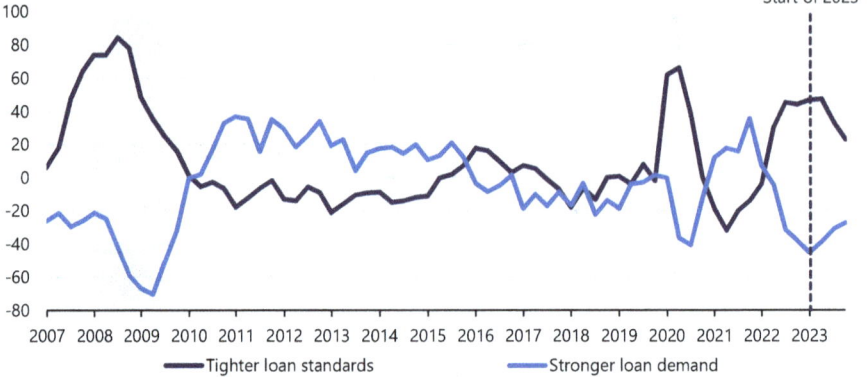

— Tighter loan standards   — Stronger loan demand

Council of Economic Advisers

Source: Federal Reserve Board.
Note: This figure shows the net percentage of domestic banks that are tightening standards for or are increasing demand for business loans, weighted by banks' outstanding loan balances from the Federal Reserve's Senior Loan Officer Opinion Survey on Bank Lending Practices. Gray bars indicate recessions.
2024 Economic Report of the President

Figure 2-28. Bond Returns and Unrealized Gains/Losses

Billions of dollars

Start of 2023   *Percent*

▓ Losses on held-to-maturity securities (left axis)   ▓ Losses on available-for-sale assets (left axis)
—◆— S&P U.S. bond index returns (right axis)

Council of Economic Advisers

Sources: Federal Deposit Insurance Corporation (FDIC); Standard & Poor's (S&P).
Note: Unrealized losses are from the FDIC 2023:Q3 quarterly banking profile, table 7. Data are quarterly.
2024 Economic Report of the President

asset volatility rose as bank shares—shown in blue in figure 2-29, panel A—sharply underperformed the broader market. Amid the bank failures, the 10-year Treasury yield fell by more than half a percentage point as investors fled to safety, and the MOVE index (the Merrill Lynch Option Volatility Estimate index), a popular measure of expected future Treasury market volatility, spiked to its highest point since the pandemic-induced financial market turmoil in March 2020. The navy line in figure 2-29, panel A,

Figure 2-29. Treasury Volatility and Market Conditions

A. MOVE Treasury Volatility Index and Bank Subindex

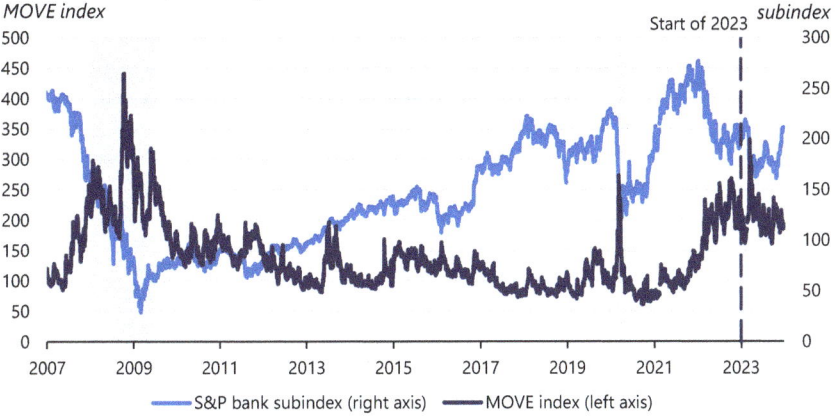

A. MOVE Treasury Volatility Index and Bank Subindex

MOVE index / Bank subindex / Start of 2023

S&P bank subindex (right axis) — MOVE index (left axis)

B. Market Credit Conditions

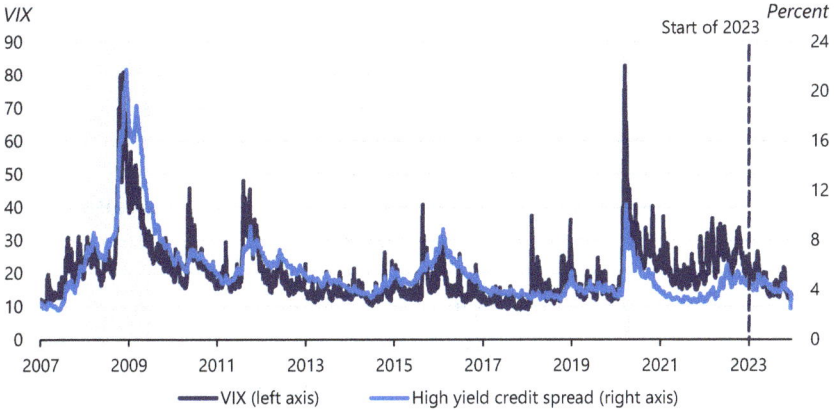

VIX / Percent / Start of 2023

VIX (left axis) — High yield credit spread (right axis)

Council of Economic Advisers
Sources: Bank of America; Bloomberg.
Note: The MOVE index is published by the Intercontinental Exchange. The index measures the implied yield volatility of a basket of one-month options on 2-year, 5-year, 10-year, and 30-year Treasury securities. The bank share price subindex is for the level 2 banks industry group of the Standard and Poor's (S&P) 500 index. The VIX is published by the Chicago Board of Options Exchange. The index measures the implied volatility of a basket of one-month options on the S&P 500 equity market price index. Gray bars indicate recessions.
2024 Economic Report of the President

illustrates the strong negative relationship between the measure of Treasury yield volatility and bank share prices, underscoring the importance of interest rate movements for the health of banks' balance sheets. The Federal Reserve rapidly introduced a new lending facility in 2023—the Bank Term Funding Program—which is aimed at alleviating pressure for banks to sell high-quality, fixed-income securities at a loss, and the Federal Deposit Insurance Corporation, the Federal Reserve, and Treasury—in consultation with the President—stepped in with a comprehensive guarantee for customers' deposits in Silicon Valley Bank and Signature Bank, an action that

Figure 2-30. Nominal and TIPS Treasury Yield Curves

Percent

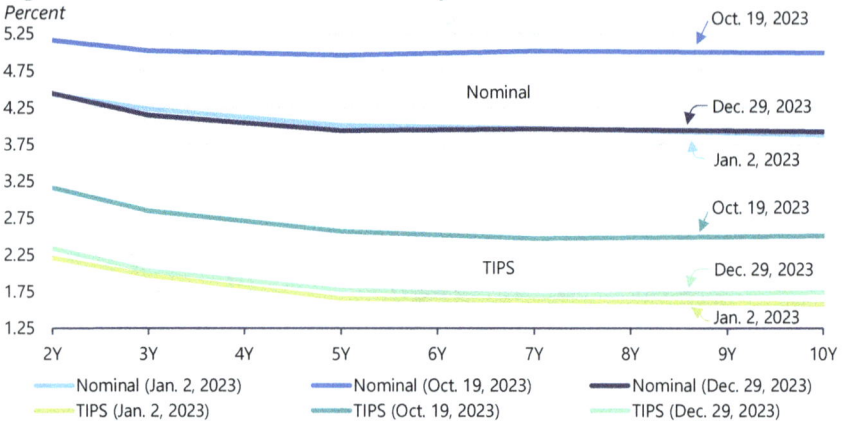

Council of Economic Advisers
Source: Bloomberg.
Note: TIPS = Treasury Inflation-Protected Securities. The figure shows real and nominal yield curves and their changes over the year.
2024 Economic Report of the President

stemmed financial contagion. By the year's end, the tightening started to reverse course. Credit spreads narrowed, and, as shown by the VIX, implied volatility on equities declined (figure 2-29, panel B), which was also consistent with persistently robust data on economic activity.

Real Rates as the Driver of Higher Long-Term Rates

Long-maturity real yields, as proxied by Treasury Inflation-Protected Securities (TIPS), rose and then declined, roughly in tandem with nominal Treasury yields during 2023 (figure 2-30), indicating that inflation expectations likely changed little and that most of the nominal yield change was attributable to the real component in rates.[19]

The causes behind changes in real rates are often uncertain, and 2023 proved to be no exception—with particular uncertainty about why rates rose so sharply but then declined. Figure 2-31 illustrates real term rates as a component of nominal rates. Suggested explanations for the initial, sharp increase in real rates include tighter monetary policy; a higher expected neutral real rate (the theoretical interest rate that neither stimulates nor slows the economy); and the difference in return demanded by investors to hold long-maturity securities relative to short-maturity ones, also referred

---

[19] Strictly speaking, the nominal minus TIPS yield spread only measures the inflation compensation to investors, which is also affected by differential liquidity of TIPS relative to nominal securities and the risk premium that investors may price for inflation, and so is not a direct measure of inflation expectations. Estimates of these effects from the model of D'Amico, Kim, and Wei (2018) show that break-even rates underestimated expected inflation by about 10 basis points, on average, during 2023.

Figure 2-31. Components of Nominal Rates

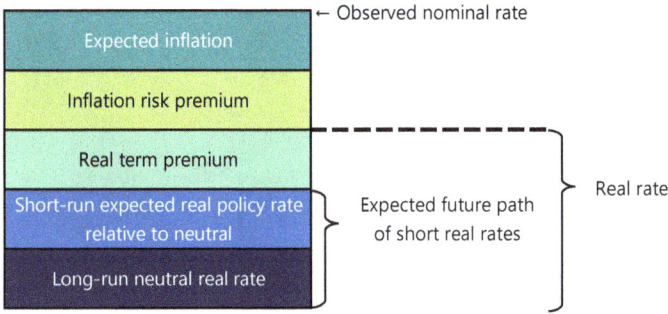

Council of Economic Advisers
Source: CEA analysis.
2024 Economic Report of the President

to as the "term premium." However, these factors fail to fully explain why long-maturity, risk-free real rate increases largely reversed in the latter part of the year, making it difficult to forecast how these rates will evolve in the future. Identifying the drivers of rate movements is difficult because concepts such as the neutral rate and term premia are not directly observable in asset prices. Surveys and term structure models can be used to estimate the various components that constitute nominal and real interest rates (Kim and Wright 2005; D'Amico, Kim, and Wei 2018).

A Higher Expected Path for the Real Policy Rate

As the Federal Reserve increased its target rate in 2022 and 2023, estimates of the expected path of near-term policy unsurprisingly shifted from below neutral—stimulative—to above neutral—restrictive. As the nominal policy rate rose to its highest level since 2001, the estimated real policy rate reached its highest level since the global financial crisis and also became restrictive for the first time in the postcrisis period.

Expectations for increasingly tight monetary policy over most of 2023 (figure 2-32, panel A) resulted in part from a series of economic data releases that showed marked labor market resilience and buoyant consumption, which surprised forecasters throughout the year. Figure 2-32, panel B, shows the total and average changes in the 10-year Treasury yield, clustered around major data releases: nonfarm payrolls, unemployment insurance claims, consumer confidence, and core CPI inflation. It incorporates both positive and negative changes in the 10-year yield, and it filters out days of Federal Open Market Committee meetings or other major nondata events with a market impact. Jobless claims, which are released weekly, showed the largest cumulative contribution to rising 10-year Treasury yields in 2023—the dark green bar in the figure—while the monthly inflation data

Figure 2-32. Federal Funds Rate and Federal Funds Futures Rates

A. Realized Policy Rate and Shift in Expected Policy Rate

Percent

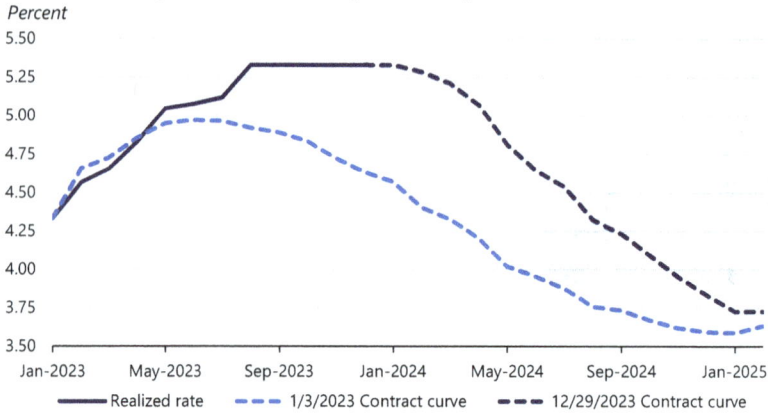

Realized rate — — — 1/3/2023 Contract curve — — — 12/29/2023 Contract curve

B. Change in the 10-Year Yield Around Data Release Surprises

Basis points   *Basis points*

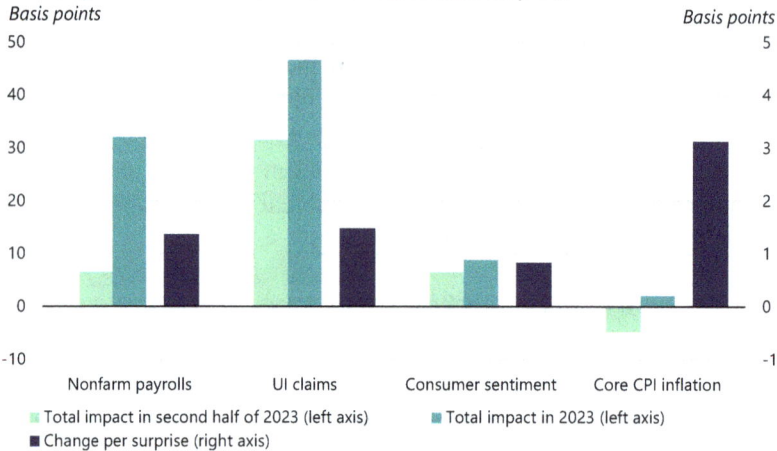

■ Total impact in second half of 2023 (left axis)   ■ Total impact in 2023 (left axis)
■ Change per surprise (right axis)

Council of Economic Advisers

Sources: Bloomberg; CEA calculations.
Note: UI = unemployment insurance; CPI = Consumer Price Index. In panel A, expectations are derived from federal funds futures contracts as of 12/29/2023 and 1/3/2023. Realized rates are monthly averages of the daily federal funds effective rate. In panel B, data release surprises are classified as any time the data differ from expectations. Change per surprise is a predicted value, measured in standard deviations from the median of surveyed expectations.
2024 Economic Report of the President

demonstrated the largest impact per surprise.[20] The difference between the light and dark green bars gives the impact over the first half of the year alone. The estimates show that the unexpected part of payroll releases had

---

[20] The estimates given here are from an event study regression of the change in 10-year Treasury yields in a 1-day window, as given in economic data releases on the surprise component of the news. The 1-day window starts with the closing price on the date before the announcement and ends with the closing price on the announcement date. The surprise component is the difference between the realized outcome and the median Bloomberg survey expectation, scaled by the standard deviation of submitted survey expectations.

a disproportionate impact on rising yields during the first half of the year, whereas jobless claims contributed relatively more in the latter half of 2023, even with the sharp drop in yields toward the end of the year.

In mid-December 2023, the Federal Open Market Committee released a statement and forecast on markets that was widely interpreted as signaling that, barring any data surprises, policy tightening had peaked and the next move would be a policy rate cut (Federal Reserve 2023a; Federal Reserve, Federal Open Market Committee 2023). Figure 2-32, panel A, provides a snapshot of the market-implied, expected short-run path of the federal funds rate, showing the upward trajectory of the target policy rate during 2023 (solid navy line in the figure) and the expected path of the target rate as captured at the end of the year (dashed navy line). Despite the end-of-year shift to expected easing, the anticipated path of the policy rate remained higher than it had been at the start of 2023 (dashed blue line).

The Term Premium

The rising Treasury term premium further drove term rates higher during 2023. Conceptually, the real term premium is the component of the long-maturity, risk-free real rate that is not explained by the expected future path of short-maturity real rates (figure 2-31). The 10-year Treasury term premium was largely negative from 2019 to 2021, according to most estimates, before rising to be occasionally positive amid the growing interest rate environment, a pattern that persisted during 2023.

Several types of risks could have supported the term premium in 2023. As interest rates rise, bond prices fall, though the relationship is not one-for-one. The pricing of duration risk recognizes that the longer the maturity of the bond (all else remaining equal), the larger the price decline per percentage-point increase in the interest rate. The risk of capital loss for an investor needing to sell a bond before maturity motivates them to demand a higher term premium. A possible contributor to a higher real term premium is greater near-term uncertainty about medium- to long-maturity real rates, which could stem from investor uncertainty about the Federal Reserve's future policy rate. Heightened expected rate volatility, as policy expectations rapidly shift, could amplify the pricing of duration risk in bond term premia. The MOVE index—as noted above, a measure of expected future Treasury rate volatility (figure 2-29, panel A)—rose along with rates across maturities and term premium estimates starting in late 2021. In March 2023, the MOVE index temporarily spiked to its highest level since the peak of the financial crisis in 2008 amid interest rate risk-related banking stresses. The index ended the year within the range it has been since 2021, which is still relatively high compared with the post–financial crisis period.

Potential Risks for the Outlook

Before long-maturity, real risk-free rates later declined—particularly compared with the negative real rates for the 2 years before the start of policy tightening—the dramatic shift to a real risk-free return above 2 percent produced some expected outcomes and posed some challenges and potential risks. Structural changes in markets and the economy may have changed the ways that firms and individuals respond to higher rates since the United States was last in a similar rate environment, about 15 years ago. Additionally, the speed at which organizations can now adjust to shocks adds an additional degree of uncertainty to the outlook.

Figure 2-33. U.S. Debt by Type and Holder

A. U.S. Debt Shares Outstanding Net of Federal Reserve Holdings
Percent of total debt

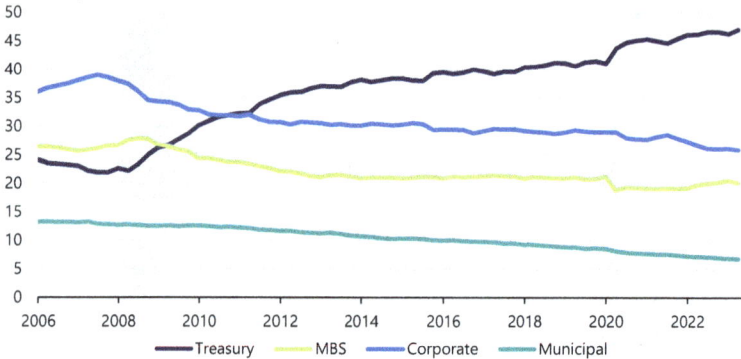

Treasury — MBS — Corporate — Municipal

B. Domestic Holders of Treasury and Corporate Debt as of 2023:Q3
Billions of dollars

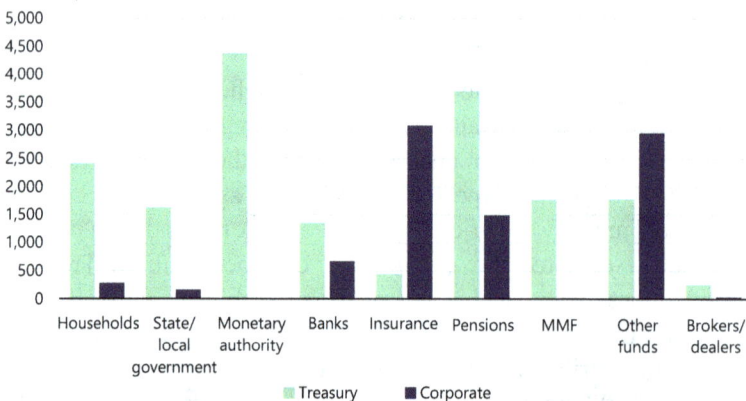

Treasury — Corporate

Council of Economic Advisers

Source: Federal Reserve Board.
Note: MBS = mortgage-backed securities. MMF = money market fund. Data are from the Federal Reserve's financial accounts. Only large categories of U.S. holders are shown. The "other funds" category includes mutual funds, closed-end funds and exchange-traded funds. Household category includes non-profit holdings. Corporate bond holdings include foreign bonds. Gray bars indicate recessions.
2024 Economic Report of the President

Treasury debt has constituted the largest portion of U.S.-issued debt since overtaking corporate debt in 2011, as illustrated in figure 2-33, panel A. Pension funds, other investment funds, and insurers are among the top holders of the two largest debt categories: Treasury and corporate securities, as illustrated in figure 2-33, panel B. Depending on the structure of the fund, the possibility of losses or rapid investor redemptions could subject some of these entities to a quickly changing risk profile. Those with relatively short-maturity holdings, such as money market funds holding primarily Treasury bills, will be less exposed as the prices of longer-duration securities are more sensitive to changes in interest rates. Although banks are not the top holders of Treasury securities, concentrated holdings could still pose risks, especially for less-diversified financial institutions such as small and regional banks.

Higher real interest rates increase the risk of adverse events for leveraged entities, whether public or private. According to the most recent data filed with the Securities and Exchange Commission, hedge funds' holdings of debt securities reached a historic high, constituting more than one-third of their total assets (Federal Reserve 2023b). Mark-to-market losses are not realized losses, but market volatility or an interruption of income could force asset liquidations at a loss that spirals into a credit event. The banking stresses of this past March served as a reminder of these risks—and the importance of vigilance in periods of transition.

Higher real rates also increase the risk of adverse movements in future stock prices, as share valuations adjust to higher competing real returns. When real risk-free rates are negative, investors can earn a positive real return only by investing in riskier assets than Treasury debt, such as stocks. Over the past 10 years, the average real risk-free rate has been about 0.3 percent, providing a low hurdle rate for equities. By the end of 2023, the real risk-free rate was above 1.5 percent (figure 2-34, panel B), substantially increasing the minimum real return that investors would require from riskier assets.

The Standard & Poor's (S&P) 500 equity index rose about 25 percent in 2023 (figure 2-34, panel A), and the average price-to-earnings ratio per share for S&P 500 companies rose slightly more. Price gains were therefore attributable to higher share valuations rather than improved earnings, on average. The inverse of the price-to-earnings ratio, the earnings-to-price ratio, is a common proxy for the expected equity return. The intuition is that earnings will either be paid out to the investor in dividends or will be reinvested to boost future growth (Campbell and Shiller 2001). The return that remains after subtracting the real risk-free rate is called the equity risk premium. The average equity risk premium for the S&P 500 index, using the 10-year TIPS yield as a proxy for the real rate, ended the year at about 2.65 percent, far below its 10-year average, much of which was attributable to the

Figure 2-34. Equity Risk Premium

A. Equity Risk Premium and the S&P 500 Index

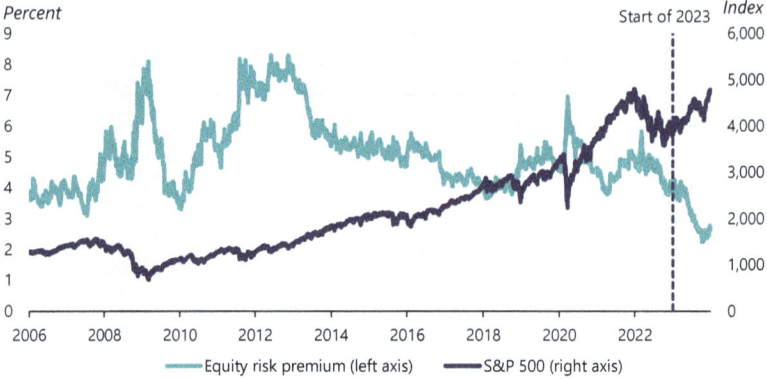

Percent / Index / Start of 2023

Legend: — Equity risk premium (left axis) — S&P 500 (right axis)

B. Equity Risk Premium and 10-Year TIPS Yield

Percent / Percent / Start of 2023

Legend: — Equity risk premium (left axis) — 10-year TIPS yield (right axis)

Council of Economic Advisers
Source: Bloomberg.
Note: S&P = Standard & Poor's; TIPS = Treasury Inflation-Protected Securities. Equity risk premium is a measure of the average equity yield minus the real risk-free rate. Gray bars indicate recessions.
2024 Economic Report of the President

sharp rise in the real rate, as shown in figure 2-34, panel B. The figure also illustrates how, in 2023, the estimated equity risk premium fell below its level from just before the 2008 financial crisis. A sharp correction in equity valuation, implying a higher earnings-to-price ratio, could dent consumption and potentially destabilize markets. However, a more modest and gradual decrease could bring the equity risk premium back in line with historic values relatively seamlessly.

Higher rates naturally raise the Treasury's debt-servicing costs for new issuances, regardless of the component in yields that is responsible for the increase. However, the implications of higher rates for future debt and GDP, which can make higher debt-servicing costs more or less sustainable, depends on the primary drivers of rising rates. For example, an expected rise in the neutral real rate—perhaps prompted by faster trend productivity growth—could reflect factors that would also boost GDP, and thus potentially moderate the debt-to-GDP ratio, all else remaining equal. However, a higher term premium—which weighs on investments without any expected offsetting productivity gain—is an unambiguous net drag on economic activity.

The Forecast for the Years Ahead

The Biden-Harris Administration finalized the latest version of its official economic forecast on November 9, 2023, with data available through November 3. The forecast provides the Administration's projections of key economic variables over the next 11 years, from 2024 to 2034, as illustrated in table 2-2. Because more 2023 data have become available during the interval between when this forecast was finalized and the publication of this *Report*, the official forecast discussed in this chapter may differ from current estimates for 2023. Indeed, since the forecast was finalized, inflation has fallen slightly more than expected and interest rates have declined, while employment and economic activity have remained robust—suggesting that, if the forecast were finalized today, it would likely show lower interest rates, with continued progress on inflation, growth, and employment. This overall forecast is a critical input to the President's Fiscal Year 2025 Budget,

Table 2-2. Economic Projections, 2022–34

Year	Percent Change (Q4-to-Q4)			Level (percent)			
		Inflation Measures		Unemployment Rate		Interest Rates	
	Real GDP	GDP Price Index	CPI	Annual	Q4	3-Month T-Bills	10-Year T-Notes
Actual							
2022	0.7	6.4	7.1	3.6	3.6	2.0	3.0
2023	3.1	2.6	3.2	3.6	3.8	5.1	4.0
Forecast							
2023	2.6	3.0	3.4	3.6	3.8	5.1	4.1
2024	1.3	2.3	2.5	4.0	4.1	5.1	4.4
2025	2.0	2.1	2.3	4.0	4.0	4.0	4.0
2026	2.0	2.1	2.3	3.9	3.9	3.3	3.9
2027	2.0	2.1	2.3	3.9	3.8	3.1	3.8
2028	2.0	2.1	2.3	3.8	3.8	2.9	3.8
2029	2.1	2.1	2.3	3.8	3.8	2.8	3.7
2030	2.2	2.1	2.3	3.8	3.8	2.8	3.7
2031	2.2	2.1	2.3	3.8	3.8	2.7	3.7
2032	2.2	2.1	2.3	3.8	3.8	2.7	3.7
2033	2.2	2.1	2.3	3.8	3.8	2.7	3.7
2034	2.2	2.1	2.3	3.8	3.8	2.7	3.7

Council of Economic Advisers

Sources: Bureau of Economic Analysis, Bureau of Labor Statistics; Department of the Treasury; Office of Management and Budget; CEA calculations.

Note: The forecast is based on data available as of November 3, 2023; actual data for 2023 arrived later. The interest rate on 3-month (91-day) Treasury bills is measured on a secondary-market discount basis.

2024 Economic Report of the President

informing many Federal agencies' budget projections and forecasted tax revenues.

All economic forecasts are subject to considerable uncertainties that affect the range of potential outcomes. As the forecast was finalized, prominent sources of uncertainty included supply chain disruptions, progress on disinflation, rising interest rates, and geopolitical issues that risked spillover effects on the global trade of essential commodities. In a change from recent years' forecasts, the COVID-19 pandemic is no longer expected to be a major impediment to economic growth. Vaccinations, increasing immunity, and new treatments have combined to stabilize fatalities, which averaged 206 per day during 2023, down from daily averages of 1,255 and 670 during 2021 and 2022, respectively (CDC n.d.).

In the first full forecast year, 2024, real GDP is expected to grow at 1.3 percent, lower than the potential rate, as interest rates remain high and inflation recedes. Starting in 2025, the President's policies on infrastructure, care, human capital, and immigration reform are expected to increase the growth rate of both potential and actual GDP. During the budget window's final five years, beginning in 2030, the forecast accounts for the decreasing downward pull on the labor force participation rate stemming from the baby boom generation's retirements. Because of the boost from the President's policies, together with the diminishing downward demographic pull, potential GDP growth is expected to be stronger relative to the period 2006–23.

The inverse relationship between the change in the unemployment rate and the growth rate is known as Okun's Law.[21] Figure 2-35 shows the four-quarter change in the unemployment rate against the five-quarter change in real output. This relationship accounts for 83 percent of the variance in the unemployment rate from 2006 through 2022.[22] The rate of real potential output growth is estimated as the rate of real GDP growth consistent with a stable unemployment rate—represented where the regression line crosses the x axis, at 1.73 percent, with a standard deviation of ±0.2 percentage point.

The consensus view of potential real GDP growth during the next 11 years is similar to this backward-looking, Okun's Law–based estimate (figure 2-35). Expected year over year growth averages 1.8 percent in the Blue Chip panel's latest survey of private professional forecasters' long-term expectations in October 2023. The Administration's forecasted pace for

---

[21] Former CEA Chairman Arthur Okun proposed what came to be known as Okun's Law in 1962 (Okun 1962). When GDP grows faster than its potential rate, the unemployment rate falls, and when real output grows more slowly than its potential rate, the unemployment rate rises. In its simple first-difference specification, Okun's Law takes the form $\Delta UR = \beta(y^* - y)$, where ΔUR is the change in the unemployment rate, and y^* and y are the rates of potential real GDP growth and of actual real GDP growth, respectively. β and y^* are estimated coefficients, where β should be between 0 and 1, and y^* is the estimated rate of potential real GDP growth.

[22] Complete data for 2023 were not available when this *Report* went to press.

Figure 2-35. Estimation of Potential Output Growth by Okun's Law, 2006–22

Four-quarter change in the unemployment rate (percentage points)

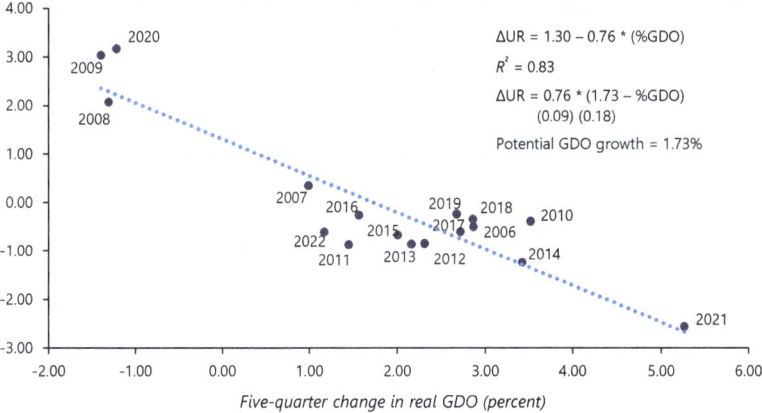

$\Delta UR = 1.30 - 0.76 * (\%GDO)$

$R^2 = 0.83$

$\Delta UR = 0.76 * (1.73 - \%GDO)$
(0.09) (0.18)

Potential GDO growth = 1.73%

Five-quarter change in real GDO (percent)

Council of Economic Advisers

Sources: Bureau of Labor Statistics; Bureau of Economic Analysis; CEA calculations.
Note: GDP = gross domestic product; GDI = gross domestic income; GDO = gross domestic output. GDO is the average of GDP and GDI. The x axis plots five-quarter average growth of GDO through Q4 of each year, with Q4 of year *t* and Q4 of year *t*-1 each receiving 1/8 weights while Q1, Q2, and Q3 receive 1/4 weights.
2024 Economic Report of the President

long-term real GDP growth exceeds the consensus pace, largely because, as is common practice in Administration forecasts, it anticipates the effects of growth-inducing policies in the budget that have not yet been enacted, and possibly because the Blue Chip forecast does not anticipate the diminishing downward pull of baby boomers' retirements.

The Near Term

The Biden-Harris Administration expects lower-than-potential output in 2024, reflecting ongoing fiscal consolidation and the legacy of tight monetary policy. Real GDP growth during the four quarters of 2024 is expected to be 1.3 percent, slightly slower than the 1.7 percent potential estimate extrapolated from Okun's Law, and the unemployment rate is expected to edge up to 4.1 percent by Q4. Compared with the October 2023 Blue Chip consensus forecast (the latest available when the Administration finalized its forecast) of 0.9 percent real GDP growth, and a 4.3 percent consensus unemployment rate by the year end, the Administration's forecast was slightly optimistic. In comparison, however, with the February 2024 Blue Chip forecast, the latest as this *Report* goes to press, in which real GDP was revised up and the unemployment rate was revised down, the Administration's forecast is closer to the latest consensus.

CPI inflation is projected to fall further, from an expected 3.4 percent during the four quarters of 2023 to 2.5 percent during 2024. CPI inflation tends to run higher than PCE inflation; thus, a 2.5 percent CPI inflation rate is roughly consistent with a 2.2 percent PCE inflation rate. Inflation, as measured by the price index for GDP, meanwhile, is expected to fall from a forecasted 3.0 percent rate during 2023 to 2.3 percent during 2024.

As inflation descends back to the target, the unemployment rate drifts up slightly, reaching a peak of 4.1 percent in 2024:Q4. The unemployment rate is then expected to edge lower, eventually falling—by 2027:Q4—to 3.8 percent, the rate that the Administration considers to be consistent with stable inflation in the long term.

Yields on 10-year Treasury notes rose about 1 percentage point from May 2023—when the previous (Mid-Session Review) Administration forecast was finalized—to early November 2023, when the fall forecast was finalized—even though, as discussed above, long-term rates retraced much of that increase by the end of 2023. The Administration has therefore substantially increased its near-term (2024) forecast of two interest rates—those for the 91-day Treasury bill (T-bill) and for the 10-year Treasury note. These interest rates are expected to average 5.1 and 4.4 percent, respectively, in 2024, representing a decline from their October 2023 levels, a bit less of a decline than that projected by the Blue Chip consensus panel in October. The implicit forecast from the October futures market was similar to the Administration's forecast of T-bill rates in 2024, but the futures market implicitly forecasted higher yields on 10-year Treasury notes. The Administration expects these interest rates to slowly decline over the first five forecast years, eventually plateauing at 2.7 percent for the T-bill and 3.7 percent for the 10-year Treasury note, rates that are slightly higher than the Blue Chip consensus of 2.6 percent and 3.5 percent, respectively, but are substantially lower than what was reflected in October 2023 values from market futures.

Although the Administration has substantially increased its forecast of output growth in 2023 relative to the Mid-Session Review, the effect on real GDP is partly offset by downward revisions to expected growth in 2024 and 2025. After adjusting for the September 2023 benchmark revision to the National Income and Product Accounts, the level of real GDP has been upwardly revised (relative to the Mid-Session Review) by about 1 percent from 2025 and thereafter.[23]

The Long Term

In contrast to the near-term outlook, the Biden-Harris Administration's long-term forecast for real GDP growth exceeds the Blue Chip consensus forecast by an average of 0.3 percentage point a year during the 10 years between 2025 and 2034. As is the common practice in the Administration's forecasts, the forecast assumes that the President's proposed economic

---

[23] Because the benchmark adjustment to real GDP has affected levels and growth rates since 2012, the calculations here cumulate growth rates only since 2022:Q4.

Figure 2-36. The Evolution of the U.S. Population's Age Composition

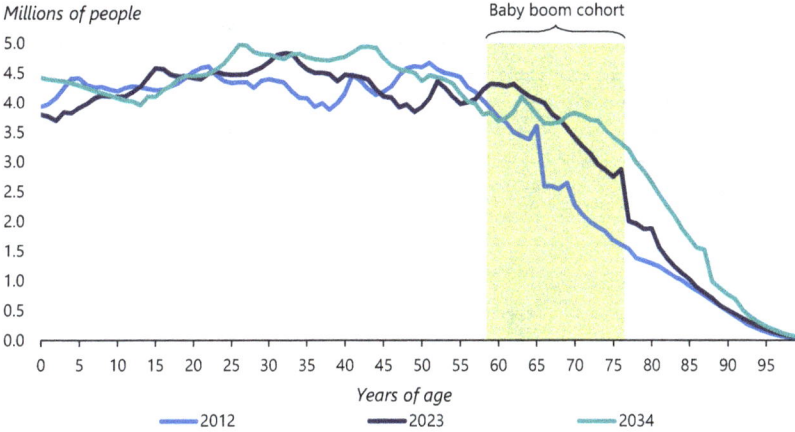

Council of Economic Advisers
Source: Social Security Administration.
Note: The U.S. Social Security population differs slightly from the U.S. civilian noninstitutional population.
2024 Economic Report of the President

policies—including a range of programs to enhance human capital formation, provide childcare, and reform immigration policy—will be enacted, modestly boosting the average annual rate of potential real GDP growth during the period 2030–34.

Demographics affect the long-term forecast in several ways (figure 2-36). The Administration recognizes that the baby boom cohort's retirements are likely to wane during the last seven years of the budget window (2028–34), easing the downward pressure on labor force participation. This pressure began in 2008, when the oldest baby boomers (those born in 1946) first reached the Social Security early retirement age of 62, and this downward pressure for continued declines in the participation rate will have been almost halved by 2028, when the youngest members of the cohort turn 66. During the past five years, this demographic force has lowered the growth of the labor force participation rate and potential real GDP growth by about 0.4 percentage point a year; but during the period 2029–34, the downward force is expected to lessen to only about 0.2 percentage point a year—an improvement of 0.2 percentage point (chapter 3 provides an in-depth analysis of these demographic trends).

The supply-side components of long-run growth are shown in table 2-3, over both history and forecast.[24] The civilian, noninstitutional population age 16 years and above is expected to grow by an average annual rate

_____

[24] Because many components of these growth rates are erratic in the short run, table 2-3 documents historical growth rates for long intervals from business-cycle peak to business-cycle peak. The exception is column 5, the interval between the last business-cycle peak, for 2019:Q4 through 2023:Q3 (the last available quarter when this forecast was finalized).

Table 2-3. Supply-Side Components of Actual and Potential Real Output Growth, 1953–2034

Component	Growth Rate (percentage points)					
	1953:Q2 to 2019:Q4	1990:Q3 to 2001:Q1	2001:Q1 to 2007:Q4	2007:Q4 to 2019:Q4	2019:Q4 to 2023:Q3	2023:Q3 to 2034:Q4
	(1)	(2)	(3)	(4)	(5)	(6)
1 Civilian noninstitutional population, age 16+	1.4	1.2	1.1	1.0	0.6	0.7
2 Labor force participation rate	0.1	0.1	−0.3	−0.3	−0.2	−0.1
3 Employed share of the labor force	0.0	0.1	0.1	0.1	0.0	0.0
4 Average weekly hours (nonfarm business)	−0.2	0.0	−0.2	−0.1	−0.2	0.0
5 Output per hour (productivity, nonfarm business)	2.1	2.4	2.4	1.5	1.3	1.7
6 Output per worker differential: GDO vs. nonfarm	−0.3	−0.3	−0.6	−0.4	0.4	−0.2
7 Sum: Actual real GDO	3.0	3.5	2.4	1.8	1.8	2.0

Council of Economic Advisers
Sources: Bureau of Labor Statistics; Bureau of Economic Analysis; Department of the Treasury; Office of Management and Budget; CEA calculations.
Note: GDP = gross domestic product. Gross domestic output (GDO) is the average of GDP and gross domestic income. Real GDO and real nonfarm business output are measured as the average of income- and product-side measures. The output-per-worker differential (row 6) is the difference between output-per-worker growth in the economy as a whole (GDO divided by household employment), and output-per-worker growth in the nonfarm business sector. All contributions are in percentage points at an annual rate. The forecast jumps off from data available on November 3, 2023. The total may not add up due to rounding. The periods 1953:Q2, 1990:Q3, 2001:Q1, 2007:Q4, and 2019:Q4 are all quarterly business-cycle peaks. Population, labor force, and household employment have been adjusted for discontinuities in the population series.
2024 Economic Report of the President

of 0.7 percent from 2023 to 2034, which is below the average 1.0 percent annual growth rate from 2007 to 2019.[25] Much of this expected growth is likely to result from immigration.[26]

The demographic factors weighing on the labor force participation rate's continued decline will be largely offset over the projection period by the Administration's human capital and childcare policy proposals. The workweek is, meanwhile, projected to stabilize after a long period of decline driven by the entry of women into the workforce and the declining share of manufacturing in total employment. These factors are less likely to dominate the path of the workweek than in past years.

The employed share of the labor force is projected to remain close to its current level, and therefore makes no net contribution over the forecast horizon. Productivity growth (measured as output per hour) is projected to grow at an average 1.7 percent a year over the 11-year forecast interval, somewhat more slowly than its 2.1 percent long-term average but faster than the 1.5 percent growth rate during the 2007–19 business cycle. Finally, the output per worker differential—the difference between the output per person for the economy as a whole and the output per person in the nonfarm business sector—is expected to be negative, which largely is a consequence of the national income accounting convention that productivity does not grow in the government or household sectors. Although the differential is therefore most often negative over long periods, it is projected here to be less negative in the projection period than over the other long periods given

---

[25] The civilian, noninstitutional population excludes individuals who are incarcerated or are living in mental health facilities or homes for seniors, or who are on active duty in the Armed Forces. Projected population growth rates are sourced from demographers at the Social Security Administration (2023a).
[26] See the forecast from the Office of the Social Security Actuary at the Social Security Administration (2023b).

in the table, because of the projected declining share of government in total output.

The real GDP forecast represents the sum of three primary layers: (1) a baseline projection, developed through an Okun's Law analysis; (2) an adjustment to this baseline to accommodate the labor force participation rate differing during the forecast interval from its behavior during the estimation interval; and (3) an increase to potential GDP growth to reflect the effects of the Administration's pro-growth policies. When the baseline projection of 1.7 percent potential growth, the 0.2-percentage-point adjustment due to the baby boom cohort's retirements slowing, and the 0.3-percentage-point increase attributable to pro-growth Administration policies are summed, this results in the Administration's projected 2.2 percent a year real GDP growth rate during the budget window's final five years.

★ ★ ★ ★ ★ ★

Chapter 3

Population, Aging, and the Economy

Death rates in the United States have declined over the past century, leading Americans to live longer, healthier lives, on average, than ever before. Birthrates have declined, as well, though less steadily and with a short-lived increase in the mid-20th century.

Declining birthrates and death rates arose in the context of expansions in educational and labor market opportunities, progress toward gender equity, and technological advancements in medicine and public health. Today, they imply a slowing of U.S. population growth that is unprecedented in the country's history.

The impact of this and the other demographic trends that are the subject of this chapter will have important effects on our Nation and our economy. They form the backdrop for how the subjects of other chapters in this *Report*—such as the labor market, artificial intelligence, climate, and housing—will play out. How these changes affect Americans will depend on the Nation's institutions and policy environment. Some demographic trends call for immediate responses. Increases in drug overdose deaths and worsening maternal mortality are urgent issues that demand decisive action. Other demographic patterns—like the decline in U.S. fertility to historically low levels and the growth of seniors' share of the population—are important to understand to help the Nation anticipate, plan for, and manage the changes.

An aging population implies fiscal challenges for social safety net programs—like Medicare, Medicaid, and Social Security—as the working share of the population declines. Low fertility also implies that immigration policy will play an increasingly important role in shaping the growth and composition of the U.S. population and labor force. Without positive net migration, the U.S. population is projected to begin shrinking by about 2040 (U.N. DESA 2022a; CBO 2024).

This chapter begins by describing fertility and mortality trends and their causes. Some trends, like the acute spike in deaths during the COVID-19 pandemic, are short-lived. Others, like the trend toward smaller families and childlessness in American households, are likely to persist due to diffuse and slow-moving social, political, and economic changes. The persistent trends imply that the U.S. population will continue to age, and the chapter discusses what the aging U.S. population will mean for the U.S. labor force, consumer demand patterns, productivity, saving and borrowing, the care economy, and the fiscal future.

Declining Fertility in the 21st Century

The United States has experienced a sharp decline in birthrates since 2009. This decline mirrors trends among other advanced economies in recent decades. A trend toward smaller families has been widespread among Americans, with U.S. women from varied backgrounds and demographic groups choosing to have fewer children and waiting until later in life to have them than at any other time in the country's history (Aragão et al. 2023; Smock and Schwartz 2020). This section describes these trends and their economic causes in order to better anticipate whether these patterns are temporary or likely to persist over the coming decades. A key theme of this section is that the widespread, long-run declines in U.S. birthrates—and birthrates worldwide—are rooted in improvements in living standards, wages, and opportunities.

U.S. Fertility Since the Global Financial Crisis

Declining U.S. fertility is not new, but rather the continuation of a long-run trend that accelerated after the global financial crisis (Bailey and Hershbein 2018).[1] An intuitive summary measure of fertility is the total fertility rate (TFR), which describes the number of children a woman would have if she followed the age-specific childbearing patterns in her country at a given point in time. For example, a TFR of 2.0 would indicate that over a lifetime,

---

[1] "Fertility" in this chapter refers to measured birthrates. It is separate from the medical concept of "infertility."

Figure 3-1. Fertility Rates by Race and Hispanic Origin, 2003–22

Annual births per 1,000 women

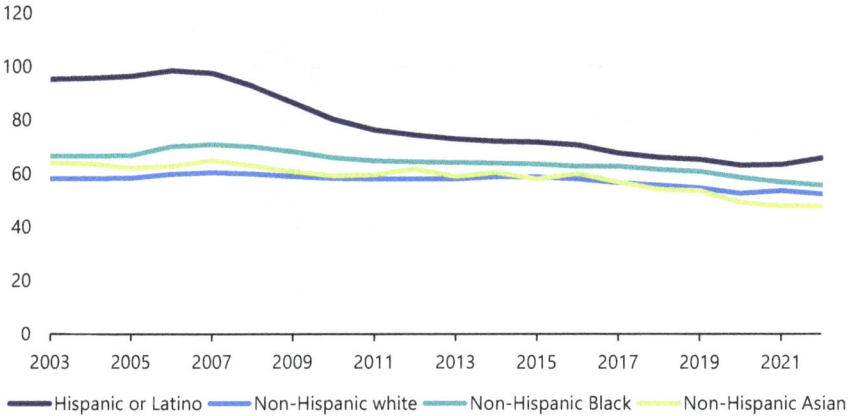

Hispanic or Latino · Non-Hispanic white · Non-Hispanic Black · Non-Hispanic Asian

Council of Economic Advisers
Source: Centers for Disease Control and Prevention WONDER.
Note: Annual births per 1,000 women age 15–44 years in the given year. Race and Hispanic origin refer to the mother. Gray bars indicate recessions.
2024 Economic Report of the President

a woman following the typical patterns of birth in her place and time would have two children. Any TFR below 2.0 is known as "subreplacement," meaning that the population would eventually shrink in the absence of migration.[2]

The U.S. TFR fell from 2.12 in 2007 to 1.67 in 2022 (Hamilton, Martin, and Ventura 2009; Hamilton, Martin, and Osterman 2022). The decrease after the global financial crisis was driven more by a decline in the number of families with any children than by shrinking family sizes among those with some children (Kearney, Levine, and Pardue 2022). The pattern coincides with broad societal changes in marriage and childbearing norms (Parker and Minkin 2023).

The decline in fertility has been across all groups defined by race, ethnicity, and nativity. However, before the global financial crisis, some demographic groups differed significantly in fertility rates. In 2007, fertility rates among Hispanic women were about 40 percent higher than those of Black, non-Hispanic women and about 60 percent higher than those of white, non-Hispanic women. By 2019, the rates had largely converged (see figure 3-1).

Figure 3-2 shows that women today are more likely to delay childbearing than their predecessors. The figure plots age-specific fertility rates (i.e.,

---

[2] "Replacement-level fertility" is slightly above 2.0 and varies across time and place. It accounts for naturally occurring sex ratio imbalances at birth and the fact that not all people will survive through their childbearing years. In all places and times, fertility below 2.0 is subreplacement.

Figure 3-2. Age-Specific Fertility Rates Over Time

Annual births per 1,000 women

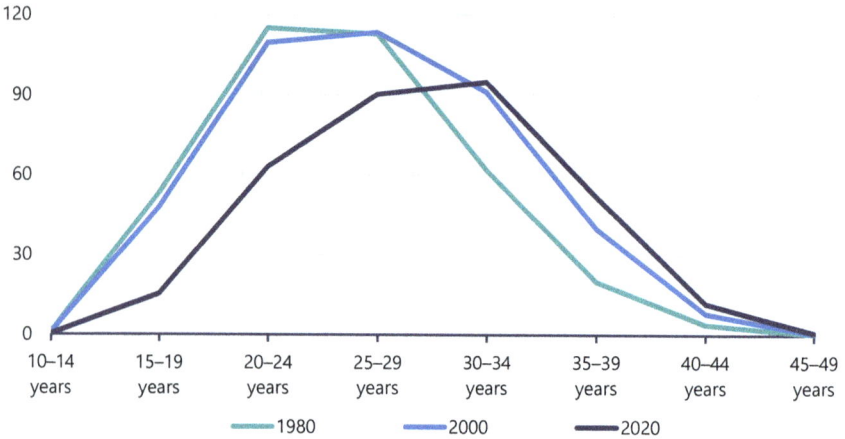

Council of Economic Advisers
Source: National Center for Health Statistics.
Note: National births per 1,000 women for each age group. In the periods plotted, all States are represented.
2024 Economic Report of the President

annual births per thousand women observed in each age group), indicating how the childbearing age profile has shifted rightward over the past several decades. As recently as 2006–11, age-specific fertility was highest in the 25–29 age group (Erbabian, Osorio, and Paulson 2022). As of the latest data from 2022, the rates are highest among women age 30–34. Overall, figure 3-2 implies both fewer births and an older average maternal age when giving birth in 2020, relative to past decades.

Figure 3-2 shows that fertility among women in their late 30s and 40s has been climbing for the past four decades. With improved access to contraception and the growth of assisted reproductive technology (ART)—a blanket term referring to medical procedures designed to help achieve a pregnancy (CDC 2019a)—more women are having children at later ages. The growth of and access to ART help women and families achieve their desired number of children, including later in life. In 2020, more than 74,000 (2 percent) of the roughly 3.6 million infants born in the United States were conceived with ART (CDC 2022). The number of healthy women who froze their eggs, an approach to delaying childbearing, rose from roughly 7,000 in 2016 to about 12,000 in 2020, a more than 70 percent increase (Kolata 2022). Based on growing ART use in other advanced economies (Chambers et al. 2021; Lazzari, Gray, and Chambers 2021), this technology is likely to play an increasingly important role in the United States, enabling some women to achieve their desired families at older ages and helping some

Figure 3-3. Total Fertility Rate in the United States and Other High-Income Countries and Regions, 1950–2021

Annual live births per woman

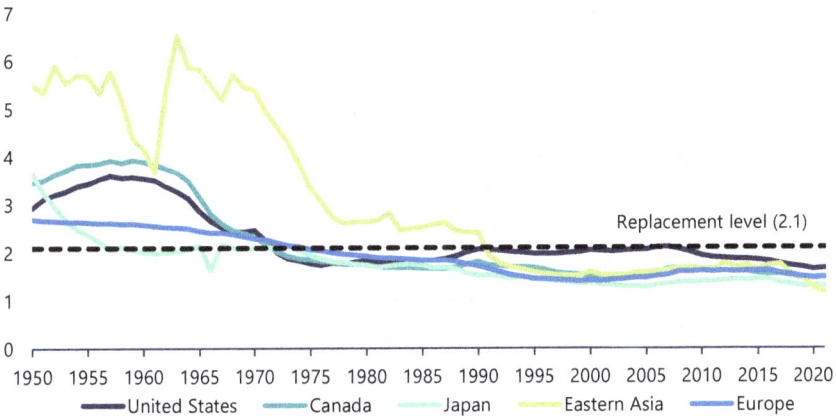

Replacement level (2.1)

United States Canada Japan Eastern Asia Europe

Council of Economic Advisers
Source: United Nations, *World Population Prospects 2022*.
Note: Gray bars indicate recessions.
2024 Economic Report of the President

young women delay childbearing with greater assurance of eventual successful pregnancies.

Low Fertility: A Global Trend

Though the recent downturn in birthrates since the global financial crisis has attracted significant attention, U.S. fertility has declined over a much longer span. Figure 3-3 plots TFR for the United States, Canada, Japan, Eastern Asia, and Europe. The figure shows that the rate has decreased in the United States, from roughly 3.6 in 1960, near the peak of the U.S. baby boom, to about 1.7 in 2021 (U.N. DESA 2022a).

The U.S. trend is in line with global fertility rate declines. In the mid–20th century, global TFR was 4.9. The global average has decreased to 2.3 children per woman in 2021 (U.N. DESA 2022a). Two-thirds of the global population is estimated to now live in a country with below-replacement fertility (Spears 2023), and the world population is projected to begin shrinking this century (Spears et al. 2023; U.N. DESA 2022a). The overall global fertility rate masks large variations across countries in both their current levels and transition paths, with the advanced European and East Asian economies displaying lower fertility than average.[3]

[3] The social, political, and economic implications of China's low fertility have garnered significant attention, particularly in 2023, when its total population was surpassed by India's (U.N. DESA 2023). But low fertility is a global phenomenon, and today even India's fertility is below replacement level (Spears 2023).

The experiences of other advanced economies offer clues to the United States' potential demographic future. In Europe, TFR declined from 2.7 in 1950 to 1.5 in 2021 (U.N. DESA 2022a). Since late in the 20th century, some of the world's lowest fertility rates have been found in major Asian economies. China, South Korea, and Japan—countries with diverse economic, policy, and social environments—are all characterized by low fertility rates today. Japan, with a TFR of 1.3, has been below replacement level for decades, along with Brazil, Canada, Chile, Germany, Thailand, and others.

Other countries' historical experiences are evidence that low fertility rates do not automatically rebound. The average fertility rate in Europe slowly declined in the second half of the 20th century. More recent trends suggest that the United States is also converging toward the general pattern of subreplacement fertility typical in high-income countries. Although 2021 U.S. fertility rates remained above those of European and East Asian countries, the global demographic trend suggests that U.S. rates may continue to decline in coming decades (PWI 2023).

Opportunity Cost

Decisions over whether and when to be a parent and what type of family to build are deeply personal and complex. Among adults without children who reported that they probably will not ever have children, survey evidence from Pew reveals diverse, multilayered explanations for not wanting children, some based on difficulties or constraints. Respondents listed financial reasons, medical reasons, concerns over the state of the world, and concerns over climate change (Brown 2021). (See box 3-1 for a discussion of how slowing U.S. population growth relates to current climate challenges.) Respondents who were already parents offered similar reasons, along with age, for not wanting more children. Yet the most common answer given in both groups was that these adults simply did not *want* to have children (or to have more children).

Economic analysis, even if it cannot capture the full texture of these decisions, can be helpful in understanding some of the underlying forces driving fertility trends. Decisions about having children are, after all, in part economic. Research suggests that birthrates are mostly pro-cyclical, rising in economic expansions and declining during downturns. But temporary economic conditions like recessions primarily affect *when* women have children, rather than how many they have over their lifetime or *if* they have them at all (Sobotka, Skirbekk, and Philipov 2011). Similarly, although media and popular sources suggest that children's direct costs explain falling birthrates (e.g., Picchi 2022; Hill 2021), researchers have found that rising costs for housing and childcare, while certainly having an impact on

Box 3-1. Climate and Population Growth

The past century has been a period of rapid growth in productivity, living standards, and population size in the United States and globally. It has also been a period of unprecedented increases in greenhouse gas (GHG) emissions from fossil fuel combustion, agriculture, and land use changes. The economics of reducing greenhouse gas emissions are more fully discussed in chapter 6 of this *Report*. This box focuses narrowly on how policy can decouple population size from environmental harm and explains why slowing population growth is no reason to relent on policy efforts aimed at reducing GHG emissions and climate harms.

The elasticity of emissions with respect to population size (i.e., how much emissions increase for each additional person) has never been constant, in part because it interacts critically with environmental policies, which are continuously changing the relationship between population size, prosperity, and environmental harm. For example, the Montreal Protocol, which was joined by the United States and 45 other countries in 1987, has dramatically reduced U.S. chlorofluorocarbon emissions that had been depleting the protective stratospheric ozone layer (EPA 2007). Similarly, the U.S. Acid Rain Program—a part of the 1990 amendments to the Clean Air Act—reduced U.S. sulfur dioxide emissions by 94 percent from 1990 to 2021. As of 2022, the emissions, which had contributed to air pollution and acid rain, were at their lowest point ever (EPA 2022). These successes demonstrate that when the United States and other governments choose to confront environmental challenges, a choice the Biden-Harris Administration has explicitly made, policy can significantly reduce linkages between population and environmental degradation.

The slowing and eventual reversal of global population growth that analysts forecast (Spears 2023) does not relieve the United States of the urgent need for environmental policy actions. While slowing population growth implies decreased emissions relative to a higher-fertility counterfactual, the demographic change is not large enough in magnitude to substitute for decisive policy action on GHGs (Kuruc et al. 2023).

Because of policy action today, led by the Biden-Harris Administration, the emissions elasticity with respect to population will continue to shrink in coming decades. The Inflation Reduction Act, which was signed into law by President Biden in 2022, is the most ambitious investment in combating the climate crisis to date. Together with the Bipartisan Infrastructure Law of 2021 and other enacted policies, it will help to lower U.S. GHG emissions to an estimated 40 percent below their 2005 level by 2030 (DOE 2022). These and other climate-focused Administration initiatives will fundamentally alter how Americans and U.S. economic activity affect the environment. A child born today is expected to live through 2100. The carbon footprint of that lifetime will be influenced by energy, transportation, agriculture, and land-use policy choices made now.

families, cannot account for the decline in fertility rates in the United States (Kearney, Levine, and Pardue 2022).

Researchers have long sought to understand the economic determinants of fertility. Canonical work by Gary Becker (1960) understood individuals' or families' demand for children as weighing the personal satisfaction that children bring parents against the time and monetary opportunity costs of parenting. Becker's insights remain relevant today, although the conceptual framework of opportunity costs is not sufficiently precise to make quantitative predictions about how particular changes in educational opportunities or wage rates will affect a country's TFR. Nonetheless, this understanding is consistent with birthrates falling over time in places where real income has risen relatively quickly (PWI 2023). Rising real income makes the cost of inputs like food and shelter more affordable in dollar terms (i.e., an income effect), while making parenting overall less affordable in terms of the opportunity cost of raising children (i.e., a substitution effect). The two effects push fertility decisions in opposite directions. Desired and realized family sizes declining over the last half century suggests that the substitution effect has dominated.

In the United States, young women's labor market expectations have been transformed dramatically over the last 50 years as part of a revolution in college and professional degree attainment, labor force participation, and the rising age of first marriage (Goldin 2004). In concert with these significant social and economic improvements, desires and decisions on childbearing have evolved. Women in their 20s and mid-30s are frequently in crucial career development periods, which drives up fertility's opportunity cost (Goldin and Mitchell 2017). Box 3-2 discusses the relationship between reproductive autonomy and female labor force participation, and box 3-3 discusses abortion access.

The expansion of opportunities over the past 50 years, including opportunities to combine and balance career and family, is a significant social and economic achievement. The Biden-Harris Administration is committed to improving options for working parents. The Administration has repeatedly called on Congress to create and fund a national comprehensive paid family and medical leave program, which would support parents' bonding with a new child by easing the financial pressure to immediately return to work after a birth or adoption.

Enhancing access to high-quality, affordable childcare is another channel through which policymakers can support working parents and caregivers, particularly women (Herbst 2022; Morrissey 2017). The Biden-Harris Administration's efforts and investments in supporting childcare have been comprehensive. During the COVID-19 pandemic, the Administration allocated a historic $24 billion to the childcare industry through the American Rescue Plan. A previous analysis by the CEA documented that these

Box 3-2. Reproductive Autonomy and Labor Market Participation

In 1968, only about 30 percent of women age 20 to 21 years said they expected to be working by age 35. By 1975, this share approximately doubled, to about 65 percent (Goldin 2004). The ability to choose whether and when to have a child is essential for women's ability to fully participate in the market economy. It is thus no coincidence that the period of rapidly increasing female labor force participation a half century ago corresponds to a period of rapidly improving reproductive health care options, especially hormonal birth control and the constitutional right to choose under *Roe v. Wade*.

A large body of research finds access to reproductive health care has benefits reaching into the labor market and beyond. These include reduced teenage pregnancies, delayed marriage, and improved educational attainment (Goldin and Katz 2002; Bailey 2006; Guldi 2008; Hock 2007; Bailey, Hershbein, and Miller 2012; Boonstra 2014; Myers 2017).

The Biden-Harris Administration believes reproductive rights are critical to maintaining the social, political, and economic progress of the past decades. The Affordable Care Act (ACA), by requiring most plans to cover contraception with no patient cost sharing, significantly advanced access to contraception (HHS 2022). The Administration has built on the ACA's foundation, including by introducing enhanced subsidies for purchasing marketplace coverage in the Inflation Reduction Act and strengthening the contraception coverage provisions of the ACA (White House 2023f).

Box 3-3. Abortion Access and Fertility After *Dobbs v. Jackson Women's Health Organization*

Access to reproductive health care is critical for women's health and has the potential to affect demographic change. In its 2022 decision in *Dobbs v. Jackson Women's Health Organization*, the U.S. Supreme Court overturned the precedent of *Roe v. Wade*, which in 1973 had recognized a constitutional right to choose. The Dobbs decision enabled States to enact new restrictions on abortion and newly enforce existing restrictions, including outright bans (Nash and Guarnieri 2022). Other States passed legislation to protect and advance access to reproductive health care, and voters in several States have voted in defense of reproductive rights through ballot initiatives.

More than one in three women of reproductive age (15–44) live in a State with an abortion ban (Shepard, Roubein, and Kitchener

2022; Myers et al. 2023). Although these laws vary by State, millions of women currently live in a State with a total ban; other States may allow access to abortion in very limited circumstances, such as when a woman's health is at risk or when the pregnancy is a result of rape or incest. In these and other States with abortion restrictions, health clinics that provide contraception and other essential health services have shuttered, eliminating critical points of care, including for other forms of reproductive health care (McCann and Walker 2023; Nash and Guarnieri 2022). State bans are also influencing medical professionals' geographic decisions over residency and practice plans (Edwards 2023; Woodcock et al. 2023), adding to the potential for shortages in the obstetrics and gynecology workforce in these States.

Because State abortion bans have eliminated or severely restricted access to abortion in many States, many women have been forced to travel across State lines to get the care they need. Figure 3-i shows the average travel time faced by women seeking abortion care from certain restrictive States, based on data from Myers and others (2023). The figure compares access from March 2022, which was before the *Dobbs* decision was issued, to September 2023. Because a large contiguous block of southern States has abortion bans in effect, travel times to the nearest provider have more than tripled in several southern States (this figure does not account for any potential international travel).

Appreciating the historic linkage between access to reproductive health care and economic opportunities, family formation, and fertility patterns since the 1970s (Myers 2017; Goldin and Katz 2002), it is

Figure 3-i. Changes in Travel Time to Nearest Provider, 2021–23

Average travel time in driving hours

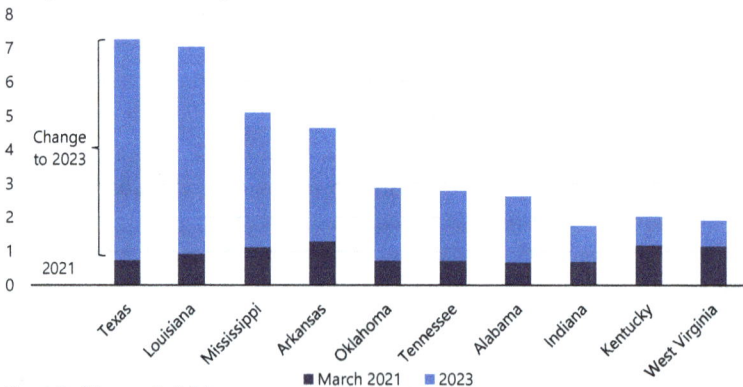

Council of Economic Advisers

Sources: Abortion Access Dashboard; CEA calculations.
Note: Driving times have been weighted by the reproductive-age female population. This figure does not account for potential international travel.
2024 Economic Report of the President

important to understand what effects the *Dobbs* decision could have on these outcomes. Research has shown that when women are denied an abortion, that denial has serious consequences for their well-being and results in adverse financial circumstances and family outcomes (Foster et al. 2018; Foster 2021; Miller, Wherry, and Foster 2023). For women who have been able to access abortion care since *Dobbs*, there may have been added economic, social, and personal costs due to longer travel, stress, delay, expense, and time away from work (Lindo and Pineda-Torres 2020). Finally, abortion restrictions also pose significant risks for maternal health, including the health of women who experience miscarriages, ectopic pregnancies, or other pregnancy complications and may be denied or receive delayed care—ultimately threatening their health and lives (Howard and Sneed 2023; Sellers and Nirappil 2022).

To address the devastating consequences that the *Dobbs* decision has had on women across the country, the President has called on Congress to pass a Federal law restoring the protections of *Roe v. Wade* (White House 2022c). In the meantime, the Biden-Harris Administration has taken executive action to protect access to the full spectrum of reproductive health care. In the wake of *Dobbs*, the President issued two Executive Orders and a Presidential Memorandum directing a comprehensive slate of actions to protect access to reproductive health care services, including access to emergency medical care and medication abortion. In June 2023, the President issued a third Executive Order to strengthen access to high-quality, affordable contraception, a critical aspect of reproductive health care (White House 2023g). The Administration remains fully committed to implementing these directives and defending reproductive rights.

While the effects of the *Dobbs* decision on the health and well-being of women are clear, the loss of abortion access resulting from the decision may ultimately have only a small effect on birthrates. The Congressional Budget Office estimates a roughly 1 percent increase in birthrates annually as a result of the new legal landscape (CBO 2023a). The relatively small impact on aggregate birthrates is in part due to anticipated changes in patterns of sexual behavior, contraception use, and how people access abortion care. Early research analyzing the effects of the *Dobbs* decision suggests that roughly three-fourths to four-fifths of people seeking abortions in the first half of 2023 were able to obtain them, despite bans (Dench, Pineda-Torres, and Myers 2023). In the aggregate, early data suggest that U.S. abortions were above pre-*Dobbs* levels one year after the decision (WeCount 2023), despite the added hardships and barriers to care erected in States where abortions are banned.

funds stabilized employment for childcare workers, reduced out-of-pocket expenses for families paying for care, and helped hundreds of thousands of mothers enter the workforce or return to work (CEA 2023a). In the President's Fiscal Year 2024 Budget, he called for $400 billion over 10 years to dramatically expand access to childcare for families with young children, while increasing childcare workers' pay. Under the President's plan, most families would pay no more than $10 per day for childcare. In April 2023, the President also signed a historic Executive Order directing his Administration to expand access to affordable, high-quality care and provide increased support for care workers and family caregivers through existing Federal programs (White House 2023a).

Mortality: Uneven Progress in the 21st Century

Mortality rates are critical determinants of the population's age structure, and thus have an impact on aggregate economic outcomes. But more importantly, longevity is intrinsically valuable. To quote Cutler, Deaton, and Lleras-Muney (2006, 97): "The pleasures of life are worth nothing if one is not alive to experience them."

U.S. life expectancy has increased by nearly 30 years since the turn of the 20th century.[4] The escape from premature death to longer, healthier lives is an accomplishment built on improvements in knowledge, nutrition, sanitation, and public health infrastructure (e.g., childhood vaccinations), as well as advances in medical science targeting chronic disease (Deaton 2014). Senior Americans are living longer than in past decades, and infant or childhood death, which was commonplace in the United States a century ago, is now a rare tragedy. Figure 3-4 charts this progress.[5]

Although the long arc of progress is clear, longevity improvements have stalled in recent years. Over the decade before the COVID-19 pandemic, life expectancy was essentially flat, as shown in the figure 3-4 detail. The stall does not reflect an upper biological limit on longevity. Life expectancies in other advanced economies have continued to increase above the U.S. level (Schwandt et al. 2021; Heuveline 2023). The patterns of U.S. mortality over the past decade are nuanced. Young and middle-age U.S. adults have experienced mortality setbacks due to increases in deaths from external causes, including guns, vehicle accidents, and drug overdoses. Gun deaths among children have risen and are now the leading cause of death among children

---

[4] For a given population, life expectancy captures how long members of a hypothetical cohort would live on average if its members were exposed to the population's mortality risks over their lifetimes.

[5] Figure 3-4 shows that the annual variability in life expectancy declined after the 1940s. Reductions in parasitic and infectious diseases, the introduction of commercially available penicillin, and the distribution of the first civilian flu vaccines in the United States were all likely contributors. But a change in how life expectancy data were calculated beginning in 1948 is responsible for some of the declining variance and renders pre and post comparisons difficult (Smith and Bradshaw 2006).

Figure 3-4. Life Expectancy at Birth, 1900–2022

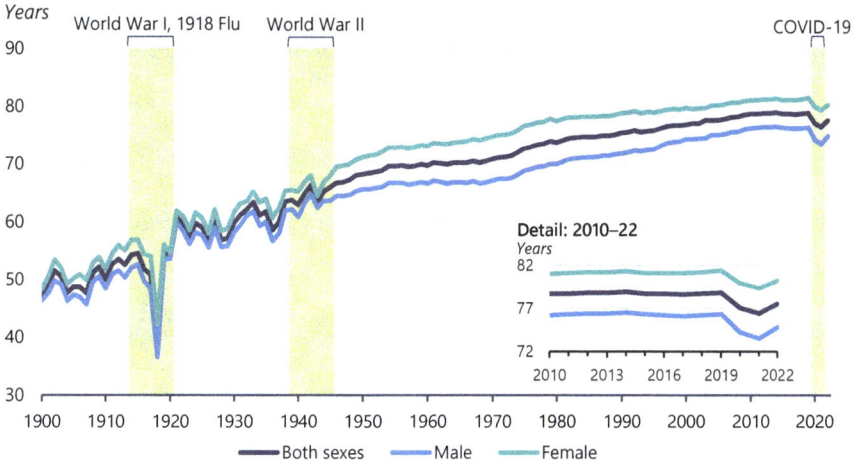

Council of Economic Advisers
Source: National Center for Health Statistics.
Note: The data for 2022 are provisional.
2024 Economic Report of the President

and teenagers 1 to 19 years of age (CDC 2023a). Meanwhile, seniors and infants have experienced continuing, gradual mortality improvements. The net effect of these forces, among others, was essentially unchanged male and female life expectancy for several years before the onset of the COVID-19 pandemic.

U.S. mortality trends are driven by three broad cause-of-death categories: infectious disease, external causes, and chronic illness.[6] All three categories are amenable to public interventions that can help improve longevity, though each requires different policy responses.

Infectious Disease: The Importance of Vaccinations

For much of the past century, deaths from infectious disease have declined. Influenza and pneumonia deaths per capita have decreased nearly 80 percent since 1950. Infant and child mortality rates from infectious disease have been especially responsive to public policy, driven down by childhood vaccinations and other public health infrastructure improvements, including in sanitation, water filtration and chlorination, and public education on infant care and hygiene (Cutler and Miller 2005; Cutler, Deaton, and Lleras-Muney 2006; Bhatia, Krieger, and Subramanian 2019). (See box 3-4.)

COVID-19 caused a major setback in infectious disease mortality. Total U.S. deaths increased by 19 percent from 2019 to 2020 when the

---

[6] External causes of death, per the definition from the Centers for Disease Control and Prevention (CDC), include unintentional injury, poisoning (including overdose), and complications of medical or surgical care (CDC 2019b).

pandemic began, causing life expectancy to fall abruptly (Sabo and Johnson 2022). Life expectancy fell for a second year, from 77.0 in 2020 to 76.4 in 2021, before rebounding to 77.5 in 2022 (Xu et al. 2022; Arias et al. 2023).

The United States' experience in responding to COVID-19 illustrates the role policy and public health authorities play in controlling infectious disease. Upon taking office, the Biden-Harris Administration immediately accelerated and improved vaccine distribution planning, resulting in the largest adult vaccination program in U.S. history and leading to 270 million individuals receiving a COVID-19 vaccine by May 2023. Federal efforts also helped distribute 750 million free COVID-19 tests by shipping them directly to 80 million households (HHS 2023a).

After the Biden-Harris Administration's successful vaccine and booster rollout, COVID-19 deaths slowed dramatically. Today, the public health emergency seems to be exiting its acute phase. COVID-19 hospitalizations were down 91 percent from January 2021 to May 2023, and deaths were down 95 percent over the same period (HHS 2023a). At the pandemic's peak, weekly COVID-19-related deaths reached almost 26,000. As of September 2023, this number was about 1,400 (CDC 2023b).

Progress has also continued against other sources of infectious disease mortality. Respiratory syncytial virus (RSV) is a highly contagious virus that causes illness and up to 10,000 deaths annually in the United States, primarily among infants and seniors (CDC 2023c). In May 2023, the Food and Drug Administration approved the world's first RSV vaccine. It approved a second vaccine later the same month. These advances promise continued mortality reductions for infants and senior citizens, including by protecting infants with vaccines administered to mothers during the in-utero period (Fleming-Dutra et al. 2023).

Unfortunately, vaccination, one of the most potent tools available to combat infectious disease, has become politically polarized and surrounded by misinformation. Vaccine skepticism is also a headwind to continued improvement in infant and child well-being. Although 88 percent of Americans maintain confidence in the net benefits of child vaccinations for measles, mumps, and rubella (Funk et al. 2023), there are worrying signs. In a poll assessing support for mandatory measles, mumps, and rubella vaccinations among schoolchildren, the trend was essentially flat at high levels in recent years for Democratic and Democratic-leaning respondents but down from 79 to 57 percent between October 2019 and March 2023 for Republican and Republican-leaning respondents (Funk et al. 2023).

Continuing long-run improvements in the health of American families will require maintaining public health priorities like the Biden-Harris Administration's emphasis on childhood and senior vaccinations. Today, the Administration continues ongoing, cross-agency efforts to combat misinformation, offering vaccine education and outreach efforts in rural

Box 3-4. Infant and Maternal Mortality

The story of early life mortality in the United States is one of continual, if uneven, progress. Infant mortality—the number of deaths in the first 12 months of life occurring for every 1,000 live births—has declined since the late 19th century (Lee 2007). In the early 1900s, the infant mortality rate was 100 (CDC 1999), meaning that 1 out of 10 children died in their first year of life. By 2021, the most recent year for which complete data are available, the rate had declined nearly 95 percent, to 5.4 (Ely and Driscoll 2023). Broadening the scope to early child mortality beyond infancy reveals a similar pattern: At the turn of the 20th century, more than 20 percent of U.S. children did not live to age 5, while today the share is less than 1 percent (Gapminder 2022). Figure 3-ii charts infant mortality since the mid-1990s, showing that the 2022 rate was 19 percent lower than it was two decades earlier (Ely and Driscoll 2023).

U.S. infant mortality has demonstrated a steady decline over the past decades and, despite a rise from 5.44 to 5.60 between 2021 and 2022, remains near its historic low. It is still unclear what role the COVID-19 public health emergency has played in the recent uptick. Yet the United States lags behind other advanced economies on this metric (Bronstein, Wingate, and Brisendine 2018). The United States has the sixth-highest infant mortality rate among countries that belong to the Organization for Economic Cooperation and Development (OECD 2021). In 2019, before the COVID-19 pandemic's health care disruptions and social upheavals, the U.S. infant mortality rate was 5.58 (Ely and Driscoll 2023). Other advanced economies had infant mortality rates

Figure 3-ii. U.S. Infant Mortality Rate, 1995–2022

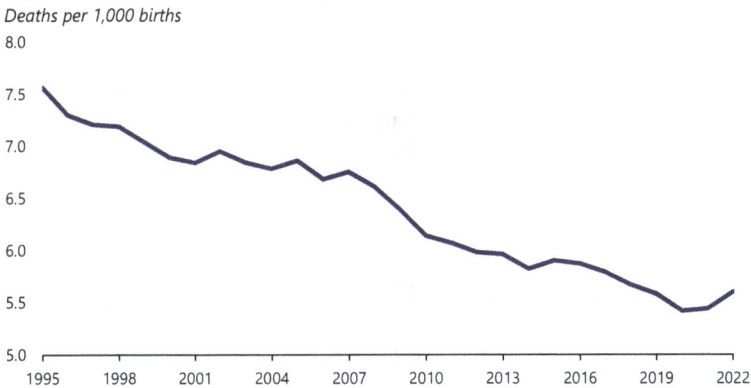

Deaths per 1,000 births

Council of Economic Advisers
Source: Centers for Disease Control and Prevention.
Note: The death rate is deaths per 1,000 live births. Gray bars indicate recessions.
2024 Economic Report of the President

that were substantially lower; for example, 1.9 in Japan and 3.7 in the United Kingdom (OECD 2021).

The United States performs similarly poorly in international comparisons of maternal mortality (i.e., deaths of pregnant and post-partum women for every 100,000 births). Maternal mortality accounted for about 1,200 U.S. deaths in 2021, compared with about 100,000 overdoses and 700,000 heart disease deaths during the same year. The rate nearly doubled from 2018 to 2021, going from roughly 17 to 33 deaths per 100,000 live births, though the contribution of COVID-19 to this trend is yet unclear (Hoyert and Miniño 2023). (Maternal mortality statistics from earlier years are not directly comparable due to a data coding change; see NVSR 2020. Previously reported increases in mater-nal mortality over the period 2002–18 were an artifact of new coding practices that were slowly diffusing across States, rather than reflective of an actual worsening of mortality in consistently applied calculations; see Joseph et al. 2021.)

What explains the relatively poor outcomes for babies and mothers in the United States? Researchers have noted that cross-country differ-ences in birthweight and gestational age account for a significant share of the infant mortality gap (Chen, Oster, and Williams 2016). Because infant health indicators like birthweight are often indicative of moth-ers' well-being during gestation, the results point to the importance of maternal health.

Black women have alarmingly high rates of maternal mortality, two to three times the rate of white women, and have experienced the largest increase in the rate in the past several years (Hoyert and Miniño 2023). Poverty contributes to both infant and maternal mortality (Turner, Danesh, and Moran 2020; Kennedy-Moulton et al. 2023), but, critically, differences in infant and maternal health across racial and ethnic groups cannot be explained simply by differential poverty incidence. Elevated mortality among U.S. Black women and their infants is greater than can be accounted for by income (Kennedy-Moulton et al. 2023). Research suggests that a combination of higher likelihood of preexisting condi-tions, higher likelihood of adverse pregnancy outcomes, and racial bias/discrimination all contribute to higher Black maternal mortality (Lister et al. 2019).

Recognizing the importance of maternal health, and the gaps in our understanding of women's health more broadly, the Biden-Harris Administration released a blueprint for addressing maternal mortality and reducing these disparities in 2022 (White House 2022d).

Progress on maternal health and closing racial mortality gaps is possible. Black Americans experienced significant mortality improve-ments across age, sex, and cause-of-death categories during the two decades beginning in 1990, especially in low-income areas (Schwandt et al. 2021). This progress shrank the Black/white mortality gap even as white mortality also improved. Improved access to health care is critical, and the Biden-Harris Administration is committed to improving maternal health and expanding insurance coverage. The American Rescue Plan, which was signed into law by President Biden, established a new State option to extend Medicaid coverage for low-income postpartum women from 60 days after childbirth to one year (White House 2021). As of December 2023, 41 States and D.C. have implemented the one-year postpartum coverage extension, and extensions are pending in several other States (KFF 2024).

communities (HHS 2021; White House 2022a). The Administration has also worked to reduce financial barriers to vaccines, including via the Inflation Reduction Act's provision to remove cost sharing among Medicare Part D and Medicaid beneficiaries for all adult vaccines recommended by the Centers for Disease Control and Prevention (CDC).

External Causes: Setbacks in Midlife Mortality

Whereas infectious disease disproportionately affects the very young and old, deaths from external causes disproportionately affect older children and middle-aged adults. This contrast highlights the difficulty in telling a simple, singular story of mortality trends in America. Today, rates of death from external causes—which include motor vehicle accidents, homicides, suicides, and drug overdoses—are rising for young and middle-aged people in the United States. Drug overdose deaths have risen in recent years to become the largest category within the external cause group (Lawrence et al. 2023; CDC WONDER n.d.). In 2021, drug overdoses were the leading cause of death for Americans between age 25 and 44 and the fourth leading cause for those between 45 and 64, after cancer, heart disease, and COVID-19 (CDC WONDER n.d.).

Figure 3-5 charts changes in mortality across all age groups due to accidents and overdoses, along with other leading causes of death. External causes, which have received significant attention due in part to pioneering work by Case and Deaton (2015), are the largest category of deaths among individuals between age 1 and 44. The rising trend in overdoses and accidental deaths apparent in figure 3-5 is a matter for serious public concern.

Research has found that the history of widespread legal opioid prescription is driving the present U.S. overdose epidemic (Cutler and Glaeser 2021). The increase in opioid deaths in the mid-1990s was linked to aggressive promotional targeting of OxyContin by pharmaceutical companies to

Figure 3-5. Selected Leading Causes of Death, 1950–2021

Annual deaths per 100,000 people, age-adjusted

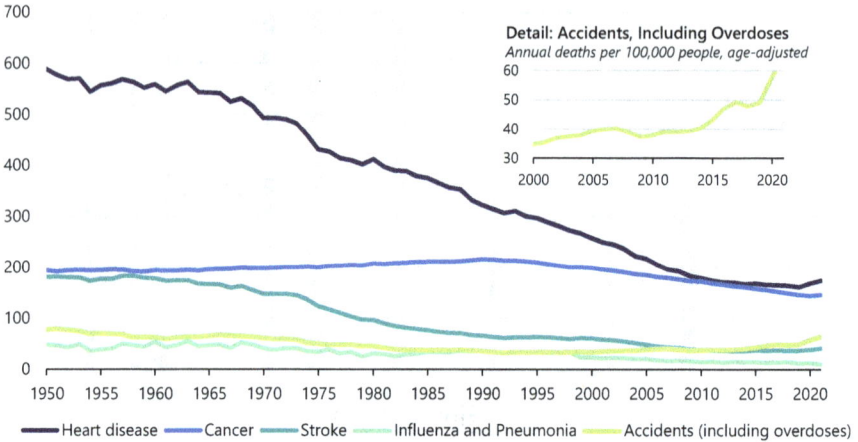

Detail: Accidents, Including Overdoses
Annual deaths per 100,000 people, age-adjusted

Heart disease ■ Cancer ■ Stroke ■ Influenza and Pneumonia ■ Accidents (including overdoses)

Council of Economic Advisers

Sources: National Center for Health Statistics; Centers for Disease Control and Prevention WONDER.
Note: Accidents refer to all "unintentional injuries," which include accidental overdoses. Gray bars indicate recessions.
2024 Economic Report of the President

States with less prescription oversight and more prescribers than their peers (Alpert et al. 2022; Arteaga and Barone 2023). Researchers further found that competition for patients among health care professionals led to looser opioid prescriptions (Currie, Li, and Schnell 2023).[7]

Even as State and Federal policymakers began to recognize opioids' harm and address their overprescription and abuse, demand for opioids remained strong because of the group of people already suffering from addiction. The demand fueled an increased supply of prescription opioid substitutes—first heroine, and later fentanyl (Giltner et al. 2022; Alpert, Powell, and Pacula 2018). And the shift in supply to more dangerous illegal opioids accelerated fatal overdose rates (Lancet 2022).

The Biden-Harris Administration's National Drug Control Strategy makes saving lives the Administration's "North Star" (White House 2022b). Several medicines approved by the U.S. Food and Drug Administration are effective in treating opioid use disorder. Seeking and receiving treatment, including Medication Assisted Treatment, is associated with significantly improved outcomes (Mancher and Leshner 2019). Promoting widespread availability of treatment and helping individuals successfully navigate into treatment is a critical component of the Administration's strategy. Further, in March 2023, the Food and Drug Administration approved the first

---

[7] One paper finds that physicians with stricter prescribing standards become more careful about prescribing opioids when diversion—the possibility of misuse either by a patient or a different unintended user—is a risk (Schnell 2022). These findings suggest an important role of physicians with more lax prescribing standards.

over-the-counter naloxone nasal spray, which has been shown to be a critical tool for preventing fatal opioid overdoses (HHS 2023b). In August 2023, the Biden-Harris Administration announced $450 million in new funding to tackle opioid-related overdose deaths (White House 2023b); more than $80 million will help rural communities respond to overdose risks (HHS 2023c).

Chronic Disease: Progress Through Innovation and Health Care Access

Chronic disease still claims the most American lives each year. While external causes of death matter most before age 45, most deaths occur after 45, when chronic disease dominates as the leading cause. Historically, progress against chronic disease has depended on advances in medical innovation and health insurance coverage that makes effective treatment accessible.

Heart disease deaths declined in the second half of the 20th century (see figure 3-5). Health behavior trends, particularly reductions in smoking, played an important role (Cutler, Glaeser, and Rosen 2009; CDC 2014; DeCicca and McLeod 2008; Evans, Farrelly, and Montgomery 1996). Innovation also led to new medicines to control hypertension and cholesterol and new treatments like stents and bypass surgeries. Longer lives from fewer heart disease deaths were initially accompanied by a slow rise in cancer deaths. Cancer death rates peaked in 1991, both as a consequence of smoking trends (ACS 2023) and because declines in heart disease allowed people to survive longer, exposing them to additional cancer risk (Honoré and Lleras-Muney 2006). Since the 1990s, cancer deaths have declined. Still, the disease remains the second leading cause of death for people age 65 and above across all race and ethnicity groups and for both men and women.

Progress on chronic disease mortality has been positive, though slow and uneven, in the past decade. Overall mortality and life expectancy above age 65 improved from 2010 to 2019, before the COVID-19 public health emergency. Further progress is possible, and the Biden-Harris Administration has led several initiatives aimed at addressing chronic disease. President Biden's Cancer Moonshot initiative affirms the critical work of continuing progress against cancer, including expanding access to and technology for screenings, building on the successful human papillomavirus vaccine to prevent cancers before they start, and strategically allocating Federal funds. The Cancer Moonshot also expands the U.S. Patent and Trademark Office's program to expedite patents for cancer treatment innovations (White House 2023c).

In November 2023, President Biden established the first-ever White House Initiative on Women's Health Research (White House 2023d) to address the consequences of the historic underfunding of research on women's health, especially for communities that have been historically excluded from research, including women of color and women with disabilities (White House 2023e). The initiative will address midlife health and chronic conditions connected to aging, among other areas. Decades of research based on men has led to significant research gaps in women's health compared with men's, masking differences that can be critical for women's health outcomes—for example, because women and men experience different heart attack symptoms, traditional diagnostic tools geared toward men can lead to misdiagnoses for women (Mehta et al. 2016).

Medical treatment can only benefit those who receive it, which highlights the importance of health insurance coverage for progress on morbidity and mortality. There is now a large body of research evidence that health insurance expansions in general—and the specific health insurance expansions created by the Affordable Care Act (ACA) and supported by the Biden-Harris Administration—have improved health and saved lives. Earlier Medicaid expansions were found to reduce infant and child mortality (Currie and Gruber 1996; Goodman-Bacon 2018), and researchers have shown that the ACA's expansions of Medicaid and Marketplace coverage have reduced adult mortality (Goldin, Lurie, and McCubbin 2021; Miller, Johnson, and Wherry 2019). Further, a wider body of work has documented improvements, resulting from the ACA, in health care access and utilization; self-reported physical and mental health; chronic disease; and maternal and neonatal health (Guth, Garfield, and Rudowitz 2020; Soni, Wherry, and Simon 2020).

The Biden-Harris Administration is committed to ensuring health care access through expanded insurance coverage. In early 2023, the share of individuals with no health insurance coverage fell to an all-time low of 7.7 percent (HHS 2023d). Today, Insurance Marketplace enrollment is at an all-time high, thanks in part to the Inflation Reduction Act's enhanced subsidies for purchasing coverage.

Aging and the Economy

Birth, death, and net migration patterns determine a population's age structure. Today, the U.S. population is aging; the age profile of the population is shifting toward relatively fewer younger people and more seniors than in past decades. Aging societies present challenges, including in terms of funding social insurance systems, meeting seniors' social and infrastructure needs, and adapting to a reduced labor force as a share of the overall population.

The United States is not alone in facing these challenges. Societies around the world are aging because of low fertility rates (World Economic Forum 2022). During the rapid population growth characterizing most of the 20th century, most advanced economies' population age distributions were bottom heavy, featuring a large share of young people and tapering at increasingly old ages. The demographic transition to low fertility and mortality implies that the United States now faces an age distribution more heavily tilted toward older ages. The result is an age "pillar," rather than the "pyramid" of the past. Figure 3-6 shows the near-term aging challenge the United States faces. Whereas the over-65 population was 12 percent of the total in 2000, it is expected to account for 21 percent in 2040.

Confronting Sustained Low Fertility

All forecasts contain uncertainty, which can compound for population projections extending several generations into the future.[8] Yet, over time frames of 10 to 20 years, population projections can be made relatively precisely.[9] Unforeseen social and economic changes may affect long-term desired family sizes and mortality rates, but the most likely near future for the United States is one of sustained low fertility and an aging population, similar to what is shown in figure 3-6.

Population forecasters do not anticipate a significant rebound in fertility rates, with the U.N. World Population Prospects' medium projection estimating U.S. TFR holding at 1.71 by the end of the century (U.N. DESA 2022b), about equal to the 2022 rate. Similarly, the Congressional Budget Office (CBO) projects no substantial rebound to above-replacement fertility. It projects that fertility rates through the middle of the century will level off at 1.7 (CBO 2024). The Census projects fertility to decline further, slowly converging to 1.52 over the next 100 years (Census 2023a). While the United Nations, CBO, and Census differ in the details of their assumptions and methodologies, they all imply a 2040 population pillar like the one shown in figure 3-6.

There are several convergent reasons to plan for the possibility of sustained low fertility embodied in these projections. First, the phenomenon of low fertility is partially rooted in social and economic progress, including improved educational and labor market opportunities. The direct costs and opportunity costs of childbearing and parenting are likely to persist. Second, the projections for the U.S. to remain below replacement are consistent with earlier fertility trends in Europe and East Asia. Finally, in recent years, U.S. fertility projections have tended to be revised downward, not upward, over

---

[8] For example, technological breakthroughs in geriatric medicine could extend longevity beyond current projections and further invert the age pyramid.

[9] Over time frames of 10 to 20 years, the already-existing population tends to determine population forecast outcomes in predictable ways. For example, there is little room for error in projecting the number of people 50 years of age a decade from now, based on the population of those 40 today, given the already-low mortality rates in the relevant age interval. The U.N. population projections used in this chapter have been shown to be relatively precise (Ritchie 2023) over these forecasting time frames.

Figure 3-6. U.S. Age Distributions for Men and Women

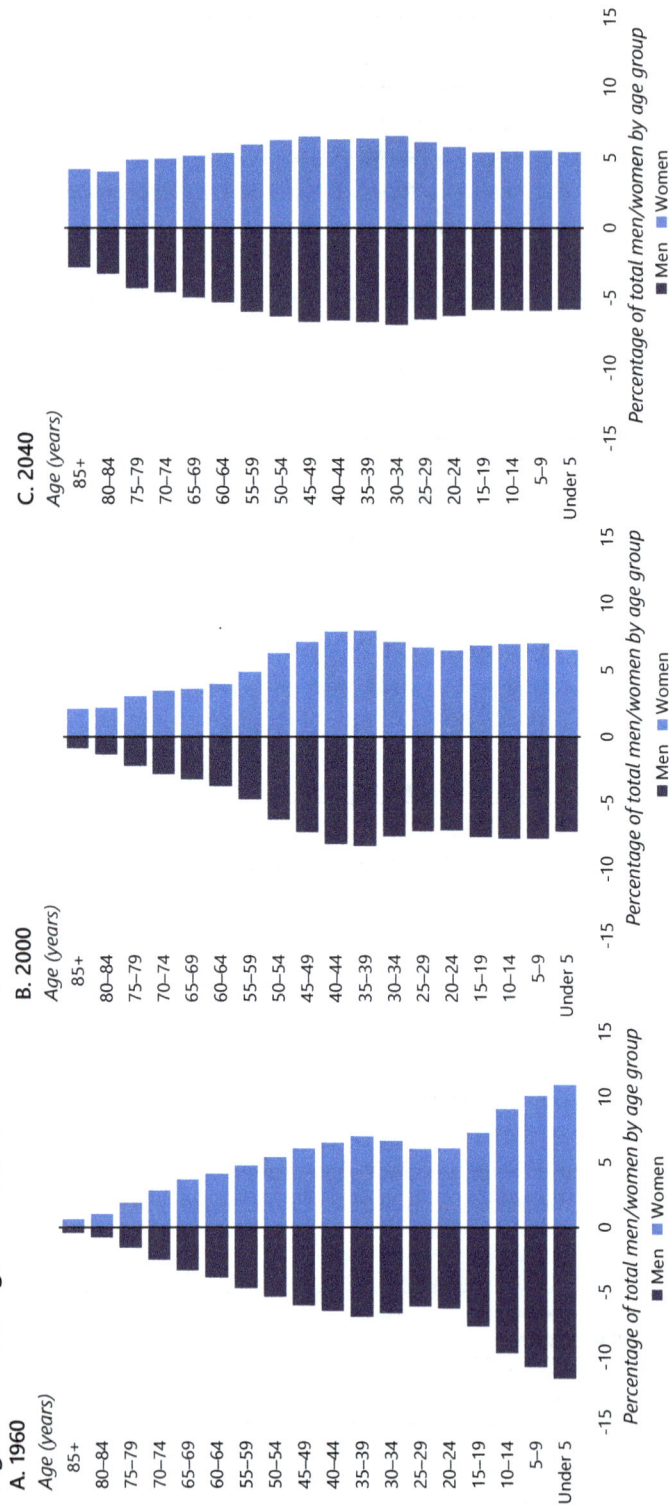

A. 1960

Age (years)

85+
80–84
75–79
70–74
65–69
60–64
55–59
50–54
45–49
40–44
35–39
30–34
25–29
20–24
15–19
10–14
5–9
Under 5

-15   -10   -5   0   5   10   15

Percentage of total men/women by age group

■ Men   ■ Women

B. 2000

Age (years)

85+
80–84
75–79
70–74
65–69
60–64
55–59
50–54
45–49
40–44
35–39
30–34
25–29
20–24
15–19
10–14
5–9
Under 5

-15   -10   -5   0   5   10   15

Percentage of total men/women by age group

■ Men   ■ Women

C. 2040

Age (years)

85+
80–84
75–79
70–74
65–69
60–64
55–59
50–54
45–49
40–44
35–39
30–34
25–29
20–24
15–19
10–14
5–9
Under 5

-15   -10   -5   0   5   10   15

Percentage of total men/women by age group

■ Men   ■ Women

Council of Economic Advisers

Sources: Census Bureau; Congressional Budget Office; CEA calculations.
Note: Data for 2040 are from long-term demographic projections.
2024 Economic Report of the President

time. For example, in 2012 the United Nations projected that long-run U.S. TFR would converge to 2.0, but updated this to 1.7 in 2022 (U.N. DESA 2012, 2022a). The CBO's 2019 demographic outlook placed long-run TFR at 1.9 but updated this to 1.7 in its 2024 outlook (CBO 2019, 2024). The Census's 2017 projection included a national convergence to a TFR of 2.0, but updated this to 1.5 in 2023 (Census 2018, 2023a). For these reasons, below-replacement fertility in the United States may persist, as it has in most of the world's advanced economies. Policy deliberations and decisions should be made with these dynamics in mind.

A Role for Immigration in Filling Workforce Gaps

One immediate implication of the changing age distribution is a slowdown in U.S. labor force growth. The size of the labor force is consequential along a number of dimensions. Because labor force growth and productivity growth are components of the economy's capacity growth rate, a labor force that is growing more slowly implies slower overall growth.[10] The labor force also constitutes a large part of the tax base supporting U.S. entitlement programs. Between 2023 and 2052, the population age 25 to 54 is projected to grow at an average annual rate of 0.2 percent, well below its 1 percent growth between 1980 and 2021. This rate is also below the senior population's projected 1.2 percent growth between 2023 and 2052 (CBO 2022).

Historically, immigration has contributed to smaller occupational and geographic labor force gaps. The foreign-born population in the United States is responsive to local employment shocks and differential employment growth across labor markets (Blau and Mackie 2017), driven by immigrants' relatively high geographic mobility (Basso and Peri 2020). Since the COVID-19 pandemic, foreign-born workers have been critical across industries, particularly food services and agriculture (CEA 2023b). They also help fill essential positions that are often not filled by local workers due to skill mismatch, among other issues (Hooper 2023), and they facilitate labor market participation among high-skilled native U.S. women by starting new companies, creating new jobs, and lowering the price of market-provided household services (Azoulay et al. 2022; Cortés 2023).

Patterns of recent immigration and U.S. fertility have combined such that recent labor force growth has been—and anticipated future growth will be—substantially attributable to foreign-born workers. Between 2000 and 2017, 43 percent of U.S. labor force growth was attributable to immigrants (Basso and Peri 2020). Immigrants contribute to the U.S. labor force beyond the proportion of their total numbers because they are more likely to be of

[10] For a fixed productivity growth path, a slower-growing labor force implies lower per capita GDP growth if the labor force declines as a fraction of the population. In other words, what matters for GDP per capita is the number of workers per capita, a metric that is declining in an aging population (see figure 3-8).

Figure 3-7. Total Population through 2100

U.S. population, millions

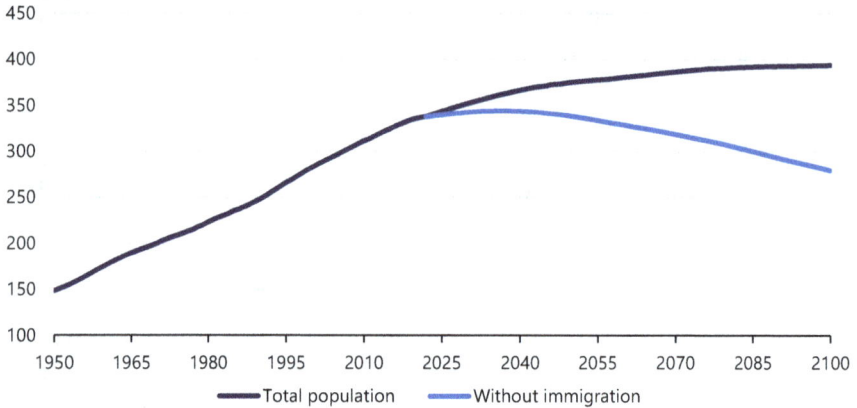

Council of Economic Advisers
Sources: United Nations World Population Projections (2022), medium variant.
Note: The medium variant estimation was used to compute immigration population projections.
2024 Economic Report of the President

working age and have full-time jobs than their U.S.-born peers. In 2016, 78 percent of immigrants were between 18 and 64 years of age; meanwhile, 59 percent of individuals born in the United States were in that age group (Vespa, Medina, and Armstrong 2020).

Figure 3-7 shows the projected U.S. population with and without net migration through the end of the century. The population would begin shrinking within 14 to 16 years in the absence of immigration—in 2038, based on U.N. projections (pictured); and in 2040, per CBO projections (CBO 2024). If immigration follows the pattern of past decades, the U.S. population would reach nearly 400 million at the end of the century.

Overall, immigration generates important net benefits for the U.S. economy, including through positive effects on productivity, entrepreneurship, and scientific innovation (Hunt and Gauthier-Loiselle 2010; Peri 2012; Prato 2022; Azoulay et al. 2022). Nonetheless, immigration's costs and benefits can be distributed unequally among stakeholders and regions (Hooper 2023). Although most studies have found that the wage effects of immigrants on natives are small and on either side of zero, immigration may place downward pressure on the wages of some low-paid workers (Butcher and Card 1991; Borjas 2003; Card 2009; Peri and Sparber 2009; Ottaviano and Peri 2012). While the country as a whole benefits from the economic activity and productivity boost immigration provides, local areas with recently arrived immigrants or immigrants with relatively lower educational attainment are likely to face immediate fiscal costs due to lower tax revenue generated per capita and additional draws on public services, especially

Figure 3-8. U.S. Old Age Dependency Ratio through 2050

Number of seniors age 65+ for every 100 people age 20–64

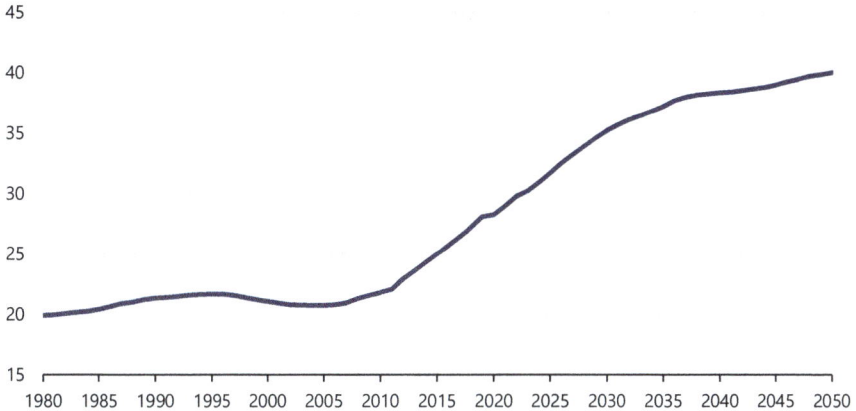

Council of Economic Advisers
Sources: Census Bureau; Congressional Budget Office; CEA calculations.
Note: The dependency ratio is calculated as the number of people age 65 years and over for every 100 people age 20–64.
2024 Economic Report of the President

K-12 education (Edelberg and Watson 2023; Blau and Mackie 2017). The Biden-Harris Administration recently took steps to extend the Temporary Protected Status of Venezuelan migrants and accelerate work authorization processing. This policy ensures that migrants can build sustainable lives and enter the formal work sector, where they can contribute to State and local income tax bases.

The Old Age Dependency Ratio: A Race Between Aging and Productivity Growth

An aging population increases pressure on Federal deficits and debts (Sheiner 2018). As people age and retire, they shift from contributing to government revenue via taxes paid on labor income to receiving Social Security and Medicare benefits. The lifecycle patterns and the country's evolving age structure complicate issues of fair resource allocation across generations. At the birth-cohort level, Social Security retirement support pays out roughly the amount each generation contributes, though progressive redistribution occurs within generations (Steuerle, Carasso, and Cohen 2004; Steuerle and Smith 2023). Through Medicare, individuals receive significantly more on average over a lifetime than they pay in via taxes (Sabelhaus 2023; Steuerle and Smith 2023), largely because medical technologies and treatments improve rapidly over time, raising the standard of care and real spending.

Figure 3-8 depicts one of the central forces governing the relationship between the population's age structure and benefit program financing. The old age dependency ratio, defined here as the number of individuals age

65 years and over for each 100 people age 20–64, has increased rapidly in recent years with the baby boom generation's ongoing retirement.[11] Between 2024 and 2050, this ratio will increase by 30 percent. After that, it will likely continue to increase, though more slowly, nearly doubling between 2024 and the end of the century.

The extent of the fiscal challenge posed by the old age dependency ratio depends not only on the share of working age people in the labor force but also on workers' productivity. Labor productivity is measured by the economic output generated for each hour worked. It grows over time with human capital improvements, labor-augmenting physical capital, and technological progress, making society wealthier per capita.

How will changes in the U.S. old age dependency ratio likely compare with changes in productivity growth? Many observers have noted a recent slowdown in productivity growth (e.g., Syverson 2017; Dieppe 2020), and some evidence suggests that an aging population decreases the pace of productivity gains (Maestas, Mullen, and Powell 2016), including by reducing startup activity (Karahan, Pugsley, and Şahin 2019). Yet even modest productivity growth could outpace the dependency ratio's growth. For example, labor productivity in the nonfarm business sector in 2023 was 1.5 times its value in 2000 (BLS 2023a), meaning that an hour of labor today produces 50 percent more output than an hour of labor in 2000. This implies an annualized 1.8 percent rate of real growth over this period. The Bureau of Labor Statistics projects that labor productivity growth will be slightly lower, at 1.7 percent, from 2020 to 2030 (BLS 2021). Either growth rate would dramatically outpace the 30 percent old age dependency ratio increase expected by 2050, an annualized change of 0.8 percent. Thus, even very modest labor productivity growth acts as an important countervailing force to concerns about dependency ratios.[12] Box 3-5 discusses the role of human capital investments in productivity growth.

Economic growth theory suggests that unprecedented U.S. and global population decline may also have important scale effects. The historical timing of global population growth (over humanity's long history) corresponds closely with per capita productivity growth. Growth theorists consider the link important: "Virtually all theories of economic growth predict a positive

---

[11] This standard definition of the old age dependency ratio uses available binned age data. It is meant to proxy, rather than exactly describe, average working lifetimes. For example, it ignores that the normal retirement age for persons born in 1960 and later is 67 and that age 20 is an imprecise marker for when full-time labor force participation may begin.

[12] Nonetheless, a doubling of labor productivity would not imply that the tax revenue associated with a single worker could support twice as many seniors. That is in part because living standards and the costs of maintaining seniors also increase over time. For example, initial Social Security benefits are wage-indexed to reflect the general rise in the standard of living that occurred during an individual's lifetime (SSA 2023a). Thus, real initial Social Security benefits increase over time as productivity rises.

relationship between population size and productivity" (Peters 2022, 1). Specialization, trade, and the nonrival nature of innovation and knowledge all imply channels running from larger populations to higher per capita living standards (Jones and Romer 2010). A key concept linking larger populations and rising per capita living standards is the production of nonrival goods (Romer 2018; Jones 2019), which are unique, in that one person's use of them does not deplete the amount available to others. Such goods include knowledge, like germ theory and calculus, and practical inventions, such as water chlorination, internet communication protocols, and modified RNA vaccines (the first of which were approved and deployed in response to the COVID-19 pandemic). The total stock of knowledge and ideas therefore equals the per capita stock, and a world with a declining population may miss out on some critical innovations that make everyone better off (Jones 2022).

Declining population numbers also affect the intrafamily burden of care work. Aging populations need care, and the burden often falls on family members. Low fertility implies that a decreasing number of children and grandchildren can participate in the intergenerational compact of family care. For example, if the United States held at its present TFR of 1.66 indefinitely, then an average of 0.7 grandchildren would be born for every grandparent in the long run. This would be a different future of care than the past generations of Americans have experienced, on average. Technological advances, including artificial intelligence, may someday ease the strain, but the human burden of care remains an unsolved problem today (see box 3-6).

Aging and the Fiscal Outlook

Social Security and Medicare are the two main Federal assistance programs for seniors in the United States, though Medicaid plays an increasingly important role in long-term care as the payer for 6 in 10 nursing home residents (CBPP 2020). Entitlement programs are projected to be an important driver of long-term increases in fiscal outlays over the next three decades, accounting for more than 40 percent of noninterest spending in 2053, up from less than 30 percent in 2023 (CBO 2023b).

Today, Social Security provides income support to roughly one-fifth of the population, or 67 million beneficiaries. By 2050, about one-quarter of the population is expected to receive benefits, boosting Social Security spending to 6 percent of gross domestic product (GDP), up from 5.2 percent currently (SSA 2023b).

As a growing share of the population transitions from the labor force to retirement, total Medicare costs will also rise. Roughly one-third of the projected increase in health care program expenditures as a share of GDP through 2053 will be attributable to the population's aging (CBO 2023b).

Box 3-5. Investing in Productivity through Human Capital

As the ratio of workers to the overall population declines due to age structure changes in the United States, the Biden-Harris Administration is committed to policies that accelerate productivity growth, facilitating more real output despite fewer workers. Investing in human capital via health and educational inputs during childhood is one of the clearest paths to increased productivity.

Research documents that educational investments in children and young people raise productivity and contribute to aggregate economic growth (Valero 2021; Hanushek and Wößmann 2010). High-quality childcare has also been shown to be important for outcomes such as school readiness, cognitive skill development, and employment and earnings in later life (Deming 2009; Duncan and Magnuson 2013; Campbell et al. 2014; Gray-Lobe, Pathak, and Walters 2022). Similarly, research has shown that providing health care to children through Medicaid and the Children's Health Insurance Program has a positive impact on human capital and confers long-term benefits (Cohodes et al. 2016; Brown, Kowalski, and Lurie 2020; Miller and Wherry 2019; Goodman-Bacon 2021; Arenberg, Neller, and Stripling 2020). Early investments in human capital tend to compound, meaning that individuals who benefit from early investments gain more from later investment than they would have otherwise (Cunha and Heckman 2007; Johnson and Jackson 2019).

Consistent with these findings, a comparative analysis of public programs shows that policies directly investing in children at young ages—including via childcare, K-12 education, health care, and housing—offer the highest return on public investment (Hendren and Sprung-Keyser 2020). These policies tend to increase employment and earnings later in life, increasing tax revenue and/or decreasing government transfers. For example, even setting aside the direct benefits of Medicaid to its beneficiaries, Medicaid expansions to children often more than pay for themselves, affecting beneficiary productivity enough to net returns in excess of the initial program cost. Analysts estimate that Medicaid generates up to $2 in discounted future tax revenue for each $1 spent expanding the program to more children (Ash et al. 2023).

Given the productivity returns, investments in children are often a win-win. The Child Tax Credit is a critical direct investment. The failure of Congress to respond to the President's call to renew the expanded Child Tax Credit for 2022 caused 3 million children to fall into poverty in 2022 (CEA 2023c). As the United States increasingly relies on improved labor productivity in the face of an aging population, disinvestments in children are a costly policy error.

Box 3-6. Long-Term Care

Demand for long-term care will be increasingly important as the U.S. population ages. Today, a mix of paid caregivers in long-term facilities and in-home and community-based services—as well as informal unpaid caregivers, who are often family members, friends, and neighbors—provide the country's senior care (Osterman 2017). The care workforce is composed of more than 37.1 million unpaid (BLS 2023b) and 4.7 million paid providers (PHI 2022), with women constituting the majority (BLS 2022). In 2021, family caregivers' unpaid economic contributions were valued at $600 billion (Reinhard et al. 2023).

Addressing the needs of the senior population and younger family members supporting them requires providing better access to affordable institutional care and continuing to expand home and community-based services to best accommodate individual preferences.

As the primary payer for long-term care services, Medicaid has an important role to play. Home- and community-based services have grown from making up less than 20 percent of Medicaid's long term care spending in 1995 to more than 50 percent today (Grabowski 2021). As of 2020, roughly 75 percent of the 5.6 million Medicaid long-term care enrollees used services under the home- and community-based services model (Chidambaram and Burns 2023). The Biden-Harris Administration has championed expanding home-based options in proposed budgets and Executive Orders. The Administration has also made historic investments in improving long-term care quality and standards (White House 2023a).

Long-term care improvements matter not only for seniors and their loved ones but also for the labor market. Increasing formal care access and affordability either in an individual's home or a nursing facility helps alleviate the burden on unpaid caregivers and improves labor market participation (AARP 2020; Schmitz and Westphal 2017). With increased access to formal home-based care, adult children of parents in need are less likely to drop out of the labor force and more likely to work full time over longer periods than they otherwise would (Shen 2023; Coe, Goda, and Van Houtven 2023). One study finds that for every three daughters with a senior parent receiving formal home-based care through Medicaid, the substitution to formal care causes one daughter to work full time who would not have otherwise (Shen 2023). As long-term care demand rises, the Federal Government must therefore continue investing in caregiving to improve the senior population's well-being and maintain a strong overall labor force.

Figure 3-9. Annual Medicare Spending per Beneficiary

2021 dollars

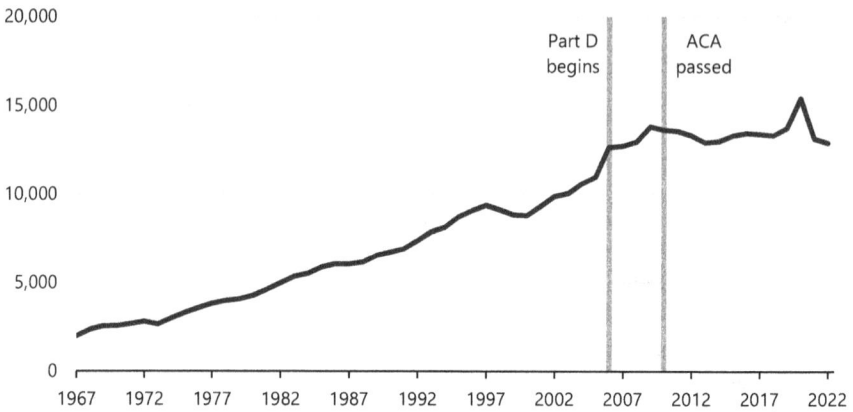

Council of Economic Advisers

Sources: Centers for Medicare and Medicaid Services 2023 Medicare Trustees Report; CEA calculations.
Note: ACA = Affordable Care Act. Per-beneficiary spending is calculated as total expenditures divided by total enrollment, including Parts A, B, C, and D. Deflated using CPI-U.
2024 Economic Report of the President

Medicare, with 86 percent of its recipients being at least 65 years of age, is projected to account for more than 60 percent of Federal health expenditures in 2053. Demographic changes will exacerbate budget deficits and the projected depletion of the Medicare and combined Social Security Trust Funds beginning 2031 and 2034, respectively (CMS 2023a; SSA 2023c).[13] The trust fund calculations, however, rely on assumptions using current laws. Outside observers have suggested altering program structures in terms of revenues or benefits (e.g., Lee and Edwards 2002; Sheiner 2018). The Affordable Care Act of 2010 made such an adjustment via the Additional Medicare Tax on high earners, and the President's 2024 budget proposed to increase taxes on earned and unearned income above $400,000 as part of a package to further extend Medicare's solvency (IRS 2024; U.S. Department of the Treasury 2023).

Against this backdrop, Medicare's slower-than-expected spending in the past decade has been a fiscal bright spot. The growth rate in real Medicare spending per beneficiary declined from 6.6 percent between 1987 and 2005 to 2.2 percent between 2013 and 2019 (CBO 2023c). Figure 3-9 plots how Medicare spending per beneficiary has evolved over the past several decades.

Several phenomena have contributed to the slowdown in Medicare cost growth: lower-than-expected growth in prescription drug expenditures,

---

[13] The combined Social Security Trust Fund refers to the Old-Age and Survivors Insurance Trust Fund and the Disability Insurance Trust Fund.

due to both generic drug entry after exclusivity expiration and the introduction of fewer new drugs (CBO 2023c); declines in hospitalizations for acute cardiovascular events, due in part to more effective medications (Cutler et al. 2019); a slowdown in the diffusion and adoption of expensive new health care technologies (Smith, Newhouse, and Cuckler 2022); and the influence of the ACA (Buntin et al. 2022). In particular, the ACA's payment reforms for Medicare providers and private Medicare Advantage insurers were an important source of savings (White, Cubanski, and Neuman 2014; CEA 2016).

One way to understand the massive importance of this slowdown in cost growth is to consider the difference in future outlays between a scenario in which per capita Medicare spending is held at a projected real GDP per capita growth rate of 1.6 percent,[14] and a scenario in which per capita Medicare spending resumes its 1980–2005 growth trend (a 3.5 percent annualized growth rate). The difference in trajectory, combined with the Medicare-supported population growing to 87 million by 2050, would add up to a difference of about $14 trillion (in 2021 dollars) between 2024 and 2050 (CMS 2023b).

Real per capita Medicare spending growth has stalled, but this is unlikely to persist indefinitely. As medical technology advances, Americans will expect Medicare to cover expensive new treatments and cures that extend and improve life. Past growth in treatments and cures has been dramatic. For example, in 1960, when real per capita U.S. health care spending was less than 10 percent of what it is today (NHEA 2023), no doctor had ever performed an angioplasty to clear a blocked artery, administered combination chemotherapy to treat cancer, or been able to prescribe a biologic drug or synthetic insulin. The improvements since then have reduced mortality and allowed people with serious chronic conditions to live flourishing lives. The coming decades will likely bring similar breakthroughs, and society must plan for ways to pay for them.

The Inflation Reduction Act is placing and will continue to place downward pressure on the drug component of Medicare spending. It requires drug companies to pay back Medicare if they raise prices faster than inflation. And beginning in 2026, Medicare will pay reduced negotiated prices for some drugs for the first time in the program's history. This is an important advance, as the United States has historically paid twice as much as other advanced economies for the same pharmaceutical products (Mulcahy et al. 2022).[15] Figure 3-10 compares drug prices in the United States and other

---

[14] The projected real GDP per capita growth rate is based on a longer-term projection of the real GDP growth rate from CBO and population projections from the Census (CBO 2023b; Census 2023b).
[15] The U.S. drug prices shown in figure 3-10 reflect estimates of net prices, subtracting estimated average rebates.

Figure 3-10. Global Prescription Drug Prices, U.S. Net Price Adjustment, 2018

Country-specific prescription drug prices versus U.S. drug prices; index: United States = 100

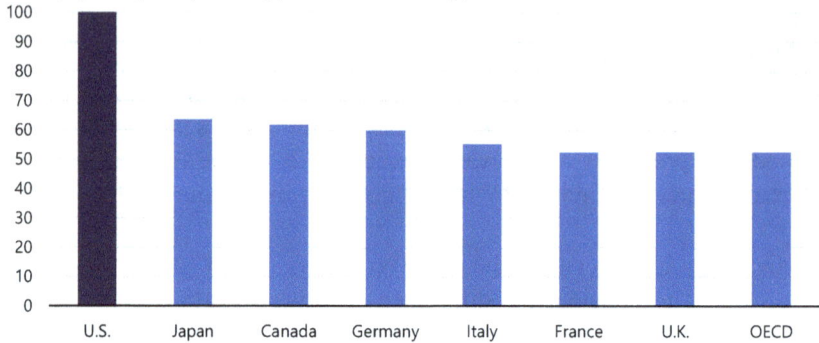

Council of Economic Advisers
Sources: Office of Assistant Secretary for Planning and Evaluation, Department of Health and Human Services; IQVIA MIDAS; CEA calculations.
Note: OECD = Organization for Economic Cooperation and Development. Here, "OECD" means 32 OECD comparison countries combined. U.S. prices are set to 100. Only some prescriptions sold in each country contribute to bilateral comparisons. In this figure, U.S. drug prices reflect estimates of net prices, subtracting estimated average rebates.
2024 Economic Report of the President

countries. The IRA-authorized negotiation process will use the United States' leverage as an important customer to get concessions on price—just as other nations have long done, and as the Department of Veterans Affairs and Department of Defense have done for years (GAO 2013). The list of drugs subject to price negotiations will expand in the future, driving overall Medicare drug spending down and narrowing the gap between U.S. drug prices and those in other advanced economies.

Planning for the Demographic Future

Rates of birth, death, and migration will govern the demographic future of the United States, with wide-ranging effects (see box 3-7). Acute mortality crises, including the opioid epidemic and COVID-19, are amenable to policy solutions, and life expectancy improvements overall will depend on public health initiatives, medical innovation, and support for public and private insurance coverage. Future improvements in health and longevity are likely to move along two axes: (1) addressing the rise in deaths due to external causes, particularly drug overdoses; and (2) investing in the fight against chronic disease.

Policy has little direct relationship with birthrates (Brainerd 2014; Sobotka, Matysiak and Brzozowska 2019). Because low fertility has its origins in improved opportunities, especially among women, it is likely to persist indefinitely. Readiness for the coming demographic changes will require attention and planning—including realistic assessments of the likely speed of these changes and of the potential role of immigration in dampening this new demographic transition. Now is the time for U.S. policymakers to seriously confront the implications of shifting population patterns and to plan responsibly.

Box 3-7. Consumption and Investment in an Aging Society

As the U.S. population skews older, aggregate consumption patterns change. Nonhousing expenditures—such as transportation, clothing, and food purchased away from home—largely follow a hump-shaped pattern over the life cycle; they are lowest during early entry into the labor force (under 25 years of age), highest during peak working age (from 45 to 54), and decline upon retirement (over 65) (Foster 2015). Health care consumption, including hospitalizations and prescription drug use, increases dramatically with age (Hales et al. 2019).

Aging has upstream effects on the labor market, as employment shifts across economic sectors to accommodate demand changes. The Bureau of Labor Statistics projects the health care and social assistance sector will add 2.1 million jobs over the next 10 years, growing faster than any other sector (BLS 2023c). Health care support occupations are projected to account for one out of every six new jobs during the coming decade.

The shifting age distribution also affects aggregate spending, borrowing, and saving. The canonical life-cycle hypothesis model predicts that people consider their expected income stream and desired onsumption and make informed decisions to smooth lifetime consumption (Modigliani and Brumberg 1954). The smoothing choices are typically characterized by demand for borrowing at young ages and saving for retirement during middle age. These behaviors imply that as people age, their wealth tends to increase, even excluding the equity of durable goods like housing and vehicles. Wealth balances typically decline only at the highest ages, suggesting that the overall aging of the U.S. population has likely increased the aggregate supply of loanable funds.

The cross-sectional expenditure data shown in figure 3-iii confirm this expectation. In 2022, the rate of saving for consumers under 25 was essentially zero, on average, according to the Consumer Expenditure Survey. The rate was higher for middle-aged Americans, peaking at 17.4 percent for those age 45 to 54, and negative for older Americans, reaching –12 percent for people 75 and above. Research suggests that the movement of baby boomers into their prime saving years increased the aggregate saving rate by about 2 percentage points in the period 1980–90 (Dynan, Edelberg, and Palumbo 2009).

Because of its impact on rates of saving and aggregate loanable funds, demographic change can also influence real interest rates, putting downward pressure on the natural interest rate as aging cohorts save for

Figure 3-iii. Savings Rates and Wealth in 2022, by Age Group

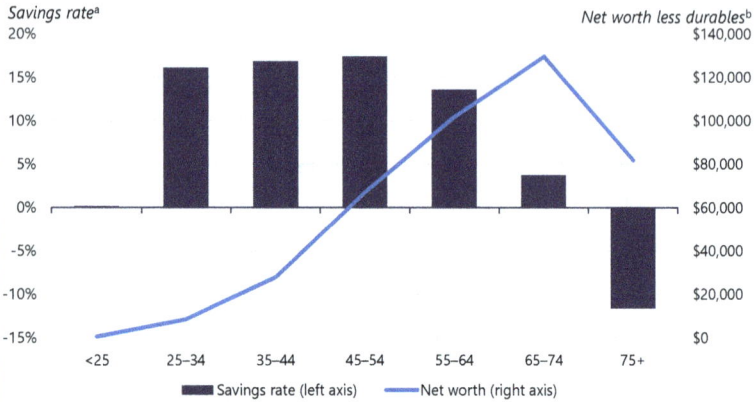

Savings rate[a]

Net worth less durables[b]

Savings rate (left axis) ——— Net worth (right axis)

Council of Economic Advisers

Sources: Bureau of Economic Analysis; CEA calculations.
[a] The savings rate = 1 – Total Expenditures / After-Tax Income in the CEX.
[b] Median net worth of families with heads in each age range, less housing equity and net vehicle equity (total vehicle value less total vehicle loan balances).
2024 Economic Report of the President

retirement. In a steady state, cohorts moving through their life cycles would have no time-varying impact. However, the baby boom generation is disproportionately large, and the United States is transitioning to increasingly low fertility rates and long lives after retirement, changes that will affect aggregate outcomes. Carvalho, Ferrero, and Nechio (2017) argue that life-expectancy increases leading to increased savings have, in particular, driven down real interest rates. Gagnon, Johannsen, and Lopez-Salido (2016) estimate that demographic factors are responsible for a 1.25-percentage-point decline in real interest rates in the United States since 1980. An inflection point exists where the savings rate declines and wealth begins shrinking, but as figure 3-iii shows, the declines tend to occur well past age 65. Although the last of the baby boomers will soon enter the negative-saving life-cycle period, the process that places upward pressure on interest rates will unfold gradually. Retirees consume only a fraction of their total savings each year, with the bulk carried forward and reinvested. This implies the current downward pressure on natural interest rates may therefore persist for an extended period.

★ ★ ★ ★ ★ ★

Chapter 4

Increasing the Supply of Affordable Housing: Economic Insights and Federal Policy Solutions

The Biden-Harris Administration believes that every American should have access to safe and affordable housing (White House 2023a). Where people live determines their available housing quality and amenities, such as labor market access, transportation options, schools, protection from crime, environmental quality, and social networks—all of which affect their quality of life and intergenerational economic mobility (Chetty and Hendren 2018). However, the housing supply has failed to keep up with demand over the last several decades, leading to a nationwide shortage of 1.5 to 3.8 million homes and driving up the cost of housing (Calanog, Metcalfe, and Fagan 2023; Khater, Kiefer, and Yanamandra 2021; Lee, Kemp, and Reina 2022). As a result, 45 percent of renters are now cost-burdened, meaning that they spend 30 percent or more of their family income on rent, more than twice the share who were cost-burdened in 1960 (Ruggles et al. 2023).

Economic analyses of housing markets identify at least two frictions restricting supply: (1) land-use regulations and zoning restrictions that limit what can be built, and (2) rising input costs associated with construction (Khater, Keifer, and Yanamandra 2021). While some land-use regulations can be a reasonable part of community planning—for example, keeping factories away from schools or ensuring that parks are situated near residential areas—many other building regulations—for example, limiting housing density and building heights, or imposing minimum lot sizes or parking requirements—can create artificial barriers that hinder growth and drive up the cost of housing. These policies arise naturally from a local decision-making process that is influenced by homeowners, who prefer higher home prices, and account for the local costs of increased housing, such as more congestion, but they fail to account for any regional or national benefits. This classic market failure negatively affects individuals in neighboring communities and potential new residents.

The costs of these housing restrictions reach across neighborhoods. Housing shortages can lead to inefficiently low levels of labor mobility and human capital investment, affecting both individual well-being and the macroeconomy. Research shows that relaxing local land-use regulations increases migration, allowing workers to relocate from low- to high-productivity regions, and boosts aggregate output (Peri 2012; Moretti 2012). Moreover, homeownership is a wealth-building tool with a long tradition in the United States, and restrictive housing policies are an important factor explaining class and racial gaps in wealth and economic outcomes (Rothstein 2017). Increasing the housing supply, especially when combined with policies that directly support the production of affordable rental and ownership units, can increase access and equity for groups with few financial resources, increase overall wealth, and reduce disparities across groups (Carroll and Cohen-Kristiansen 2021).

This chapter focuses on the major causes and consequences of the United States' long-standing shortage of housing—and especially affordable housing—as well as Federal policy's ability to alleviate these issues. While there are policy levers at all levels of government, this chapter focuses on Federal policy. For example, public funds could be tied to zoning reforms and used to reduce financing constraints for affordable housing developments, and workforce training could increase the supply of labor used to construct housing. The first section illustrates the magnitude and trends in the housing supply shortage over the last six decades. The second and third sections discuss the causes and consequences of housing shortages. The fourth section highlights several areas where Federal policy can equitably boost the housing supply and alleviate rising housing unaffordability.

Magnitude and Trends

Housing costs are demanding a growing share of household budgets in the United States. At the same time, the U.S. housing market faces a long-run supply shortage.

Figure 4-1. Housing Price Index versus Wage Index, 1975–2023

Index: 2000:Q1 = 100

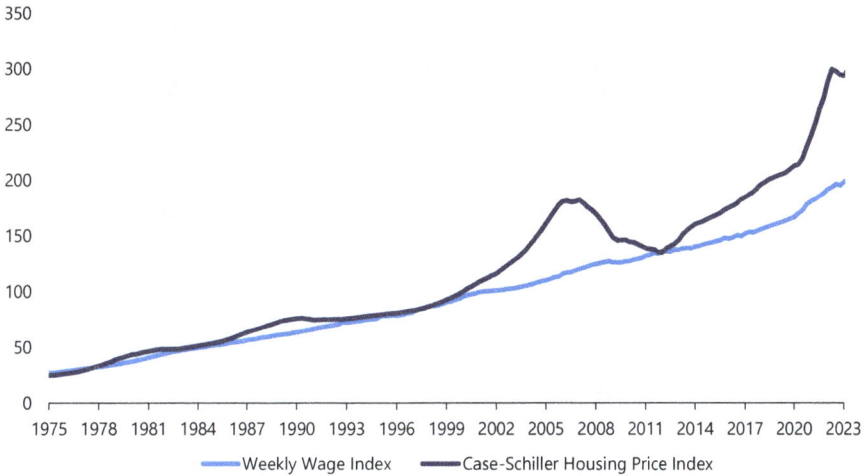

Council of Economic Advisers

Sources: Bureau of Labor Statistics (Quarterly Census of Employment and Wages); CEA calculations.
Note: Weekly Wage Index has been smoothed using a 4-quarter moving average. Gray bars indicate recessions.
2024 Economic Report of the President

Unaffordable Housing

Figure 4-1 shows that housing price increases have outpaced wage growth in the last 20 years. Between 2000 and the early 2020s, housing prices tripled while household income doubled; in other words, the price of housing rose by 50 percent more than household income in the last 20 years.[1] Of course, increased spending on housing could be a rational consumption choice. Some people will choose to spend more on housing in exchange for lower nonhousing consumption because they prefer better housing amenities, like

---

[1] Figure 4-1 reports changes in the housing price index. To provide additional context for the level of rental expenses during this period: the median rent in 1960, 1980, 2000, and 2020 was, respectively, $544, $692, $867, and $1,086, measured in 2022 dollars; and the 25th percentile of rent in 1960, 1980, 2000, and 2020 was $445, $479, $595, and $735.

a nicer location or a newer structure. But the steadily rising financial burden of housing over many decades suggests that for many families, expensive housing is not a proactive choice but rather a trend they are increasingly forced to accept.

The share of households burdened by housing expenses has risen steadily over the last 60 years. A common benchmark for describing rent-burdened households is the income share spent on housing (i.e., rent/mortgage, utilities, and other housing needs) (Cromwell 2022).[2] The U.S. Department of Housing and Urban Development defines families as rent-burdened if this share exceeds 30 percent;[3] and severely rent-burdened if households spend more than half their income on housing. Figure 4-2 shows the share of renter households that spend more than 30 percent, 40 percent, and 50 percent of their income on rent. For each measure, the share has more than doubled since the 1960s. Today, nearly 45 percent of renters are rent-burdened and nearly 24 percent of renters are severely rent-burdened.

Figure 4-2. Renter Households That Spent More Than 30 Percent of Family Income on Rent, 1960–2022

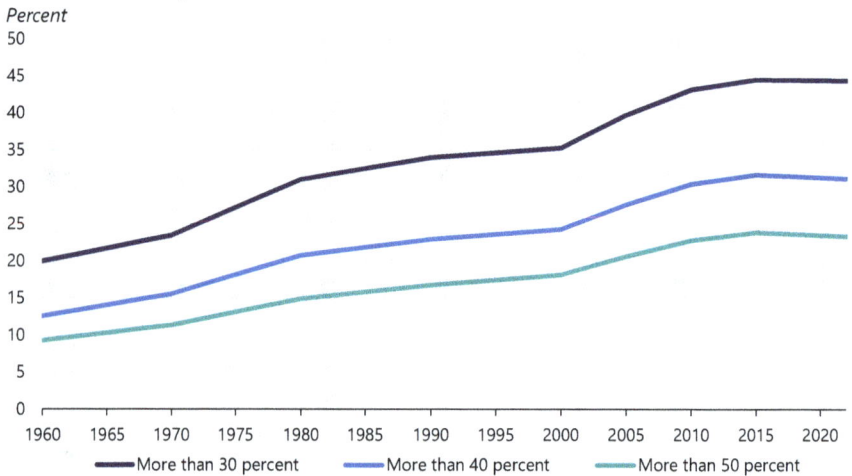

Council of Economic Advisers
Sources: Census Bureau (American Community Survey); CEA calculations.
Note: The data for years after 2000 are averaged in 5-year bins. Gray bars indicate recessions.
2024 Economic Report of the President

---

[2] Owners are typically excluded from the cost-burdened analysis because monthly mortgage payments that reduce the principal are a transfer to savings.
[3] This benchmark is based on public housing rent limits, which originated with the Brooke Amendment in 1969 and were last updated in the 1980s.

The financial burden of housing can also be illustrated by the number of work hours required to pay for housing. Figure 4-3 reports the minimum monthly work hours required to pay for monthly median rental rate housing in 2002, 2012, and 2022. Estimates are shown separately for households earning the median wage, the Federal minimum wage, and the wages that put someone at 100 percent of the Federal poverty level for single-adult households with no children.[4] Median wage earners had to work nearly 55 hours to pay for monthly housing costs in 2002, or more than one week per month based on a 40-hour work week; this number grew to more than 70 hours in 2022, or slightly less than two weeks of work. Households earning the Federal minimum wage had to work 110 hours to pay for housing in 2002, or nearly three quarters of the monthly hours worked by full-time workers. This number increased to 180 hours in 2022, suggesting that more than a full month of minimum-wage work is now required to pay for median rental-rate housing. In other words, median rental-rate housing has become increasingly out-of-reach for low-wage workers, and even median-wage

Figure 4-3. Minimum Monthly Hours of Work Needed to Pay for Median Monthly Rent

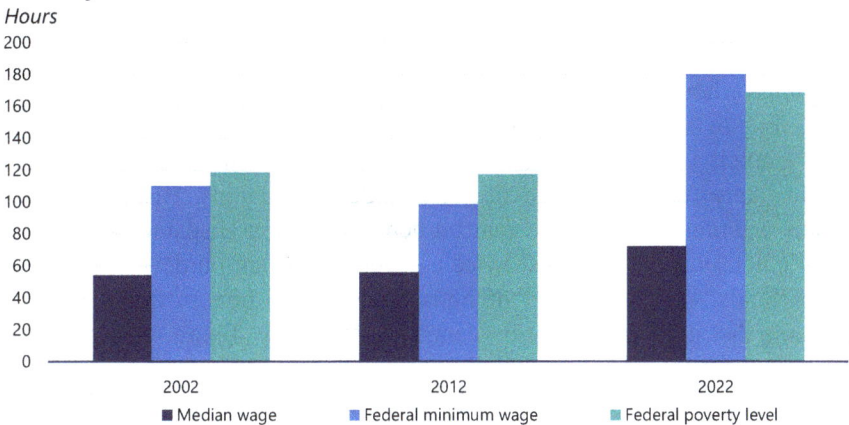

Council of Economic Advisers
Sources: Bureau of Labor Statistics; Census Bureau; Department of Labor; CEA calculations.
Note: Real median rent in 2002, 2012, and 2022, respectively: $923, $914, and $1306. The Federal poverty level is the poverty level for a single individual with no children. Effective July 2009, the Federal minimum wage was raised to $7.25. Unlike in 2002 or 2012, the Federal minimum wage led to income below the Federal poverty level in 2022.
2024 Economic Report of the President

---

[4] The minimum number of hours of work required to pay for median monthly rent is calculated as median monthly rent divided by hourly wage for workers that earn the median monthly earnings, the Federal minimum wage, or 100 percent of the Federal poverty level. For workers earning the median monthly earnings or 100 percent of the Federal poverty level, monthly earnings are converted to hourly earnings by assuming a that an employee works 160 hours per month, a typical full-time schedule.

Figure 4-4. Share of Households That Are Rent-Burdened by Household Head Characteristics, 2022

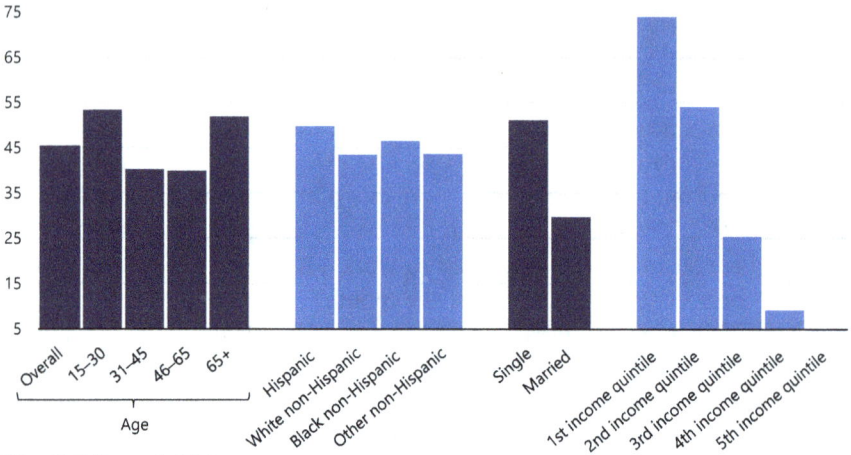

Percent

Council of Economic Advisers
Sources: Census Bureau (American Community Survey); CEA calculations.
Note: A household is defined as rent burdened if the share of family income spent on rent is more than 30 percent.
2024 Economic Report of the President

workers must devote a considerable share of their monthly earnings toward housing expenses. Many households have little disposable income after paying for housing.

Figure 4-4 reports the share of rent-burdened households by age, race and ethnicity, marital status, and income in 2022. Younger households are more likely to be rent-burdened than older households, Hispanic households are more likely to be rent-burdened than non-Hispanic households, single households are almost twice as likely to be rent-burdened as married households, and 74 percent of households in the bottom quintile of the income distribution are rent burdened. Additionally, figure 4-5 reports the share of rent-burdened households by geographic region and population density, as well as for households in the largest U.S. cities. While some variation emerges based on demographic and geographic characteristics, a large fraction of households across the entire country are rent burdened. Rent-burdened households are not just located in urban centers or in coastal States: 45 percent of rural households are rent-burdened, as are 44 and 40 percent of households in the South and Midwest, respectively.

The Housing Supply Shortage

Years of insufficient new construction relative to household formation have led to a housing supply shortage (Khater, Keifer, and Yanamandra 2021). Estimates of the stock of the total housing shortage range from 1.5 million (Calanog, Metcalfe, and Fagan 2023) to 3.8 million (Khater, Keifer, and

Figure 4-5. Share of Households That Are Rent-Burdened by Geography, 2022
Percent

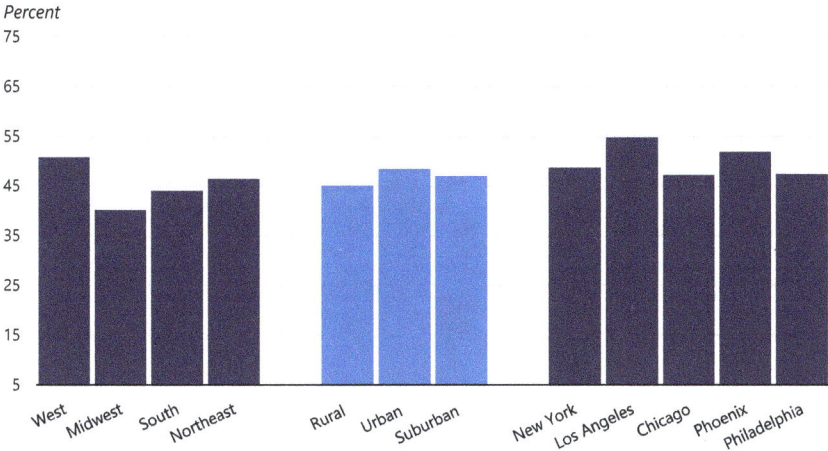

Council of Economic Advisers
Sources: Census Bureau (American Community Survey); CEA calculations.
Note: A household is defined as rent-burdened if the share of family income spent on rent is more than 30 percent. The cities chosen for the graph are among the largest six cities in the U.S. by population as of 2022. Houston is not shown here as it is not recorded in the 2022 American Community Survey data.
2024 Economic Report of the President

Yanamandra 2021), and the annual flow of the shortage of units under construction is estimated to be 100,000 (Parrott and Zandi 2021).

Increased housing demand is driven by a growing economy and a growing population. In recent decades, however, housing production has fallen dramatically. As figure 4-6 shows, quarterly housing starts per 1,000 people (shown in navy blue) fell from 22–40 units between 1963 and 1980 to 15–21 units between 1990 and 2005. Figure 4-6 also shows quarterly single-family housing starts in light blue. Single-family housing starts were relatively flat between 1963 and 2005 (averaging 10–18 units per 1,000 people). All types of housing starts fell sharply after the global financial crisis and have not yet recovered to pre-2007 levels.

A decline in new housing construction has been concurrent with the reduced availability of relatively small "starter homes" and low-cost rental units. As illustrated in figure 4-7, the fraction of all new single-family homes under 1,400 square feet declined from nearly 40 percent in the early 1970s to about 7 percent in the early 2020s. Moreover, the supply of low-cost rental units, measured as the share of rental units with contract rent below the maximum amount affordable for households in the lowest quintile of the income distribution, fell from 26.7 percent in 2011 to 17.1 percent in 2021 after adjusting for inflation. This is equivalent to the loss of 3.9 million affordable units in the last decade (Joint Center for Housing Studies 2023).

Figure 4-6. U.S. Housing Production, 1963–2022

Housing starts per 1,000 people

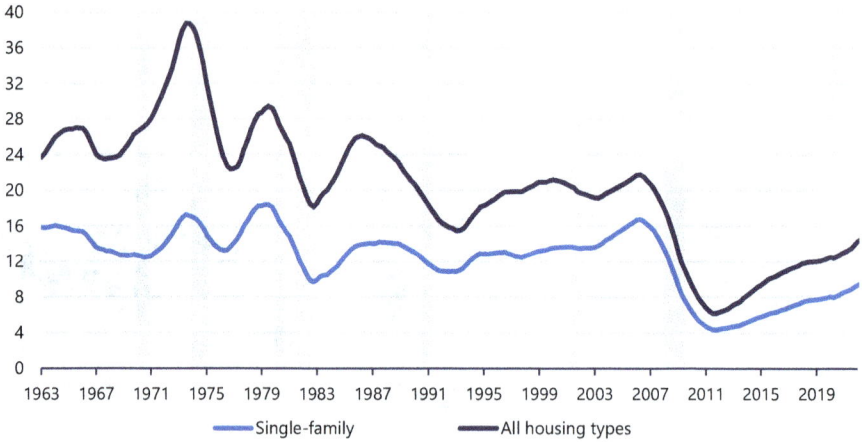

Council of Economic Advisers
Sources: Census Bureau; CEA calculations.
Note: The quarterly data are smoothed using a 3-year moving average. Gray bars indicate recessions.
2024 Economic Report of the President

Figure 4-7. Share of New Single-Family Homes under 1,400 Square Feet, 1973–2022

Percent

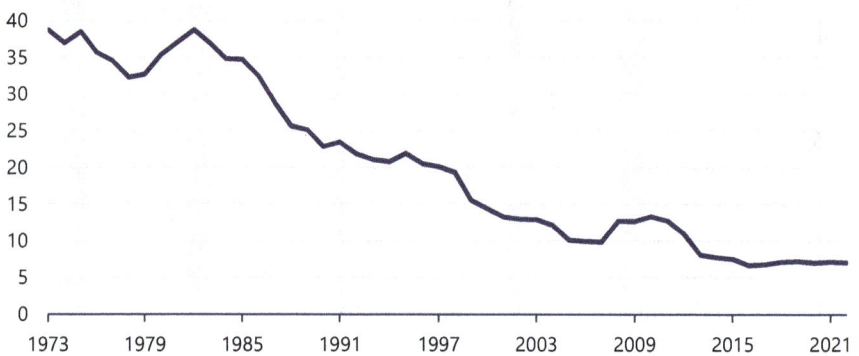

Council of Economic Advisers
Sources: Census Bureau; CEA calculations.
Note: The data shows the share of completed new single family homes that are under 1,400 square feet. Gray bars indicate recessions.
2024 Economic Report of the President

Causes of Housing Supply Shortages

The incentives of several key stakeholders inform economic models of housing markets that predict a constrained housing supply. First, homeowners typically seek to maximize their home's value. Second, local governments have an incentive to raise public funds to maximize the welfare of their constituents—among other things—which is generally linked to land value through property taxation. Third, developers and landowners seek to maximize their profit from economic development of residential and commercial real estate. These incentives jointly determine land value within a community through zoning and land-use regulations, which generally enrich insiders (i.e., existing property owners) at the expense of outsiders (i.e., renters and would-be property owners) (Fischel 2001).

Economic models make several predictions about how stakeholder incentives influence changes to land-use regulations, the housing supply, and housing prices (Ortalo-Magne and Prat 2014; Hilber and Robert-Nicoud 2013; Glaeser, Gyourko, and Saks 2005). Locations with more homeowners than renters have stricter housing supply regulations than their counterparts, and the regulations tighten as homeowners' political influence grows (Fang, Stewart, and Tyndall 2023). Regulations reduce the price elasticity of the housing supply; in other words, the supply of housing is less responsive to market prices in markets with more regulation.

Research consistently finds that increasingly stringent zoning restrictions lead to lower housing construction and a lower price elasticity of the housing supply, while decreasingly stringent zoning restrictions lead to higher housing construction costs and a higher price elasticity of the housing supply (Baum-Snow 2023; Gyourko and Molloy 2015; Stacy et al. 2023; Landis and Reina 2021). The relationship between zoning restrictiveness and housing prices is more nuanced: tighter zoning restrictions lead to more expensive housing, often by requiring new homes to be larger and occupy larger lots (Gyourko and McCulloch 2023). More relaxed zoning restrictions lead to a higher supply of smaller, lower-cost housing, and, in at least some instances, can lead to lower prices and rents or slower growth in rents among existing housing (Crump et al. 2020; Been, Ellen, and O'Regan 2023; Baum-Snow 2023; Greenaway-McGrevy 2023).

Broadly, local decision-making processes lead to at least two cascading housing market failures. The first is of negative externalities, which predict too much land-use regulation relative to the social optimum because homeowners, developers, and local governments do not account for the welfare cost of these regulations for individuals in neighboring communities or would-be residents. The excessive regulations lead to an incomplete housing market, where the private sector does not create enough supply to meet demand. Corrective policy at the State or Federal level can help bridge the gap between housing supply and demand.

Figure 4-8. Housing Prices and Construction Costs, 1980–2022

Inflation-adjusted index

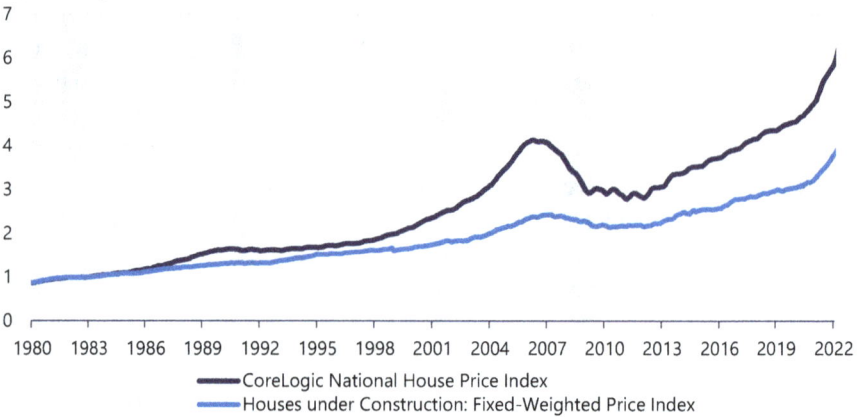

CoreLogic National House Price Index
Houses under Construction: Fixed-Weighted Price Index

Council of Economic Advisers

Sources: Census Bureau; CoreLogic; CEA calculations.
Note: Both price indices are adjusted for inflation using the Personal Consumption Expenditures price index (core services excluding housing), reindexed to 1982 = 100. The data are not seasonally adjusted. Gray bars indicate recessions.
2024 Economic Report of the President

The Wedge Between Price and Construction Cost: Land Value

The causes and consequences of housing supply shortages in the United States can be understood within the context of the housing market's pricing efficiency, or the relationship between price and cost. As shown in figure 4-8, physical construction costs have quadrupled since the 1980s, accelerated by an increase in labor and material costs (Khater, Keifer, and Yanamandra 2021; CBRE 2022), while construction sector productivity has fallen (Goolsbee and Syverson 2023). Also seen in figure 4-8, housing prices have increased more quickly than construction costs. Between 1980 and the early 2020s, housing prices grew by over sixfold, or about 50 percent more than the fourfold increase in construction costs. Economists attribute the growing gap between housing prices and physical construction costs in the U.S. housing market to land prices, which largely reflect the impact of restrictive land-use regulations (Gyourko and Molloy 2015).

Zoning and Land-Use Regulations: Effects on the Housing Supply

Exclusionary zoning policies are a subset of local land-use regulations that can constrain the housing supply and thus decrease affordability. Examples include prohibitions on multifamily homes, height limits, minimum lot sizes, square footage minimums, and parking requirements—each of which functions to constrain housing and population density. Researchers estimate that loosening land-use restrictions would lead to a small but significant increase in the metropolitan housing supply over the next decade (Stacy et al. 2023).

Some zoning laws date back to the late 1800s, when city planners were concerned about fire hazards, access to light and outdoor air, or proximity to industry (Fischel 2004). While some zoning laws were intended to improve the quality of life for poor and vulnerable families, others were designed to discriminate against minority groups and raise property prices in suburban and urban neighborhoods (Rigsby 2016; Mangin 2014). Some of the first zoning laws appeared in about 1917, when the Supreme Court banned explicit race-based segregation in zoning ordinances in *Buchanan v. Warley* (Rothstein 2017). Scholars have shown that certain zoning practices enabled cities to continue race-based segregation (Gray 2022; Kahlenberg 2023). Box 4-1 provides additional detail on the history of zoning laws and their effects on racial and ethnic minorities.

Single-family zoning is imposed on most residentially zoned land across the country and constitutes 70 percent of all U.S. residential zoning (Frank 2021). Minimum lot size requirements force developers to build homes on larger lots than the market would otherwise provide (Gyourko, Hartley, and Krimmel 2019; Furth and Gray 2019). For example, 81 percent of Connecticut land requires a minimum of 1 acre lots (Bronin 2023). Research finds that doubling minimum lot sizes increases sale prices by 14 percent and rents by 6 percent, while intensifying residential segregation (Song 2021). Recent zoning changes allowing multifamily housing in Boston and Minneapolis–Saint Paul has led to increased housing supply, desegregation, and increased shares of Black and Hispanic residents (Resseger 2022; Furth and Webster 2022).

Another important land-use regulation concerns minimum parking requirements, which dictate a minimum number of off-street spaces per housing unit or business. However, studies have shown the requirements often exceed what is needed to meet demand, leading to large shares of land devoted to parking lots. For example, 30 percent of downtown Detroit is dedicated to parking, compared with 12 percent in Los Angeles and 4 percent in Chicago (Sorens 2023; Chester et al. 2015; Kaufmann 2023). Parking requirements impose space requirements beyond lot sizes, reducing the housing supply and increasing the cost of housing (WGI 2021). Research has found that parking requirements in Los Angeles reduce the number of units in apartment buildings by 13 percent (Shoup 2014). A Seattle reform that reduced parking requirements was found to be associated with developers building 40 percent less parking than would have been required before the reform, resulting in 18,000 fewer parking spaces and saving an estimated $537 million in construction costs, ultimately leading to lower-priced housing (Gabbe, Pierce, and Clowers 2020).

Box 4-1. A Brief History of Exclusionary Zoning Laws in the United States

Some of the earliest zoning ordinances were enacted in the mid to late 1800s to isolate nuisance land use, such as by slaughterhouses, from residential areas. Under the guise of further resident protection, however, other ordinances were implemented that isolated racial and ethnic minorities. For example, the historic "Chinese laundry" regulations allowed many white proprietors to be licensed while excluding Chinese business owners (Howells 2022).

In 1910, Baltimore enacted one of the first zoning laws that explicitly segregated neighborhoods by suggesting that the ordinances protected the public. The Supreme Court's 1917 *Buchanan v. Warley* decision struck down explicitly racist zoning laws (Howells 2022).

In the wake of *Buchanan v. Warley*, communities began implicitly segregating by race with new forms of zoning. Single-family zoning in Berkeley, California, in early 1910s attempted to prohibit "Negroes and Asiatics" from living in certain areas, and the strategy began to spread across the country (Barber 2019). Single-family zoning also prohibited apartment buildings and other types of affordable housing, leading to increased class segregation (Gray 2022). Saint Louis introduced zoning designed to preserve homes in areas unaffordable to most Black families in 1919, and the city often changed areas' zoning designations from residential to industrial once numerous Black families moved in (Rothstein 2014). Similarly, Seattle's 1923 zoning laws changed many areas with a large number of Black or Chinese American families from residential to commercial (Twinam 2018). The Supreme Court upheld various zoning restrictions, including against multifamily housing, in *Euclid v. Ambler* (Supreme Court 1926), furthering class-based discrimination. The new zoning rules restricted new housing levels and made prices unaffordable for low income and most nonwhite households (CEA 2021).

In the 1920s, the Secretary of Commerce, Herbert Hoover, published "A Zoning Primer," which encouraged States to allow municipalities to adopt exclusionary zoning (Gries 1922). The 1923 Standard State Zoning Enabling Act provided model legislation that States could pass to give municipalities zoning power; eventually, all States gave municipalities the right to determine local zoning regulations (Flint 2022). The number of cities with zoning rules increased by 1,246 additional municipalities between 1916 and 1936 (Fischel 2004).

The 1970s saw a second wave of zoning in response to (1) the 1968 Fair Housing Act, which attempted to clamp down on discrimination by race and other factors, as communities responded by increasing economically discriminatory zoning; and (2) the growing importance of real estate within household financial portfolios. By the 2000s, more than 30,000 local governments in the United States had their own zoning rules (Kahlenberg 2023). In recent decades, America's neighborhoods have continued to be segregated by race and income (Loh, Coes, and Buthe 2020).

One analysis found that 40 percent of Manhattan buildings could not be built today because they do not conform to zoning codes (Bui, Chaban, and White 2016). Dense city centers would be almost impossible to build with modern minimum parking requirements, and many new developments are only approved after receiving special permits or variances to circumvent zoning rules (Bui, Chaban, and White 2016; Gray 2022). Other factors restricting the housing supply include mandatory public hearings, fees and exactions, environmental review, design standards, lot configuration requirements, building size regulations, rising insurance costs, and occupancy rules (Bronin 2023). Each regulation restricts what developers can build, increases time-to-construction and structure costs, and leads many would-be housing projects to be financially infeasible.

Additional Constraints

New multifamily housing development, whether for renter- or owner-occupied units, is a complex, long-run capital investment process that is highly sensitive to the macroeconomic environment. The projects involve various development costs, including (1) physical construction ("hard") costs, (2) project design and development ("soft") costs, and (3) land costs. Developers draw project financing from a combination of debt and equity that require different rates of return from completed projects, imposing minimum profitability thresholds and tying private development to interest rate fluctuations. At the same time, most revenue for multifamily rental development comes from rent charged to tenants, which is related to local land-use regulations. Box 4-2 describes the calculus behind financing housing development projects—this calculus is sometimes referred to as "penciling the deal."

Demographic shifts in the American population affect both housing supply and demand. For example, a sharp increase in life expectancy during the last century—combined with the aging of the baby boom generation—has increased the demand for housing among older Americans (*Berkeley Economic Review* 2019). In addition, to the extent that homeowners choose not to move as they age, this will tend to reduce the rate of repeat sales for the current stock of homes, reducing the supply of available homes. Changes in fertility and international immigration have also affected housing demand.

Box 4-2. Penciling the Deal: The Math Behind Developing Rental Housing with LIHTC

New multifamily development projects are characterized by large upfront costs and long-run investment returns. Most of the revenue generated by housing developments comes from rent charged to tenants, as determined by local market conditions. The Low-Income Housing Tax Credit (LIHTC) enables developers to meet these upfront costs and charge less rent, making units affordable for 30 years after construction.

Developers balance future revenue streams against development and financing costs to determine whether a property is worth constructing; in other words, whether the deal "pencils out" (Garcia 2019). Development costs can be grouped into three categories: (1) hard physical construction costs, including labor and materials; (2) soft costs (e.g., fees, financing, consulting, taxes, title, and insurance); and (3) land acquisition costs, including those associated with closing (e.g., environmental studies and resolving zoning issues). While local market conditions vary across the United States, land costs generally comprise 10–20 percent of total costs, soft costs comprise 20–30 percent, and hard costs comprise 60–70 percent. Local land-use regulations, such as zoning restrictions, parking requirements, and density restrictions, can all increase development costs (Urban Institute 2016; Hoyt and Schuetz 2020).

To finance projects, developers obtain funding from debt and equity. Debt typically comprises most of the funding, with loan-to-cost ratios of 50 to 75 percent (Urban Institute 2016; Garcia 2019; RCN Capital n.d.). Historically, interest rates have fluctuated between 4 and 8 percent. Equity, mostly from private investors, fills the gap between debt and project costs. Housing development equity is a relatively risky investment class due to the time required for projects to generate revenue. At a high level, equity investors compare the return on cost—the ratio of the project's first year net operating income to its costs—with local capitalization rates. Local capitalization rates capture the average rates of return on alternative housing projects and typically range between 3 and 6 percent. According to one analysis, differences of 1 to 1.5 percent between the return on cost and capitalization rates would incentivize private investment (Garcia 2019; JPMorgan Chase 2022).

For example, on a $20 million project, the building could be financed with $13 million in loans—which require $780,000 in debt service payments, assuming a 6 percent interest rate—and $7 million in private equity, which require $455,000 in returns to be attractive based on typical market capitalization rates. Assuming a per-unit rent that equals the nationwide median, the structure can have, at most, 136 units; this structure could generate a 6.5 percent capitalization rate in 10 years. These units would be affordable for a tenant who earns the median income in 2022 ($74,755), but they would be unaffordable for low-income households. For example, households in the bottom 20th percentile of the income distribution can spend, at most, $765 in monthly rent in order to not be considered cost-burdened, about half the nation-wide median monthly rent ($1,300). Developers can privately choose to designate some units as affordable by charging below-market-rate rent, but to maintain profitability, they must raise rent on the remaining units.

Affordable housing can reduce the net operating income of a hous-ing development project and threaten its viability. The LIHTC offers an incentive to construct affordable housing by providing tax credit equity in exchange for affordable unit construction. Among other requirements, projects must meet one of three income tests to be eligible:

A. At least 20 percent of the units are occupied by tenants with an income of 50 percent or less of area median income (AMI), adjusted for family size.

B. At least 40 percent of the units are occupied by tenants with an income of 60 percent or less of AMI, adjusted for family size.

C. At least 40 percent of the units are occupied by tenants with income averaging no more than 60 percent of AMI, and no units are occupied by tenants with income greater than 80 percent of AMI, adjusted for family size.

The LIHTC provides a 10-year stream of annual credits based on a housing project's construction costs equal to either 30 or 70 percent of the present value of the qualified basis, depending on whether the project was approved for the competitive or noncompetitive allocation (Tax Policy Center n.d.). The LIHTC is one of the few tax programs that allows for credits to be bought and sold on a secondary market. In particular, developers can sell their tax credits to investors who are better able to take advantage of the LIHTC and other project-related tax benefits to reduce their tax liability. Credits are typically sold by developers at a discount, which fluctuated between $0.85 and $0.90 on the $1 as of 2021, to reflect the time-value of money (Kimura 2022). The tax equity investors typically take a passive role, receiving the benefits but not participating in day-to-day decision-making.

In the case of the $20 million building, if 20 percent of the units are set aside for low-income tenants, as specified by income test A above, and the LIHTC credits were awarded competitively, the LIHTC program can provide $1.4 million in equity, assuming that investors are willing to purchase credits at a discount of $0.85 on $1. With this tax equity, only $5.6 million in private equity is needed, which will require 7 percent fewer returns from rent to cover financing costs.

Figure 4-i compares the per-unit rent in the affordable and remain-ing units with and without the LIHTC and under two scenarios: (1) 20 percent of units affordable at 50 percent of the nationwide median

Figure 4-i. Rent Comparisons Under Different Funding Scenarios

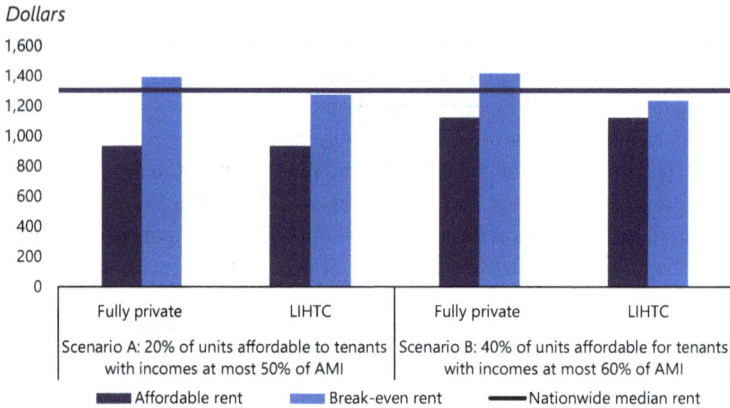

Dollars

Fully private	LIHTC	Fully private	LIHTC
Scenario A: 20% of units affordable to tenants with incomes at most 50% of AMI		Scenario B: 40% of units affordable for tenants with incomes at most 60% of AMI	

■ Affordable rent   ■ Break-even rent   — Nationwide median rent

Council of Economic Advisers

Sources: Census Bureau (2022); CEA calculations.
Note: LIHTC = Low Income Housing Tax Credit; AMI = Area Median Income. The figure illustrates calculations for a $20 million hypothetical building.
2024 Economic Report of the President

income; and (2) 40 percent of units affordable at 60 percent of the nationwide median. As shown, the LIHTC program allows developers to allocate units to low-income renters without cross-subsidizing via increased rent on the remaining units. If developers instead choose to fund affordable units privately, for example, in order to satisfy an inclusionary zoning requirement, the building's remaining units would need to be rented at above the market rate, as characterized in figure 4-i, based on the nationwide median rent for illustrative purposes, for the developer to break even on costs. This funding scenario, however, introduces additional risk as the developer would have no guarantee of demand for the above-market-rate units.

Researchers estimate that the combined effect of changes in life expectancy, international immigration, urbanization, and fertility can account for 41 percent of the observed housing price increase from 1970 to 2010 and forecast an additional increase of 5 to 19 percent in housing prices through 2050 (Gong and Yao 2022). Likewise, research finds that a 1-percentage-point increase in the current birthrate would increase housing prices by 4 to 5 percent in 25 to 30 years (Francke and Korevaar 2022). Moreover, foreign-born household heads are projected to be the primary source of new housing demand by 2040 (Nguyen 2015).

Housing Supply Shortages: Consequences for Welfare, Economic Mobility, and Aggregate Output

Even in functional housing markets, income variation across households implies that low-income households face higher housing cost burdens than those with a higher income. When land-use restrictions drive supply constraints, growing housing demand in cities and neighborhoods leads to more expensive housing, rather than new housing development (Baum-Snow 2023). The resulting housing shortages manifest as lower vacancy rates and higher prices and rents relative to wage growth. As the gap widens between market prices and production costs, more households experience housing insecurity, which negatively affects individual welfare and economic mobility (Been et al. 2011; Taylor 2018).

Neighborhood Choice, Individual Welfare, and Economic Mobility

Prices affect not only the type of housing in which individuals choose to live, but also where they live. The latter decision is tied to a bundle of local amenities, including access to jobs and transportation, schools, exposure to crime, environmental quality, health care access, and social networks. Importantly, neighborhood choice shapes children's long-run educational and economic outcomes, and neighborhood environment affects adult health and well-being (Chetty and Hendren 2018; Chyn and Katz 2021).

Property taxes typically fund public schools; the greater the tax base per capita, the more funds are available for education. Children from high-income households tend to live in expensive neighborhoods and, therefore, have access to higher quality schools. Housing near high-scoring public schools costs on average 2.4 times more, or nearly $11,000 more per year, than housing near low-scoring schools (Rothwell 2012). Few affordable housing options exist near high-quality schools (DiSalvo and Yu 2023), which reduces the number of low-income, as well as Black and Hispanic, students attending them, and exacerbates intergenerational inequality (Ihlanfeldt 2019). Black and Hispanic students attending more segregated schools are less likely to graduate from high school and attend college than their peers attending less segregated schools, and they are less likely to work and more likely to have low earnings as adults (Gould Ellen, De la Roca, and Steil 2015).

Economic models, such as that developed by Tiebout (1956), suggest that beyond valuing neighborhoods for their schools, households "vote with their feet" and choose neighborhoods that best match their preferences. However, because housing markets are incomplete and affordable houses are often not available in neighborhoods with high-quality amenities, rising housing prices push low-income households toward areas with few amenities.

Housing supply constraints can affect demographic shifts in the American population. For instance, young adults primarily demand entry-level and lower-priced housing. As a result, shortages in the entry-level market sector are felt most by young adults. Research has shown household formation rates decreased in recent years as a result of increased housing prices: a 1 percent increase in housing prices decreases household formation by almost 5 percent for young adults (Kiefer, Atreya, and Yanamandra 2018). Consistent with this finding, homeownership rates have been declining over time for young adults (Goodman, Choi, and Zhu 2023).

Wealth Accumulation

Homeownership has long been a common path to wealth accumulation in the United States, with returns being especially high for those who can afford expensive homes (Wolff 2022). As a result, housing supply restrictions have implications for wealth accumulation (La Cava 2016). Figure 4-9 reports homeownership rates and median net family worth by income, age, race and ethnicity, and geography. Generally, patterns in homeownership rates according to these characteristics are correlated with wealth patterns. Higher-income, older, and white non-Hispanic households are more likely to own their homes and have accumulated more wealth than other groups.

Intergenerational wealth transfers interact with homeownership. For example, individuals are about 8 percentage points more likely to become

Figure 4-9. Homeownership Rate and Median Net Family Worth, 2022

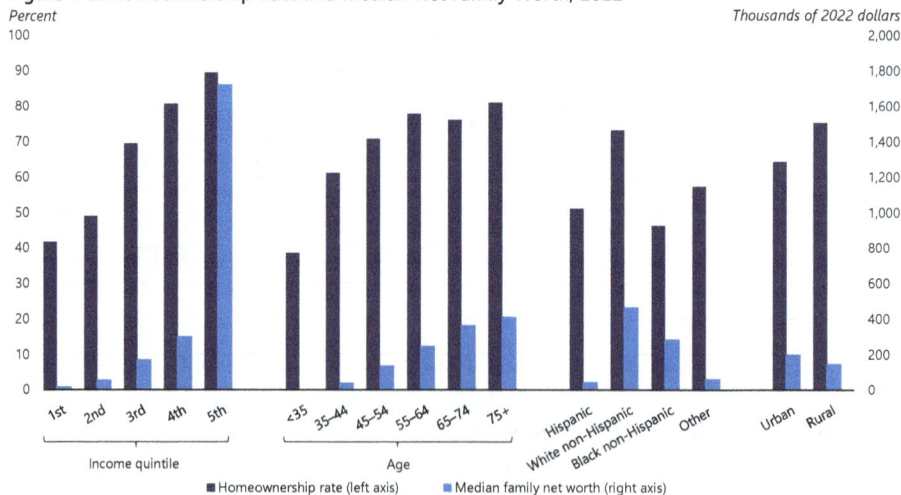

Council of Economic Advisers
Sources: Survey of Consumer Finances; Census Bureau; CEA calculations.
Note: The values for the fifth income quintile are calculated by averaging over data reported for 80–89.9 and 90–100 income quintiles.
2024 Economic Report of the President

homeowners if their parents are homeowners rather than nonhomeowners (Choi, Zhu, and Goodman 2018). Because housing is the main source of wealth for most households, disparities in homeownership rates and valuations across groups are likely to lead to differences in wealth accumulation (figure 4-9). In particular, generations of discrimination in the housing market have created a substantial racial wealth gap in America; one paper estimates that, on average, Black Americans had 17 cents for every $1 in wealth white Americans had in 2019 (Derenoncourt et al. 2023). Many researchers show that these trends are likely to be perpetuated into the future (Derenoncourt et al. 2023; Aaronson, Hartley, and Mazumder 2023). Black and Hispanic homeowners also face an assessment bias in the value of their homes, creating further household wealth disparities by race and ethnicity (Avenancio-Leon and Howard 2022).

Income Shocks, Housing Instability, and Homelessness

Homeownership and home values affect households' ability to withstand income shocks. Black and Hispanic households were disproportionately affected by the foreclosure crisis after the global financial crisis and the financial hardship related to the COVID-19 pandemic (Reid et al. 2016; Bayer et al. 2016; Gerardi et al. 2021; Cornelissen and Pack 2023; Hermann et al. 2023). Foreclosures cause sustained housing instability and make future homeownership difficult, in addition to inflicting other forms of financial distress (Diamond, Guren, and Tan 2020).

While homeowners benefit from rising housing costs in their own neighborhood, the 35 percent of households who rent their home do not (Ruggles et al. 2023), and low-income residents who do not own their home face the threat of eviction. Eviction orders, which are increasingly likely after earnings declines and employment losses, increase homelessness and further reduce future earnings, durable consumption, and credit access (Collinson et al. 2023). Children are at the greatest risk for eviction, and extensive research suggests they are substantially and lastingly harmed by housing instability (Graetz et al. 2023). Finally, housing stability, quality, safety, and affordability are all associated with improved health outcomes (Taylor 2018).

Evidence suggests that regional variation in housing costs and availability explains regional variation in homelessness (Aldern and Colburn 2022). Counter to intuition, poverty rates are lower in places with higher rates of homelessness (Aldern and Colburn 2022). Homelessness is strongly correlated with median rent at the city or county level; one study shows that a $100 increase in median rent is associated with a 15 percent rise in homelessness in metropolitan areas (Byrne et al. 2016). Moreover, evidence suggests that higher homelessness rates are not associated with higher

Figure 4-10. Components of Year-on-Year Headline CPI Inflation, 2013–23

Percentage points

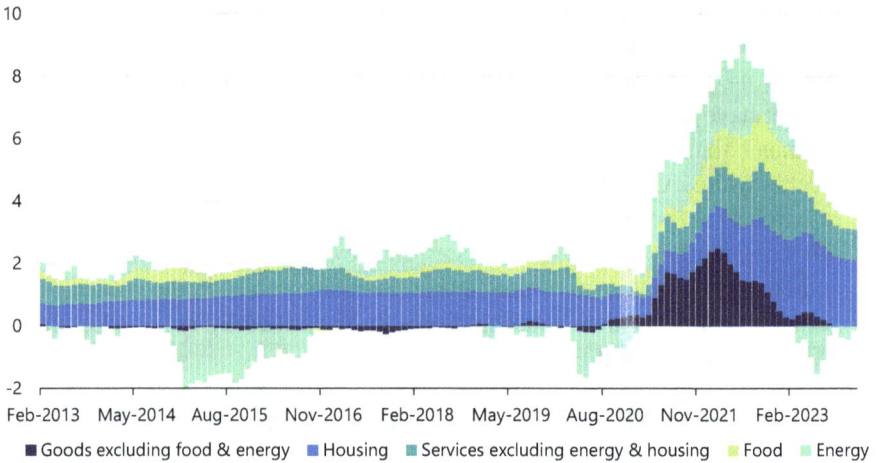

Legend: ■ Goods excluding food & energy ■ Housing ■ Services excluding energy & housing ■ Food ■ Energy

Council of Economic Advisers
Sources: Bureau of Labor Statistics; CEA calculations.
Note: Gray bars indicate recessions.
2024 Economic Report of the President

incidence of mental health issues, substance abuse, or generosity of the local safety net (Aldern and Colburn 2022). A statewide California study finds that 75 percent of homeless residents remain in the county where they last had housing (Benioff Homelessness and Housing Initiative 2023).

Implications for Inflation and Aggregate Growth

A constricted housing supply across regions creates migration frictions that can lead to a geographic labor misallocation (Ganong and Shoag 2017). All else being equal, workers should migrate from low to high productivity cities until productivity, and therefore wages, equalizes across cities. If high-productivity cities also have a constrained housing supply, fewer workers can respond to productivity and wage incentives. Recent evidence suggests that many workers might not move to places with higher wages because higher housing costs completely offset any increase in wages (Card, Rothstein, and Yi 2023).

Housing supply restrictions also exacerbate inflation. When measured by the Consumer Price Index (CPI), inflation reflects changes over time in the price paid for a market basket of consumer goods and services, including food, energy, and housing. Housing expenses—the single largest basket component—have accounted for at least 25 percent of the CPI basket since 1993. Figure 4-10 depicts a decade of inflation trends, including a decomposition of the market basket's core components. As the level of housing prices has increased, the contribution of housing to CPI has increased simultaneously (CEA 2023a). High housing inflation partially reflects a shift in housing demand—for example, increased working from home—paired with an already-constrained housing supply (Mischke et al. 2023). Housing inflation has steadily declined since the spring 2023 peak, and as a result, annual inflation declined to 3.4 percent at the end of 2023.

Federal Policy's Role

The three prominent frictions related to long-run housing supply shortages and affordability issues are (1) locally determined land-use regulations, which lead to exclusionary zoning; (2) financing and other construction costs that increase the cost of producing housing; and (3) the spatial mismatch of workers and jobs, which reduces aggregate output. These three costs motivate multiple Federal policy solutions.

Although much of housing supply policy is local, the Federal Government can affect national priorities through various mechanisms. For example, the government can help address long-standing implicit and explicit discriminatory zoning practices. To this end, the Federal Government can align its agency resources and policy priorities to promote zoning reforms that reduce barriers that limit what can be built. Likewise, the Federal purse can be used to advance existing agency priorities and launch new initiatives to alleviate housing supply constraints, increase the production of affordable units, and address the Nation's growing affordability challenges.

A central goal of the Biden-Harris Administration is an economy in which every American has access to a safe and affordable home. On one hand, demand-side policies, including direct subsidies to cost-burdened households, can help address acute affordability issues. Box 4-3 describes several important examples. On the other hand, supply-side policies that directly boost housing construction are an integral part of the solution.

Zoning Reforms: Expanding the Housing Supply and Increasing Affordability

Local zoning and land-use restrictions are a long-standing, fundamental hurdle for increasing the housing supply. Under these restrictions, housing supply shortages have become increasingly salient, with a growing share of household budgets dedicated to housing. Reducing barriers to the housing supply can lead to several benefits: increased housing production, economic growth, job creation, reduced class and racial segregation, and increased climate resiliency through reduced sprawl and commuting times. Fortunately, momentum is building for zoning reforms, and numerous policy changes have been enacted at the State and local levels. Examples, detailed in box

Box 4-3. Assistance for Housing Demand

Even in a functioning housing market with abundant supply, many low-income families still struggle to afford housing. Federal policies can help families close the gap between housing expenditures and personal financial resources. The Federal Government can provide financial assistance to individuals directly and also enact policies to decrease the price of housing.

The Federal Government uses several assistance programs to help low-income families access affordable housing, including Project-Based Rental Assistance, Public Housing, and housing vouchers. The Section 8 Housing Choice Voucher Program, administered by HUD in partnership with local public housing agencies, is one of the largest Federal housing programs (Center on Budget and Policy Priorities 2017). The program generally caps families' housing costs at 30 percent of their income, helping 2.3 million low-income households annually, while also reducing evictions and homelessness (HUD 2023d, 2023i). Almost three-quarters of families receiving housing vouchers have children (Center on Budget and Policy Priorities 2017). Households using vouchers were once young relative to the general population but have steadily become older (Reina and Aiken 2022). Many voucher households live in high-poverty and low-opportunity areas, where vouchers are more often accepted; however, only about one in four voucher-eligible households actually receive and use a voucher, due to the lack of program funding (Gould Ellen 2018). When families use vouchers to move to low poverty neighborhoods, children's long-run outcomes improve in the form of higher college attendance rates and adult earnings (Chetty, Hendren, and Katz 2016).

Recognizing that funding limitations constrain the number of households able to receive rental assistance, President Biden's Fiscal Year 2024 Budget proposed expanding rental assistance to well over 200,000 additional households through $2.4 billion in additional funding for the voucher program, as well as $22 billion in mandatory funding to provide guaranteed housing to extremely low income veterans and youth transitioning out of foster care (White House 2023c; HUD 2024b).

Federal financial assistance to families in the form of cash, tax credits, and in-kind benefits like the Supplemental Nutrition Assistance Program (known as SNAP) can help alleviate some of the financial burden of housing. For instance, the temporarily expanded 2021 Child Tax Credit (CTC) helped families maintain stable housing by alleviating other financial burdens (CEA 2023b; Pilkauskas, Michelmore, and Kovski 2023).

The Rural Housing Service of the U.S. Department of Agriculture (USDA) offers direct and guaranteed loans to help low-income rural residents buy and maintain housing. In 2022, USDA's Single Family

Housing Direct Loan Program obligated $1.3 billion to underwrite and service mortgages for low-income families that often face credit constraints. Additionally, USDA obligated $13.1 billion in mortgage loan guarantees to help provide moderate- to low-income rural residents an opportunity to realize the dream of homeownership (USDA 2024).

In a housing market with sufficient supply, demand-side assistance can be very effective. However, in a housing market with a constrained supply, these policies may lead to increased rent prices for some rental units, possibly directing some of the benefits to landlords and property owners rather than renters (Diamond, McQuade, and Qian 2018).

4-4, include initiatives allowing construction of multifamily housing in areas previously zoned for single-family homes, expanding homeowners' right to construct and rent out accessory dwelling units, and abolishing minimum parking requirements (Greene and González-Hermoso 2019; Parking Reform Network n.d.). Federal policy could build on these successes to help cities and States continue their reforms.

Federal dollars can create incentives for State and local policymakers to meet housing policy goals. For instance, the Pathways to Removing Obstacles to Housing (PRO Housing) program sponsored by the Department of Housing and Urban Development (HUD) will award $85 million in competitive grants to communities with plans to remove barriers to affordable housing and production in 2024 (HUD 2023b). In addition, President Biden has called for $20 billion to create a first-of-its-kind fund that will award planning and housing capital grants to State and local jurisdictions to expand the housing supply and lower housing costs for lower- and middle-income households (as described in the forthcoming Fiscal Year 2025 Budget, per the U.S. Department of the Treasury). Further, HUD's 2023 publication *Policy & Practice* collects and disseminates evidence-based insights drawn from State and local housing policy initiatives. HUD also recently announced $4 million in grant funding to support research studying zoning and land-use reforms, and a $350,000 award through the Research Partnerships program to support the development of the "National Zoning Atlas" to "close data gaps that limit our understanding of the relationship between zoning and segregation, affordability, and other outcomes of interest" (HUD 2023j, 2023g). HUD has further reinforced the 1968 Fair Housing Act's goal of "Affirmatively Furthering Fair Housing" with a rule that would require recipients of HUD funding to work to overcome patterns of segregation, promote fair housing choice, eliminate disparities in opportunities, and foster inclusive communities free from discrimination (HUD 2023a).

Box 4-4. State and Local Zoning: Recent Steps

Zoning is one of the most significant regulatory powers of local government, and research shows reform can unlock economic growth and opportunity (Flint 2022). Zoning reforms that are likely to increase housing supply include allowing more multifamily housing to be built (especially near public transportation hubs), legalizing accessory dwelling units (ADUs), and eliminating minimum parking requirements, minimum lot sizes, minimum square feet requirements, and density restrictions. None of these reforms prevent new single-family home construction; rather, the changes prevent municipalities from requiring only single-family homes.

Some steps taken in recent years include:

- Buffalo became the first major U.S. city to abolish minimum parking requirements in 2017 (Poon 2017). Recently, more cities have followed suit, including Anchorage, San Jose, and Gainesville. Other cities, such as San Diego, made incremental steps in the same direction by eliminating parking requirements near public transit (Wamsley 2024; Khouri 2022).
- Minneapolis banned single-family exclusive zoning in 2018, and Charlotte enacted a similar policy in 2021 (Grabar 2018; Brasuell 2021). At the State level, Oregon, California, and Washington enacted such policies in 2018, 2021, and 2023, respectively (Garcia et al. 2022; Gutman 2023).
- California has enacted multiple policies intended to grow housing supply in recent years. The State has legalized ADUs statewide, allowed duplexes and lot splits in single-family zones, and allowed mixed-income, multifamily housing in all residential areas (Skelton 2021; Gray 2022). At the same time, California has eliminated minimum parking requirements at transit stations statewide (Khouri 2022). California has also set up a Regional Housing Needs Allocation process, whereby local jurisdictions must produce housing and land use plans to comply with State housing targets (California Department of Housing and Community Development 2023).
- Connecticut has enacted significant policy changes, requiring its cities and towns to "affirmatively further fair housing" in their zoning, promote diverse housing options, legalize ADUs, and cap minimum parking requirements (Flint 2022).
- Montana enacted several changes in 2023 aimed at making housing more affordable and reducing sprawl into rural and agricultural areas (State of Montana Governor's Office 2023). These pro-housing changes include allowing duplexes, ADUs, and apartment-style housing, while also speeding up permitting approvals (Dietrich 2023).

- In 2022, Maine passed legislation to allow ADUs and duplexes in residential zones, and legalized quadplexes in "designated growth areas" (SMPDC 2023).
- In Massachusetts, a program known as MBTA Communities, signed in 2021, requires cities and towns to allow multifamily housing near transit stations, with a minimum density of 15 units per acre (Commonwealth of Massachusetts 2023). Fairfax County, Virginia, is taking similar steps, such as easing height and density restrictions near transit stations (Merchant 2016).
- Vermont legalized duplexes in all residential neighborhoods, as well as triplexes and quadruplexes in all areas served by municipal sewer and water infrastructure in 2023 (Brasuell 2023).

In addition to HUD's efforts, the U.S. Department of Transportation (DOT) manages several large grant programs that improve transportation connections, including connections to affordable housing and funding for land-use reform. For example, the Reconnecting Communities and Neighborhoods Program offers grant funding for capital construction, community planning, and regional partnerships that prioritize disadvantaged communities, improve access to daily needs, foster equitable development, and reconnect communities (DOT 2023). The Areas of Persistent Poverty Program awards competitive grants to finance projects including those that improve transit facilities, technologies, and transit service in areas of persistent poverty or in historically disadvantaged communities (FTA 2023). In addition, the Economic Development Administration has updated its guidance to emphasize efficient land use as part of the agency's grantmaking authority (White House 2023a). Many of these efforts are connected with the Administration's Housing Supply Action Plan, which provides incentives for local zoning reforms by tying these reforms to Federal grant process scoring (White House 2022). Together, these policies prioritize and direct Federal spending toward increasing the housing supply and affordability, especially in locations close to public transportation.

Reducing Supply Constraints with Federal Taxes and Other Subsidies

Addressing home affordability requires both short-term and long-term solutions. To unlock supply and increase access in the short run, the Biden-Harris Administration has called for a series of new policies designed to lower costs for homeowners and homebuyers. This includes a temporary mortgage payment relief tax credit for first-time homebuyers, which can increase access to homeownership during this period of historically high mortgage interest rates (as described in the forthcoming Fiscal Year 2025 Budget, per the U.S. Department of the Treasury). It includes down payment assistance to first-generation homebuyers, which can increase access for families that have not benefited from the generational wealth accumulation associated with homeownership (HUD 2024a). Further, it includes a temporary tax credit targeting low- and middle-income homeowners who sell their starter homes, which can unlock inventory in the starter-home market that is currently facing an acute supply shortage (as described in the forthcoming Fiscal Year 2025 Budget, per the U.S. Department of the Treasury). Finally, to reduce the value gap between rehabilitation costs and postconstruction home values for single-family homes in distressed neighborhoods, it includes new funding to subsidize rehabilitation expenses (White House 2023d). These funds can increase the likelihood that homes are rehabilitated before sale, making it easier to attract homebuyers and boosting revitalization efforts in these neighborhoods.

To address supply issues in the long run requires making progress on both cost and access. However, these policies take time to show progress. President Biden has called for a new Project-Based Rental Assistance Program to fund long-term contracts with private owners to rent new affordable units to America's neediest families (White House 2023c). The Federal Government has also directly reduced the cost of building affordable housing by subsidizing construction expenses through the tax code.

The largest construction subsidy, the LIHTC, has funded one in five of all new multifamily units since 1987 and has created more than 3.5 million affordable rental units (HUD 2023e). The LIHTC awards developers a stream of Federal tax credits over a 10-year period after a project is placed in service. In exchange, developers must designate a subset of units as rent restricted for low-income households. Box 4-2 provides additional details on the LIHTC, including how it helps close the gap between profitability and the investment returns required for investors to fund the project.

Figure 4-11 shows the financial characteristics of LIHTC unit tenants in 2021. LIHTC provides housing for households with very low incomes: 24 percent had an annual income below $10,000, and 56 percent had an income below $20,000. The program benefits a diverse group of households: roughly one-quarter are white, another quarter are Black, and one-tenth self-identify as Hispanic/Latino. The statistics suggest that the LIHTC program effectively targets vulnerable families.[5] Still, nearly 40 percent of tenants spend more than 30 percent of their income on rent (HUD 2021).

---

[5] While HUD collects demographic information describing households residing in each LIHTC property, these data are incomplete because a universal list of buildings placed in service that received LIHTC is not publicly available. Improving the collection of these data would permit HUD to more completely portray the scope of the LIHTC portfolio and its residents.

Figure 4-11. Financial Characteristics of LIHTC Unit Tenants, 2021

Percentage of households in LIHTC units

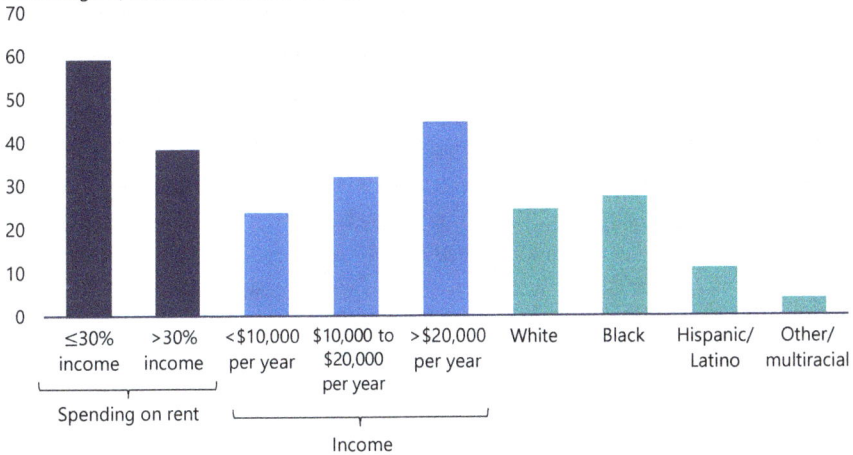

Council of Economic Advisers

Sources: U.S. Department of Housing and Urban Development; CEA calculations.
Note: LIHTC = Low-Income Housing Tax Credit. The "other/multiracial category" includes those reporting race as Asian, American Indian/Alaska Native, Native Hawaiian or Other Pacific Islander, other, and multiple races. The shares within each category do not sum to 100 percent due to missing or unreported data.
2024 Economic Report of the President

LIHTC-funded developments make an impact on both families and neighborhoods, according to multiple studies of the program's benefits (Baum-Snow and Marion 2009; Eriksen and Rosenthal 2010). Evidence from Chicago demonstrates that LIHTC-assisted developments have positive spillover effects on local property values (Voith et al. 2022). Home price appreciation contributes to wealth accumulation for neighborhood residents and increases funding for public services, but it can also make localities inaccessible for financially disadvantaged families. At the same time, LIHTC-assisted developments are associated with reductions in violent crime through neighborhood revitalization (Freedman and Owens 2011). One study estimates that the program's aggregate welfare benefits in low-income areas are $116 million via property value appreciation, declines in crime, and the inflow of racially diverse individuals (Diamond and McQuade 2019). Further, access to affordable housing via LIHTC units gives families and their children the stability required for regular health care access and is associated with decreased rates of child abuse and neglect (Gensheimer et al. 2022; Shanahan et al. 2022).

However, there is also evidence that new LIHTC projects may increase owner turnover rates and crowd out private rental construction (Baum-Snow and Marion 2009; Eriksen and Rosenthal 2010). Still, the Administration believes the program can help improve housing affordability and supply, and President Biden's Fiscal Year 2025 Budget calls for roughly $30 billion to expand and enhance the program. The President's 2022 Housing Supply Action Plan called for LIHTC reforms, including a now-finalized Treasury rule allowing developers to average incomes across some, rather than all, households in a given property to incentivize more mixed-income developments (White House 2022; Internal Revenue Service 2022).

The Historic Tax Credit subsidizes the rehabilitation of historic properties, including those that result in a new or renovated housing supply.[6] Since its inception in 1976, the program has rehabilitated more than 300,000 housing units and has created 343,000 new housing units, 192,000 of which are low- and moderate-income units (U.S. Department of the Interior 2022). In Fiscal Year 2021, the National Park Service certified 1,063 historic rehabilitation projects to revitalize abandoned and underutilized buildings; nearly 80 percent of them were located in economically distressed areas (U.S. Department of the Interior 2021). The National Park Service has also shown that Historic Tax Credit–related rehabilitation projects provide a better return on investment than equal investments in new construction (U.S. Department of the Interior 2020).

Federal housing tax subsidies can help achieve long-term housing supply goals and affect the U.S. economy's climate impact. Buildings account for 29 percent of all U.S. greenhouse gas emissions (Leung 2018). Estimates suggest that rehabilitated structures produce 50–75 percent fewer carbon emissions than new construction (Gupta, Martinez, and Nieuwerburgh 2023). The Inflation Reduction Act has committed $9 billion in tax credits, rebates, workforce training, and funding opportunities to transform existing homes into green homes and construct new, environmentally friendly residential spaces (Martin 2022). Currently, the commercial real estate market, with high office vacancy rates and rising loan delinquencies, is in a position to be transformed into usable and financially prudent residential spaces (Sorokin 2023; DBRS Morningstar 2023; White House 2023b).

In addition to tax subsidies, the Federal Government provides several block grants to State and local jurisdictions to assist in affordable housing development. HUD's Community Development Block Grant Program (CDBG) can support the acquisition and rehabilitation of housing for low- and moderate-income individuals. In Fiscal Year 2022, the CDBG State and local grantees allocated more than $920 million to housing activities, including public housing modernization and single- and multifamily home rehabilitation (HUD 2022). Recently, HUD issued additional guidance on how to make use of CDBG funds to further develop "decent, accessible, equitable, and affordable housing," providing specific ways that grantees can best make use of CDBG funds (HUD 2023h). HUD also administers the

---

[6] The Historic Tax Credit is a colloquial name for the Rehabilitation Tax Credit, which was made available under section 47 of the Internal Revenue Code.

HOME Investment Partnerships Program, the largest Federal block grant program that provides funding exclusively to increase access to an adequate, affordable housing supply for low-income households (CRS 2021). Since 1992, HOME appropriations have cumulatively totaled nearly $45 billion, with annual appropriations ranging between about $1 billion and $2 billion. The funds have supported completion of more than 1.3 million affordable housing units (HUD 2023c).

Expanding Manufactured Home Delivery and Financing to Address Rural Housing Constraints

Manufactured housing costs 45 percent less to build per square foot than site-built housing due to efficient production technologies that take advantage of economies of scale (Freddie Mac n.d.). Manufactured homes, which are required to comply with HUD-promulgated Manufactured Home Construction and Safety Standards, are energy efficient, safe, and designed to withstand natural disasters, inclement weather, and fires (Freddie Mac 2022; Code of Federal Regulations 2023). As a result, they may help provide affordable housing units and alleviate supply constraints, especially in rural communities.

Manufactured housing has a higher share of total owner- and renter-occupied housing in rural communities than in more densely populated areas (Layton 2023). However, efforts to expand the manufactured housing supply face hurdles driven by land-use regulations. Although the HUD-promulgated manufactured housing building code preempts State and local design and construction code, local land-use regulations often restrict the placement of manufactured homes, either implicitly or explicitly (HUD 2023f). For example, some jurisdictions have zoning requirements that limit manufactured housing to specific zoning districts, and other jurisdictions may have minimum home size requirements that preclude manufactured housing (Freddie Mac 2022). In addition, minimum lot size and parking regulations increase land costs and price manufactured homeowners out of the market. Federal efforts to encourage the adoption of improved State and local zoning policies could serve as a financial incentive to promote these kinds of reforms as well.

Barriers to manufactured home financing dampen demand. The traditional government-sponsored mortgage enterprises, specifically Fannie Mae and Freddie Mac, cannot purchase and guarantee loans for manufactured homes because their owners do not typically own the land on which they sit. Instead, owners must take out a so-called chattel loan, which, relative to a mortgage, has higher interest rates, shorter repayment periods, and fewer consumer finance protections (CFPB 2021). These loans can be prohibitively costly for low-income families (Goodman and Ganesh 2018). In light of this, Fannie Mae and Freddie Mac have identified the financing of manu-factured and rural housing among the activities targeted by their 2022–24 Duty to Serve Plans, including the plan to begin purchasing loans titled as personal property in 2024 and to increase the purchase of loans titled as real property (FHFA 2022).[7]

Conclusion

Housing shortages and unaffordability have risen over the last 60 years, in large part because of local land-use policies that restrict housing density and what can be built. These effects are felt most by low-income and vulnerable families, which are increasingly priced out of the housing market. Because many amenities are bundled with housing and neighborhoods, housing supply shortages inhibit economic mobility for millions of Americans. Investing in the housing supply and producing affordable units opens the door for upward mobility and increases overall economic growth.

Persistent market failures in the housing market create a role for gov-ernment. Demand-side assistance can help households facing affordability constraints. In addition, the Federal Government has encouraged efforts to increase supply-side policies that incentivize local zoning reform, reduce exclusionary zoning via grants and other spending, and directly subsidize affordable unit construction through programs like LIHTC. While the efforts have made a difference, the housing market still faces an acute supply short-age and declining affordability. Ultimately, meaningful change will require State and local governments to reevaluate the land-use regulations that reduce the housing supply.

Fortunately, local, State, and Federal policies can boost the housing supply through incentivized changes to zoning policies, tax credits that subsidize construction costs for affordable units, and other block grants that prioritize affordable unit construction. By taking further steps to address the country's housing supply shortage, the United States will be richer, our citizens will be more financially stable, and our environment will be greener.

---

[7] The Safety and Soundness Act provides that the "Government-Sponsored Entities" have a "duty to serve underserved markets," specifying that the enterprises "shall provide leadership to the market in developing loan products and flexible underwriting guidelines" to improve access and equity in the mortgage financing market.

Chapter 5

International Trade and Investment Flows

After a period of rapid globalization during the 1990s and early 2000s, global goods trade and financial flows showed signs of plateauing in the decade after the global financial crisis due to a combination of factors, including sluggish recoveries after the crisis and diminished opportunities to further disburse production across borders. Still, the global economy remains inextricably linked—even in the face of large economic shocks and rising geopolitical tensions—with the U.S. economy continuing to play a leading role. The United States is the world's second-largest trading country, with more than $7 trillion in combined goods and services exports and imports in 2022, and it remains both the largest source of and destination for foreign direct investment (USTR 2022a; OECD 2023a).

There are well-documented gains from trade and cross-border investment flows. The benefits of global integration include lower inflation, a greater variety of goods and services, more innovation, higher productivity, good jobs for American workers in exporting sectors, foreign direct investment in U.S. industries, and a higher likelihood of achieving our climate goals (Bernstein 2023). However, policymakers must continue to pay careful attention to negative effects associated with global integration and some trade policies. First and foremost, global integration can disproportionately affect certain groups of workers and communities through employment and earnings losses when facing rising import competition. These distributional effects are further complicated by differing commercial standards and practices, with some countries using unfair labor practices (e.g., forced or child labor) or environmentally-degrading manufacturing techniques that are not fully captured in prices and create an unfair and uneven global production landscape that can distort and stymie competition. To mitigate the negative consequences of trade and investment flows for both workers and communities, international policies (e.g., trade agreements and economic frameworks) can seek to promote high-level standards (e.g., fair labor practices), and domestic policies (e.g., social safety nets and education or reskilling programs) can be adapted to focus needed resources on workers who are adversely affected by global integration.

By reorienting trade and foreign investment policy to center on workers, the Biden-Harris Administration's policy agenda continues to define and elevate the standards by which trade and foreign investment are conducted, and it serves as a mechanism for achieving broader economic goals. These goals include confronting unfair trade practices, elevating labor and environmental standards (USTR 2022b), and building cooperative and beneficial economic relationships with U.S. partner countries (CEA 2023a). For example, the Indo-Pacific Economic Framework is an innovative economic framework that promotes inclusive growth by advancing higher economic standards, building supply chain resiliency, facilitating and capturing the economic opportunities that relate to addressing climate change, fighting corruption, supporting efficient tax administration, and promoting high-standard labor commitments. Another example is the United States–Mexico–Canada Agreement's Rapid Response Labor Mechanism, which promotes the right of free association and collective bargaining rights by workers (USTR 2023a). Since 2021, this mechanism has been used to protect labor rights at multiple different facilities, and thus it has had an impact on thousands of workers in Mexico (U.S. Department of Labor 2023; USTR 2023a).

While the longer-term outlook for U.S. trade and investment flows remains uncertain, early signs of important shifts have begun materializing. Supply chains are being rewired in patterns consistent with near-shoring and friend-shoring. Trade in many services sectors has proved resilient to the effects of the COVID-19 pandemic and is growing. Foreign investors are contributing to a historic ramping up of domestic manufacturing in critical sectors, including advanced technologies and clean energy. In particular, a disproportionate number of announced foreign investments in clean energy projects are being located in regions of the country that experienced more pronounced losses in manufacturing employment in the 1990s and early 2000s.

After describing the evolution of global integration over the past three decades, this chapter surveys signs that, though still robust, goods trade integration has slowed for many economies since the global financial crisis. It then explores how the U.S. trade and investment landscapes have changed in recent years, and it investigates the centrality of global value chains for understanding shifts in trade and investment that are consistent with near-shoring and friend-shoring. Finally, it discusses trade and foreign investment's costs and benefits for U.S. workers, consumers, and communities—highlighting how the Biden-Harris Administration's economic and trade frameworks and partnerships harness global integration's benefits while mitigating its costs.

Long-Term Trends in Trade and Foreign Investment

The liberalization of goods trade and cross-border financial markets—a trend sometimes characterized as "hyperglobalization" (Rodrik 2011)—was a defining economic story of the 1990s and early 2000s.[1] However, it largely stagnated after the global financial crisis and, while 2021 and 2022 saw a rebound, global goods trade integration remained below its 2008 peak and may level off once again as goods consumption normalizes in the aftermath of the COVID-19 pandemic. The cessation of hyperglobalization has given

---

[1] Major liberalization episodes include the integration of former Soviet countries in the early 1990s with the rest of the global economy, the creation of the World Trade Organization in 1995, and China's accession to the World Trade Organization in 2001 (Aiyar et al. 2023).

Figure 5-1. Trade in Goods as a Percent of GDP, 1995–2022

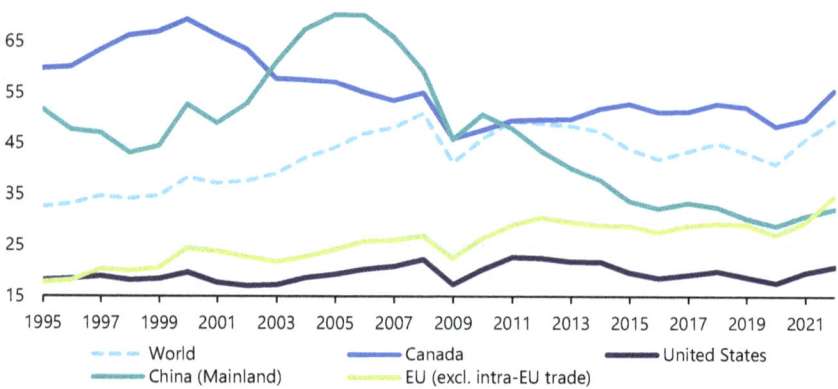

Percentage of GDP

Council of Economic Advisers

Sources: International Monetary Fund; CEA calculations.
Note: Data were only available through 2022. EU trade excludes trade between EU countries, which includes all countries that were members as of 2022. The data for 1995 and 1996 are from the former Belgium-Luxembourg Economic Union.
2024 Economic Report of the President

way to what some have termed "slowbalization" (*Economist* 2021; Nathan, Galbraith, and Grimberg 2022).[2]

Global Integration Slowed After the Global Financial Crisis, Following Earlier Decades of Rapid Growth

Global goods trade integration—the total value of goods exports and imports as a share of gross domestic product (GDP)—rose steadily, from 33 to 51 percent, between 1995 and 2008 (figure 5-1).[3] Figure 5-1 also shows that the extent and timing of the slowdown in goods trade integration differs across economies, and the future outlook remains considerably uncertain. China's decline in goods trade integration since 2006—an outsized 38-percentage-point drop—is the primary driver for the observed slowing in global goods trade integration, and reflects the country's shift away from importing intermediate inputs and in favor of domestic sources for its production

---

[2] There is a notable exception—trade in commercial services excluding travel and transportation (e.g., business services and telecommunications) grew much faster than goods between 1990 to 2023 and shows no sign of slowing (Baldwin 2022). This continuing rise in cross-border digital activity has been associated with the idea of "newbalization," indicating the changing nature of globalization with a slowdown in flows of tangible goods while intangible flows (e.g., of digital services and cross-border data) accelerate (Nathan, Galbraith, and Grimberg 2022). Meanwhile, measuring trade incorporating information on both freight and distance traveled compared with value shows an increasing trend in global trade, in part reflecting the growing importance of commodities like critical minerals (which weigh more than comparable manufactured products like toys) and can only be sourced from distant locations (Ganapati and Wong 2023; Zumbrun 2023).

[3] The economics literature describes the share of trade relative to GDP as trade openness.

processes (Constantinescu, Mattoo, and Ruta 2018). Canada's peak goods trade integration in 2000 likewise preceded many other economies' turning points. While the European Union (excluding intrabloc trade) also experienced a dip after the global financial crisis, unlike comparable economies, the slowdown in its goods trade integration has not been as marked and has not yet reached a discernible peak.[4]

The United States' trend line of overall goods trade integration differs from the other economies shown in figure 5-1 in two respects. First, during the steady increase of goods trade integration in the 1990s and early 2000s, U.S. trade integration remained well below the world average and that of most other major economies. Second, the United States' decline in goods trade integration since the global financial crisis has been far smaller than China's decline. Given that U.S. goods trade integration remains below global averages and that of peer economies, figure 5-1 suggests there may be additional scope to increase America's trade with the global economy. As this chapter discusses, the United States' goods trade integration has generated benefits for American workers and consumers, as well as for U.S. growth; however, it has also created important vulnerabilities. These trade-offs underline the strong role for policy to minimize adverse distributional consequences and maximize the benefits (e.g., supply chain resiliency and lower prices) from greater trade openness, as discussed in more depth later in this chapter.

The discussion above of trade in goods is just one dimension of global integration. Cross-border financial flows—which include flows in securities (e.g., stocks and bonds) and in foreign direct investment (FDI), referring to a firm or individual's investment in a commercial interest in another country—are another key mechanism of global integration (Loungani and Razin 2001; OECD 2024).[5] Unlike cross-border securities flows, which tend to be highly volatile, FDI typically signals longer-term and often more productive investment, and it can take the form of expanding or acquiring an existing foreign-owned company or starting a new enterprise in a foreign country.

Global FDI flows as a share of GDP have also exhibited signs of slowing across many economies since the global financial crisis (figure 5-2).[6]

---

[4] Including intra-EU trade, the EU's global goods integration is far higher, at roughly 85 percent of GDP in 2022 (vs. 35 percent excluding intra-EU trade), given that almost 60 percent of total EU cross-border trade on average is between countries within the bloc.

[5] Another channel for global integration is immigration (the cross-border movement of people), which is beyond the scope of this chapter. Other forms of cross-border financial flows include remittances and financial transactions (e.g., development aid transfers).

[6] FDI flows are reported based on the geographic location of the investor, meaning that a foreign entity's investment in a U.S. firm counts as an inflow to the United States even if (on net) the entity removed more money from the country than it put into the country that year. In the event that transactions that decrease a foreign entity's investment in a U.S. firm outweigh transactions that increase the entity's investments, the FDI inflow would be recorded as negative to the United States.

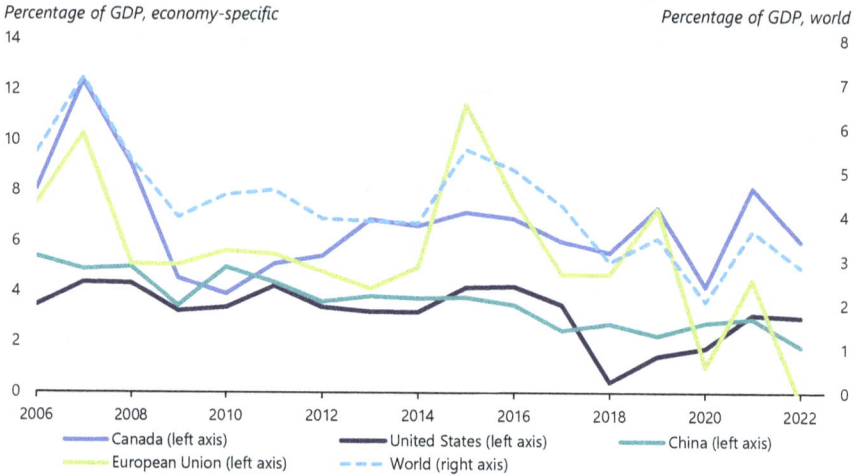

Figure 5-2. Total Foreign Direct Investment Flows as a Percentage of GDP, 2006–22

Percentage of GDP, economy-specific

Percentage of GDP, world

Council of Economic Advisers

Sources: Organization for Economic Cooperation and Development; CEA calculations.

Note: This figure shows the sum of inflows and outflows of foreign direct investment relative to gross domestic product (GDP) for selected economies.

2024 Economic Report of the President

While the United States has experienced a muted recovery since 2018, total FDI flows remain below levels seen immediately before the crisis. But as the lynchpin of the global financial system, the United States is still highly financially integrated with the global economy according to several metrics, including FDI (Bertaut, von Beschwitz, and Curcuru 2023; OECD 2023b).

The slowing integration trends through 2020 have been widespread, making an impact on countries at diverse stages of development and often facing different economic shocks (figures 5-1 and 5-2). Both cyclical factors (high-frequency developments often associated with business cycles, e.g., temporary declines in demand) and secular factors (structural, slower-moving phenomena, e.g., technological change) help to explain these trends.

Cyclical factors include sluggish recoveries since the global financial crisis in advanced economies that have weighed on global aggregate demand, and the impact of the crisis on the financial and corporate sectors, which were compelled to address vulnerabilities in their balance sheets by deleveraging and rebuilding capital buffers (Aiyar et al. 2023). And just as some economies reached their pre-2008 unemployment levels roughly a decade later, a new set of cyclical shocks surfaced—including the COVID-19 pandemic and Russia's further invasion of Ukraine—each of which had an adverse impact on global financial conditions and complicated trade flows.

Secular factors include a slowdown in production fragmentation, or the unbundling of tasks across borders, also known as global value chains

(GVCs) (Timmer et al. 2016). Because multinationals play a central role in both trade integration and FDI (Qiang, Liu, and Steenbergen 2021), a reduction in the pace of GVC creation helps explain the stagnation shown by both measures. Other secular factors include China's slowdown in growth and decline in share of trade relative to GDP; in the 21st century, China's annual GDP growth rate reached a high in 2007, roughly coinciding with a peak in the country's trade integration, and has since been persistently lower. Ongoing geopolitical tensions and rising national security concerns have also resulted in an increase in trade sanctions, with the highest share of global trade affected by sanctions since at least 1950 (WTO 2023a).

The combination of factors described above are generating important shifts in the extent and intensity of interlinkages with cross-border supply chains—known as GVC participation—and sourcing. Two GVC participation measures signal these shifts, some of which began with the global financial crisis and have accelerated in recent years (WTO 2021). First, the extent of China's and the United States' use of imported inputs for the production of their exports has declined since the global financial crisis (see figure 5-3, panel A).[7]

Second, the United States' and European Union's shares of content in other countries' domestic final demand dropped across many of the selected economies between 2009 and 2019; in contrast, China's content in these countries' domestic final demand increased (figure 5-3, panel B).[8] For example, the share of U.S. value added in Mexico's domestic final demand fell by 4 percentage points between 2009 and 2019, and in contrast, China's share increased by 7 percentage points. And while the share of U.S. value added in India's domestic final demand increased by 1 percentage point between 2009 and 2019, China's share of value added increased by 6 percentage points over the same period. The shares of U.S. and European Union value added in China's domestic final demand remained unchanged over this period.

Putting the two sets of findings together suggests that U.S. exports had a lower value share of foreign-produced components in 2019 compared with 2009, while other countries became more dependent on China as a source of inputs in their domestic consumption. Lower cross-border connectedness may risk reducing the gains from trade and FDI for the U.S. economy.

---

[7] The measure of foreign value-added content of overall exports is also called "backward GVC participation" (WTO 2022).

[8] The share of foreign value added in countries' domestic final demand reflects how much value added in goods and services purchased in other countries' domestic markets originates from abroad and shows a "domestic economy's relative connectedness to production in other countries and regions—independent of whether or not there are direct imports from foreign (upstream) industries" (OECD 2021). Indicators of forward GVC participation that measure domestic value added sent to other countries as a share of overall exports paint a more sanguine picture but do not offset the multitude of indicators pointing to a generalized slowdown in GVC participation (OECD 2023c).

Figure 5-3. Indicators of Global Value Chain Participation

A. Foreign Content in Countries' Exports as a Share of Total Exports, 1995–2020

Percent

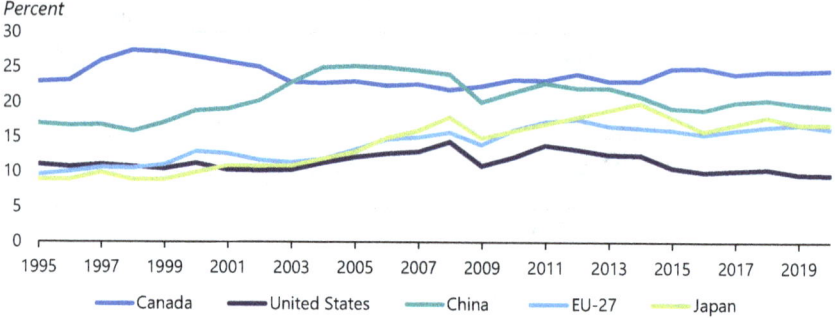

Legend: Canada, United States, China, EU-27, Japan

B. Change in Share of Foreign Value Added in Domestic Final Demand, 2009–19

Percentage points

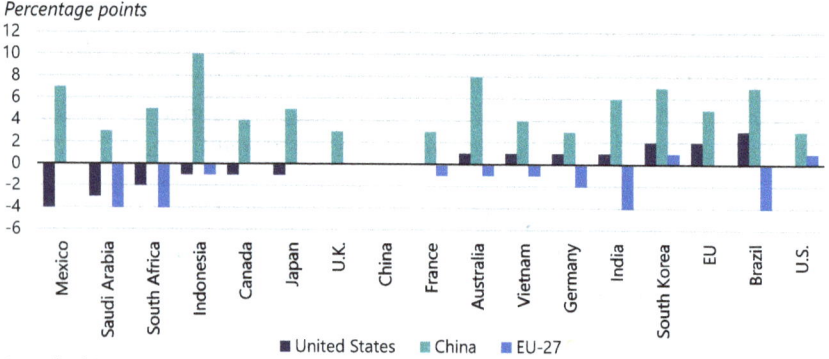

Countries (left to right): Mexico, Saudi Arabia, South Africa, Indonesia, Canada, Japan, U.K., China, France, Australia, Vietnam, Germany, India, South Korea, EU, Brazil, U.S.

Legend: United States, China, EU-27

Council of Economic Advisers

Sources: Organization for Economic Cooperation and Development; CEA calculations.

Note: In panel A, the underlying indicator represents the import content of a country's gross exports and is a measure of global value chain integration. In panel B, the underlying indicator represents the amount of foreign value added (from the United States, China, and the EU-27, respectively) reflected in domestic final goods or services demand in various countries as a share of total foreign value added in countries' domestic final demand; the figure shows changes in the share from 2009 to 2019.

2024 Economic Report of the President

The complexity of the current international environment for global trade and FDI flows points to considerable uncertainty for the future out-look. Despite supply chain pressures during the COVID-19 pandemic, U.S. goods trade proved resilient and supply chains had begun to normalize (CEA 2023b); U.S. consumption also remained strong in 2023 (see chapter 2 of this *Report*). Together with policy actions that are also promoting shifts in supply chains, these factors may boost global integration. But at the same time, the ongoing pandemic recovery may be masking the impact of secular headwinds, and still-developing shifts in supply chains may introduce new obstacles (e.g., higher costs) to greater integration.

Figure 5-4. Real Quarterly Trade in Goods, Actual versus Forecasted, 1992–2023

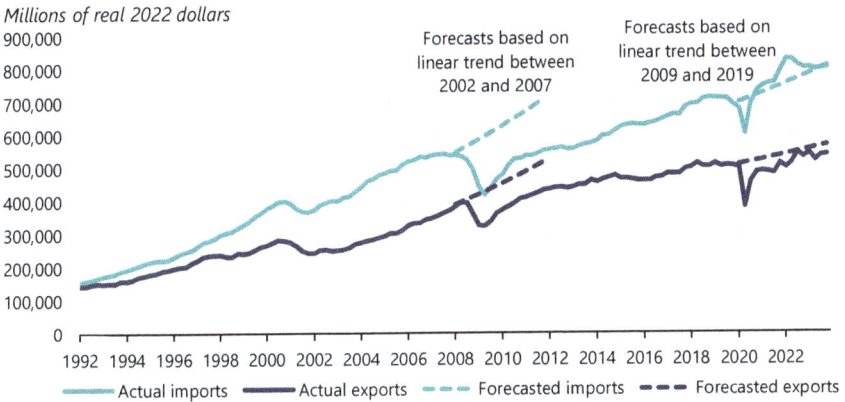

Millions of real 2022 dollars

Forecasts based on linear trend between 2002 and 2007

Forecasts based on linear trend between 2009 and 2019

Actual imports — Actual exports — Forecasted imports — Forecasted exports

Council of Economic Advisers

Sources: Bureau of Economic Analysis; CEA calculations.
Note: Actuals were deflated to 2022 dollars using import/export price indexes. Post-2007:Q4 forecast based on linear trend in each series from 2002:Q1 to 2007:Q4; post-2019:Q4 forecast based on linear trend in each series from 2009:Q3 to 2019:Q4. Trade data are on a balance of payments basis. Gray bars indicate recessions.
2024 Economic Report of the President

U.S. Trade Growth Tracks Global Trends: Signs of a Recent Slowdown and Recovery

U.S. trade growth has broadly tracked global trade growth over the past three decades (WTO 2023b). Between 1993 and 2023, U.S. trade in goods and services grew at an average annual rate of 4.4 percent, which was faster than the average annual rate of 2.4 percent growth for the U.S. economy.[9]

As with broader economic activity, U.S. trade flows are often broken out into two major categories: goods trade and services trade. Goods trade includes the importing or exporting of tangible products (e.g., automobiles and cell phones), while services trade includes the importing or exporting of intangible products (e.g., tourism and insurance). Demand for goods and services is driven by different forces, as exemplified by pandemic-induced shutdowns and work-from-home mandates that led to increased demand for household goods and a sharp decline in demand for such services as dining-in restaurants and international travel (CEA 2023a). Historically, services trade has been less sensitive than goods trade to macroeconomic shocks. Real trade flows underscore this point. Figures 5-4 and 5-5 compare actual trade flows (in goods and services, respectively) with alternative paths, forecasting continued growth at pre–global financial crisis linear trend rates after the start of the crisis and at 2009–19 linear trend rates after the start of the pandemic. The negative demand shock during and after the crisis depressed

---

[9] The real GDP growth rate for 2023 was calculated as the simple average of the annualized real growth rate over the period 2023:Q1–2023:Q3.

Figure 5-5. Real Quarterly Trade in Services, Actual versus Forecasted, 1992–2023

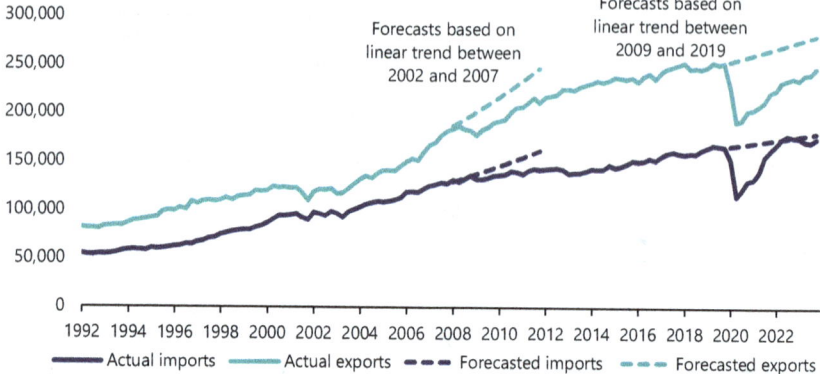

Council of Economic Advisers

Sources: Bureau of Economic Analysis; CEA calculations.
Note: Actuals were deflated to 2022 dollars using import/export price indexes. Post-2007:Q4 forecast based on linear trend in each series from 2002:Q1 to 2007:Q4; post-2019:Q4 forecast based on linear trend in each series from 2009:Q3 to 2019:Q4. Trade data are on a balance of payments basis. Gray bars indicate recessions.
2024 Economic Report of the President

both goods and services trade flows; however, the impact was more muted for services trade flows. The slowdown in U.S. goods trade growth (particularly in goods imports) was therefore a key driver of the plateauing in overall U.S. trade flows after the crisis.

Unlike during the global financial crisis, trade in both goods and services collapsed in 2020 due to mobility restrictions motivated by public health precautions that drove supply chain disruptions and brought global travel to a sudden halt (OECD 2022; IMF 2022). After the pandemic, goods trade flows recovered rapidly, especially for U.S. imports, which soon rose above the trend forecasted before the pandemic and returned to this trend in late 2023. U.S. goods exports recovered more slowly, but are near their forecasted trend. These recovery paths offer reason for cautious optimism that in 2024, both goods exports and imports will remain in line with their trends before the pandemic (figure 5-4).

The outlook for services—namely, services exports—is more uncertain (for a definition of services, see BEA 2023a). Services imports (including American travel abroad) recovered to their growth trend before the pandemic by early 2022 but slowed in the early part of 2023 and are near their long-term trend (figure 5-5). Services exports have not yet returned to their long-term trend. However, there are reasons for optimism. Services exports exhibited positive growth throughout 2023 and, on a monthly basis, reached a historic high in November 2023 (U.S. Census Bureau 2023). And services export sectors—including the financial sector, telecommunications, computer and information services, and intellectual property (e.g., patent and

Figure 5-6. U.S. Services Exports by Broad Product Categories, 1999–2023

Billions of real 2022 dollars
300

Billions of real 2022 dollars
1,200

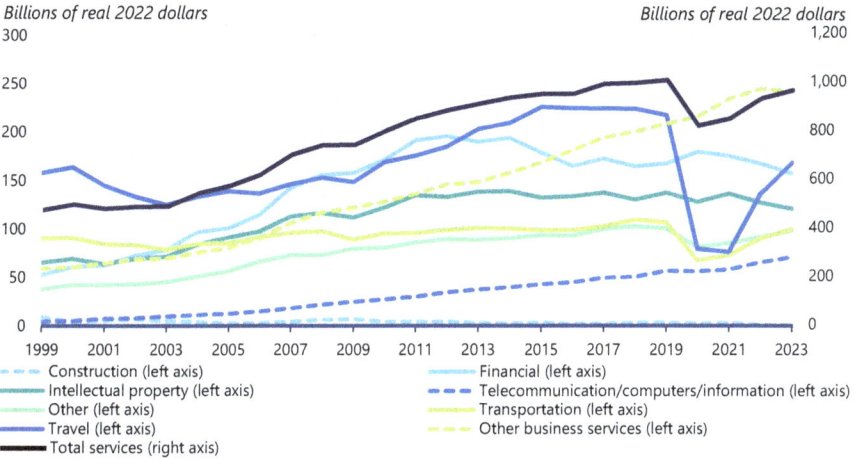

- - - Construction (left axis)
——— Intellectual property (left axis)
——— Other (left axis)
——— Travel (left axis)
——— Total services (right axis)
——— Financial (left axis)
- - - Telecommunication/computers/information (left axis)
——— Transportation (left axis)
- - - Other business services (left axis)

Council of Economic Advisers

Sources: Bureau of Economic Analysis; CEA calculations.
Note: Dashed lines indicate types of services that did not experience declines during recessions. "Other" includes maintenance and repairs, insurance, personal/cultural/recreational services, and government goods and services. Trade data are on a balance of payments basis. Gray bars indicate recessions.
2024 Economic Report of the President

trademark licensing), and other business services (including services related to research and development, computer and data processing, engineering, and services that cover management of construction projects)—were largely unaffected by the pandemic (figure 5-6). This is important because these collectively represent high-value-added activities in which the United States continues to maintain a comparative advantage (Baccini, Osgood, and Weymouth 2019).

Within services, telecommunications, computer and information services, and other business services have grown steadily and were especially resilient during the three recessions between 1999 and 2023. Two factors explain this resiliency. First, services trade is often governed by long-term contracts that are not easily changed without long lag times. Second, services trade represents an extreme form of highly agile, "just in time" production: inventories do not present obstacles in the event of a shock, and resources can be redirected quickly toward other goals (Miroudot 2022).

Travel (foreign spending on travel to the United States) and transportation (revenues from airplanes and ocean carriers for transporting freight and passengers) exports accounted for most of the pandemic-era drop; travel has yet to recover to its level before the pandemic. Travel advisories and health restrictions exacerbated these weaknesses, suggesting that lifting these restrictions can play a role in helping travel exports recover at a faster pace.[10] Transportation exports are closely linked to the exporting of merchandise freight (BEA 2018), and goods exports recovered more slowly than goods imports—dragging the recovery of transportation services exports after the pandemic. Transportation services exports also include revenue from transporting passengers and are, as a result, closely linked to commercial and business travel. While both sectors are improving as travel restrictions loosen, business travel has recovered more slowly, with large businesses having to cut back on travel—motivated in part by an interest in reducing carbon emissions (Georgiadis et al. 2023).

The United States' sluggish trade growth in 2023 mirrors global developments. From a cyclical perspective, the slowdown in U.S. goods imports may be partly attributable to the postpandemic normalization toward services consumption (including nontradable services like restaurants and tradable services like travel), away from goods consumption (U.S. Department of the Treasury 2023; CEA 2023a, chap. 2). Higher U.S. interest rates and associated borrowing costs are also likely to affect goods imports negatively, since durable goods such as cars, home furnishings, and capital goods are often purchased using borrowed funds (Romei 2023). Both goods and services exports are negatively affected by slower growth in foreign markets like Europe and China and by higher interest rates, which together are leading to lower external demand for U.S. exports. From a secular perspective, the slowdown in trade could also reflect longer-term factors, including compositional changes in GVCs. The near-term outlook for overall U.S. trade growth remains uncertain, in light of the many factors at play.

U.S. Trade Deficits Are Driven by Aggregate Saving and Investment Patterns

A country's overall trade balance is the difference in value between its imports and exports. A country that imports more than it exports runs a trade deficit, while a country that exports more than it imports runs a trade surplus. The United States is a net exporter of services and a net importer of goods. Because the magnitude of its goods deficit far outweighs that of its services surplus, overall, the United States has run a trade deficit since the early 1990s (figure 5-7). In 2022, the annual value of the U.S. goods trade deficit reached an all-time high and expanded as a percentage of GDP, and

---

[10] For example, while flights between the United States and China—a major source of U.S. tourist arrivals—were slated to increase from 48 a week to 70 a week beginning in November 2023, these figures remain well below the 340 flights a week that connected the countries before the pandemic (Bloomberg 2023). Still, developments suggest continued expansion in services exports as pandemic-era travel policies ease further; e.g., China lifted its ban on group travel to the United States in August 2023, which will allow large-scale tour groups to once again visit the United States (Cheng 2023).

Figure 5-7. U.S. Trade Balances and Real Growth, 1992–2023

Percentage of GDP   *Percent, year-over-year*

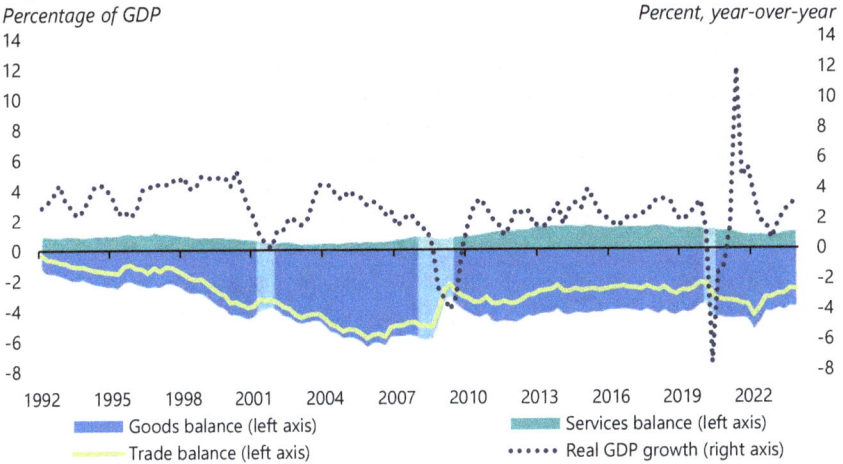

Goods balance (left axis)   Services balance (left axis)
Trade balance (left axis)   •••••• Real GDP growth (right axis)

Council of Economic Advisers
Sources: Bureau of Economic Analysis; CEA calculations.
Note: Trade data are on a balance of payments (BOP) basis. Real GDP is seasonally adjusted at an annualized rate. Gray bars indicate recessions.

the U.S. services trade surplus contracted as a percentage of GDP. These trends started to reverse more recently, with the 2023 U.S. annual trade deficit contracting by nearly 19 percent compared with 2022.

Trade deficits can elicit negative attention if the presumption is that the GDP accounting identity (where negative net exports—exports minus imports—are subtracted from GDP) describes the totality of the relationship between trade and growth. Trade deficits are also sometimes associated with import competition, which has historically generated concentrated employment losses for certain groups of workers. However, the connections between trade deficits, economic growth, and employment are closely tied to broader macroeconomic conditions. For example, when an economy is operating at full employment, a rising trade deficit can be a pressure-release valve, providing needed supplies of imported goods and services that help prevent overheating (Baker 2014). Moreover, imports complement domestic spending on American goods and services, so that their negative accounting impact on GDP is partially offset by the domestic value added generated,

Box 5-1. Trade Balances and Capital Flows—Fundamental Drivers

Overall trade balances. The fundamental drivers of a country's overall trade balance are its relative saving and investment rates—both public and private (Ghosh and Ramakrishnan 2024). Countries with lower domestic saving than domestic investment (likely as a result of low domestic saving rates, high domestic investment rates due to attractive economic opportunities, or a combination of the two) tend to run trade deficits and accompanying current account deficits (where the current account balance is defined as the trade balance plus net foreign investment income plus net transfer payments from foreign income sources like worker remittances and foreign aid). The trade balance typically accounts for the bulk of the current account balance and is highly correlated with it, so, for expositional simplicity, we focus on the trade balance. Trade deficits are necessarily matched by capital and financial account surpluses (the net inflows of foreign lending necessary to finance the trade deficit)—as is the case with the United States.

There are several schools of thought on what drives the United States' trade deficit. One emphasizes a supply-side view, where much of the onus for the United States' capital and financial account surplus and trade deficit can be placed on other countries' *excess supply of savings* or foreign saving gluts (Bernanke 2005; Pettis 2017; Klein and Pettis 2020). Under this framing, the United States absorbs disproportionately large inflows of capital from countries where saving rates are relatively high. This can occur due to both government policies (e.g., large foreign reserve acquisitions, exchange rate management to influence currency values, and suppression of consumption to boost internal savings) and myriad other factors (including weak social safety nets or demographics) (Devadas and Loayza 2018). When saving is too high relative to investment, this can result in weak demand for imports and capital outflows to other countries, potentially causing distortive financial bubbles in recipient countries (McBride and Chatzky 2019). By emphasizing foreign influences on domestic trade balances, this view downplays the impact of domestic saving and investment. Under this model, excess saving flowing from one country to another would tend to lower the receiving country's interest rate and appreciate its currency, leading to lower saving, higher investment, and a larger trade deficit.

A second school of thought emphasizes a demand-side view (e.g., Knight and Scacciavillani 1998). According to this theory, countries can have *excess demand for saving* due to their outsized productive investment opportunities compared with available domestic saving. Needed inflows are imported via net sales of assets to foreigners (e.g., sales of Treasuries and securities and FDI inflows). These large net capital inflows allow for a level of consumption and investment that

Figure 5-i. U.S.–China Trade Deficit, 2009–22

Trade balance as a percentage of GDP

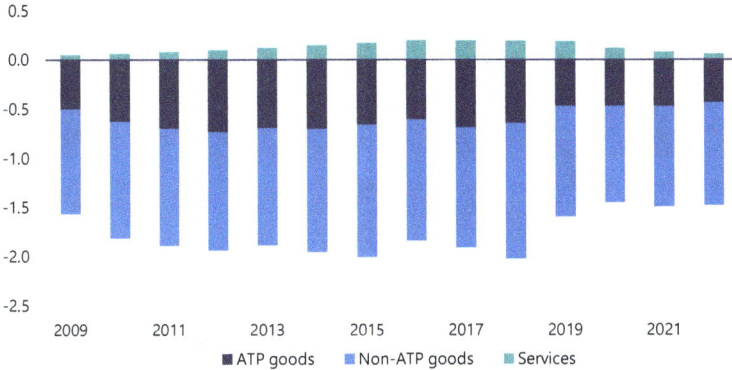

■ ATP goods ■ Non-ATP goods ■ Services

Council of Economic Advisers
Sources: Census Bureau; CEA calculations.
Note: ATP = advanced technology products. Trade data are on a balance of payments basis.
2024 Economic Report of the President

could not otherwise occur; with access to these foreign countries' excess savings, domestic households, firms, and government all benefit by incurring lower borrowing costs. Over time, such investments can yield strong returns and higher productivity—allowing them to service their accumulated debts and potentially generating trade surpluses (Obstfeld and Rogoff 1996).

Of course, together with other explanations—for example, Caballero, Farhi, and Gourinchas (2017) on safe asset shortages—the excess savings and excess demand views may all play a role and interact in ways that can be problematic in some cases, particularly if excess foreign funding supports excess demand that fuels unproductive, distortionary investment. An oft-cited example is the U.S. housing bubble of the early 2000s, when excess foreign saving helped inflate a real estate bubble that crashed with devastating and lasting consequences (Jørgensen 2023).

Bilateral trade balances. A country's overall deficit is the sum of its bilateral balances, of which some generally will be negative and some positive. While the overall balance reflects the macroeconomic factors that determine saving and investment, bilateral imbalances can reflect a comparative advantage—with systematic heterogeneity across different goods and services (IMF 2019). As an example, figure 5-i divides the U.S.-China deficit into services and two broad product-group categories: advanced technology product (ATP) goods and non-ATP goods. ATP goods include products that embody advanced technologies in biotechnology, life science, opto-electronics, information and communications, electronics, flexible manufacturing, advanced materials, aerospace, weapons, and nuclear technology (Abbott et al. 1989). Two-thirds of the ratio between the goods trade deficit and GDP is driven by trade in non-ATP goods, and the United States has a long-standing, albeit small, surplus with China in services—highlighting the role of comparative advantage in determining the U.S.-China bilateral deficit, with the United States showing relative advantage in technology-intensive production technologies and services sectors compared with China. China has a comparative advantage in non-ATP goods.

along with downward pressure on inflation.[11] Trade, including via higher imports, can also boost the productivity of importing firms and the broader economy by supporting higher growth (CEA 2015a). Data support this view; the U.S. trade deficit tends to be countercyclical and is largest during periods of strong GDP growth because the same drivers of increased domestic demand (including savings and investment rates) also tend to fuel increased import demand (CEA 2015b). Box 5-1 discusses these fundamental drivers and the trade-offs from running large deficits, including how excessive foreign savings flowing into a country can fuel unproductive, distortionary investments over time (Bernanke 2005).

The United States Leads in Global FDI Flows

The United States is the largest source of and destination for FDI flows globally.[12] Over 20 percent of both U.S. FDI inflows and outflows in 2022 were targeted at cross-border manufacturing investments (OECD 2023b; BEA 2023b). In addition to providing another source of financing for domestic investments, FDI tends to increase wages and productivity in target firms (Hale and Xu 2016) and can also generate positive spillovers

---

[11] The COVID-19 pandemic offers an instructive anecdote. Imports surged during lockdowns, allowing consumption of goods to increase and help buoy the recovery (Higgins and Klitgaard 2021). A large share of final expenditures on imported goods is generated domestically, as shown by Hale et al. (2019): "Nearly half of the amount we spend on imported goods stays in the United States to pay for the local component of the retail price of these goods. . . . Almost half of the total expenditures on imports is embedded in the production of U.S. goods and services that use imported intermediate inputs. Taking all of these factors into account, import content in total [personal consumption expenditures] was just over 10% in 2017. The high share of local content means that imports generate a number of transportation and retail jobs that might or might not be as numerous if these goods were produced in the United States."

[12] Global comparison based on data from the first half of 2023 (OECD 2023b).

across U.S. firms within an industry (Keller and Yeaple 2009).[13] Reflecting long-standing trends, the large majority of U.S. FDI flows are either destined for or originate from the country's closest trading partners. For example, in 2022, Canada and countries in Europe accounted for 79 percent of inward U.S. FDI flows and 65 percent of outward U.S. FDI flows (BEA 2023c).

FDI flows are less volatile across time than cross-border securities flows, but they still tend to fluctuate (Lipsey 2000). In order to smooth out some of the volatility, figure 5-8 shows the three-quarter moving average of quarterly U.S. FDI-to-GDP inflows and outflows, as well as linear trend lines for each series before and after the global financial crisis. The smoothed series still shows sizable fluctuations in FDI flows, often dur-

Figure 5-8. U.S. FDI Flows as a Percentage of GDP, 1990:Q1–2023:Q2

Three-quarter moving average (percent)

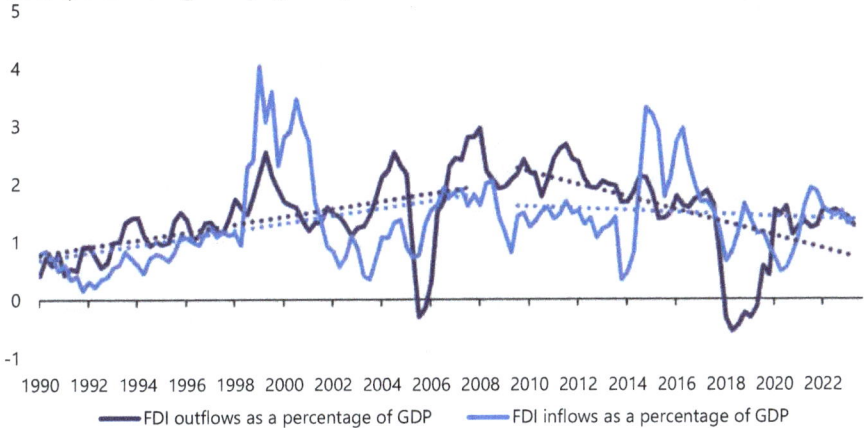

Council of Economic Advisers

Sources: Bureau of Economic Analysis; CEA calculations.
Note: FDI = foreign direct investment. The moving average is centered on each quarter. Gray bars indicate recessions.
Linear trend lines (dotted lines) are based on periods before and after the global financial crisis.
2024 Economic Report of the President

ing nonrecessionary periods, which reflect the acyclicity of FDI flows in

---

[13] FDI often correlates with the arrival not only of technological advances but also other intangible assets, including novel managerial approaches and production processes, technical know-how, and lessons from learning-by-doing in a cross-border setting (Branstetter 2006). FDI can also promote trade through creating new cross-border commercial connections, and FDI's effects on productivity can result in increased domestic and global competitiveness for a firm and its peers. But absorptive capacity, including an educated workforce and sufficient research and development investment, is needed for a country to reap the benefits of FDI (Blomström, Kokko, and Mucchielli 2003). Evidence from the United States signals that horizontal productivity spillovers across firms in an industry tend to be strongest in high-tech industries and for firms most distant from the productivity frontier. These effects accounted for between 8 to 19 percent of U.S. manufacturing productivity growth during the late 1980s and early 1990s (Keller and Yeaple 2009).

advanced markets (BIS 2017). Explanations for such fluctuations are often unique to each episode and flow type. For example, the decline in U.S. FDI outflows in 2018 has been attributed to a dramatic reduction in reinvested earnings (retained profits) abroad due to a regulatory change in the tax treatment of offshore profits.[14] During that same year, a large portion of the decline in U.S. FDI inflows was attributed to the reincorporation of a single technology solutions provider—Broadcom; changes to the ownership structure reclassified the firm's U.S. affiliate as a U.S.-headquartered company, making its associated transactions no longer cross-border (Tabova 2020).

Taking a longer view, U.S. FDI outflows have broadly been on a downward path since the global financial crisis due to many of the same cyclical and secular headwinds that have had an impact on trade flows (see the linear trends shown in figure 5-8) (UNCTAD 2023). Since 2022, they have largely leveled off as a share of GDP. FDI inflows as a share of GDP fell 19 percent from 2021 to 2022—more than double the median post–global financial crisis year-on-year declines but smaller than the large declines in the early 2000s and mid-2010s.[15] The 2022 drop was primarily driven by a fall in cross-border mergers and acquisitions, as tighter global financial conditions and uncertainty in financial markets caused borrowing costs to increase (UNCTAD 2023).

Aggregate flows mask the different types of foreign investment transactions, including those that expand an economy's production capacity through new facilities or expanded existing facilities. Capacity-expanding FDI flows into manufacturing have, for instance, partially offset aggregate weak FDI trends, both globally and in the United States.[16]

The United States was the largest destination for capacity-expanding FDI in 2022 (UNCTAD 2023). FDI expenditures in new U.S. establishments and expansions of existing facilities were concentrated in manufacturing, which represented almost two-thirds of total new FDI first-year expenditures in 2022 (BEA 2023d).[17] This concentration of new FDI investments in

---

[14] As noted by Tabova (2020), "For most of the period prior to 2018, reinvested earnings accounted for the majority of [flows of U.S. direct investment abroad, USDIA]. The drop in USDIA in 2018 is driven by the drop in reinvested earnings as a result of the 2017 [Tax Cuts and Jobs Act] that eliminated the tax incentive to keep earnings abroad and led to U.S. companies repatriating a large part of their accumulated earnings abroad."

[15] After the global financial crisis, and measuring year-on-year percentage changes at a quarterly frequency, FDI outflows to GDP declined at a median rate of −2.3 percent and FDI inflows to GDP declined at a rate of −7.9 percent.

[16] According to UNCTAD (2023), capacity-expanding FDI announcements grew by 64 percent year on year, to $1.2 trillion globally in 2022, rising by 37 percent in advanced markets and more than doubling in developing countries.

[17] The Bureau of Economic Analysis's (2023d) survey of new FDI in the United States identifies capacity-expanding transactions that create new U.S. establishments and the building of new physical facilities by existing U.S. affiliates of foreign-owned firms, as well as other transactions from foreign investors for new acquisitions of U.S. businesses.

Figure 5-9. Real FDI in U.S. Manufacturing New Establishments and Expansions, 2014–22

Billions of 2022 dollars

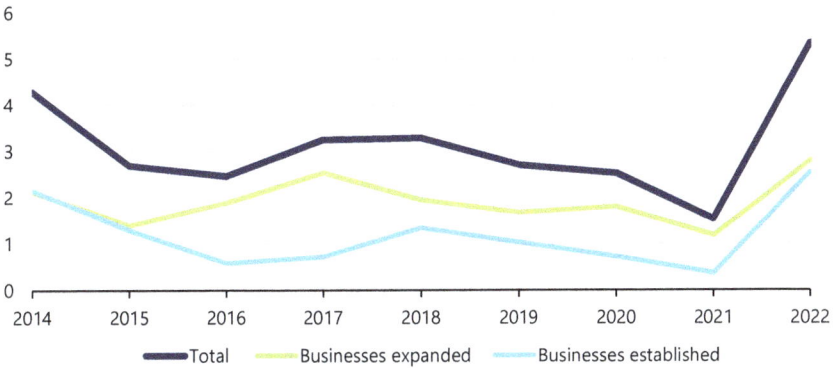

Total   Businesses expanded   Businesses established

Council of Economic Advisers
Sources: Bureau of Economic Analysis; Bureau of Labor Statistics; CEA calculations.
Note: Series were deflated using the Producer Price Index: Total Manufacturing (2022 = 100). New FDI refers to transactions that create new U.S. establishments and the building of new facilities by existing U.S. affiliates of foreign-owned firms. First-year expenditures include expenditures in the year in which the transaction occured.
2024 Economic Report of the President

manufacturing deviates from earlier years; the manufacturing sector's average share of capacity-expanding FDI spending from 2014 to 2021 was less than one-third. FDI flows in new U.S. manufacturing production capacity increased 247 percent from 2021 to 2022, reaching $5.3 billion and reversing a multiyear downward trend that began in 2019 (figure 5-9).[18]

These new foreign investments in manufacturing projects in the United States are concentrated in strategically important sectors, including advanced technologies and clean energy; foreign investments in computer and electronic products (including semiconductor manufacturing) were among the largest, at $1.8 billion of capacity-expanding FDI flows in 2022 (BEA 2023d).[19] There has also been a sizable number of announced FDI

---

[18] In 2022, expenditures outperformed the average from before the pandemic (2014–19) by a factor of 1.7.

[19] Looking at more speculative planned investment expenditures, the increase in capacity-expanding FDI in the computer and electronics sector is striking, rising from $17 *million* in 2021 to $54 *billion* in 2022 in real terms and representing roughly two-thirds of 2022's planned capacity-expanding manufacturing FDI.

Box 5-2. The U.S. High-Capacity Battery Supply Chain and the Complementary Role of Domestic and Trade Policies

Battery supply chains in the United States illustrate the importance of international trade partnerships in complementing domestic legislation to achieve clean energy goals. The high-capacity battery supply chain is characterized by five main value chains: (1) raw material production, (2) material refinement and processing, (3) material manufacturing and cell fabrication, (4) battery pack and end-use product manufacturing, and (5) battery end of life and recycling (White House 2021b).

The 2022 Inflation Reduction Act (IRA) offers critical support to clean energy industries, particularly the high-capacity battery value chain for electric vehicles and energy storage. The Advanced Manufacturing Production Tax Credit (45X) and Advanced Energy Project Investment Tax Credit (48C) can allay almost a third of capital investment faced by battery manufacturers (Mehdi and Morenhout 2023). In 2023, under the Bipartisan Infrastructure Law (BIL), the Department of Energy allocated $1.9 billion to build and expand commercial-scale facilities to extract and process battery materials (e.g., lithium and graphite) and produce components (U.S. Department of Energy 2023).

Provision of tax credits under the IRA and public funding under BIL are designed to "crowd in" private sector investments (Boushey 2023). Between July 1, 2022, and June 30, 2023, the U.S. economy received a total of $213 billion in new investments in the clean energy

Figure 5-ii. Battery Investments as a Share of Total Actual Manufacturing Investments, 2021–23

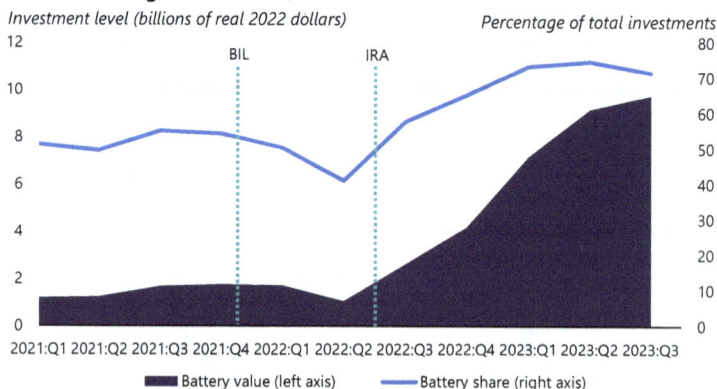

Council of Economic Advisers
Sources: Clean Investment Monitor; CEA calculations.
Note: BIL = Bipartisan Infastructure Law; IRA = Inflation Reduction Act.
2024 Economic Report of the President

Table 5-i. Percentage of Imports to the United States in the High-Capacity Battery Supply Chain by Top Partner Countries

Year	China (percent)	South Korea (percent)	Japan (percent)	Canada (percent)
2021	25.3	11.6	16.1	18.6
2022	33.9	14.7	14.2	12.4
2023	37.4	17.8	13.6	10.2

Council of Economic Advisers
Sources: Trade Data Monitor; CEA calculations.
Note: This table displays the percentage share of imported products in the high-capacity battery supply chain from the top four partner countries. The "battery supply chain" is defined by the set of 10-digit HS codes identified as inputs and lithium-ion batteries and parts by the Department of Commerce (2023). The top-four country ranking is based on 2022 import values.
2024 Economic Report of the President

Table 5-ii. Percentage of Imports by Raw Materials and Lithium-Ion Battery Parts by Top Sources, 2021–23

Imports	China (percent)	South Korea (percent)	Japan (percent)	Canada (percent)
Raw Materials	8.0%	33.8%	47.1%	98.1%
Lithium-Ion Batteries and Parts	92.0%	66.2%	52.9%	1.9%

Council of Economic Advisers
Sources: Trade Data Monitor; CEA calculations.
Note: This table displays the percentage share of imported products in the high-capacity battery supply chain from the top four partner countries. The "battery supply chain" is defined by the set of 10-digit HS codes identified as inputs and lithium-ion batteries and parts by the Department of Commerce (2023). The top-four country ranking is based on 2022 import values.
2024 Economic Report of the President

Table 5-iii. Ford Motor Company's Investment Announcements in High-Capacity Battery Materials, 2022–23

Materials Being Supplied	Material Supplier (Country)	Arrangement
Nickel	Vale (Indonesia) and Zhejiang Huayou Cobalt (China);	Joint venture
	BHP Nickel West (Australia)	Agreement
Lithium	Ioneer (United States);	Agreement
	Lake Resources (Argentina)	Agreement

Council of Economic Advisers
Source: Reuters.
2024 Economic Report of the President

sector, representing a 37 percent increase from the prior year (Bermel et al. 2023). Within manufacturing, actual investments in batteries accounted for the largest share—72 percent—of total manufacturing investments in 2023:Q3 (figure 5-ii).

The most critical metals for producing lithium-ion batteries are lithium, cobalt, nickel, manganese, and graphite (Tracy 2022). Access to these metals and related battery materials is fundamental to building a flourishing U.S. battery supply chain. Globally, China controls most of the market for mining and processing of critical battery materials (International Energy Agency 2022). China's share of imports to the United States of products in the battery supply chain has been steadily increasing since 2021 (table 5-i).

Among the top source countries, most battery supply chain imports from China and South Korea are of lithium-ion batteries and parts, most battery supply chain imports from Canada are of raw materials, and battery supply chain imports from Japan are more evenly distributed between battery components and raw materials (table 5-ii). Company announcements also provide tangible insights into planned domestic and international investments to secure battery raw materials from miners and refiners (table 5-iii). For example, Ford Motor Company has recently entered into various arrangements to secure battery raw materials, as table 5-iii shows.

In the long run, a suite of bilateral agreements and frameworks to promote climate goals between the United States and partner countries are expected to pave the way to achieve diversification of sources for critical minerals. The U.S.-Japan Critical Minerals Agreement enables the countries to develop and strengthen critical minerals supply chains using best practices in labor and environmental standards (USTR 2023f); the Australia–United States Climate, Critical Minerals, and Clean Energy Transformation Compact is designed to coordinate on several issues vital to clean energy and critical minerals supply chains (White House 2023a); and the Minerals Security Partnership, with 13 countries, targets financial and diplomatic support for projects along the minerals supply chain (U.S. Department of State n.d.)

investments in clean energy in recent years (Bermel et al. 2023).[20] While these projects are in earlier stages of planning or implementation than the FDI projects discussed above, and therefore are more speculative, foreign investors nevertheless account for one-third of all clean energy announcements. Of $154 billion in announcements over the period 2021:Q1–2023:Q2, $51 billion in announcements stems from companies with headquarters abroad. South Korean and Japanese firms account for some of the largest announcements in clean energy (including electric vehicles and batteries), while Canadian firms plan to invest in critical minerals projects. Box 5-2 highlights the complementary roles of international and domestic policies in promoting a more resilient battery supply chain, including through FDI investments.

---

[20] This is based on the Clean Investment Monitor (2024), a joint project of Rhodium Group and the Massachusetts Institute for Technology's Center for Energy and Environmental Policy Research. The data set includes detailed metadata for manufacturing, utility-scale energy, and industrial facilities. All included facilities have investments during the time horizon 2021:Q1–2023:Q2. Investments fall into one of four camps: announced (excluding announcements of "intent," without specifying a particular location and committing resources); under construction or postconstruction but not yet operating; operating or offline but planned to return to operation; and canceled, retired, or offline, with no plans to return to operation. Joint ventures, investments in utilities, and canceled investments were dropped.

The near-term outlook for FDI inflows remains uncertain. While the Biden-Harris Administration's industrial strategy is attracting foreign investment in capacity-expanding manufacturing projects in strategic sectors like clean energy and advanced technology, inflationary pressures in partner countries have led to higher interest rates and tightening global financial conditions (IMF 2023). Global economic conditions will continue shaping the flows of cross-border mergers and acquisitions—a major component of FDI flows.

The Rise of Global Value Chains and Early Signs of Reallocation

Global value chains are essential for understanding several important trends: How trade and FDI have changed since the 1990s, the recent attention on promoting supply chain resilience through greater supplier diversification, and multinational corporations' central role in concentrating production. GVCs allow for the production of a single good to take place across several countries, and for firms to specialize in the assembly of specific intermediate goods according to their comparative advantage (World Bank 2020). In 2009, for example, a Boeing plant in Everett, Washington, assembled Boeing's 787 Dreamliner from parts sourced from around the world: The wings were sourced from Japan, the horizontal stabilizers from Italy, the wingtips from South Korea, and the engines from the United Kingdom (Shenhar et al. 2016). Each country added value to the production of the aircraft along the chain.

Two key developments allowed GVCs to gain such prominence in global trade: the wave of trade liberalization (including decreases in tariff rates), which was led by the United States and other major economies in the 1990s and early 2000s (Brainard 2001; Aiyar and Ilyina 2023); and the reduced costs of coordinating across distant locations, which were driven by the information and communications technology revolution (Baldwin 2016). Lower communication costs also facilitated the transfer of knowledge both within and across firm boundaries, and allowed firms to locate production facilities away from their headquarters—even across national borders (Fort 2017). Firms have taken advantage of these changes—and also of advances in transportation technologies—to unbundle their production processes into tasks performed at different locations, leveraging varying factor costs to achieve greater efficiencies.[21]

---

[21] However, benefits of offshoring in lower production costs may be offset by higher coordination costs (Grossman and Rossi-Hansberg 2008). For example, the Boeing Company cited complexities coordinating across its global supply chain for delays in developing the 787 Dreamliner (Peterson 2011).

Multinational firms—themselves fueled by the information and communications revolution—have been particularly adept at taking advantage of cross-border input cost differentials. By establishing foreign affiliates through FDI, these firms can mediate trade with both foreign subsidiaries (within-firm trade) and unaffiliated firms (arm's-length trade) within GVCs (OECD 2018). Multinational firms accounted for, respectively, 65 percent and 60 percent of U.S. goods exports and imports on average between 1997 and 2017 (Kamal, McCloskey, and Ouyang 2022).[22] And within-firm trade accounts for a large share of multinationals' total trade flows: In 2022, one-third (33.7 percent) of U.S. exports and almost half (46.6 percent) of U.S. imports by value were between multinational parent firms and their affiliates or related parties (U.S. Census Bureau 2022).[23] The growth of trade within multinational firms (i.e., flows between parents and affiliates) underscores the highly fragmented nature of production.[24]

Global supply chains' prevalence in U.S. production can also be observed in the high share of intermediate goods or imported input trade in the United States (figure 5-10).[25] Industrial supplies (e.g., lumber and steelmaking materials) and capital goods (e.g., drilling equipment)—typically, inputs into final goods—are highly positively correlated with GVC trade and accounted on average for over half of imports between 1992 and 2022 (Hummels, Ishii, and Yi 2001; Baldwin and López-González 2014). The import share of industrial materials grew more than that of any other product group between 1992 through the onset of the global financial crisis in 2008, showcasing how multinationals' FDI and the establishment of GVC linkages can support greater trade flows.

---

[22] Multinationals are major contributors to the U.S. economy, especially in the manufacturing sector, accounting for 70 percent of all domestic manufacturing employment, more than 50 percent of all nonresidential capital expenditures, and more than 80 percent of all the industrial research and development performed in the United States that underpins innovative output (Foley, Hines, and Wessel 2021, chap. 1).

[23] "Exports: Title 15 of USC Chapter 9, Section 301" of the Foreign Trade Regulations defines a related party transaction as one "involving trade between a U.S. principal party in interest and an ultimate consignee where either party owns directly or indirectly 10 percent or more of the other party." "Imports: Title 19 of USC Chapter 4, Section 1401a (g)(1)" of the Tariff Act of 1930 defines related persons as including "any person directly or indirectly owning, controlling, or holding with power to vote, 5 percent or more of the outstanding voting stock or shares of any organization and such organization." (See https://www.ecfr.gov/current/title-19/chapter-I/part-152.)

[24] Two-way, related-party trade—where the multinational parent or affiliate sends partially finished goods for processing, after which they are shipped back—is one possible indication of production fragmentation. Other arrangements, however, including those in which the affiliate ships finished goods to the parent without any shipments from the parent—or vice versa—are also possible (Ramondo, Rappoport, and Ruhl 2016).

[25] End use is a commodity classification system that identifies merchandise based on principal use rather than the physical characteristics of the merchandise (U.S. Census Bureau 2012). A complete list is available at census.gov/foreign-trade/reference/codes/enduse/imeumstr.txt. The Bureau of Economic Analysis developed the concept of end use demand for balance of payments purposes.

Figure 5-10. U.S. Goods Imports by End Use, 1990–2023
Trillions of 2022 dollars

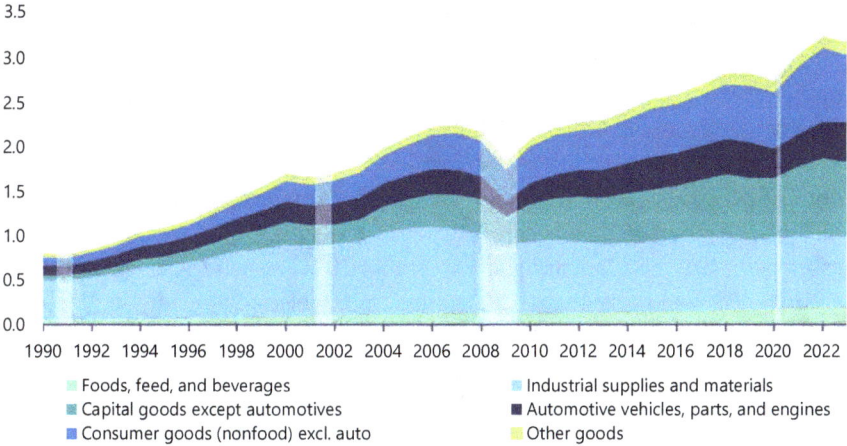

Legend:
- Foods, feed, and beverages
- Capital goods except automotives
- Consumer goods (nonfood) excl. auto
- Industrial supplies and materials
- Automotive vehicles, parts, and engines
- Other goods

Council of Economic Advisers
Sources: Census Bureau; Bureau of Economic Analysis; CEA calculations.
Note: Trade data are on a Census basis. Deflated using industry-specific import price indexes. Gray bars indicate recessions.
2024 Economic Report of the President

The fact that GVC participation appears to have slowed since the global financial crisis is also reflected in the intermediate trade data. The imported share of U.S. industrial supplies and materials declined from 43 percent in 2008 to 25 percent in 2022—a decline inextricably linked to stagnation in post–global financial crisis trade flows (figure 5-10). Decreased cross-border investment, due to an extended deleveraging process, translated into less investment in establishing new GVC linkages. And while the economics literature shows that higher FDI flows are associated with stronger "backward," or upstream, GVC linkages (Fernandes, Kee, and Winkler 2020), there are still positive signs of the United States' participation in downstream or forward value chains. According to the Organization for Economic Cooperation and Development's (OECD 2023c) measure of U.S. domestic value added in foreign countries' exports, the United States' forward value-added contributions as a share of foreign countries' gross exports increased from 24 percent in 2008 to 27 percent in 2020. Together with other indicators, these patterns indicate a slowdown in GVC participation but not a wholesale retreat.

Early Evidence of Supplier Reallocation in 2023

While GVCs offer many benefits, successive economic shocks in recent years, including those caused by the COVID-19 pandemic and Russia's further invasion of Ukraine, illustrate their vulnerability. Supply chain bottlenecks can generate substantial economic disruptions, especially when firms concentrate reliance on a single producer (Baldwin and Freeman 2022; CEA 2022, chap. 6). And in the past three decades, the manufacturing of intermediate goods has become highly geographically concentrated. In 1995, China was the top industrial input supplier to about 5 percent of U.S. manufacturing sectors; by 2018, that share had climbed to over 60 percent (Baldwin, Freeman, and Theodorakopoulos 2023).

Concentration of suppliers can lead to effects that can be felt both domestically and abroad. The recent global semiconductor shortage, for instance, exacerbated a nearly 30 percent decline in U.S. motor vehicle assemblies between January and September 2021, and the average American auto worker lost more than 2 work hours per week as a result—tantamount to a 6 percent weekly pay cut (Bernstein 2023). Meanwhile, pandemic-related supply chain disruptions exacerbated higher prices in the United States (Santacreu and LaBelle 2022) and had negative effects on real GDP (Bonadio et al. 2020). Along with increased onshoring, diversification to include multiple locations and suppliers, especially for critical nodes in supply chains, can increase the resilience of the production chain and minimize exposure to economic and security risks (Iakovou and White 2020; Shih 2020; IMF 2022).[26]

Some early evidence suggests that this sort of supplier diversification is already under way in the United States. While the European Union, Mexico, Canada, and China remain the United States' top trading partners for both exports and imports, the composition of U.S. trade vis-à-vis each of these partners has shifted (figure 5-11). Between 2017 and 2023, China's share of U.S. imports declined by almost 8 percentage points, from 21.6 percent to 13.9 percent. By the beginning of 2023, Mexico had become the United States' top trading partner—having increased its share of U.S. imports by 2 percentage points since 2017—and U.S. import shares from South Korea, Canada, Germany, and Vietnam have also increased.

With respect to advanced technology products (ATP)—which include semiconductors—the share of U.S. imports from China has decreased by almost 14 percentage points (figure 5-12).[27] Vietnam experienced the largest increase in ATP import shares, followed by Taiwan, Ireland, and Germany.

---

[26] Diversification through onshoring should similarly guard against concentrated reliance on a small set of domestic suppliers. For example, the United States relies almost exclusively on domestic sources for its infant formula. When a domestic U.S. infant formula facility was temporarily closed in 2022, domestic supply declined dramatically. Policymakers navigated this crisis by taking various actions to facilitate formula imports by a factor of 17 (WTO 2023a). Nonetheless, supplier diversification may not achieve supply chain resiliency if shocks are global and are correlated across locations (Goldberg and Reed 2023).

[27] ATP include products that embody advanced technologies in biotechnology, life science, opto-electronics, information and communications, electronics, flexible manufacturing, advanced materials, aerospace, weapons, and nuclear technology (Abbott et al. 1989).

Figure 5-11. Percentage Change in U.S. Import Share, by Country, 2017–23

Change in import share (percentage points)

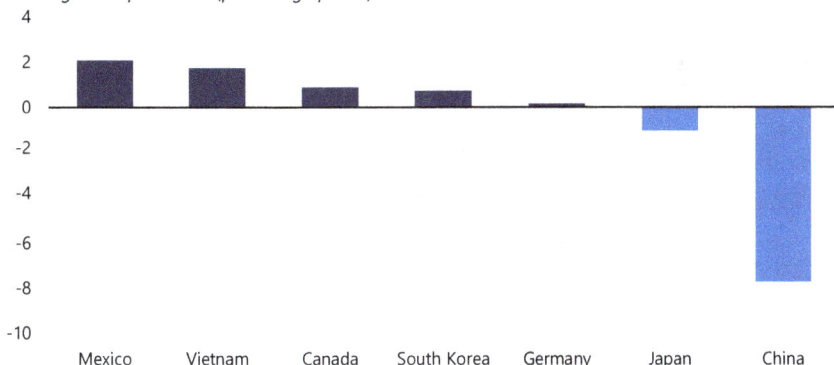

Council of Economic Advisers
Sources: Trade Data Monitor; CEA calculations.
Note: These changes were calculated using nominal import values between 2017 and 2023. These countries were selected based on having the highest import shares in 2023 and largest changes in import shares between 2017 and 2023.
2024 Economic Report of the President

Figure 5-12. Percentage Change in U.S. Import Share of Advanced Technology Products, by Country, 2017–23

Change in import share (percentage points)

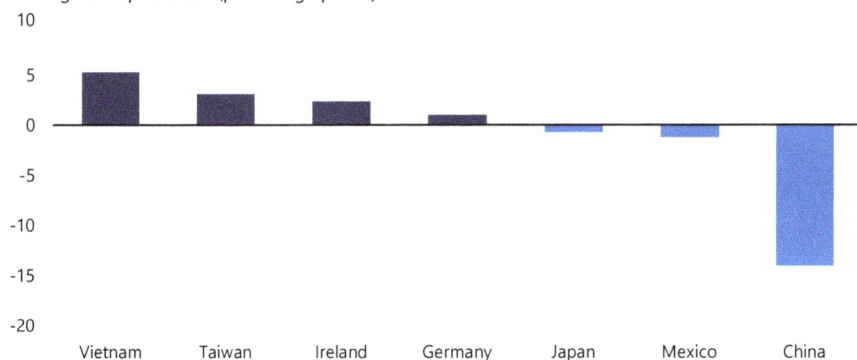

Council of Economic Advisers
Sources: Trade Data Monitor; CEA calculations.
Note: Advanced Technology Products (ATP) definition from U.S. Census Bureau. Calculated using nominal ATP import values between 2017 and 2023. These countries were selected based on having the highest ATP import shares in 2023 and largest changes in ATP import shares between 2017 and 2023.
2024 Economic Report of the President

These compositional changes took place both in response to U.S. trade policy and longer-term factors in China, including rising unit labor costs (Yang, Zhu, and Ren 2023) and declining FDI (Bloomberg 2023). Mexico's and Canada's gains in overall U.S. market share are consistent with patterns of near-shoring, while the other countries gaining share are also trusted partners—consistent with notions of friend-shoring. The marked increase in Vietnam's share of ATP imports, for instance, is consistent with the U.S.-Vietnam Comprehensive Strategic Partnership's goals, including to promote resiliency in semiconductor supply chains (White House 2023b). These reallocations have also broadly been larger in industries that faced higher U.S. import tariffs on goods sourced from China (Freund et al. 2023).

Recent shifts should however be interpreted with caution, for several reasons. First, reallocation may result in increasing costs in the form of higher import prices from alternative locations, at least in the short term. Since 2017, U.S. import prices from Vietnam, Mexico, South Korea, Taiwan, and Singapore have increased in sectors that faced a decline in the U.S. share of imports from China (Alfaro and Chor 2023). Second, while diversification in import sources is under way, U.S. supply chains still remain closely, albeit indirectly, linked with China. Countries that have gained the most U.S. market share between 2017 and 2022 are also deeply engaged in supply chains with China (Freund et al. 2023).[28] These ongoing engagements suggest that global value chains have lengthened to include several Asian economies, particularly when linking China and the United States (Qiu, Shin, and Zhang 2023). Some of these dynamics may reflect underlying fundamentals (including rising labor costs and policy uncertainty), but they may also reflect a higher likelihood of increased transshipments and circumvention of U.S. trade restrictions (Hancock 2023).

The Costs and Benefits of Global Integration for Workers, Consumers, and Communities

Classical trade models highlight how trade can improve aggregate economic efficiency but also lead to a redistribution of income across factors of production in a manner that can increase inequality. Aggregate welfare gains arise from comparative advantage, specialization, and trade across countries based on advantaged goods and services. In any given country, increased specialization leads to a relative increase in labor demand and wages for workers in advantaged sectors over those in less-advantaged sectors.[29] Foreign direct investment, including through multinationals, can also shape wage inequality through higher relative demand for more specialized labor—including demand for college-educated workers or labor demand that evidences a skill bias (Feenstra and Hanson 1997; Hale and Xu 2016). In short, the presence of unambiguous overall welfare gains from

---

[28] The members of the Indo-Pacific Economic Framework received about one-third of their imports from and sent about a fifth of their exports to China in 2021 (Dahlman and Lovely 2023). This framework includes these countries: Australia, Brunei Darussalam, Fiji, India, Indonesia, Japan, South Korea, Malaysia, New Zealand, the Philippines, Singapore, Thailand, and Vietnam.

[29] The factor-based Heckscher-Ohlin model provides one example. However, other models, like the Specific Factors model, also generate winners and losers among workers based on factors of production that are specific (or fixed) to export or import sectors.

global integration does not imply that everyone will benefit from these gains equally—some workers will explicitly lose. Therefore, trade and investment policies should facilitate maximizing the benefits of robust trade and foreign investment flows while concurrently mitigating integration's negative effects, in conjunction with domestic redistribution policies.

Global Integration and Inequality

The evidence for the impact of increased U.S. trade and foreign investment flows on inequality reveals a complex set of patterns. Shifts in U.S. labor demand based on increased specialization and the associated diversification of production processes (e.g., via offshoring) have generated distributional consequences, particularly for domestic manufacturing employment. Between 1993 and 2011, total nonfarm employment increased by roughly 21 million workers; however, manufacturing employment declined by almost 30 percent, or 5 million workers (BLS 2023a, 2023b). To understand the decline in manufacturing employment, two primary factors have been examined empirically: The trade-based view identifies import competition leading to labor-intensive industries moving abroad, while the technology-based view identifies innovations in production techniques—including automation—that reduced or changed the nature of labor demand (e.g., shifting from demand for production workers to college-educated service workers). Disentangling the potential explanations requires overcoming acute empirical challenges, since these forces are often complementary and reinforce one another (Fort, Pierce, and Schott 2018). While the literature suggests that both factors played a role (e.g., Galle and Lorentzen 2021), this subsection highlights causal results from the trade-based explanation.

Part of the steep decline in U.S. manufacturing employment since 2000 has been linked to the sharp rise in Chinese import competition—a dynamic referred to as the "China shock" (Autor, Dorn, and Hanson 2013).[30] While there remains an active debate on the share of U.S. manufacturing job losses that can be ascribed to increased Chinese imports, there is a broader

---

[30] Close to a fifth (16 percent) of the decline in manufacturing employment between 2000 and 2007 has been attributed to the rise in import competition from China (Caliendo, Dvorkin, and Parro 2019). Firms that reorganized activities away from the production of machinery, electronics, or transportation equipment and toward wholesale, professional services (including research and development), and management drove almost a third of the negative manufacturing employment decline between 1990 and 2015 (Bloom et al. 2019). Several factors have been analyzed to understand the surge in U.S. imports from China during this period, including the United States granting China permanent normal trade relations in 2000, China's accession to the World Trade Organization in 2001, reduced trade and investment policy uncertainty associated with these policy actions, and China's own trade and domestic reforms (e.g., tariff reductions and privatizations) (Lincicome and Anand 2023).

consensus on its unequal distributional employment implications.[31] The shock grew during the 2000s and plateaued in 2010; however, its adverse local employment effects persisted through the next decade (Autor, Dorn, and Hanson 2021). Critically, the decline in manufacturing employment was not evenly distributed across workers or space. On one hand, losses were concentrated in geographic areas that were more reliant on import-competing industries and where workers had lower levels of formal educational attainment—especially the South and Midwest (Autor, Dorn, and Hanson 2013). On the other hand, regions with higher levels of formal educational attainment experienced employment gains during this period—largely localized in services sectors (Bloom et al. 2019).[32] These dynamics comport with long-term shifts that occurred within U.S. manufacturing firms: greater outsourcing via participation in GVCs and increased automation that led to a reorientation away from physical production processes toward the provision of intellectual services (e.g., research and development, design, and logistical services) (Fort, Pierce, and Schott 2018).

Import competition from China was also accompanied by a substantial fall in U.S. consumer prices, with disproportionate benefits accruing to low- and middle-income households because they have higher shares of tradable goods like food and apparel in their consumption baskets (Fajgelbaum and Khandelwal 2016; Russ, Shambaugh, and Furman 2017). Causal estimates suggest that a 1-percentage-point increase in Chinese import penetration led to a decline in consumer price inflation of 1 to 2 percentage points—largely reflecting indirect pro-competitive cost effects, where greater foreign competition induces domestic firms to lower markups and thus further drives down prices (Jaravel and Sager 2019).[33] Considering the modeled impact of increased Chinese import penetration across U.S. geographic regions, Galle, Rodríguez-Clare, and Yi (2023) find that almost 90 percent of the U.S. population saw an increase in purchasing power, with those regions that saw

---

[31] For examples of studies that find smaller effects of the China shock on U.S. manufacturing employment than Autor, Dorn, and Hanson (2013), see Jakubik and Stolzenburg (2020) and De Chaisemartin and Lei (2023). Studies that also incorporate downstream supply chain effects in addition to direct competition effects have found positive local employment effects of the China shock (Wang et al. 2018); Antràs, Fort, and Tintelnot (2017) find that firms that increased their use of Chinese imported intermediates also simultaneously increased their sourcing of domestic inputs and increased their production.

[32] Formal educational attainment is defined as the percentage of the total population with a college degree in 1990, using the Decennial Census. Manufacturing workers who transitioned to the services sectors associated with lower educational attainment (e.g., retail) have been found to have experienced nominal earnings declines (Pierce, Schott, and Tello-Trillo 2023).

[33] These results have been corroborated in the broader trade literature (e.g., Bai and Stumpner 2019; Amiti et al. 2020).

Figure 5-13. Pro-Poor Bias in Gains from Trade in the United States (Percent Welfare Gain)

Absolute welfare changes relative to autarky

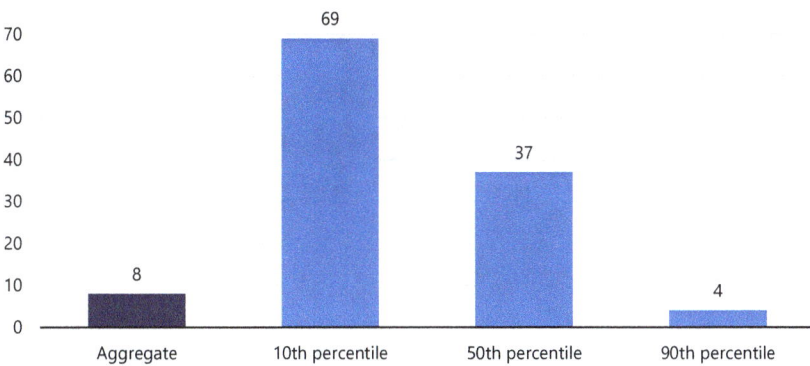

Council of Economic Advisers
Source: Fajgelbaum and Khandelwal (2016, table V).
2024 Economic Report of the President

purchasing power losses being spatially correlated with regions that also saw a loss in manufacturing employment from the China shock.[34]

The results, showing that trade with China has benefited most Americans' purchasing power, are consistent with a larger body of evidence on the benefits from trade with all countries—again, with disproportionate benefits accruing to lower-income households.[35] For example, the average U.S. household has been shown to gain 8 percent in purchasing power from trade compared with a counterfactual autarky (Fajgelbaum and Khandelwal 2016).[36] However, the lowest-income U.S. households gain the most, at 69 percent (figure 5-13).

Recent trends in foreign direct investment may contribute to boosting manufacturing activity and reducing inequality, including for communities disproportionately affected by the China shock. Figure 5-14 maps histori-cal manufacturing employment changes across commuting zones over the period 1990–2007. Areas that incurred higher job losses are indicated in darker shades of gray. The bubbles are sized to correspond to the magnitude of announced clean energy projects since 2021 and are colored to indicate the investor's headquarters country. Areas that experienced larger historical

---

[34] The authors find that the worst-affected areas experienced average losses as large as four times the average overall gain in purchasing power.

[35] There is also a literature documenting welfare increases due to greater access to varieties of goods through trade (e.g., Broda and Weinstein 2006; Melitz and Trefler 2012).

[36] The authors develop a general equilibrium model that considers the distributional effects of international trade on the cost of living (the expenditure channel). Distributional effects through workers' earnings (the earnings channel) are not explicitly modeled to enable a focus on unequal gains through the expenditure channel only.

Figure 5-14. FDI in Clean Energy Projects between 2021:Q1 and 2023:Q2, by Investor Headquarter Country, and Decline in Manufacturing Employment between 1990 and 2007 (Percentage of Working-Age Population)

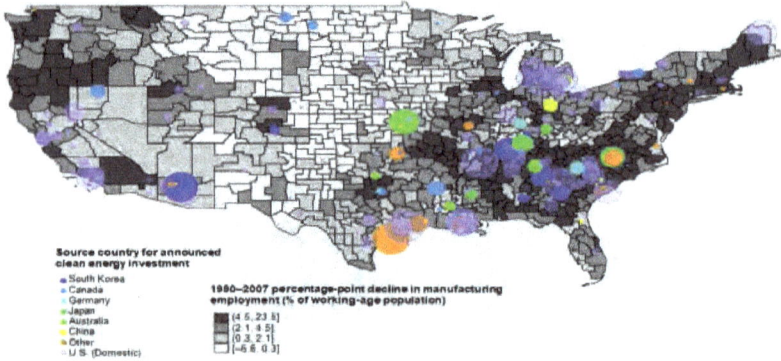

Source country for announced clean energy investment
- South Korea
- Canada
- Germany
- Japan
- Australia
- China
- Other
- U.S. (Domestic)

1990–2007 percentage-point decline in manufacturing employment (% of working-age population)
- (4.5, 23.8]
- (2.1, 4.5]
- (0.3, 2.1]
- [-5.6, 0.3]

Council of Economic Advisers
Sources: Clean Investment Monitor; Autor, Dorn, and Hanson (2013); CEA calculations.
Note: Darker gray regions represent areas that incurred higher historical job losses. Bubbles—representing announced clean energy projects between 2021:Q1 to 2023:Q2—are sized according to the magnitude of the project and colored to indicate the country in which investors' headquarters are located. Regions are defined as commuting zones (USDA).
2024 Economic Report of the President

losses in manufacturing employment have attracted a higher concentration (both in number and size) of announced clean energy FDI projects.

Figure 5-15 illustrates the statistically significant correlations between commuting zones with larger historical manufacturing employment losses and the number and value of clean energy FDI projects announced since 2021. These relationships hold when the data set is expanded to include all announced clean energy projects, suggesting that domestic clean energy projects are likewise disproportionately locating in vulnerable communities, which is consistent with early evidence from Van Nostrand and Ashenfarb (2023).[37] The key drivers of location choice and whether these investments will improve labor market and socioeconomic outcomes in these geographies remain high-priority topics for future research.

Trading Firms and Job Creation

GVCs have created strong interconnections between exporting and importing—which are often performed by the same firms. Among goods traders, averaged over the period 1992–2021, firms that both export and import goods account for a plurality of total U.S. private sector employment (36 percent), followed by firms that only export goods (8 percent) and firms that only import goods (6 percent) (figure 5-16). The majority of employment at goods traders is by large firms (defined as those employing 500 or more

---

[37] For all projects (both FDI and domestic), the correlations between the number and value of projects with historical manufacturing employment declines are both significant at the 1 percent level.

Figure 5-15. Correlations Between Historical Declines in Manufacturing Employment between 1990 and 2007 and the Total Number and Value of Recently Announced Clean Energy Projects between 2021:Q1 and 2023:Q2

A. Decline in Manufacturing Employment and Number of FDI Projects

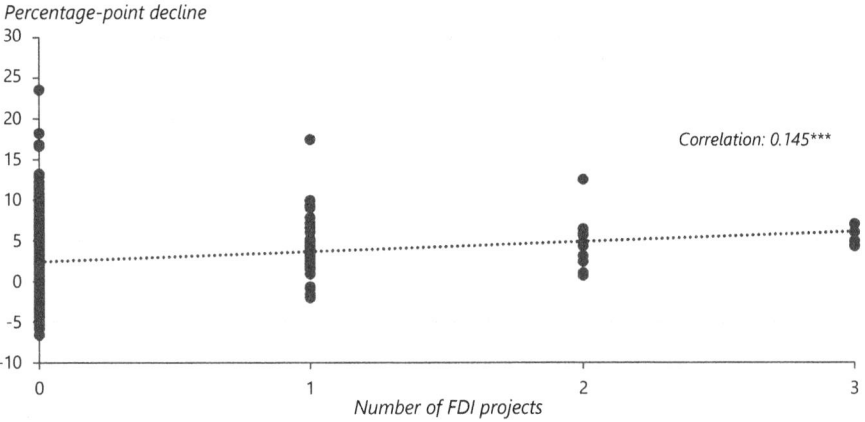

B. Decline in Manufacturing Employment and Total Value of FDI Projects

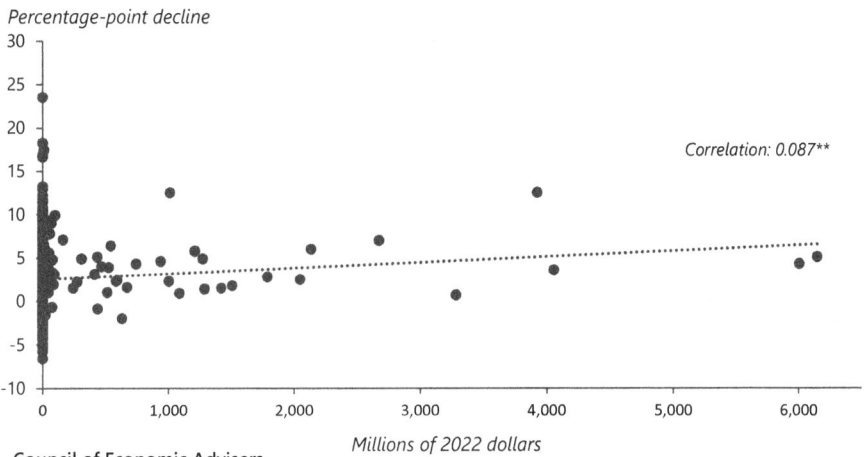

Council of Economic Advisers

Sources: Autor, Dorn, and Hanson (2013); Clean Investment Monitor; CEA calculations.
Note: The decline in manufacturing employment from 1990 to 2007 is calculated as a percentage of the working-age population for 722 commuting zones. Projects are classified as foreign direct investment (FDI) if the associated company headquarters could be traced to a foreign country. Only projects announced between 2021:Q1 and 2023:Q2 are included. Stars denote statistical significance at the 5 percent (**) and 1 percent (***) levels or lower.
2024 Economic Report of the President

workers); in contrast, the majority of employment at nontraders is by small firms (those employing fewer than 500 workers). Nevertheless, small firms directly engaged in the goods trade account for almost 10 percent of national employment.

About 1.3 million small firms were estimated to be exporting goods in 2021—with the potential for almost an equal number of additional small

Figure 5-16. Goods Trader and Employment by Firm Size, 1992–2021 Average

Percentage of employment

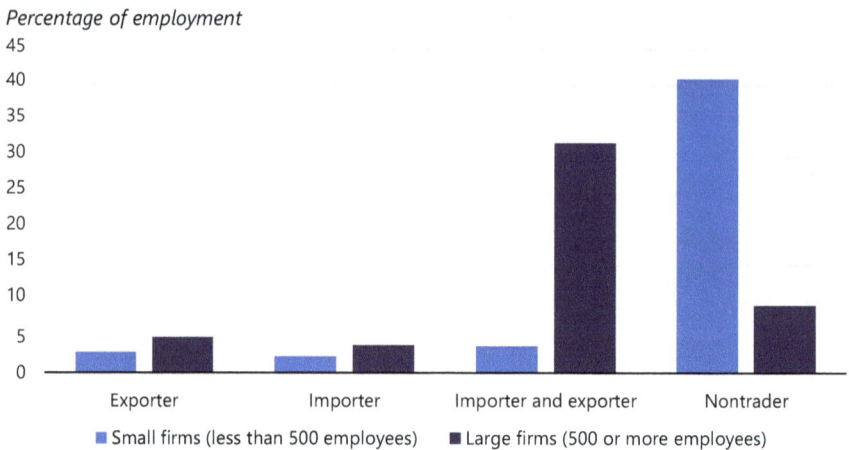

Small firms (less than 500 employees) Large firms (500 or more employees)

Council of Economic Advisers
Sources: Census Bureau; CEA calculations.
2024 Economic Report of the President

businesses to begin exporting based on the tradability of the industries in which they operate (U.S. Small Business Administration 2023a, 2023b). Increased opportunities to export may accrue disproportionately to smaller regions in the United States. While large metropolitan areas (including New York City and Los Angeles) account for large volumes of U.S. exports, the most export-intensive regions (with the highest shares of exports to regional GDP) include relatively less populous cities like Wichita, Detroit, Youngstown, and Houston (Parilla and Muro 2017).

Goods traders' contribution to net job creation has grown over recent years: During the 2001–7 period, goods traders accounted for only 10 percent of total net job creation; but between 2008 and 2019, that figure rose to 60 percent. Overall, goods traders were responsible for almost 40 percent of net job creation in the U.S. economy between 1992 and 2019 (Handley, Kamal, and Ouyang 2021).[38] These statistics underscore the changing nature of the U.S. production landscape, where both exports and imports support domestic jobs.[39]

---

[38] Handley, Kamal, and Ouyang (2021) document that vast majority of goods-traders' contribution to net job creation is driven by the opening of new establishments, particularly, in services-providing sectors like wholesale, retail, business and professional services. These patterns hint at the complementarity between manufacturing and services activities as well as the sectoral diversity in job creation tied to trade participation.

[39] See Fort (2023) for an in-depth discussion of U.S. firms' organization of goods production across firm and country boundaries.

Mitigating the Challenges of Global Integration

The classical Ricardian trade model—that the concept of comparative advantage allows all countries to access goods produced by the most efficient and lowest-cost producers, increase their aggregate consumption, and ultimately benefit from trade, even if a single country produces all goods more efficiently in absolute terms—is based on several assumptions that may not hold in the real world (Ricardo 1817). One such assumption is that workers are frictionlessly mobile between sectors. When the costs of transitioning to sectors where a country has a relative cost advantage are high, domestic producers in import-competing sectors lose out—as do their workers—even if overall consumption rises. Meanwhile, the classical Ricardian model conceives of comparative advantage only with respect to monetary costs. American workers and consumers may place a high value on the consumption of foreign goods that adhere to high environmental and labor standards, but adherence to such standards is not well captured by cost signals. To make trade fair and beneficial for all, trade and foreign investment policies need to explicitly consider distributional, environmental, and labor rights in their design.

The Biden-Harris Administration's approach to trade and investment partnerships centers on promoting middle-class prosperity, reducing inequality, addressing climate risks, and advancing fair competition (USTR 2023b). It aims to raise labor standards, adopt sustainable environmental practices, bolster supply chain resilience, and minimize national security risks through more U.S.-based production in certain sectors while concurrently supporting ongoing robust trade and investment flows with U.S. partners. This approach encompasses a combination of economic frameworks and regional partnerships:

- *United States–Mexico–Canada Agreement* (USMCA) *Rapid Response Labor Mechanism:* The USMCA modernized the North American Free Trade Agreement and includes new labor obligations, such as the innovative rapid response mechanism, which provides for expedited enforcement of workers' rights of free association and collective bargaining at the facility level (USTR 2023a). Since 2021, the United States has invoked the mechanism 18 times to seek Mexico's review at 17 different facilities.[40] As a result, the United States has achieved improved outcomes for thousands of Mexican workers—millions of dollars have been paid to workers, more workers are represented by independent unions, there have been more free and fair union elections, and unions have successfully negotiated for higher wages and improved policies at facilities.[41] These developments are

---

[40] We thank USTR colleagues for sharing the rapid response mechanism's statistics that are current through December 20, 2023.
[41] Based on review of all USMCA cases (U.S. Department of Labor 2023).

consistent with studies finding that labor-related cooperation provisions specific to trade union rights in the context of preferential trade agreements improve compliance with requirements for enforcing collective labor rights (Sari, Raess, and Kucera 2016).

• *Indo-Pacific Economic Framework* (IPEF): This is an economic framework between the United States and 13 member countries: Australia, Brunei Darussalam, Fiji, India, Indonesia, Japan, South Korea, Malaysia, New Zealand, the Philippines, Singapore, Thailand, and Vietnam (USTR n.d.–a). IPEF comprises four pillars: trade, supply chains, a clean economy (including clean energy, decarbonization, and infrastructure), and a fair economy (including tax and anticorruption). The trade pillar aims to enhance resilience, sustainability, and inclusivity through a variety of provisions, including high-standard labor and environment commitments (USTR n.d.–b). The supply chains pillar aims to build resilient supply chains through multiple initiatives, including the development of criteria for critical sectors, the promotion of supply chain diversification, and establishing channels for information sharing and crisis response mechanisms (U.S. Department of Commerce 2022). The clean economy pillar aims to further the climate goals articulated under the Paris Agreement through a variety of cooperative actions, including sharing best practices on the commercialization and deployment of clean energy technologies and mobilizing private sector investment in emission-reducing projects (U.S. Department of Commerce 2023a). The fair economy pillar aims to strengthen domestic legal frameworks to accelerate progress on various international standards related to reducing corruption and bribery and promoting efficient tax administration (U.S. Department of Commerce 2023b). Collectively, these pillars promote inclusive growth by advancing higher economic standards, building supply chain resiliency, addressing climate change, fighting corruption, and promoting high-standard labor commitments.

• *U.S.-Taiwan Initiative on 21st-Century Trade:* The first agreement under this trade initiative covers areas of customs administration and trade facilitation aimed at reducing red tape for U.S. exporters. These include good regulatory practices and domestic services regulation, such as streamlining licenses for firms seeking to operate abroad and promoting fair competition opportunities. Anticorruption provisions address issues including money laundering, and denial of entry for foreign public officials who have committed specified corruption offenses. They also promote cross-border trade and investment, information sharing, and exchanging best practices in finance and other areas for small and medium-sized enterprises (USTR 2023c). A second round of negotiations commenced in August 2023, focusing on agriculture, labor, and the environment (USTR 2023d).

• *U.S.-Kenya Strategic Trade and Investment Partnership* (STIP): STIP is an initiative to pursue high-standard commitments in selected areas (including agriculture, anticorruption, digital trade, the environment and climate change action, regulatory practices, endorsing workers' rights and protections, and trade facilitation and customs procedures, among other focus areas) intended to increase investment; promote sustainable and inclusive economic growth; benefit workers, consumers, and businesses (including small and medium-sized enterprises); and promote African regional economic integration (USTR 2022c, 2023e).

- *Regional partnerships:* The Administration has focused on building closer partnerships with regions across continents. Two examples, spanning Europe and Africa, are highlighted here:

—*U.S.-EU Trade and Technology Council:* This council includes two working groups focused on securing supply chains and addressing global trade challenges (White House 2021a). One group, which focuses on secure supply chains, aims to advance resilience and security in supply chains and create coordination mechanisms to avoid disruptions (U.S. Department of Commerce 2023c). The other group, which focuses on global trade challenges, aims to address issues of nonmarket economic policies and practices, promote the development of emerging technologies by avoiding new and unnecessary product and service barriers, promote and protect labor rights, and address other trade and environment issues (USTR 2021).

—*African Growth and Opportunity Act* (AGOA): AGOA is a unilateral U.S. trade preference program that provides duty-free access to the U.S. market for certain exports from countries in Sub-Saharan Africa that meet AGOA's eligibility criteria. Thirty-two countries currently qualify in 2024 (USTR n.d.–c). Eligibility encourages countries to make continual progress on economic benchmarks (e.g., having a market-based economy); political benchmarks (e.g., the rule of law, political pluralism, and anticorruption efforts); poverty reduction (e.g., via job creation in exporting sectors); and the protection of labor rights (e.g., prohibitions against child labor and protections of the rights to organize and bargain collectively). Countries must also not engage in gross violations of internationally recognized human rights or activities that undermine U.S. national security or provide support for acts of international terrorism (USTR 2022d).

Conclusion

The decades-long trend of steady increases in global trade and foreign direct investment plateaued after the global financial crisis. Nonetheless, the United States remains the world's second-largest trader after China, and the largest country with respect to FDI flows. U.S. trade and foreign investment patterns in 2022 and 2023 reflect a combination of cyclical and secular factors, in addition to the Biden-Harris Administration's policy agenda—all of which are interacting in novel ways to show signs of positive developments (including an increase in U.S. supply chain resilience and increasing FDI inflows into the U.S. manufacturing sector), along with reasons for caution (including services exports remaining below trends before the pandemic).

While the future outlook for U.S. trade and investment flows remains uncertain, the Administration is continuing to pursue a worker-centered trade agenda by reviewing trade policies for their impact on, and consequences for, American workers. This policy approach also aims to harness the benefits of trade while reversing the jobs and earnings displacements that beset too many American communities for decades. These ongoing actions are helping to rebuild these communities, not by walling off international trade but by leveraging its benefits while managing its costs for American workers.

★ ★ ★ ★ ★ ★

Chapter 6

Accelerating the Clean Energy Transition

The clean energy transition is under way. Its end goal is an innovative, cutting-edge U.S. economy powered by cheap, reliable, and secure clean energy sources and technologies. In this future, various aspects of the economy—the electricity that powers it, the cars and planes that move people and goods, the products and foods we consume—will be provided without the harm of air pollution and climate change. The production of clean energy will also create new sources of economic growth, employment, and prosperity, furthering American competitiveness throughout the 21st century to meet global demand for clean energy technologies.

Contrast this future with the Nation's past reliance on fossil fuels, a dependence that has come at significant costs. The use of fossil fuels—responsible for 68 percent of total historical human-induced carbon dioxide emissions—has given rise to climate change (Friedlingstein et al. 2020). The global average temperature has already risen more than 1 degree Celsius (1.8 degrees Fahrenheit) since the preindustrial period, and is projected to reach 2.4 to 5 degrees Celsius (4.3 to 9 degrees Fahrenheit) by 2100 if no further action is taken (Kriegler et al. 2017; IEA 2023a).

The cost of inaction is high, with damage from climate change already starting to mount. In 2023, the United States experienced an unprecedented 28 weather- and climate-related disasters with losses of at least $1 billion each (NOAA 2024). Some insurers are starting to pull out of home insurance markets due to the high costs of covering climate-related disasters (CEA 2023a). Additional warming is expected to further damage human health, productivity, living standards, and food security, driving mass migration and

Figure 6-1. U.S. Net Total Greenhouse Gas Emissions, with Emissions Reduction Goals

Millions of metric tons of CO_2 equivalent

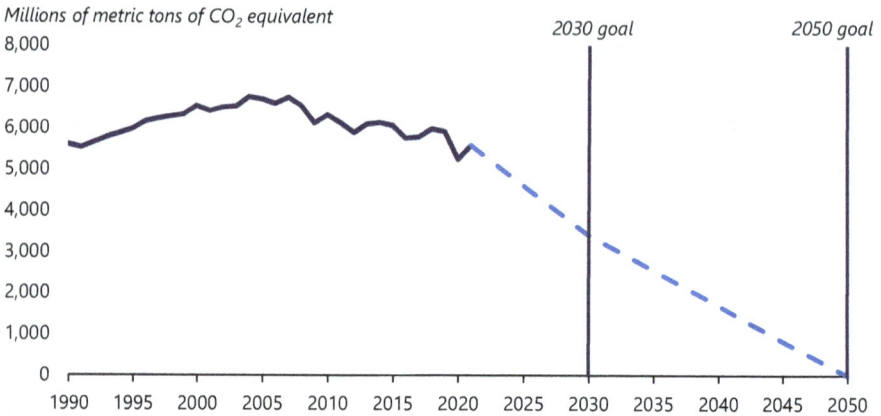

Council of Economic Advisers
Sources: U.S. Environmental Protection Agency; CEA calculations.
Note: Dotted segments represent pathways to achieving 2030 and 2050 emissions reduction goals. The measure "millions of metric tons of CO_2 equivalent" scales each gas by its global warming potential relative to CO_2.
2024 Economic Report of the President

worsening social and political instability, among other social and economic outcomes, and inequities therein (Carleton et al. 2022; Burke, Hsiang, and Miguel 2015; Schlenker and Roberts 2009; Hsiang et al. 2013, 2023; Marvel et al. 2023). This is further compounded by the harmful health consequences of local air pollution due to continued burning of fossil fuels (Lelieveld et al. 2019). To avoid these costs, policymakers must induce a rapid energy transition from fossil fuels to clean energy sources.

Decarbonizing the U.S. economy is an immense undertaking. A combination of private and public investments triggered by Federal, State, and local climate policies are already moving in this direction (CEA 2023a; White House 2022; OMB 2023; California Legislature 2023; NYC Department of Buildings 2023). Between 2005 and 2021, U.S. greenhouse gas (GHG) emissions fell by 17 percent, as shown in figure 6-1 (UNFCCC 2023), a remarkable annualized rate for a major industrial economy during a period of economic growth (OECD 2023).[1] Yet this pace is still not fast enough

---

[1] GHG emissions also fell across the European Union during this period, but under a regulated declining cap on emissions (UNFCCC 2024b; European Environment Agency 2023).

to meet Paris Agreement commitments seeking to limit global warming to 1.5 degrees Celsius (UNFCCC 2024a). To achieve the midway goal of a 50 percent emissions reduction relative to 2005, the United States must lower its annual emissions by 6 percent on average between 2021 and 2030, and must further accelerate emissions reductions after 2030.[2]

Achieving decarbonization rapidly enough to avoid growing physical damage from climate change will require deploying commercially available clean energy technologies—like solar and wind power, electric vehicles, and heat pumps—at even faster rates (IEA 2023b). To reach net zero emissions by 2050, the United States will need to act across all sectors of the economy. For example, the United States may need to double its share of electricity generated by non-carbon-emitting sources to roughly 75 percent by 2030 (National Academies 2021). Furthermore, more than half of global emissions reductions by 2050 will need to come from technologies that are yet to be invented or commercialized (IEA 2023b).

Faster decarbonization can be achieved in part by accelerating two complementary recent developments. First, the electricity sector needs to shift away from fossil fuels. Much of recent U.S. GHG reduction comes from the electricity sector (dark teal line, figure 6-2). A large share of emissions reductions in the electricity sector to date have been the result of displacing coal-fired generation with clean energy and natural gas (figure 6-3). The electricity sector must now accelerate its transition from using fossil fuels, including natural gas, to clean energy. At the same time, given a cleaner source of electricity, a shift toward electrification in other sectors—such as the transportation, industrial, commercial, and residential sectors—would be an effective way to help lower emissions across the economy. Both tasks are long-term shifts in the type of energy that powers the U.S. economy.

---

[2] This CEA calculation assumes a constant-percentage annual GHG emissions decline between observed 2021 U.S. GHG emissions and the Administration's 2030 U.S. GHG emissions target.

Figure 6-2. U.S. Emissions per Sector, 1990–2021

Millions of metric tons of CO_2 equivalent

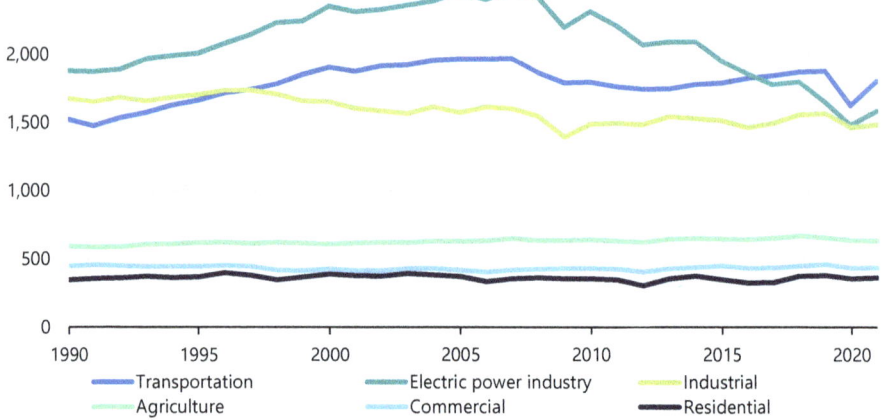

Council of Economic Advisers
Source: U.S. Environmental Protection Agency (2023).
2024 Economic Report of the President

Figure 6-3. U.S. Electricity Generation by Energy Source, 1990–2021

Electric power generated (billion KWh)

Total emissions from electric power industry (millions of metric tons of CO_2 equivalent)

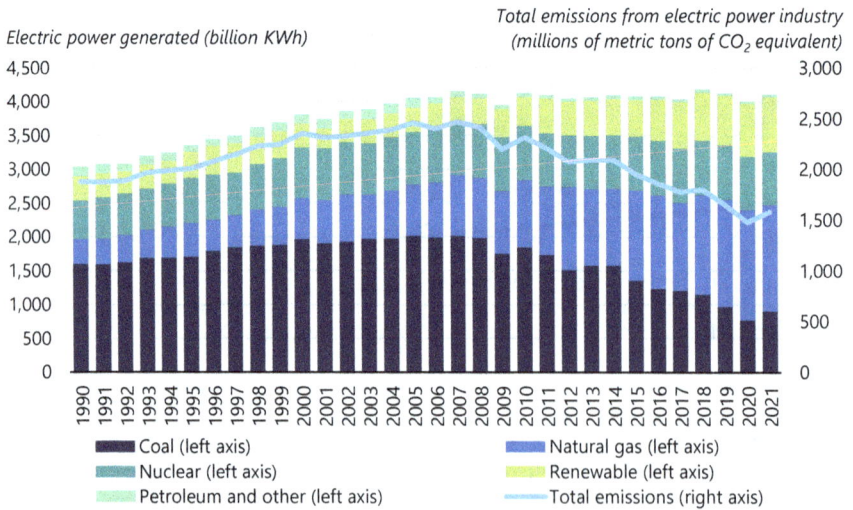

Council of Economic Advisers
Sources: U.S. Energy Information Administration; U.S. Environmental Protection Agency.
2024 Economic Report of the President

Economists characterize such broad transitions as structural change: long-term evolutions in an economy's composition, whether through inputs or outputs, from an established set of economic activities to a set of emerging ones. Structural change underlies many major moments in economic development; past examples include the transition from agriculture to manufacturing during the Industrial Revolution and the more recent shift from manufacturing to services in advanced economies. The clean energy transition—moving an economy primarily based on fossil fuels to one powered by clean energy sources and technologies—can also be viewed through this lens.

The structural change perspective provides a foundation for understanding the forces that will determine the direction, pace, and endpoint in the transition from one energy system to another. It also offers a lens for identifying the specific investments needed for accelerating the transition from an energy system based on fossil fuels to one based on clean energy. For example, in the electricity sector, the decline in capital costs for clean energy has increasingly made it competitive with fossil-based electricity, yet some new electricity capacity still uses natural gas (Lazard 2023; EIA 2023a). This is in part because some types of clean electricity, such as solar, require complementary technologies, like batteries, to be available during all parts of the day. A structural change perspective highlights how the transition can be accelerated through complementary investments in battery storage, along with lowering siting and transmission costs, enabling renewable energy to better substitute for fossil fuels by supplying electricity throughout the day.

Also embedded in a structural change perspective is the notion of path dependence. Fossil fuels dominate today's market not only because they have historically been cheaper, due in part to Federal policies and subsidies implemented in the past, but also because they have accumulated historical economic advantages that are difficult for emerging clean energy technologies to surmount. However, this path dependence cuts both ways. Policies that provide a sufficient push for clean energy technologies to overcome fossil fuels' historically accumulated advantage can alter the need for future government intervention. That is, putting the economy on a clean energy path will make it easier to achieve long-term decarbonization. As that happens, policy interventions need not be permanent: Once an economy has built up sufficient economic advantage in clean energy, private market incentives can sustain the clean energy transition.

By considering a subset of clean energy sources and technologies—including wind, solar, electric vehicles (EVs), and batteries—through the economics of structural change, this chapter provides a framework for understanding the clean energy transition and the policies that can accelerate it.[3] However, this framework, like any, is not comprehensive, and does not address every element of the Biden-Harris Administration's whole-of-government approach to climate policy. It is also an incomplete account of the benefits of the clean energy transition, such as avoiding climate damage, lowering air pollution and energy prices, creating high-quality jobs, and fostering economic competitiveness. Instead, the narrower task of this chapter is to offer an economic lens for understanding the path toward the clean energy transition and how it can be achieved.

The chapter's first section provides an overview of structural change and how economists have applied the framework to explain important moments in economic development. It then provides a taxonomy of the various factors that can push or pull against structural change and thus determine the direction, rate, and end point of long-term transitions. The section then discusses market failures and economic frictions under which government intervention may be needed when the direction and pace of market-driven structural change are not in line with society's goals.

---

[3] This framework also applies to nuclear, hydropower, and technologies such as carbon capture and storage and direct air capture that lower net GHG emissions.

The second section applies the structural change framework to the clean energy transition, discussing various ways in which the transition represents a distinct case of structural change—and the ensuing set of unique challenges and opportunities. The push-and-pull factors discussed in the first section are then mapped onto specific issues in the clean energy transition.

The third section describes how specific policies enacted by the Biden-Harris Administration are strategically targeting these push-and-pull factors to accelerate the clean energy transition. These and other efforts can build a U.S. clean energy economy that benefits workers and communities, avoiding the worst economic consequences of climate inaction.

The Economics of Structural Change

This section introduces structural change as a broad economic concept and delineates the various push-and-pull forces that determine the direction and speed of structural change. Market failures and other economic frictions may inhibit the socially optimal direction and rate of structural change, justifying government intervention. The structural change lens shows how policy interventions, if successful, need not be permanent; once properly directed, an economy has the momentum to carry forward that transition on its own.

What Is Structural Change?

The transition to a net zero economy requires structural change. Structural change refers to long-term (as opposed to short-term, cyclical) changes in the composition of an economy, from an established activity to an emerging one. Of particular interest are the direction and the pace of this change, as well as the final composition of the economy. Embedded in a structural change perspective is the notion of path dependence: that historical economic dependence continues to exert influence today (Nelson and Winter 1985). Once the process of structural change begins, it can gather momentum on its own without much further impetus.

History is rich with examples of structural change, many of which were considered important turning points in economic development. For instance, structural change in the allocation of labor from agricultural to industrial activity characterized the Industrial Revolution (Nurkse 1952; Rao 1952; Lewis 1954; Ranis and Fei 1961). Similarly, much attention has been given to the shift in labor shares from industrial to service-oriented activities during the latter half of the 20th century (Autor, Levy, and Murnane 2003; Acemoglu and Autor 2011).

Redirection of capital—both physical and financial—also characterizes major historical transitions. During World War II, economies around the world redirected domestic production from consumer durables—such as automobiles and home appliances—to tanks, airplanes, and artillery. From February 1942 until the end of the war, U.S. commercial auto production ceased, and auto assembly lines were repurposed to produce 80 percent of U.S. tanks and more than half of all aircraft engines (Gropman 1996). From 1940 to 1943, U.S. national defense gross investment rose from $13.2 billion to $517.9 billion (in 2022 dollars), representing an enormous financial real-location.[4] Such redirection of resources transformed the trajectory of U.S. innovation for decades thereafter (see box 6-1).

These and other historical examples have led to a rich intellectual tradition in economics examining the drivers and consequences of structural change (Johnston 1970; McMillan and Rodrik 2011; Autor, Dorn, and Hanson 2013; Herrendorf, Rogerson, and Valentinyi 2014). Unlike more static frameworks, this literature focuses on transitional dynamics and their drivers. In doing so, it builds on macroeconomic models, but with an added focus on understanding the composition of an economy and how it changes.

Determinants of Structural Change

The structural change framework focuses on understanding the forces that shape—or reshape—the composition of an economy, whether through inputs, outputs, or both. These forces can push or pull against structural change, the balance of which determines the direction, speed, and end point of an economy's transition from an established activity to an emerging one. This section details such push-and-pull forces.

Productivity spillovers arise under many circumstances. Spillovers within a sector can occur at the individual level in the form of learning-by-doing (Arrow 1962; Lucas 1988) or at the sectoral level through technological or knowledge spillovers (Romer 1990; Acemoglu 2002; Acemoglu et al. 2012). Regardless of the mechanism, productivity spillovers within a sector favor the established economic activity and allow that advantage to strengthen over time, making the emerging economic activity increasingly unlikely to replace the established activity. Spillovers across sectors can, however, accelerate structural change, particularly when knowledge and technologies developed for an established sector can be applied to an emerging sector (Bloom, Schankerman, and Van Reenen 2013). Government-supported research efforts during the World War II mobilization effort, for example, had spillovers onto postwar innovation that enabled the

---

[4] This is from CEA calculations using data from the Bureau of Economic Analysis.

Box 6-1. World War II and Technological Change

The U.S. government has played a critical role in enabling past periods of rapid technological change, including during World War II, when the Federal Government established the Office of Scientific Research and Development (OSRD), an expansion of the then–recently created National Research Defense Committee and a predecessor to the National Science Foundation. This new office would eventually invest more than $9 billion (in 2022 dollars) in research and development (R&D) between 1940 and 1945 to develop innovations in radar technology, military weapons, and pharmaceuticals, among other sectors. Unlike previous models of public investment in R&D, the OSRD's novel approach channeled investments to hubs of applied research while facilitating partnerships and collaborations between public, private, and academic researchers (Gross and Sampat 2023a). Despite its brief existence, the OSRD bent the path of U.S. technical innovation for decades to follow, as a potential template for the clean energy transition.

Many of the technological advancements generated by OSRD support had direct civilian applications despite originally being intended for military use. For example, while penicillin cells were discovered in 1928, neither industry nor government had pursued their use as an antibiotic until the OSRD began investigating them for military applications in the early 1940s. After demonstrating its success in the military, the government released penicillin for commercial use in 1945 (Quinn 2013).

Recent evidence on the large-scale shock to research activity during World War II from the OSRD program suggests that public investment can have a sustained, long-term impact on subsequent innovation. Technology hubs that received the greatest R&D investment from the program during World War II realized 40–50 percent more patent-based innovation activity per year by 1970 (Gross and Sampat 2023a). World War II–era Federal investment in industrial activity and the ensuing mobilization also led to a sectoral shift in the composition of manufacturing activity toward industries like lumber, chemicals, rubber, stone, metals, machinery, and transportation equipment (Jaworski 2017).

These effects on future innovation were primarily driven by spillovers and agglomeration economies, in which co-located firms mutually benefit from the sharing of ideas, infrastructure, and other assets (Duranton and Puga 2004). Gross and Sampat (2023a) find that these effects were approximately double in clusters centered on a highly ranked university. That firms and other research institutions (including government labs) later located in these hubs also suggests spillover benefits from regionalized innovation activity. Roughly 40 years after World War II, industrial clusters that received the OSRD's R&D investment saw 90 percent higher employment in those manufacturing industries as well as additional manufacturing business formation (Gross and Sampat 2023a).

The research demands necessitated by World War II are similar in scope to those required to address climate change. Gross and Sampat (2023b) argue that unlike the Manhattan Project or the Apollo Program—which were focused on singular technological goals for singular customers—World War II demanded a portfolio-based approach to technological innovations for a variety of end users. In this regard, the authors note a parallel between the R&D investment approach of the OSRD and the scope of today's energy transition needs. But while the challenges are similar in scope, the broad-based structural transformation necessary to address climate change may require investment at an even greater scale.

development of information technologies and biomedical advances (see box 6-1).

An economy's composition may reflect *relative input prices* between established and emerging inputs. These include both the price of the input itself and any complementary capital, land, or other material inputs associated with the input of interest. Relative adoption tilts toward the input with lower contemporaneous prices. But in the presence of within-sector productivity spillovers, that tilt may be muted. For a new input, technology, or sector to become dominant, lower relative contemporaneous prices may not fully overcome the productivity advantage the established activity has built up over time. For example, high efficiencies in some forms of fossil fuel use from decades of experience would lead to lower adoption of renewables even if electricity from renewables were cheaper today than from fossil fuels.

Factor mobility can also accelerate structural change. Factor mobility refers to the ease with which factors of production—labor, capital equipment, or materials—can be allocated across different economic activities. For example, when workers in established sectors have skills that are attractive in emerging sectors, these workers can switch jobs across sectors—and relocate geographically if moving costs are low—without acquiring much additional education or retraining. Likewise, capital that can be redeployed readily across established and emerging sectors—for example, if a factory can shift from being powered by fossil fuels to clean energy—can help accelerate structural change. But when factors of production cannot be easily reallocated, the rate of structural change may be slow.

Structural change is often shaped by the degree of *substitutability* between existing technologies and those replacing them. Emerging economic activity must compete for consumers with existing activity. When an emerging sector's output perfectly substitutes for that of an established sector, consumers will more readily adopt goods from the new sector (Acemoglu 2002). However, when the new product is not a direct substitute, complementary investments are necessary to ensure the new good has similar—if not better—attributes than the established good. For example, complementary investments in battery storage alongside clean energy sources for electricity will enable electricity supplied from clean sources at all hours of the day, as is currently provided by the established electricity generation mix (IRENA 2019).

New goods can also offer *quality or attribute improvements* that induce added demand. In many sectors, the adoption of new product categories is hastened in part by consumer demand for improved attributes, new use cases, or simply novelty.

Market Failures and Policy Implications

Policymakers and the public may in some cases decide that structural change is occurring in the wrong direction or too slowly. This is justified in the presence of canonical market failures. Externalities, for instance—whereby economic activity imposes costs and benefits onto others without consequences for the actor generating the activity—can lead markets to underprovide a public good (e.g., innovation) or overprovide a public bad (e.g., pollution or GHG emissions). Sector-level economies of scale that require coordination across complementary inputs may also prevent emerging sectors from overcoming the initial hurdle of competing with established sectors.

Policymakers can address these market failures with familiar economic policy tools, including input and output taxes designed to "internalize" the externality, along with subsidies and public research-and-development (R&D) investments. But government interventions differ in one fundamental way when structural change dynamics are at play: They can create lasting change via path dependence. As such, to the extent that these interventions are successful, they need not be permanent. Provided that an intervention is sufficiently large to redirect an economy toward a more socially desirable composition, the intervention may no longer be needed once enough momentum has been built (Acemoglu 2002; Acemoglu et al. 2012, 2016; Meng 2023).

Structural change's key implication—the ability to use policy interventions to permanently alter the direction of change toward a different composition of the economy—may be attractive from a political economy perspective. But because path dependence cuts both ways, it also places added importance on well-targeted policy interventions that direct the economy toward an efficient use of cost-effective inputs. Policies that promote costly technologies may lead to a locking in of those technologies, making a future redirection toward more cost-effective alternatives harder to accomplish. The momentum inherent in economies undergoing structural change amplifies the importance of correctly promoting cost-effective technologies.

Structural Change and the Clean Energy Transition

The structural change framework and the push-and-pull forces articulated in the first section provide a lens to understand opportunities and challenges for accelerating the clean energy transition. Energy is an essential input for nearly every form of economic activity, and it has undergone various transitions over the past few centuries. As society invents new technologies, energy sources—and the form energy takes—change. Before the Industrial Revolution, labor—both human and animal—was the primary energy input for the production of goods and services. The Industrial Revolution unleashed a new and disembodied source of energy: fossil fuels. And the introduction of steam-powered, and then electricity-powered energy brought a transition in how the economy utilized fossil fuels (Devine 1982).

To lay out how the clean energy transition can be viewed through a structural change lens, this section examines the various push-and-pull forces that can accelerate or delay the clean energy transition. While these forces are explored in isolation, policies must target these economic forces simultaneously to achieve the required speed and scale of an economy-wide clean energy transition, as discussed in the third section.

The Costs of Fossil Fuels

Fossil fuels—coal, oil, and natural gas—provide energy through combustion, and in doing so release air pollutants, toxins, and climate-damaging greenhouse gases such as carbon dioxide (CO_2) and methane. In 2021, 92 percent of U.S. anthropogenic CO_2 emissions could be attributed to the combustion of fossil fuels (EIA 2023b).

Understanding the economic challenges of transitioning from fossil fuels to clean energy sources begins with understanding how fossil fuels came to be dominant and deeply embedded in the global and U.S. economies. Because energy is central to both national and economic security, fossil fuel providers benefited from government subsidies to secure strategic geopolitical alliances beginning in the late 19th century. U.S. government support, itself the result of political lobbying, aided fossil fuels in becoming the primary sources of American energy (Victor 2009) (see box 6-2). This is not a uniquely American phenomenon: Fossil fuels became a relatively cheap source of energy globally in part because they have been heavily subsidized.

In addition to government support, the technical characteristics of fossil fuels and their availability further shaped the energy system that emerged in the global economy. Fossil fuels are abundant, energy-dense, and found in many parts of the world. They are also transportable carriers of energy: A piece of coal can be mined in one location and shipped elsewhere to readily meet that location's energy demand, leading to global markets for many fossil fuels and associated infrastructure as well as competitive price pressures. Additional technical qualities aid fossil fuels' competitiveness even when they are not the final energy carrier. For instance, use of some fossil fuels, like natural gas, can be readily ramped up and down for electricity generation, helping balance aggregate electricity supply and demand nearly instantaneously (EIA 2012).

Clean Energy Opportunities and Challenges

Fossil fuels are not the only energy source, and they are far from the most abundant one; sunlight and wind are freely available around the planet. Aside from their critical role in mitigating GHG emissions and air pollution, clean energy technologies have many economic and national security benefits. Because they do not rely on costly fuel inputs, these technologies have

---

Box 6-2. Fossil Fuel Subsidies

A key challenge for the clean energy transition is the cost competitiveness of renewable energy sources compared with the fossil fuel sources they are replacing—a challenge made particularly difficult because the U.S. government has long subsidized fossil fuel production. These subsidies have largely been enacted through the tax code. Since the introduction of the modern Federal income tax in 1913, fossil fuel producers have received unique deductions, effectively shifting risk and losses from oil and gas producers to taxpayers.

The largest fossil fuel subsidies focus on defraying the risks of investment for producers. One major provision involves the deduction of intangible drilling costs—which include wages and preparatory work conducted to drill an oil well—amounting to 60–80 percent of total drilling costs, according to one estimate. Oil producers may deduct 70 percent of these costs immediately, rather than over the lifetime of the well, as is common with standard business expenditures (CRFB 2013). Also subsidized are the costs to explore new wells, despite novel technologies that significantly reduce the risks of drilling unprofitable or nonproducing wells. As recently as 2004, the Federal Government

---

introduced new tax instruments to support investment in drilling capacity (U.S. Congress 2004).

Production is also subsidized, for instance, in the form of a percentage depletion. Independent oil producers are permitted to write off 15 percent of gross income on the first 1,000 barrels they produce a day, and this deduction rises to 25 percent for marginal wells during periods of low prices. Because this deduction is based on gross income, its value can exceed the total value of the producer's investment in the well (CRS 2021). While these provisions target independent producers (those without integrated refining capacity), this represents over 80 percent of U.S. crude oil production (Golding and Kilian 2022).

While estimates vary, one valuation assesses the total producer benefit from the Federal Government's fossil fuel subsidies at $62 billion, on average, annually (Kotchen 2021). This benefit substantially incentivizes production and the entry of new fossil fuel producers at the margin, particularly when oil prices are low, and the subsidies' total contributions to domestic production are estimated to be substantial (Erickson et al. 2017). Over the past 20 years, these subsidies have fueled the development of unconventional projects through the shale boom, with potential benefits to oil producers of up to $4 a barrel (Erickson and Achakulwisut 2021). One study estimates that at oil prices of $50 per barrel, fossil fuel subsidies could be responsible for up to 20 percent of U.S. crude oil production through 2050, while contributing 6 billion metric tons of CO_2 emissions (Erickson et al. 2017).

These subsidies to fossil fuels, both direct and indirect, have greatly promoted domestic production of natural gas and oil for more than a century. Their scope and longevity demonstrate both the Federal Government's ability to support energy production and the extent to which the oil and gas sectors have benefited from such support. As the country looks to accelerate the adoption of nonemitting energy sources, fossil fuel subsidies are also an obstacle to a rapid clean energy transition. As such, President Biden has repeatedly urged Congress to remove these subsidies, most recently in his 2024 budget proposal, in order to recover billions for taxpayers while winding down policy interventions that slow the clean energy transition (OMB 2023).

near-zero marginal costs of generation and can, in the long run with continued technological advances, lower energy prices. Due to its cost advantages, solar is already the fastest growing source of energy in the United States and in the world (EIA 2024a; IEA 2023c). Clean energy technologies can also reduce volatility in energy markets and enhance energy security (Cox, Beshilas, and Hotchkiss 2019). Studies have also shown clean energy to be more resilient than fossil fuels in the event of a natural disaster (Chang 2023; Esposito 2021).

And yet, despite the benefits of clean energy and the need to transition away from fossil fuels to address climate change, many parts of the world have been slow in adopting clean energy technologies that produce energy from these abundant and free resources—or have not adopted them at all (IRENA 2023). In some cases, this may be because clean energy technologies require inputs that are costly or exhibit low mobility. In other settings, complementary technologies are needed for clean energy to serve as a better substitute for fossil fuels. To understand what may accelerate or delay the clean energy transition, this section maps the push-and-pull forces—productivity spillovers, input prices, factor mobility, and substitutability—articulated abstractly in the chapter's first section, onto specific features of the clean energy transition.

Productivity spillovers and declining capital cost curves. Technologies tend to become cheaper as experience with their production increases, consistent with the presence of productivity spillovers. This dynamic likely characterizes the clean energy sector. Despite high initial costs, increased manufacturing capacity and deployment of clean energy technologies have been associated with lowering costs as a result of learning and investments in process innovation (Nemet 2019).

The role of path dependence in productivity spillovers and declining capital cost curves can be illustrated through the history of clean energy technologies over the past century. In a number of cases, despite having near-zero marginal costs, high capital costs—alongside ongoing government subsidies for fossil fuels—made clean energy more expensive than energy derived from fossil fuels. For example, while in the early 20th century, electric wind turbines were common across rural America, in the two decades after President Roosevelt's rural electrification programs brought cheaper fossil-fuel-based electricity to rural areas, every American wind power company went out of business (Pasqualetti, Righter, and Gipe 2004). Solar photovoltaic (PV) panels, first developed in the 1950s to power space satellites, were unable to compete commercially for decades, and were restricted to niche applications such as calculators and solar-powered radios (Nemet 2019). Electric vehicles enjoyed an early boom around the turn of the 20th century, after the discovery of electromagnetism and the invention of the rechargeable battery allowed them to capture 38 percent of the (albeit very small) U.S. automotive market. However, advances in the combustion engine and the growing cost-competitiveness of fossil fuels—a result partially of public subsidies—quickly led to the dominance of internal combustion engine vehicles (Guarnieri 2012).

In the future, as clean energy technologies develop and disseminate, costs are likely to decline as a result of economies of scale and

Figure 6-4. Capital Cost Curves for PV Solar and Onshore Wind, 2000–2020

2020 dollars per megawatt-hour, logarithmic scale

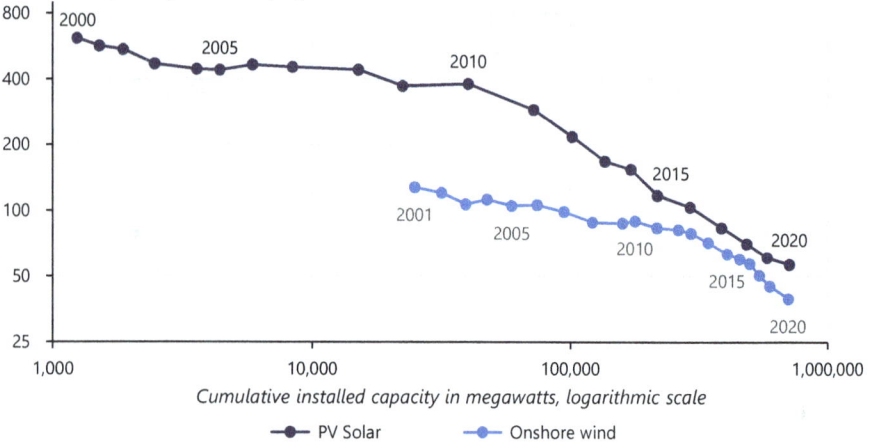

Council of Economic Advisers
Sources: International Renewable Energy Agency (2023); Nemet (2019).
Note: Logarithmic scale shows the relationship between a 50 percent drop in capital costs and a 1,000 percent increase in installed capacity.
2024 Economic Report of the President

learning-by-doing. Economies of scale will move clean technologies down the average cost curve while learning-by-doing will shift down the average cost curve itself as productivity increases. Together, these forces should lead to lower costs at higher levels of output. However, if new technologies cannot compete with existing energy technologies, they will be unable to advance to mass production and experience the cost declines associated with scale economies and learning effects (Hart 2020). This could result from a lack of policies to spur demand, the competitiveness of established technologies, or some combination of both. Indeed, as shown in figure 6-4, it was not until the start of this century that clean energy's capital costs began declining dramatically, coinciding with when many governments around the world began supporting its deployment (Nemet 2019).

Land, transmission, and supply chain costs. Capital costs of clean energy for electricity have fallen dramatically over recent decades and are now often lower than those of fossil fuels (Lazard 2023). These cost advantages notwithstanding, there are other inputs incurred when changing from a fossil-fuel-based to a clean-energy-based system. Electricity from renewable energy has different land use requirements, necessitates investments in transmission infrastructure, and relies on different raw materials than fossil-fuel-based electricity. This implies that the total input cost of clean energy relative to fossil fuels may still not be low enough for markets on their own to deliver a structural transition.

Clean energy electricity generation can be more land-intensive than fossil fuel generation, even after accounting for land used in fossil fuel extraction and distribution (Gross 2020; Van Zalk and Behrens 2018). Utility-scale solar and land-based wind power generation requires large quantities of contiguous land. By one estimate, the capacity necessary to complete the U.S. net zero transition with current technologies could take over 250,000 square miles, roughly the area of Texas (Nature Conservancy 2023). While some of this renewable capacity can be installed on existing land uses—as in the case of rooftop solar—replacing the fossil-fuel-based energy system will likely require repurposing land specifically for clean energy. Siting, the process of picking locations for projects, can also incur political risks. Local interest groups have sued and taken political action against renewable projects, with opposition rising rapidly in recent years, raising the cost of installation (Bryce 2023; Brooks and Liscow 2023).

Siting clean energy installations on cheaper land away from population centers can mitigate these concerns, but may prompt an additional cost: the need to transmit renewable energy generation to load centers. Current transmission regulations also create an externality: The cost of adding a marginal transmission line is often borne by the marginal generator connecting onto the grid—even though the extra transmission line benefits all connected generators (Sankaran, Parmar, and Collison 2021). One recent analysis argues that inadequacies in the current U.S. transmission system—which in some parts of the country fails to connect regions with high solar and wind potential—may lower renewable energy adoption by 65 percent by 2030 (Jenkins et al. 2022). And for planned renewable generation that can connect to existing transmission lines, the average wait time for grid connection is currently 3.5 years (RMI 2022).

Clean energy technologies require different inputs than do fossil fuel technologies, which may be less raw-material-intensive in the construction of generation facilities but require ongoing fuel supplies (IEA 2023b). Wind generation uses over 5 metric tons of zinc per new megawatt of generation capacity, while solar PV uses about 4 metric tons of rare earth metals. By contrast, a new megawatt of natural gas generation capacity uses only about 1 metric ton of metal. Similarly, EV production requires over six times the critical minerals compared with what is needed for producing internal combustion engines, owing primarily to the large quantities of graphite, cobalt, nickel, and lithium used in batteries, though that difference will narrow as battery recycling programs ramp up (IEA 2023b; Riofrancos et al. 2023). Global supply chains can drive down input costs for clean energy technologies, but that may require government intervention. While the United States is currently developing domestic capacity in this area, mining these materials and transporting them requires, in some cases, creating new supply chains and forming new trade relationships (IEA 2023b).

Labor mobility. The clean energy transition will require a shift in the labor market, with workers leaving fossil fuel jobs and entering clean energy jobs. The extent to which labor is mobile across locations and sectors will play an important role in the clean energy transition. These frictions are not unique to the clean energy transition; they affect any process of structural change.

The clean energy sector will require more highly skilled workers (IEA 2022). Globally, about 45 percent of energy workers were in occupations requiring tertiary education as of 2019, compared with only about one-quarter across the U.S. economy. In 2022, more than 80 percent of U.S. clean energy employers reported at least "some difficulty" finding qualified workers (DOE 2023a), compared with about 75 percent of firms across the economy (Manpower Group 2022). In an industry survey, 89 percent of U.S. solar companies reported difficulties finding skilled labor, citing competition, small applicant pools, and applicants' lack of training, experience, and technical skills (IREC 2022). Demand for workers in clean energy sectors continues to increase (DOE 2023a). Indeed, in some sectors, such as transportation, manufacturing clean energy technologies may be more labor-intensive than manufacturing fossil-fuel-based counterparts (Cotterman, Fuchs, and Whitefoot 2022), but that may not apply in all cases.

Geographic immobility may also slow transitions from fossil fuel to clean energy jobs (Lim, Aklin, and Frank 2023). While some fossil fuel and clean energy skills overlap (IEA 2022), fossil fuel and clean energy jobs are often not in the same places. For instance, approximately one-third of recently laid-off coal miners in Appalachia—some of them third-generation employees—have not moved since job displacement, despite the lack of clean energy job opportunities nearby (Greenspon and Raimi 2022; Weber 2020).

This clean energy labor demand presents an economic opportunity, but also requires overcoming skill mismatch with the current workforce. Some of this demand may be met by workers currently employed in fossil fuel sectors. But so long as these workers are able to find employment more generally in an economy as large as the United States', a one-to-one match between fossil and clean industries' labor pools may not be needed (Curtis, O'Kane, and Park 2023). The likelihood of working at a clean firm conditional on having worked for a fossil fuel firm in the previous year was extremely low as of 2019, suggesting an important potential role for work-force development programs and place-based incentives (Colmer, Lyubich, and Voorheis 2023).

Finally, fossil fuel extraction also has local fiscal effects (Raimi et al. 2023). Excise and royalty taxes on fossil fuel extraction provide a major source of local tax revenue, supporting employment in local schools, hospitals, and other public services. An important consideration is whether and how revenue from local fossil fuel taxes can be replaced by proceeds from investments in clean energy or other industrial sectors.

Substitutability. Electricity from clean energy sources like wind and solar is not available at all times of the day, unlike electricity from fossil fuels. This variability of renewable energy can be solved through complementary investments in battery storage and other solutions—including nuclear and hydropower—which makes electricity from clean energy a better substitute for electricity from fossil fuels. For example, to make clean energy dispatchable at all hours of the day, battery storage can be deployed in a manner that incentivizes batteries to be charged when renewables are abundant and discharged when they are not.

Likewise, electric vehicle range—though it is improving rapidly—can present a barrier to EV adoption. To date, most EVs have a lesser range than cars powered by internal combustion engines. Recent surveys show that the majority of EV owners have a second, nonelectric vehicle—and drive that second vehicle more (Davis 2023). As a result, actual EV usage is less than half of what State regulators typically assume (Burlig et al. 2021). While there remain challenges for the substitution of EVs for internal combustion engine vehicles, solutions already exist and more are emerging. These include carmakers installing larger battery packs, improvements in battery technology, and progress on the building out of a robust EV charging network, which is currently under way.

In the extreme case of no substitutability between energy technologies, demand can fail to materialize. Solar PV cells present an early case study of missing demand. When silicon solar cells were first developed by Bell Labs in 1954, they were too expensive for many commercial applications. The U.S. government long remained their main buyer for use in satellites and defense applications (Nemet 2019). Today, hydrogen as an energy feedstock faces similar challenges in industrial settings, where some existing equipment and processes for using fossil fuels cannot be used for hydrogen. Complementary capital investments will be needed to generate demand for hydrogen as an energy feedstock (CEA 2023b).

Financing the Speed and Scale of the Clean Energy Transition

While past structural changes have tended to move on their own timelines, the biggest challenges for the clean energy transition are the required speed and scale. As noted above, global temperatures are already rising and the economic damage is growing. The United States and other countries need to decarbonize across their economies through the rapid deployment of existing clean energy technologies and investments in new technological solutions.

The energy transition has significant financing needs that require accelerating private sector investments. Private investments in clean energy technologies have grown in recent years (White House 2023). However, as a result of impediments common to structural change, they can be riskier and less profitable than alternative investments. Removing such obstacles to rapid structural change in the energy sector can accelerate the pace at which financial markets fund the energy transition on their own. Conceptually, this financing issue is not distinct from other challenges for the clean energy transition discussed above; rather, it is a consequence of many of these impediments existing simultaneously.

On the supply side, novel clean energy technologies can have difficulty accessing traditional capital markets relative to other industries because of greater perceived credit risk (Armitage, Bakhtian, and Jaffe 2023). Novel technologies may experience large cost uncertainties as a result of construction timing and delays, uncertainty about future revenue streams, and manufacturing cost overruns due to a lack of production experience. Traditional financial institutions may also have less capacity to assess risk for nascent technologies, making them reluctant to underwrite projects (IEA 2021c).

Clean energy projects confront an additional set of challenges: They must demonstrate initial commercial viability before being widely adopted. Early-stage financiers are often unable or unwilling to provide the substantial initial capital this demonstration requires (Ghosh and Nanda 2010). Financing risks can further limit early-stage investment. Nanda, Younge, and Fleming (2015) document how energy projects' financing needs and profiles are riskier and more capital-intensive than those in other high-growth industries, such as software and information technology. Potential early-stage investors may refrain from investing in clean energy companies if they anticipate that the technology will likely not receive mid-stage financing in the "valley of death," whereby market demand is insufficient for large-scale deployment (Nanda and Rhodes-Kropf 2016).

Demand-side factors can also slow financing for the energy transition. For example, investors in venture-financed energy start-ups have historically realized fewer exit opportunities compared with those in industries like biotechnology, semiconductors, and information technology, where established markets exist for start-up firms even before they have demonstrated commercial viability for their products (Ghosh and Nanda 2010). Energy companies and utilities have in the past often been reluctant to acquire start-ups with unproven technologies (Nanda, Younge, and Fleming 2015). Even as venture capital investment in clean energy has increased over time (CTVC 2023), venture capital firms may remain hesitant to invest in capital-intensive energy projects when the exit opportunities are limited in the short run, because such investments may require repeated capital injections over long periods of time to see a product through to market (Van den Heuvel and Popp 2022; Fontana and Nanda 2023). Creating a more favorable exit environment for start-ups can help mobilize private sector investment in these sectors.

In the transition to a new energy system, uncertainty about the broader market for clean energy can inhibit private sector investment, creating an opportunity for the public sector to send a durable demand signal. Lerner and Nanda (2020) argue that understanding market demand is an important prerequisite for early-stage companies to succeed. According to the authors, software and service-based businesses have shorter development timelines, and technological advancements allow these types of companies to ascertain market demand faster. Compared with software- and service-based businesses, clean energy companies may have more difficulty forecasting or demonstrating the demand certainty that would make them attractive to investors.

In summary, the balance of the economic push-and-pull forces affecting the clean energy transition today may limit private sector investment from reaching the necessary scale required to meet decarbonization goals, even as progress has been made. The next section turns to the role that government can play in catalyzing a faster transition to the net zero economy.

The Role of the Public Sector

Due to the market failures and economic frictions discussed in the first section, government intervention is necessary to reach net zero emissions. Governments have long made investments in developing clean energy technologies, though not always with the intent of reducing GHG emissions. In the 1970s, large-scale public investments in wind and solar R&D, which came about primarily in reaction to shortages and high prices in the oil market, were major forays into this space (Pirani 2018; CRS 2018; Nahm 2021). Since then, governments around the world have amplified support for clean energy, increasingly to accelerate the transition to a net zero economy.

Government intervention is critical to solving classic market failures, such as pollution and knowledge externalities. When it comes to structural change, such interventions are fundamentally about changing the direction and pace of transitions. Because economic incentives do not yet fully encourage replacing the existing, fossil-fuel-based energy system with one based on clean energy, government intervention can alter such incentives. But importantly, from a structural change lens, those interventions need not be permanent; once sufficient momentum builds in favor of the clean energy transition, the private sector could continue the transition, even without continued government involvement (see box 6-3).

Figure 6-5 illustrates this argument. Emissions in the absence of a policy intervention are shown as the dashed green line, declining—as in the case of recent U.S. GHG emissions—albeit not fast enough to meet net

Figure 6-5. Schematic: GHG Emissions with and without Structural Change Dynamics

Greenhouse gas emissions

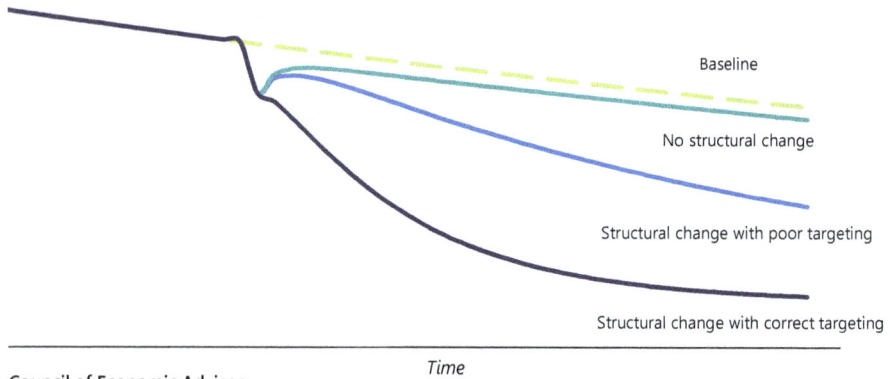

Baseline

No structural change

Structural change with poor targeting

Structural change with correct targeting

Time

Council of Economic Advisers

Source: CEA calculations.
Note: GHG = greenhouse gas. In the absence of structural change dynamics, a temporary policy intervention would lower GHG emissions but not their growth rate (solid teal line) relative to the no-policy trajectory (dashed green baseline). In the presence of structural change, a temporary policy would lower the growth rate of GHG emissions. The added decline in GHG emissions is faster when the policy correctly targets technologies (solid dark navy line) than when targeting is poor (solid lighter blue line).
2024 Economic Report of the President

zero goals. Consider first an economy without structural change dynamics. A temporary policy intervention lowers the level of GHG emissions over time but not the growth rate, as illustrated by the solid teal line. As a consequence, emissions continue changing at the same pace as before the policy. For such an economy, achieving net zero emissions requires permanent policy intervention. This trajectory contrasts with an economy featuring structural change dynamics, as shown by the solid blue lines in the figure. A policy under this scenario can permanently lower emissions' growth rate by building path dependence into clean energy sources, generating momentum that maintains the clean energy transition even after the policy is lifted. That is, under structural change, long-term decarbonization can be achieved with policy interventions that eventually allow private market incentives to sustain the clean energy transition without continued government intervention.

The rate at which emissions decline depends on how well the policy targets cost-effective technologies and GHG reduction options that can compete with fossil-fuel-based technologies to become self-sustaining. Policies that target poorly (the solid light blue line in the figure) may lead to lock-in of more costly technologies, ultimately making the economy's redirection toward the adoption of clean energy technologies more difficult and expensive than with better targeting (solid navy line).

This path dependence can emerge from economic conditions, but can also have political origins. A growing literature has documented that climate policies can help strengthen economic and consumer interest groups

Box 6-3. The Public Sector's Role in Accelerating Structural Change: The Case of South Korea

The transformation of South Korea's heavy and chemical industries (HCI) sector since the 1970s is an example of export-led structural change. After the devastation of the Korean War of the early 1950s, South Korea turned to a broad export-based economic strategy in the 1960s and early 1970s, giving preferential trade policy treatment to any exporting firm. In 1973, in response to defense concerns, the South Korean government restricted this policy to HCI firms, providing extensive loan subsidies from domestic financial institutions. The state additionally instituted performance standards for subsidy recipients, relying on export targets and eschewing financial indicators of firm performance. Although this policy system was short-lived, lasting only until 1979, it had a sharp effect on South Korean industrial production in the decades that followed (Lane 2022).

This sector-specific public intervention resulted in a steep increase in the productivity of HCI firms, both during the 1973–79 period of direct industrial strategy and afterward (Lane 2022). The share of HCI exports remained above pre-1973 levels well after 1979, and remains above those levels today (Lane 2022; Choi and Levchenko 2021; OEC 2023). Major present-day South Korean exports—such as Samsung semiconductors and Hyundai cars—were first produced between 1973 and 1979, and production grew sharply through the 1980s.

Government policies during this period helped spur structural change, which had previously stalled due to frictions and market failures. Before the intervention, South Korea's HCI sector suffered from a financing problem: Western financial institutions were reluctant to provide loans to Korean plants (Amsden 1992). The South Korean government spurred investment with subsidized loans that resemble the investment tax credits underlying modern clean energy investment. And because local demand was not sufficient to sustain growth in the targeted industries, the South Korean government then supported exports, allowing cheaper capital and privileged regulatory status for exporting firms. The government's last intervention was to build human capital—essential due to the complexity of HCI manufacturing—by developing and promoting an extensive engineering education pipeline (Amsden 1992).

The success of South Korea's HCI sector can be linked to the country's industrial strategy during this period. The government's temporary intervention was sufficient to shift the direction of investment and establish comparative advantage over the long term in a previously undistinguished industry. Today, many of the component industries of the HCI drive, such as motor vehicles and shipbuilding, remain pillars of the South Korean economy. The program's success suggests that public intervention can be critical to overcoming obstacles to rapid structural change.

that make policies more difficult to reverse. For instance, policies that yield widespread economic benefits, such as by creating new industrial sectors and sources of employment, can be politically costly to reverse and therefore are more likely to stay in place across administrations (Meckling and Nahm 2021; Meckling et al. 2015). Conversely, the absence of policy certainty will lead to underinvestment if potential entrants become unsure of the subsidies or taxes they may encounter years down the road (Noailly, Nowzohour, and van den Heuvel 2022). Studies have documented that frequent expirations of renewable energy production and investment tax credits—as well as short-term extensions—have a negative impact on the development of a domestic wind industry (Lewis and Wiser 2007; DOE 2022a).

Finally, public sector interventions work best when governments directly support desired outcomes rather than require firms to adopt specific processes or market behaviors (Rodrik 2014). For example, to increase renewable energy adoption in the power sector, government interventions would ideally either subsidize renewable energy or tax fossil fuel emissions—without mandating where, how, or what type of renewable energy is built, as in the case of technology-neutral tax credits. Furthermore, to meet research and development goals—which may otherwise face private financing challenges—governments could invest in well-diversified portfolios covering large suites of potential new technologies rather than pick a handful of firms and products, anticipating that some technologies may ultimately fail while others succeed. These interventions can provide certainty to the private sector while allowing flexibility for new innovations. They can help mitigate the potential effects of incomplete information, particularly during a transition to emerging technologies, and address the difficulty of acquiring accurate information in the face of rent-seeking by firms.

In order to accelerate the clean energy transition, the supply- and demand-side policies highlighted below take account of these considerations. These interventions must also be coordinated because they are part of a broader, multipolicy approach that simultaneously enhances the push forces and removes the pull forces behind the clean energy transition.

Supply-Side Policies

Enhancing productivity spillovers. Government can induce the creation of new technologies. Basic research can lead to breakthrough technologies that generate high economic returns (National Research Council 2001), but because private returns are significantly smaller than public returns, private investors tend to underinvest in basic research (Lucking, Bloom, and Van Reenen 2020). This pattern is particularly pronounced in the energy sector, where the private sector has historically underinvested in basic R&D (Nemet and Kammen 2007).

The U.S. government has therefore long supported basic research, and remains the world's largest funder of energy research (IEA 2023d; Sandalow et al. 2022). The Bipartisan Infrastructure Law (BIL)—enacted as the Infrastructure Investment and Jobs Act (Public Law 117-58), along with the 2020 Energy Act (Public Law 116-260, div. Z)—more than triples the Department of Energy's annual funding for energy programs and includes a significant expansion of funds for R&D (DOE 2022b). Such public investments in research will yield global knowledge and productivity spillovers that can accelerate the energy transition (Berkes, Manysheva, and Mestieri 2022). Nonetheless, current public investments in energy R&D still fall short of the levels required to meet climate targets, given that key technologies needed to reduce costs and decarbonize industrial sectors have yet to become commercialized (see box 6-4). Current U.S. public energy R&D spending remains below the amount spent in the aftermath of the oil crises of the 1970s (Gallagher and Anadon 2022).

Lowering capital, land, and transmission costs. Certain clean energy technologies, like solar PV cells, have already seen significant declines in capital costs. However, newer technologies—such as grid-scale battery storage, hydrogen electrolyzers, carbon capture and storage, direct air capture, and advanced modular nuclear reactors—still face high capital costs (DOE 2023c).

Public sector interventions, including loan guarantees, can lower capital costs for clean energy technologies. The Department of Energy's Clean Energy Financing Program, which provides loan guarantees for innovative clean energy technologies—and which was recently scaled up under the Inflation Reduction Act (IRA) of 2022 (Public Law 117-169)—is an example of such a public sector intervention. Such programs can lower the future cost of renewable technologies through learning-by-doing (Arkolakis and Walsh 2023) and by encouraging complementary private investments required to achieve the net zero economy (Heintz 2010; Juhász, Lane, and Rodrik 2023). Loan guarantees can lower the risks inherent in financing clean energy projects, thereby increasing the availability of capital (Bachas, Kim, and Yannelis 2021; CRS 2012). They can also provide an information signal to private financiers to further de-risk projects and "crowd in" private capital—shortening the time frame by which clean energy technologies become bankable (DOE 2023e). One analysis of the Department of Energy's early-stage grants to high-tech clean energy start-up firms finds a positive effect on future financing from the private sector (Howell 2017). Another study finds that young firms in Germany that received public investment were more likely to access bank loans, and that this effect was particularly pronounced in sectors that were "information-opaque" (Hottenrott, Lins, and Lutz 2017).

Box 6-4. The Need for Global Climate Collaboration

Solving climate change is an inherently global challenge, for which the United States' clean energy transition is only one part of the solution. The world will avoid dangerous climate change only if other countries also undertake similar structural transformations. In 2022, the United States accounted for 14 percent of global GHG emissions; China's share was 31 percent. Collectively, major powers have the potential to substantially curb emissions: The United States, China, the EU-27, Brazil, Russia, and India together accounted for more than 60 percent of global emissions in 2022 (Friedlingstein 2023).

U.S. investments in clean energy technologies could drive down global production costs (Way et al. 2022; Larsen et al. 2023) and encourage innovation worldwide (Berkes, Manysheva, and Mestieri 2022). But even accounting for these investments and their global spillovers, the world is projected to fall short of the manufacturing and deployment capacity necessary to meet global climate goals. For example, while the world is expected to develop sufficient or near-sufficient manufacturing capacity for EV batteries and solar modules by 2030 to stay on track for global net zero emissions by 2050 (IEA 2021a), global manufacturing capacity of wind turbines, heat pumps, and other key technologies is likely lagging behind the necessary pace to meet decarbonization goals (figure 6-i).

There is an urgent need for other governments to join the United States in rapidly accelerating their clean energy transitions. In the United States and elsewhere, strategic public sector intervention to remove impediments to structural change in the energy transition can generate the necessary buy-in from the private sector to yield clean energy technologies that will be cheaper than their carbon-emitting counterparts.

Figure 6-i. Projected and Target Global Manufacturing Capacity, 2030

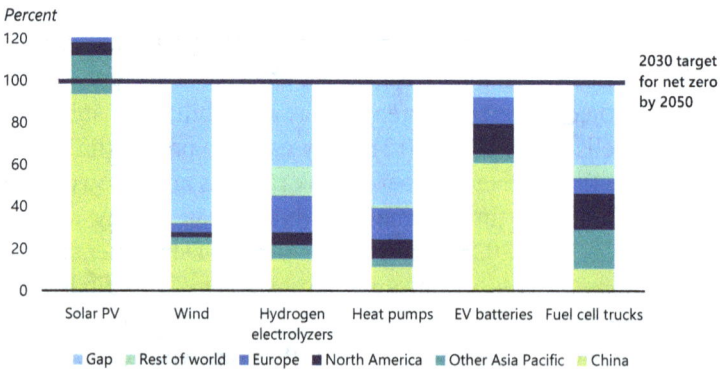

Percent

2030 target for net zero by 2050

Legend: Gap, Rest of world, Europe, North America, Other Asia Pacific, China

Categories: Solar PV, Wind, Hydrogen electrolyzers, Heat pumps, EV batteries, Fuel cell trucks

Council of Economic Advisers

Sources: International Energy Agency; CEA calculations.

Note: "Manufacturing capacity" refers to the maximum rated output of facilities for producing a given technology, as distinguished from the capacity of the technologies themselves once deployed. Capacity is stated on an annual basis for the final product.

2024 Economic Report of the President

However, lowered capital costs for clean technologies may be insufficient if other input costs remain high. The land requirements of some clean energy technologies imply added costs—and often this demand occurs in agriculturally productive areas (van de Ven et al. 2021). Governments can help navigate this trade-off, especially in the case of wind farms. Each turbine has a relatively small footprint (Denholm et al. 2009), and incentivizing the use of arable space between wind turbines for agriculture dramatically lessens a wind farm's land requirements. Likewise, policies can encourage solar co-location with agriculture. While growing crops under solar PV is still a nascent practice, tax breaks and direct subsidies could scale it up (Boyd 2023), potentially through the resources provided by the IRA for the U.S. Department of Agriculture's Rural Energy for America Program.

High land prices can also be mitigated by building renewable energy generation away from agriculturally productive areas. But these locations tend to be far from population centers where electricity demand is highest, and new renewables projects are limited by the transmission capacity of the section of the grid to which they are connected. Expanding transmission is therefore an important complement to building new clean energy generation capacity. New transmission is needed both within and across regions of the country (DOE 2023d). The BIL allocates $2.5 billion to specific projects to this end. Absent such investment in transmission as well as in distribution, increased electrification will strain the existing grid.

Increasing labor mobility. Governments can play a central role in removing labor market frictions that could otherwise impede the clean energy transition (CEA 2021). Initiatives that address both skill needs and mismatch in the labor market, along with geographic immobility, are particularly necessary to accelerate the energy transition.

Workforce development programs are needed to train the next generation of workers in the clean energy sector and to retrain workers transitioning from the fossil fuel industry. Government initiatives that standardize education to include training on clean energy technologies are critically important—particularly for multicraft work like rooftop solar installation, which requires knowledge of carpentry, roofing, metal work, electrical, and information technology (IREC 2023). Programs that create pathways between education, training, entry-level jobs, and long-term careers are necessary to ensure long-term job quality and retention. Recent Federal policies reflect the importance of establishing a pipeline from apprenticeships to entry-level jobs. The IRA, for instance, introduced a bonus adder on top of a wide range of tax credits in the power, manufacturing, and transportation sectors for eligible firms that provide prevailing wages and employ qualified apprentices for certain construction, alteration, and repair work. Moreover, the creation of new apprenticeship programs provides an opportunity to accelerate economic growth by ensuring that workers—and in particular women—who have been historically underrepresented in the energy sector have access to the jobs of the future. Women represent less than 20 percent of employed workers in both the clean and fossil fuel sectors (Colmer, Lyubich, and Voorheis 2023).

Government interventions in retraining programs can support workers currently in the fossil fuel sector, retraining them for either the clean energy sector or other industries (Katz et al. 2022; Hanson 2023). Hyman (2022) provides evidence that deliberately targeting labor immobility during market disruptions can increase the likelihood that workers will switch industries—and improve workers' outcomes. In the context of the clean energy transition, estimates for the costs of retraining programs vary (Louie and Pearce 2016), but may be minor relative to the overall costs of the transition (Vanatta et al. 2022).

Government programs addressing geographic immobility can complement workforce development programs. Such programs can provide funding to construct clean energy manufacturing facilities close to their fossil-fuel-based counterparts, or provide moving allowances to help workers relocate (Vanatta et al. 2022; Pollin and Callaci 2016). The Department of Energy, for instance, announced $15.5 billion in funding for the conversion of existing automotive manufacturing facilities to support the EV supply chain (DOE 2023b). Policies can also support communities where local tax revenues have historically depended on fossil fuel industries (International Renewable Energy Age 2023).

Demand-Side Policies

Boosting demand over longer horizons. Because private investors are reluctant to fund the commercialization of new energy technologies, government interventions can create a long-term demand signal. Such interventions can prevent novel clean energy technologies from being stranded in the "valley of death" (Nemet 2019).

Production and investment tax credits for clean energy installations can boost demand for these technologies. The United States has employed some form of a production tax credit since 1992 to generate demand for a wide variety of renewable energy technologies, all without favoring specific firms (CRS 2020). Under the IRA, production and investment tax credits for clean energy will be technology-neutral by 2025—production of any type of energy with sufficiently low emissions will receive the same tax breaks. Both subsidies are available without a total tax expenditure limit until 2032, or when U.S. GHG emissions from electricity reach a certain threshold, creating a durable market signal incentivizing the use of renewable energy for electricity.

Such policies have proven effective in mobilizing private sector financing in other contexts. One paper finds that such demand-side policies shore up durable market demand and help mobilize private sector investments—particularly venture capital—toward clean energy innovation (van den Heuvel and Popp 2022). And in the pharmaceutical industry, demand-side policies (also known as "demand-pull" policies) have helped to mobilize biomedical R&D when market incentives to do so are weak (Glennerster and Kremer 2000; Global Trade Funding n.d.). Likewise, advance market commitments have enabled greater production of pharmaceutical products—such as vaccines—in markets without mature market demand (Kremer, Levin, and Snyder 2020; Berndt et al. 2006).

Improving substitutability. In the power sector, battery storage technologies provide one avenue for alleviating variability concerns and making renewable energy a better substitute for fossil fuels. Grid-connected battery storage is rapidly increasing in the United States. In 2023, the United States deployed 16 gigawatts (GW) of grid-connected battery capacity, with another 15 GW planned for 2024 (EIA 2024b). To meet net zero goals, the United States needs about 131 GW of grid-scale storage by 2050, according to models (Narich et al. 2021). Policies encouraging additional deployment are likely to lower costs further (NREL 2023). These policies include investment tax credits for battery adoption and production tax credits for battery manufacturing—both of which are provided under the IRA.

Batteries installed on electricity grids should be charged when wholesale electricity prices are low and discharged when these prices rise. Assuming the marginal electricity generator uses renewable energy when prices are low and fossil fuels when prices are high, tax incentives for batteries will result in reduced GHG emissions by replacing electricity from fossil fuels with electricity from renewables. If low electricity prices instead coincide with deriving marginal electricity from fossil fuels, battery incentives could lead to increased GHG emissions (Hittinger and Azevedo 2015; Pimm et al. 2019; Beuse et al. 2021). Policies that tie investment tax credits for batteries only to grids with a positive within-day correlation between wholesale prices and marginal emissions would ensure that battery expansion coincides with GHG reductions.

Better substitutability between clean energy and fossil fuels also ensures that clean energy subsidies deliver both lower electricity prices and GHG reductions. This is because clean energy subsidies have composition and scale effects (Baumol and Oates 1988). They make clean energy cheaper relative to fossil fuels, tilting the composition of electricity toward clean energy and lowering GHG emissions, all else remaining equal. Clean energy subsidies also increase the overall scale of electricity consumption by making electricity cheaper, increasing all energy inputs, including fossil fuels, and thus possibly GHG emissions, all else remaining equal (Casey, Jeon, and Traeger 2023). When clean energy and fossil fuels are better substitutes, as with greater battery deployment, the composition effect dominates over the scale effect and clean energy subsidies both reduce emissions and lower electricity prices (Hassler et al. 2020; Casey, Jeon, and Traeger 2023).

Likewise, policies that make EVs more substitutable with internal combustion engines—either by improving range or increasing charging convenience—can accelerate their adoption. The IRA's production tax credit for battery manufacturing is aimed at driving down the cost of production, which can improve range. The investment tax credit for household adoption of battery storage under the IRA and the $7.5 billion allocated for building a national high-speed EV charger network under the BIL are designed to increase charging convenience.

Coordinating Supply and Demand

The necessary scale and speed of the clean energy transition requires coordinating supply and demand policies. Demand for clean energy technologies often requires complementary and simultaneous supply-side investments in different technologies and supporting infrastructure. As noted above, EVs are dependent on a charging infrastructure. Some consumers are reluctant to invest in EVs before an adequately convenient supply of chargers is installed, while investments in chargers are unprofitable before consumers collectively purchase a sufficient fleet of EVs (Li et al. 2017). Prior research has suggested that supply-side investments—such as subsidies for the EV charging infrastructure—should be developed in tandem with direct EV subsidies (Cole et al. 2023; Rapson and Muehlegger 2022; Dimanchev et al. 2023).

Similar network effects and coordination problems exist in the switch to new fuels, like clean hydrogen, which require investments in the technologies for both production and demand (Armitage, Bakhtian, and Jaffe 2023). In addition to retrofitting facilities to use hydrogen as a feedstock, midstream infrastructure, including pipelines and storage, will be essential for maturing the clean hydrogen industry—in addition to investments in the technology used for hydrogen production (U.S. Department of Energy 2023c). The current short-term availability of infrastructure to transport, store, and distribute hydrogen is often cited as a constraint on industry growth, especially given the challenges of co-locating production and end use (Zacarias and Nakano 2023).

The public sector can play a significant coordinating role, incentivizing demand while ensuring adequate supply to establish new markets. When future demand is uncertain, firms may find investing in the necessary production technology or infrastructure more challenging, in part because financing is more difficult to obtain under such conditions. However, in the absence of adequate supply, investments in technologies and infrastructure to create demand are often also difficult to justify. Policy interventions can resolve such coordination challenges. For example, offtake contracts—to purchase an agreed-upon quantity at a price often determined ahead of production—are often a prerequisite for project financing. Loan underwriters therefore commonly ask to see offtake contracts before approving debt financing (Global Trade Funding n.d.). The Department of Energy is currently establishing a demand-side support program that provides offtake certainty—through contracts with, for instance, hydrogen producers and buyers—for projects in the Regional Clean Hydrogen Hubs program funded by the BIL (U.S. Department of Energy 2023).

Conclusion

Decarbonizing the global economy—in addition to mitigating the effects of climate change—provides new economic opportunities. The shift to clean energy can lower energy prices, offer greater energy security, reduce volatility in energy markets, mitigate local air pollution, and create new sources of employment in emerging sectors. Switching to clean energy also offers a generational opportunity for the United States to further its economic competitiveness in the innovative sectors of the 21st century. This chapter has explained in detail how to achieve these objectives through structural change, presenting an economic framework for understanding the factors that can accelerate the clean energy transition. It has further highlighted specific government interventions that can remove obstacles to the transition and create opportunities for the private sector to drive new sources of green growth.

The Biden-Harris Administration is strategically targeting these high-return investments. On the supply side, examples of this approach include the Department of Energy's expanded funding for energy programs and R&D through the BIL, which serves to accelerate innovation spillovers and drive down capital costs for emerging technologies where private sector investments are still insufficient. Similarly, the IRA includes loan guarantees for innovative clean energy technologies to mitigate risk for clean energy projects and to unlock new private financing. Both the BIL and the IRA support the construction of new clean energy manufacturing facilities in communities with preexisting fossil fuel industry presence, thereby reducing labor market frictions by helping workers transition to the clean energy sector (U.S. Department of the Treasury 2023).

On the demand side, the IRA, among many other of its provisions, employs tax credits for renewable energy installation and for household adoption of electric vehicles, renewable energy generation, and heat pumps. The duration of these tax credits boosts demand for clean energy technologies over longer time horizons sufficient for enabling scale economies and learning-by-doing. Battery incentives under the IRA can also accelerate the clean energy transition in the power sector by making renewable energy sources less variable and thus a better substitute for fossil fuels. By simultaneously pursuing these interventions, the clean energy agenda of the Biden-Harris Administration is jointly addressing the supply- and demand-side challenges needed to ensure a rapid clean energy transition.

Although the scale and urgency of the clean energy transition present unique challenges, this transition ultimately shares many features with prior government- and market-led transformations. In the process of reaching net zero emissions, both governments and private actors will need to grapple with how to transform an economy powered by fossil fuels to one powered by clean energy. A structural change framework helps illuminate how to achieve this shift, through targeted government investments that lower the cost of clean energy and their complementary inputs and technologies, as well as through programs that enable the transition to help both workers and their communities. Such successful interventions could pay large dividends for decades to come, putting the U.S. economy on a path toward a future where energy is clean, cheap, reliable, and secure.

Chapter 7

An Economic Framework for Understanding Artificial Intelligence

Artificial intelligence (AI) systems touch the lives of virtually every American. They range from simple systems like text autocorrect to complex algorithms capable of setting prices, driving cars, and writing essays. In recent years, AI systems have advanced rapidly as recent developments in computing, data availability, and machine learning models have simultaneously come together to produce rapid improvements. Still, much remains unknown. Agrawal, Gans, and Goldfarb (2022) suggest that AI is in "the between times," where society has begun to see the technology's potential but has not come close to fully realizing it. While AI's capabilities will depend in part on the technology itself, its effects will be shaped by economic, regulatory, and social pressures. How society deploys this technology and what technology-specific guardrails are implemented will be critical factors in determining both the breadth and magnitude of its effects.

Economic incentives play a central role in how decisions are made. An economic framework, combined with a basic understanding of AI technology, allows us to make predictions about when, how, and why AI may be adopted. While such a framework can also tell us what broader effects AI adoption may have, applying economic insights to an evolving and proliferating technology like AI is especially challenging. However, it is also especially valuable, because decisions made at the onset of a new technology have a greater influence on its eventual impact. This chapter begins with a basic discussion of the technology and then examines how the inputs to AI have changed, with a particular focus on the concept of diminishing returns and the key role of data in AI systems. Next, it examines the economic incentives for AI development and adoption, including on macroeconomic outcomes like productivity. The chapter's third section adapts standard economic models to explore AI's potential effects on labor markets across the earnings distribution, demographic groups, industries, and geographic areas, updating previous work with new data and augmenting it with a novel analysis based on not only exposure to AI but also the complexity of each task. Finally, the fourth section examines important economic issues for upcoming policy choices related to the law and regulations, competition issues, and social outcomes (e.g., how technology interacts with existing inequalities like racial discrimination).

Toward "Intelligent" Automation

Since Adam Smith's first observations about how machinery allowed for the division of labor, economists have studied the economic effects of technology (Smith 1776). Many technologies—like Smith's example of specialization by workers in a pin factory—enable more output from the same inputs. Some technologies, however, enable an increase in capital to reduce labor. Economists call this class of technologies automation (Brozen 1957; Zeira 1998; Acemoglu and Restrepo 2018).[1] This definition of automation is broader than factory machines and computers, and includes technologies that have been in place for centuries. For example, according to this definition, a windmill set up to grind wheat would be a kind of automation. These kinds of technologies can have broad effects—including on prices, wages, input usage, and output—which in turn may resonate throughout the economy.[2] As discussed later in the chapter, a wide range of potential uses of AI entail this kind of capital-for-labor substitution, making it an automation technology.

To understand the incentives for AI's development and adoption, it is necessary to have a basic common understanding of the technology. The field of AI is broad and changing quickly. What follows is a stylized representation of basic concepts that may not be applicable to every circumstance.

---

[1] In some cases, automation technologies simply replace existing labor. In most cases, however, automation technologies allow for greater output than before, and in some cases, they may allow for the creation of products that would never be economically viable to create by hand.

[2] While this definition's emphasis on the word "substitution" might suggest that automation technologies invariably reduce employment, this need not be the case. Because automation technologies make certain production steps faster and cheaper, they can increase overall demand for both the product being made and related products. Additionally, labor is generally required to create and maintain such technologies.

Although definitions of AI vary across fields and purposes, AI systems are generally understood to take in data and,[3] through statistical or computational techniques, make predictions.[4] Some have called them "prediction machines" (Agrawal, Gans, and Goldfarb 2018). In many cases, predictions are used to inform recommendations or determine how other components of the system will act. For example, AI systems have been developed to solve challenging scientific problems, and they are widely used to set prices and rank job candidates. In other cases, as with some generative AI models, these predictions themselves are simply aggregated to form an output.[5] In this context, predictions are far broader than forecasting the future, and can indeed be about practically anything for which reliable data can be obtained.

The ability to make predictions often allows improved decision-making, even in the face of uncertainty. As a result, AI systems can automate more tasks than prior technologies and improve the work quality of existing processes. For example, stamping machines automate the creation of certain kinds of metal parts, but automated systems may have struggled to handle situations where the production process had inherent variation, like harvesting produce. Today, an AI-augmented system might use sensor data to predict when fruit is ripe and how to detach it, allowing that production process to be further automated (Zhou et al. 2022). Likewise, autocorrect systems are an example of how AI increases the quality of work. Originally, these systems relied on lists of often-mistyped words and their correct spelling. When the software detected misspellings, it suggested a correction. Advanced autocorrect systems using AI employ dictionaries, information about what all users tend to type, and data from individual users' past typing activities to predict what they intend to type (Lewis-Kraus 2014). As a result, the systems detect not only misspellings but also incorrect words.

Figure 7-1 portrays a stylized diagram of how AI systems interact with traditional automation in order to emphasize key ideas relevant to the economic discussion.[6] During training, an algorithm is applied to data

---

[3] In this context, data can refer to any machine-readable information and is not limited to the kinds of datasets that economists might be most familiar with. It can potentially include digitally encoded text, images, sound, video, information on real-time human input, simulation feedback, and many other categories of information.

[4] For example, Executive Order 14110 (2023) defines AI systems as those that "use machine- and human-based inputs to perceive real and virtual environments; abstract such perceptions into models through analysis in an automated manner; and use model inference to formulate options for information or action." It defines an AI model as something that "implements AI technology and uses computational, statistical, or machine-learning techniques to produce outputs from a given set of inputs."

[5] Executive Order 14110 (2023) defines generative AI as "the class of AI models that emulate the structure and characteristics of input data in order to generate derived synthetic content. This can include images, videos, audio, text, and other digital content."

[6] Of particular note, figure 7-1 emphasizes the role of data in AI, though in many cases it might be more accurate to more generally refer to inputs.

Figure 7-1. A Stylized Diagram of How AI Extends Automation with Prediction

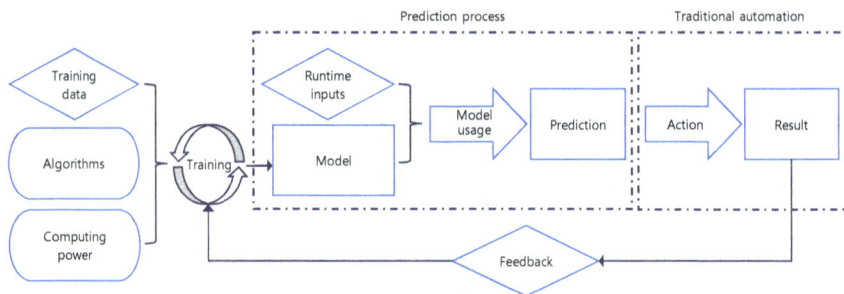

Council of Economic Advisers
2024 Economic Report of the President

using computing power.[7] In some instances, this training process can be quite complex and involve many iterations; often, it includes validation and testing steps, which are not shown in the figure. The training process produces a model, which is combined with data at the time it is used to create a prediction. Such predictions, however, are rarely useful until they are applied in some way. In typical AI systems, one or more predictions are used to take actions automatically. For example, a large language model might make many predictions about individual words based upon a user's request, and then the system aggregates them into one output to display. The same kind of model in a different context, such as customer service, might not only respond to the user but also issue a refund. Finally, the results may be evaluated to create feedback to help further refine the model in the future, and some systems learn continuously to further improve performance and prevent degradation.

As figure 7-1 illustrates, AI systems can integrate multiple sources of data, often at different points and for different purposes. For example, in the diagram, data may enter the system at the training, runtime, and feedback stages. In some cases, human input can be an important part of development as well (Amershi et al. 2014; Mosqueira-Rey et al. 2022; Ouyang et al. 2022).[8] AI's reliance on data raises unique economic issues, including ones related to competition and transparency. These issues are discussed in more detail later in the chapter.

Figure 7-1 also illustrates that having the requisite algorithm, data, and computational power to make predictions is a necessary but not sufficient condition for AI-based automation. For example, even after a model

---

[7] Some types of AI systems—for example, systems that rely on coded rules rather than machine learning—may not make use of training data (e.g., Taddy 2019).

[8] In some cases, a large amount of human input has been important in fine-tuning models to ensure acceptable performance, and serious concerns have been raised about the pay and working conditions of those workers (Perrigo 2023; Bartholomew 2023).

is developed for self-driving cars, it may not be deployed in older cars that lack the sophisticated sensors necessary to collect the requisite data while being driven. Similarly, practical limitations on actions may limit the scope of AI deployment. For example, many tasks involving flexible materials have proven very difficult for robots to handle (Billard and Kragic 2019). AI systems may ameliorate these problems, but such physical limitations may continue to prevent the automation of tasks even where the system has sufficient predictive power. Finally, in some cases, translating prediction into action may require making decisions that we are unwilling or unable to fully delegate to AI due to ethical or other concerns (Agrawal, Gans, and Goldfarb 2018).

Prediction Is Improving but Faces Constraints

In general, prediction quality can be thought of as the output of an economic production function. Developers choose an option from a variety of different algorithms, each of which can be optimized subject to the developer's constraints, such as development time, data availability, or budget for computational resources. Economists represent these kinds of situations where agents are maximizing an objective subject to restrictions as constrained optimization problems (Mas-Colell, Whinston, and Green 1995). Typically, in a constrained optimization setting, not all constraints are equally binding, and some may not be binding at all. As an extreme example, a complete lack of data on a problem could render a lack of computational resources irrelevant. Of course, these constraints are constantly changing as new data become available, as computational resources become cheaper, and as research develops more efficient algorithms and other innovations.[9] The relationship between design and development choices (e.g., algorithms, data, and computational resources) and prediction quality is thus complex and varies from situation to situation. In part because of the complex interactions of these constraints, predictions about AI's future capabilities have often been wrong (Armstrong, Sotala, and Ó hÉigeartaigh 2014).

It is potentially more informative to look at how AI performs various tasks. Figure 7-2 shows the performance of the best available AI model in each year on a number of benchmarks, rescaled to compare with human performance on the same test. Comparing AI's performance with human performance in this way is potentially useful for understanding if and when AI systems may be deployed as a substitute for labor, although researchers have raised serious concerns about these kinds of benchmarks, both in the way they aggregate performance (e.g., Burnell et al. 2023) and in the way

---

[9] Research can also alter these constraints in other ways. For example, a great deal of work in both machine learning and econometrics is done to find ways to compensate for data limitations, often at the cost of increased computational requirements.

Figure 7-2. AI Capabilities Over Time and Across Tasks

Test scores of AI relative to human performance

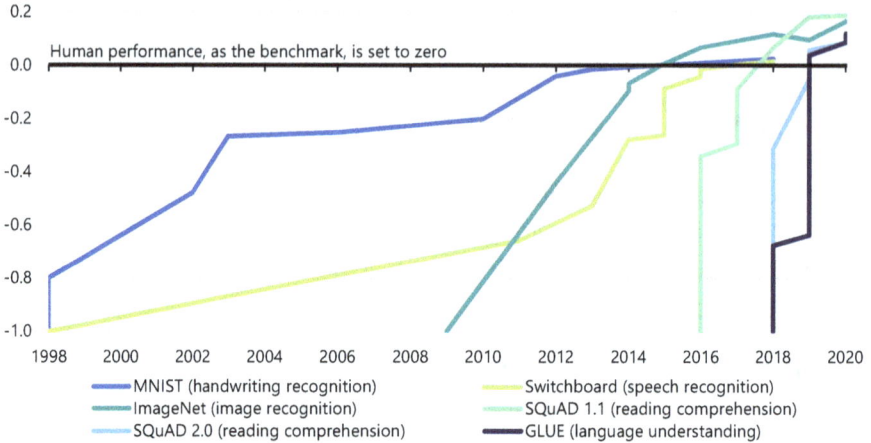

Human performance, as the benchmark, is set to zero

Legend:
- MNIST (handwriting recognition)
- ImageNet (image recognition)
- SQuAD 2.0 (reading comprehension)
- Switchboard (speech recognition)
- SQuAD 1.1 (reading comprehension)
- GLUE (language understanding)

Council of Economic Advisers

Sources: Adapted from Hutson (2022), based on Kiela et al. (2021); CEA calculations.
Note: MNIST = Modified National Institute of Standards and Technology; SQuAD = Stanford Question Answering Dataset; GLUE = General Language Understanding Evaluation. Benchmark performance is scaled so that −1 is initial performance and 0 is human performance.
2024 Economic Report of President

selected metrics may create the fictious appearance of sudden large performance improvements (Schaeffer, Miranda, and Koyejo 2023).

Figure 7-2 shows that AI systems have approached human performance at very different rates across the various benchmarks. In some cases, the progress of AI was significantly influenced by data availability (e.g., Xiong et al. 2016; Sharifani and Amini 2023). Because of the way in which they naturally produce and share digital information, the Internet and smartphones have been important data sources. Similarly, small, cheap sensors have dramatically changed data availability in industrial and maintenance operations. These complementary technologies have been especially important in creating the volume of data necessary to train modern AI systems, and especially foundation models.

In most economic optimization problems, the marginal value of an input (data, computational resources, etc.) tends to decrease as more of it is used, as measured by the amount of output in quantity, quality, or otherwise. In other words, adding more of something may help the situation, but it takes more and more of that resource to generate the same increase in benefits as before. As a simple example, hiring workers to work in an empty factory may rapidly improve production, but over time the workers will begin to get in each other's way. This phenomenon is widely observed in economics, including in returns to capital, income growth across countries, and even research activity (Solow 1956; Mankiw, Romer, and Weil 1992; Kortum

1997; Bloom et al. 2020). In extreme cases, more of an input can make the problem worse. One such example, in software engineering, is given in *The Mythical Man-Month* (Brooks 1975).

Many AI models have also exhibited evidence of diminishing returns (Hestness et al. 2017; Kaplan et al. 2020; Zhai et al. 2022). While in some cases it is possible to improve the performance effect of an input (e.g., via new data-pruning methods; see Sorscher et al. 2022), these techniques typically do not change the underlying diminishing relationship (Muennighoff et al. 2023).

Just because the marginal value of each additional input tends to fall does not imply that performance is fundamentally limited. Adding more of every input—if they are available—can continue to produce substantial gains, as can finding new kinds of inputs (e.g., new kinds of data). And large enough changes in inputs may shift which class of algorithms or models perform best. For example, large language models became viable when sufficient data and computational resources became available, in turn spurring researchers to develop further technical innovations like transformer-based architecture or more specialized hardware (Vaswani et al. 2017; Bommasani et al. 2021; Dally, Keckler, and Kirk 2021). But the speed of continued progress is likely to be heavily dependent on the rate at which we continue to produce new innovations rather than simply by virtue of ever-increasing computational or data resources (Jones 2022; Philippon 2022).

Garbage In, Garbage Out

Data are key informational inputs into AI systems, and they are central to the way AI performs. AI systems make informed predictions because they use the correlations embedded in data. Many different changes have contributed to improvements in AI systems, including improvements in algorithms and increased availability of computational resources. Nonetheless, developers of AI-based prediction models continue to grapple with many of the same data-related challenges that statisticians and econometricians have faced for decades.[10] To understand AI technology as a whole, it is helpful to understand the unique role that data and data-related constraints play.

The scale and quality of available data directly affect the performance of AI, but a large quantity of data alone is not sufficient. Prediction models typically perform well in situations that look much like the data they are trained on. In contrast, rare or novel circumstances where the past is a poor guide to the future make prediction more challenging, as do data limitations

---

[10] These fields are very much related. Economists borrowed a large number of techniques from statisticians in the early days of econometrics; and in the late 1990s and early 2000s, many computer scientists adopted statistics and econometric techniques like Bayesian updating. While it can be challenging to collaborate because these different fields approach problems in different ways and have very different jargon, past collaborations have yielded substantial improvements.

that might not immediately be apparent. In situations with poor or incomplete data, models may be simultaneously highly confident and wrong in their predictions (e.g., DeVries and Taylor 2018). For example, concerns arise when input data are systematically biased. An AI system that is trained without accounting for the bias is nearly certain to reproduce it. Many current facial recognition applications face this problem, and an overreliance on AI facial recognition technology could exacerbate discrimination (e.g., Najibi 2020; Buolamwini and Gebru 2018; Raji et al. 2020a). (See box 7-1.) Additionally, in some instances, people may intentionally feed an AI system manipulated data so as to undermine its function (Shan et al. 2023). Such attacks can be more difficult to detect and reverse than more traditional methods of interference. After training is completed, isolating and removing the impact of poor-quality data can prove challenging and expensive, and may be only partially successful.[11] For all these reasons, curation of data is generally important for AI systems, just as it is for most technology firms.[12]

Data are unlike natural resources, such as iron or copper; they are often drawn from users. User data include things such as the words they publish in books or on social media, as well as records of the things they do, typically captured by now ubiquitous electronic devices. AI enables predictions to be individualized in ways that rules-based algorithmic approaches do not. Such personalization can allow firms to create customized products or recommendations, and these tailored products can benefit consumers. However, AI can also be used in ways that harm consumers through price discrimination, by suggesting products or services sold by the AI company that may not best meet a consumer's needs, or through the exploitation of behavioral biases (e.g., Gautier, Ittoo, and Cleynenbreugel 2020; Engler 2021). Many social media companies, for example, design their products to maximize engagement rather than entertainment or education, even when such engagement can be harmful (e.g., Luca 2015; Braghieri, Levy, and Makarin 2022). As consumers learn about AI-related targeting, they may abandon products or change their behavior, undermining the technology's value (e.g., Garbarino and Maxwell 2010; Nunan and Di Domenico 2022).

---

[11] Researchers continue to make progress on so-called unlearning methods to address the issue of unwanted data, though many approaches have been shown to have limited performance in practice (Kuramanji et al. 2023; Zhang et al. 2024). The implications of successful unlearning are also relevant for issues such as individual privacy protection (Neel and Chang 2023).

[12] In many cases, data have scaled up more quickly than firms' ability to curate them. While AI-powered curation may improve the situation, AI systems may also make the situation worse. For example, while some AI systems may help firms decide which content to publish, other AI systems may increase the volume of proposed content requiring review (Edwards 2023).

Box 7-1. AI and Equity/Discrimination

Many artificial intelligence applications use data generated by humans to predict how individuals will behave. While these data can give AI considerable power and utility, they also allow it to replicate many of humanity's worst biases. The capacity of AI to lead to discrimination—whether inadvertently or intentionally—poses new challenges for enforcement of existing anti-discrimination policies.

Economists have shown that discriminatory behavior can have many sources. Even in the absence of any intentional prejudgment (what economists call prejudice), discrimination based on statistical inference can be harmful (e.g., Lang and Spitzer 2020). Users of predictive algorithms have already faced this problem, including hiring managers who found they were favoring male candidates (Dastin 2018), potential employers who advertised job posts less heavily to women (Lambrecht and Tucker 2019), and health care systems that favored white patients over Black patients in predicting care needs (Obermeyer et al. 2019), among many other examples. These effects may arise from the biases of AI model developers, or inadvertently from previously unrecognized patterns in the data. The lack of transparency in sophisticated AI algorithms may compound the issue (e.g., Chesterman 2021; Hutson 2021). Even if AI providers remove obviously biased or prejudicial content from their training data, discrimination based on subtle statistical patterns is still likely (Barocas and Selbst 2016).

An additional challenge is ill intent among the users of AI models. AI's opaque methods could provide cover for prejudiced entities to use AI in numerous discriminatory ways, such as firms combining AI with surveillance to predict, deter, and punish union organizing activity, or landlords using AI to discriminate against potential tenants based on their predicted demographics. Evidence suggests that illegal behavior is already widespread in these contexts (McNicholas et al. 2019; Christensen and Timmins 2023), and users will likely adopt AI tools to continue their discriminatory practices and obfuscate their intent.

AI-abetted discrimination could harm individuals in the labor market, in housing markets, in financial transactions, and anywhere else predictive algorithms are used. Often, discrimination may only be observable through sophisticated analysis of AI methods and outputs. Regulatory measures to help identify discrimination in critical markets are necessary. The Biden-Harris Administration's Blueprint for an AI Bill of Rights emphasizes the importance of protection from algorithmic discrimination, and its recent Executive Order has identified key agencies within the Federal Government to develop the tools and issue guidance or regulations needed to combat it (White House 2022, 2023a).

Nonetheless, widespread AI adoption means that identifying and rooting out discrimination will remain an ongoing process. Researchers who study the auditing of AI algorithms generally conclude that a multifaceted approach is necessary, including a clear identification of objectives and metrics, transparency about the audit process, and a proactive consideration of how auditability can be incorporated into AI models in multiple stages (Guszcza et al. 2018; Raji et al. 2020b; Mökander et al. 2021; Costanza-Chock, Raji, and Buolamwini 2022). Explicit methods to identify discriminatory capabilities and strengthen AI guardrails are also likely to be a key component of a comprehensive antidiscrimination strategy (e.g., Ganguli et al. 2022). Some of these methods may themselves use AI, since predictive algorithms may be useful in detection of discrimination (e.g., Kleinberg et al. 2018). Reducing discrimination may also involve encouraging some forms of AI adoption. For example, algorithmic decision-making has been observed to reduce disparities in some lending contexts (Bartlett et al. 2022).

From the Technological Frontier to Reality

There are a number of different ways to measure the economic impact of a technology. How widely is it deployed? How does the production process change for existing products and services? What new products and services are created, and what old products and services decline or disappear? Of particular interest to economists and policymakers is the idea of productivity, the notion that we can do more with the same resources. Recent evidence suggests that large productivity increases driven by AI are possible in some specific contexts (e.g., Brynjolfsson, Li, and Raymond 2023).[13] And though such forecasts are notoriously challenging, economic analysts have already begun to update their forecasts to account for the potential of more rapid growth brought about by AI (e.g., Goldman Sachs 2023; Chui et al. 2023). A more fulsome answer to all these questions requires understanding not only AI's theoretical capabilities but also how AI systems might be used.

Adoption Is Difficult and Invariably Lags the Technological Frontier

Before a new technology can have real-world effects, it needs to be adopted by individuals and businesses. This process is costly and difficult, and thus the scale of adoption largely depends on weighing these costs against the potential benefits. AI has been an active area of computational research since the 1950s (Newell 1983), and many types of AI have been widely deployed (e.g., Maslej et al. 2023). At the same time, in many industries AI

---

[13] Precise measurement of productivity within firm environments can be challenging, but studies in controlled settings also suggest the potential for sizable productivity improvements in other contexts (e.g., Peng et al. 2023; Noy and Zhang 2023).

adoption has been low and has skewed heavily toward large and young firms (Acemoglu et al. 2022). In addition, some impressive advances in AI have been very recent, and it takes time for firms to observe progress and adapt.

Furthermore, technologies are rarely adopted at an even rate. Instead, early adoption is slow, as users and firms work through the challenges. It then proceeds more quickly as these challenges are overcome and economies of scale drive down costs (Hall and Khan 2003). Adoption can lag invention by decades, and differences in the surrounding circumstances can substantially change adoption timelines. For example, more than 90 percent of American households had microwaves within 30 years of their invention (Roser, Ritchie, and Mathieu 2023). In contrast, it was more than 100 years before flush toilets reached the same 90 percent threshold. Because the devices depended on running water, adoption was delayed until people had indoor plumbing.

Early adoptions of a technology often happen where it is least complicated to deploy. One of the earliest commercial AI success stories was in identifying credit card fraud. In this case, data were widely available, the key task clearly depended on prediction, the action to be taken was straightforward, and the costs and benefits of prediction quality could be readily quantified (Ryman-Tubb, Krause, and Garn 2018; Agrawal, Gans, and Goldfarb 2022). Similarly, in recent years, AI systems aimed at improving customer service have developed rapidly because the data were previously being collected, the functionality could easily be added to existing software, and customer service involves many low-complexity tasks (Xu et al. 2020; Brynjolfsson, Li, and Raymond 2023; Chui et al. 2023). These kinds of early projects using a technology have positive spillover effects for the technology as a whole, both because they are proof that the technology can be effective in a real-world setting and because they create valuable human capital—in the form of knowledge about how to adapt business practices to use the technology. The markets for AI are already adapting, with investment and start-up activity both increasing in recent years (Maslej et al. 2023). Businesses specializing in cloud computing and AI deployment have also since emerged, lowering costs and expanding adoption.

With AI, there are a variety of additional potential impediments to adoption—consider five. First, even when data are available to train an AI system, there may be additional data-related constraints on adoption. Many firms may not yet collect the necessary data for certain AI implementations, and they may face substantial challenges in beginning to do so. In other cases, systems do not receive feedback sufficient to judge the quality of their own predictions after they have been made. Finally, even when the data exist, legal restrictions like copyright may prevent their use.[14] Until these

---

[14] Copyright and other related issues are discussed in more detail later in this chapter.

data-related constraints on adoption are resolved, firms may have difficulty implementing AI. This likely explains some of the uneven adoption across industries and firms, as large firms are more able to invest in data collection and incumbent firms may not yet have completed their digital transformation (Verhoef et al. 2021).

Second, because predictions can be wrong, AI systems introduce an additional kind of risk. Risk is often a major factor in technology adoption; when stakes are high, risk-averse firms may be less willing to make needed investments or use inputs with uncertain returns (Roosen and Hennessy 2003; Whalley 2011).[15] Often, the distribution of potential payoffs for business decisions is not just uncertain but also ambiguous, in that firms do not know the potential set of outcomes and their probabilities. Ambiguity makes prediction more difficult, and research has shown the condition has a range of effects on firms' willingness to develop or adopt new technologies (Knight 1921; Beauchêne 2019). Risk and ambiguity related to liability assignment is a prominent example discussed later in the chapter.

Third, many potential AI applications exhibit network effects, in which the use of the technology by one party increases its value to others. One way in which these network effects can arise is by increasing the amount of feedback data from users, which in turn increases the quality of predictions for everyone (Gregory et al. 2021). Adoption can also lead to network effects by reducing coordination costs, such as vehicular communications systems that simplify the set of predictions that autonomous cars would need to make if they were widely adopted (Arena and Pau 2019).

Fourth, integrating AI systems with humans has unique challenges related to incentives, job design, and communication. For example, some processes may work best when AI systems handle routine decision-making, like highway driving, and humans handle unusual situations, like construction zones. But without guardrails, the human may be tempted to leave too much to the AI system or may accidentally fail to intervene (e.g., fall asleep at the wheel) (Athey, Bryan, and Gans 2020; Herrmann and Pfeiffer 2023).

Fifth and finally, permanent or indefinite limits to AI's adoption are possible for many reasons, including those unrelated to the technology. Institutional quality issues, coordination problems, and financial frictions can all delay or halt technological adoption (e.g., Parente and Prescott 1994; Foster and Rosenzweig 2010).

---

[15] Some scholars have argued that the fields of AI and machine learning have a serious problem with reproducibility because of the complexity and nuances of the problems, which may provide a further incentive for firms to delay adoption (Kapoor and Narayanan 2023).

AI Has the Potential to Be Even More Transformative in the Future

In the past, many innovations' biggest effects came from enabling people to structure entire productive processes differently and from spurring complementary inventions, not from performing individual tasks at a lower cost (David 1990; Brynjolfsson, Hui, and Liu 2019; Agrawal, Gans, and Goldfarb 2022). Consider the migration of factories from steam power to electricity. Steam power required vertical factories oriented around shafts used to power machines. Even when electricity became less expensive than steam power, adoption remained slow and unsteady because replacing the machines was capital intensive for only a modest ongoing benefit. In the long run, the largest gains from electricity were not from direct cost savings, but rather arose because firms were no longer required to locate their factories next to steam plants or design them vertically (Du Boff 1967). Realizing these gains, however, required building entirely new factories and power plants, and developing complementary technologies, all of which required even more capital and time. Similarly, the widespread adoption of automobiles and subsequent construction of the interstate highway system did not just increase the number of car trips consumers took; it changed where people lived (Biggs 1983; Eschner 2017).

AI is a general-purpose technology (GPT), like electricity and computers (Brynjolfsson, Rock, and Syverson 2021). Key hallmarks of these technologies are that they improve over time and lead to complementary inventions (Bresnahan and Trajtenberg 1995). Because of these similarities, the effects of AI are also likely to be larger and more wide-reaching than the initial use cases would suggest. While some services have been redesigned on the basis of AI, and some new technologies have been built with AI from the ground up, many systems and processes that could be redesigned to take advantage of AI have not yet been updated (McElheran et al. 2023). Firms that invest in AI are showing signs of increased product innovation, but they do not yet show evidence of process innovations that might arise from a more thorough restructuring of their operations (Babina et al. 2024).

In addition, AI technology continues to evolve in transformative ways. For example, many recent developments in AI have come not from increasingly specialized models but rather from foundation models, which are trained on very large volumes of data and are adaptable to many different tasks (Bommasani et al. 2021). This stands in seeming contrast to one of the earliest and best-known ideas in economics: that gains from specialization are a fundamental force behind economic growth (Smith

1776; Ricardo 1817).[16] However, a further investigation suggests that the rise of broad foundation models is consistent with the same forces that yield specialization in other contexts. Gains from specialization are bounded not only by the size of markets but also by training costs, transaction costs, the need for workers to synchronize, and other frictional forces in the economy (Becker and Murphy 1994; Bolton and Dewatripont 1994; Costinot 2009). The degree of specialization ultimately depends on how these costs compare with the potential benefits: if costs are high, then relatively little specialization is likely to occur. In the case of AI-induced automation, coordination costs between computer systems are often low compared with coordination costs between humans, especially as the scale increases. However, training costs for foundational AI models are currently high, which likely limits overall specialization. One way to reduce such costs is to train models on targeted subsets of data (e.g., Kaddour et al. 2023), but many such applications may not yet make economic sense. Another approach is to fine-tune models in specialized ways after their initial training (Min et al. 2023).

This approach is widely used, but research is ongoing as to how effective this method is compared with or in concert with specialization at the training stage (e.g., Kumar et al. 2022). In addition, as discussed earlier in the chapter, some systems continue fine-tuning after deployment, though updating models over time may cause them to behave in unpredictable ways (e.g., Chen et al. 2022; Chen, Zaharia, and Zou 2023). Finally, specialization may be integrated in more limited ways—for example, through multi-tiered production processes with generalized and specialized components (Garicano 2000; Ling et al. 2023). The outcomes from ongoing AI research in these areas may have large implications for future AI adoption, market structure, and competition; later in this chapter, there is further discussion of AI market structure and competition. Alternatively, decreases in computational costs or other methodological improvements may make specialized generative models more economically viable over time (e.g., Leffer 2023).

Finally, AI may also drive changes outside the markets where it is directly employed. In some areas, AI may allow automation of a wide variety of tasks that might not have historically been regarded as prediction-centered. For example, farmers can make conditions more hospitable for bees to increase plant pollination, and researchers are attempting to create AI-powered robotic pollinators for this purpose (Cherney 2021). Conversely, just as automobiles undermined the buggy whip industry (Levitt 2004) and smartphones have decreased demand for printed maps, technology can make

---

[16] Subsequent research has identified specific economic mechanisms that encourage specialization, such as differences in inputs or skill endowments, gains from human capital deepening, and consumer tastes for variety (Krugman 1981; Ohlin and Heckscher 1991; Becker and Murphy 1992). Similarly, AI researchers have identified cross-country patterns of comparative advantage as one reason AI might be specialized (Mishra et al. 2023).

products obsolete. In this case, AI may partially or entirely eliminate the need for products that exist primarily due to insufficient prediction capabilities. For example, many stores and warehouses carry substantial inventories because they are unable to predict what customers will demand. If improved prediction capabilities can substantially reduce the need for such storage, there may be substantial reductions in the necessary land and infrastructure. In short, AI may increase consumption of some products and decrease consumption of others. This same dynamic, complementing in some places while substituting in others, is also important in the labor market, and is further explored later in the chapter.

When Will We Know the Future Has Arrived?

The scale and scope of AI's effects on the economy will be influenced by the development and adoption issues discussed earlier in the chapter. But even after invention and adoption, there can be substantial delays before a technology's effects are captured in macroeconomic statistics like productivity. Thus, there is still considerable uncertainty—not only about when the future effects of AI will be felt but also when economic statistics will reflect them.

In 1987, the Nobel Prize–winning economist Robert Solow said that computers were everywhere except in the productivity statistics. As figure 7-3 shows, faster productivity growth actually did appear in the data, just not until roughly two decades later, during a period of widespread Internet adoption. Thus, it is uncertain whether the productivity increase was simply delayed or whether the invention of a complementary technology was a

Figure 7-3. Nonfarm Labor Productivity Growth, 1975–2010 (5-year moving average)

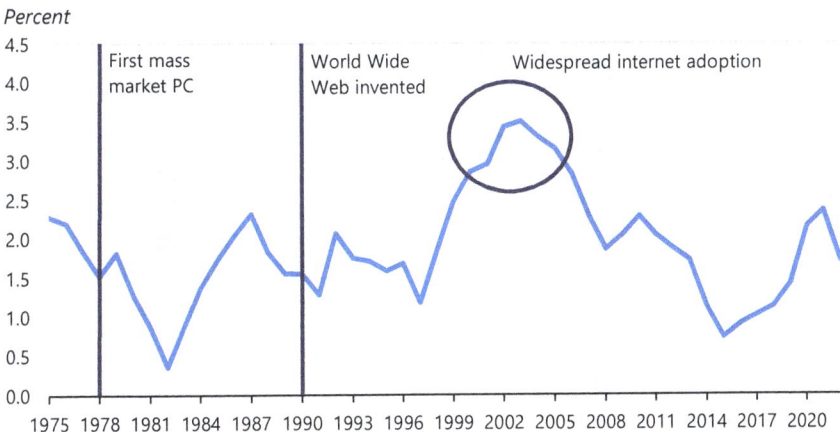

Council of Economic Advisers
Sources: Bureau of Labor Statistics; CEA calculations.
Note: Gray bars indicate recessions.
2024 Economic Report of President

necessary prerequisite. Productivity also eventually returned to its earlier trend, which suggests that it was more of a level shift than a structural growth shift. Consistent with past experience, current productivity statistics do not suggest an immediate uplift in productivity resulting from AI.

Some have argued that instead of a delayed effect, this pattern is the result of a measurement issue common to general-purpose technologies (Brynjolfsson, Rock, and Syverson 2021). These technologies initially require large investments, particularly in intangible and thus unmeasurable assets like new business practices and employee knowledge. Investments in a new technology may also crowd out other productive work or other potential productivity-increasing investments. As a result, there may be a considerable period when expenditures are measured but benefits are not.

Ultimately, the evidence is inconclusive. It may be a while before the full effects of AI are felt, and even longer before we can confidently observe it in economic statistics. Moreover, a productivity boom is not guaranteed. The current excitement over generative AI may fade if developers and users discover that its drawbacks are insurmountable, if few new data are available to power improvements, or if it turns out to be difficult to monetize the technology. Furthermore, how deeply AI becomes integrated into the economy depends not only on technological progress but also on institutional and regulatory issues. These topics are discussed more fully later in this chapter. (See box 7-2.)

Box 7-2. Government Applications of AI

One way that AI can increase productivity and improve individuals' well-being is by using it to improve the Federal Government. Numerous administrative and regulatory processes could benefit from the adoption of AI. The recent Executive Order directs agencies throughout the government to identify and implement beneficial uses (White House 2023a). The order also encourages agencies to take steps to attract and retain the AI talent necessary for adoption to take place.

Prediction, evaluation, and routine content generation are core components of many government processes. Often, these tasks are performed via labor-intensive methods, and AI could make these operations more efficient by automating their most routine components. Applications for government benefits are one such example. Most applications for benefits do not involve fraud, and many can be processed with little human labor. However, application reviews must be thorough enough to detect and disincentivize fraudulent activity, and so considerable human labor is used. Thoughtful application of AI could improve

---

fraud detection in two ways, by detecting fraud directly, and by filtering and processing clearly non-fraudulent applications so that employees can more effectively target their fraud-detection efforts.

Government AI adoption will look different than private sector adoption because of the unique challenges the government faces. For example, private firms are often not required to protect privacy and confidentiality to the same extent as the Federal government (e.g., GAO 2018). Performance standards that would be acceptable in a commercial environment may be insufficient for sophisticated or sensitive government applications. In addition, many government activities simply have no private sector analog. Commercial solutions and private sector innovation will undoubtedly play a role in government AI adoption, but the government may only realize the full benefits of AI by tailoring applications to suit its unique needs.

Another reason to encourage government AI adoption is that positive externalities are likely to result. Government innovations have a long history of being repurposed to benefit other sectors of the economy. Many current AI applications are only possible because of technologies like GPS that arose from government research and development. Private sector AI innovation has been rapid in recent years, but numerous limitations remain. The government is well positioned to be a leader in developing solutions to outstanding problems precisely because it faces so many unique situations.

Institutions such as the Defense Advanced Research Projects Agency (DARPA) have long embodied a model of mission-focused innovation to considerable success (e.g., Bonvillian 2018). Similar research agencies are found throughout the government and are already engaged in targeted AI research. However, potential AI applications are dispersed throughout many organizations, and spillovers between agencies tackling similar problems are likely. New interagency councils along with existing cross-government programs such as the U.S. Digital Service are an initial step to ensuring that knowledge sharing within the government remains a priority.

Government adoption of AI is not without risk. For example, automating too many processes too quickly could result in a lack of accountability and access to key services, in addition to public sector job losses. But with these risks comes the opportunity for the government to lead by example. Adoption that is done thoughtfully, with input from current workers and other stakeholders, will lead to better outcomes and allow the government to develop the key institutional knowledge necessary to create good policy (Kochan et al. 2023).

AI and the Labor Market

What does AI's ability to undertake tasks previously performed by humans mean for labor and the labor market? On net, will AI complement workers, yielding increased jobs, productivity, and prosperity? Or will prediction models substitute for human labor, yielding a world where fewer people are needed to work, but also where fewer people can contribute to the economy while also earning a living?

Although AI is a comparatively new technology, the notion of "technological unemployment" is hundreds of years old. Numerous 18th- and 19th-century economists hypothesized that technology would displace workers by substituting for their labor (Mokyr, Vickers, and Ziebarth 2015). During the Great Depression, John Maynard Keynes predicted that within a century, individuals would work no more than 15 hours a week, and that the innate desire to work would lead to many workers performing small tasks so they could remain at least nominally employed (Keynes 1930).[17]

Figure 7-4 shows that so far, these predictions have not proven true. Prime-age labor participation remains near long-term highs, matched only by a brief period in the late 1990s. The average prime-age worker has worked close to 40 hours a week for decades. Some have noted that increased life spans have reduced overall time spent working over the life cycle, and that working conditions have improved considerably (e.g., Zilibotti 2007). Nonetheless, while Keynes accurately predicted massive average income increases, he failed to recognize how ever-increasing demand for consumer goods and other forces would keep people from working fewer hours.[18]

This historical evidence suggests that caution is warranted in making predictions about technology's impact on the future of the labor force. Moreover, mistaken predictions in this area have not been random: They have overwhelmingly incorrectly predicted substitution instead of complementarity (Autor 2015). To be fair, the adaptations of workers and firms to technological change and increased wealth are difficult to foresee.

---

[17] CEOs and Nobel laureates have recently made nearly identical predictions about AI shortening the work week (Taub and Levitt 2023; Rees 2023).

[18] Economists have highlighted many features of the economy that may discourage workers from reducing their hours despite higher average incomes over time. Relative product quality or status comparisons may lead consumer demand to track higher purchasing power (e.g., Frank 2008). Increased wage inequality may be associated with an increase in the return to additional hours of work (e.g., Freeman 2008). Performance-related compensation systems and increased competitive pressures may make hours reductions more costly (Freeman 2008). Increasing income volatility may lead individuals to increase their labor supply as insurance against future economic shocks (Heathcote, Storesletten, and Violante 2010). Changes to work attributes may have made time spent at work more pleasant, and individuals may value the social or intellectual components of work (e.g., Cowen 2017). Nonetheless, recent empirical evidence from inheritances and lottery winners in the United States suggests that the work-reducing impact of greater wealth is substantial, and is stronger among individuals with higher incomes (Brown, Coile, and Weisbenner 2010; Golosov et al. 2021).

Figure 7-4. Employment-Population Ratio and Weekly Work Hours, 1976–2022

Percentage of working-age population employed

Hours worked per week

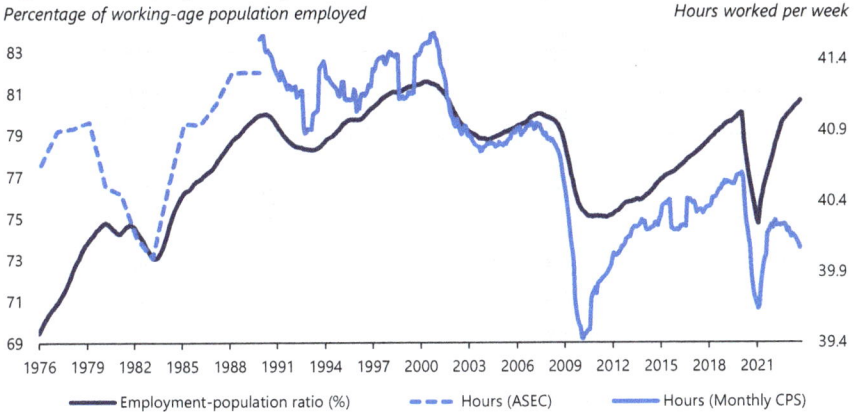

──── Employment-population ratio (%)   ─ ─ ─ Hours (ASEC)   ──── Hours (Monthly CPS)

Council of Economic Advisers

Sources: Current Population Survey; Bureau of Labor Statistics; CEA calculations.
Note: CPS = Current Population Survey; ASEC = CPS Annual Social and Economic Supplements. Working-age population refers to the population between the age of 25 and 54 years. The employment-population ratio is a 12-month moving average. ASEC hours are a measure of hours worked in the last week. Monthly CPS hours are a measure of hours worked in the last week from the basic monthly CPS. Gray bars indicate recessions.
2024 Economic Report of President

Still, technological change has greatly affected workers over time through their occupations, the tasks they perform, and the payment they receive. Economic frameworks characterize the forces behind these prior effects, and in doing so they also provide suggestive evidence of the impact that AI may have in the future.

In the next subsection, the CEA considers several leading frameworks used by economists to study the impact of technological change in recent decades. Although data limitations make it difficult to attribute this impact to individual technologies, predictions from these frameworks align with the observed patterns of economic change stemming from the widespread adoption of general-purpose technologies like computers and the Internet.[19] A common theme among these frameworks is that technologies make an impact on different groups of workers differently, in large part because they perform different tasks. The ability of AI to perform additional tasks may mean that its effects will differ from the effects of automation in the past.

_____

[19] Technologies tend to be adopted in the circumstances where they are especially valuable, and multiple technologies tend to be in use simultaneously; these features make isolating a single technology's effects difficult or impossible in most circumstances without further assumptions. In one well-known example, researchers found that they could not empirically distinguish the purported large effects of the computer from the effects of the pencil (DiNardo and Pischke 1997). In limited cases, researchers can exploit exogenous variation in adoption brought about by other policies to help isolate the impact of a specific technology. For example, this approach has been used to suggest that broadband Internet adoption complements workers performing abstract tasks, and substitutes for workers performing routine tasks (Akerman, Gaarder, and Mogstad 2015).

In response to this concern, the CEA uses information about the current task content of occupations to provide suggestive evidence about the occupations and workers that may be affected by AI in the future. As noted throughout, the analysis presented has similarities to other analyses found in the recent literature. The CEA's measure of occupational AI exposure is closely related to and extends the recent analysis by the Pew Research Center (Kochhar 2023), and many of its conclusions are similar. However, all predictions of the future are inherently speculative, because they are based on the models and data that exist today. The assumptions that go into this analysis may later prove to be erroneous. And many open questions cannot yet be answered, or cannot be answered with the available data. The particular concern of data limitations is discussed later in the chapter.

Modeling the Effect of Technological Change on Labor Markets

Though technological changes are often complex, a simple framework can often explain their effects on employment and earnings. The model of skill-biased technological change (SBTC) is one influential example. This model is based on the notion that technology increases the relative demand for highly educated workers over time (generally proxied by a college education). The SBTC model conceives of "skill" very narrowly, and it abstracts away from other features of labor markets such as unemployment. The benefit of these simplifications is that they allow the model to succinctly describe the relationship between technological change and wage patterns: When the relative demand for highly educated labor grows more quickly than the relative supply of labor from highly educated workers, the relative wages of these workers rise compared with those of workers without college degrees. This model suggests that the growing college wage premium over the past several decades is a result of demand for educated workers increasing faster than their supply. Skill-biased technological change is sometimes characterized as a race between education and technology; the more technological change outpaces the supply of educated workers, the more workers' wages rise (Goldin and Katz 2007).

Figure 7-5 demonstrates this point; inflation-adjusted weekly earnings for working-age men and women with graduate degrees have risen more than 60 percent since 1964, while earnings for workers with less education have increased more slowly. In fact, 75 percent of the rise in earnings inequality from 1980 to 2000, measured as the log of hourly wage variance, can be explained by the increase in the college wage premium alone (Autor, Goldin, and Katz 2020). Figure 7-5 also shows that a model of ever-increasing demand for highly educated labor is incomplete; the flatness of the college premium over the last two decades, especially for men, and the comparatively rapid wage growth among those who did not receive a

Figure 7-5. Cumulative Changes in Real Weekly Earnings by Education for Men and Women

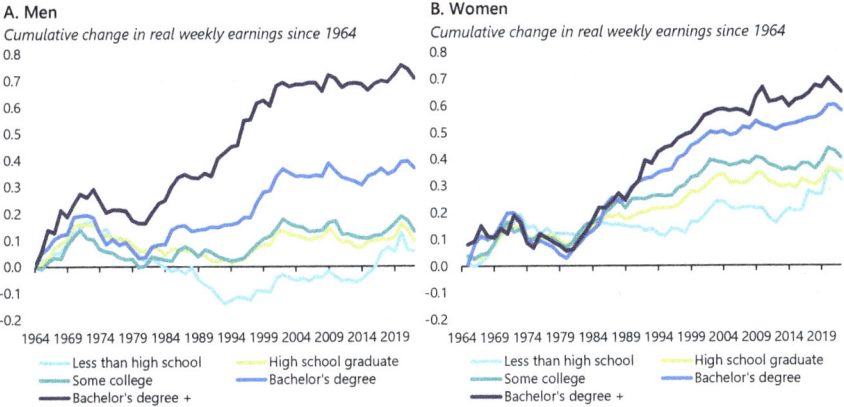

A. Men

Cumulative change in real weekly earnings since 1964

B. Women

Cumulative change in real weekly earnings since 1964

Legend:
— Less than high school
— Some college
— Bachelor's degree +
— High school graduate
— Bachelor's degree

Council of Economic Advisers

Sources: Current Population Survey; CEA calculations.
Note: Data are cleaned and analyzed following Autor (2019). Full-time, full-year workers between the age of 18 and 64 are used and education categories are harmonized using the procedures described by Autor, Katz, and Kearney (2008). All earnings are deflated by the chain-weighted (implicit) price deflator for personal consumption expenditures.
2024 Economic Report of President

high school degree over the past decade, do not align with a purely demand-driven SBTC explanation.

The SBTC framework is hampered by two limitations: (1) it conceives of "skill" as a one-dimensional attribute, typically proxied by education, and (2) it does not explain why technological change increases the relative demand for educated workers. As an example of the first limitation, the SBTC framework would classify workers in occupations like stenographers, typists, and paralegals similarly, based on their average level of educational attainment. However, following personal computer adoption, paralegals saw both earnings and employment rise (i.e., demand for the job increased), while typists and stenographers saw their employment dwindle. In contrast, many occupations that require manual labor (e.g., roofers) perform their work much as they have for decades, with relatively stable employment and modest real earnings growth in recent years. These distinctions are especially salient when considering AI's predictive and generative capabilities; jobs that rely on predictions or routine generation are more readily affected by AI than others that do not involve these tasks.

To overcome the limitations of the SBTC model, researchers have suggested an alternative framework that uses a richer notion of workers' characteristics, categorizing workers by the task composition of their occupations (Autor, Levy, and Murnane 2003). Such models typically divide tasks along two characteristic dimensions: whether they are routine or nonroutine and whether they are manual or analytic. Technological change has led to the automation of many routine tasks. Workers who performed these tasks have seen their employment and earnings opportunities decline.

Workers performing nonroutine manual tasks have been less affected by recent technological changes, while those performing nonroutine analytic tasks have been made more productive, as technology complements their work. Because the workers performing nonroutine tasks are often at the extremes of the earnings distribution, while workers performing routine tasks are often in the middle, the model suggests that technology can cause labor market polarization.

Research finds evidence of U-shaped job polarization in employment and earnings, particularly for the 1980–2005 period (Autor and Dorn 2013).[20] Evidence also suggests that polarization happens inconsistently over short periods, with employment and earnings growth often concentrated on one side or another of the occupational wage distribution (e.g., Mishel, Shierholz, and Schmitt 2013). Figure 7-6 shows that during the period of peak productivity growth in the early 2000s, most employment growth was near the bottom of the occupational wage distribution, even as real earnings declined among that same group. In contrast, more recent data from 2015 to 2019 show quite different growth patterns.[21] Nearly all growth in employment shares occurred in the top quintile of occupations, and real earnings growth was broad based, though slightly stronger among low-earning occupations than others.

Figure 7-6. Smoothed Changes in Employment and Earnings Across Occupational Wage Distribution

A. Smoothed Changes in Employment by Occupational Wage Percentile

100x change in employment share

B. Smoothed Changes in Real Log Wages by Occupational Wage Percentile

100x change in real hourly log wage

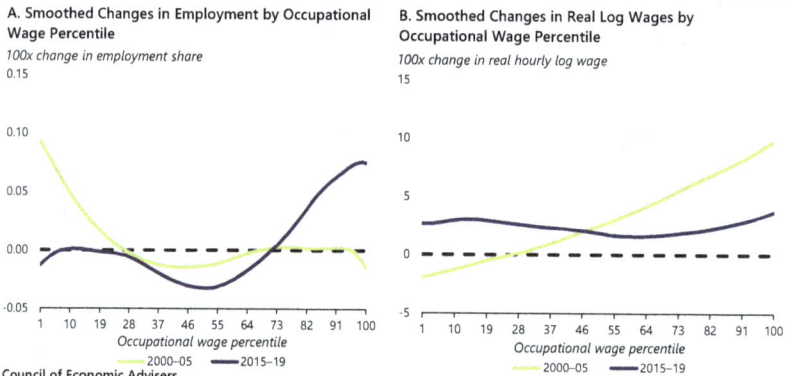

Council of Economic Advisers

Sources: American Community Survey; CEA calculations.
Note: Following Autor and Dorn (2013), occupations are ranked by initial mean wage and are grouped into percentiles weighted by aggregate hours. Analysis uses full-time, full-year workers between the age of 18 and 64.
2024 Economic Report of the President

---

[20] While this pattern is often attributed to computerization, other research has suggested that the pattern may have begun even earlier, and that it could be linked to a broader shift from manufacturing to services employment (Bárány and Siegel 2018).

[21] The CEA ends its analysis of employment and earnings changes across the occupational distribution in 2019 because of the lingering effects of the COVID-19 pandemic in more recent data.

Both periods show employment share reductions at the middle of the earnings distribution, aligning with a core task-based model prediction. The patterns also suggest a nuanced interpretation of the SBTC model. The rapid adoption of computers and information technology in the early 2000s appears to have increased demand for workers in high-wage occupations more rapidly than their available supply could adjust. The pattern of strong demand for high-wage workers has continued; but in recent years, the supply of workers to these occupations has also grown more rapidly. The proportion of the population age 25 years and above who have completed at least four years of college increased by 12 percentage points from 2000 to 2022, from 26 to 38 percent (Census 2023). Even as job polarization has pushed workers into occupations at the earnings distribution extremes over some periods, relative supply's ability to catch up with relative demand in recent years has enabled increasingly stable earnings growth across the earnings distribution. The patterns also suggest that if AI continues or intensifies the trend of strong demand growth for high-wage workers, then continued rapid supply growth will be necessary to sustain broad-based earnings gains.[22]

Modification and additions to this task-based framework have recognized that occupations and tasks are not static. In 2018, more than 60 percent of employment was in jobs that did not exist in 1940 (Autor et al. 2022). New work tends to be concentrated in cities and in occupations with higher average levels of education (Lin 2011; Autor et al. 2022). As new technologies emerge, workers begin performing entirely new tasks, gaining a comparative advantage by complementing the technology. Some tasks cease to be performed by humans, but the new tasks can keep people employed even in the face of rapid technological change. Instead of a race between education and technology, the "new task formation" framework characterizes the labor market as a race between human and machine (Acemoglu and Restrepo 2018).

The new task formation framework is especially promising for understanding AI and other recent technological shifts. For example, the framework is robust enough to explain why few people now work as telephone operators, while data scientist and wind turbine service technician are among the occupations projected to grow fastest in coming years (Price 2019; BLS 2023). It also explains why the share of total income going to workers has declined in some recent periods of technological change but has

---

[22] Conversely, AI could make training workers easier in ways that moderate this pattern. For example, Brynjolfsson, Li, and Raymond (2023) find that the largest productivity gains in their context came from improvements among novice or less skilled workers. It may be that in this context, current AI systems are most useful for training such workers. Furthermore, it may be that an AI system trained on data from existing workers is simply unable to do better than the best of those existing workers.

risen at others: Technology automates and creates new tasks simultaneously (Acemoglu and Restrepo 2019).

Occupation-Specific Effects of AI

The technological change literature discussed above generally concludes that technology affects workers through a mix of complementarity and substitution. Some workers typically benefit from technological change, either because the evolving technology provides new labor market opportunities for them or because it enhances their productivity in their current job. Conversely, some are harmed, typically due to job displacement. Predicting the impact on a given occupation requires identifying whether it is exposed to AI via its particular mix of activities, and also whether, on net, AI complements or substitutes for human performance of those activities.

Researchers have made several attempts to identify and explore the occupations AI is most likely to affect. Surveying individuals about what they expect is one approach. A second approach is to classify occupations by task or activity content (e.g., Frey and Osborne 2017; Felten, Raj, and Seamans 2021; Brynjolfsson, Mitchell, and Rock 2018; Kochhar 2023; Ellingrud et al. 2023). Other researchers have compared the results of this approach to an AI system's predictions of what its own impact will be (Eloundou et al. 2023). Each approach is limited in its ability to measure and predict AI's impact on future economic activity. For example, the occupational content measures used by these papers are generally retrospective and are not necessarily based on actual exposure to deployed AI. No single measure should be considered definitive.

The CEA begins its analysis by considering the specific activities performed in each occupation, and the importance of these activities for the occupation. The Department of Labor's Employment and Training Administration collects this information as part of its O*NET (n.d.) database. The CEA follows the Pew Research Center (Kochhar 2023) in identifying 16 work activities with high exposure to AI. CEA researchers then construct a measure of these activities' relative importance compared to all other work activities.[23] The measure is then used to identify a subset of occupations in which AI-exposed activities are particularly central to the performance of the work. Workers in such occupations are plausibly the

---

[23] Although the CEA identifies the same AI-exposed work activities as Pew, the relative importance measure used by the CEA differs slightly. In particular, it relies on normalizing the importance scales for each activity across occupations, then measuring relative importance as the difference between the average normalized importance of AI-exposed activities and all other activities. Following Pew, the top 25 percent of occupations according to the measure are identified as AI-exposed. Among these occupations, AI-exposed work activities are at least 0.25 standard deviation more important to the performance of the occupation than the average for other activities.

ones most likely to be affected by AI, whether positively through complementarity, or negatively through substitution or displacement.[24]

To explore the potential for complementarity versus substitution, the CEA also considers a key feature of automation: Labor-substitution is easiest and cheapest in situations where complexity and difficulty are low. Working with AI in a complementary fashion may be more effective in complicated and challenging jobs.[25] The CEA captures the distinction by using responses to a separate O*NET question about the degree of difficulty or complexity at which each work activity must be performed for each job. Survey respondents are asked to indicate the level of activity performance requirements for their job, and are provided reference anchors that characterize the difficulty and complexity associated with different levels.[26] CEA researchers then divide the set of AI-exposed occupations into two groups based on whether their performance requirements for AI-exposed activities are above or below the average across all occupations. Although this measure is coarse, it reflects the underlying relationship between the difficulty of an activity and its ability to be fully automated.

These measures of occupation-level exposure and potential for substitution allow the CEA to study AI's potential effects across the earnings distribution, demographic groups, industries, and geographic regions. The CEA's analysis examines the occupations most likely to be exposed to AI in comparison with all other occupations. However, there are important differences within high and low exposure and activity performance categories from which this analysis abstracts, and the results are contingent on the exposure threshold chosen.[27] As such, while this approach provides some important insights about who is more or less likely to be affected, it does not tell us how widespread these effects will be on the labor market as a whole.

---

[24] In addition to affecting levels of employment and earnings, AI could affect job quality in numerous ways. The potential for occupations to experience these changes is also likely correlated with the exposure measure presented here.

[25] Task or activity complexity has been shown to complicate decision-making and increase its information demands, which may determine automation possibilities (e.g., Byström and Järvelin 1995; Sintchenko and Coiera 2003). Recent research has also suggested that task complexity plays a role in whether AI is adopted for activities such as customer service and medical decision-making (Fan et al. 2020; Xu et al. 2020). Other recent research on AI exposure has suggested that potential complementarity can be measured using other O*NET information on work contexts and job zones (Pizzinelli et al. 2023).

[26] The O*NET questionnaire asks respondents to report the activity performance level needed to perform their job on a 7-point scale, with benchmarks at the low end, midpoint, and high end. For example, in the AI-exposed activity "Evaluating Information to Determine Compliance," "Review forms for completeness" scores a 1, "Evaluate a complicated insurance claim for compliance with policy terms" receives a 4, and "Make a ruling in court on a complicated motion" scores a 6. See Peterson et al. (1995) for further details on the survey design.

[27] The percentage of employees who are exposed to AI directly depends on the threshold chosen. However, the CEA's analysis suggests that the economic and demographic distribution of effects is relatively insensitive to that choice.

With this caveat in mind, figure 7-7 groups occupations into deciles based on the average earnings of workers, and then reports the percentage of workers within each decile who are employed in AI-exposed occupations. Similar to the task-based model's predictions, employment exposure is not monotonic. The most significant AI exposure levels correspond to occupations in the lower-middle portion of the earnings distribution, in the third and fourth deciles. However, more than a quarter of workers in the top two deciles are employed in AI-exposed occupations as well.

The addition of information about the required level of activity performance adds additional context regarding possible complementarity or substitution. Although AI-exposed activities are relatively central to each examined job, individuals in high-earning occupations are more likely to be required to perform AI-exposed activities at a higher level of complexity or difficulty than those in low-earning jobs. Because implementing AI as a human substitute is more costly and/or challenging for complex and difficult tasks, the analysis implies that AI may more quickly be able to substitute for employment in the lower-middle portion of the earnings distribution. To the extent that workers in some occupations can work in conjunction with AI to raise their productivity, the analysis provides suggestive evidence that such occupations may already have higher-than-average wages.

In figure 7-8, CEA researchers examine AI exposure across demographic groups. Previous research has suggested that AI exposure increases with education, that it is least concentrated among young workers, and that

Figure 7-7. Employment in High-AI-Exposed Occupations by Earnings Decile

Percentage of employment within decile

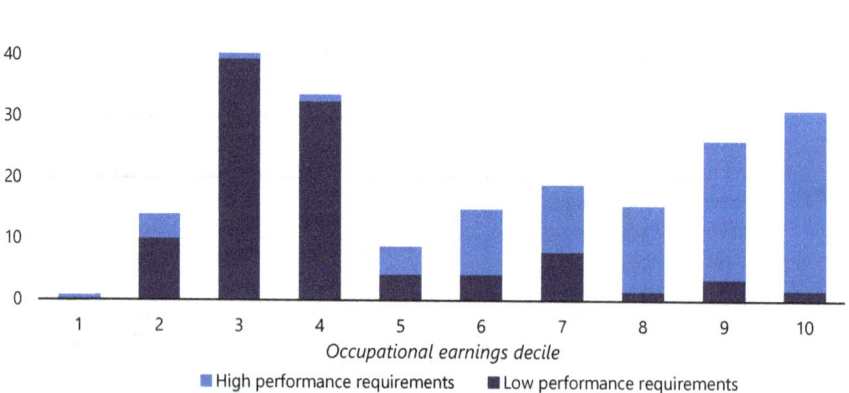

■ High performance requirements   ■ Low performance requirements

Council of Economic Advisers

Sources: American Community Survey; Department of Labor; Pew Research Center; CEA calculations.
Note: Deciles are calculated using mean occupational earnings of workers who are full-time, full-year workers age 16 plus. Performance requirements are captured using the O*NET data measuring degree of difficulty or complexity at which a high-AI-exposed work activity is performed within an occupation. High (low) indicates an average degree of difficulty above (below) the median.
2024 Economic Report of the President

it is somewhat more prevalent among women, as well as among white and Asian workers (Kochhar 2023). Using its own occupation-level exposure metric, the CEA largely replicates these findings. As in figure 7-7, the CEA considers how AI-exposed workers whose jobs have lower performance requirements differ from AI-exposed workers as a whole. This analysis suggests that the demographic characteristics of workers negatively affected by AI may be somewhat different from those of individuals simply exposed to AI. For example, many high school graduates lacking four-year degrees have jobs that are highly AI exposed and that have relatively low performance requirements. A similar fraction of college graduates are exposed to AI, but their performance requirements are higher on average, and so they may be less at risk of displacement. Similarly, while women are only slightly more exposed to AI than men, they are more likely to have high exposure with low performance requirements, suggesting that women may be at higher risk of displacement.

The findings shown in figures 7-7 and 7-8 suggest that AI may be a skill-biased technology, increasing relative demand for workers with high levels of education in high-earning occupations. They also suggest that AI could exacerbate aggregate income inequality if it substitutes for employment in lower-wage jobs and complements higher-wage jobs. The possibility of increased inequality from AI has been widely discussed among economists studying the topic (e.g., Korinek and Stiglitz 2018; Furman and Seamans 2019; Acemoglu 2021). However, such an interpretation of the

Figure 7-8. Share of Workers in High-AI-Exposure Occupations by Demographic

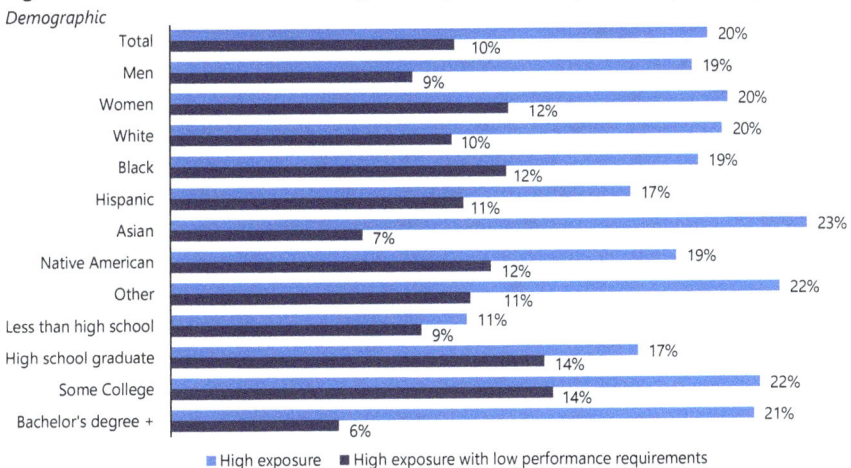

Demographic

Demographic	High exposure with low performance requirements	High exposure
Total	10%	20%
Men	9%	19%
Women	12%	20%
White	10%	20%
Black	12%	19%
Hispanic	11%	17%
Asian	7%	23%
Native American	12%	19%
Other	11%	22%
Less than high school	9%	11%
High school graduate	14%	17%
Some College	14%	22%
Bachelor's degree +	6%	21%

■ High exposure ■ High exposure with low performance requirements

Council of Economic Advisers

Sources: American Community Survey; Department of Labor; Pew Research Center; CEA calculations.
Note: Analysis uses full-time, full-year workers age 16 plus. Performance requirements are captured using the O*NET data measuring degree of difficulty or complexity at which a high-AI-exposed work activity is performed within an occupation. Low indicates an average degree of difficulty below the median.
2024 Economic Report of the President

evidence presented here should be made cautiously. As the historical analysis given earlier in the chapter demonstrates, supply-and-demand forces both play a role in determining patterns of wages and employment. Nonetheless, the possibility of increased inequality resulting from AI adoption may inform policy responses.

More generally, the economic and demographic breakdowns of figures 7-7 and 7-8 suggest possible effects, but they simplify a complex reality. For example, figure 7-8 does not imply that the 10 percent of workers who have high AI exposure and low performance requirements will inevitably lose their jobs. Rather, the measures shown identify the occupations and workers who perform the tasks that are most likely to change as a result of AI. The implications for jobs and workers may be quite nuanced.

For example, most jobs remain a collection of tasks of which only a portion can be automated. AI may allow humans to focus on other tasks, fundamentally changing their jobs without reducing the use of their labor. For example, if AI eventually allows school buses to drive themselves, children may still need someone on the bus to watch them, ensure they behave, and ensure they enter and exit safely. In other words, AI-led automation might fundamentally change the school bus driver's job, but it is unlikely to eliminate the job. Similarly, airplanes still have pilots, despite autopilot systems having automated some of their tasks for more than a century (Chialastri 2012).

Additionally, even among workers within an occupation, the extent of automation may be highly context dependent. Different AI models may be deployed in different situations, tailored to unique goals in ways that allow them to succeed at different tasks. An AI model that can replace human performance of tasks in some contexts might require extensive human assistance in others, or it may not be economically viable to adopt (e.g., Svanberg et al. 2024).

More broadly, there are reasons to believe that integrating humans and AI may often prove more effective than using either alone. Having multiple approaches to prediction and problem solving often produces better results than any one approach on its own. Diversity of thought can improve human decision-making (Post et al. 2015), and prediction techniques may benefit by combining multiple different machine learning approaches (Webb and Zheng 2004; Dong et al. 2020; Naik et al. 2023). Emerging research suggests that this principle extends to the combination of human and AI approaches as well (Zirar, Ali, and Islam 2023; Hitsuwari et al. 2023).

Finally, these measures of AI exposure are based on the tasks that future AI systems are believed to be well suited to perform. As AI technology develops, it may change in ways that lead it to automate a different set of tasks than existing measures foresee.

A more precise understanding of how AI affects specific occupations, industries, demographic groups, and geographic regions will be critical for constructing appropriate policy responses. Researchers continue to develop and refine their frameworks to predict the potential effects of AI. As evidence of AI's effects emerges, these frameworks will evolve to incorporate the new information. At the same time, the limitations of available data and testable frameworks will continue to constrain researchers' quest for understanding.

Evidence for AI's Effects

Economists have already begun measuring AI's adoption, and they are looking for signs of its impact on the labor market. Although uncertainty remains, some patterns have emerged. First, AI adoption is driven by larger and more productive firms. While the percentage of businesses adopting or integrating AI directly is still small, these firms employ a sizable share of workers (Acemoglu et al. 2022; Kochhar 2023). Note that survey measures of technology usage are likely to provide an underestimate of AI's ongoing impact on firms; whether businesses adopt AI directly or not, many of the products and services they purchase and use implement AI. For example, online advertising platforms, navigation systems, and recommendation systems all commonly implement AI and have been widely adopted.

Limited evidence also suggests AI's impact on labor market decision-making. For example, commuting zones with greater industrial robot adoption in the 1990s and 2000s saw reduced employment and wage growth, and these effects can be distinguished from the simultaneous impact of import competition (Acemoglu and Restrepo 2020). Though robots are only one form of automation, and not all robots use AI extensively, predicting a robot's surroundings and interactions with others is often critical to its use. Businesses with task structures exposed to AI showed a rapid increase in AI-related job vacancy postings through the 2010s, but they simultaneously reduced hiring of non-AI-related positions, which could indicate the substitution of AI for human labor (Acemoglu et al. 2020). Evidence from Dutch employers suggests that workers whose jobs are displaced by automation are less likely to be working and more likely to retire than their peers (Bessen et al. 2023). Collectively, these papers suggest that a mix of complementarity to and substitution from AI is likely already happening.

Using the occupation-level exposure measure discussed earlier in this chapter, the CEA is also able to identify what percentage of workers in each industry are most likely to be exposed to AI, and whether these workers have high or low performance requirements that could be associated with complementarity or substitution. The two panels of figure 7-9 plot these measures against recent changes in employment growth relative to the long

Figure 7-9. Industry AI Exposure versus Payroll Employment Growth Relative to Long-Run Trends

A. AI-Exposed Employment with High Performance Requirements

Difference in growth rate of payroll employment from 2023 to annualized rate between 2007 and 2019 (percentage points)

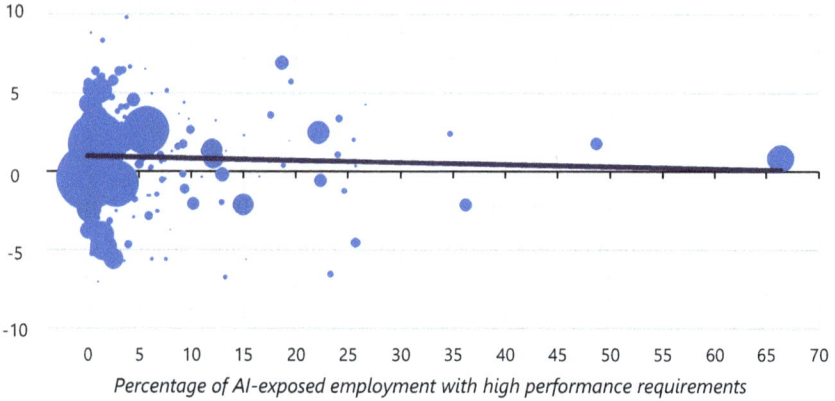

Percentage of AI-exposed employment with high performance requirements

B. AI-Exposed Employment with Low Performance Requirements

Difference in growth rate of payroll employment from 2023 to annualized rate between 2007 and 2019 (percentage points)

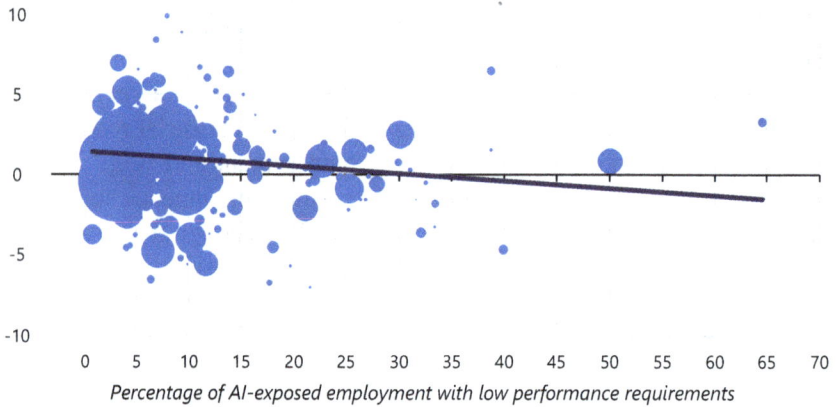

Percentage of AI-exposed employment with low performance requirements

Council of Economic Advisers

Sources: Bureau of Labor Statistics (Occupational Employment and Wage Statistics); Pew Research Center; CEA calculations.
Note: Occupations are matched to the most detailed industry data available in the Current Employment Statistics. Point sizes are proportional to industry employment and linear predictions are weighted by industry employment. These outliers are not shown: 213, support activities for mining; 313, textile mills; 3132, fabric mills; 3361, motor vehicle manufacturing; and 3212, veneer, plywood and engineered wood product manufacturing.
2024 Economic Report of the President

run trend from 2007 to 2019. The figure demonstrates three things: (1) most industries and most workers still have relatively low exposure; (2) employment in AI-exposed occupations is dispersed across industries, with only a handful of small industries having most of their employment in highly exposed occupations; and (3) relatively little evidence of heterogeneity by performance requirements has emerged. In particular, the similarity of the relationship plotted in the two panels suggests that neither large-scale complementarity to nor substitution from AI is taking place. Industries with a high share of exposed employment saw slightly less rapid employment growth in 2023 relative to long-run patterns, but thus far AI exposure has little explanatory power.

Preparing Institutions for AI

Productivity gains make society richer by allowing it to do more with fewer resources. The new economic activity permitted by AI can, in principle, provide the potential for everyone to be better off than they were before. However, a world where AI increases everyone's living standards is not guaranteed. Institutions and regulatory environments have important effects on the ways that technologies are developed and deployed, and on how their effects are felt. Just as strong but flexible institutions were necessary for the Industrial Revolution (e.g., Mokyr 2008), and as poor institutions still limit development in much of the world (e.g., Acemoglu, Johnson, and Robinson 2005), so too will details of the U.S. institutional environment dictate both how widely AI is adopted and who benefits from it.

The Federal Government's role goes beyond ensuring that the gains brought about by AI are widely shared. It must also ensure that the costs to harmed individuals are addressed. To the extent that AI may displace some employees, evidence shows that workers are likely to experience significant negative effects. These effects may be sizable even if the labor market remains strong and despite the fact that most workers eventually find new jobs (Davis and von Wachter 2011). However, AI's potential harm is broader than its impact on affected workers. Loss of consumer privacy, reduced market competition, and increased inequality are all potential consequences of AI that the government can help manage (e.g., Acemoglu 2021). The potential use of AI by malicious actors is also a concern—and one reason the Biden-Harris Administration has begun taking specific steps to develop best practices and secure the nation's infrastructure (White House 2023a).

Many new technologies affect only a single market or a few products. AI has applications touching most industries and markets, likely including some that do not yet exist. Also, the inputs to many AI models include data generated from vast swaths of economic activity. Outlining every way in which the institutional environment affects AI is therefore impossible. Still, it is worth considering the broad economic forces at issue and some of the ways the economy's institutions must be reexamined to ensure they can manage an economy in which AI is a fundamental feature.

Ownership, Liability, and Regulation

The usefulness of AI arises from its ability to make predictions, automate tasks, or generate outputs that humans value. However, these same characteristics that make AI systems useful often raise important questions about both intellectual property rights and liability. This has been true of AI systems in the past, and the rapid rise of generative AI systems has expanded the scope of issues. For example, a number of recent copyright infringement lawsuits have challenged AI companies' argument that generative AI systems can be trained on copyrighted materials under fair use provisions (Appel, Neelbauer, and Schweidel 2023; CRS 2023a; Sag 2023; Setty 2023; Oremus and Izadi 2024). Similarly, creators have contested the training of AI systems on their creative works, and celebrities have contested the use of AI to replicate their likenesses from their personal traits (Kadrey et al. v. Meta Platforms 2023; Horton 2023; Kahveci 2023). Furthermore, scholars have begun to weigh numerous AI-related challenges to the boundaries of liability law, such as generative AI systems that could produce defamatory speech, self-driving cars that could harm pedestrians, or AI systems that could be used to commit crimes (Brown 2023; Gless, Silverman, and Weigend 2016; King et al. 2020). The way these issues are resolved will alter incentives for content creators, platforms, and end users. Thus, the decisions that regulators and the legal system make will be a critical element in determining whether and how AI is adopted and deployed (e.g., Brodsky 2016; Sobel 2017), and may have an impact on competition as well (e.g., Tirole 2023; Volokh 2023). An economic framing of ownership and liability provides key insights for regulators in adapting to the challenges presented by AI.

In a strict legal sense, ownership of AI inputs and systems is generally not in question.[28] However, the contemporary economic conception of ownership is considerably broader. Rather than focusing on the absolute rights of owners to possess an asset themselves, economists emphasize that the value of ownership derives from the capabilities it provides: the ability to select the use of an asset, to prohibit its use by others, and to form contracts around this use (e.g., Alchian 1965; Barzel and Allen 2023).[29] Regulations and legal constraints place limits on ownership, either by limiting what owners can do or by limiting what owners can prevent others from doing. For the

---

[28] Regarding AI outputs, courts have considered cases in which an individual applied for patent or copyright protections for AI outputs, and have generally ruled that such ownership rights are not available to outputs generated by AI without human involvement (e.g., *Thaler v. Vidal* 2022; *Thaler v. Perlmutter* 2023).

[29] Extensive legal scholarship has also considered the nature of ownership, and is characterized by multiple competing approaches. Economic thought has played a role in outlining the benefits and drawbacks to each approach, although many economically salient features of ownership are not strictly dependent on the legal theory applied (e.g., Coase 1960; Honoré 1961; Bell and Parchomovsky 2005; Merrill and Smith 2011; Smith 2012; and Medema 2020).

same reason, ownership rights and liability assignments are only economically meaningful to the extent that they can be enforced (e.g., Calabresi and Melamed 1972).

The incentives created by ownership rights have very broad economic effects. For example, the incentives of ownership are fundamental to determining how and why firms form, and to how product markets and financial markets are structured (e.g., Grossman and Hart 1986; Aghion and Bolton 1992). Similarly, the ability to profit from new technologies is critical not only for their development but also for economic growth as a whole (e.g., Aghion and Howitt 1992). Even in cases where strict legal ownership is not in question, regulatory choices that change the incentives around ownership may have sizable effects on overall market competition, as well as on the path of technology development itself. With AI in particular, the incentives of ownership will shape developers' decisions to invest in advancing AI's technological frontier, companies' decisions to deploy or commercialize AI applications, and many other consequential decisions.

A particularly economically important capability of owners is that they can form contracts related to the assets they own. Through these contracts, the owners of assets can assign many or most of their specific rights and responsibilities to others to reduce economic inefficiencies. Consider, for example, an out-of-town landlord who contracts with a local management company to find tenants and fix things that break. In some cases, clear assignment of property rights and contracts are sufficient for markets to achieve economic efficiency (Coase 1960). However, transaction costs, uncertainty, private information, and other common features of the economy can cause contract mechanisms to break down (e.g., Medema 2020). Writing contracts that efficiently address all situations may be too costly to be practicable. Moreover, unexpected or unplanned situations may also arise for which writing contracts is impossible. Because the owner remains the residual claimant (Fama and Jensen 1983), they bear both the positive and negative consequences that may result. In these circumstances, contracts are said to be incomplete, and market mechanisms may fail to achieve efficient outcomes. Owners adapt to some market failures by forming firms, or by merging or otherwise integrating to mitigate the problem (Williamson 1971; Grossman and Hart 1986). Integrations can be beneficial when they address market failures, but they also have the potential to undermine competition (e.g., Broussard 2009). In many other cases, only government regulations are capable of alleviating market failures.

The potential for incomplete contracts and associated issues related to AI is high, for several reasons. First, the technology is developing rapidly. Many specific ways in which AI will be used are still uncertain, as are the consequences of those uses. Moreover, many of the most useful AI applications must make predictions in novel environments with limited relevant training data. In such situations, even thoughtfully developed AI models are prone to unanticipated behavior. The existence of this possibility can cause potentially serious market failures (Hart 2009). Second, data inputs often originate from user activity, so negotiating directly with each user could lead to high transaction costs. A similar concern exists regarding AI models that are trained on copyrighted works from many different authors (e.g., Samuelson 2023). Also, AI providers often have considerable private information about how their models operate, which can be used to tilt contracts away from economic efficiency and in providers' favor and can prevent agreements from being reached at all (Kennan and Wilson 1993; McKelvey and Page 1999). For these and other reasons, the markets for AI technology are especially susceptible to failure, so laws or regulations that address those failures are needed to strike an economically efficient balance between AI's benefits and costs.

A related incomplete contracts issue arises because AI-created work may not be subject to copyright or other intellectual property protection (e.g., *Thaler v. Vidal* 2022; *Thaler v. Perlmutter* 2023). Intellectual property rights narrow the residual, and the lack of such rights means that restrictions on the use of AI outputs will be largely driven by contract law. When laws do not otherwise assign ownership of an asset, then the government becomes the de facto residual claimant, setting rules that manage its use and bearing responsibility for the consequences. Efficient management of common assets is often possible, although it poses unique challenges (Ostrom 1990; Frischmann, Marciano, and Ramello 2019).

Another way in which laws and regulations create incentives is through the assignment of liability. Often, liability is determined separately from ownership. However, the two concepts are linked because ownership often conveys some forms of liability, because liability is commonly transferred or constrained through contracts, and because the economic incentives of liability assignments depend on their ability to be enforced. A lengthy literature in law and economics considers the economic foundations of liability law (Calabresi 2008; Landes and Posner 1987; Shavell 2004). Major concepts from this literature—such as the economic benefit of assigning liability to the "cheapest cost avoider" to disincentivize harm efficiently—have proven influential in recent legal decisions related to digital technologies (e.g., Sharkey 2022).

When laws and regulations have an impact on ownership rights or potential liability, they often strike a delicate balance between multiple incentives. For example, when patent laws assign ownership rights, they balance the incentive to create and benefit from one's creation against the incentive to adopt and benefit from previous creations (Scotchmer 1991). Other intellectual property laws, like copyright and trademark laws, balance similar incentives. And libel laws balance the potential benefits of information dissemination against the costs of harmful misinformation (Dalvi and Refalo 2008). As technology evolves, the nature of these incentive forces can change as well, so regulations may need to be updated to establish a new balance.

Interpretations of laws have adapted substantially to accommodate the extensive technological changes of the past. For example, interpretations of the "fair use" doctrine in copyright law have depended on the technology available at the time; in recent decades, this doctrine has been interpreted to look at how transformative the new use is in order to accommodate new technologies like Internet search (Gordon 1982; Netanel 2011; Authors Guild v. Google 2015). Similarly, the interpretation of tort law has evolved repeatedly to accommodate technological changes, such as the rise of mechanized transportation and factory production (Gifford 2018). Although such adaptations may be encouraging, the ways in which existing laws and regulations can be adapted to AI is, in many cases, still an open question.

Even in cases where existing laws or regulations can adapt, there may also be other economic benefits from a proactive approach. For example, defining explicit liability rules before the situation arises can improve economic efficiency by reducing uncertainty about how liability will be assigned, narrowing the residual and creating incentives as it does so. One such case may be the liability issues related to autonomous AI systems whose actions unexpectedly harm someone (e.g., Gifford 2018; Diamantis, Cochran, and Dam 2023). Likewise, enacting more specific regulations about AI liability may also reduce the costliness of enforcement, which can improve economic incentives (Mookherjee and Png 1992). Other regulations, such as regulations that encourage increased transparency in AI systems, could also ease enforcement of liability law and improve incentives (e.g., Llorca et al. 2023).

Scholars have already identified a few specific policies as potential targets for reform. For example, in recent years some researchers have suggested adjusting or limiting patent protection to incentivize innovation more effectively (Boldrin and Levine 2013; Bloom, Van Reenen, and Williams 2019). Others have argued that the inability to patent AI-generated inventions will weaken innovation incentives (e.g., Dornis 2020). Recent empirical evidence has generally found that patenting does encourage start-up success and later innovation, but not necessarily in all markets (Gaulé 2018; Farre-Mensa, Hegde, and Ljungqvist 2019; Sampat and Williams 2019). This suggests that the limits to patentability associated with AI could be a substantial concern for innovation in some fields. Conversely, there is less evidence of a problem with AI innovation itself. Although thousands of AI-related patents are filed each year (Miric, Jia, and Huang 2022), private companies have released the algorithms used by multiple popular large-language-model AI frameworks as freely distributed open source software.

The companies' competitive strategies are often multifaceted, but they frequently appear to rely more heavily on their access to data, their ability to integrate AI into other products, or positive network effects from adoption than on the exclusive rights patent protection can provide (Heaven 2023; Boudreau, Jeppesen, and Miric 2022).

Additionally, existing regulation of Internet activity delineates between the creators of content and the platforms and providers who serve that content to consumers. Under current law, providers are shielded from liability in most circumstances for content they serve but do not create, while they are also given latitude to moderate the content (e.g., CRS 2024). Online generative AI services blur the conceptual distinctions underpinning this law. When a generative AI summarizes an article and posts it online instead of a human, is the AI a content creator? If so, are AI algorithm operators themselves liable for harm like defamation that may originate in the initial article? Holding operators liable for such uses of their technology could greatly limit generative AI adoption, even in places where it is beneficial (Perault 2023). Conversely, the link between AI data inputs and outputs is often opaque; in such situations, if AI systems operators are not held liable, then enforcement of liability against other parties may be impracticable (Bambauer and Surdeanu 2023).

In summary, many of AI's most profound potential effects are closely linked to the ways in which it tests existing delineations of ownership rights and liability. Economics has a long history of demonstrating just how important those choices about ownership rights and liability can be. As policymakers and courts consider their options for addressing AI-related issues, they will benefit from taking these economic forces into account.

Competition and Market Structure

Competition creates incentives that increase economic welfare and, as President Biden has stressed, lower costs. It pushes firms to lower prices, raise wages, and create higher-quality products (the combination of lower prices and higher wages suggests that competition can reduce economic rents that occur amid insufficient competition). And although its relationship with innovation is complicated, competition generally encourages innovation at the technological frontier (Aghion et al. 2005; Bloom, Van Reenen, and Williams 2019). In markets without robust competition, firms have the ability to increase their own profits or advance their other interests at the expense of others by raising prices, reducing production, or strategically underinvesting in quality, customer service, or innovation. Because lower competition is typically associated with higher profits, firms may be incentivized to merge, to foreclose rivals, or to take other actions in order to undermine competition. Mergers and some types of conduct that reduce competition are illegal under antitrust laws, but the government also shapes markets and influences competition through regulation and its own conduct as a market participant.

As last year's *Economic Report of the President* discussed, the economics of competition are particularly complex in digital markets (CEA 2023). AI is widely used in many of these digital markets, including to set prices in platform markets, to optimize content on social media, and to optimize inventory levels. However, because of their widespread and growing adoption, AI systems are also present in many markets outside digital platforms.

In all these cases, the addition of AI can have positive or negative effects on competition. In many cases, it can create better products and lower costs. In some cases, the adoption of AI systems can also increase competition by making it easier for new firms to enter or by lowering switching costs. For example, AI-powered machine translation can reduce language barriers, allowing greater international competition (Brynjolfsson, Hui, and Liu 2019). Similarly, AI can alleviate other barriers by making it easier to convert computer code from one language to another, or enter into software development (e.g., Roziere et al. 2020; Weisz et al. 2022; Peng et al. 2023). Conversely, AI integrations might inappropriately reduce competition by increasing the barriers to switching providers and thus locking in customers who use their services. Data or integration methods locked to proprietary AI models, for example, can create such barriers.

AI can also be used as a tool for either tacit or explicit collusion that can harm competition. AI systems may make it less costly for firms to closely track and respond to the behavior of rivals or facilitate sharing competitively sensitive information to which competing firms otherwise would not be privy, factors that make it easier to sustain collusion (Tirole 1988). They may also make it simpler for firms to engage in complex multimarket interactions that also can facilitate collusion (Bernheim and Whinston 1990). Recent research suggests that these pricing algorithms may actually learn collusion as the optimal outcome of their profit-maximizing algorithm (Calvano et al. 2020; Johnson and Sokol 2020; Abada and Lambin 2023).

"Learning by doing" is an economically important process in many markets (e.g., Arrow 1962; Thompson 2010), and it has particularly important implications for competition in many AI markets. On one hand, such learning improves the product, creating positive network effects that can, in turn, attract more users and lead to a virtuous cycle that benefits consumers (Gregory et al. 2021). On the other hand, the same network effects that can create product improvements can also drive smaller firms out of the market, leaving a market with only a handful of dominant players. And, in the long run, such network effects may also dampen future innovation and competition by raising barriers to entry. Even entrants that have better or more efficient underlying technology may struggle to attract users if they lack the data to appropriately tailor their products (Werden 2001; Farrell and Klemperer 2007). Finally, some AI systems automate feedback loops to continuously improve, in effect automating the learning-by-doing process. Such automation likely strengthens network effects, in turn increasing potential consequences, both positive and negative.

In addition to AI's effects on other markets, competition between AI providers will be important for AI's deployment and ultimate impact. In some markets, entry costs are relatively modest, data are widely available, and network effects are not too strong. In such markets, competition may be robust and involve many small providers. Similarly, some AI systems will be developed internally by firms that do not specialize in the technology, but who use it to support their overall business. Multitiered integrations are also likely, such as for systems in which general-purpose models interface with other, more specialized add-on tools.[30] In other cases, however, some combination of high entry costs, data availability, and network effects may drive markets toward having only a small number of players. Markets for generative AI products, which require huge amounts of data and computing power to train, may be particularly prone to this issue, with some even suggesting that such markets may naturally trend toward monopoly (Narechania 2022). There is an inherent economic trade-off between the cost of entry and the benefits of increased competition, but appropriate government policy can help ensure that a monopoly outcome is not a foregone conclusion.

Competition inside a market is also affected by competition in adjacent markets. For example, even if there are many aluminum can suppliers, competition may be weak if there is only one supplier of the aluminum itself. In this way, supply chains are only as competitive as their least competitive link, a so-called competitive bottleneck. Firms may also participate in multiple markets through vertical integration or exclusive contracting. In such situations, firms may use a dominant position in one market to undermine competition in another (Ordover, Saloner, and Salop 1990; Moresi and Schwartz 2021). Furthermore, self-preferencing by vertically integrated firms can result in inferior technologies being adopted even in the long run (Katz and Shapiro 1986).

Scholars have suggested that all these concerns may be particularly acute in digital platforms and AI markets (Athey and Scott Morton 2022; Vipra and Korinek 2023). For example, many AI-related products have been built by organizations with ties to existing large technology firms that themselves are increasingly vertically integrated across the AI stack. Similarly, some inputs necessary to create AI systems are controlled by a small number

---

[30] For example, several foundation model providers have released libraries that allow their services to be easily integrated into other software, including other AI models (e.g., Anthropic 2024; OpenAI 2024).

of companies, raising concerns about the potential for competitive bottle-necks. For example, the design, production, and equipment used to produce the specialty chips needed to power AI computing are each controlled by a handful of firms, as is the provision of cloud computing (Narechania and Sitaraman 2023).

AI policy will have a large role in ensuring healthy and competitive markets, protecting consumers of AI outputs, workers who use AI systems, and other market participants. Competition-aware policy can avoid inadvertently increasing barriers to entry while ensuring that some providers are not unduly favored over others. Antitrust enforcement will play a critical role, but so too will other government policies.

Broadly, ex ante regulation or other policies can improve efficiency relative to ex post antitrust enforcement by offering certainty to businesses and avoiding costly ex-post remedies (Ottaviani and Wickelgren 2011). At the same time, such ex ante policies could backfire if poorly conceived or executed. Developing standards in an open and transparent manner can avoid inadvertently favoring a market's incumbents or making it difficult for smaller firms to comply or enter.

Similarly, freely available and portable data may encourage a competitive landscape and ensure that gains from data are widely distributed. Market participants often have an incentive to maintain proprietary data. Data can be copied at low cost, and productive improvements from data may be easily replicated, so firms are likely to compete away gains from publicly available sources. However, reliance on proprietary data could cause fragmented AI markets to emerge. If each firm can access only a small portion of the available data, AI systems may not function as well as they otherwise could. This has been an ongoing problem in pharmaceutical research (Schneider et al. 2020) and is increasingly an issue on the Internet, where content and user data are often locked into proprietary tools and applications. Increased availability of public data, such as that produced by the Federal Government, may encourage more competition. Restrictions on what data may remain proprietary and appropriate regulations on how AI companies can use the data collected from their users may do the same.

Additionally, policies that encourage portability and interoperability can reduce barriers to competition (Brown 2020). Market providers generally have an incentive to reduce customer switching, and systems that encourage locking in may be developed to gain an anticompetitive advantage. Interoperability requirements make switching providers easier, reducing firms' ability to gain an advantage through lock-in. In labor markets, firm strategies—such as noncompete agreements, training repayment agreements, and other methods—can tie workers to specific firms; however, these tactics could also limit competition in markets for AI skills. The sophisticated skills needed to develop and work with AI systems can only be put to best use throughout the economy if workers can transition freely in competitive labor markets, and so policies that reduce labor market barriers could improve competition in markets for AI itself.

Finally, sharing competitively sensitive information through AI systems can undermine competition and pose risks to firms under existing antitrust laws. Government efforts to educate firms about these risks and to promote sound antitrust compliance policies can reduce the possibility that AI technologies will be used to lessen competition.

In summary, the policies needed to encourage competition go well beyond the traditional tools of merger or monopolization analysis. Competition will be affected by the choices the Federal Government makes to regulate AI and its markets. The correct approach requires consideration of the sophisticated ways in which individual markets interact with the technological landscape and learning lessons from past instances in which new technologies were not regulated to promote competition at the outset. The Biden-Harris Administration has released new competition guidance encouraging the Federal Government's agencies to consider these issues in their analyses of regulations (OMB 2023a), and the Office of Management and Budget (OMB 2023b) has encouraged agencies to consider competition in their use and procurement of AI tools. This holistic framing may be particularly important as the role of AI in the economy grows. (See box 7-3.)

Labor Market Institutions

AI has real potential to transform the labor market. The empirical case for permanent market displacement is limited, but the transition to an economy that thoroughly incorporates AI could displace many workers from their existing jobs, create many new types of jobs, and affect the work of others dramatically. What labor market features will be most important to protecting workers in the transition, and what features will help ensure they are prepared to use AI?

In part, policies that reduce AI's disruptive effects on labor markets are the same ones that encourage efficient and responsible AI investment. Encouraging innovation, reducing regulatory uncertainty, and supporting needed human capital investment are all important goals of AI policy. Responsible stewardship of the economy as a whole is also important, as the negative effects on workers of job displacement are considerably magnified by weak economic conditions (Davis and von Wachter 2011).

In practice, the negative effects of technological and regulatory change are often quite concentrated on specific industries, occupations, and geographic regions. The experience of trade liberalization has shown that negative effects of job displacement can persist for many years and spill over to local economies (Autor, Dorn, and Hanson 2013, 2021). Many policy

Box 7-3. What Can Voluntary AI Agreements Accomplish?

The Biden-Harris Administration announced voluntary agreements covering cybersecurity, algorithmic discrimination, output watermarking, and other issues with seven leading artificial intelligence companies in July 2023; the agreement now covers fifteen companies (White House 2023b). The agreements were a step toward creating the first AI-specific guidelines and guardrails at a critical time. They demonstrated not only the industry participants' interest and willingness to work toward the common good, but also their belief that it is possible to make progress through open dialogue, unilateral action, and social norms. Still, the agreements are unlikely to be a long-term solution.

Meaningful voluntary commitments are rare in the private sector. If taking an action is in a firm's unilateral interest, no commitment is necessary. If the action is not in the firm's unilateral best interest, the company will have an incentive to avoid making such a commitment.

The features that make agreements meaningful can also provide the incentive to change course later. For example, the existence of a voluntary agreement can create opportunities for new entrants. These new firms may decline to make the commitment and may use that flexibility to outcompete committed firms (Brau and Carraro 1999). Existing firms may respond to competition by dropping out of an agreement or abandoning its limiting principles.

The recent voluntary agreement covers major players in generative AI. These markets feature many barriers to entry (Federal Trade Commission 2023), making them a relatively favorable environment for voluntary agreements to form and be sustained. Other AI market segments that lack similar barriers may be less amenable to voluntary cooperation.

options for addressing AI substitution are similar to those suggested in the context of past economic shocks.

Recent trade shocks have predominantly affected people in areas that became subject to new import competition. Analogously, AI's effects are likely to be felt most acutely in places where AI-exposed workers live. The CEA has mapped its occupation-level measure of AI exposure to workers' places of residence, showing where exposure is most likely to have localized effects. As figure 7-10 indicates, in the most AI-exposed regions, the average worker's neighborhood is more than three times as dense as it is in the least exposed regions. However, the story is somewhat different for workers whose jobs have low performance requirements. Both the most exposed and least exposed areas to this type of work are relatively dense, and less dense areas are often in the middle of the exposure distribution.

The evidence suggests that AI's effects are likely to be felt most strongly in urban areas. This finding is consistent with other recent research demonstrating that a preponderance of innovation, along with a large fraction of new work, occurs in cities (Lin 2011; Gruber, Johnson, and Moretti 2023). Conversely, to the extent that exposure with a low average level of required activity performance captures the possibility of job substitution, the evidence suggests that only a subset of urban areas may experience negative effects from widespread job displacement. Prior research suggests one likely reason for the pattern: Occupational segregation is high, and overall economic residential segregation has increased over time (Florida and Mellander 2015; Bischoff and Reardon 2013). While some workers in urban areas may become more productive as a result of AI, others could be displaced, and the two sets of workers may live in different neighborhoods, with differing implications for policy. And although greater job access in dense urban labor markets may make it relatively easy for workers to weather economic disruptions, evidence also suggests that at the local level, the effect of competing with many displaced individuals can outweigh the effect of increased nearby opportunities (Haller and Heuermann 2020). In short, although evidence about geographically concentrated AI exposure is limited, there is reason to believe that targeted place-based policies could play a useful role, much as they play a role in other contexts such as clean energy transitions (CEA 2022).

Figure 7-10. Average Population Density by Decile of Geographic AI Exposure
Weighted average population per square mile

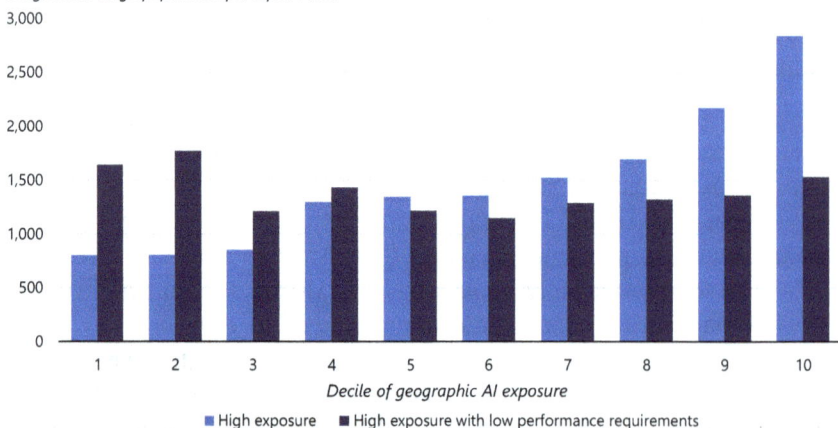

Decile of geographic AI exposure

■ High exposure   ■ High exposure with low performance requirements

Council of Economic Advisers

Sources: American Community Survey; Department of Labor; Pew Research Center; CEA calculations.
Note: Average density is the population-weighted geometric mean density of each workers' census tract of residence. Geographic units are public-use microdata areas. Average population per square mile is the population-weighted geometric mean density of Census tracts in each unit. Analysis uses full-time, full-year workers age 16 plus. Performance requirements are captured using the O*NET data measuring degree of difficulty or complexity at which a high AI-exposed work activity is performed within an occupation. Low indicates an average degree of difficulty below the median.
2024 Economic Report of the President

Individual firms will play a major role in training their employees to work with AI, particularly in cases where firms use customized systems or adopt foundation models in unique ways. However, government can help ensure that the training benefits workers. Economists distinguish general human capital, which can be put to broad productive use, and firm-specific human capital, which is not portable. Because many AI models are purpose-built for a particular firm's needs, many of the skills workers need to use the models will likely be firm-specific or learned on the job. Economic theory has shown that firm-specific human capital gives employers labor market power over their employees and can allow them to keep wages low (Acemoglu and Pischke 1998). In contrast, because general human capital is portable, it gives employers no additional market power, and firms have a lower incentive to invest in it.

The Biden-Harris Administration has made record investments to encourage general human capital training through registered apprenticeships—and recently proposed to further expand and modernize the National Apprenticeship System (White House 2023c; DOL 2023b). Registered apprenticeships provide firms with resources to invest in workers' skills and provide opportunities for workers to learn on the job with a mentor while getting paid. They also establish standards to ensure the resulting human capital is portable and of high quality. Firms propose and register an apprenticeship program in an approved occupation; the set of apprenticeable occupations already includes many that are likely to work with AI technologies. Through increased flexibility, improved processes, and better data collection, the proposed improvements to the Registered Apprenticeship System would help to ensure that workers can develop the skills they need to work with AI.

Unions can also help develop workers' skills and protect their livelihoods. Unions counteract the effects of employers' labor market power and have been shown to yield increased worker training (Booth and Chatterji 1998; Green, Machin, and Wilkinson 1999). More generally, giving workers a voice in how AI is used may help ensure that they benefit from its use. Collective bargaining has empowered workers to secure protections related to the use of AI, such as the protections for screenwriters and actors secured in their respective union contracts (WGAW 2023; SAG-AFTRA 2023). The engagement of frontline workers on the development of AI could also have beneficial effects on the successful deployment of these systems (Kochan et al. 2023). Unions can also have many other economic effects, including positive effects on compensation for workers, as well as effects on firm incentives to substitute capital for labor and to engage in research and development (e.g., Hirsch 2004; Knepper 2020; U.S. Department of the Treasury 2023). The net effect of these incentives on AI adoption is unclear and is likely to depend on the particular structure of unionized industries (Haucap and Wey 2004).

The Federal Government can help ensure workers displaced by AI are prepared to take their next steps in the economy both indirectly and directly through Federal investment and programs. One critical indirect mechanism that exists to ensure smooth labor transitions is the unemployment insurance program. Unemployment insurance keeps workers economically stable, and it encourages them to find new employment rather than leave the labor force. Finding new, high-quality jobs for displaced workers may take time, and a flexible unemployment insurance system allows workers to search for higher-paying and better jobs (Chetty 2008; Schmieder, von Wachter, and Bender 2012; Nekoei and Weber 2017).

The government can also help workers transition to new careers directly by combining unemployment insurance with explicit training and reemployment services. This approach is currently embodied by the Reemployment Services and Eligibility Assessment Grants program (DOL 2023c). It has also been used to assist workers losing their jobs to foreign competition via the Trade Adjustment Assistance (TAA) Program, which has expired for new beneficiaries.[31] Recent research using worker-level administrative data suggests that displaced workers who are approved for TAA increase their cumulative earnings by tens of thousands of dollars in the years following the program (Hyman 2022). This research also finds suggestive evidence that the skills learned from TAA may depreciate over time, an area of concern as AI technology rapidly evolves. Policymakers could build upon lessons learned from TAA to revitalize and expand a program for displaced workers that accommodates AI-related displacement as a way to ensure that workers remain in the labor force and are able to work productively with AI. (See box 7-4.)

Measuring AI and Its Effects

A common thread among the various questions and policies outlined above is that they require observability. If the government cannot observe the ways and extents to which AI is being used, it may be difficult to enforce existing laws and to target and implement new regulations. Similarly, the government is constrained in its ability to assist workers who are displaced by AI if it cannot observe who these workers are. Policies that improve observability or increase data collection may have a high impact if they allow the government to identify AI adoption when it occurs, distinguish AI-generated outputs from human-generated ones, and measure more precisely the economic effects of AI.

---

[31] See CRS (2023b). The TAA program's termination provisions took effect in July 2022 after Congress declined to renew funding for the program.

Box 7-4. Should AI Be Taxed?

Artificial intelligence has the capacity to increase productivity, but it may do so while displacing many workers from their current jobs or exacerbating inequality. Technology industry leaders, the European Parliament, and others have therefore suggested taxing the use of AI and related technologies. They argue that an AI tax could fund training for displaced workers and potentially reduce overall inequality (Quartz 2017; European Parliament Committee on Legal Affairs 2017; Abbott and Bogenschneider 2018).

Economists generally consider the proposed AI tax analogously to other taxes on capital as a production factor. Because some capital is durable, deciding whether to invest in it may impact productivity and growth in the future. Correspondingly, a tax that disincentivizes capital investment has the potential to be especially costly. The concern is especially salient for general purpose technologies like AI, as one of their functions is to increase existing capital's reusability (Aghion, Howitt, and Violante 2002). A lengthy literature has considered the optimal rate of capital taxation for balancing economic growth against other features of the economy and of existing tax policy (e.g., Diamond and Saez 2011; Saez and Stantcheva 2018). Rich frameworks that incorporate borrowing constraints, uncertainty, and other real-world features typically find that the optimal way to fund fiscal policy is through a mix of taxes, including on capital.

Economists have recently considered how an additional tax on AI adoption could affect both impacted workers and overall economic well-being. The effective U.S. capital taxation rate has declined in recent years, which some have argued could encourage excessive negative employment impacts through automation (Acemoglu, Manera, and Restrepo 2020). However, these researchers also argue that setting appropriate capital and labor tax rates may sufficiently ensure that excessive automation does not occur, as increased AI-specific tax rates only serve a purpose if it is infeasible to alter these broader capital tax rates. Other recent research considers technology's declining cost trend and its differential effect on present versus future workers. These papers find that taxing AI in excess of other capital can be beneficial in the short run but not in the long run (Guerreiro, Rebelo, and Teles 2022; Thuemmel 2022).

How might taxation affect AI-related innovation itself? Evidence from historical patent data suggests that inventors respond to taxation-based incentives, both in how much they innovate and in where they do so (Akcigit et al. 2021). Software-related patents, including for AI technology, comprise roughly half of those issued today, and this patenting activity is particularly geographically clustered (Chattergoon and Kerr 2021). Taxes on AI adoption and innovation may therefore have implications for overall growth, place-based policies, and other initiatives.

Observing AI adoption and measuring its effects is inherently challenging. This is in part because firms that adopt AI do so in many ways. They may have service contracts with large technology providers, make use of purchased or open source tools with proprietary data, engage in in-house model development, or purchase inputs for which AI is only one component. AI models may be large, in the sense of containing many parameters and being trained on large volumes of data, or they may be small. And, the potential negative effects of AI may be closely linked to the model's actions, or they may be further afield in upstream or downstream markets. Nonetheless, the Federal Government is taking and has taken steps to improve observability of AI adoption.

To address certain risks to safety and security, the recent Executive Order identifies reporting thresholds for very large AI models based on the number of arithmetic operations used to train them (White House 2023a). These thresholds may be well suited to identify providers in certain segments of the AI market in the future, such as large language models. Identifying such providers may be sufficient to identify and address some kinds of AI-related risks. At the same time, substantively all effects from AI adoption so far—including negative effects, such as discrimination—have been associated with models that did not meet these thresholds (e.g., Brown et al. 2020). More generally, in many economic contexts, there is little reason to believe that the potential for negative effects from an AI model is proportional to its underlying scale. So, although arithmetic reporting thresholds have value, and additional thresholds could be implemented in the future, other approaches are also necessary to address the wide range of AI-related risks.

The Executive Order also directs agencies to consider methods of identifying AI-generated outputs such as watermarking and content detection. These approaches could help observe and measure some types of AI usage. If watermarking requirements are sufficient to identify the origins of an AI output, then harmful outputs can also be traced back to their creators. However, the practical uses of watermarking are likely limited to generative AI outputs that are widely distributed. Many other uses of AI in economic activity are not directly observable outside the firms where they occur. Also, enforcement of watermarking requirements may be difficult unless the generative AI models used to produce these outputs have already been identified, or an alternative method of content detection is successfully implemented.

A complementary approach may be to identify the workers and other parties who are most likely to be affected by AI. Surveys of firms already collect some information about AI adoption (Zolas et al. 2020), and data from administrative processes are used to produce many other economic statistics that could be useful. However, current gaps in data collection significantly limit some uses of these data. For example, occupation is a key dimension along which exposure to AI is likely to have a labor market impact, so policies that target vulnerable or displaced workers based on their occupation could play an important role in the overall policy responses to AI.[32] However, linking workers with their occupations consistently is challenging. Surveys that include occupation are subject to substantial measurement error, and programs such as unemployment insurance often have difficulty collecting this information in a standardized way (Fisher and Houseworth 2013; DOL 2023a). Furthermore, even the best sources of administrative data on workers in the United States do not include information on their occupations. Additional administrative processes or enhanced surveys may address gaps in government data collection, making it easier to implement policies that effectively target and assist affected workers.

Conclusions and Open Questions

AI has the potential to increase economic well-being. Like many previous technologies, it will do so by transforming the economy in both expected and unexpected ways. Economic theory demonstrates that the changes have the capacity to benefit everyone, but recent empirical evidence shows that broad-based benefits are not guaranteed. Sensible policies to encourage responsible innovation, protect consumers, empower workers, encourage competition, and help affected workers adjust are critical.

Many open questions remain, and the Biden-Harris Administration is working continuously to seek answers to these questions and incorporate the lessons it learns into its regulatory and policy responses. In 2022, the White House's Office of Science and Technology Policy released its Blueprint for an AI Bill of Rights, which highlights five principles covering many of the most pressing concerns about AI (White House 2022). Agencies throughout the Federal Government are taking steps to implement the blueprint's recommendations. The National AI Advisory Committee, launched in May 2022, has engaged leaders from industry and academia to consider major policy questions and make recommendations (NAIAC 2023). The National Institute of Standards and Technology has launched the U.S. AI Safety Institute to enable collaboration on safety and security standards (NIST 2023). And the President's Executive Order 14110 has identified key government agencies and bodies to oversee and advise on numerous other AI-related issues. The order directs the identified organizations to study AI-related needs and make recommendations for additional tools required to address them (White House 2023a).

---

[32] For example, policies that target specific occupations could in many cases reduce the administrative burden and practical difficulty of demonstrating displacement.

The future path of technological change is always uncertain, but the Biden-Harris Administration is working to ensure that the Nation's institutions and policies are prepared for the changes that AI will bring. As AI's role in the economy grows, the Federal Government will need to continually evaluate its institutional framework. Only by thinking broadly about AI and its effects can society balance the technology's potential for harm against its many possible benefits.

★ ★ ★ ★ ★ ★

References

Chapter 1

Aaronson, S., M. Daly, W. Wascher, and D. Wilcox. 2019. *Okun Revisited: Who Benefits Most from a Strong Economy?* Finance and Economics Discussion Series 2019-072. Washington: Board of Governors of the Federal Reserve System. https://doi.org/10.17016/FEDS.2019.072.

Aaronson, S., F. Galbis-Reig, T. Cajner, C. Smith, B. Fallick, and W. Wascher. 2014. "Labor Force Participation: Recent Developments and Future Prospects." *Brookings Papers on Economic Activity* 2: 197–275. https://muse.jhu.edu/pub/11/article/577366/pdf.

Ashenfelter, O., Card, D., Farber, H., and Ransom, M. 2022. "Monopsony in the Labor Market: New Empirical Results and New Public Policies." *Journal of Human Resources* 57. https://doi.org/10.3368/jhr.monopsony.special-issue-2022-introduction.

Autor, D., A. Dube, and A. McGrew. 2023. *The Unexpected Compression: Competition at Work in the Low Wage Labor Market.* NBER Working Paper 31010. Cambridge, MA: National Bureau for Economic Research. https://www.nber.org/papers/w31010.

Baker, D., and J. Bernstein. 2013. *Getting Back to Full Employment: A Better Bargain for Working People.* Washington: Center for Economic Policy Research. https://cepr.net/documents/Getting-Back-to-Full-Employment_20131118.pdf.

Barlevy, G. J. Faberman, B. Hobijn, and A. Şahin. 2023. *The Shifting Reasons for Beveridge-Curve Shifts.* NBER Working Paper 31783. Cambridge, MA: National Bureau of Economic Research. https://doi.org/10.3386/w31783.

Barnichon, R., and A. Shapiro. 2022. "What's the Best Measure of Economic Slack?" *Federal Reserve Bank of San Francisco Economic Letter*, no. 4. https://www.frbsf.org/wp-content/uploads/sites/4/el2022-04.pdf.

Barrero, J., N. Bloom, S. Davis, B. Meyer, and E. Mihaylov. 2022. *The Shift to Remote Work Lessens Wage-Growth Pressures.* NBER Working Paper 30197. Cambridge, MA: National Bureau of Economic Research. https://www.nber.org/papers/w30197.

Benigno, P., and G. Eggertsson. 2023. *It's Baaack: The Surge in Inflation in the 2020s and the Return of the Non-Linear Phillips Curve.* NBER Working Paper 31197.

Cambridge, MA: National Bureau of Economic Research. https://www.nber.org/papers/w31197.

Berger, D., K. Herkenhoff, and S. Mongey. 2022. "Labor Market Power." *American Economic Review* 112, no. 4: 1147–93. https://doi.org/10.1257/aer.20191521.

Bernstein, J. 2012. "Raise the Economy's Speed Limit." *New York Times*, December 5. https://www.nytimes.com/2012/12/06/opinion/a-slow-growth-rate-is-the-real-threat.html?_r=0.

Bernstein, J., and K. Bentele. 2019. "The Increasing Benefits and Diminished Costs of Running a High-Pressure Labor Market." Center on Budget and Policy Priorities. https://www.cbpp.org/sites/default/files/atoms/files/5-15-19fe.pdf.

Bjelland, M., B. Fallick, J. Haltiwanger, and E. McEntarfer. 2011. "Employer-to-Employer Flows in the United States: Estimates Using Linked Employer-Employee Data." *Journal of Business and Economic Statistics* 29, no. 4: 493–505. https://ideas.repec.org/a/bes/jnlbes/v29i4y2011p493-505.html.

Blanchard, O., A. Domash, and L. Summers. 2022. "Bad News for the Fed from the Beveridge Space." Peterson Institute for International Economics, Policy Brief 22–7. http://dx.doi.org/10.2139/ssrn.4174601.

BLS (U.S. Bureau of Labor Statistics). 2024. "Annual Work Stoppages Involving 1,000 or More Workers, 1947–Present." https://www.bls.gov/web/wkstp/annual-listing.htm.

Bok, B., C. Nekarda, N. Petrosky-Nadeau, and R. Crump. 2023. *Estimating Natural Rates of Unemployment: A Primer.* Working Paper 2023–25. San Francisco: Federal Reserve Bank of San Francisco. https://doi.org/10.24148/wp2023-25.

Bosler, C., and N. Petrosky-Nadeau. 2016. "Job-to-Job Transitions in an Evolving Labor Market." *Federal Reserve Board of San Francisco Economic Letter*, no. 34. https://www.frbsf.org/wp-content/uploads/el2016-34.pdf.

Burdett, K., and D. Mortensen. 1998. "Wage Differentials, Employer Size, and Unemployment." *International Economic Review* 39, no. 2: 257–73. https://www.jstor.org/stable/2527292.

Cajner, T., J. Coglianese, and J. Montes. 2021. *The Long-Lived Cyclicality of the Labor Force Participation Rate.* Finance and Economics Discussion Series 2017-047. Washington: Board of Governors of the Federal Reserve System. https://doi.org/10.17016/FEDS.2021.047.

Cajner, T., T. Radler, D. Ratner, and I. Vidangos. 2017. *Racial Gaps in Labor Market Outcomes in the Last Four Decades and over the Business Cycle.* Finance and Economics Discussion Series 2017-01. Washington: Board of Governors of the Federal Reserve System. https://doi.org/10.17016/FEDS.2017.071.

Card, D., A. Cardoso, J. Heining, and P. Kline. 2018. "Firms and Labor Market Inequality: Evidence and Some Theory." *Journal of Labor Economics* 36, no. S1. https://doi.org/10.1086/694153.

CEA (Council of Economic Advisers). 2014. 'The Labor Force Participation Rate Since 2007: Causes and Policy Implications." https://obamawhitehouse.archives.gov/sites/default/files/docs/labor_force_participation_report.pdf.

———. 2016a. *Economic Report of the President*. Washington: U.S. Government Publishing Office. https://www.whitehouse.gov/wp-content/uploads/2021/07/2016-ERP.pdf.

———. 2016b. "Labor Market Monopsony: Trends, Consequences, and Policy Responses." https://obamawhitehouse.archives.gov/sites/default/files/page/files/20161025_monopsony_labor_mrkt_cea.pdf.

———. 2021. "The Pandemic's Effect on Measured Wage Growth." https://www.whitehouse.gov/cea/written-materials/2021/04/19/the-pandemics-effect-on-measured-wage-growth/.

———. 2022. *Economic Report of the President*. Washington: U.S. Government Publishing Office. https://www.whitehouse.gov/wp-content/uploads/2022/04/ERP-2022.pdf.

———. 2023a. "Disinflation Explanation: Supply, Demand, and Their Interaction." https://www.whitehouse.gov/cea/written-materials/2023/11/30/disinflation-explanation-supply-demand-and-their-interaction.

———. 2023b. *Economic Report of the President*. Washington: U.S. Government Publishing Office. https://www.whitehouse.gov/wp-content/uploads/2023/03/ERP-2023.pdf.

———. 2023c. "Did Stabilization Funds Help Mothers Get Back to Work After the COVID-19 Recession?" Working Paper. https://www.whitehouse.gov/wp-content/uploads/2023/11/Child-Care-Stabilization.pdf.

Charles, K., and J. Guryan. 2008. "Prejudice and Wages: An Empirical Assessment of Becker's *The Economics of Discrimination*." *Journal of Political Economy* 116, no. 5: 773–809. https://doi.org/10.1086/593073.

Crump, R., S. Eusepi, M. Giannoni, and A. Şahin. 2019. *A Unified Approach to Measuring U**. NBER Working Paper 25930. Cambridge, MA: National Bureau of Economic Research. https://doi.org/10.3386/w25930.

Crump, R., C. Nekarda, and N. Petrosky-Nadeau. 2020. *Unemployment Rate Benchmarks*. Finance and Economics Discussion Series 2020-072. Washington: Board of Governors of the Federal Reserve System. https://doi.org/10.17016/FEDS.2020.072.

Cumming, C. 2021. "The Importance of Anti-Discrimination Enforcement for a Fair and Equitable U.S. Labor Market and Broadly Shared Economic Growth." Washington Center for Equitable Growth. https://equitablegrowth.org/wp-content/uploads/2022/01/122121-anti-discrimination-enf-ib.pdf.

Daly, M., and B. Hobijn. 2017. "Composition and Aggregate Real Wage Growth." *American Economic Review* 107, no. 5: 349–52. https://doi.org/10.1257/aer.p20171075.

Daly, M., B. Hobijn, A. Şahin, and R. Valletta. 2011. "A Rising Natural Rate of Unemployment: Permanent or Transitory?" Working Paper, Tinbergen Institute. https://www.frbsf.org/wp-content/uploads/wp11-05bk.pdf.

Davis, S., J. Faberman, and J. Haltiwanger. 2013. "The Establishment-Level Behavior of Vacancies and Hiring." *Quarterly Journal of Economics* 128, no. 2: 581–622. https://doi.org/10.1093/qje/qjt002.

DiNardo, J., N. Fortin, and T. Lemieux. 1996. "Labor Market Institutions and the Distribution of Wages, 1973–1992: A Semiparametric Approach." *Econometrica* 64, no.5: 1001–44. https://doi.org/10.2307/2171954.

Elsby, M., R. Michaels, and D. Ratner. 2015. "The Beveridge Curve: A Survey." *Journal of Economic Literature* 53, no. 3: 571–630. https://doi.org/10.1257/jel.53.3.571.

Faccini, R., and L. Melosi. 2023. *Job-to-Job Mobility and Inflation.* Chicago Fed Working Paper 2023-03. Chicago: Federal Reserve Bank of Chicago. https://www.chicagofed.org/publications/working-papers/2023/2023-03.

Figura, A., and C. Waller. 2022. "What Does the Beveridge Curve Tell Us About the Likelihood of a Soft Landing?" FEDS Notes. Board of Governors of the Federal Reserve System. https://doi.org/10.17016/2380-7172.3190.

Fleischman, C., and J. Roberts. 2011. "From Many Series, One Cycle: Improved Estimates of the Business Cycle from a Multivariate Unobserved Components Model." FEDS Working Paper 2011-46. Board of Governors of the Federal Reserve System. https://papers.ssrn.com/sol3/papers.cfm?abstract_id=1957379.

Furman, J., and W. Powell. 2021. "What Is the Best Measure of Labor Market Tightness?" Peterson Institute for International Economics, Realtime Economics. https://www.piie.com/blogs/realtime-economic-issues-watch/what-best-measure-labor-market-tightness.

Galbraith, J. 2001. "The Surrender of Economic Policy." *American Prospect*, December 19. https://prospect.org/economy/surrender-economic-policy/.

Ganong, P., and D. Shoag. 2017. "Why Has Regional Income Convergence in the U.S. Declined?" *Journal of Urban Economics* 102: 76–90. https://doi.org/10.1016/j.jue.2017.07.002.

Gittleman, M. 2022. "The 'Great Resignation' in Perspective." U.S. Bureau of Labor Statistics, *Monthly Labor Review*. https://doi.org/10.21916/mlr.2022.20.

Haltiwanger, J., H. Hyatt, L. Khan, and E. McEntarfer. 2018. "Cyclical Job Ladders by Firm Size and Firm Wage." *American Economic Journal: Macroeconomics* 10, no. 2. 52–85. https://doi.org/10.1257/mac.20150245.

Hansen, S., P. Lambert, N. Bloom, S. Davis, R. Sadun, and B. Taska. 2023. *Remote Work Across Jobs, Companies, and Space.* NBER Working Paper 31007. Cambridge, MA: National Bureau of Economic Research. https://doi.org/10.3386/w31007.

Hazell, J., J. Herreño, E. Nakamura, and J. Steinsson. 2022. "The Slope of the Phillips Curve: Evidence from U.S. States." *Quarterly Journal of Economics* 137, no. 3: 1299–344. https://doi.org/10.1093/qje/qjac010.

Historical Register: Containing and Impartial Relation of All Transactions, Foreign and Domestick 16. 1731. London: Sun Fire Office.

Hobjin, B., and A. Şahin. 2021. *Maximum Employment and the Participation Cycle.* NBER Working Paper 29222. Cambridge, MA: National Bureau of Economic Research. https://doi.org/10.3386/w29222.

Hornstein, A., M. Kudlyak, and F. Lange. 2014. "Measuring Resource Utilization in the Labor Market." *Economic Quarterly* 100, no. 1: 1–21. https://www.richmondfed.org/-/media/RichmondFedOrg/publications/research/economic_quarterly/2014/q1/pdf/hornstein.pdf.

Karahan, F., R. Michaels, B. Pugsley, A. Şahin, and R. Schuh. 2017. "Do Job-to-Job Transitions Drive Wage Fluctuations over the Business Cycle?" *American Economic Review* 107, no. 5: 353–57. https://doi.org/10.1257/aer.p20171076.

Kline, P., E. Rose, and C. Walters. 2022. "Systemic Discrimination Among Large U.S. Employers." *Quarterly Journal of Economics* 137, no. 4: 1963–2036. https://doi.org/10.1093/qje/qjac024.

Kudlyak, M. 2017. "Measuring Labor Utilization: The Non-Employment Index." *Federal Reserve Bank of San Francisco, Economic Letter*, no. 8. https://www.frbsf.org/wp-content/uploads/sites/4/el2017-08.pdf.

Kurtulus, F. 2015. "The Impact of Affirmative Action on the Employment of Minorities and Women: A Longitudinal Analysis Using Three Decades of EEO-1 Filings." *Journal of Policy Analysis and Management* 35, no. 1: 34–66. https://doi.org/10.1002/pam.21881.

Lang, K., and J. Lehmann. 2012. "Racial Discrimination in the Labor Market: Theory and Empirics." *Journal of Economic Literature* 50, no. 4: 959–1006. https://doi.org/10.1257/jel.50.4.959.

Manning, A. 2003. *Monopsony in Motion: Imperfect Competition in Labor Markets.* Princeton, NJ: Princeton University Press. https://press.princeton.edu/books/paperback/9780691123288/monopsony-in-motion.

———. 2021. "Monopsony in Labor Markets: A Review." *ILR Review* 74, no. 1: 3–26. https://doi.org/10.1177/0019793920922499.

McLeay, M., and S. Tenreyro. 2019. *Optimal Inflation and the Identification of the Phillips Curve.* NBER Working Paper 25892. Cambridge, MA: National Bureau of Economic Research. https://doi.org/10.3386/w25892.

Miller, C., and E. Tedeschi. 2019. "Single Mothers Are Surging Into the Work Force." *New York Times*, May 29. https://www.nytimes.com/2019/05/29/upshot/single-mothers-surge-employment.html.

Moscarini, G., and F. Postel-Vinay. 2017. "The Relative Power of Employment-to-Employment Reallocation and Unemployment Exits in Predicting Wage Growth." *American Economic Review* 107, no. 5: 364–68. https://doi.org/10.1257/aer.p20171078.

Mukoyama, T. 2014. "The Cyclicality of Job-To-Job Transitions and Its Implications for Aggregate Productivity." *Journal of Economic Dynamics and Control* 39: 1–17. https://doi.org/10.1016/j.jedc.2013.12.004.

Paul, M., W. Darity, and D. Hamilton. 2018. "The Federal Job Guarantee: A Policy to Achieve Permanent Full Employment." Center on Budget and Policy Priorities, Policy Futures. https://www.cbpp.org/research/ the-federal-job-guarantee-a-policy-to-achieve-permanent-full-employment.

Pissarides, C. 2000. *Equilibrium Unemployment Theory*, 2nd ed. Cambridge, MA: MIT Press. https://mitpress.mit.edu/9780262533980/ equilibrium-unemployment-theory/.

Powell, J. 2018. "Speech by Chairman Powell on Monetary Policy in a Changing Economy." Board of Governors of the Federal Reserve System. https://www. federalreserve.gov/newsevents/speech/powell20180824a.htm.

Reifschneider, D., W. Wascher, and D. Wilcox. 2015. *Aggregate Supply in the United States: Recent Developments and Implications for the Conduct of Monetary Policy.* Finance and Economics Discussion Series 2013-77. Washington: Board of Governors of the Federal Reserve System. https://doi.org/10.17016/ FEDS.2013.77.

Sanchez Cumming, C. 2021. "The Importance of Anti-Discrimination Enforcement for a Fair and Equitable U.S. Labor Market and Broadly Shared Economic Growth." Washington Center for Equitable Growth. https://equitablegrowth.org/ wp-content/uploads/2022/01/122121-anti-discrimination-enf-ib.pdf.

Shroyer, A., and V. Gaitán. 2019. "Four Reasons Why Employers Should Care About Housing." Urban Institute, Housing Matters. https://housingmatters.urban.org/ articles/four-reasons-why-employers-should-care-about-housing.

Solon, G., R. Barsky, and J. Parker. 1994. "Measuring the Cyclicality of Real Wages: How Important is Composition Bias." *Quarterly Journal of Economics* 109, no. 1: 1–25. https://doi.org/10.2307/2118426.

Spriggs, W. 2015. "The Case of Women: Why the Fed Isn't Close to Achieving Full Employment and Shouldn't Be Discussing Raising Interest Rates." Seattle Medium. https://seattlemedium.com/ the-case-of-women-why-the-fed-isnt-close-to-achieving-full-employment-and-shouldnt-be-discussing-raising-interest-rates.

———. 2017. "Testimony Prepared for U.S. House of Representatives on a Mandate for Full Employment." 115th Congress, First Session. https://www.congress. gov/115/meeting/house/105846/witnesses/HHRG-115-BA20-Wstate-SpriggsW-20170404.pdf.

Staiger, D., J. Stock, and M. Watson. 1997. "The NAIRU, Unemployment and Monetary Policy." *Journal of Economic Perspectives* 11, no. 1: 33–49. https://www. aeaweb.org/articles?id=10.1257/jep.11.1.33.

Stansbury, A., and L. Summers. 2020. *The Declining Worker Power Hypothesis: An Explanation for the Recent Evolution of the American Economy.* NBER

Working Paper 27193. Cambridge, MA: National Bureau of Economic Research. https://doi.org/10.3386/w27193.

Tomaskovic-Devey, D., C. Zimmer, K. Stainback, C. Robinson, T. Taylor, and T. McTague. 2006. "Documenting Desegregation: Segregation in American Workplaces by Race, Ethnicity, and Sex, 1966–2023." *American Sociological Review* 71, no. 4: 565–88. https://doi.org/10.1177/000312240607100403.

Topel, R., and M. Ward. 1992. "Job Mobility and the Careers of Young Men." *Quarterly Journal of Economics* 107, no. 2: 439–79. https://www.jstor.org/stable/2118478.

U.S. Census Bureau. 2017. "Job-to-Job (J2J) Flows 101." https://lehd.ces.census.gov/doc/j2j_101.pdf.

U.S. Department of the Treasury. 2022. "The State of Labor Market Competition." https://home.treasury.gov/system/files/136/State-of-Labor-Market-Competition-2022.pdf.

Wolfers, J. 2019. "Okun Revisited: Who Benefits Most from a Strong Economy? Comment." *Brookings Papers on Economic Activity*, Spring, 385–97. https://par.nsf.gov/servlets/purl/10440910.

Yeh, C., C. Macaluso, and B. Hershbein. 2022. "Monopsony in the U.S. Labor Market." *American Economic Review* 112, no. 7: 2099–138. https://doi.org/10.1257/aer.20200025.

Yellen, J. 2014. "Speech by Chair Yellen on Labor Market Dynamics and Monetary Policy." Board of Governors of the Federal Reserve System. https://www.federalreserve.gov/newsevents/speech/yellen20140822a.htm.

———. 2016. "Speech by Chair Yellen on Macroeconomic Research After the Crisis." Board of Governors of the Federal Reserve System. https://www.federalreserve.gov/newsevents/speech/yellen20161014a.htm.

Chapter 2

Ajello, A., M. Cavallo, G. Favara, W. Peterman, J. Schindler, and N. Sinha. 2023. "A New Index to Measure U.S. Financial Conditions." Board of Governors of the Federal Reserve System, FEDS Notes. https://www.federalreserve.gov/econres/notes/feds-notes/a-new-index-to-measure-us-financial-conditions-20230630.html.

Aksoy, C., J. Barrero, N. Bloom, S. Davis, M. Dolls, and P. Zarate. 2022. *Working from Home Around the World*. NBER Working Paper 30466. https://doi.org/10.3386/w30446.

Asdourian, E., G. Nabors, L. Stojanovic, and L. Sheiner. 2024. "Hutchins Center Fiscal Impact Measure." https://www.brookings.edu/articles/hutchins-center-fiscal-impact-measure/.

Barrero, J., N. Bloom, and S. Davis. 2023. "The Evolution of Work from Home." *Journal of Economic Perspectives*, September 3. https://www.aeaweb.org/articles?id=10.1257/jep.37.4.23.

Blau, F., and L. Kahn. 2013. *Female Labor Supply: Why Is the U.S. Falling Behind?* NBER Working Paper 18702. Cambridge, MA: National Bureau of Economic Research. https://doi.org/10.3386/w18702.

BLS (U.S. Bureau of Labor Statistics). 2024. "Job Openings and Labor Turnover Survey." https://www.bls.gov/jlt/.

Campbell, J., and R. Shiller. 2001. *Valuation Ratios and the Long-Run Stock Market Outlook: An Update.* NBER Working Paper 8221. Cambridge, MA: National Bureau of Economic Research. https://doi.org/10.3386/w8221.

CDC (U.S. Centers for Disease Control and Prevention). No date. "COVID-19 Update for the United States." https://covid.cdc.gov/covid-data-tracker/.

CEA (Council of Economic Advisers). 2015. *Economic Report of the President.* Washington: U.S. Government Publishing Office. https://www.whitehouse.gov/wp-content/uploads/2021/07/2015-ERP.pdf.

———. 2023a. *Did Stabilization Funds Help Mothers Get Back to Work After the COVID-19 Recession?* Working Paper. https://www.whitehouse.gov/wp-content/uploads/2023/11/Child-Care-Stabilization.pdf.

———. 2023b. "Disinflation Explanation: Supply, Demand, and their Interaction." https://www.whitehouse.gov/cea/written-materials/2023/11/30/disinflation-explanation-supply-demand-and-their-interaction/.

Cheremukhin, A., and P. Restrepo-Echavarria. 2024. *The Dual Beveridge Curve.* Federal Reserve Bank of Saint Louis, Working Paper 2022-021. https://www.dallasfed.org/research/papers/2022/wp2221.

Conference Board. 2024. "U.S. Leading Indicators." https://www.conference-board.org/topics/us-leading-indicators.

Congressional Budget Office. No date. "Budget and Economic Data." https://www.cbo.gov/data/budget-economic-data.

D'Amico, S., D. Kim, and M. Wei. 2018. "Tips from TIPS: The Informational Content of Treasury Inflation-Protected Security Prices." *Journal of Financial and Quantitative Analysis* 53, no. 1: 395–436. https://www.jstor.org/stable/26591911.

Elsby, M., R. Michaels, and D. Ratner. 2015. "The Beveridge Curve: A Survey." *Journal of Economic Literature* 53, no. 3: 571–630. https://doi.org/10.1257/jel.53.3.571.

Federal Reserve. 2023a. "Federal Reserve Issues: FOMC Statement." Board of Governors of the Federal Reserve System. https://www.federalreserve.gov/monetarypolicy/fomcpresconf20231213.htm.

———. 2023b. "Enhanced Financial Accounts." Board of Governors of the Federal Reserve System. https://www.federalreserve.gov/releases/efa/efa-hedge-funds.htm.

Federal Reserve, Federal Open Market Committee. 2023. "Summary of Economic Projections." December 13. https://www.federalreserve.gov/monetarypolicy/files/fomcprojtabl20231213.pdf.

Federal Reserve Bank of Atlanta. 2024. "Wage Growth Tracker." Center for Human Capital Studies, Data & Tools. https://www.atlantafed.org/chcs/wage-growth-tracker.

Figura, A., and C. Waller. 2022. "What Does the Beveridge Curve Tell Us About the Likelihood of a Soft Landing?" FEDS Notes. https://doi.org/10.17016/2380-7172.3190.

Hartman, M. 2022. "Why Republican Consumers Are Glum and Democrats Upbeat." Marketplace. https://www.marketplace.org/2022/08/31/why-republican-consumers-are-glum-and-democrats-upbeat/.

Herbstman, J., and S. Brave. 2023. "Persistently Pessimistic: Consumer and Small Business Sentiment After the Covid Recession." Federal Reserve Bank of Chicago, Chicago Fed Letter 490. https://www.chicagofed.org/publications/chicago-fed-letter/2023/490.

Hirsch, P. 2012. "Consumer Confidence vs. Consumer Sentiment." Marketplace. https://www.marketplace.org/2012/08/28/consumer-confidence-vs-consumer-sentiment/.

Kim, D., and J. Wright. 2005. *An Arbitrage-Free Three-Factor Term Structure Model and the Recent Behavior of Long-Term Yields and Distant-Horizon Forward Rates.* Finance and Economics Discussion Series 2005-33. Washington: Board of Governors of the Federal Reserve System. https://doi.org/10.2139/ssrn.813267.

Mas, A., and A. Pallais. 2017. "Valuing Alternative Work Arrangements." *American Economic Review* 107, no. 12: 3722–59. https://doi.org/10.1257/aer.20161500.

Mongey, S., and J. Horwich. 2023. "Are Job Vacancies Still as Plentiful as They Appear? Implications for the 'Soft Landing.'" Federal Reserve Bank of Minneapolis. https://www.minneapolisfed.org/article/2023/are-job-vacancies-still-as-plentiful-as-they-appear-implications-for-the-soft-landing.

Moscarini, G., and F. Postel-Vinay. 2017. "The Relative Power of Employment-to-Employment Reallocation and Unemployment Exits in Predicting Wage Growth." *American Economic Review* 107, no. 5: 364–68. https://doi.org/10.1257/aer.p20171078.

Okun, A. 1962. "Potential GNP: Its Measurement and Significance." American Statistical Association, *Proceedings of the Business and Economic Statistics Section*, 89–104.

O'Kane, C. 2023. "Photo of Connecticut McDonald's $18 Big Mac Meal Sparks Debate Online." CBS News. https://www.cbsnews.com/news/mcdonalds-prices-big-mac-sparks-expensive-menu-darien-connecticut-debate-online/.

Social Security Administration. 2023a. "Social Security Program Data." https://www.ssa.gov/OACT/HistEst/Population/2023/Population2023.html.

———. 2023b. "Table V.A2: Immigration Assumptions, Calendar Years 1940–2100." 2023 OASDI Trustees Report. https://www.ssa.gov/OACT/TR/2023/lr5a2.html.

U.S. Census Bureau. No date. "Quarterly Survey of Plant Capacity Utilization (QPC)."
https://www.census.gov/programs-surveys/qpc.html.

White House. 2022. "Fact Sheet: CHIPS and Science Act Will Lower Costs, Create Jobs,
Strengthen Supply Chains, and Counter China." https://www.whitehouse.gov/
briefing-room/statements-releases/2022/08/09/
fact-sheet-chips-and-science-act-will-lower-costs-create-jobs-strengthen-supply-
chains-and-counter-china/.

———. No date. "Investing in America: cleanenergy.gov." https://www.whitehouse.gov/
cleanenergy/.

Yellen, J. 2015. "Inflation Dynamics and Monetary Policy." Transcript of Philip Gamble
Memorial Lecture, University of Massachusetts Amherst. https://www.federal-
reserve.gov/newsevents/speech/yellen20150924a.htm.

Chapter 3

AARP. 2020. "Caregiving in the United States." https://www.aarp.org/content/dam/aarp/
ppi/2020/05/full-report-caregiving-in-the-united-states.doi.10.26419-
2Fppi.00103.001.pdf.

ACS (American Cancer Society). 2023. "Cancer Facts & Figures 2023." https://www.
cancer.org/content/dam/cancer-org/research/cancer-facts-and-statistics/annual-
cancer-facts-and-figures/2023/2023-cancer-facts-and-figures.pdf.

Alpert, A., W. Evans, E. Lieber, and D. Powell. 2022. *Origins of the Opioid Crisis and Its
Enduring Impacts*. NBER Working Paper 26500. Cambridge, MA: National
Bureau for Economic Research. https://doi.org/10.3386/w26500.

Alpert, A., D. Powell, and R. Pacula. 2018. "Supply-Side Drug Policy in the Presence of
Substitutes: Evidence from the Introduction of Abuse-Deterrent Opioids."
American Economic Journal: Economic Policy 10, no. 4: 1–35. https://doi.
org/10.1257/pol.20170082.

Alvarez, P. 2022. "What Does the Global Decline of the Fertility Rate Look Like?" World
Economic Forum. https://www.weforum.org/agenda/2022/06/
global-decline-of-fertility-rates-visualised/.

Aragão, C., K. Parker, S. Greenwood, C. Baronavski, and J. Mandapat. 2023. "The
Modern American Family." Pew Research Center. https://www.pewresearch.
org/social-trends/2023/09/14/the-modern-american-family/.

Arenberg, S., S. Neller, and S. Stripling. 2020. "The Impact of Youth Medicaid Eligibility
on Adult Incarceration." Forthcoming, *American Economic Journal: Applied
Economics*. https://www.aeaweb.org/articles?id=10.1257/app.20200785.

Arias, E., K. Kochanek, J. Xu, and B. Tejada-Vera. 2023. "Provisional Life Expectancy
Estimates for 2022." Centers for Disease Control and Prevention: National Vital
Statistics System. https://www.cdc.gov/nchs/data/vsrr/vsrr031.pdf.

Arteaga, C., and V. Barone. 2023. "A Manufactured Tragedy: The Origins and Deep Ripples of the Opioid Epidemic." Working paper. https://viquibarone.github.io/baronevictoria/Opioids_ArteagaBarone.pdf.

Ash, E., W. Carrington, R. Heller, and G. Hwang. 2023. "Exploring the Effects of Medicaid During Childhood on the Economy and the Budget." Working paper, Congressional Budget Office. https://www.cbo.gov/system/files/2023-10/59231-Medicaid.pdf.

Azoulay, P., B. Jones, J. Kim, and J. Miranda. 2022. "Immigration and Entrepreneurship in the United States." *American Economic Review* 4, no. 1: 71–88. https://doi.org/10.1257/aeri.20200588.

Bailey, M. 2006. "More Power to the Pill: The Impact of Contraceptive Freedom on Women's Life Cycle Labor Supply." *Quarterly Journal of Economics*. https://doi.org/10.1093/qje/121.1.289.

Bailey, M., and B. Hershbein. 2018. "U.S. Fertility Rates and Childbearing in American Economic History, 1800–2010." In *The Oxford Handbook of American Economic History*, 1: 75–100, ed. L. Cain, P. Fishback, and P. Rhode. New York: Oxford University Press. https://doi.org/10.1093/oxfordhb/9780190882617.013.21.

Bailey, M., B. Hershbein, and A. Miller. 2012. "The Opt-In Revolution? Contraception and the Gender Gap in Wages." *American Economic Journal: Applied Economics* 4, no. 3: 225–54. https://doi.org/10.1257/app.4.3.225.

Basso, G., and G. Peri. 2020. "Internal Mobility: The Greater Responsiveness of Foreign-Born to Economic Conditions." *Journal of Economic Perspectives* 34, no. 3: 77–98. https://doi.org/10.1257/jep.34.3.77.

Becker, G. 1960. "An Economic Analysis of Fertility." In *Demographics and Economic Change in Developed Countries*, 209–40. New York: Columbia University Press. http://www.nber.org/chapters/c2387.

Bhatia, A., N. Krieger, and S. Subramanian. 2019. "Learning from History About Reducing Infant Mortality: Contrasting the Centrality of Structural Interventions to Early-20th-Century Successes in the United States to Their Neglect in Current Global Initiatives." *Milbank Quarterly* 97, no. 1: 285–345. https://doi.org/10.1111/1468-0009.12376.

Blau, F., and C. Mackie. 2017. *The Economic and Fiscal Consequences of Immigration.* Washington: National Academies Press. https://doi.org/10.17226/23550.

BLS (U.S. Bureau of Labor Statistics). 2021. "Employment Projections: 2020–2030." https://www.bls.gov/news.release/archives/ecopro_09082021.pdf.

———.2022. "Over 16 Million Worked in Health Care and Social Assistance in 2021." https://www.bls.gov/opub/ted/2022/over-16-million-women-worked-in-health-care-and-social-assistance-in-2021.htm.

———.2023a. "Nonfarm Business Sector: Labor Productivity (Output per Hour) for All Workers [OPHNFB]." https://fred.stlouisfed.org/series/ophnfb.

———. 2023b. "Unpaid Eldercare in the United States: News Release." https://www.bls. gov/news.release/elcare.htm.

———.2023c. "Employment Projections: 2022–2032 Summary." https://www.bls.gov/ news.release/ecopro.nr0.htm.

Boonstra, H. 2014. "What Is Behind the Declines in Teen Pregnancy Rates?" *Guttmacher Policy Review* 17, no. 3. https://www.guttmacher.org/gpr/2014/09/ what-behind-declines-teen-pregnancy-rates.

Borjas, G. 2003. "The Labor Demand Curve Is Downward Sloping: Reexamining the Impact of Immigration on the Labor Market." *Quarterly Journal of Economics* 118, no. 4: 1335–74. http://www.jstor.org/stable/25053941.

Brainerd, E. 2014. "Can Government Policies Reverse Undesirable Declines in Fertility?" *IZA World of Labor* 23. https://doi.org/10.15185/izawol.23.

Bronstein, J., M. Wingate, and A. Brisendine. 2018. "Why Is the U.S. Preterm Birth Rate So Much Higher Than the Rates in Canada, Great Britain, and Western Europe?" *International Journal of Health Services* 48, no. 40: 622–40. https:// doi.org/10.1177/0020731418786360.

Brown, A. 2021. "Growing Share of Childless Adults in U.S. Don't Expect to Ever Have Children." Pew Research Center. https://www.pewresearch.org/short-reads/2021/11/19/growing-share-of-childless-adults-in-u-s-dont-expect-to-ever-have-children/.

Brown, D., A. Kowalski, and I. Lurie. 2020. "Long-Term Impacts of Childhood Medicaid Expansions on Outcomes in Adulthood." *Review of Economic Studies* 87, no. 2: 792–821. https://doi.org/10.1093/restud/rdz039.

Buntin, M., S. Freed, P. Lai, K. Lou, and L. Keohane. 2022. "Trends in and Factors Contributing to the Slowdown in Medicare Spending Growth, 2007–2018." *JAMA Health Forum* 3, no. 12. https://doi.org/10.1001/ jamahealthforum.2022.4475.

Butcher, K., and D. Card. 1991. "Immigration and Wages: Evidence from the 1980's." *American Economic Review* 81, no. 2: 292–96. http://www.jstor.org/ stable/2006872.

Campbell, F., G. Conti, J. Heckman, S. Moon, R. Pinto, E. Pungello, and Y. Pan. 2014. "Early Childhood Investments Substantially Boost Adult Health." *Science* 28:1478–85. https://doi.org/ 10.1126/science.1248429.

Card, D. 2009. "Immigration and Inequality." *American Economic Review* 99, no. 2: 1–21. https://pubs.aeaweb.org/doi/pdf/10.1257/aer.99.2.1.

Carvalho, C., A. Ferrero, and F. Nechio. 2017. "Demographic Transition and Low U.S. Interest Rates." Federal Reserve Bank of San Francisco, FRBSF Economic Letter 2017-27. https://www.frbsf.org/wp-content/uploads/sites/4/el2017-27.pdf.

Case, A., and A. Deaton. 2015. "Rising Morbidity and Mortality in Midlife Among White Non-Hispanic Americans in the 21st Century." *Proceedings of the National*

Academy of Sciences 112, no. 49: 15078–83. https://doi.org/10.1073/pnas.1518393112.

CBO (Congressional Budget Office). 2019. "CBO's Projections of Demographic and Economic Trends." In *The 2019 Long-Term Budget Outlook*. https://www.cbo.gov/system/files?file=2019-06/55331-Appendix_A.pdf.

———. 2022. "The Demographic Outlook: 2022 to 2052." https://www.cbo.gov/publication/57975.

———. 2023a. "The Demographic Outlook: 2023 to 2053." https://www.cbo.gov/publication/58612.

———. 2023b. "The 2023 Long-Term Budget Outlook." https://www.cbo.gov/publication/59331.

———. 2023c. "CBO's Projections of Federal Health Care Spending." https://www.cbo.gov/system/files/2023-03/58997-Whitehouse.pdf.

———. 2024. "The Demographic Outlook: 2024 to 2054." https://www.cbo.gov/publication/59697.

CBPP (Center on Budget and Policy Priorities). 2020. "Policy Basics: Introduction to Medicaid." https://www.cbpp.org/research/policy-basics-introduction-to-medicaid.

CDC (Centers for Disease Control and Prevention). 1999. "Achievements in Public Health, 1900–1999: Healthier Mothers and Babies." https://www.cdc.gov/mmwr/preview/mmwrhtml/mm4838a2.htm.

———. 2014. "Smoking and Cardiovascular Disease." https://www.cdc.gov/tobacco/sgr/50th-anniversary/pdfs/fs_smoking_cvd_508.pdf.

———. 2019a. "What Is Assisted Reproductive Technology?" https://www.cdc.gov/art/whatis.html.

———. 2019b. "QuickStats: Percentage of Deaths from External Causes, by Age Group—United States, 2017." *Morbidity Mortal Weekly Report* 68: 710. http://dx.doi.org/10.15585/mmwr.mm6832a7.

———. 2022. "State-Specific Assisted Reproductive Technology Surveillance." https://www.cdc.gov/art/state-specific-surveillance/2020/index.html.

———. 2023a. "Summary of Initial Findings from CDC-Funded Firearm Injury Prevention Research." https://www.cdc.gov/violenceprevention/firearms/firearm-research-findings.html.

———. 2023b. "COVID Data Tracker: Trends in United States COVID-19 Hospitalizations, Deaths, Emergency Department (ED) Visits, and Test Positivity by Geographic Area." https://stacks.cdc.gov/view/cdc/137422.

———. 2023c. "Respiratory Syncytial Virus Infection (RSV): RSV Surveillance & Research." https://www.cdc.gov/rsv/research/index.html.

———. No date. "CDC WONDER." https://wonder.cdc.gov.

CEA (Council of Economic Advisers). 2016. "The Economic Record of the Obama Administration: Reforming the Health Care System." https://obamawhitehouse. archives.gov/sites/default/files/page/files/20161213_cea_record_healh_care_ reform.pdf.

———. 2023a. "Did Stabilization Funds Help Mothers Get Back to Work After the COVID-19 Recession?" Working Paper. https://www.whitehouse.gov/ wp-content/uploads/2023/11/Child-Care-Stabilization.pdf.

———. 2023b. "The Labor Supply Rebound from the Pandemic." https://www.white-house.gov/cea/written-materials/2023/04/17/ the-labor-supply-rebound-from-the-pandemic/.

———. 2023c. "The Anti-Poverty and Income-Boosting Impacts of the Enhanced CTC." https://www.whitehouse.gov/cea/written-materials/2023/11/20/ the-anti-poverty-and-income-boosting-impacts-of-the-enhanced-ctc/.

Census (U.S Census Bureau). 2018. "Methodology, Assumptions, and Inputs for the 2017 National Population Projections." https://www2.census.gov/programs-surveys/ popproj/technical-documentation/methodology/methodstatement17.pdf.

———. 2023a. "Methodology, Assumptions, and Inputs for the 2023 National Population Projections." https://www2.census.gov/programs-surveys/popproj/technical-documentation/methodology/methodstatement23.pdf.

———. 2023b. "2023 National Population Projections." https://www.census.gov/data/ tables/2023/demo/popproj/2023-summary-tables.html.

Chambers, G., S. Dyer, F. Zegers-Hochschild, J. de Mouzon, O. Ishihara, M. Banker, R. Mansour, M. Kupka, and G. Adamson. 2021. "International Committee for Monitoring Assisted Reproductive Technologies World Report: Assisted Repro-ductive Technology, 2014." *Human Reproduction* 36, no. 11: 2921–34. https:// doi.org/10.1093/humrep/deab198.

Chen, A., E. Oster, and H. Williams. 2016. "Why Is Infant Mortality Higher in the United States Than in Europe?" *American Economic Journal: Economic Policy* 9, no.2: 89–124. https://doi.org/10.1257/pol.20140224.

Chidambaram, P., and A. Burns. 2023. "How Many People Use Medicaid Long-Term Services and Supports and How Much Does Medicaid Spend on Those People?" KFF. https://www.kff.org/medicaid/issue-brief/ how-many-people-use-medicaid-long-term-services-and-supports-and-how-much-does-medicaid-spend-on-those-people/.

CMS (Centers for Medicare & Medicaid Services). 2023a. "National Health Expenditure Data." https://www.cms.gov/oact/tr/2023.

———. 2023b. "2023 Medicare Trustee Report." https://www.cms.gov/ research-statistics-data-and-systemsstatistics-trends-and-reportsreportstrustfund-strusteesreports/2021-2022.

Coe, N., G. Goda, and C. Van Houtven. 2023. "Family Spillovers and Long-Term Care Insurance." *Journal of Health Economics* 90: 102781. https://doi.org/10.1016/j. jhealeco.2023.102781.

Cohodes, S., D. Grossman, S. Kleiner, and M. Lovenheim. 2016. "The Effect of Child Health Insurance Access on Schooling: Evidence from Public Insurance Expansions." *Journal of Human Resources* 51, no. 3: 727–59. https://doi.org/10.3368/jhr.51.3.1014-6688r1.

Cortés, P. 2023. *Immigration, Household Production, and Native Women's Labor Market Outcomes: A Survey of a Global Phenomenon.* NBER Working Paper 31234. Cambridge, MA: National Bureau for Economic Research. https://doi.org/10.3386/w31234.

Cunha, F., and J. Heckman. 2007. "The Technology of Skill Formation." *American Economic Review* 97, no. 2: 31–47. https://doi.org/10.1257/aer.97.2.31.

Currie, J., and J. Gruber. 1996. "Health Insurance Eligibility, Utilization of Medical Care, and Child Health." *Quarterly Journal of Economics* 111, no. 2: 431-66. https://doi.org/10.2307/2946684.

Currie, J., A. Li, and M. Schnell. 2023. "The Effects of Competition on Physician Prescribing." Working paper. https://static1.squarespace.com/static/572372e7c2ea51b309e9991a/t/64aeceef4539e40f84b240d3/1689177840601/CLS_062123.pdf.

Cutler, D., A. Deaton, and A. Lleras-Muney. 2006. "The Determinants of Mortality." *Journal of Economic Perspectives* 20, no. 3: 97–120. https://doi.org/10.1257/jep.20.3.97.

Cutler, D., K. Ghosh, K. Messer, T. Raghunathan, S. Stewart, and A. Rosen. 2019. "Explaining the Slowdown in Medical Spending Growth among the Elderly, 1999–2012." *Health Affairs* 38, no. 2: 222–29. https://doi.org/10.1377/hlthaff.2018.05372.

Cutler, D., and E. Glaeser. 2021. "When Innovation Goes Wrong: Technological Regress and the Opioid Epidemic." *Journal of Economic Perspectives* 35, no. 4: 171–96. https://doi.org/10.1257/jep.35.4.171.

Cutler, D., E. Glaeser, and A. Rosen. 2009. "Is the U.S. Population Behaving Healthier?" In *Social Security Policy in a Changing Environment*, 423–42, ed. J. Brown, J. Liebman, and D. Wise. Chicago: University of Chicago Press. https://doi.org/10.7208/chicago/9780226076508.003.0013.

Cutler, D., and G. Miller. 2005. "The Role of Public Health Improvements in Health Advances: The Twentieth-Century United States." *Demography* 42, no. 1: 1–22. https://www.jstor.org/stable/1515174.

Deaton, A. 2014. *The Great Escape: Health, Wealth, and the Origins of Inequality.* Princeton, NJ: Princeton University Press. https://press.princeton.edu/books/hardcover/9780691153544/the-great-escape.

DeCicca, P., and L. McLeod. 2008. "Cigarette Taxes and Older Adult Smoking: Evidence from Recent Large Tax Increases." *Journal of Health Economics* 27, no. 4: 918–29. https://doi.org/10.1016/j.jhealeco.2007.11.005.

Deming, D. 2009. "Early Childhood Intervention and Life-Cycle Skill Development: Evidence from Head Start." *American Economic Journal: Applied Economics* 1: 111–34. https://doi.org/10.1257/app.1.3.111.

Dench, D., M. Pineda-Torres, and C. Myers. 2023. *The Effects of the Dobbs Decision on Fertility*. IZA Discussion Paper 16608. Bonn: Institute of Labor Economics. https://docs.iza.org/dp16608.pdf.

Dieppe, A. 2020. "The Broad-Based Productivity Slowdown, in Seven Charts." World Bank Blogs. https://blogs.worldbank.org/developmenttalk/broad-based-productivity-slowdown-seven-charts.

DOE (U.S. Department of Energy). 2022. "The Inflation Reduction Act Drives Significant Emissions Reductions and Positions America to Reach Our Climate Goals." https://www.energy.gov/sites/default/files/2022-08/8.18%20InflationReductionAct_Factsheet_Final.pdf.

Duncan, G., and K. Magnuson. 2013. "Investing in Preschool Programs." *Journal of Economic Perspectives* 27: 109–32. https://doi.org/10.1257/jep.27.2.109.

Dynan, K., W. Edelberg, and M. Palumbo. 2009. "The Effects of Population Aging on the Relationship among Aggregate Consumption, Saving, and Income." *American Economic Review* 99, no. 2: 380–86. https://doi.org/10.1257/aer.99.2.380.

Edelberg, W., and T. Watson. 2023. "Immigration Impact Index." Brookings Institution. https://www.brookings.edu/articles/immigration-impact-index/.

Edwards, E. 2023. "Abortion Bans Could Drive Away Young Doctors, New Survey Finds." NBC News. https://www.nbcnews.com/health/health-news/states-abortion-bans-young-doctors-survey-rcna84899.

Ely, M., and A. Driscoll. 2023. "Infant Mortality in the United States, 2021: Data from the Period Linked Birth/Infant Death File." Centers for Disease Control and Prevention, National Vital Statistics System. https://www.cdc.gov/nchs/data/nvsr/nvsr72/nvsr72-11.pdf.

EPA (U.S. Environmental Protection Agency) 2007. "Achievements in Stratospheric Ozone Protection Progress Report." https://www.epa.gov/sites/default/files/2015-07/documents/achievements_in_stratospheric_ozone_protection.pdf.

———. 2022. "Sulfur Dioxide Trends." https://www.epa.gov/air-trends/sulfur-dioxide-trends.

Erbabian, M., V. Osorio, and M. Paulson. 2022. "Measuring Fertility in the United States." Penn Wharton Budget Model. https://budgetmodel.wharton.upenn.edu/issues/2022/7/8/measuring-fertility-in-the-united-states.

Evans, W., M. Farrelly, and E. Montgomery. 1996. *Do Workplace Smoking Bans Reduce Smoking?* NBER Working Paper 5567. Cambridge, MA: National Bureau for Economic Research. https://doi.org/10.3386/w5567.

Fleming-Dutra, K., J. Jones, L. Roper, M. Prill, I. Ortega-Sanchez, D. Moulia, M. Wallace, M. Godfrey, K. Broder, N. Tepper, O. Brooks, P. Sánchez, C. Kotton, B. Mahon, S. Long, and M. McMorrow. 2023. "Use of the Pfizer Respiratory

Syncytial Virus Vaccine During Pregnancy for the Prevention of Respiratory Syncytial Virus–Associated Lower Respiratory Tract Disease in Infants: Recommendations of the Advisory Committee on Immunization Practices—United States, 2023." Centers for Disease Control and Prevention, *MMWR Morbidly Mortality Weekly Report* 72: 1115–22. https://www.cdc.gov/mmwr/volumes/72/wr/mm7241e1.htm.

Foster, A. 2015. "Consumer Expenditures Vary by Age." Bureau of Labor Statistics: Beyond the Numbers. https://www.bls.gov/opub/btn/volume-4/consumer-expenditures-vary-by-age.htm.

Foster, D. 2021. *The Turnaway Study: Ten Years, a Thousand Women, and the Consequences of Having—or Being Denied—an Abortion.* New York: Simon & Schuster. https://www.simonandschuster.com/books/The-Turnaway-Study/Diana-Greene-Foster/9781982141578.

Foster, D., M. Biggs, L. Ralph, C. Gerdts, S. Roberts, and M. Glymour. 2018. "Socioeconomic Outcomes of Women Who Receive and Women Who Are Denied Wanted Abortions in the United States." *American Journal of Public Health* 112, no. 9: 1290–96. https://doi.org/10.2105/ajph.2017.304247.

Funk, C., A. Tyson, B. Kennedy, and G. Pasquini. 2023. "Americans' Largely Positive Views of Childhood Vaccines Hold Steady." Pew Research Center. https://www.pewresearch.org/science/wp-content/uploads/sites/16/2023/05/PS_2023.05.16_vaccines_REPORT.pdf.

Gagnon, E., B. Johannsen, and J. López-Salido. 2021. "Understanding the New Normal: The Role of Demographics." *IMF Economic Review* 69, no. 2: 357–90. https://doi.org/10.1057/s41308-021-00138-4.

GAO (U.S. Government Accountability Office). 2013. "Prescription Drugs Comparison of DOD and VA Direct Purchase Prices." https://www.gao.gov/assets/gao-13-358.pdf.

Gapminder. 2022. "Child Mortality Rate, Under Age 5." https://www.gapminder.org/data/documentation/gd005/.

Giltner, A., A. Evans, C. Cicco, S. Leach, and W. Rowe. 2022. "Fentanyl Analog Trends in Washington, D.C., Observed in Needle-Exchange Syringes." *Forensic Science International* 338: 111393. https://doi.org/10.1016/j.forsciint.2022.111393.

Goldin, C. 2004. *From the Valley to the Summit: The Quiet Revolution That Transformed Women's Work.* NBER Working Paper 10335. Cambridge, MA: National Bureau for Economic Research. https://doi.org/10.3386/w10335.

Goldin, C., and L. Katz. 2002. "The Power of the Pill: Oral Contraceptives and Women's Career and Marriage Decisions." *Journal of Political Economy* 110, no. 4: 730–70. https://doi.org/10.1086/340778.

Goldin, J., I. Lurie, and J. McCubbin. 2021. "Health Insurance and Mortality: Experimental Evidence from Taxpayer Outreach." *Quarterly Journal of Economics* 136, no. 1: 1–49. https://doi.org/10.1093/qje/qjaa029.

Goldin, C., and J. Mitchell. 2017. "The New Life Cycle of Women's Employment: Disappearing Humps, Sagging Middles, Expanding Tops." *Journal of Economic Perspectives* 31, no. 1: 161–82. https://doi.org/10.1257/jep.31.1.161.

Goodman-Bacon, A. 2018. "Public Insurance and Mortality: Evidence from Medicaid Implementation." *Journal of Political Economy* 126, no. 1: 216–62. https://doi.org/10.1086/695528.

———. 2021. "The Long-Run Effects of Childhood Insurance Coverage: Medicaid Implementation, Adult Health, and Labor Market Outcomes." *American Economic Review* 111, no. 8: 2550–93. https://doi.org/10.1257/aer.20171671.

Grabowski, D. 2021. "The Future of Long-Term Care Requires Investment in Both Facility- and Home-Based Services." *Nature Aging* 1: 10–11. https://doi.org/10.1038/s43587-020-00018-y.

Gray-Lobe, G., P. Pathak, C.R. Walters. "The Long-Term Effects of Universal Preschool in Boston." 2022. *Quarterly Journal of Economics* 138, no. 1: 363–411. https://doi.org/10.1093/qje/qjac036.

Guldi, M. 2008. "Fertility Effects of Abortion and Birth Control Pill Access for Minors." *Demography* 45, no. 4: 817–27. https://www.jstor.org/stable/25651477.

Guth, M., R. Garfield, and R. Rudowitz. 2020. "The Effects of Medicaid Expansion Under the ACA: Studies from January 2014 to January 2020." Kaiser Family Foundation. https://www.kff.org/report-section/the-effects-of-medicaid-expansion-under-the-aca-updated-findings-from-a-literature-review-report/.

Hales, C., J. Servais, C. Martin, and D. Kohen. 2019. "Prescription Drug Use Among Adults Aged 40–79 in the United States and Canada." NCHS Daily Brief 347. https://www.cdc.gov/nchs/data/databriefs/db347-h.pdf.

Hamilton, B., J. Martin, and E. Osterman. 2023. "VSRR 028: Births: Provisional Data for 2022." https://doi.org/10.15620/cdc:127052.

Hamilton, B., J. Martin, and S. Ventura. 2009. "Births: Preliminary Data for 2007." *National Vital Statistics Reports* 57, no 12. https://www.cdc.gov/nchs/data/nvsr/nvsr57/nvsr57_12.pdf.

Hanushek, E., and L. Wößmann. 2010. "Education and Economic Growth." In *Economics of Education*, 60–67, ed. D. Brewer and P. McEwan. New York: Academic Press. https://shop.elsevier.com/books/economics-of-education/brewer/978-0-08-096530-7.

Hendren, N., and B. Sprung-Keyser. 2020. "A Unified Welfare Analysis of Government Policies*." *Quarterly Journal of Economics* 135, no. 3: 1209–1318. https://doi.org/10.1093/qje/qjaa006.

Herbst, C. 2022. "Child Care in the United States: Markets, Policy, and Evidence." *Journal of Policy Analysis and Management* 42, no. 1: 255–304. https://doi.org/10.1002/pam.22436.

Heuveline, P. 2023. "The COVID-19 Pandemic and the Expansion of the Mortality Gap between the United States and Its European Peers." *Plos One* 18, no. 3. https://doi.org/10.1371/journal.pone.0283153.

HHS (U.S. Department of Health and Human Services). 2021. "Confronting Health Misinformation." https://www.hhs.gov/sites/default/files/surgeon-general-misinformation-advisory.pdf.

———. 2022. "New HHS Report Shows National Uninsured Rate Reached All-Time Low in 2022." https://www.hhs.gov/about/news/2022/08/02/new-hhs-report-shows-national-uninsured-rate-reached-all-time-low-in-2022.html.

———. 2023a. "Fact Sheet: End of the COVID-19 Public Health Emergency." https://www.hhs.gov/about/news/2023/05/09/fact-sheet-end-of-the-covid-19-public-health-emergency.html.

———. 2023b. "The Biden-Harris Administration Takes Critical Action to Make Naloxone More Accessible and Prevent Fatal Overdoses from Opioids Like Fentanyl." https://www.hhs.gov/about/news/2023/03/29/biden-harris-administration-takes-critical-action-make-naloxone-more-accessible-prevent-fatal-overdoses-opioids-fentanyl.html.

———. 2023c. "Biden Harris Administration Invests More Than $80 Million to Help Rural Communities Respond to Fentanyl and Other Opioid Overdose Risks." Health Resources and Services Administration. https://www.hrsa.gov/about/news/press-releases/rcorps-2023-awards.

———. 2023d. "National Uninsured Rate Reaches an All-Time Low in Early 2023." https://www.aspe.hhs.gov/reports/national-uninsured-rate-reaches-all-time-low-early-2023.

Hill, A. 2021. "'I Had Second Thoughts': The Gen Z-ers Choosing Not to Have Children." *Guardian*, April 23. https://www.theguardian.com/society/2021/apr/23/i-had-second-thoughts-the-gen-z-ers-choosing-not-to-have-children.

Hock, H. 2007. "The Pill and the College Attainment of American Women and Men." Working paper, Florida State University. https://coss.fsu.edu/econpapers/wpaper/wp2007_10_01.pdf.

Honoré, B., and A. Lleras-Muney. 2006. "Bounds in Competing Risks Models and the War on Cancer." *Econometrica* 74, no. 6: 1675–98. https://doi.org/10.1111/j.1468-0262.2006.00722.x.

Hooper, K. 2023. "What Role Can Immigration Play in Addressing Current and Future Labor?" Migration Policy Institute. https://www.migrationpolicy.org/research/immigration-addressing-labor-shortages.

Howard, J., and T. Sneed. 2023. "Texas Woman Denied an Abortion tells Senators She 'Nearly Died on their Watch.'" CNN. https://www.cnn.com/2023/04/26/health/abortion-hearing-texas-senators-amanda-zurawski/index.html.

Hoyert, D., and A. Miniño. 2023. "Maternal Mortality Rates in the United States, 2021." Centers for Disease Control and Prevention, National Center for Health

Statistics. https://www.cdc.gov/nchs/data/hestat/maternal-mortality/2021/maternal-mortality-rates-2021.pdf.

Hunt, J., and M. Gauthier-Loiselle. 2010. 'How Much Does Immigration Boost Innovation?" *American Economic Journal: Macroeconomics* 2, no. 2: 31–56. https://doi.org/10.1257/mac.2.2.31.

IRS (U.S. Internal Revenue Service). 2024. "Affordable Care Act Tax Provisions." https://www.irs.gov/affordable-care-act/affordable-care-act-tax-provisions.

Johnson, R., and C. Jackson. 2019. "Reducing Inequality through Dynamic Complementarity: Evidence from Head Start and Public School Spending." *American Economic Journal: Economic Policy* 11, no. 4: 310–49. https://doi.org/10.1257/pol.20180510.

Jones, C. 2019. "Paul Romer: Ideas, Nonrivalry, and Endogenous Growth." *Scandinavian Journal of Economics* 121, no. 3: 859–83. https://doi.org/10.1111/sjoe.12370.

———. 2022. "The End of Economic Growth? Unintended Consequences of a Declining Population." *American Economic Review* 112, no. 11: 3489–527. https://doi.org/10.1257/aer.20201605.

Jones, C., and P. Romer. 2010. "The New Kaldor Facts: Ideas, Institutions, Population, and Human Capital." *American Economic Journal: Macroeconomics* 2, no. 1: 224–45. https://doi.org/10.1257/mac.2.1.224.

Joseph, K., A. Boutin, S. Lisonkova, G. Muraca, N. Razaz, S. John, A. Mehrabadi, Y. Sabr, C. Ananth, and E. Schisterman. 2021. "Maternal Mortality in the United States: Recent Trends, Current Status, and Future Considerations." *Obstetrics Gynecology* 137, no.5: 763–71. https://doi.org/10.1097/AOG.0000000000004361.

Karahan, F., B. Pugsley, and A. Şahin. 2019. *Demographic Origins of the Startup Deficit.* NBER Working Paper 25874. Cambridge, MA: National Bureau for Economic Research. https://doi.org/10.3386/w25874.

Kearney, M., P. Levine, and L. Pardue. 2022. "The Puzzle of Falling U.S. Birth Rates since the Great Recession." *Journal of Economic Perspectives* 36, no. 1: 151–76. https://www.econ.umd.edu/sites/www.econ.umd.edu/files/pubs/jep.36.1.151.pdf.

Kennedy-Moulton, K., S. Miller, P. Persson, M. Rossin-Slater, L. Wherry, and G. Aldana. 2023. *Maternal and Infant Health Inequality: New Evidence from Linked Administrative Data.* NBER Working Paper 30693. Cambridge, MA: National Bureau for Economic Research. https://doi.org/10.3386/w30693.

KFF (Kaiser Family Foundation). 2024. "Medicaid Postpartum Coverage Extension Tracker." https://www.kff.org/medicaid/issue-brief/medicaid-postpartum-coverage-extension-tracker/.

Kolata, G. 2022. "'Sobering' Study Shows Challenges of Egg Freezing." *New York Times.* https://www.nytimes.com/2022/09/23/health/egg-freezing-age-pregnancy.html.

Kuruc, K., S. Vyas, M. Budolfson, M. Geruso, and D. Spears. 2023. "Population Decline: Too Slow for the Urgency of Climate Solutions." University of Texas at Austin, Population Wellbeing Initiative. https://sites.utexas.edu/pwi/files/2023/11/Vienna_authors.pdf.

Lancet. 2022. "Managing the Opioid Crisis in North America and Beyond." Vol. 399, no. 10324: 495. https://doi.org/10.1016/s0140-6736(22)00200-8.

Lawrence, W., N. Freedman, J. McGee-Avila, A. González, Y. Chen, M. Emerson, G. Gee, E. Haozous, A. Haque, M. Inoue-Choi, S. Jackson, B. Lord, A. Nápoles, E. Pérez-Stable, J. Vo, F. Williams, and M. Shiels. 2023. "Trends in Mortality from Poisonings, Firearms, and All Other Injuries by Intent in the U.S., 1999–2020." *JAMA Internal Medicine* 183, no. 8: 849–56. https://doi.org/10.1001/jamainternmed.2023.2509.

Lazzari, E., E. Gray, and G. Chambers. 2021. "The Contribution of Assisted Reproductive Technology to Fertility Rates and Parity Transition: An Analysis of Australian Data." *Demographic Research* 45: 1081–96. https://doi.org/10.4054/demres.2021.45.35.

Lee, K. 2007. "Infant Mortality Decline in the Late 19th and Early 20th Centuries: The Role of Market Milk." *Perspectives in Biology and Medicine* 50, no. 4: 585–602. https://doi.org/10.1353/pbm.2007.0051.

Lee, R., and R. Edwards. 2002. "The Fiscal Effects of Population Aging in the U.S.: Assessing the Uncertainties." *Tax Policy and the Economy* 16: 141–80. https://www.nber.org/books-and-chapters/tax-policy-and-economy-volume-16/fiscal-effects-population-aging-us-assessing-uncertainties.

Lindo, J., and M. Pineda-Torres. 2020. *New Evidence on the Effects of Mandatory Waiting Periods for Abortion.* NBER Working Paper 26228. Cambridge, MA: National Bureau for Economic Research. https://doi.org/10.3386/w26228.

Lister, R., W. Drake, B. Scott, and C. Graves. 2019. "Black Maternal Mortality: The Elephant in the Room." *World Journal of Gynecology & Women's Health* 3, no. 1. https://www.ncbi.nlm.nih.gov/pmc/articles/PMC7384760/.

Livingston, G., and D. Cohn. 2010. "The New Demography of American Motherhood." Pew Research Center, Social & Demographic Trends Project. https://www.pewresearch.org/social-trends/2010/05/06/the-new-demography-of-american-motherhood/.

Maestas, N., K. Mullen, and D. Powell. 2016. "The Effect of Population Aging on Economic Growth, The Labor Force and Productivity." Working Paper, RAND Labor & Population. https://www.rand.org/content/dam/rand/pubs/working_papers/WR1000/WR1063-1/RAND_WR1063-1.pdf.

Mancher, M., and A. Leshner. 2019. "The Effectiveness of Medication-Based Treatment for Opioid Use Disorder." In *Medications for Opioid Use Disorder Save Lives*, ed. M. Mancher and A. Leshner. Washington: National Academies Press. https://doi.org/10.17226/25310.

McCann, A., and A. Walker. 2023. "Dozens of Abortion Clinics Have Closed Since *Roe v. Wade* Was Overturned." *New York Times.* https://www.nytimes.com/interactive/2023/06/22/us/abortion-clinics-dobbs-roe-wade.html.

Mehta, L., T. Beckie, H. DeVon, C. Grines, H. Krumholz, M. Johnson, K. Lindley, V. Vaccarino, T. Wang, K. Watson, and N. Wenger. 2016. "Acute Myocardial Infarction in Women." *Circulation*, vol. 133, no. 9. https://www.ahajournals.org/doi/10.1161/CIR.0000000000000351.

Miller, S., N. Johnson, and L. Wherry. 2019. *Medicaid and Mortality: New Evidence from Linked Survey and Administrative Data.* NBER Working Paper 26081. Cambridge, MA: National Bureau for Economic Research. https://doi.org/10.3386/w26081.

Miller, S., and L. Wherry. 2019. "The Long-Term Effects of Early Life Medicaid Coverage." *Journal of Human Resources* 54, no. 3: 785–824. https://doi.org/10.3368/jhr.54.3.0816.8173r1.

Miller, S., L. Wherry, and D. Foster. 2023. "The Economic Consequences of Being Denied an Abortion." *American Economic Journal: Economic Policy* 15, no. 1: 394–437. https://doi.org/10.1257/pol.20210159.

Modigliani, F., and R. Brumberg. 1954. "Utility Analysis and the Consumption Function." In *The Collected Papers of Franco Modigliani*, ed. F. Modigliani. Cambridge, MA: MIT Press. https://doi.org/10.7551/mitpress/1923.001.0001.

Morrissey, T. 2017. "Child Care and Parent Labor Force Participation: A Review of the Research Literature." *Review of Economics of the Household* 15, no. 1: 1–24. https://doi.org/10.1007/s11150-016-9331-3.

Mulcahy, A., C. Whaley, M. Gizaw, D. Schwam, N. Edenfield, and A. Becerra-Ornelas. 2022. "International Prescription Drug Price Comparisons: Current Empirical Estimates and Comparisons with Previous Studies." Health and Human Services Department, Office of the Assistant Secretary for Planning and Evaluation. https://aspe.hhs.gov/reports/international-prescription-drug-price-comparisons.

Myers, C. 2017. "The Power of Abortion Policy: Reexamining the Effects of Young Women's Access to Reproductive Control." *Journal of Political Economy* 125, no. 6: 2178–2224. https://doi.org/10.1086/694293.

Myers, C., L. Bennett, F. Vale, and A. Nieto. 2023. "Abortion Access Dashboard." https://experience.arcgis.com/experience/6e360741bfd84db79d5db774a1147815.

Nash, E., and I. Guarnieri. 2022. "13 States Have Abortion Trigger Bans—Here's What Happens When *Roe* Is Overturned." Guttmacher Institute. https://www.guttmacher.org/article/2022/06/13-states-have-abortion-trigger-bans-heres-what-happens-when-roe-overturned.

NHEA (National Health Expenditure Data). 2023. "National Health Expenditure Data." https://www.cms.gov/data-research/statistics-trends-and-reports/national-health-expenditure-data.

OECD (Organization for Economic Cooperation and Development). 2021. "Health at a Glance 2021: OECD Indicators." https://doi.org/10.1787/7a7afb35-en.

Osterman, P. 2017. *Who Will Care for Us? Long-Term Care and the Long-Term Workforce.* New York: Russell Sage Foundation. https://www.russellsage.org/publications/who-will-care-us-0.

Ottaviano, G., and G. Peri. 2012. "Rethinking the Effect of Immigration on Wages." *Journal of the European Economic Association* 10, no 1:152–97. https://doi.org/10.1111/j.1542-4774.2011.01052.x.

Parker, K., and R. Minkin. 2023. "Public Has Mixed Views on the Modern American Family." Pew Research Center. https://www.pewresearch.org/social-trends/2023/09/14/public-has-mixed-views-on-the-modern-american-family/.

Peri, G. 2012. "The Effect of Immigration on Productivity: Evidence from U.S. States." *Review of Economics and Statistics* 94, no. 1: 348–58. https://doi.org/10.1162/REST_a_00137.

Peri, G., and C. Sparber. 2009. "Task Specialization, Immigration, and Wages." *American Economic Journal: Applied Economics*, 1 no. 3: 135–69. https://doi.org/10.1257/app.1.3.135.

Peters, M. 2022. "Market Size and Spatial Growth—Evidence from Germany's Post-War Population Expulsions." *Econometrica* 90, no. 5: 2357–96. https://doi.org/10.3982/ecta18002.

PHI (Paraprofessional Healthcare Institute). 2022. "Direct Care Workers in the United States." https://www.phinational.org/wp-content/uploads/2022/08/DCW-in-the-United-States-2022-PHI.pdf.

Picchi, A. 2022. "It Now Costs $310,000 to Raise a Child: 'Something Has to Give.'" CBS News. https://www.cbsnews.com/news/raising-a-child-costs-310000/.

Prato, M. 2022. "The Global Race for Talent: Brain Drain, Knowledge, Transfer, and Growth." Working Paper, World Bank. https://thedocs.worldbank.org/en/doc/35e299dda0bce4645403a3418356b405-0050022023/original/prato-global-race-talent-november2022.pdf.

PWI (Population Wellbeing Initiative, University of Texas at Austin). 2023. "Projections of Long-Term Population Decline for the United States: Causes, Consequences, and Responses to Sustained Low Birth Rates." PWI Policy Discussion Paper. https://sites.utexas.edu/pwi/us_long-term_population_decline/.

Reinhard, S., S. Caldera, A. Houser, and R. Choula. 2023. "Valuing the Invaluable: 2023 Update." AARP Public Policy Initiative. https://doi.org/10.26419/ppi.00082.006.

Ritchie, H. 2023. "The U.N. Has Made Population Projections for More Than 50 Years—How Accurate Have They Been?" OurWorldInData.org. https://ourworldindata.org/population-projections.

Romer, P. 2018. "Prize Lecture: On the Possibility of Progress." Nobel Prize in Economics. https://www.nobelprize.org/prizes/economic-sciences/2018/romer/lecture/.

Sabelhaus, J. 2023. "Will Population Aging Push Us Over a Fiscal Cliff?" Aspen Institute Economic Strategy Group. https://www.economicstrategygroup.org/publication/population-aging-fiscal-cliff/.

Sabo, S., and S. Johnson. 2022. "Pandemic Disrupted Historical Mortality Patterns, Caused Largest Jump in Deaths in 100 Years." U.S. Census Bureau. https://www.census.gov/library/stories/2022/03/united-states-deaths-spiked-as-covid-19-continued.html.

Schmitz, H., and M. Westphal. 2017. "Informal Care and Long-Term Labor Market Outcomes." *Journal of Health Economics* 56: 1–18. https://doi.org/10.1016/j.jhealeco.2017.09.002.

Schnell, M. 2022. "Physician Behavior in the Presence of a Secondary Market: The Case of Prescription Opioids." Working paper. https://static1.squarespace.com/static/572372e7c2ea51b309e9991a/t/62a361101fa2c47a22943335/1654874393320/Schnell_06102022.pdf.

Schwandt, H., J. Currie, M. Bär, J. Banks, P. Bertoli, A. Bütikofer, S. Cattan, B. Chao, C. Costa, L. González, V. Grembi, K. Huttunen, R. Karadakic, L. Kraftman, S. Krutikova, S. Lombardi, P. Redler, C. Riumallo-Herl, A. Rodríguez-González, K. Salvanes, P. Santana, J. Thuilliez, E. Doorslaer, T. Ourti, J. Winter, B. Wouterse, and A. Wuppermann. 2021. "Inequality in Mortality between Black and White Americans by Age, Place, and Cause and in Comparison to Europe, 1990 to 2018." *Proceedings of the National Academy of Sciences of the United States of America* 118, no. 40. https://doi.org/10.1073/pnas.2104684118.

Sellers, F., and F. Nirappil. 2022. "Confusion Post-*Roe* Spurs Deals, Denials for Some Lifesaving Pregnancy Care." *Washington Post*. https://www.washingtonpost.com/health/2022/07/16/abortion-miscarriage-ectopic-pregnancy-care/.

Sheiner, L. 2018. *The Long-Term Impact of Aging on the Federal Budget.* Hutchins Center Working Paper 40. Washington: Brookings Institution. https://www.brookings.edu/wp-content/uploads/2018/01/wp405.pdf.

Shen, K. 2023. "Who Benefits from Public Financing of Home-Based Long Term Care? Evidence from Medicaid." Working Paper, SSRN. http://dx.doi.org/10.2139/ssrn.4523279.

Shepard, K., R. Roubein, and C. Kitchener. 2022. "1 in 3 American Women Have Already Lost Abortion Access; More Restrictive Laws Are Coming." *Washington Post*. https://www.washingtonpost.com/nation/2022/08/22/more-trigger-bans-loom-1-3-women-lose-most-abortion-access-post-roe/.

Smith, D., and B. Bradshaw. 2006. "Variation in Life Expectancy During the Twentieth Century in the United States." *Demography* 43: 647–57. https://doi.org/10.1353/dem.2006.0039.

Smith, S., J. Newhouse, and G. Cuckler. 2022. *Health Care Spending Growth Has Slowed: Will the Bend in the Curve Continue?* NBER Working Paper 30782. Cambridge, MA: National Bureau for Economic Research. https://doi.org/10.3386/w30782.

Smock, P., and C. Schwartz. 2020. "The Demography of Families: A Review of Patterns and Change." *Journal of Marriage and Family* 82, no. 1: 9–34. https://doi.org/10.1111/jomf.12612.

Sobotka, T., V. Skirbekk, and D. Philipov. 2011. "Economic Recession and Fertility in the Developed World." *Population and Development Review* 37, no. 2: 267–306. https://doi.org/10.1111/j.1728-4457.2011.00411.x.

Soni, A., L. Wherry, and K. Simon. 2020. "How Have ACA Insurance Expansions Affected Health Outcomes? Findings from the Literature." *Health Affairs* 39, no. 3: 371–78. https://doi.org/10.1377/hlthaff.2019.01436.

Spears, D. 2023. "The World's Population May Peak in Your Lifetime; What Happens Next?" *New York Times.* https://www.nytimes.com/interactive/2023/09/18/opinion/human-population-global-growth.html.

Spears. D., S. Vyas, G. Weston, and M. Geruso. 2023. "Long-Term Population Projections: Scenarios of Low or Rebounding Fertility." Working Paper, SSRN. https://dx.doi.org/10.2139/ssrn.4534047.

SSA (U.S. Social Security Administration). 2023a. "National Average Wage Index." https://www.ssa.gov/oact/cola/AWI.html.

———. 2023b. "2023 OASDI Trustees Report." https://www.ssa.gov/OACT/TR/2023/VI_G2_OASDHI_GDP.html.

———. 2023c. "The 2023 Annual Report of the Board of Trustees of the Federal Old-Age and Survivors Insurance and Federal Disability Insurance Trust Funds." https://www.ssa.gov/oact/TR/2023/tr2023.pdf.

Steuerle, C., A. Carasso, and L. Cohen. 2004. "How Progressive Is Social Security and Why?" Urban Institute. 2004. https://www.urban.org/sites/default/files/publication/57666/311016-how-progressive-is-social-security-and-why-.pdf.

Steuerle, C., and K. Smith. 2023. "Social Security & Medicare Lifetime Benefits and Taxes: 2022." Urban Institute and Brookings Institution, Tax Policy Center. https://www.taxpolicycenter.org/publications/social-security-medicare-lifetime-benefits-and-taxes-2022/full.

Syverson, C. 2017. "Challenges to Mismeasurement Explanations for the U.S. Productivity Slowdown." *Journal of Economic Perspectives* 31, no. 2: 165–86. https://doi.org/10.1257/jep.31.2.165.

Turner, N., K. Danesh, and K. Moran. 2020. "The Evolution of Infant Mortality Inequality in the United States, 1960–2016." *Science Advances* 6, no. 29. https://doi.org/10.1126/sciadv.aba5908.

U.N. DESA (United Nations, Department of Economic and Social Affairs, Population Division). 2012. "2012 Revision." https://population.un.org/wpp/Download/Archive/Standard/.

———. 2022a. *World Population Prospects 2022.* https://population.un.org/wpp/.

———. 2022b. *Methodology Report: World Population Prospects 2022.* https://population.un.org/wpp/Publications/Files/WPP2022_Methodology.pdf.

———. 2023. "India Overtakes China as the World's Most Populous Country." Policy Brief 153. https://www.un.org/development/desa/dpad/publication/un-desa-policy-brief-no-153-india-overtakes-china-as-the-worlds-most-populous-country.

U.S. Department of the Treasury. 2023. "General Explanations of the Administration's Fiscal Year 2024 Revenue Proposals." https://home.treasury.gov/system/files/131/General-Explanations-FY2024.pdf.

Valero, A. 2021. *Education and Economic Growth.* CEP Discussion Paper 1764. London: Centre for Economic Performance. https://files.eric.ed.gov/fulltext/ED614082.pdf.

Vespa, J., L. Medina, and D. Armstrong. 2020. "Demographic Turning Points for the United States: Population Projections for 2020 to 2060." U.S. Census Bureau. https://www.census.gov/content/dam/Census/library/publications/2020/demo/p25-1144.pdf.

WeCount. 2023. "#WeCount Report April 2022 to June 2023." Society of Family Planning. https://societyfp.org/wp-content/uploads/2023/10/WeCountReport_10.16.23.pdf.

White, C., J. Cubanski, and T. Neuman. 2014. "How Much of the Medicare Spending Slowdown Can be Explained? Insights and Analysis from 2014." Issue Brief, Kaiser Family Foundation. https://files.kff.org/attachment/issue-brief-how-much-of-the-medicare-spending-slowdown-can-be-explained-insights-and-analysis-from-2014.

White House. 2021. "Fact Sheet: Vice President Kamala Harris Announces Call to Action to Reduce Maternal Mortality and Morbidity." https://www.whitehouse.gov/briefing-room/statements-releases/2021/12/07/fact-sheet-vice-president-kamala-harris-announces-call-to-action-to-reduce-maternal-mortality-and-morbidity/.

———. 2022a. "Fact Sheet: The Biden Administration's Historic Investments to Create Opportunity and Build Wealth in Rural America." https://www.whitehouse.gov/briefing-room/statements-releases/2022/03/01/fact-sheet-the-biden-administrations-historic-investments-to-create-opportunity-and-build-wealth-in-rural-america/.

———. 2022b. "National Drug Control Strategy." https://www.whitehouse.gov/wp-content/uploads/2022/04/National-Drug-Control-2022Strategy.pdf.

———. 2022c. "Fact Sheet: President Biden to Sign Executive Order Protecting Access to Reproductive Health Care Services." https://www.whitehouse.gov/

briefing-room/statements-releases/2022/07/08/
fact-sheet-president-biden-to-sign-executive-order-protecting-access-to-repro-
ductive-health-care-services/.

———. 2022d. "White House Blueprint for Addressing the Maternal Health Crisis."
https://www.whitehouse.gov/wp-content/uploads/2022/06/Maternal-Health-
Blueprint.pdf.

———. 2023a. "Fact Sheet: Biden-Harris Administration Announces Most Sweeping Set
of Executive Actions to Improve Care in History." https://www.whitehouse.gov/
briefing-room/statements-releases/2023/04/18/
fact-sheet-biden-harris-administration-announces-most-sweeping-set-of-execu-
tive-actions-to-improve-care-in-history/.

———. 2023b. "ICYMI: Biden-Harris Administration Announces $450M to Support
President Biden's Unity Agenda Efforts to Beat the Overdose Epidemic & Save
Lives." https://www.whitehouse.gov/ondcp/briefing-room/2023/09/01/
icymi-biden-%E2%81%A0harris-administration-announces-450m-to-support-
president-bidens-unity-agenda-efforts-to-beat-the-overdose-epidemic-save-lives.

———. 2023c. "The President and First Lady's Cancer Moonshot." https://www.white-
house.gov/cancermoonshot/.

———. 2023d. "Fact Sheet: President Joe Biden to Announce First-Ever White House
Initiative on Women's Health Research, an Effort led by First Lady Jill Biden
and the White House Gender Policy Council." https://www.whitehouse.gov/
briefing-room/statements-releases/2023/11/13/
fact-sheet-president-joe-biden-to-announce-first-ever-white-house-initiative-
on-womens-health-research-an-effort-led-by-first-lady-jill-biden-and-the-white-
house-gender-policy-council/.

———. 2023e. "Remarks as Prepared for Delivery by First Lady Jill Biden on a Press
Call Announcing White House Initiative on Women's Health Research." https://
www.whitehouse.gov/briefing-room/speeches-remarks/2023/11/13/
remarks-as-prepared-for-delivery-by-first-lady-jill-biden-on-a-press-call-
announcing-white-house-initiative-on-womens-health-research/.

———. 2023f. "Fact Sheet: One Year In, President Biden's Inflation Reduction Act Is
Driving Historic Climate Action and Investing in America to Create Good
Paying Jobs and Reduce Costs." https://www.whitehouse.gov/briefing-room/
statements-releases/2023/08/16/
fact-sheet-one-year-in-president-bidens-inflation-reduction-act-is-driving-
historic-climate-action-and-investing-in-america-to-create-good-paying-jobs-
-and-reduce-costs/.

———. 2023g. "Fact Sheet: President Biden Issues Executive Order on Strengthening
Access to Contraception." https://www.whitehouse.gov/briefing-room/state-
ments-releases/2023/06/23/
fact-sheet-president-biden-issues-executive-order-on-strengthening-access-to-
contraception/.

Woodcock, A., G. Carter, J. Baayd, D. Turok, J. Turk, J. Sanders, M. Pangasa, L. Gawron, and J. Kaiser. 2023. "Effects of the Dobbs v Jackson Women's Health Organization Decision on Obstetrics and Gynecology Graduating Residents' Practice Plans." *Obstetrics & Gynecology* 142, no. 5: 1105–11. https://doi.org/10.1097/AOG.0000000000005383.

Xu, J., S. Murphy, K. Kochanek, and E. Arias. 2022. "Mortality in the United States, 2021." Centers for Disease Control and Prevention, National Center for Health Statistics. https://www.cdc.gov/nchs/products/databriefs/db456.htm.

Chapter 4

Aaronson, D., D. Hartley, and B. Mazumder. 2021. "The Effects of the 1930s HOLC 'Redlining' Maps." *American Economic Journal: Economic Policy* 13, no. 4: 355–92. https://doi.org/10.1257/pol.20190414.

Aldern, C. and G. Colburn. 2022. *Homelessness Is a Housing Problem: How Structural Factors Explain U.S. Patterns*. Berkeley: University of California Press. https://homelessnesshousingproblem.com/.

Avenancio-Leon, C., and T. Howard. 2022. "The Assessment Gap: Racial Inequalities in Properly Taxation." *Quarterly Journal of Economics* 137, no. 3: 1383–1434. https://doi.org/10.1093/qje/qjac009.

Barber, J. 2019. "Berkeley Zoning Has Served for Many Decades to Separate the Poor from the Rich and Whites from People of Color." *Berkeleyside*. https://www.berkeleyside.org/2019/03/12/berkeley-zoning-has-served-for-many-decades-to-separate-the-poor-from-the-rich-and-whites-from-people-of-color.

Baum-Snow, N. 2023. "Constraints on City and Neighborhood Growth: The Central Role of Housing Supply." *Journal of Economic Perspective* 37, no. 2: 53–74. https://doi.org/10.1257/jep.37.2.53.

Baum-Snow, N., and J. Marion. 2009. "The Effects of Low-Income Housing Tax Credit Developments on Neighborhoods." *Journal of Public Economics* 93: nos. 5–6: 654–66. https://doi.org/10.1016/j.jpubeco.2009.01.001.

Bayer, P., F. Ferreira, and S. Ross. 2016. "The Vulnerability of Minority Homeowners in the Housing Boom and Bust." *American Economic Journal: Economic Policy* 8, no. 1: 1–27. http://dx.doi.org/10.1257/pol.20140074.

Been, V., I. Ellen, and K. O'Regan. 2023. "Supply Skepticism Revisited." NYU Law and Economics Research Paper. https://ssrn.com/abstract=4629628.

Been, V., I. Ellen, A. Schwartz, L. Stiefel, and M. Weinstein. 2011. "Does Losing Your Home Mean Losing Your School? Effects of Foreclosures on the School Mobility of Children." *Regional Science and Urban Economics* 41: 407–14. https://nyuscholars.nyu.edu/en/publications/does-losing-your-home-mean-losing-your-school-effects-of-foreclos.

Benioff Homelessness and Housing Initiative. 2023. "Executive Summary of the California Statewide Study of People Experiencing Homelessness." University of California, San Francisco. https://homelessness.ucsf.edu/sites/default/files/2023-06/CASPEH_Executive_Summary_62023.pdf.

Berkeley Economic Review. 2019. "Baby Boomers and the Future of Homeownership in the United States." https://econreview.berkeley.edu/baby-boomers-and-the-future-of-homeownership-in-the-united-states/.

Brasuell, J. 2021. "Charlotte's New, Controversial Comprehensive Plan to End Single-Family Zoning." Planetizen. https://www.planetizen.com/news/2021/06/113893-charlottes-new-controversial-comprehensive-plan-end-single-family-zoning.

———. 2023. "Vermont Latest State to Preempt Single-Family Zoning." Planetizen. https://www.planetizen.com/news/2023/06/123767-vermont-latest-state-preempt-single-family-zoning.

Bronin, S. 2023. "Zoning by a Thousand Cuts." *50 Pepperdine Law Review* 719. https://dx.doi.org/10.2139/ssrn.3792544.

Bui, Q., M. Chaban, and J. White. 2016. "40 Percent of the Buildings in Manhattan Could Not Be Built Today." *New York Times*, May 20. https://www.nytimes.com/interactive/2016/05/19/upshot/forty-percent-of-manhattans-buildings-could-not-be-built-today.html.

Byrne, T., E. Munley, J. Fargo, A. Montgomery, and D. Culhane. 2016. "New Perspectives on Community-Level Determinants of Homelessness." *Journal of Urban Affairs* 35, no. 5: 607–25. https://doi.org/10.1111/j.1467-9906.2012.00643.x.

Calanog, V., T. Metcalfe, and K. Fagan. 2023. "The Outlook for the Housing Market." *Moody's Analytics*, Quarterly Analysis. https://cre.moodysanalytics.com/insights/research/q42022-the-outlook-for-the-housing-market/.

California Department of Housing and Community Development. 2023. "Regional Housing Needs Allocation (RHNA)." https://www.hcd.ca.gov/planning-and-community-development/regional-housing-needs-allocation.

Card, D., J. Rothstein, and M. Yi. 2023. *Location, Location, Location.* NBER Working Paper 31587. Cambridge, MA: National Bureau of Economic Research. https://doi.org/10.3386/w31587.

Carroll, D., and R. Cohen-Kristiansen. 2021. "Evaluating Homeownership as the Solution to Wealth Inequality." Federal Reserve Bank of Cleveland, "Economic Commentary." https://www.clevelandfed.org/publications/economic-commentary/2021/ec-202122-evaluating-homeownership-as-the-solution-to-wealth-inequality.

CBRE (Coldwell Banker Richard Ellis). 2022. "2022 U.S. Construction Cost Trends." https://www.cbre.com/insights/books/2022-us-construction-cost-trends#:~:text=CBRE%27s%20new%20Construction%20Cost%20Index,material%20costs%20continue%20to%20rise.

CEA (Council of Economic Advisers). 2021. "Exclusionary Zoning: Its Effect on Racial Discrimination in the Housing Market." https://www.whitehouse.gov/cea/written-materials/2021/06/17/exclusionary-zoning-its-effect-on-racial-discrimination-in-the-housing-market/.

———. 2023a. "An Update on Housing Inflation in the Consumer Price Index." https://www.whitehouse.gov/cea/written-materials/2023/04/27/update-on-housing-inflation-in-cpi/.

———. 2023b. "The Anti-Poverty and Income-Boosting Impacts of the Enhanced CTC." https://www.whitehouse.gov/cea/written-materials/2023/11/20/the-anti-poverty-and-income-boosting-impacts-of-the-enhanced-ctc/.

CFPB (Consumer Financial Protection Bureau). 2021. "Manufactured Housing Finance: New Insights from the Home Mortgage Disclosure Act Data." https://files.consumerfinance.gov/f/documents/cfpb_manufactured-housing-finance-new-insights-hmda_report_2021-05.pdf.

Chester, M., et al. 2015. "Parking Infrastructure: A Constraint on or Opportunity for Urban Redevelopment? A Study of Los Angeles County Parking Supply and Growth." https://www.tandfonline.com/doi/full/10.1080/01944363.2015.1092879.

Chetty, R., and N. Hendren. 2018. "The Impacts of Neighborhoods on Intergenerational Mobility I: Childhood Exposure Effects." *Quarterly Journal of Economics* 133, no. 3: 1107–62. https://doi.org/10.1093/qje/qjy007.

Chetty, R., N. Hendren, and L. Katz. 2016. "The Effects of Exposure to Better Neighborhoods on Children: New Evidence from the Moving to Opportunity Experiment." *American Economic Review* 106, no. 4: 855–902. https://doi.org/10.1257/aer.20150572.

Choi, J., J. Zhu, and L. Goodman. 2018. "Is Homeownership Inherited? A Tale of Three Millennials." Urban Institute. https://www.urban.org/urban-wire/homeownership-inherited-tale-three-millennials.

Chyn, E., and L. Katz. 2021. "Neighborhoods Matter: Assessing the Evidence for Place Effects." *Journal of Economic Perspectives* 35, no. 4: 197–222. https://doi.org/10.1257/jep.35.4.197.

Code of Federal Regulations. 2023. "Title 24: Housing and Urban Development." https://www.ecfr.gov/current/title-24/subtitle-B/chapter-XX.

Collinson, R., J. Humphries, N. Mader, D. Reed, D. Tannenbaum, and W. Dijk. 2023. *Eviction and Poverty in American Cities.* NBER Working Paper 30382. Cambridge, MA: National Bureau of Economic Research. https://www.nber.org/papers/w30382.

Commonwealth of Massachusetts. 2023. "Multi-Family Zoning Requirement for MBTA Communities." Executive Office of Housing and Livable Communities. https://www.mass.gov/info-details/multi-family-zoning-requirement-for-mbta-communities.

Center on Budget and Policy Priorities. 2017. "United States Housing Choice Vouchers Fact Sheet." https://www.cbpp.org/sites/default/files/atoms/files/3-10-14hous-factsheets_us.pdf.

Cornelissen, S., and L. Pack. 2023. "Immigrants' Access to Homeownership in the United States: A Review of Barriers, Discrimination, and Opportunities." Joint Center for Housing Studies at Harvard University. https://www.jchs.harvard.edu/sites/default/files/research/files/harvard_jchs_immigrant_homeownership_cornelissen_pack_2023.pdf.

Cromwell, M. 2022. "Housing Costs a Big Burden on Renters in Largest U.S. Counties." U.S. Census Bureau, America Counts. https://www.census.gov/library/stories/2022/12/housing-costs-burden.html.

CRS (Congressional Research Service). 2021. "An Overview of the HOME Investment Partnerships Program." https://sgp.fas.org/crs/misc/R40118.pdf.

Crump, S., T. Mattos, J. Schuetz, and L. Schuster. 2020. "Fixing Greater Boston's Housing Crisis Starts with Legalizing Apartments Near Transit." Brookings Institution. https://www.brookings.edu/articles/fixing-greater-bostons-housing-crisis-starts-with-legalizing-apartments-near-transit/.

DBRS Morningstar. 2023. "DBRS Morningstar CMBS Monthly Highlights—June Remittance: Delinquency and Special Servicing Rates Move Higher on Continued Office Underperformance." https://www.dbrsmorningstar.com/research/417134.

Derenoncourt, E., C. Kim, M. Kuhn, and M. Schularick. 2023. "Wealth of Two Nations: The U.S. Racial Wealth Gap, 1860–2020." *Quarterly Journal of Economics.* https://doi.org/10.1093/qje/qjad044.

Desegregate Connecticut. No date. "FAQS." https://www.desegregatect.org/faqs.

Diamond, R., A. Guren, and R. Tan. 2020. *The Effect of Foreclosures on Homeowners, Tenants, and Landlords.* NBER Working Paper 27358. Cambridge, MA: National Bureau of Economic Research. https://doi.org/10.3386/w27358.

Diamond, R., and T. McQuade. 2019. "Who Wants Affordable Housing in Their Backyard? An Equilibrium Analysis of Low-Income Property Development." *Journal of Political Economy* 3: 1063–1117. https://doi.org/10.1086/701354.

Diamond, R., T. McQuade, and F. Qian. 2018. *The Effects of Rent Control Expansion on Tenants, Landlords, and Inequality: Evidence from San Francisco.* NBER Working Paper 24181. Cambridge, MA: National Bureau of Economic Research. https://www.nber.org/system/files/working_papers/w24181/w24181.pdf.

Dietrich, E. 2023. "Homeowner Group Files Court Challenge Against Pro-Construction Housing Laws." *Montana Free Press.* https://montanafreepress.org/2023/12/15/homeowner-group-files-court-challenge-against-pro-construction-housing-laws/.

DiSalvo, R., and J. Yu. 2023. "Housing Affordability and School Quality in the United States." *Journal of Housing Economics* 60. https://doi.org/10.1016/j.jhe.2023.101933.

DOT (U.S. Department of Transportation). 2023. "Reconnecting Communities and Neighborhoods Grant Program." https://www.transportation.gov/grants/rcnprogram.

Eriksen, M., and S. Rosenthal. 2010. "Crowd Out Effects of Place-Based Subsidized Rental Housing: New Evidence from the LIHTC Program." *Journal of Public Economics* 94, nos. 11–12: 953–66. https://doi.org/10.1016/j.jpubeco.2010.07.002.

Fang, L., N. Stewart, and J. Tyndall. 2023. "Homeowner Politics and Housing Supply." *Journal of Urban Economics* 138. https://doi.org/10.1016/j.jue.2023.103608.

FHFA (Federal Housing Finance Agency). 2022. "Duty to Serve Underserved Markets Plan." https://sf.freddiemac.com/docs/pdf/marketing-materials/freddie-mac-underserved-markets-plan.pdf.

Fischel, W. 2001. *The Homevoter Hypothesis: How Home Values Influence Local Government Taxation, School Finance, and Land-Use Policies*. Cambridge, MA: Harvard University Press. https://www.hup.harvard.edu/catalog.php?isbn=9780674015951.

———. 2004. "An Economic History of Zoning and a Cure for Its Exclusionary Effects." *Urban Studies* 41. https://doi.org/10.1080/0042098032000165271.

Flint, A. 2022, "The State of Local Zoning: Reforming a Century-Old Approach to Land Use." Lincoln Institute of Land Policy. https://www.lincolninst.edu/publications/articles/2022-12-state-local-zoning-reform.

Frank, T. 2021. "End to Single-Family Zoning in Berkeley Forces Us to Reflect on Our Past." Sierra Club, San Francisco Bay, blog. https://www.sierraclub.org/san-francisco-bay/blog/2021/06/end-single-family-zoning-berkeley-forces-us-reflect-our-past.

Francke, M., and M. Korevaar. 2022. "Baby Booms and Asset Booms: Demographic Change and the Housing Market." Working paper, SSRN. https://dx.doi.org/10.2139/ssrn.3368036.

Freddie Mac. 2022. "Could More Inclusive Zoning for Manufactured Homes Help Address the Current Housing Supply Gap?" Single-Family Division. https://sf.freddiemac.com/articles/insights/could-more-inclusive-zoning-for-manufactured-homes-help-address-the-current-housing-supply-gap.

———. No date. "Manufactured Housing." Single-Family Division. https://sf.freddiemac.com/working-with-us/affordable-lending/duty-to-serve/manufactured-housing.

Freedman, M., and E. Owens. 2011. "Low-Income Housing Development and Crime." *Journal of Urban Economics* 70, nos. 2–3: 115–31. https://doi.org/10.1016/j.jue.2011.04.001.

FTA (Federal Transit Administration). 2023. "Areas of Persistent Poverty Program." https://www.transit.dot.gov/grant-programs/areas-persistent-poverty-program.

Furth, S., and N. Gray. 2019. "Do Minimum-Lot-Size Regulation Limit Housing Supply in Texas?' Mercatus Center at George Mason University. https://www.mercatus.org/publications/urban-economics/do-minimum-lot-size-regulations-limit-housing-supply-texas.

Furth, S., and M. Webster. 2022. "Single-Family Zoning and Race: Evidence from the Twin Cities." Working paper, Mercatus Center at George Mason University. https://www.mercatus.org/research/working-papers/single-family-zoning-and-race-evidence-twin-cities.

Gabbe, C., G. Pierce, and G. Clowers. 2020. "Parking Policy: The Effects of Residential Minimum Parking Requirements in Seattle." *Land Use Policy* 91: 104053. https://doi.org/10.1016/j.landusepol.2019.104053.

Ganong, P., and D. Shoag. 2017. "Why Has Regional Income Convergence in the U.S. Declined?" *Journal of Urban Economics* 102: 76–90. https://doi.org/10.1016/j.jue.2017.07.002.

Garcia, D. 2019. "Making It Pencil: The Math Behind Housing Development." UC Berkeley Terner Center for Housing Innovation. https://ternercenter.berkeley.edu/wp-content/uploads/pdfs/Making_It_Pencil_The_Math_Behind_Housing_Development.pdf.

Garcia, D., et al. 2022. "Unlocking the Potential of Missing Middle Housing." Terner Center at UC Berkeley. https://ternercenter.berkeley.edu/wp-content/uploads/2022/12/Missing-Middle-Brief-December-2022.pdf.

Gensheimer, S., M. Eisenberg, D. Hindman, A. Wu, and C. Pollack. 2022. "Examining Health Care Access and Health of Children Living in Homes Subsidized by the Low-Income Housing Tax Credit." *Health Affairs* 41, no. 6: 883–92. https://doi.org/10.1377/hlthaff.2021.01806.

Gerardi, K., L. Lambie-Hanson, and P. Willen. 2021. "Racial Differences in Mortgage Refinancing, Distress, and Housing Wealth Accumulation during COVID-19." Federal Reserve Bank of Boston, "Current Policy Perspectives." https://www.bostonfed.org/publications/current-policy-perspectives/2021/racial-differences-in-mortgage-refinancing-distress-and-housing-wealth-accumulation-during-covid-19.aspx.

Glaeser, E., J. Gyourko, and R. Saks. 2005. "Why Have Housing Prices Gone Up?" *American Economic Review* 95, no. 2: 329–33. https://doi.org/10.1257/000282805774669961.

Gong, Y., and Y. Yao. 2022. "Demographic Changes and the Housing Market." *Regional Science and Urban Economics* 95. https://www.sciencedirect.com/science/article/abs/pii/S0166046221000946

Goodman, L., J. Choi, and J. Zhu. 2023. "The 'Real' Homeownership Gap between Today's Young Adults and Past Generations Is Much Larger Thank You Think." Urban Institute, *Urban Wire*. https://www.urban.org/urban-wire/real-homeownership-gap-between-todays-young-adults-and-past-generations-much-larger-you.

Goodman, L., and B. Ganesh. 2018. "Challenges to Obtaining Manufactured Home Financing." Urban Institute. https://www.urban.org/sites/default/files/publication/98687/challenges_to_obtaining_manufactured_home_financing_0.pdf.

Goolsbee, A., and C. Syverson. *The Strange and Awful Path of Productivity in the U.S. Construction Sector.* NBER Working Paper 30845. Cambridge, MA: National Bureau of Economic Research. https://doi.org/10.3386/w30845.

Gould Ellen, I. 2018. "What Do We Know About Housing Choice Vouchers?" NYU Furman Center. https://furmancenter.org/files/fact-sheets/HousingChoiceVouchers_ige.pdf.

Gould Ellen, I., J. De la Roca, and J. Steil. 2015. "Black and Latino Segregation and Socioeconomic Outcomes." NYU Furman Center Research Brief. https://furmancenter.org/research/publication/black-and-latino-segregation-and-socioeconomic-outcomes.

Grabar, H. 2018. "Minneapolis Confronts Its History of Housing Segregation." *Slate*, December 7. https://slate.com/business/2018/12/minneapolis-single-family-zoning-housing-racism.html.

Graetz, N., C. Gershenson, P. Hepburn, S. Porter, D. Sandler, and M. Desmond. 2023. "A Comprehensive Demographic Profile of the U.S. Evicted Population." 2023. *Proceedings of the National Academy of Sciences* 120, no. 41: e2305860120. https://www.pnas.org/doi/10.1073/pnas.2305860120.

Gray, M. 2022. *Arbitrary Lines: How Zoning Broke the American City and How to Fix It.* Washington: Island Press. https://www.theatlantic.com/ideas/archive/2022/10/california-accessory-dwelling-units-legalization-yimby/671648/.

Greenaway-McGrevy, R. 2023. *Can Zoning Reform Reduce Housing Costs? Evidence from Rents in Auckland.* Economic Policy Centre Working Paper 016. Auckland: University of Aukland Business School. https://cdn.auckland.ac.nz/assets/business/about/our-research/research-institutes-and-centres/Economic-Policy-Centre--EPC-/WP016.pdf.

Greene, S., and J. González-Hermoso. 2019. "How Communities Are Rethinking Zoning to Improve Housing Affordability and Access to Opportunity." Urban Institute, *Urban Wire.* https://www.urban.org/urban-wire/how-communities-are-rethinking-z.oning-improve-housing-affordability-and-access-opportunity.

Gries, J. 1922. "A Zoning Primer by the Advisory Committee on Zoning." U.S. Department of Commerce. https://www.govinfo.gov/content/pkg/GOVPUB-C13-cf208d8ed0dda43ed677acd6cad8be81/pdf/GOVPUB-C13-cf208d8ed0dda43ed677acd6cad8be81.pdf.

Gupta, A., C. Martinez, and S. Van Nieuwerburgh. 2023. *Converting Brown Offices to Green Apartments.* NBER Working Paper 31530. Cambridge, MA: National Bureau of Economic Research. http://www.nber.org/papers/w31530.

Gutman, A. 2023. "WA House Passes Bill Banning Single-Family Zoning." *Seattle Times*, March 7. https://www.seattletimes.com/seattle-news/politics/wa-house-passes-bill-banning-single-family-zoning/.

Gyourko, J., J. Hartley, and J. Krimmel. 2019. *The Local Residential Land Use Regulatory Environment Across U.S. Housing Markets: Evidence from a New Wharton Index.* NBER Working Paper 26573. Cambridge, MA: National Bureau of Economic Research. https://doi.org/10.3386/w26573.

Gyourko, J., and S. McCulloch. 2023. *Minimum Lot Size Restrictions: Impacts on Urban Form and House Price at the Border.* NBER Working Paper 31710. Cambridge, MA: National Bureau of Economic Research. https://www.nber.org/papers/w31710.

Gyourko, J., and R. Molloy. 2015. "Regulation and Housing Supply." In *Handbook of Regional and Urban Economics*, ed. G. Duranton, J. Vernon Henderson, and W. Strange. Oxford: Elsevier. https://www.sciencedirect.com/science/article/abs/pii/B9780444595317000193.

Hermann, A., S. Wedeen, W. Airgood-Obrycki, and C. Herbert. 2023. "The Geography of Renter Financial Distress and Housing Insecurity During the Pandemic." Joint Center for Housing Studies of Harvard University. https://www.jchs.harvard.edu/research-areas/working-papers/geography-renter-financial-distress-and-housing-insecurity-during.

Hilber, C., and F. Robert-Nicoud. 2014. "On the Origins of Land Use Regulations: Theory and Evidence from U.S. Metro Areas." *Journal of Urban Economics* 75, no. 1. https://www.sciencedirect.com/science/article/abs/pii/S0094119012000666.

Howells, R. 2022. "The History of Zoning Laws in America." *Politically Speaking*, February 8. https://medium.com/politically-speaking/the-history-of-zoning-laws-in-america-9babd157bc29.

Hoyt, H., and J. Schuetz. 2020. "Flexible Zoning and Streamlined Procedures Can Make Housing More Affordable." https://www.jchs.harvard.edu/blog/flexible-zoning-and-streamlined-procedures-can-make-housing-more-affordable.

Hsieh, C., and E. Moretti. 2019. "Housing Constraints and Spatial Misallocation." *American Economic Journal: Macroeconomics* 11, no. 2: 1–39. https://doi.org/10.1257/mac.20170388.

HUD (U.S. Department of Housing and Urban Development). 2021. "Tenants in LIHTC Units as of December 31, 2021." https://www.huduser.gov/portal/Datasets/lihtc/2021-LIHTC-Tenant-Tables.pdf.

———. 2022. "CDBG Activity Expenditure Reports." Community Development Block Grant Programs. https://view.officeapps.live.com/op/view.aspx?src=https%3A%2F%2Ffiles.hudexchange.info%2Fresources%2Fdocuments%2FCDBG_Expend_NatlAll.xlsx&wdOrigin=BROWSELINK.

———. 2023a. "HUD Announces New Proposed 'Affirmatively Furthering Fair Housing' Rule, Taking a Major Step Towards Rooting Out Long-Standing Inequities in Housing and Fostering Inclusive Communities." https://www.hud.gov/press/press_releases_media_advisories/HUD_No_23_013.

———. 2023b. "Pathways to Removing Obstacles to Housing (PRO Housing)." https://www.hud.gov/program_offices/comm_planning/pro_housing.

———. 2023c. "HOME Program Funding, Commitments, and Disbursements." Office of Community Planning and Development. https://files.hudexchange.info/reports/published/HOME_Prod_Natl_20230831.pdf.

———. 2023d. "Housing Choice Vouchers Fact Sheet." https://www.hud.gov/topics/housing_choice_voucher_program_section_8.

———. 2023e. "Low-Income Housing Tax Credit (LIHTC): Property-Level Data." Office of Policy Development and Research. https://www.huduser.gov/portal/datasets/lihtc/property.html.

———. 2023f. "The Office of Manufactured Housing Programs." https://www.hud.gov/program_offices/housing/mhs.

———. 2023g. "HUD Takes Action to Highlight and Research Land Use and Zoning Reforms." https://www.hud.gov/press/press_releases_media_advisories/hud_no_23_072.

———. 2023h. "Notice CPD-2023-10." https://www.hud.gov/sites/dfiles/OCHCO/documents/2023-10cpdn.pdf.

———. 2023i. "Tenant-Based Rental Assistance." https://www.hud.gov/sites/dfiles/CFO/documents/2024_CJ_Program_Template_-_TBRA.pdf.

———. 2023j. "FY 2023 Increasing the Supply of Affordable Housing through Off-Site Construction and Pro-Housing Reforms Research Grant Program Pre and Full Application NOFO." https://www.hud.gov/program_offices/spm/gmomgmt/grantsinfo/fundingopps/fy2023_increasing.

———. 2024a. "HUD 2024 Congressional Justifications." https://www.hud.gov/sites/dfiles/CFO/documents/2024-HUD-Congressional-Justifications.pdf.

———. 2024b. "Mandatory Affordable Housing Programs." https://www.hud.gov/sites/dfiles/CFO/documents/2024_Mandatory_Affordable_Housing_Programs.pdf

Ihlanfeldt, K. 2019. "The Deconcentration of Minority Students Attending Bad Schools: The Role of Housing Affordability within School Attendance Zones Containing Good Schools." *Journal of Housing Economics* 43: 83–101. https://www.sciencedirect.com/science/article/abs/pii/S1051137718300718.

Internal Revenue Service. 2022. "Section 42, Low-Income Housing Credit Average Income Test Regulations." 87 *FR* 61489. https://www.federalregister.gov/documents/2022/10/12/2022-22070/section-42-low-income-housing-credit-average-income-test-regulations.

Joint Center for Housing Studies. 2023. "The State of the Nation's Housing 2023." https://www.jchs.harvard.edu/sites/default/files/reports/files/Harvard_JCHS_The_State_of_the_Nations_Housing_2023.pdf.

JPMorgan Chase. 2022. "Cap Rates, Explained." https://www.jpmorgan.com/insights/real-estate/commercial-term-lending/cap-rates-explained.

Kahlenberg, R. 2023. *Excluded: How Snob Zoning, NIMBYism, and Class Bias Build the Walls We Don't See.* New York: PublicAffairs. https://www.hachettebookgroup. com/titles/richard-d-kahlenberg/excluded/9781541701465/?lens=publicaffairs.

Kaufmann, J. 2023. "Downtown Chicago Is a Downer for Drivers." Axios Chicago. https://www.axios.com/local/chicago/2023/04/21/chicago-downtown-parking.

Khater, S., L. Kiefer, and V. Yanamandra. 2021."Housing Supply: A Growing Deficit." 2021. Freddie Mac, Research Note. https://www.freddiemac.com/research/ insight/20210507-housing-supply.

Khouri, A. 2022. "California Bans Mandated Parking Near Transit to Fight High Housing Prices, Climate Change." *Los Angeles Times*, September 23. https://www. latimes.com/california/story/2022-09-23/ newsom-bill-banning-parking-requirement-transit-housing-climate-change.

Kiefer, L., A. Atreya, and V. Yanamandra. 2018. "Why Is Adulting Getting Harder? Young Adults and Household Formation." Freddie Mac, Insight. https://www. freddiemac.com/research/insight/20180316-adulting.

Kimura, D. 2022. "Steady LIHTC Pricing Expected for First Half of 2022." *Affordable Housing Finance*, March 7. https://www.housingfinance.com/finance/ steady-lihtc-pricing-expected-for-first-half-of-2022_o.

La Cava, G. 2016. "Housing Prices, Mortgage Interest Rates and the Rising Share of Capital Income in the United States." BIS Working Paper 572. Bank for International Settlements. https://ssrn.com/abstract=2814142.

Landis, J., and V. Reina. 2021. "Do Restrictive Land Use Regulations Make Housing More Expensive Everywhere?" *Economic Development Quarterly* 35, no. 4: 305–24. https://doi.org/10.1177/08912424211043500.

Layton, D. 2023. "Manufactured Housing Is a Good Source of Unsubsidized Affordable Housing—Except When It's Not: High-Level and Specific Policy Recommendations (Part 3)." NYU Furman Center, *The Stoop.* https://furmancenter.org/ thestoop/entry/ manufactured-housing-is-a-good-source-of-unsubsidized-affordable-housing-except-when-its-not-high-level-and-specific-policy-recommendations-part-3.

Lee, Y., P. Kemp, and V. Reina. 2022. "Divers of Housing (Un)affordability in the Advanced Economies: A Review and New Evidence." *Housing Studies* 37, no. 10: 1739–52. https://doi.org/10.1080/02673037.2022.2123623.

Leung, J. 2018. "Decarbonizing U.S. Buildings." Center for Climate and Energy Solutions. https://www.c2es.org/wp-content/uploads/2018/06/ innovation-buildings-background-brief-07-18.pdf.

Loh, T., C. Coes, and B. Buthe. 2020. "Separate and Unequal: Persistent Residential Segregation Is Sustaining Racial and Economic Injustice in the U.S." Brookings. https://www.brookings.edu/articles/ trend-1-separate-and-unequal-neighborhoods-are-sustaining-racial-and-economic-injustice-in-the-us/.

Mangin, J. 2014. "The New Exclusionary Zoning." *Stanford Law & Policy Review* 25. https://law.stanford.edu/wp-content/uploads/2018/03/mangin_25_stan._l._poly_rev_91.pdf.

Martin, C. 2022. "The Inflation Reduction Act Will Reduce Household Energy Insecurity—but It Could Do More." Metropolitan Policy Program at Brookings. https://www.brookings.edu/articles/the-inflation-reduction-act-will-reduce-household-energy-insecurity-but-it-could-do-more/.

Merchant, C. 2016. "A Zoning Change in Fairfax Will Allow More Density." *Greater Greater Washington*, June 29. https://ggwash.org/view/41968/a-zoning-change-in-fairfax-will-allow-more-density.

Mischke, J., et al. 2023. "Empty Spaces and Hybrid Places: The Pandemic's Lasting Impact on Real Estate." McKinsey Global Institute. https://www.mckinsey.com/mgi/our-research/empty-spaces-and-hybrid-places/.

Moretti, E. 2012. *The New Geography of Jobs*. New York: Liveright / Houghton Mifflin Harcourt. https://books.google.com/books/about/The_New_Geography_of_Jobs.html?id=br0S54w0u_sC.

Nguyen, M. 2015. "The Intersection of Immigration and Housing Policies: Implications for the U.S. Housing Market and Economy," *Housing Policy Debate* 25: 796–98. https://doi.org/10.1080/10511482.2015.1043084.

Office of Policy Development and Research. 2023. *Policy & Practice*. U.S. Department of Housing and Urban Development. https://www.huduser.gov/Portal/Policy-and-Practice.html.

Ortalo-Magne, F., and A. Prat. 2014. "On the Political Economy of Urban Growth: Homeownership versus Affordability." *American Economic Journal: Microeconomics* 6, no. 1: 410–42. https://www.jstor.org/stable/43189657.

Parking Reform Network. No date. "Mandates Map." https://parkingreform.org/resources/mandates-map/.

Parrott, J., and M. Zandi. 2021. "Overcoming the Nation's Daunting Housing Supply Shortage." Urban Institute. https://www.urban.org/sites/default/files/publication/103940/overcoming-the-nations-daunting-housing-supply-shortage_0.pdf.

Peri, G. 2012. "The Effect of Immigration on Productivity: Evidence from U.S. States." *Review of Economics and Statistics* 94, no. 1: 348–58. http://www.jstor.org/stable/41349180.

Pilkauskas, N., K. Michelmore, and N. Kovski. 2023. *The 2021 Child Tax Credit, the Living Arrangements and Housing Affordability of Families with Low Incomes*. NBER Working Paper 31339. Cambridge, MA: National Bureau of Economic Research. https://doi.org/10.3386/w31339.

Poon, L. 2017. 'Buffalo Becomes First City to Bid Minimum Parking Goodbye." Bloomberg. https://www.bloomberg.com/news/articles/2017-01-09/buffalo-is-the-first-to-abandon-minimum-parking-requirements-citywide.

RCN Capital. No date. "Multifamily and Commercial Real Estate Loan Ratios." https://rcncapital.com/blog/multifamily-and-commercial-real-estate-loan-ratios.

Reid, C., D. Bocian, W. Li, and R. Quercia. 2016. "Revisiting the Subprime Crisis: The Dual Mortgage Market and Mortgage Defaults by Race and Ethnicity." *Journal of Urban Affairs.* https://www.tandfonline.com/doi/full/10.1080/07352166.2016.1255529?scroll=top&needAccess=true.

Reina, V., and C. Aiken. 2022. "Moving to Opportunity, or Aging in Place? The Changing Profile of Low-Income and Subsidized Households and Where They Live." *Urban Affairs Review* 58, no. 2: 454–92. https://doi.org/10.1177/1078087420969895.

Resseger, M. 2022. "The Impact of Land Use Regulation on Racial Segregation: Evidence from Massachusetts Zoning Borders." Working paper, Mercatus Center at George Mason University. https://www.mercatus.org/research/working-papers/impact-land-use-regulation-racial-segregation-evidence-massachusetts-zoning.

Rigsby, E. 2016. "Understanding Exclusionary Zoning and Its Impact on Concentrated Poverty." Century Foundation. https://tcf.org/content/facts/understanding-exclusionary-zoning-impact-concentrated-poverty/?agreed=1.

Rothstein, R. 2014. "The Making of Ferguson: Public Policies at the Root of its Troubles." Economic Policy Institute. https://files.epi.org/2014/making-of-ferguson-final.pdf.

———. 2017. *The Color of Law: A Forgotten History of How Our Government Segregated America.* New York: Liveright. https://www.epi.org/publication/the-color-of-law-a-forgotten-history-of-how-our-government-segregated-america/.

Rothwell, J. 2012. "Housing Costs, Zoning, and Access to High Scoring School." Metropolitan Policy Program at Brookings. https://www.brookings.edu/articles/housing-costs-zoning-and-access-to-high-scoring-schools/.

Ruggles, S., S. Flood, S. Sobek, D. Backman, A. Chen, G. Cooper, S. Richards, R. Rogers, and M. Schouweiler. 2023. IPUMS USA: Version 14.0. Data set, Minneapolis. https://doi.org/10.18128/D010.V14.0.

Shanahan, M., A. Austin, C. Durrance, S. Martin, J. Mercer, D. Runyan, and C. Runyan. 2022. "The Association of Low-Income Housing Tax Credit Units and Reports of Child Abuse and Neglect." *American Journal of Preventive Medicine* 62, no. 5: 727–34. https://doi.org/10.1016/j.amepre.2021.11.020.

Shoup, D. 2014. "The High Cost of Minimum Parking Requirements." *Parking Issues and Policies* 5: 87–113. https://www.emerald.com/insight/content/doi/10.1108/S2044-994120140000005011./full/html.

Skelton, G. 2021. "Don't Be Fooled: California's New Housing Laws Make Significant Changes to Zoning." *Los Angeles Times.* https://www.latimes.com/california/story/2021-09-22/skelton-sb9-housing-single-family-zoning.

SMPDC (Southern Maine Planning and Development Commission). 2023. "Housing Legislation LD 2003." https://smpdc.org/ld2003.

Song, J. 2021. "The Effects of Residential Zoning in U.S. Housing Markets." SSRN. https://dx.doi.org/10.2139/ssrn.3996483.

Sorens, J. 2023. "Abolish Parking Minimums. Yes, All of Them." American Institute for Economic Research, *Daily Economy*. http://www.aier.org/article/abolish-parking-minimums-yes-all-of-them/.

Sorokin, O. 2023. "Office Vacancy Rates in 2022." National Association of Realtors, *Economists' Outlook*. https://www.nar.realtor/blogs/economists-outlook/office-vacancy-rates-in-2022.

Stacy, C., C. Davis, Y. Freemark, L. Lo, G. MacDonald, V. Zheng, and R. Pendall. 2023. "Land-Use Reforms and Housing Costs: Does Allowing for Increased Density Lead to Greater Affordability?" Urban Institute. https://www.urban.org/research/publication/land-use-reforms-and-housing-costs.

State of Montana Governor's Office. 2023. "Governor Gianforte Announces Bold, Transformational Pro-Housing Zoning Reform." https://news.mt.gov/Governors-Office/Governor_Gianforte_Announces_Bold_Transformational_Pro-Housing_Zoning_Reform.

Supreme Court of the United States. 1926. *Village of Euclid v. Ambler Realty Co.*, 272 U.S. 365. https://supreme.justia.com/cases/federal/us/272/365/.

Tax Policy Center. No date. "Briefing Book." https://www.taxpolicycenter.org/briefing-book/what-low-income-housing-tax-credit-and-how-does-it-work.

Taylor, L. 2018. "Housing and Health: An Overview of the Literature." *Health Affairs.* https://www.healthaffairs.org/do/10.1377/hpb20180313.396577/.

Tiebout, C. 1956. "A Pure Theory of Local Expenditures." *Journal of Political Economy* 64. https://www.journals.uchicago.edu/doi/10.1086/257839.

Twinam, T. 2018. "The Long-Run Impact of Zoning: Institutional Hysteresis and Durable Capital in Seattle, 1920–2015." *Regional Science and Urban Economics* 73: 155–69. https://doi.org/10.1016/j.regsciurbeco.2018.08.004.

Urban Institute. 2016. "The Cost of Affordable Housing: Does It Pencil Out?" https://apps.urban.org/features/cost-of-affordable-housing/.

U.S. Census Bureau. 2023. "Homeownership Rate in the United States [RHORUSQ156N]." FRED, Federal Reserve Bank of Saint Louis. https://fred.stlouisfed.org/series/RHORUSQ156N.

USDA (U.S. Department of Agriculture). 2024. "2024 USDA Explanatory Notes, Rural Housing Service." https://www.usda.gov/sites/default/files/documents/32-2024-RHS.pdf.

U.S. Department of the Interior. 2020. "Annual Report on the Economic Impact of the Federal Historic Tax Credits for Fiscal Year 2020." National Park Service,

Technical Preservation Services. https://www.nps.gov/subjects/taxincentives/upload/report-2020-economic-impact.pdf.

———. 2021. "Annual Report on the Economic Impact of the Federal Historic Tax Credits for Fiscal Year 2021." National Park Service, Technical Preservation Services. https://www.nps.gov/subjects/taxincentives/upload/report-2021-economic-impact.pdf.

———. 2022. "Federal Tax Incentives for Rehabilitating Historic Buildings: Annual Report for Fiscal Year 2022." National Park Service, Technical Preservation Services. https://www.nps.gov/subjects/taxincentives/upload/report-2022-annual.pdf.

U.S. Department of the Treasury. 2023a. "General Explanations of the Administration's Fiscal Year 2024 Revenue Proposals." https://home.treasury.gov/system/files/131/General-Explanations-FY2024.pdf.

———. 2023b. "Tax Expenditures FY2024 Update." https://home.treasury.gov/system/files/131/Tax-Expenditures-FY2024-update.pdf.

Voith, R., J. Liu, S. Zielenbach, A. Jakabovics, B. An, S. Rodnyansky, A. Orlando, and R. Bostic. 2022. "Effects of Concentrated LIHTC Development on Surrounding House Prices." *Journal of Housing Economics* 56: 101838. https://doi.org/10.1016/j.jhe.2022.101838.

Wamsley, L. 2024. "From Austin to Anchorage, U.S. Cities Opt to Ditch Their Off-Street Parking Minimums." NPR. https://www.npr.org/2024/01/02/1221366173/u-s-cities-drop-parking-space-minimums-development.

WGI. 2021. "Parking Structure Cost Outlook for 2021." https://publications.wginc.com/parking-structure-construction-cost-outlook-2021.

White House. 2022. "President Biden Announces New Actions to Ease the Burden of Housing Costs." https://www.whitehouse.gov/briefing-room/statements-releases/2022/05/16/president-biden-announces-new-actions-to-ease-the-burden-of-housing-costs/.

———. 2023a. "Biden-Harris Administration Announces Actions to Lower Housing Costs and Boost Supply." https://www.whitehouse.gov/briefing-room/statements-releases/2023/07/27/biden-harris-administration-announces-actions-to-lower-housing-costs-and-boost-supply/.

———. 2023b. "Fact Sheet: Biden-Harris Administration Takes Action to Create More Affordable Housing by Converting Commercial Properties to Residential Use." https://www.whitehouse.gov/briefing-room/statements-releases/2023/10/27/fact-sheet-biden-harris-administration-takes-action-to-create-more-affordable-housing-by-converting-commercial-properties-to-residential-use/.

———. 2023c. "Fact Sheet: President Biden's Budget Lowers Housing Costs and Expands Access to Affordable Rent and Home Ownership." https://www.whitehouse.gov/omb/briefing-room/2023/03/09/

fact-sheet-president-bidens-budget-lowers-housing-costs-and-expands-access-to-affordable-rent-and-home-ownership/.

———. 2023d. "White House Announces New Actions on Homeownership." https://www.whitehouse.gov/briefing-room/statements-releases/2023/10/16/white-house-announces-new-actions-on-homeownership/.

Wolff, E. 2022. *Heterogenous Rates of Return on Homes and Other Real Estate: Do the Rich Do Better? Do Black Households Do Worse?* NBER Working Paper 30543. Cambridge, MA: National Bureau of Economic Research. https://doi.org/10.3386/w30543.

Chapter 5

Abbott, T., R. McGuckin, P. Herrick, and L. Norfolk. 1989. "Measuring the Trade Balance in Advanced Technology Products." Working paper, Center for Economic Studies. https://www2.census.gov/ces/wp/1989/CES-WP-89-01.pdf.

Aiyar, S., J. Chen, C. Ebeke, R. Garcia-Saltos, T. Gudmundsson, A. Ilyina, A. Kangur, T. Kunaratskul, S. Rodriguez, M. Ruta, T. Schulze, G. Soderberg, and J. Trevino. 2023. "Geoeconomic Fragmentation and the Future of Multilateralism." https://www.imf.org/en/Publications/Staff-Discussion-Notes/Issues/2023/01/11/Geo-Economic-Fragmentation-and-the-Future-of-Multilateralism-527266.

Aiyar, S., and A. Ilyina. 2023. "Charting Globalization's Turn to Slowbalization After Financial Crisis." https://www.imf.org/en/Blogs/Articles/2023/02/08/charting-globalizations-turn-to-slowbalization-after-global-financial-crisis.

Alfaro, L., and D. Chor. 2023. *Global Supply Chains: The Looming "Great Realloca-tion."* NBER Working Paper 31661. Cambridge, MA: National Bureau of Economic Research. https://doi.org/10.3386/w31661.

Amiti, M., M. Dai, R. Feenstra, and J. Romalis. 2020. "How Did China's WTO Entry Affect U.S. Prices?" *Journal of International Economics* 126. https://doi.org/10.1016/j.jinteco.2020.103339.

Antràs, P., T. Fort, and F. Tintelnot. 2017. "The Margins of Global Sourcing: Theory and Evidence from U.S. Firms." *American Economic Review* 107, no. 9: 2514–64. https://doi.org/10.1257/aer.20141685.

Autor, D., D. Dorn, and G. Hanson. 2013. "The China Syndrome: Local Labor Market Effects of Import Competition in the United States." *American Economic Review* 103, no. 6: 2121–68. http://dx.doi.org/10.1257/aer.103.6.2121.

———. 2021. *On the Persistence of the China Shock.* NBER Working Paper 29401. Cambridge, MA: National Bureau for Economic Research. https://doi.org/10.3386/w29401.

Baccini, L., I. Osgood, and S. Weymouth. 2019. "The Service Economy: U.S. Trade Coalitions in an Era of Deindustrialization." *Review of International Organiza-tions* 14: 261–96. https://doi.org/10.1007/s11558-019-09349-x.

Bai, L., and S. Stumpner. 2019. "Estimating U.S. Consumer Gains from Chinese Imports." *American Economic Review: Insights* 1, no. 2: 209–24. https://doi.org/10.1257/aeri.20180358.

Baker, D. 2014. "The Trade Deficit: The Biggest Obstacle to Full Employment." Center on Budget and Policy Priorities. https://www.cbpp.org/sites/default/files/atoms/files/4-2-14fe-baker.pdf.

Baldwin, R. 2016. *The Great Convergence: Information Technology and the New Globalization.* Cambridge, MA: Harvard University Press. https://doi.org/10.2307/j.ctv24w655w.

———. 2022. "The Peak Globalization Myth, Part 4: Services Trade Did Not Peak." CEPR-VoxEU. https://cepr.org/voxeu/columns/peak-globalisation-myth-part-4-services-trade-did-not-peak.

Baldwin, R., and R. Freeman. 2022. "Risks and Global Supply Chains: What We Know and What We Need to Know." *Annual Review of Economics* 14: 153–80. https://doi.org/10.1146/annurev-economics-051420-113737.

Baldwin, R., R. Freeman, and A. Theodorakopoulos. 2023. "Hidden Exposure: Measuring U.S. Supply Chain Reliance." *Brookings Papers on Economic Activity*, Fall. https://www.brookings.edu/wp-content/uploads/2023/09/2_Baldwin-et-al_unembargoed.pdf.

Baldwin, R., and J. López-González. 2014. "Supply-Chain Trade: A Portrait of Global Patterns and Several Testable Hypotheses." *World Economy* 38, no. 11: 1682–721. https://doi.org/10.1111/twec.12189.

BEA (U.S. Bureau of Economic Analysis). 2018. "A Guide to BEA's Services Surveys." https://www.bea.gov/system/files/2018-04/surveysu.pdf.

———. 2023a. "U.S. International Economic Accounts: Concepts and Methods." https://www.bea.gov/system/files/2023-06/iea-concepts-methods-2023.pdf.

———. 2023b. "Table 6.1. U.S. International Financial Transactions for Direct Investment." https://www.bea.gov/data/intl-trade-investment/international-transactions.

———. 2023c. "Table 6.2: U.S. International Financial Transactions for Direct Investment by Country and Industry." https://www.bea.gov/data/intl-trade-investment/international-transactions.

———. 2023d. "New Foreign Direct Investment in the United States, 2022." News release. https://www.bea.gov/news/2023/new-foreign-direct-investment-united-states-2022.

Bermel, L., J. Chen, B. Deese, M. Delgado, L. English, Y. Garcia, T. Houser, A. Khan, J. Larsen, N. Stewart, and H. Tavarez. 2023. "The Clean Investment Monitor: Tracking Decarbonization Technology in the United States." Rhodium Group. https://assets-global.website-files.com/64e31ae6c5fd44b10ff405a7/6500f1718b8bc3b49a69d333_The%20Clean%20Investment%20Monitor_Tracking%20Decarbonization%20in%20the%20US.pdf.

Bernanke, B. 2005. "Remarks by Governor Ben S. Bernanke at the Sandridge Lecture, Virginia Association of Economists, Richmond, Virginia, on the Global Saving Glut and the U.S. Current Account Deficit." https://www.federalreserve.gov/boarddocs/speeches/2005/200503102/.

Bernstein, J. 2023. "Remarks by Chair Jared Bernstein at the Economic Policy Institute." Transcript of speech at Economic Policy Institute, Washington, September 28. https://www.whitehouse.gov/cea/written-materials/2023/09/28/remarks-by-chair-jared-bernstein-at-the-economic-policy-institute-washington-d-c/.

Bertaut, C., B. von Beschwitz, and S. Curcuru. 2023. "'The International Role of the U.S. Dollar,' Post-COVID Edition." https://www.federalreserve.gov/econres/notes/feds-notes/the-international-role-of-the-us-dollar-post-covid-edition-20230623.html.

BIS (Bank for International Settlements). 2017. "BIS 87th Annual Report." https://www.bis.org/publ/arpdf/ar2017e_ec.pdf.

Blomström, M., A. Kokko, and J. Mucchielli. 2003. "The Economics of Foreign Direct Investment Incentives." In *Foreign Direct Investment on the Real and Financial Sector of Industrial Counties*, 37–60. https://doi.org/10.1007/978-3-540-24736-4_3.

Bloom, N., K. Handley, A. Kurmann, and P. Luck. 2019. "The Impact of Chinese Trade on U.S. Employment: The Good, The Bad, and The Debatable." Meeting Papers 1433. Society for Economic Dynamics. https://red-files-public.s3.amazonaws.com/meetpapers/2019/paper_1433.pdf.

Bloomberg. 2023. "China Is Having a Hard Time Wooing Foreign Investors Back." November 7. https://www.bloomberg.com/news/articles/2023-11-08/china-is-having-a-hard-time-wooing-foreign-investors-back.

BLS (U.S. Bureau of Labor Statistics). 2023a. "All Employees, Manufacturing [MANEMP]." https://fred.stlouisfed.org/series/MANEMP.

———. 2023b. "All Employees, Total Nonfarm [PAYEMS]." https://fred.stlouisfed.org/series/PAYEMS.

Bonadio, B., Z. Huo, A. Levchenko, and N. Pandalai-Nayar. 2020. *Global Supply Chains in the Pandemic*. NBER Working Paper 27224. Cambridge, MA: National Bureau for Economic Research. https://doi.org/10.3386/w27224.

Boushey, H. 2023. "The Economics of Public Investment Crowding in Private Investment." White House Briefing Room Blog. https://www.whitehouse.gov/briefing-room/blog/2023/08/16/the-economics-of-public-investment-crowding-in-private-investment/.

Brainard, L. 2001. "Trade Policy in the 1990s." Brookings Institution. https://www.brookings.edu/articles/trade-policy-in-the-1990s/.

Branstetter, L. 2006. "Is Foreign Direct Investment a Channel of Knowledge Spillovers? Evidence from Japan's FDI in the United States." *Journal of International Economics* 68, no. 2: 325–44. https://doi.org/10.1016/j.jinteco.2005.06.006.

Broda, C., and D. Weinstein. 2006. "Globalization and the Gains from Variety." *Quarterly Journal of Economics* 121, no. 2: 541–85. https://doi.org/10.1162/qjec.2006.121.2.541.

Caballero, R., E. Farhi, and P. Gourinchas. 2017. "The Safe Assets Shortage Conundrum." *Journal of Economic Perspectives* 31, no 3: 29–46. https://doi.org/10.1257/jep.31.3.29.

Caliendo, L., M. Dvorkin, and F. Parro. 2019. "Trade and Labor Market Dynamics: General Equilibrium Analysis of the China Trade Shock." *Econometrica* 87, no. 3: 741–835. https://doi.org/10.3982/ECTA13758.

CEA (Council of Economic Advisers). 2015a. "The Economic Benefits of U.S. Trade." https://obamawhitehouse.archives.gov/sites/default/files/docs/cea_trade_report_final_non-embargoed_v2.pdf.

———. 2015b. *Economic Report of the President.* Washington: U.S. Government Publishing Office. https://www.whitehouse.gov/wp-content/uploads/2021/07/2015-ERP.pdf.

———. 2022. *Economic Report of the President.* Washington: U.S. Government Publishing Office. https://www.whitehouse.gov/wp-content/uploads/2022/04/ERP-2022.pdf.

———. 2023a. *Economic Report of the President.* Washington: U.S. Government Publishing Office. https://www.whitehouse.gov/wp-content/uploads/2023/03/erp-2023.pdf.

———. 2023b. "Issue Brief: Supply Chain Resilience." https://www.whitehouse.gov/cea/written-materials/2023/11/30/issue-brief-supply-chain-resilience/.

Cheng, S. 2023. "China Lifts Ban on Group Tours to U.S. and Other Countries, in Boost to Global Travel Industry." *Wall Street Journal*, August 10. https://www.wsj.com/articles/china-lifts-ban-on-group-tours-to-u-s-and-other-countries-in-boost-to-global-travel-industry-1b467c78.

Clean Investment Monitor. 2024. Rhodium Group & MIT's Center for Energy and Environmental Policy Research. https://www.cleaninvestmentmonitor.org/.

Constantinescu, C., A. Mattoo, and M. Ruta. 2018. "The Global Trade Slowdown: Cyclical or Structural?" *World Bank Economic Review* 34, no. 1: 121–42. https://doi.org/10.1093/wber/lhx027.

Dahlman, A., and M. Lovely. 2023. "U.S.-Led Effort to Diversify Indo-Pacific Supply Chains Away from China Runs Counter to Trends." Peterson Institute for International Economics, Realtime Economics. https://www.piie.com/blogs/realtime-economics/us-led-effort-diversify-indo-pacific-supply-chains-away-china-runs-counter.

De Chaisemartin, C., and Z. Lei. 2023. "More Robust Estimators for Instrumental-Variable Panel Designs, with an Application to the Effect of Imports from China on U.S. Employment." Working paper, Social Science Research Network. https://dx.doi.org/10.2139/ssrn.3802200.

Devadas, S., and N. Loayza. 2018. "When Is a Current Account Deficit Bad?" Research and Policy Briefs, World Bank. https://openknowledge.worldbank.org/server/api/core/bitstreams/8edf9fe5-f97b-55d9-aa21-2a52c8d513bc/content.

Economist. 2021. "Globalisation Has Faltered." January 29. https://www.economist.com/briefing/2019/01/24/globalisation-has-faltered.

Fajgelbaum, P., and A. Khandelwal. 2016. "Measuring the Unequal Gains from Trade." *Quarterly Journal of Economics* 131: no. 3: 1113–80. https://doi.org/10.1093/qje/qjw013.

Feenstra, R., and G. Hanson. 1997. "Foreign Direct Investment and Relative Wages: Evidence from Mexico's Maquiladoras." *Journal of International Economics* 42, nos. 3–4: 371–93. https://doi.org/10.1016/S0022-1996(96)01475-4.

Fernandes, A., H. Kee, and D. Winkler. 2020. "Determinants of Global Value Chain Participation: Cross-Country Evidence." *World Bank Economic Review* 36, no. 2: 329–60. https://doi.org/10.1093/wber/lhab017.

Foley, C., J. Hines, and D. Wessel. 2021. "Multinational Activity in the Modern World." In *Global Goliaths: Multinational Corporations in the 21st Century Economy,* ed. C. Foley, J. Hines, and D. Wessel, 1–32. Washington: Brookings Institution Press. https://repository.law.umich.edu/cgi/viewcontent.cgi?article=1427&context=book_chapters.

Fort, T. 2017. "Technology and Production Fragmentation: Domestic versus Foreign Sourcing." *Review of Economic Studies* 84, no. 2: 650–87. https://doi.org/10.1093/restud/rdw057.

———. 2023. "The Changing Firm and Country Boundaries of U.S. Manufacturers in Global Value Chains." *American Economic Association* 37, no. 3: 31–58. https://doi.org/10.1257/jep.37.3.31.

Fort, T., J. Pierce, and P. Schott. 2018. "New Perspectives on the Decline of U.S. Manufacturing Employment." *Journal of Economic Perspectives* 32, no. 2: 47–72. https://www.aeaweb.org/articles?id=10.1257/jep.32.2.47.

Freund, C., A. Mattoo, A. Mulabdic, and M. Ruta. 2023. "Natural Disasters and the Reshaping of Global Value Chains." *IMF Economic Review* 70, no. 3: 590–623. https://doi.org/10.1057/s41308-022-00164-w.

Galle, S., A. Rodríguez-Clare, and M. Yi. 2023. "Slicing the Pie: Quantifying the Aggregate and Distributional Effects of Trade." *Review of Economic Studies* 90, no. 1: 331–75. https://doi.org/10.1093/restud/rdac020.

Galle, S., and L. Lorentzen. 2021. "The Unequal Effects of Trade and Automation across Local Labor Markets." SSRN. https://dx.doi.org/10.2139/ssrn.3800962.

Ganapati, S., and W. Wong. 2023. *How Far Goods Travel: Global Transport and Supply Chains from 1965–2020.* NBER Working Paper 31167. Cambridge, MA: National Bureau for Economic Research. https://www.nber.org/papers/w31167.

Georgiadis, P., M. O'Dwyer, I. Smith, S. Morris. 2023. "Business Travel Recovery Stalls as Companies Seek to Cut Costs and Emissions." *Financial Times*. https://www.ft.com/content/ea564d48-6dfd-4c7f-b28b-c2028bbc2fe8.

Ghosh, A., and U. Ramakrishnan. 2024. "Current Account Deficits." International Monetary Fund, Back to Basics. https://www.imf.org/en/Publications/fandd/issues/Series/Back-to-Basics/Current-Account-Deficits.

Goldberg, P., and T. Reed. 2023. *Is the Global Economy Deglobalizing? And If So, Why? And What Is Next?* NBER Working Paper 31115. Cambridge, MA: National Bureau for Economic Research. https://doi.org/10.3386/w31115.

Grossman, G., and E. Rossi-Hansberg. 2008. "Trading Tasks: A Simple Theory of Offshoring." *American Economic Review* 98, no. 5: 1978–97. https://doi.org/10.1257/aer.98.5.1978.

Hale, G., B. Hobijn, F. Nechio, and D. Wilson. 2019. "How Much Do We Spend on Imports?" Federal Reserve Bank of San Francisco, Economic Letters. https://www.frbsf.org/economic-research/publications/economic-letter/2019/january/how-much-do-we-spend-on-imports/.

Hale, G., and M. Xu. 2016. *FDI Effects on the Labor Markets of Host Countries*. Federal Reserve Bank of San Francisco, Working Paper 2016-25. https://doi.org/10.24148/wp2016-25.

Hancock, T. 2023. "U.S. Trade Data Overstates Decoupling from China, Report Says." Bloomberg, October 12. https://www.bloomberg.com/news/articles/2023-10-12/us-trade-data-overstates-decoupling-from-china-gavekal-says.

Handley, K., F. Kamal, and W. Ouyang. 2021. "A Long View of Employment Growth and Firm Dynamics in the United States: Importers vs. Exporters vs. Non-Traders." Working Paper, Center for Economic Studies. https://www2.census.gov/ces/wp/2021/CES-WP-21-38.pdf.

Higgins, M., and T. Klitgaard. 2021. "How Much Have Consumers Spent on Imports During the Pandemic?" Federal Reserve Bank of New York, Liberty Street Economics. https://libertystreeteconomics.newyorkfed.org/2021/10/how-much-have-consumers-spent-on-imports-during-the-pandemic/.

Hummels, D., J. Ishii, and K. Yi. 2001. "The Nature and Growth of Vertical Specialization in World Trade." *Journal of International Economics* 54, no. 1: 75–96. https://doi.org/10.1016/s0022-1996(00)00093-3.

Iakovou, E., and C. White. 2020. "How to Build More Secure, Resilient, Next-Gen U.S. Supply Chains." Brookings Institution. https://www.brookings.edu/articles/how-to-build-more-secure-resilient-next-gen-u-s-supply-chains/.

IMF (International Monetary Fund). 2019. "The Drivers of Bilateral Trade and the Spillovers from Tariffs." In *World Economic Outlook*, April. https://www.elibrary.imf.org/display/book/9781484397480/ch004.xml.

———. 2022. "Global Trade and Value Chains during the Pandemic." In *World Economic Outlook*, April. https://www.elibrary.imf.org/display/book/9781616359423/CH004.xml.

———. 2023. "Global Financial Stability Report." https://www.imf.org/en/Publications/GFSR/Issues/2023/10/10/global-financial-stability-report-october-2023?cid=pr-com-AM2023-GFSREA2023002.

International Energy Agency. 2022. "Global Supply Chains of EV Batteries." https://iea.blob.core.windows.net/assets/4eb8c252-76b1-4710-8f5e-867e751c8dda/Global-SupplyChainsofEVBatteries.pdf.

Jakubik, A., and V. Stolzenburg. 2020. "The 'China Shock' Revisited: Insights from Value Added Trade Flows." *Journal of Economic Geography* 21, no. 1: 67–95. https://doi.org/10.1093/jeg/lbaa029.

Jaravel, X., and E. Sager. 2019. *What Are the Price Effects of Trade? Evidence from the U.S. and Implications for Quantitative Trade Models.* CEP Discussion Paper 1642. London: Centre for Economic Performance. https://cep.lse.ac.uk/pubs/download/dp1642.pdf.

Jørgensen, P. 2023. "The Global Savings Glut and the Housing Boom." *Journal of Economic Dynamics and Control* 146. https://doi.org/10.1016/j.jedc.2022.104563.

Kamal, F., J. McCloskey, W. Ouyang. 2022. "Multinational Firms in the U.S. Economy: Insights from Newly Integrated Microdata." Working Paper, U.S. Census Bureau. https://www2.census.gov/ces/wp/2022/CES-WP-22-39.pdf.

Keller, W., and S. Yeaple. 2009. "Multinational Enterprises, International Trade, and Productivity Growth: Firm Level Evidence from the United States." *Review of Economics and Statistics* 91, no. 4: 821–31. https://doi.org/10.1162/rest.91.4.821.

Klein, M., and M. Pettis. 2020. *Trade Wars Are Class Wars: How Rising Inequality Distorts the Global Economy and Threatens International Peace.* New Haven, CT: Yale University Press. https://www.jstor.org/stable/j.ctv10sm96m.

Knight, M., and F. Scacciavillani. 1998. "Current Accounts: What Is Their Relevance for Economic Policymaking?" Working Paper, International Monetary Fund. https://www.imf.org/external/pubs/ft/wp/wp9871.pdf.

Lincicome, S., and A. Anand. 2023. "The 'China Shock' Demystified: Its Origins, Effects, and Lessons for Today." CATO Institute, Defending Globalization: Economics. https://www.cato.org/publications/china-shock.

Lipsey, R. 2000. "Foreign Direct Investment and the Operations of Multinational Firms." National Bureau of Economic Research, Reporter. https://www.nber.org/reporter/winter-2000/1/foreign-direct-investment-and-operations-multinational-firms.

Loungani, P., and A. Razin. 2001. "How Beneficial Is Foreign Direct Investment for Developing Countries?" *Finance and Development* 38, no. 2. https://www.imf.org/external/pubs/ft/fandd/2001/06/loungani.htm.

McBride, J., and A. Chatzky. 2019. "The U.S. Trade Deficit: How Much Does It Matter?" Council on Foreign Relations. https://www.cfr.org/backgrounder/us-trade-deficit-how-much-does-it-matter.

Mehdi, A., and T. Moorenhout. 2023. "The IRA and the U.S. Battery Supply Chain: One Year On." Center on Global Energy Policy at Columbia University School of International and Public Affairs. https://www.energypolicy.columbia.edu/publications/the-ira-and-the-us-battery-supply-chain-one-year-on/.

Melitz, M., and D. Trefler. 2012. "Gains from Trade When Firms Matter." *Journal of Economic Perspectives* 26, no. 2: 91–118. http://dx.doi.org/10.1257/jep.26.2.91.

Miroudot, S. 2022. "Resilience in Services Value Chains." Council on Economic Policies Blog. https://www.cepweb.org/resilience-in-services-value-chains/.

Nathan, A., G. Galbraith, and J. Grimberg. 2022. "(De)Globalization Ahead?" Goldman Sachs Global Macro Research Newsletter. https://www.goldmansachs.com/intelligence/pages/top-of-mind/de-globalization-ahead/report.pdf.

Obstfeld, M., and K. Rogoff. 1996. *Foundations of International Macroeconomics.* Cambridge, MA: MIT Press. https://mitpress.mit.edu/9780262150477/foundations-of-international-macroeconomics/.

OECD (Organization for Economic Cooperation and Development). 2018. "Multinational Enterprises and Global Value Chains." https://www.oecd-ilibrary.org/industry-and-services/multinational-enterprises-and-global-value-chains_194ddb63-en;jsessionid=YO7EGol9Lb2iPwdAAYF_-ZXVzkslnGe1ksbgX1AF.ip-10-240-5-163.

———. 2021. "Guide to OECD's Trade in Value Added Indicators." https://www.oecd-ilibrary.org/docserver/58aa22b1-en.pdf?expires=1707515380&id=id&accname=ocid49017102b&checksum=FA3625888B88ACB19AB5EBDB5E292537.

———. 2022. "International Trade During the COVID-19 Pandemic: Big Shifts and Uncertainty." https://www.oecd.org/coronavirus/policy-responses/international-trade-during-the-covid-19-pandemic-big-shifts-and-uncertainty-d1131663/.

———. 2023a. "Foreign Direct Investment Statistics: Data, Analysis and Forecasts." https://www.oecd.org/investment/statistics.htm.

———. 2023b. "FDI in Figures." https://www.oecd.org/daf/inv/FDI-in-Figures-October-2023.pdf.

———. 2023c. "Trade in Value Added." https://www.oecd.org/sti/ind/measuring-trade-in-value-added.htm.

———. 2024. "Foreign Direct Investment (FDI)." https://www.oecd-ilibrary.org/finance-and-investment/foreign-direct-investment-fdi/indicator-group/english_9a523b18-en.

Parilla, J., and M. Muro. 2017. "U.S. Metros Most Exposed to a Trump Trade Shock." Brookings Institution. https://www.brookings.edu/articles/u-s-metros-most-dependent-on-trade/.

Peterson, K. 2011. "Boeing Says Learned from Outsourcing Issues with 787." Reuters, January 20. https://www.reuters.com/article/boeing-idUSN1916381720110120/.

Pettis, M. 2017. "Why a Savings Glut Does Not Increase Savings." Carnegie Endowment for International Peace. https://carnegieendowment.org/chinafinancialmarkets/69838.

Pierce, J., P. Schott, and C. Tello-Trillo. 2023. *Trade Liberalization and Labor-Market Gains: Evidence from U.S. Matched Employer-Employee Data.* Working Paper CES-22-42. Suitland, MD: Center for Economic Studies. https://sompks4.github.io/public/newlehd_114.pdf.

Qiang, C., Y. Liu, and V. Steenbergen. 2021. "Multinational Corporations Shape Global Value Chain Development." In *An Investment Perspective on Global Value Chains*, ed. C. Qiang, Y. Liu, and V. Steenbergen, 62–107. Washington: World Bank. https://elibrary.worldbank.org/doi/abs/10.1596/978-1-4648-1683-3_ch2.

Qiu, H., H. Shin, and L. Zhang. 2023. "Mapping the Realignment of Global Value Chains." Working Paper, Bank for International Settlements. https://www.bis.org/publ/bisbull78.pdf.

Ramondo, N., V. Rappoport, and K. Ruhl. 2016. "Intrafirm Trade and Vertical Fragmentation in U.S. Multinational Corporations." *Journal of International Economics* 98: 51–59. https://doi.org/10.1016/j.jinteco.2015.08.002.

Ricardo, D. 1817. *On the Principles of Political Economy, and Taxation.* Cambridge: Cambridge University Press. https://www.cambridge.org/core/books/on-the-principles-of-political-economy-and-taxation/5C17BF2152379956950601EFE05AE14F.

Rodrik, D. 2011. *The Globalization Paradox: Democracy and the Future of the World Economy.* New York: W. W. Norton. https://drodrik.scholar.harvard.edu/publications/globalization-paradox-democracy-and-future-world-economy.

Romei, V. 2023. "Global Trade Falls at Fastest Pace Since Pandemic." *Financial Times.* https://www.ft.com/content/36982601-b799-4166-9e6b-39533efbdfdf?emailId=7ca6f95a-051d-4797-bfd5-6a835f9a1c1d&segmentId=2785c52b-1c00-edaa-29be-7452cf90b5a2.

Russ, K., J. Shambaugh, and J. Furman. 2017. "U.S. Tariffs Are an Arbitrary and Regressive Tax." Centre for Economic Policy Research, VoxEU Column. https://cepr.org/voxeu/columns/us-tariffs-are-arbitrary-and-regressive-tax.

Santacreu, A., and J. LaBelle. 2022. "Global Supply Chain Disruptions and Inflation during the COVID-19 Pandemic." *Federal Reserve Bank of Saint Louis Review* 104, no. 2: 78–91. https://doi.org/10.20955/r.104.78-91.

Sari, D., D. Raess, and D. Kucera. 2016. "Do PTAs Including Labor Provisions Reduce Collective Labor Rights Violations? The Role of Labor Cooperation Provisions." Working paper, Swiss Network for International Studies. https://www.peio.me/wp-content/uploads/2016/12/PEIO10_paper_63.pdf.

Shenhar, A., V. Holzmann, B. Melamed, and Y. Zhao. 2016. "The Challenge of Innovation in Highly Complex Projects: What Can We Learn from Boeing's Dreamliner Experience?" *Project Management Journal* 47: 62–78. https://journals.sagepub.com/doi/10.1002/pmj.21579.

Shih, W. 2020. "Global Supply Chains in a Post-Pandemic World." *Harvard Business Review*. https://hbr.org/2020/09/global-supply-chains-in-a-post-pandemic-world.

Tabova, A. 2020. "What Happened to Foreign Direct Investment in the United States?" Federal Reserve Board, FEDS Notes. https://www.federalreserve.gov/econres/notes/feds-notes/what-happened-to-foreign-direct-investment-in-the-united-states-20200213.html.

Timmer, M., B. Los, R. Stehrer, and G. de Vries. 2016. *An Anatomy of the Global Trade Slowdown Based on the WIOD 2016 Release*. GGDC Research Memorandum GD-162. Groningen, Netherlands: Groningen Growth and Development Center. https://ideas.repec.org/p/gro/rugggd/gd-162.html.

Tracy, B. 2022. "Critical Minerals in Electric Vehicle Batteries." Congressional Research Service. https://crsreports.congress.gov/product/pdf/R/R47227.

UNCTAD (United Nations Conference on Trade and Development). 2023. "World Investment Report 2023." https://unctad.org/system/files/official-document/wir2023_en.pdf.

U.S. Census Bureau. 2012. "Trade Term: End-Use." https://www.census.gov/newsroom/blogs/global-reach/2012/03/end-use-trade-term-of-the-month-2.html.

———. 2022. "U.S. Goods Trade: Imports and Exports by Related-Parties, 2022." https://www.census.gov/foreign-trade/Press-Release/related_party/rp22.pdf.

———. 2023. "Monthly U.S. International Trade in Goods and Services, December 2023." https://www.census.gov/foreign-trade/current/index.html.

U.S. Department of Commerce. 2022. "Ministerial Statement for Pillar III of the Indo-Pacific Economic Framework for Prosperity." https://www.commerce.gov/sites/default/files/2022-09/Pillar-III-Ministerial-Statement.pdf.

———. 2023a. "Fact Sheet: Substantial Conclusion of Negotiations on Groundbreaking IPEF Clean Economy Agreement." https://www.commerce.gov/sites/default/files/2023-11/US-Factsheet-SF-Pillar-III.pdf.

———. 2023b. "Fact Sheet: Substantial Conclusion of Negotiations of an Innovative IPEF Fair Economy Agreement." https://www.commerce.gov/sites/default/files/2023-11/US-Factsheet-SF-Pillar-IV.pdf.

———. 2023c. "U.S.-EU Joint Statement of the Trade and Technology Council." https://www.commerce.gov/news/press-releases/2023/05/us-eu-joint-statement-trade-and-technology-council.

U.S. Department of Energy. 2023. "Department of Energy Celebrates Two Years of President Biden's Historic Investment in America's Clean Energy Future." https://www.energy.gov/articles/

department-energy-celebrates-two-years-president-bidens-historic-investment-americas-clean.

U.S. Department of Labor. 2023. "USMCA Cases." https://www.dol.gov/agencies/ilab/our-work/trade/labor-rights-usmca-cases.

U.S. Department of State. No date. "Minerals Security Partnership." https://www.state.gov/minerals-security-partnership/.

U.S. Department of the Treasury. 2023. "Economy Statement by Eric Van Nostrand, Acting Assistant Secretary for Economic Policy, for the Treasury Borrowing Advisory Committee July 31, 2023." https://home.treasury.gov/news/press-releases/jy1661.

U.S. Small Business Administration. 2023a. "Report with Eight Deliverables for Project to Support Small Business Administration (SBA) to Identify the Total Addressable Market of Small Business Exporters." https://www.sba.gov/sites/default/files/2023-02/SBA%20Total%20Addressable%20Market%20Study%20FINAL-508%20%281%29.pdf.

———. 2023b. "SBA Research Sheds Light on Small Business Exporters." https://www.sba.gov/article/2023/mar/14/sba-research-sheds-new-light-small-business-exporters.

USTR (Office of the U.S. Trade Representative). 2021. "U.S.-EU Trade and Technology Council Inaugural Joint Statement." https://ustr.gov/about-us/policy-offices/press-office/press-releases/2021/september/us-eu-trade-and-technology-council-inaugural-joint-statement.

———. 2022a. "Countries & Regions." https://ustr.gov/countries-regions.

———. 2022b. "Fact Sheet: 2021 President's Trade Agenda and 2020 Annual Report." https://ustr.gov/sites/default/files/files/reports/2021/2021%20Trade%20Agenda/2021%20Trade%20Report%20Fact%20Sheet.pdf.

———. 2022c. "United States and Kenya Announce the Launch of the U.S.-Kenya Strategic Trade and Investment Partnership." https://ustr.gov/about-us/policy-offices/press-office/press-releases/2022/july/united-states-and-kenya-announce-launch-us-kenya-strategic-trade-and-investment-partnership.

———. 2022d. "2022 Biennial Report on the Implementation of the African Growth and Opportunity Act." https://ustr.gov/sites/default/files/files/reports/2022/2022AGOAImplementationReport.pdf.

———. 2023a. "Chapter 31, Annex A: Facility-Specific Rapid-Response Labor Mechanism." https://ustr.gov/issue-areas/enforcement/dispute-settlement-proceedings/fta-dispute-settlement/usmca/chapter-31-annex-facility-specific-rapid-response-labor-mechanism.

———. 2023b. "2023 Trade Policy Agenda and 2022 Annual Report of the President of the United States on the Trade Agreements Program." https://ustr.gov/sites/default/files/2023-02/2023%20Trade%20Policy%20Agenda%20and%202022%20Annual%20Report%20FINAL%20(1).pdf.

———. 2023c. "Agreement Between the American Institute in Taiwan and the Taipei Economic and Cultural Representative Office in the United States Regarding Trade Between the United States of America and Taiwan." https://ustr.gov/sites/default/files/2023-05/AIT-TECRO%20Trade%20Agreement%20May%202023.pdf.

———. 2023d. "United States and Taiwan Hold Second Negotiating Round for the U.S.-Taiwan Initiative on 21st-Century Trade." https://ustr.gov/about-us/policy-offices/press-office/press-releases/2023/august/united-states-and-taiwan-hold-second-negotiating-round-us-taiwan-initiative-21st-century-trade-1.

———. 2023e. "U.S.-Kenya Strategic Trade and Investment Partnership Summary of Texts Proposed by the U.S. Side." https://ustr.gov/sites/default/files/2023-05/U.S.-Kenya%20STIP%20Chapter%20Summaries%20May%202023.pdf.

———. 2023f. "United States and Japan Sign Critical Minerals Agreement." https://ustr.gov/about-us/policy-offices/press-office/press-releases/2023/march/united-states-and-japan-sign-critical-minerals-agreement.

———. No date–a. "Indo-Pacific Economic Framework for Prosperity." https://ustr.gov/ipef.

———. No date–b. "Ministerial Text for Trade Pillar of the Indo-Pacific Economic Framework for Prosperity." https://ustr.gov/sites/default/files/2022-09/IPEF%20Pillar%201%20Ministerial%20Text%20(Trade%20Pillar)_FOR%20PUBLIC%20RELEASE%20(1).pdf.

———. No date–c. "African Growth and Opportunity Act (AGOA)." https://ustr.gov/issue-areas/trade-development/preference-programs/african-growth-and-opportunity-act-agoa.

Van Nostrand, E., and M. Ashenfarb. 2023. "The Inflation Reduction Act: A Place-Based Analysis." https://home.treasury.gov/news/featured-stories/the-inflation-reduction-act-a-place-based-analysis.

Wang, Z., S. Wei, X. Yu, and K. Zhu. 2018. *Re-examining the Effects of Trading with China on Local Labor Markets: A Supply Chain Perspective.* NBER Working Paper 24886. Cambridge, MA: National Bureau of Economic Research. https://doi.org/10.3386/w24886.

White House. 2021a. "U.S.-EU Trade and Technology Council Inaugural Joint Statement." https://www.whitehouse.gov/briefing-room/statements-releases/2021/09/29/u-s-eu-trade-and-technology-council-inaugural-joint-statement/.

———. 2021b. "Building Resilient Supply Chains, Revitalizing American Manufacturing, and Fostering Broad-Based Growth." https://www.whitehouse.gov/wp-content/uploads/2021/06/100-day-supply-chain-review-report.pdf.

———. 2023a. "Australia–United States Climate, Critical Minerals and Clean Energy Transformation Compact." https://www.whitehouse.gov/briefing-room/statements-releases/2023/05/20/

australia-united-states-climate-critical-minerals-and-clean-energy-transforma-
tion-compact/.

———. 2023b. "Fact Sheet: President Joseph R. Biden and General Secretary Nguyen
Phu Trong Announce the U.S.-Vietnam Comprehensive Strategic Partnership."
https://www.whitehouse.gov/briefing-room/statements-releases/2023/09/10/
fact-sheet-president-joseph-r-biden-and-general-secretary-nguyen-phu-trong-
announce-the-u-s-vietnam-comprehensive-strategic-partnership/.

World Bank. 2020. *World Development Report 2020: Trading for Development in the Age
of Global Value Chains*. Washington: World Bank. https://doi.
org/10.1596/978-1-4648-1457-0.

WTO (World Trade Organization). 2021. "Global Value Chain Development Report
2021." https://www.wto.org/english/res_e/booksp_e/00_gvc_dev_
report_2021_e.pdf.

———. 2022. "Trade in Value Added and Global Value Chains: Country Profiles Explanatory Notes." https://www.wto.org/english/res_e/statis_e/miwi_e/
Explanatory_Notes_e.pdf.

———. 2023a. "World Trade Report." https://www.wto.org/english/res_e/booksp_e/
wtr23_e/wtr23_e.pdf.

———. 2023b. "Evolution of Trade Under the WTO: Handy Statistics." https://www.wto.
org/english/res_e/statis_e/trade_evolution_e/evolution_trade_wto_e.htm.

Yang, L., Y. Zhu, and F. Ren. 2023. "Does Government Investment Push up Manufacturing Labor Costs? Evidence from China." *Humanities and Social Sciences
Communications* 10, no. 1. https://doi.org/10.1057/s41599-023-02180-1.

Zumbrun, J. 2023. "Is Globalization in Decline? A New Number Contradicts the
Consensus." Wall Street Journal, November 3. https://www.wsj.com/economy/
global/
is-globalization-in-decline-a-new-number-contradicts-the-consensus-
60df8ecf?mod=djemRTE_h.

Chapter 6

Acemoglu, D. 2002. "Directed Technical Change." *Review of Economic Studies* 69, no. 4:
781–809. https://doi.org/10.1111/1467-937X.00226.

Acemoglu, D., P, Aghion, L. Bursztyn, and D. Hemous. 2012. "The Environment and
Directed Technical Change." *American Economic Review* 102, no. 1: 131–66.
https://doi.org/10.1257/aer.102.1.131.

Acemoglu, D., U. Akcigit, D. Hanley, and W. Kerr. 2016. "Transition to Clean Technology." *Journal of Political Economy* 124, no. 1: 52–104. https://doi.
org/10.1086/684511.

Acemoglu, D., and D. Autor. 2011. "Chapter 12: Skills, Tasks and Technologies—Implications for Employment and Earnings." In *Handbook of Labor Economics*, 4B,

ed. O. Ashenfelter and D. Card. Amsterdam: Elsevier Science. https://www.
sciencedirect.com/science/article/abs/pii/S0169721811024105.

Amsden, A. 1992. *Asia's Next Giant: South Korea and Late Industrialization*. Oxford:
Oxford University Press. https://doi.org/10.1093/0195076036.001.0001.

Arkolakis, C, and C. Walsh. 2023. *Clean Growth*. NBER Working Paper 31615.
Cambridge, MA: National Bureau for Economic Research. https://doi.
org/10.3386/w31615.

Armitage, S., N. Bakhtian, and A. Jaffe. 2023. *Innovation Market Failures and the
Design of New Climate Policy Instruments*. NBER Working Paper 31622.
Cambridge, MA: National Bureau for Economic Research. https://doi.
org/10.3386/w31622.

Arrow, K. 1962. "The Economic Implications of Learning by Doing." *Review of
Economic Studies* 29, no. 3: 155–73. https://doi.org/10.2307/2295952.

Autor, D., D. Dorn, and G. Hanson. 2013. "The China Syndrome: Local Labor Market
Effects of Import Competition in the United States." *American Economic
Review* 103, no. 6: 2121–68. https://doi.org/10.1257/aer.103.6.2121.

Autor, D., F. Levy, and R. Murnane. 2003. "The Skill Content of Recent Technological
Change: An Empirical Exploration." *Quarterly Journal of Economics* 118, no.
4: 1279–333. https://doi.org/10.1162/003355303322552801.

Bachas, N., O. Kim, and C. Yannelis. 2021. "Loan Guarantees and Credit Supply."
Journal of Financial Economics 139: 872–94. https://www.sciencedirect.com/
science/article/abs/pii/S0304405X20302361.

Baumol, W., and W. Oates. 1988. *The Theory of Environmental Policy*. Cambridge:
Cambridge University Press. https://books.google.com/
books?hl=en&lr=&id=32-r0N8l9BgC&oi=fnd&pg=PR7&dq=baumol+and+oate
s+1988&ots=P3N0jyJZwI&sig=sZmDlJUPsVMTaFFUm6PqZVRqKHA.

Berkes, E., K. Manysheva, and M. Mestieri. 2022. "Global Innovation Spillovers and
Productivity: Evidence from 100 Years of World Patent Data." Working
paper, Federal Reserve Bank of Chicago. https://www.chicagofed.org/
publications/working-papers/2022/2022-15.

Berndt, E., R. Glennerster, M. Kremer, J. Lee, R. Levine, G. Weizsäcker, and H.
Williams. 2006. "Advance Market Commitments for Vaccines against
Neglected Diseases: Estimating Costs and Effectiveness." *Health Economics*
16, no. 5: 491–511. https://doi.org/10.1002/hec.1176.

Beuse, M., B. Steffen, M. Dirksmeier, and T. Schmidt. 2021. "Comparing CO2 Emissions
Impacts of Electricity Storage Across Applications and Energy Systems." *Joule*
5, no. 6: 1501–20. https://doi.org/10.1016/j.joule.2021.04.010.

Bloom, N., M. Schankerman, and J. Van Reenen. 2013. "Identifying Technology Spillovers and Product Market Rivalry." *Econometrica* 81, no. 4: 1347–93. https://
doi.org/10.3982/ECTA9466.

Boushey, H. 2023. "The Economics of Public Investment Crowding in Private Investment." White House Blog. https://www.whitehouse.gov/briefing-room/blog/2023/08/16/the-economics-of-public-investment-crowding-in-private-investment/

Boyd, M. 2023. "The Potential of Agrivoltaics for the U.S. Solar Industry, Farmers, and Communities." U.S. Department of Energy Solar Energy Technologies Office Blog. https://www.energy.gov/eere/solar/articles/potential-agrivoltaics-us-solar-industry-farmers-and-communities.

Brooks, L., and Z. Liscow. 2023. "Infrastructure Costs." *American Economic Journal: Applied Economics* 15, no. 2: 1–30. https://doi.org/10.1257/app.20200398.

Burke, M., S. Hsiang, and E. Miguel. 2015. "Global Non-Linear Effect of Temperature on Economic Production." *Nature* 527, no. 7577: 235–39. https://doi.org/10.1038/nature15725.

Burlig, F., J. Bushnell, D. Rapson, and C. Wolfram. 2021. "Low Energy: Estimating Electric Vehicle Electricity Use." *AEA Papers and Proceedings* 111: 430–35. https://doi.org/10.1257/pandp.20211088.

Bryce, R. 2023. "Renewable Rejection Database." https://robertbryce.com/renewable-rejection-database/.

California Legislature. 2023. "An Act Making Appropriations for the Support of the Government of the State of California and for Several Public Purposes in Accordance with the Provisions of Section 12 of Article IV of the Constitution of the State of California, Relating to the State Budget, to Take Effect Immediately, Budget Bill, Senate Bill No. 101, 2023." https://leginfo.legislature.ca.gov/faces/billTextClient.xhtml?bill_id=202320240SB101.

Carleton, T., A. Jina, M. Delgado, M. Greenstone, T. Houser, S. Hsiang, A. Hultgren, R. Kopp, K. McCusker, I. Nath, J. Rising, A. Rode, H. Kwon Seo, A. Viaene, J. Yuan, and A. Zhang. 2022. "Valuing the Global Mortality Consequences of Climate Change Accounting for Adaptation Costs and Benefits." *Quarterly Journal of Economics* 137, no. 4: 2037–105. https://doi.org/10.1093/qje/qjac020.

Casey, G., W. Jeon, and C. Traeger. 2023. *The Macroeconomics of Clean Energy Subsidies*. CESifo Working Paper 10828. https://www.cesifo.org/en/publications/2023/working-paper/macroeconomics-clean-energy-subsidies.

CEA (Council of Economic Advisers). 2021. "Innovation, Investment, and Inclusion: Accelerating the Energy Transition and Creating Good Jobs." https://www.whitehouse.gov/wp-content/uploads/2021/04/Innovation-Investment-and-Inclusion-CEA-April-23-2021-1.pdf.

———. 2023a. "Chapter 9: Opportunities for Better Managing Weather Risk in the Changing Climate." In *Economic Report of the President*. Washington: U.S. Government Publishing Office. https://www.whitehouse.gov/wp-content/uploads/2023/03/erp-2023.pdf.

———. 2023b. "The Economics of Demand-Side Support for the Department of Energy's Clean Hydrogen Hubs." https://www.whitehouse.gov/cea/written-materials/2023/07/05/the-economics-of-demand-side-support-for-the-department-of-energys-clean-hydrogen-hubs/.

Chang, R. 2023. "Renewable Energy Is the Key to Building a More Resilient and Reliable Electricity Grid." Center for American Progress. https://www.americanprogress.org/article/renewable-energy-is-the-key-to-building-a-more-resilient-and-reliable-electricity-grid/.

Choi, J., and A. Levchenko. 2021. *The Long-Term Effects of Industrial Policy*. NBER Working Paper 29263. Cambridge, MA: National Bureau of Economic Research. https://doi.org/10.3386/w29263.

Cole, C., M. Droste, C. Knittel, S. Li, and J. Stock. 2023. "Policies for Electrifying the Light-Duty Vehicle Fleet in the United States." *AEA Papers and Proceedings* 113: 316–22. https://doi.org/10.1257/pandp.20231063.

Colmer, J., E. Lyubich, and J. Voorheis. 2023. "Nice Work If You Can Get It? The Distribution of Employment and Earnings During the Early Years of the Clean Energy Transition." https://api.semanticscholar.org/CorpusID:266525460

Cotterman, T., E. Fuchs, and K. Whitefoot. 2022. "The Transition to Electrified Vehicles: Evaluating the Labor Demand of Manufacturing Conventional versus Battery Electric Vehicle Powertrains." Working paper, Carnegie Mellon University. https://dx.doi.org/10.2139/ssrn.4128130.

Cox, S., L. Beshilas, and E. Hotchkiss. 2019. "Renewable Energy to Support Energy Security." National Renewable Energy Lab. https://www.nrel.gov/docs/fy20osti/74617.pdf.

CRFB (Committee for a Responsible Federal Budget). 2013. "The Tax Break-Down: Intangible Drilling Costs" https://www.crfb.org/blogs/tax-break-down-intangible-drilling-costs.

CRS (Congressional Research Service). 2012. "Loan Guarantees for Clean Energy Technologies: Goals, Concerns, and Policy Options." https://crsreports.congress.gov/product/pdf/R/R42152.

———. 2018. "Renewable Energy R&D Funding History: A Comparison with Funding for Nuclear Energy, Fossil Energy, Energy Efficiency, and Electric Systems R&D." https://crsreports.congress.gov/product/pdf/RS/RS22858/17.

———. 2020. "The Renewable Electricity Production Tax Credit: In Brief." https://sgp.fas.org/crs/misc/R43453.pdf.

———. 2021. "Oil and Gas Tax Preferences: In Brief." https://crsreports.congress.gov/product/pdf/IF/IF11528.

CTVC. 2023. "Insights: CTVC by Sightline Climate." https://www.ctvc.co/tag/insights/.

Curtis, E., L. O'Kane, and R. Park. 2023. *Workers and the Green-Energy Transition: Evidence from 300 Million Job Transitions.* NBER Working Paper 31539. Cambridge, MA: National Bureau of Economic Research. https://doi.org/10.3386/w31539.

Davis, L. 2023. "Electric Vehicles in Multi-Vehicle Households." *Applied Economics Letters* 30, no. 14: 1909–12. https://doi.org/10.1080/13504851.2022.2083563.

Denholm, P., M. Hand, M. Jackson, and S. Ong. 2009. "Land Use Requirements of Modern Wind Power Plants in the United States." National Renewable Energy Lab, Technical Report TP-6A2-45834. https://www.nrel.gov/docs/fy09osti/45834.pdf.

Devine, W. 1982. *An Historical Perspective on the Value of Electricity in American Manufacturing.* Technical Report ORAU/IEA-82-8(M). Oak Ridge: Institute for Energy Analysis, Oak Ridge Associated Universities. https://doi.org/10.2172/6774921.

Dimanchev, E., S. Fleten, D. MacKenzie, and M. Korpås. 2023. "Accelerating Electric Vehicle Charging Investments: A Real Options Approach to Policy Design." *Energy Policy* 181. https://doi.org/10.1016/j.enpol.2023.113703.

DOE (U.S. Department of Energy). 2022a. "Wind Energy: Supply Chain Deep Dive Assessment." https://www.energy.gov/sites/default/files/2022-02/Wind%20Supply%20Chain%20Report%20-%20Final%202.25.22.pdf.

———. 2022b. "DOE Optimizes Structure to Implement $62 Billion in Clean Energy Investments from Bipartisan Infrastructure Law." https://www.energy.gov/articles/doe-optimizes-structure-implement-62-billion-clean-energy-investments-bipartisan.

———. 2023a. "United States Energy and Employment Report 2023." https://www.energy.gov/sites/default/files/2023-06/2023%20USEER%20REPORT-v2.pdf.

———. 2023b. "Biden-Harris Administration Announces $15.5 Billion to Support a Strong and Just Transition to Electric Vehicles, Retooling Existing Plants, and Rehiring Existing Workers." Press release.

———. 2023c. "Pathways to Commercial Liftoff: Clean Hydrogen." https://liftoff.energy.gov/.

———. 2023d. "National Transmission Needs Study."

———. 2023e. "Building a Bridge to Bankability." https://www.energy.gov/sites/default/files/2023-05/DOE-LPO22-PPTv03_LPO-Overview_May2023.pdf.

Duranton, G., and D. Puga. 2004. "Chapter 48: Micro-Foundations of Urban Agglomeration Economies." In *Handbook of Regional and Urban Economics*, no. 4: 2063–2117. https://doi.org/10.1016/s1574-0080(04)80005-1.

EIA (U.S. Energy Information Administration). 2012. "Today in Energy." https://www.eia.gov/todayinenergy/detail.php?id=7590.

———. 2023a. "Electricity Monthly Update: December 2022." https://www.eia.gov/electricity/monthly/update/archive/february2023/.

———. 2023b. "Energy and the Environment Explained Where Greenhouse Gases Come From." https://www.eia.gov/energyexplained/energy-and-the-environment/where-greenhouse-gases-come-from.php.

———. 2024a. "Solar and Wind to Lead Growth of U.S. Power Generation for the Next Two Years." https://www.eia.gov/todayinenergy/detail.php?id=61242.

———. 2024b. "U.S. Battery Storage Capacity Expected to Nearly Double in 2024." https://www.eia.gov/todayinenergy/detail.php?id=61202.

Erickson, P., and P. Achakulwisut. 2021. "How Subsidies Aided the U.S. Shale Oil and Gas Boom." Stockholm Environmental Institute. https://www.sei.org/publications/subsidies-shale-oil-and-gas/.

Erickson, P., A. Down, M. Lazarus, and D. Koplow. 2017. "Effect of Subsidies to Fossil Fuel Companies on United States Crude Oil Production." *Nature Energy* 2, no. 11: 891–98.

Esposito, D. 2021. "Meta-Analysis of Clean Energy Policy Models." Energy Innovation Policy & Technology LLC. https://energyinnovation.org/wp-content/uploads/2021/09/Studies-Agree-80-Percent-Clean-Electricity-by-2030-Would-Save-Lives-and-Create-Jobs-at-Minimal-Cost.pdf.

European Environment Agency. 2023. "Total Net Greenhouse Gas Emission Trends and Projections in Europe." https://www.eea.europa.eu/en/analysis/indicators/total-greenhouse-gas-emission-trends?activeAccordion=546a7c35-9188-4d23-94ee-005d97c26f2b.

Fontana, S., and R. Nanda. 2023. "Innovating to Net Zero: Can Venture Capital and Start-Ups Play a Meaningful Role?" In *Entrepreneurship and Innovation Policy and the Economy, Volume 2*, ed. B. Jones, and J. Lerner. Chicago: University of Chicago Press. https://doi.org/10.1086/723236.

Friedlingstein, P., M. O'Sullivan, M. Jones, R. Andrew, J. Hauck, A. Olsen, G. Peters, et al. 2020. "Global Carbon Budget 2020." *Earth System Science Data* 12, no. 4: 3269–340. https://doi.org/10.5194/essd-12-3269-2020.

Friedlingstein, P., M. O'Sullivan, M. Jones, R. Andrew, D. Bakker, J. Hauck, P. Landschützer, et al. 2023. "Global Carbon Budget 2023." *Earth System Science Data* 15: 5301–69. https://doi.org/10.5194/essd-15-5301-2023.

Gallagher, K., and L. Anadon. 2022. "Database on U.S. Department of Energy (DOE) Budgets for Energy Research, Development, & Demonstration (1978-2023R)." Harvard Kennedy School. https://www.belfercenter.org/publication/database-us-department-energy-doe-budgets-energy-research-development-demonstration-1.

Ghosh, S., and R. Nanda. 2010. *Venture Capital Investment in the Clean Energy Sector*. Working Paper 11-020, Harvard Business School. https://www.hbs.edu/ris/Publication%20Files/11-020_0a1b5d16-c966-4403-888f-96d03bbab461.pdf.

Glennerster, R., and M. Kremer. 2000. "A Better Way to Spur Medical Research and Development." *Regulation* 23: 34. https://papers.ssrn.com/sol3/papers. cfm?abstract_id=235870.

Global Trade Funding. No date. "Offtake Agreements, Project Finance Document Critical for Loan Approval." https://globaltradefunding.com/project-finance/project-finance-documents/offtake-agreements/.

Golding, G., and L. Kilian. 2022. "Don't Look to Oil Companies to Lower High Retail Gasoline Prices." Federal Reserve Bank of Dallas. https://www.dallasfed.org/research/economics/2022/0510.

Greenspon, J., and D. Raimi. 2022. *Matching Geographies and Job Skills in the Energy Transition*. RFF WP 22-25. Washington: Resources for the Future. https://media.rff.org/documents/WP_22-25_PnkcURf.pdf.

Gropman, A. 1996. "Mobilizing U.S. Industry in World War II: Myth and Reality." Institute for National Strategic Studies. https://apps.dtic.mil/sti/tr/pdf/ADA316780.pdf.

Gross, D., and B. Sampat. 2023a. "America, Jump-Started: World War II R&D and the Takeoff of the US Innovation System." *American Economic Review* 113, no. 12: 3323–56. https://doi.org/10.1257/aer.20221365.

———.2023b. "The World War II Crisis Innovation Model: What Was It, and Where Does It Apply?" *Research Policy* 52, no. 9: 104845. https://doi.org/10.1016/j.respol.2023.104845.

Gross, S. 2020. "Renewables, Land Use, and Local Opposition in the United States." Brookings Institution. https://www.brookings.edu/articles/renewables-land-use-and-local-opposition-in-the-united-states/.

Guarnieri, M. 2012. "Looking Back to Electric Cars." https://ieeexplore.ieee.org/xpl/conhome/6480931/proceeding.

Hanson, G. 2023. "Local Labor Market Impacts of the Energy Transition: Prospects and Policies." In *Economic Policy in a More Uncertain World*, 155–99. Washington: Aspen Economic Strategy Group. https://www.economicstrategygroup.org/wp-content/uploads/2022/12/Hanson-chapter.pdf.

Hart, D. 2020. "The Impact of China's Production Surge on Innovation in the Global Solar Photovoltaics Industry." Information Technology & Innovation Foundation. https://itif.org/publications/2020/10/05/impact-chinas-production-surge-innovation-global-solar-photovoltaics/.

Hassler, J., P. Krusell, C. Olovsson, and M. Reiter. 2020. "On the Effectiveness of Climate Policies." Working paper, Institute for International Economic Studies at Stockholm University.

Heintz, J. 2010. "The Impact of Public Capital on the US Private Economy: New Evidence and Analysis." *International Review of Applied Economics* 24, no. 5: 619–32. https://doi.org/10.1080/02692170903426104.

Herrendorf, B., R. Rogerson, and A. Valentinyi. 2014. "Chapter 6: Growth and Structural Transformation." In *Handbook of Economic Growth*, ed. P. Aghion and S. Durlauf, 855–941. Amsterdam: Elsevier Science. https://www.sciencedirect.com/science/article/abs/pii/B9780444535405000069.

Hittinger, E., and I. Azevedo. 2015. "Bulk Energy Storage Increases United States Electricity System Emissions." *Environmental Science & Technology* 49, no. 5: 3203–10. https://doi.org/10.1021/es505027p.

Hottenrott, H., E. Lins, and E. Lutz. 2018. "Public Subsidies and New Ventures' Use of Bank Loans." *Economics of Innovation and New Technology* 27, no. 8: 786–808. https://doi.org/10.1080/10438599.2017.1408200.

Howell, S. 2017. "Financing Innovation: Evidence from R&D Grants." *American Economic Review* 107, no. 4: 1136–64. https://doi.org/10.1257/aer.20150808.

Hsiang, S., M. Burke, and E. Miguel. 2013. "Quantifying the Influence of Climate on Human Conflict." *Science* 341, no. 6151: 1235367. https://doi.org/10.1126/science.1235367.

Hsiang, S., S. Greenhill, J. Martinich, M. Grasso, R. Schuster, L. Barrage, D. Diaz, et al. 2023. "Ch. 19: Economics." In *Fifth National Climate Assessment*, ed. A. Crimmins, C. Avery, D. Easterling, K. Kunkel, B. Stewart, and T. Maycock. Washington: U.S. Global Change Research Program. https://doi.org/10.7930/NCA5.2023.CH19.

Hyman, B. 2022. "Can Displaced Labor Be Retrained? Evidence from Quasi-Random Assignment to Trade Adjustment Assistance." Working Paper, U.S. Census Bureau, Center for Economic Studies. https://www2.census.gov/ces/wp/2022/CES-WP-22-05.pdf.

IEA (International Energy Agency). 2021a. "Net Zero by 2050: A Roadmap for the Global Energy Sector." https://iea.blob.core.windows.net/assets/deebef5d-0c34-4539-9d0c-10b13d840027/NetZeroby2050-ARoadmapfortheGlobalEnergySector_CORR.pdf.

———.2021b. "The Role of Critical Minerals in Clean Energy Transitions." In *World Energy Outlook*. https://www.iea.org/reports/the-role-of-critical-minerals-in-clean-energy-transitions.

———. 2021c. "The Cost of Capital in Clean Energy Transitions." https://www.iea.org/articles/the-cost-of-capital-in-clean-energy-transitions.

———. 2022. "World Energy Employment." https://iea.blob.core.windows.net/assets/a0432c97-14af-4fc7-b3bf-c409fb7e4ab8/WorldEnergyEmployment.pdf.

———. 2023a. *World Energy Outlook*. Paris: IEA. https://www.iea.org/reports/world-energy-outlook-2023.

———. 2023b. "A Renewed Pathway to Net Zero Emissions." https://www.iea.org/reports/net-zero-roadmap-a-global-pathway-to-keep-the-15-0c-goal-in-reach/a-renewed-pathway-to-net-zero-emissions.

————. 2023c. "Solar PV: Overview." https://www.iea.org/energy-system/renewables/solar-pv.

————. 2023d. "Energy Technology RD&D Budgets Data Explorer." https://www.iea.org/data-and-statistics/data-tools/energy-technology-rdd-budgets-data-explorer.

Interagency Working Group on Coal and Power Plant Communities and Economic Revitalization. 2023. "Revitalizing Energy Communities: Two-Year Report to the President." https://energycommunities.gov/wp-content/uploads/2023/04/IWG-Two-Year-Report-to-the-President.pdf.

International Renewable Energy Agency. 2023. "Renewable Power Generation Costs in 2022." Report. https://energycommunities.gov/wp-content/uploads/2023/04/IWG-Two-Year-Report-to-the-President.pdf.

IREC (Interstate Renewable Energy Council). 2022. "National Solar Jobs Census 2021." https://irecusa.org/wp-content/uploads/2022/07/National-Solar-Jobs-Census-2021.pdf.

————. 2023. "Cultivating a Diverse and Skilled Talent Pipeline for the Equitable Transition." https://irecusa.org/wp-content/uploads/2023/02/Alliance-Report-2.23-Interactive-compressed.pdf.

IRENA (International Renewable Energy Agency). 2019. "Utility-Scale Batteries: Innovation Landscape Brief." https://www.irena.org/-/media/Files/IRENA/Agency/Publication/2019/Sep/IRENA_Utility-scale-batteries_2019.pdf.

————. 2023. "Renewable Capacity Statistics 2023." https://mc-cd8320d4-36a1-40ac-83cc-3389-cdn-endpoint.azureedge.net/-/media/Files/IRENA/Agency/Publication/2023/Mar/IRENA_RE_Capacity_Statistics_2023.pdf?rev=d294915 1ee6a4625b65c82881403c2a7.

Jaworski, T. 2017. "World War II and the Industrialization of the American South." *Journal of Economic History* 77, no. 4: 1048–82. https://doi.org/10.1017/S0022050717000791.

Jenkins, J., J. Farbes, R. Jones, N. Patankar, and G. Schivley. 2022. "Electricity Transmission Is Key to Unlock the Full Potential of the Inflation Reduction Act." Rapid Energy Policy Evaluation and Analysis Toolkit Project, PowerPoint presentation. https://repeatproject.org/docs/REPEAT_IRA_Transmission_2022-09-22.pdf.

Johnston, B. 1970. "Agriculture and Structural Transformation in Developing Countries: A Survey of Research." *Journal of Economic Literature* 8, no. 2: 369–404. https://www.jstor.org/stable/2720471.

Juhász, R., N. Lane, and D. Rodrik. 2023. "The New Economics of Industrial Policy." National Bureau of Economic Research. https://drodrik.scholar.harvard.edu/sites/scholar.harvard.edu/files/dani-rodrik/files/the_new_economics_of_ip_080123.pdf.

Katz, L., J. Roth, R. Hendra, and K. Schaberg. 2022. "Why Do Sectoral Employment Programs Work? Lessons from WorkAdvance." *Journal of Labor Economics* 40, no. S1: S249–91. https://doi.org/10.1086/717932.

Kotchen, M. 2021. "The Producer Benefits of Implicit Fossil Fuel Subsidies in the United States." *Proceedings of the National Academy of Sciences* 118, no. 14: e20119691 https://www.pnas.org/doi/10.1073/pnas.2011969118.

Kremer, M., J. Levin, and C. Snyder. 2020. "Advance Market Commitments: Insights from Theory and Experience." *AEA Papers and Proceedings* 110: 269–73. https://pubs.aeaweb.org/doi/pdfplus/10.1257/pandp.20201017.

Kriegler, E., N. Bauer, A. Popp, F. Humpenöder, M. Leimbach, J. Strefler, L. Baumstark, et al. 2017. "Fossil-Fueled Development (SSP5): An Energy and Resource-Intensive Scenario for the 21st Century." *Global Environmental Change* 42: 297–315. https://doi.org/10.1016/j.gloenvcha.2016.05.015.

Lane, N. 2022. "Manufacturing Revolutions: Industrial Policy and Industrialization in South Korea." University of Oxford, Department of Economics. http://dx.doi.org/10.2139/ssrn.3890311.

Larsen, K., H. Pitt, M. Mobir, S. Movalia, A. Rivera, E. Rutkowski, and T. Houser. 2023. "Global Emerging Climate Technology Diffusion and the Inflation Reduction Act." Rhodium Group. https://rhg.com/research/emerging-climate-technology-ira/.

Lazard. 2023. "Levelized Cost of Energy Analysis +." PowerPoint presentation. https://www.lazard.com/media/2ozoovyg/lazards-lcoeplus-april-2023.pdf.

Lelieveld, J., K. Klingmüller, A. Pozzer, R. Burnett, A. Haines, and V. Ramanathan. 2019. "Effects of Fossil Fuel and Total Anthropogenic Emission Removal on Public Health and Climate." *Proceedings of the National Academy of Sciences* 116, no. 15: 7192–97. https://doi.org/10.1073/pnas.1819989116.

Lerner, J., and R. Nanda. 2020. "Venture Capital's Role in Financing Innovation: What We Know and How Much We Still Need to Learn." *Journal of Economic Perspectives* 34, no. 3: 237–61. https://doi.org/10.1257/jep.34.3.237.

Lewis, J., and R. Wiser. 2007. "Fostering a Renewable Energy Technology Industry: An International Comparison of Wind Industry Policy Support Mechanisms." *Energy Policy* 35, no. 3: 1844–57. https://doi.org/10.1016/j.enpol.2006.06.005.

Lewis, W. 1954. "Economic Development with Unlimited Supplies of Labour." *Manchester School* 22, no. 2: 139–91. https://doi.org/10.1111/j.1467-9957.1954.tb00021.x.

Li, S., L. Tong, J. Xing, and Y. Zhou. 2017. "The Market for Electric Vehicles: Indirect Network Effects and Policy Design." *Journal of the Association of Environmental and Resource Economists* 4, no. 1: 89–133. http://dx.doi.org/10.1086/689702.

Lim, J., M. Aklin, and M. Frank. 2023. "Location Is a Major Barrier for Transferring U.S. Fossil Fuel Employment to Green Jobs." *Nature Communications* 14: 5711. https://doi.org/10.1038/s41467-023-41133-9.

Louie, E., and J. Pearce. 2016. "Retraining Investment for U.S. Transition from Coal to Solar Photovoltaic Employment." *Energy Economics* 57: 295–302. https://doi.org/10.1016/j.eneco.2016.05.016.

Lucas, R. 1988. "On the Mechanics of Economic Development." *Journal of Monetary Economics* 22, no. 1: 3–42. https://doi.org/10.1016/0304-3932(88)90168-7.

Lucking, B., N. Bloom, and J. Van Reenen. 2020. "Have R&D Spillovers Declined in the 21st Century?" *Fiscal Studies* 40, no. 4: 561–90. https://doi.org/10.1111/1475-5890.12195.

Manpower Group. 2022. "The United States' 2022 Talent Shortage." https://go.manpowergroup.com/hubfs/Talent%20Shortage%202022/MPG_2022_TS_Infographic-US.pdf.

Marvel, K., W. Su, R. Delgado, S. Aarons, A. Chatterjee, M. Garcia, Z. Hausfather, et al. 2023. "Ch. 2: Climate Trends." In *Fifth National Climate Assessment*, ed. A. Crimmins, C. Avery, D. Easterling, K. Kunkel, B. Stewart, and T. Maycock. Washington: U.S. Global Change Research Program. https://doi.org/10.7930/NCA5.2023.CH2.

McMillan, M., and D. Rodrik. 2011. *Globalization, Structural Change and Productivity Growth*. NBER Working Paper 17143. Cambridge, MA: National Bureau of Economic Research. https://doi.org/10.3386/w17143.

Meckling, J., N. Kelsey, E. Biber, and J. Zysman. 2015. "Winning Coalitions for Climate Policy." *Science* 349, no. 6253: 1170–71. https://doi.org/10.1126/science.aab1336.

Meckling, J., and J. Nahm. 2021. "Strategic State Capacity: How States Counter Opposition to Climate Policy." *Comparative Political Studies* 55, no. 3: 493–523. https://doi.org/10.1177/00104140211024308.

Mendell, R., M. Einberger, and K. Siegner. 2022. "FERC Could Slash Inflation and Double Renewables with These Grid Upgrades." Rocky Mountain Institute. https://rmi.org/ferc-could-slash-inflation-and-double-renewables-grid-upgrades/.

Meng, K. 2023. *Estimating Path Dependence in Energy Transitions*. NBER Working Paper 22536. Cambridge, MA: National Bureau of Economic Research. https://doi.org/10.3386/w22536.

Nahm, J. 2021. *Collaborative Advantage: Forging Green Industries in the New Global Economy*. Oxford: Oxford University Press. https://global.oup.com/academic/product/collaborative-advantage-9780197555361.

Nanda, R., and M. Rhodes-Kropf. 2016. "Financing Risk and Innovation." *Management Science* 63, no. 4: 901–18. https://doi.org/10.1287/mnsc.2015.2350.

Nanda, R., K. Younge, and L. Fleming. 2015. "Innovation and Entrepreneurship in Renewable Energy." In *The Changing Frontier: Rethinking Science and Innovation Policy*, ed. A. Jaffe and B. Jones, 199–232. Chicago: University of Chicago Press. https://www.nber.org/system/files/chapters/c13048/c13048.pdf.

Narich, C., D. Kammen, M. Stark, T. Powers, B. Budiman, J. Szinai, and P. Hidalgo-Gonzalez. 2021. "The Role of Storage in the Path to Net Zero." Accenture and University of California-Berkeley Renewable and Appropriate Energies Lab. https://www.accenture.com/content/dam/accenture/final/a-com-migration/r3-3/pdf/pdf-144/accenture-path-to-net-zero-pov.pdf.

National Academies of Sciences, Engineering, and Medicine. 2021. *Accelerating Decarbonization of the U.S. Energy System.* Washington: National Academies Press. https://doi.org/10.17226/25932.

National Renewable Energy Lab. 2023. "Annual Technology Baseline: Utility-Scale Battery Storage." https://atb.nrel.gov/electricity/2023/utility-scale_battery_storage.

National Research Council. 2001. *Energy Research at DOE: Was It Worth It? Energy Efficiency and Fossil Energy Research 1978 to 2000.* Washington: National Academies Press. https://doi.org/10.17226/10165.

Nature Conservancy. 2023. "Power of Place National Executive Summary." https://www.nature.org/content/dam/tnc/nature/en/documents/FINAL_TNC_Power_of_Place_National_Executive_Summary_5_2_2023.pdf?itid=lk_inline_enhanced-template.

NCEI (National Centers for Environmental Information). 2024. "Billion-Dollar Weather and Climate Disasters." https://www.ncei.noaa.gov/access/billions/overview/.

Nelson, R., and S. Winter. 1985. *An Evolutionary Theory of Economic Change.* Cambridge, MA: Harvard University Press. https://www.hup.harvard.edu/books/9780674272286.

Nemet, G. 2019. *How Solar Energy Became Cheap: A Model for Low-Carbon Innovation.* Oxford: Routledge. https://www.routledge.com/How-Solar-Energy-Became-Cheap-A-Model-for-Low-Carbon-Innovation/Nemet/p/book/9780367136598?utm_source=cjaffiliates&utm_medium=affiliates&cjevent=ced8fe67678411ee8168008b0a82b82a.

Nemet, G., and D. Kammen. 2007. "U.S. Energy Research and Development: Declining Investment, Increasing Need, and the Feasibility of Expansion." *Energy Policy* 35, no. 1: 746–55. https://doi.org/10.1016/j.enpol.2005.12.012.

Nemet, G., V. Zipperer, and M. Kraus. 2018. "The Valley of Death, the Technology Pork Barrel, and Public Support for Large Demonstration Projects." *Energy Policy* 119: 154–67. https://doi.org/10.1016/j.enpol.2018.04.008.

NOAA (National Oceanic and Atmospheric Administration). 2024. "Billion-Dollar Weather and Climate Disasters." https://www.ncei.noaa.gov/access/billions/overview.

Noailly, J., L. Nowzohour, and M. van den Heuvel. 2022. *Does Environmental Policy Uncertainty Hinder Investments Towards a Low-Carbon Economy?* NBER Working Paper 30361. Cambridge, MA: National Bureau of Economic Research. https://doi.org/10.3386/w30361.

NREL (National Renewable Energy Laboratory). 2023. "Utility-Scale Battery Storage." https://atb.nrel.gov/electricity/2023/utility-scale_battery_storage.

Nurkse, R. 1952. "Some International Aspects of the Problem of Economic Development." *American Economic Review* 42, no. 2: 571–83. https://www.jstor.org/stable/1910629.

NYC Department of Buildings. 2023. "Solar Electric Generating Systems Tax Abatement Program." https://nyc-business.nyc.gov/nycbusiness/description/solar-electric-generating-systems-tax-abatement-program.

OEC (Observatory of Economic Complexity). 2021. "South Korea." https://oec.world/en/profile/country/kor.

OCED (Office of Clean Energy Demonstrations). 2023. "OCED Funding Opportunity Announcements." https://oced-exchange.energy.gov/Default.aspx#FoaId3c3d8e7f-1839-45fc-8735-c0caf87408ef.

OECD (Organization for Economic Cooperation and Development). 2023. "Greenhouse Gas Emissions." https://stats.oecd.org/Index.aspx?DataSetCode=air_ghg.

OMB (U.S. Office of Management and Budget). 2023. "Budget Exposure to Increased Costs and Lost Revenue Due to Climate Change: A Preliminary Assessment and Proposed Framework for Future Assessments." White Paper. https://www.whitehouse.gov/wp-content/uploads/2023/03/climate_budget_exposure_fy2024.pdf.

Pasqualetti, M., R. Righter, and P. Gipe. 2004. "History of Wind Energy." In *Encyclopedia of Energy*, ed. C. Cleveland, 419–33. Cambridge: Academic Press. https://www.researchgate.net/publication/265594973_History_of_Wind_Energy.

Pimm, A., E. Barbour, T. Cockerill, and J. Palczewski. 2019. "Evaluating the Regional Potential for Emissions Reduction Using Energy Storage." In *Proceedings of 2019 Offshore Energy and Storage Summit*, 1–6. https://ieeexplore.ieee.org/document/8867357.

Pirani, S. 2018. *Burning Up: A Global History of Fossil Fuel Consumption.* London: Pluto Press. https://www.jstor.org/stable/j.ctv4ncp7q.14?typeAccessWorkflow=login&seq=10.

Pollin, R., and B. Callaci. 2016. "The Economics of Just Transition: A Framework for Supporting Fossil-Fuel-Dependent Workers and Communities in the United States." Working paper, *Labor Studies Journal.* https://peri.umass.edu/publication/item/762-the-economics-of-just-transition-a-framework-for-supporting-fossil-fuel-dependent-workers-and-communities-in-the-united-states.

Quinn, R. 2013. "Rethinking Antibiotic Research and Development: World War II and the Penicillin Collaborative." *American Journal of Public Health* 103, no. 3: 426–34. https://www.ncbi.nlm.nih.gov/pmc/articles/PMC3673487/.

Raimi, D., E. Grubert, J. Higdon, G. Metcalf, S. Pesek, and D. Singh. 2023. "The Fiscal Implications of the U.S. Transition Away from Fossil Fuels." *Review of Environmental Economics and Policy* 17, no. 2: 295–315. https://doi.org/10.1086/725250.

Ranis, G., and J. Fei. 1961. "A Theory of Economic Development." *American Economic Review* 51, no. 4: 533–65. https://www.jstor.org/stable/1812785.

Rao, V. 1952. "Investment, Income and the Multiplier in an Under-Developed Economy." *Indian Economic Review* 1, no. 1: 55–67. https://doi.org/10.1177/0019466220080205.

Rapson, D., and E. Muehlegger. 2023. *The Economics of Electric Vehicles.* NBER Working Paper 29093. Cambridge, MA: National Bureau of Economic Research. https://doi.org/10.3386/w29093.

Riofrancos, T., A. Kendall, K. Dayemo, M. Haugen, K. McDonald, B. Hassan, M. Slattery, and X. Lillehei. 2023. "Achieving Zero Emissions with More Mobility and Less Mining." Climate and Community Project. https://www.climateandcommunity.org/more-mobility-less-mining.

RMI. 2022. "FERC Could Slash Inflation and Double Renewables with These Grid Upgrades." https://rmi.org/ferc-could-slash-inflation-and-double-renewables-grid-upgrades/.

Rodrik, D. 2014. "Green Industrial Policy." *Oxford Review of Economic Policy* 30, no. 3: 469–91. https://doi.org/10.1093/oxrep/gru025.

Romer, P. 1990. "Endogenous Technological Change." *Journal of Political Economy* 98, no. 5: S71–102. https://www.jstor.org/stable/2937632.

Sandalow, D., M. Meidan, P. Andrews-Speed, A. Hove, S. Qiu, and E. Downie. 2022. "Guide to Chinese Climate Policy 2022." Oxford Institute of Energy Studies, chap. 21: "Clean Energy R&D." https://chineseclimatepolicy.oxfordenergy.org/book-content/domestic-policies/clean-energy-rd/.

Sankaran, V., H. Parmar, and K. Collison. 2021. "Just & Reasonable? Transmission Upgrades Charged to Interconnecting Generators Are Delivering System-Wide Benefits." American Council on Renewable Energy. https://acore.org/wp-content/uploads/2021/10/Just_and_Reasonable.pdf.

Schlenker, W., and M. Roberts. 2009. "Nonlinear Temperature Effects Indicate Severe Damages to U.S. Crop Yields under Climate Change." *Proceedings of the National Academy of Sciences* 106, no. 37: 15594–98. https://doi.org/10.1073/pnas.0906865106.

UNFCCC (United Nations Framework Convention on Climate Change). 2023. "2023 Voluntary Supplement to the U.S. Fifth Biennial Report." https://unfccc.int/sites/default/files/resource/US_BR_Voluntary_Suplement_2023.pdf.

———. 2024a. "The Paris Agreement." https://unfccc.int/process-and-meetings/the-paris-agreement.

———. 2024b. "What Is the Kyoto Protocol?" https://unfccc.int/kyoto_protocol.

U.S. Congress. 2004. "H.R.4520: American Jobs Creation Act of 2004." https://www.congress.gov/bill/108th-congress/house-bill/4520.

U.S. Department of the Treasury. 2023. "New U.S. Department of the Treasury Analysis: Inflation Reduction Act Driving Clean Energy Investment to Underserved Communities, Communities at the Forefront of Fossil Fuel Production." https://home.treasury.gov/news/press-releases/jy1931.

Van den Heuvel, M., and D. Popp. 2022. *The Role of Venture Capital and Governments in Clean Energy: Lessons from the First Cleantech Bubble.* NBER Working Paper 29919. Cambridge, MA: National Bureau of Economic Research. https://doi.org/10.3386/w29919.

Van de Ven, D., I. Capellan-Peréz, I. Arto, I. Cazcarro, C. de Castro, P. Patel, and M. Gonzalez-Eguino. 2021. "The Potential Land Requirements and Related Land Use Change Emissions of Solar Energy." *Scientific Reports* 11. https://doi.org/10.1038/s41598-021-82042-5.

Vanatta, M., M. Craig, B. Rathod, J. Florez, I. Bromley-Dulfano, and D. Smith. 2022. "The Costs of Replacing Coal Plant Jobs with Local Instead of Distant Wind and Solar Jobs across the United States." *iScience* 25, no. 8. https://doi.org/10.1016/j.isci.2022.104817.

Van Zalk, J., and P. Behrens. 2018. "The Spatial Extent of Renewable and Non-Renewable Power Generation: A Review and Meta-Analysis of Power Densities and Their Application in the U.S." *Energy Policy* 123: 83–91. https://www.sciencedirect.com/science/article/pii/S0301421518305512.

Victor, D. 2009. "The Politics of Fossil-Fuel Subsidies." Working paper, Global Studies Initiative. https://dx.doi.org/10.2139/ssrn.1520984.

Way, R., M. Ives, P. Mealy, and J. Farmer. 2022. "Empirically Grounded Technology Forecasts and the Energy Transition." *Joule* 6, no. 9: 2057–82. https://doi.org/10.1016/j.joule.2022.08.009.

Weber, J. 2020. "How Should We Think about Environmental Policy and Jobs? An Analogy with Trade Policy and an Illustration from U.S. Coal Mining." *Review of Environmental Economics and Policy* 14. no. 1. https://doi.org/10.1093/reep/rez016.

White House. 2022. "Federal Budget Exposure to Climate Risk." https://www.whitehouse.gov/wp-content/uploads/2022/04/ap_21_climate_risk_fy2023.pdf.

Zacarias, M., and J. Nakano. 2023. "Exploring the Hydrogen Midstream: Distribution and Delivery." Center for Strategic and International Studies. https://www.csis.org/analysis/exploring-hydrogen-midstream-distribution-and-delivery.

Chapter 7

Abada, I., and X. Lambin. 2023. "Artificial Intelligence: Can Seemingly Collusive Outcomes Be Avoided?" *Management Science* 69, no. 9: 5042–65. https://doi.org/10.1287/mnsc.2022.4623.

Abbott, R., and B. Bogenschneider. 2018. "Should Robots Pay Taxes? Tax Policy in the Age of Automation." *Harvard Law & Policy Review* 12. https://heinonline.org/HOL/Page?handle=hein.journals/harlpolrv12&div=10&g_sent=1&casa_token=&collection=journals.

Acemoglu, D. 2021. *Harms of AI.* NBER Working Paper 29247. Cambridge, MA: National Bureau of Economic Research. https://doi.org/10.3386/w29247.

Acemoglu, D., G. Anderson, D. Beede, C. Buffington, E. Childress, E. Dinlersoz, L. Foster, N. Goldschlag, J. Haltiwanger, Z. Kroff, P. Restrepo, and N. Zolas. 2022. *Automation and the Workforce: A Firm-Level View from the 2019 Annual Business Survey*. NBER Working Paper 30659. Cambridge, MA: National Bureau of Economic Research. https://www.nber.org/system/files/working_papers/w30659/w30659.pdf.

Acemoglu, D., D. Autor, J. Hazell, and P. Restrepo. 2020. *AI and Jobs: Evidence from Online Vacancies.* NBER Working Paper 28257. Cambridge, MA: National Bureau of Economic Research. https://doi.org/10.3386/w28257.

Acemoglu, D., S. Johnson, and J. Robinson, 2005. "Chapter 6: Institutions as a Fundamental Cause of Long-Run Growth." In *Handbook of Economic Growth* 1: 385–472. https://doi.org/10.1016/S1574-0684(05)01006-3.

Acemoglu, D., A. Manera, and P. Restrepo. 2020. *Does the U.S. Tax Code Favor Automation?* NBER Working Paper 27052. Cambridge, MA: National Bureau of Economic Research. https://doi.org/10.3386/w27052.

Acemoglu, D. and Pischke, J. 1998. "Why Do Firms Train? Theory and Evidence." *Quarterly Journal of Economics* 113, no. 1: 79–119. https://doi.org/10.1162/003355398555531.

Acemoglu, D., and P. Restrepo. 2018. "The Race between Man and Machine: Implications of Technology for Growth, Factor Shares, and Employment." *American Economic Review* 108, no. 6: 1488–542. https://doi.org/10.1257/aer.20160696.

———. 2019. "Automation and New Tasks: How Technology Displaces and Reinstates Labor." *Journal of Economic Perspectives* 33, no. 2: 3–30. https://doi.org/10.1257/jep.33.2.3.

———. 2020. "Robots and Jobs: Evidence from U.S. Labor Markets." *Journal of Political Economy* 128, no. 6: 2188–244. https://doi.org/10.1086/705716.

Aghion, P., N. Bloom, R. Blundell, R. Griffith, and P. Howitt. 2005. "Competition and Innovation: An Inverted-U Relationship." *Quarterly Journal of Economics* 120, no. 2: 701–28. https://doi.org/10.1093/qje/120.2.701.

Aghion, P., and P. Bolton. 1992. "An Incomplete Contracts Approach to Financial Contracting." *Review of Economic Studies* 59, no. 3: 473–94. https://doi.org/10.2307/2297860.

Aghion, P., and P. Howitt. 1992. "A Model of Growth Through Creative Destruction." *Econometrica* 60, no. 2: 323–51. https://doi.org/10.2307/2951599.

Aghion, P., P. Howitt, and G. Violante. 2002. "General Purpose Technology and Wage Inequality." *Journal of Economic Growth* 7, no. 4: 315–45. https://doi.org/10.1023/A:1020875717066.

Agrawal, A., J. Gans, and A. Goldfarb. 2018. *Prediction Machines: The Simple Economics of Artificial Intelligence.* Brighton, MA: Harvard Business Review Press. https://www.predictionmachines.ai/pre-order.

————. 2022. *Power and Prediction: The Disruptive Economics of Artificial Intelligence.* Brighton, MA: Harvard Business Review Press. https://www.predictionmachines.ai/power-prediction.

Akcigit, U., J. Grigsby, T. Nicholas, and S. Stantcheva. 2021. "Taxation and Innovation in the Twentieth Century." *Quarterly Journal of Economics* 137, no. 1: 329–85. https://doi.org/10.1093/qje/qjab022.

Akerman, A., I. Gaarder, and M. Mogstad. 2015. "The Skill Complementarity of Broadband Internet." *Quarterly Journal of Economics* 130, no. 4: 1781-1824. https://doi.org/10.1093/qje/qjv028.

Alchian, A. 1965. "Some Economics of Property Rights." *Il Politico* 30, no. 4: 816–29. https://www.jstor.org/stable/43206327.

Amershi, S., M. Cakmak, W. Knox, and T. Kulesza. 2014. "Power to the People: The Role of Humans in Interactive Machine Learning." *AI Magazine* 35, no. 4: 105–20. https://doi.org/10.1609/aimag.v35i4.2513.

Anthropic. 2024. "Anthropic-SDK-Python." Code commit. https://github.com/anthropics/anthropic-sdk-python.

Appel, G., J. Neelbauer, and D. Schweidel. 2023. "Generative AI Has an Intellectual Problem." *Harvard Business Review.* https://hbr.org/2023/04/generative-ai-has-an-intellectual-property-problem.

Arena F., and G. Pau. 2019. "An Overview of Vehicular Communications." *Future Internet* 11, no. 2: 27. https://doi.org/10.3390/fi11020027.

Armstrong, S., K. Sotala, and S. Ó hÉigeartaigh. 2014. "The Errors, Insights and Lessons of Famous AI Predictions—and What They Mean for the Future." *Journal of Experimental & Theoretical Artificial Intelligence* 26, no. 3: 317–42. https://doi.org/10.1080/0952813X.2014.895105.

Arrow, K. 1962. "The Economic Implications of Learning by Doing." *Review of Economic Studies* 29, no. 3: 155–73. https://doi.org/10.2307/2295952.

Athey, S., K. Bryan, and J. Gans. 2020. "The Allocation of Decision Authority to Human and Artificial Intelligence." *AEA Papers and Proceedings* 110: 80–84. https://doi.org/10.1257/pandp.20201034.

Athey, S., and F. Scott Morton. 2022. "Platform Annexation." *Antitrust Law Journal* 84, no. 3. https://www.americanbar.org/content/dam/aba/publications/antitrust/journal/84/3/platform-annexation.pdf.

Authors Guild v. Google, Inc. 2015. U.S. Court of Appeals for the Second Circuit, No. 13-4829-cv. https://law.justia.com/cases/federal/appellate-courts/ca2/13-4829/13-4829-2015-10-16.html.

Autor, D. 2015. "Why Are There So Many Jobs? The History and Future of Workplace Automation." *Journal of Economic Perspectives* 29, no. 3: 3–30. https://doi.org/10.1257/jep.29.3.3.

Autor, D., C. Chin, A. M. Salomons, and B. Seegmiller. 2022. *New Frontiers: The Origins and Content of New Work, 1940–2018.* NBER Working Paper 30389.

Cambridge, MA: National Bureau for Economic Research. https://doi.
org/10.3386/w30389.

Autor, D., and D. Dorn. 2013. "The Growth of Low-Skill Service Jobs and the Polarization of the U.S. Labor Market." *American Economic Review* 103, no. 5:
1553–97. https://doi.org/10.1257/aer.103.5.1553.

Autor, D., D. Dorn, and G. Hanson. 2013. "The China Syndrome: Local Labor Market
Effects of Import Competition in the United States." *American Economic
Review* 103, no. 6: 2121–68. https://doi.org/10.1257/aer.103.6.2121.

———. 2021. *On the Persistence of the China Shock.* NBER Working Paper 29401.
Cambridge, MA: National Bureau of Economic Research. https://doi.
org/10.3386/w29401.

Autor, D., C. Goldin, and L. Katz. 2020. *Extending the Race Between Education and
Technology.* NBER Working Paper 26705. Cambridge, MA: National Bureau
for Economic Research. https://doi.org/10.3386/w26705.

Autor, D., F. Levy, and R. Murnane. 2003. "The Skill Content of Recent Technological
Change: An Empirical Exploration." *Quarterly Journal of Economics* 118, no.
4: 1279–1333. https://doi.org/10.1162/003355303322552801.

Babina, T., A. Fedyk, A. He, and J. Hodson. 2024. "Artificial Intelligence, Firm Growth,
and Product Innovation." *Journal of Financial Economics* 151, no. 103745.
https://doi.org/10.1016/j.jfineco.2023.103745.

Bambauer, D., and M. Surdeanu. 2023. *Authorbots.* Arizona Legal Studies Discussion
Paper 23-13. Tucson: Arizona Legal Studies Research Paper Series. https://ssrn.
com/abstract=4443714.

Bárány, Z., and C. Siegel. 2018. "Job Polarization and Structural Change." *American
Economic Journal: Macroeconomics* 10, no. 1: 57–89. https://www.aeaweb.org/
articles?id=10.1257/mac.20150258.

Barocas, S., and A. Selbst. 2016. "Big Data's Disparate Impact." *California Law Review*
104, no. 3: 671–732. https://www.jstor.org/stable/24758720.

Bartholomew, J. 2023. "Q&A: Uncovering the Labor Exploitation That Powers AI."
Columbia Journalism Review, Tow Center. https://www.cjr.org/tow_center/
qa-uncovering-the-labor-exploitation-that-powers-ai.php.

Bartlett, R., A. Morse, R. Stanton, and N. Wallace. 2022. "Consumer-Lending Discrimination in the FinTech Era." *Journal of Financial Economics* 143, no. 1: 30–56.
https://doi.org/10.1016/j.jfineco.2021.05.047.

Barzel, Y., and D. Allen. 2023. *Economic Analysis of Property Rights.* New York:
Cambridge University Press. https://www.cambridge.org/core/books/economic-
analysis-of-property-rights/6D5E9A3AA67284FD9A12379CA3028D50.

Beauchêne, D. 2019. "Is Ambiguity Aversion Bad for Innovation?" *Journal of Economic
Theory* 183: 1154–76. https://doi.org/10.1016/j.jet.2019.07.015.

Becker, G., and K. Murphy. 1994. "Chapter XI: The Division of Labor, Coordination
Costs, and Knowledge." In *Human Capital: A Theoretical and Empirical*

Analysis with Special Reference to Education, 3rd Edition. Chicago: University of Chicago Press. https://www.nber.org/books-and-chapters/ human-capital-theoretical-and-empirical-analysis-special-reference-education-third-edition.

Bell, A., and G. Parchomovsky. 2005. "A Theory of Property." *Cornell Law Review* 90, no. 3: 531–616. https://scholarship.law.cornell.edu/clr/vol90/iss3/1.

Bernheim, B., and M. Whinston. 1990. "Multimarket Contact and Collusive Behavior." *RAND Journal of Economics* 21, no. 1: 1–26. https://www.jstor.org/ stable/2555490.

Bessen, J., M. Goos, A. Salomons, and W. van den Berge. 2023. "What Happens to Workers at Firms That Automate?" *Review of Economics and Statistics*, 1–45. https://doi.org/10.1162/rest_a_01284.

Biggs, R. 1983. "The Impact of the Interstate Highway System on Nonmetropolitan Development, 1950–75." In *Beyond the Urban Fringe: Land Use Issues in Nonmetropolitan America*, ed. R. Platt and G. Macinko, 83–105. Minneapolis: University of Minnesota Press. https://books.google.com/books?hl=en&lr=&id= Nm0I8ogefv0C&oi=fnd&pg=PA83&dq=interstate+highway+system+migration &ots=jTrCdS1jud&sig=KpyxVj-EBIhO4MGC9XppYQ2nEew.

Bischoff, K., and S. Reardon. 2013. "Residential Segregation by Income, 1970–2009." Working paper, US2010 Project. https://cepa.stanford.edu/content/ residential-segregation-income-1970-2009.

Billard, A., and D. Kragic. 2019. "Trends and Challenges in Robot Manipulation." *Science*. https://www.science.org/doi/full/10.1126/science.aat8414.

Bloom, N., C. Jones, J. Van Reenen, and M. Webb. 2020. "Are Ideas Getting Harder to Find?" *American Economic Review* 110, no. 4: 1104–44. https://doi. org/10.1257/aer.20180338.

Bloom, N., J. Van Reenen, and H. Williams. 2019. "A Toolkit of Policies to Promote Innovation." *Journal of Economic Perspectives* 33, no. 3: 163–84. https://doi. org/10.1257/jep.33.3.163.

BLS (U.S. Bureau of Labor Statistics). 2023. "Fastest Growing Occupations: Occupational Outlook Handbook." https://www.bls.gov/ooh/fastest-growing.htm.

Boldrin, M., and D. Levine. 2013. "The Case Against Patents." *Journal of Economic Perspectives* 27, no. 1: 3–22. https://doi.org/10.1257/jep.27.1.3.

Bolton, P., and M. Dewatripont. 1994. "The Firm as a Communication Network." *Quarterly Journal of Economics* 109, no. 4: 809–39. https://doi. org/10.2307/2118349.

Bommasani, R., D. Hudson, E. Adeli, R. Altman, S. Arora, S. von Arx, M. Bernstein, J. Bohg, A. Bosselut, E. Brunskill, E. Brynjolfsson, S. Buch, D. Card, R. Castellon, N. Chatterji, A. Chen, K. Creel, J. Quincy Davis, D. Demszky, C. Donahue, M. Doumbouya, E. Durmus, S. Ermon, J. Etchemendy, K. Ethayarajh, L. Fei-Fei, C. Finn, T. Gale, L. Gillespie, K. Goel. N. Goodman, S. Grossman, N. Guha, T. Hashimoto, P. Henderson, J. Hewitt, D. Ho, J. Hong, K.

Hsu, J. Huang, T. Icard, S. Jain, D. Jurafsky, P. Kalluri, S. Karamcheti, G. Keeling, F. Khani, O. Khattab, P. Wei Koh, M. Krass. R. Krishna, R. Kuditipudi, A. Kumar, F. Ladhak, M. Lee, T. Lee, J. Leskovec, I. Levent, X.L. Li, X. Li, T. Ma, A. Malik, C. Manning, S. Mirchandani, E. Mitchell, Z. Munyikwa, S. Nair, A. Narayan, D. Narayanan, B. Newman, A. Nie, J. Niebles, H. Nilforoshan, J. Nyarko, G. Ogut, L. Orr, I. Papadimitriou, J. Sung Park, C. Piech, E. Portelance, C. Potts, A. Raghunathan, R. Reich, H. Ren, F. Rong, Y. Roohani, C. Ruiz, J. Ryan, C. Ré, D. Sadigh, S. Sagawa, K. Santhanam, A. Shih, K. Srinivasan, A. Tamkin, R. Taori, A. Thomas, F. Tramèr, R. Wang, W. Wang, B. Wu, J. Wu, Y. Wu, S. Xie, M. Yasunaga, J. You, M. Zaharia, M. Zhang, T. Zhang, X. Zhang, Y. Zhang, L. Zheng, K. Zhou, and P. Liang. 2021. *On the Opportunities and Risks of Foundation Models*. ArXiv Preprint ArXiv:1802.04865. Ithaca, NY: Cornell University. https://doi.org/10.48550/arXiv.2108.07258.

Bonvillian, W. 2018. "DARPA and Its ARPA-E and IARPA Clones: A Unique Innovation Organization Model." *Industrial and Corporate Change* 27, no. 5: 897–914. https://doi.org/10.1093/icc/dty026.

Booth, A., and M. Chatterji. 1998. "Unions and Efficient Training." *Economic Journal* 108, no. 447: 328–43. https://doi.org/10.1111/1468-0297.00290.

Boudreau, K., L. Jeppesen, and M. Miric. 2022. "Profiting from Digital Innovation: Patents, Copyright and Performance." *Research Policy* 51, no. 5. https://doi.org/10.1016/j.respol.2022.104477.

Braghieri, L., R. Levy, and A. Makarin. 2022. "Social Media and Mental Health." *American Economic Review* 112, no. 11: 3660–93. https://doi.org/10.1257/aer.20211218.

Brau, R., and C. Carraro. 1999. "Voluntary Approaches, Market Structure and Competition." Fondazione eni Enrico Mattei. FEEM Working Paper 53–99 https://doi.org/10.2139/ssrn.200614.

Bresnahan, T., and M. Trajtenberg. 1995. "General Purpose Technologies 'Engines of Growth'?" *Journal of Econometrics* 65, no. 1: 83–108. https://doi.org/10.1016/0304-4076(94)01598-T.

Brodsky, J. 2016. "Autonomous Vehicle Regulation." *Berkeley Technology Law Journal* 21, no. 2: 851–78. https://www.jstor.org/stable/26377774.

Brooks, F. 1996. *The Mythical Man-Month*. Boston: Addison-Wesley Professional. https://web.eecs.umich.edu/~weimerw/2018-481/readings/mythical-man-month.pdf.

Broussard, W. 2009. "The Promise and Peril of Collective Licensing." *Journal of Intellectual Property Law* 17, no. 1: 21–34. https://heinonline.org/HOL/P?h=hein.journals/intpl17&i=23.

Brown, N. 2023. "Bots Behaving Badly: A Products Liability Approach to the Chatbot-Generated Defamation." *Journal of Free Speech* 3, no. 2: 389–424. https://heinonline.org/HOL/P?h=hein.journals/jfspl3&i=389.

Brown, I. 2020. "Interoperability as a Tool for Competition Regulation." https://econpapers.repec.org/paper/osflawarx/fbvxd.htm.

Brown, J., C. Coile, and S. Weisbenner. 2010. "The Effects of Inheritance Receipt on Retirement." *Review of Economics and Statistics* 92, no. 2: 425–34. https://doi.org/10.1162/rest.2010.11182.

Brown, T., B. Mann, N. Ryder, M. Subbiah, J. Kaplan, P. Dhariwal, A. Neelakantan, P. Shyam, G. Sastry, A. Askell, S. Agarwal, A. Herbert-Voss, G. Krueger, T. Henighan, R. Child, A. Ramesh, D. Ziegler, J. Wu, C. Winter, C. Hesse, M. Chen, E. Sigler, M. Litwin, S. Gray, B. Chess, J. Clark, C. Berner, S. McClandish, A. Radford, I. Sutskever, and D. Amodei. 2020. "Language Models Are Few-Shot Learners." In *Proceedings of the 34th International Conference on Neural Information Processing Systems*, 1877–1901. NIPS'20. Red Hook, NY: Curran Associates. https://dl.acm.org/doi/abs/10.5555/3495724.3495883.

Brozen, Y. 1957. "The Economics of Automation." *American Economic Review* 47, no. 2: 339–50. https://www.jstor.org/stable/1831605.

Brynjolfsson, E., X. Hui, and M. Liu. 2019. "Does Machine Translation Affect International Trade? Evidence from a Large Digital Platform." *Management Science* 65, no. 12: 5449–60. https://doi.org/10.1287/mnsc.2019.3388.

Brynjolfsson, E., D. Li, and L. Raymond. 2023. *Generative AI at Work*. NBER Working Paper 31161. Cambridge, MA: National Bureau for Economic Research. https://doi.org/10.3386/w31161.

Brynjolfsson, E., T. Mitchell, and D. Rock. 2018. "What Can Machines Learn and What Does It Mean for Occupations and the Economy?" *AEA Papers and Proceedings* 108: 43–47. https://www.aeaweb.org/articles?id=10.1257/pandp.20181019.

Brynjolfsson, E., D. Rock, and C. Syverson. 2021. "The Productivity J-Curve: How Intangibles Complement General Purpose Technologies." *American Economic Journal: Macroeconomics* 13, no. 1: 333–72. https://doi.org/10.1257/mac.20180386.

Burnell, R., W. Schellaert, J. Burden, T. Ullman, F. Martínez-Plumed, J. Tenenbaum, D. Rutar, L. Cheke, J. Sohl-Dickstein, M. Mitchell, D. Kiela, M. Shanahan, E. Voorhees, A. Cohn, J. Leibo, and J. Hernández-Orallo. 2023. "Rethink Reporting of Evaluation Results in AI." *Science* 380, no. 6641: 136–38. https://doi.org/10.1126/science.adf6369.

Buolamwini, J., and T. Gebru. 2018. "Gender Shades: Intersectional Accuracy Disparities in Commercial Gender Classification." *Proceedings of the First Conference on Fairness, Accountability, and Transparency, PMLR* 81: 77–91. https://proceedings.mlr.press/v81/buolamwini18a.html.

Byström, K., and K. Järvelin. 1995. "Task Complexity Affects Information Seeking and Use." *Information Processing & Management* 31, no. 2: 191–213. https://doi.org/10.1016/0306-4573(95)80035-R.

Calabresi, G., and A. Melamed. 1972. "Property Rights, Liability Rules, and Inalienability: One View of the Cathedral." *Harvard Law Review* 85, no. 6: 1130–303.

https://heinonline.org/HOL/Page?handle=hein.journals/
hlr85&div=8&g_sent=1&casa_token=&collection=journals.

Calvano, E., G. Calzolari, V. Denicolò, and S. Pastorello. 2020. "Artificial Intelligence, Algorithmic Pricing, and Collusion." *American Economic Review* 110, no. 10: 3267–97. https://doi.org/10.1257/aer.20190623.

Census (U.S. Bureau of the Census). 2023. "CPS Historical Time Series Tables: Table A-1. Years of School Completed by People 25 Years and Over, by Age and Sex: Selected Years 1940–2022." https://www.census.gov/data/tables/time-series/demo/educational-attainment/cps-historical-time-series.html.

Chattergoon, B., and W. Kerr. 2021. *Winner Takes All? Tech Clusters, Population Centers, and the Spatial Transformation of U.S. Invention.* NBER Working Paper 29456. Cambridge, MA: National Bureau of Economic Research. https://doi.org/10.3386/w29456.

Chen, L., M. Zaharia, and J. Zou. 2023. *How Is ChatGPT's Behavior Changing Over Time?* ArXiv Preprint ArXiv: 2307.09009. Ithaca, NY: Cornell University. https://doi.org/10.48550/arXiv.2307.09009.

Chen, L., Z. Jin, S. Eyuboglu, C. Ré, M. Zaharia, and J. Zou. 2022. "HAPI: A Large-Scale Longitudinal Dataset of Commercial ML API Predictions." Advances in Neural Information Processing Systems 35. https://proceedings.neurips.cc/paper_files/paper/2022/hash/9bcd0bdb2777fe8c729b682f07e993f1-Abstract-Datasets_and_Benchmarks.html.

Cherney, M. 2021. "Buzz Off, Bees. Pollination Robots Are Here." *Wall Street Journal,* July 7. https://www.wsj.com/articles/buzz-off-bees-pollination-robots-are-here-11625673660?reflink=desktopwebshare_permalink.

Chetty, R. 2008. "Moral Hazard versus Liquidity and Optimal Unemployment Insurance." *Journal of Political Economy* 116, no. 2: 173–234. https://doi.org/10.1086/588585.

Chesterman, S. 2021. "Through a Glass, Darkly: Artificial Intelligence and the Problem of Opacity." *American Journal of Comparative Law* 69, no. 2: 271–94. https://doi.org/10.1093/ajcl/avab012.

Chialastri, A. 2012. "Automation in Aviation." *INTECH Open Access.* https://pdfs.semanticscholar.org/8232/21400579c2d309f84b33667cf3a7b4772d04.pdf.

Christensen, P., and C. Timmins. 2023. "The Damages and Distortions from Discrimination in the Rental Housing Market." *Quarterly Journal of Economics* 138, no. 4: 2505–57. https://doi.org/10.1093/qje/qjad029.

Chui, M., E. Hazan, R. Roberts, A. Singla, K. Smaje, A. Sukharevsky, L. Yee, and R. Zemmel. 2023. "The Economic Potential of Generative AI: The Next Productivity Frontier." McKinsey & Company. https://www.mckinsey.com/capabilities/mckinsey-digital/our-insights/the-economic-potential-of-generative-ai-the-next-productivity-frontier.

Coase, R. 1960. "The Problem of Social Cost." *Journal of Law and Economics* 56, no. 4: 837–77. https://doi.org/10.1086/674872.

CEA (Council of Economic Advisers). 2022. *Economic Report of the President.* Washington: U.S. Government Publishing Office. https://www.whitehouse.gov/wp-content/uploads/2022/04/ERP-2022.pdf.

———. 2023. *Economic Report of the President.* Washington: U.S. Government Publishing Office. https://www.whitehouse.gov/wp-content/uploads/2023/03/ERP-2023.pdf.

Costanza-Chock, S., I. Raji, and J. Buolamwini. 2022. "Who Audits the Auditors? Recommendations from a Field Scan of the Algorithmic Auditing Ecosystem." In *Proceedings of the 2022 ACM Conference on Fairness, Accountability, and Transparency*, 1571–83. New York: Association for Computing Machinery. https://doi.org/10.1145/3531146.3533213.

Costinot, A. 2009. "On the Origins of Comparative Advantage." *Journal of International Economics* 77, no. 2: 255–64. https://doi.org/10.1016/j.jinteco.2009.01.007.

Cowen, T. 2017. "Why Hasn't Economic Progress Lowered Work Hours More?" *Social Philosophy & Policy* 34, no. 2: 190–212. https://doi.org/10.1017/S0265052517000267.

CRS (Congressional Research Service). 2023a. "Generative Artificial Intelligence and Copyright Law." https://crsreports.congress.gov/product/pdf/LSB/LSB10922.

———. 2023b. "Trade Adjustment Assistance for Workers: Background and Current Status." https://crsreports.congress.gov/product/pdf/R/R47200.

———. 2024. "Section 230: An Overview." https://crsreports.congress.gov/product/pdf/R/R46751.

Dally, W., S. Keckler, and D. Kirk. 2021. "Evolution of the Graphics Processing Unit (GPU)". *IEEE Micro* 41, no. 6: 42–51. https://doi.org/10.1109/MM.2021.3113475.

Dalvi, M., and J. Refalo. 2008. "An Economic Analysis of Libel Law." *Eastern Economic Journal* 34, no. 1: 74–91. http://www.jstor.org/stable/20642394.

Dastin, J. 2018. "Insight: Amazon Scraps Secret AI Recruiting Tool That Showed Bias against Women." Reuters. https://www.reuters.com/article/amazoncom-jobs-automation/rpt-insight-amazon-scraps-secret-ai-recruiting-tool-that-showed-bias-against-women-idINL2N1WP1RO/.

David, P. 1990. "The Dynamo and the Computer: An Historical Perspective on the Modern Productivity Paradox." *American Economic Review* 80, no. 2: 355–61. https://www.jstor.org/stable/2006600.

Davis, S., and T. von Wachter. 2011. *Recessions and the Cost of Job Loss.* NBER Working Paper 17638. Cambridge, MA: National Bureau of Economic Research. https://doi.org/10.3386/w17638.

DeVries, T., and G. Taylor. 2018. *Learning Confidence for Out-of-Distribution Detection in Neural Networks.* ArXiv Preprint ArXiv:1802.04865. Ithaca, NY: Cornell University. https://doi.org/10.48550/arXiv.1802.04865.

Diamantis, M., R. Cochran, and M. Dam. 2023. "AI and the Law." In *Technology Ethics*, edited by G. Robson, and J. Tsou., 242–49. New York: Routledge. https://doi. org/10.4324/9781003189466.

Diamond, P., and E. Saez. 2011. "The Case for a Progressive Tax: From Basic Research to Policy Recommendations." *Journal of Economic Perspectives* 25, no. 4: 165–90. https://doi.org/10.1257/jep.25.4.165.

DiNardo, J., and J. Pischke. 1997. "The Returns to Computer Use Revisited: Have Pencils Changed the Wage Structure Too?" *Quarterly Journal of Economics* 112, no. 1: 291–303. http://www.jstor.org/stable/2951283.

DOL (U.S. Department of Labor). 2023a. "Employer and Occupation Sections." https:// www.dol.gov/agencies/eta/ui-modernization/improve-applications/ employer-occupation.

———. 2023b. "U.S. Department of Labor Announces Proposed Rulemaking to Modernize Registered Apprenticeship Regulations." https://www.dol.gov/news-room/releases/eta/eta20231214-0.

———. 2023c. "Reemployment Services and Eligibility Assessment Grants." https:// www.dol.gov/agencies/eta/american-job-centers/RESEA.

Dong, X., Z. Yu, W. Cao, Y. Shi and Q. Ma, 2020. "A Survey on Ensemble Learning." *Frontiers of Computer Science* 14: 241–58. https://doi.org/10.1007/ s11704-019-8208-z.

Dornis, T. 2020. "Artificial Intelligence and Innovation: The End of Patent Law as We Know It." *Yale Journal of Law & Technology* 23: 97–159. https://dx.doi. org/10.2139/ssrn.3668137.

Du Boff, R. 1967. "The Introduction of Electric Power in American Manufacturing." *Economic History Review* 20, no. 3: 509–18. https://doi.org/10.2307/2593069.

Eschner, K. 2017. "Three Ways the Interstate System Changed America." *Smithsonian Magazine*, June. https://www.smithsonianmag.com/smart-news/ three-ways-interstate-system-changed-america-180963815/.

Edwards, B. 2023. "AI-Generated Books Force Amazon to Cap E-Book Publications to 3 Per Day." Ars Technica. https://arstechnica.com/information-tech-nology/2023/09/ ai-generated-books-force-amazon-to-cap-ebook-publications-to-3-per-day/.

Ellingrud, K., S. Sanghvi, G. Dandona, A. Madgavkar, M. Chui, O. White, and P. Hasebe. 2023. "Generative AI and the Future of Work in America." McKinsey Global Institute. https://www.mckinsey.com/mgi/our-research/ generative-ai-and-the-future-of-work-in-america.

Eloundou, T., S. Manning, P. Mishkin, and D. Rock. 2023. *GPTs Are GPTs: An Early Look at the Labor Market Impact Potential of Large Language Models*. ArXiv Preprint ArXiv:2303.10130. Ithaca, NY: Cornell University. https://doi. org/10.48550/arXiv.2303.10130.

Engler, A. 2021. "Enrollment Algorithms Are Contributing to the Crises of Higher Education." Brookings Institution, AI Governance. https://www.brookings.edu/
articles/
enrollment-algorithms-are-contributing-to-the-crises-of-higher-education/.

European Parliament Committee on Legal Affairs. 2017. "Draft Report with Recommendations to the Commission on Civil Law Rules on Robotics." https://www.
europarl.europa.eu/doceo/document/JURI-PR-582443_EN.pdf.

Fama, E., and M. Jensen. 1983. "Separation of Ownership and Control." *Journal of Law
& Economics* 26, no. 2: 301–25. https://doi.org/10.2139/ssrn.94034.

Fan, W., J. Liu, S. Zhu, and P. Pardalos. 2020. "Investigating the Impacting Factors for
the Healthcare Professionals to Adopt Artificial Intelligence-Based Medical
Diagnosis Support System (AIMDSS)." *Annals of Operations Research* 294,
no. 2: 567–92. https://doi.org/10.1007/s10479-018-2818-y.

Farre-Mensa, J., D. Hegde, and A. Ljungqvist. 2019. "What Is a Patent Worth? Evidence
from the U.S. Patent 'Lottery'?" *Journal of Finance* 75, no. 2: 639–82. https://
doi.org/10.1111/jofi.12867.

Farrell, J., and P. Klemperer. 2007. "Chapter 31 Coordination and Lock-In: Competition
with Switching Costs and Network Effects." *Handbook of Industrial Organization* 3: 1967–2072. https://doi.org/10.1016/S1573-448X(06)03031-7.

Felten, E., M. Raj, and R. Seamans. 2021. "Occupational, Industry, and Geographic
Exposure to Artificial Intelligence: A Novel Dataset and Its Potential Uses."
Strategic Management Journal 42, no. 12: 2195–2217. https://doi.org/10.1002/
smj.3286.

Fisher, J., and C. Houseworth. 2013. "Occupation Inflation in the Current Population
Survey." *Journal of Economic and Social Measurement* 38, no. 3: 243–61.
https://content.iospress.com/articles/journal-of-economic-and-social-measure-
ment/jem00377.

Florida, R., and C. Mellander. 2015. "Segregated City: The Geography of Economic
Segregation in America's Metros." Martin Prosperity Institute. https://urn.kb.se/
resolve?urn=urn:nbn:se:hj:diva-28303.

Foster, A., and M. Rosenzweig. 2010. "Microeconomics of Technology Adoption."
Annual Review of Economics 2, no. 1: 395–424. https://doi.org/10.1146/
annurev.economics.102308.124433.

Frank, R. 2008. "Context Is More Important Than Keynes Realized." In *Revisiting
Keynes: Economic Possibilities for Our Grandchildren*, ed. L. Pecchi, and G.
Piga, 143–50. Cambridge, MA: MIT Press. https://andrewmbailey.com/money/
readings/pecchi.pdf.

Freeman, R. 2008. "Why Do We Work More Than Keynes Expected?" In *Revisiting
Keynes: Economic Possibilities for Our Grandchildren*, ed. L. Pecchi and G.
Piga, 135–42. Cambridge, MA: MIT Press. https://dash.harvard.edu/bitstream/
handle/1/34310002/Why-Do-We-Work-More-Keynes-Expected_MS-for-Pecchi-
Piga-VOL-4-07_0.pdf.

Frey, C., and M. Osborne. 2017. "The Future of Employment: How Susceptible Are Jobs to Computerisation?" *Technological Forecasting and Social Change* 114: 254–80. https://doi.org/10.1016/j.techfore.2016.08.019.

Frischmann, B, A. Marciano, and G. Ramello. 2019. "Retrospectives: Tragedy of the Commons after 50 Years." *Journal of Economic Perspectives* 33, no. 4: 211–28. https://doi.org/10.1257/jep.33.4.211.

FTC (U.S. Federal Trade Commission). 2023. "Generative AI Raises Competition Concerns." https://www.ftc.gov/policy/advocacy-research/tech-at-ftc/2023/06/generative-ai-raises-competition-concerns.

Furman, J., and R. Seamans. 2019. "AI and the Economy." *Innovation Policy and the Economy* 19: 161–91. https://doi.org/10.1086/699936.

GAO (U.S. Government Accountability Office). 2018. "Personal Information, Private Companies." https://www.gao.gov/blog/2018/05/01/personal-information-private-companies.

Ganguli, D., L. Lovitt, J. Kernion, A. Askell, Y. Bai, S. Kadavath, B. Mann, E. Perez, N. Schiefer, K. Ndousse, A. Jones, S. Bowman, A. Chen, T. Conerly, N. DasSarma, D. Drain, N. Elhage, S. El-Showk, S. Fort, Z. Hatfield-Dodds, T. Henighan, D. Hernandez, T. Hume, J. Jacobson, S. Johnston, S. Kravec, C. Olsson, S. Ringer, E. Tran-Johnson, D. Amodei, T. Brown, N. Joseph, S. McCandlish, C. Olah, J. Kaplan, and J. Clark. 2022. *Red Teaming Language Models to Reduce Harms: Methods, Scaling Behaviors, and Lessons Learned.* ArXiv Preprint ArXiv:2209.07858. Ithaca, NY: Cornell University. https://doi.org/10.48550/arXiv.2209.07858.

Garbarino, E., and S. Maxwell. 2010. "Consumer Response to Norm-Breaking Pricing Events in E-Commerce." *Journal of Business Research* 63, nos. 9–10: 1066–72. https://doi.org/10.1016/j.jbusres.2008.12.010.

Garicano, L. 2000. "Hierarchies and the Organization of Knowledge in Production." *Journal of Political Economy* 108, no. 5: 874–904. https://doi.org/10.1086/317671.

Gaulé, P. 2018. "Patents and the Success of Venture-Capital-Backed Startups: Using Examiner Assignment to Estimate Causal Effects." *Journal of Industrial Economics* 66, no. 2: 350–76. https://doi.org/10.1111/joie.12168.

Gautier, A., A. Ittoo, and P. Van Cleynenbreugel. 2020. "AI Algorithms, Price Discrimination and Collusion: A Technological, Economic, and Legal Perspective." *European Journal of Law and Economics* 50: 405–35. https://link.springer.com/article/10.1007/s10657-020-09662-6.

Gifford, D. 2018. "Technological Triggers to Tort Revolutions: Steam Locomotives, Autonomous Vehicles, and Accident Compensation." *Journal of Tort Law* 11, no. 1: 71–143. https://doi.org/10.1515/jtl-2017-0029.

Gless, S., E. Silverman, and T. Weigend. 2016. "If Robots Cause Harm, Who Is to Blame? Self-Driving Cars and Criminal Liability." *New Criminal Law Review* 19, no. 3: 412–36. https://doi.org/10.1525/nclr.2016.19.3.412.

Goldin, C., and L. Katz. 2007. *The Race Between Education and Technology: The Evolution of U.S. Educational Wage Differentials, 1890 to 2005.* NBER Working Paper 12984. Cambridge, MA: National Bureau for Economic Research. https://doi.org/10.3386/w12984.

Goldman Sachs. 2023. "AI May Start to Boost U.S. GDP in 2027." https://www.goldmansachs.com/intelligence/pages/ai-may-start-to-boost-us-gdp-in-2027.html.

Golosov, M., M. Graber, M. Mogstad, and D. Novgorodsky. 2021. *How Americans Respond to Idiosyncratic and Exogenous Changes in Household Wealth and Unearned Income.* NBER Working Paper 29000. Cambridge, MA: National Bureau of Economic Research. https://doi.org/10.3386/w29000.

Gordon, W. 1982. "Fair Use as Market Failure: A Structural and Economic Analysis of the Betamax Case and Its Predecessors." *J. Copyright Society USA* 30: 253. https://www.jstor.org/stable/pdf/1122296.pdf.

Green, F., S. Machin, and D. Wilkinson. 1999. "Trade Unions and Training Practices in British Workplaces." *ILR Review* 52, no. 2. https://journals.sagepub.com/doi/10.1177/001979399905200202.

Gregory, R., O. Henfridsson, E. Kaganer, and H. Kyriakou. 2021. "The Role of Artificial Intelligence and Data Network Effects for Creating User Value." *Academy of Management Review* 46, no. 3: 534–51. https://doi.org/10.5465/amr.2019.0178.

Grossman, S., and O. Hart. 1986. "The Costs and Benefits of Ownership: A Theory of Vertical and Lateral Integration." *Journal of Political Economy* 94, no. 4: 691–719. https://doi.org/10.1086/261404.

Gruber, J., S. Johnson, and E. Moretti. 2023. "Place-Based Productivity and Costs in Science." *Entrepreneurship and Innovation Policy and the Economy* 2, no. 1. https://doi.org/10.1086/723239.

Guerreiro, J., S. Rebelo, and P. Teles. 2022. "Should Robots Be Taxed?" *Review of Economic Studies* 89, no. 1: 279–311. https://doi.org/10.1093/restud/rdab019.

Guszcza, J., I. Rahwan, W. Bible, M. Cebrian, and V. Katyal. 2018. "Why We Need to Audit Algorithms." *Harvard Business Review.* https://hbr.org/2018/11/why-we-need-to-audit-algorithms.

Hall, B., and B. Khan. 2003. *Adoption of New Technology.* NBER Working Paper 9730. Cambridge, MA: National Bureau of Economic Research. https://doi.org/10.3386/w9730.

Haller, P., and D. Heuermann. 2020. "Opportunities and Competition in Thick Labor Markets: Evidence from Plant Closures." *Journal of Regional Science* 60, no. 2: 273–95. https://doi.org/10.1111/jors.12460.

Hart, O. 2009. "Hold-Up, Asset Ownership, and Reference Points." *Quarterly Journal of Economics* 124, no. 1: 267–300. https://www.jstor.org/stable/40506229.

Haucap, J., and C. Wey. 2004. "Unionisation Structures and Innovation Incentives." *Economic Journal* 114, no. 494: C149–65. https://doi.org/10.1111/j.0013-0133.2004.00203.x.

Heathcote, J., K. Storesletten, and G. Violante. 2010. "The Macroeconomic Implications of Rising Wage Inequality in the United States." *Journal of Political Economy* 118, no. 4: 681–722. https://doi.org/10.1086/656632.

Heaven, W. 2023. "The Open-Source AI Boom Is Built on Big Tech's Handouts; How Long Will It Last?" *MIT Technology Review.* https://www.technologyreview.com/2023/05/12/1072950/open-source-ai-google-openai-eleuther-meta/.

Herrmann, T., and S. Pfeiffer. 2023. "Keeping the Organization in the Loop: A Socio-Technical Extension of Human-Centered Artificial Intelligence." *AI & Society* 38: 1523–42. https://doi.org/10.1007/s00146-022-01391-5.

Hestness, J., S. Narang, N. Aredalani, G. Diamos, H. Jun, H. Kianinejad, M. Patwary, Y. Yang, and Y. Zhou. 2017. *Deep Learning Scaling Is Predictable, Empirically.* ArXiv Preprint ArXiv:1712.00409. Ithaca, NY: Cornell University. https://doi.org/10.48550/arXiv.1712.00409.

Hirsch, B. 2004. *What Do Unions Do for Economic Performance.* IZA Discussion Paper 892. Bonn: IZA Institute of Labor Economics. https://dx.doi.org/10.2139/ssrn.459581.

Hitsuwari, J., Y. Ueda, W. Yun, and M. Nomura, 2023. "Does Human–AI Collaboration Lead to More Creative Art? Aesthetic Evaluation of Human-Made and AI-Generated Haiku Poetry." *Computers in Human Behavior* 139: 107502. https://doi.org/10.1016/j.chb.2022.107502.

Honoré, A. 1961. "Ownership." In *Oxford Essays in Jurisprudence*, ed. A. Guest, 106–46. Oxford: Oxford University Press. http://fs2.american.edu/dfagel/www/OwnershipSmaller.pdf.

Horton, A. 2023. "Scarlett Johansson Takes Legal Action Against Use of Image for AI." *Guardian.* https://www.theguardian.com/film/2023/nov/01/scarlett-johansson-artificial-intelligence-ad.

Hutson, M. 2021. "The Opacity of Artificial Intelligence Makes it Hard to Tell when Decision-Making is Biased." *IEEE Spectrum* 58, no. 2: 40–45. https://ieeexplore.ieee.org/abstract/document/9340114.

Hyman, B. 2022. "Can Displaced Labor Be Retrained? Evidence from Quasi-Random Assignment to Trade Adjustment Assistance." Discussion Paper, U.S. Census Bureau, Center for Economic Studies. https://www2.census.gov/ces/wp/2022/CES-WP-22-05.pdf.

Johnson, J., and D. Sokol. 2020. "Understanding AI Collusion and Compliance." Working paper, Cambridge Handbook of Compliance. https://ssrn.com/abstract=3413882.

Jones, C. 2022. "The Past and Future of Economic Growth: A Semi-Endogenous Perspective." *Annual Review of Economics* 14: 125–52. https://doi.org/10.1146/annurev-economics-080521-012458.

Kaddour, J., J. Harris, M. Mozes, H. Bradley, R. Raileanu, and R. McHardy. 2023. *Challenges and Applications of Large Language Models.* ArXiv Preprint ArXiv:2307.10169. Ithaca, NY: Cornell University. https://doi.org/10.48550/arXiv.2307.10169.

Kadrey et al. v. Meta Platforms, Inc. 2023. U.S. District Court for the Northern District of California. https://dockets.justia.com/docket/california/candce/3:2023cv03417/415175.

Kahveci, Z. 2023. "Attribution Problem of Generative AI: A View from U.S. Copyright Law." *Journal of Intellectual Property Law & Practice* 18, no. 11: 796–807. https://doi.org/10.1093/jiplp/jpad076.

Kaplan, J., S. McCandlish, T. Henighan, T. Brown, B. Chess, R. Child, S. Gray, A. Radford, J. Wu, and D. Amodei. 2020. *Scaling Laws for Neural Language Models.* ArXiv Preprint ArXiv:2001.08361. Ithaca, NY: Cornell University. https://doi.org/10.48550/arXiv.2001.08361.

Kapoor, S., and A. Narayanan. 2023. "Leakage and the Reproducibility Crisis in Machine-Learning-Based Science." *Patterns* 4, no. 9: 100804. https://doi.org/10.1016/j.patter.2023.100804.

Katz, M., and C. Shapiro. 1986. "Technology Adoption in the Presence of Network Externalities." *Journal of Political Economy* 94, no. 4. https://www.journals.uchicago.edu/doi/abs/10.1086/261409.

Kennan, J., and R. Wilson. 1993. "Bargaining with Private Information." *Journal of Economic Literature* 31, no. 1: 45–104. https://www.jstor.org/stable/2728150.

Keynes, J. 1930. "Economic Possibilities for Our Grandchildren." In *Essays in Persuasion,* 321–32. New York: Harcourt Brace. https://doi.org/10.1007/978-1-349-59072-8_25.

King, T., N. Aggarwal, M. Taddeo, and L. Floridi. 2020. "Artificial Intelligence Crime: An Interdisciplinary Analysis of Foreseeable Threats and Solutions." *Science and Engineering Ethics* 26: 89–120. https://doi.org/10.1007/s11948-018-00081-0.

Kleinberg, J., J. Ludwig, S. Mullainathan, and C. Sunstein. 2018. "Discrimination in the Age of Algorithms." *Journal of Legal Analysis* 10: 113–74. https://doi.org/10.1093/jla/laz001.

Knepper, M. 2020. "From the Fringe to the Fore: Labor Unions and Employee Compensation." *Review of Economics and Statistics* 102, no. 1: 98–112. https://doi.org/10.1162/rest_a_00803.

Knight, F. 1921. *Risk, Uncertainty and Profit.* Cambridge, MA: Riverside Press Cambridge. https://fraser.stlouisfed.org/files/docs/publications/books/risk/riskuncertaintyprofit.pdf.

Kochan, T., B. Armstrong, J. Shah, E. Castilla, B. Likis, and M. Mangelsdorf. 2023. "Bringing Worker Voice into Generative AI." *IWER Research.* https://mitsloan.mit.edu/centers-initiatives/institute-work-and-employment-research/bringing-worker-voice-generative-ai.

Kochhar, R. 2023. "Which U.S. Workers Are Exposed to AI in Their Jobs?" Pew Research Center, Social and Demographic Trends Project. https://www.pewresearch.org/social-trends/2023/07/26/which-u-s-workers-are-more-exposed-to-ai-on-their-jobs/.

Korinek, A., and J. Stiglitz. 2019. "Artificial Intelligence and Its Implications for Income Distribution and Unemployment." In *The Economics of Artificial Intelligence: An Agenda*, 349–90. Chicago: University of Chicago Press. https://www.nber.org/system/files/chapters/c14018/c14018.pdf.

Kortum, S. 1997. "Research, Patenting, and Technological Change." *Econometrica* 65, no. 6: 1389–1419. https://doi.org/10.2307/2171741.

Krugman, P. 1981. "Intraindustry Specialization and the Gains from Trade." *Journal of Political Economy* 89, no. 5: 959–73. https://www.journals.uchicago.edu/doi/abs/10.1086/261015.

Kumar, A., A. Raghunathan, R. Jones, T. Ma, and P. Liang. 2022. *Fine-Tuning can Distort Pretrained Features and Underperform Out-of-Distribution*. ArXiv Preprint ArXiv:2202.10054. Ithaca, NY: Cornell University. https://doi.org/10.48550/arXiv.2202.10054.

Kuramanji, M., P. Triantafillou, J. Hayes, and E. Triantafillou. 2023. *Towards Unbounded Machine Unlearning*. ArXiv Preprint ArXiv:2302.09880. Ithaca, NY: Cornell University. https://doi.org/10.48550/arXiv.2302.09880.

Lambrecht, A., and C. Tucker. 2019. "Algorithmic Bias? An Empirical Study of Apparent Gender-Based Discrimination in the Display of STEM Career Ads." *Management Science* 65, no. 7: 2966–81. https://pubsonline.informs.org/doi/10.1287/mnsc.2018.3093.

Landes, W., and R. Posner. 1987. *The Economic Structure of Tort Law.* Cambridge, MA: Harvard University Press. https://chicagounbound.uchicago.edu/books/226/.

Lang, K., and A. Spitzer. 2020. "Race Discrimination: An Economic Perspective." *Journal of Economic Perspectives* 34, no. 2: 68–89. https://doi.org/10.1257/jep.34.2.68.

Leffer, L. 2023. "When It Comes to AI Models, Bigger Isn't Always Better." *Scientific American.* https://www.scientificamerican.com/article/when-it-comes-to-ai-models-bigger-isnt-always-better/.

Lewis-Kraus, G. 2014. "The Fasinatng . . . Fascinating History of Autocorrect." *Wired*, July 22. https://www.wired.com/2014/07/history-of-autocorrect/.

Levitt, T. 2004. "Marketing Myopia." *Harvard Business Review.* https://hbr.org/2004/07/marketing-myopia.

Lin, J. 2011. "Technological Adaptation, Cities, and New Work." *Review of Economics and Statistics* 93, no. 2: 554–74. https://doi.org/10.1162/REST_a_00079.

Ling, C., X. Zhao, J. Lu, C. Deng, C. Zheng, J. Wang, T. Chowdhury, Y. Li, H. Cui, X. Zhang, T. Zhao, A. Panalkar, W. Cheng, H. Wang, Y. Liu, Z. Chen, H. Chen, C. White, Q. Gu, J. Pei, and L. Zhao. 2023. *Domain Specialization as the Key to Make Large Language Models Disruptive: A Comprehensive Survey.* ArXiv Preprint ArXiv:2305.18703. Ithaca, NY: Cornell University. https://doi.org/10.48550/arXiv.2305.18703.

Llorca, D., V. Charisi, R. Hamon, I. Sánchez, and E. Gómez. 2023. "Liability Regimes in the Age of AI: A Use-Case-Driven Analysis of the Burden of Proof." *Journal of Artificial Intelligence Research* 76: 613–44. https://doi.org/10.1613/jair.1.14565.

Luca, M. 2015. "Chapter 12: User-Generated Content and Social Media." In *Handbook of Media Economics* 1: 563–92. https://doi.org/10.1016/B978-0-444-63685-0.00012-7.

Mankiw, N., D. Romer, and D. Weil. 1992. "A Contribution to the Empirics of Economic Growth." *Quarterly Journal of Economics* 107: 407–37. https://doi.org/10.2307/2118477.

Mas-Colell, A., M. Whinston, and J. Green. 1995. *Microeconomic Theory*. Oxford: Oxford University Press. https://global.oup.com/academic/product/microeconomic-theory-9780195073409?cc=us&lang=en&.

Maslej, N., L. Fattorini, E. Brynjolfsson, J. Etchemendy, K. Ligett, T. Lyons, J. Manyika, H. Ngo, J. Niebles, V. Parli, Y. Shoham, R. Wald, J. Clark, and R. Perrault. 2023. *The AI Index 2023 Annual Report*. AI Index Steering Committee, Institute for Human-Centered AI. Stanford, CA: Stanford University. https://aiindex.stanford.edu/wp-content/uploads/2023/04/HAI_AI-Index-Report_2023.pdf.

McElheran, K., J. Li, E. Brynjolfsson, Z. Kroff, E. Dinlersoz, L. Foster, and N. Zolas. 2023. *AI Adoption in America: Who, What, and Where*. NBER Working Paper 31788. Cambridge, MA: National Bureau of Economic Research. https://doi.org/10.3386/w31788.

McKelvey, R., and T. Page. 1999. "Taking the Coase Theorem Seriously." *Economics and Philosophy* 15, no. 2: 235–47. https://doi.org/10.1017/S0266267100003990.

McNicholas, C., M. Poydock, J. Wolfe, B. Zipperer, G. Lafer, and L. Loustaunau. 2019. "Unlawful: U.S. Employers Are Charged with Violating Federal Law in 41.5% of All Union Election Campaigns." Economic Policy Institute. https://www.epi.org/publication/unlawful-employer-opposition-to-union-election-campaigns/.

Medema, S. 2020. "The Coase Theorem at Sixty." *Journal of Economic Literature* 58, no. 4: 1045–128. https://doi.org/10.1257/jel.20191060.

Merrill, T., and H. Smith. 2011. "Making Coasean Property More Coasean." *Journal of Law and Economics* 54, no. S4: S77–S104. https://doi.org/10.1086/661946.

Min, B., H. Ross, E. Sulem, A. Veyseh, T. Nguyen, O. Sainz, E. Agirre, I. Heintz, and D. Roth. 2023. "Recent Advances in Natural Language Processing via Large Pre-trained Language Models: A Survey." *ACM Computing Surveys* 56, no. 2: 1–40. https://doi.org/10.1145/3605943.

Miric, M., N. Jia, and K. Huang. 2022. "Using Supervised Machine Learning for Large-Scale Classification in Management Research: The Case for Identifying Artificial Intelligence Patents." *Strategic Management Journal* 44, no. 2: 491–519. https://doi.org/10.1002/smj.3441.

Mishel, L., H. Shierholz, and J. Schmitt. 2013. "Don't Blame the Robots: Assessing the Job Polarization Explanation of Growing Wage Inequality." Working paper,

Economic Policy Institute, Center for Economic and Policy Research. https://files.epi.org/2013/technology-inequality-dont-blame-the-robots.pdf.

Mishra, S., R. Koopman, G. De Prato, A. Rao, I. Osorio-Rodarte, J. Kim, N. Spatafora, K. Strier, and A. Zaccaria. 2023. "AI Specialization for Pathways of Economic Diversification." *Scientific Reports* 13: 19475. https://doi.org/10.1038/s41598-023-45723-x.

Mökander, J., J. Morley, M. Taddeo, and L. Floridi. 2021. "Ethics-Based Auditing of Automated Decision-Making Systems: Nature, Scope, and Limitations." *Science and Engineering Ethics* 27, no. 44. https://doi.org/10.1007/s11948-021-00319-4.

Mookherjee, D., and I. Png, 1992. "Monitoring vis-a-vis Investigation in Enforcement of Law." *American Economic Review*, 556–65. https://www.jstor.org/stable/2117321.

Mokyr, J. 2008. "The Institutional Origins of the Industrial Revolution." Working paper, Northwestern University. https://faculty.wcas.northwestern.edu/jmokyr/Institutional-Origins-4.PDF.

Mokyr, J., C. Vickers, and N. Ziebarth. 2015. "The History of Technological Anxiety and the Future of Economic Growth: Is This Time Different?" *Journal of Economic Perspectives* 29, no. 3: 31–50. https://doi.org/10.1257/jep.29.3.31.

Moresi, S., and M. Schwartz. 2021. "Vertical Mergers with Input Substitution: Double Marginalization, Foreclosure, and Welfare." *Economic Letters* 202. https://doi.org/10.1016/j.econlet.2021.109818.

Mosqueira-Rey, E., E. Hernández-Pereira, D. Alonso-Ríos, J. Bobes-Bascarán, and A. Fernández-Leal. 2022. "Human-in-the-Loop Machine Learning: A State of the Art." *Artificial Intelligence Review* 56: 3005–54. https://doi.org/10.1007/s10462-022-10246-w.

Muennighoff, N., A. Rush, B. Barak, T. Le Scao, A. Piktus, N. Tazi, S. Pyysalo, T. Wolf, and C. Raffel. 2023. *Scaling Data-Constrained Language Models*. ArXiv Preprint ArXiv:2305.16264. Ithaca, NY: Cornell University. https://doi.org/10.48550/arXiv.2305.16264.

NAIAC (National Artificial Intelligence Advisory Committee). 2023. "National AI Advisory Committee." https://ai.gov/naiac/.

Naik, R., V. Chandrasekaran, M. Yuksekgonul, H. Palangi, and B. Nushi, 2023. "Diversity of Thought Improves Reasoning Abilities of Large Language Models." https://doi.org/10.48550/arXiv.2310.07088.

Najibi, A. 2020. "Racial Discrimination in Face Recognition Technology." Harvard University, Science in the News. https://sitn.hms.harvard.edu/flash/2020/racial-discrimination-in-face-recognition-technology/.

Narechania, T. 2022. "Machine Learning as Natural Monopoly." *Iowa Law Review* 7, no. 4: 1543–1614. https://ilr.law.uiowa.edu/sites/ilr.law.uiowa.edu/files/2023-02/A4_Narechania.pdf.

Narechania, T., and G. Sitaraman. 2023. "An Antimonopoly Approach to Governing Artificial Intelligence." Vanderbilt Policy Accelerator for Political Economy & Regulation. https://cdn.vanderbilt.edu/vu-URL/wp-content/uploads/sites/412/2023/10/06212048/Narechania-Sitaraman-Antimonopoly-AI-2023.10.6.pdf.pdf.

Neel, S., and P. Chang. 2023. *Privacy Issues in Large Language Models: A Survey.* ArXiv Preprint ArXiv:2312.06717. Ithaca, NY: Cornell University. https://doi.org/10.48550/arXiv.2312.06717.

Nekoei, A., and A. Weber. 2017. "Does Extending Unemployment Benefits Improve Job Quality?" *American Economic Review* 107, no. 2: 527–61. https://doi.org/10.1257/aer.20150528.

Netanel, N. 2011. "Making Sense of Fair Use." *Lewis & Clark Law Review* 15, no. 3: 715–71. https://heinonline.org/HOL/P?h=hein.journals/lewclr15&i=731.

Newell, A. 1983. "Chapter 1: Intellectual Issues in the History of Artificial Intelligence." In *Artificial Intelligence: Critical Concepts, Volume 1*, ed. R. Chrisley and S. Begeer, 25–70. Abingdon, U.K.: Taylor & Francis. apps.dtic.mil/sti/citations/ADA125318.

Noy, S., and W. Zhang. 2023. "Experimental Evidence on the Productivity Effects of Generative Artificial Intelligence." Working paper, Social Science Research Network. https://dx.doi.org/10.2139/ssrn.4375283.

Nunan, D., and M. Di Domenico. 2022. "Value Creation in an Algorithmic World: Towards an Ethics of Dynamic Pricing." *Journal of Business Research* 150: 451–60. https://doi.org/10.1016/j.jbusres.2022.06.032.

NIST (National Institute of Standards and Technology). 2023. "NIST Seeks Collaborators for Consortium Supporting Artificial Intelligence Safety." https://www.nist.gov/news-events/news/2023/11/nist-seeks-collaborators-consortium-supporting-artificial-intelligence.

Obermeyer, Z., B. Powers, C. Vogeli, and S. Mullainathan. 2019. "Dissecting Racial Bias in an Algorithm Used to Manage the Health of Populations." *Science* 366, no. 6464: 447–53. https://www.science.org/doi/10.1126/science.aax2342.

Ohlin, B., and E. Heckscher. 1991. *Heckscher-Olin Trade Theory.* Cambridge, MA: MIT Press. https://mitpress.mit.edu/9780262082013/heckscher-ohlin-trade-theory/.

OMB (U.S. Office and Management and Budget). 2023a. "Guidance on Accounting for Competition Effects When Developing and Analyzing Regulatory Actions." https://www.whitehouse.gov/wp-content/uploads/2023/10/RegulatoryCompetitionGuidance.pdf.

———. 2023b. "OMB Releases Implementation Guidance Following President Biden's Executive Order on Artificial Intelligence." https://www.whitehouse.gov/omb/briefing-room/2023/11/01/omb-releases-implementation-guidance-following-president-bidens-executive-order-on-artificial-intelligence/.

O*NET Online. No date. Database sponsored by U.S. Department of Labor. https://www.onetonline.org/.

OpenAI. 2024. "OpenAI-Python." Code commit. https://github.com/openai/openai-python.

Ordover, J., G. Saloner, and S. Salop. 1990. "Equilibrium Vertical Foreclosure." *American Economic Review* 80, no. 1: 127–42. https://www.jstor.org/stable/2006738.

Oremus, W., and E. Izadi. 2024. "AI's Future Could Hinge on One Thorny Legal Question." *Washington Post.* https://www.washingtonpost.com/technology/2024/01/04/nyt-ai-copyright-lawsuit-fair-use/.

Ostrom, E. 1990. *Governing the Commons: The Evolution of Institutions for Collective Action.* Cambridge: Cambridge University Press. https://www.cambridge.org/core/books/governing-the-commons/A8BB63BC4A1433A50A3FB92EDBBB97D5.

Ottaviani, M., and A. Wickelgren. 2011. "Ex Ante or Ex Post Competition Policy? A Progress Report." *International Journal of Industrial Organization* 29, no. 3: 356–59. https://doi.org/10.1016/j.ijindorg.2011.02.004.

Ouyang, L., J. Wu, X. Jiang, D. Almeida, C. Wainwright, P. Mishkin, C. Zhang, S. Agarwal, K. Slama, A. Ray, J. Schulman, J. Hilton, F. Kelton, L. Miller, M. Simens, A. Askell, P. Welinder, P. Christiano, J. Leike, and R. Lowe. 2022. "Training Language Models to Follow Instructions with Human Feedback." *Advances in Neural Informational Processing Systems* 35: 27730–44. https://proceedings.neurips.cc/paper_files/paper/2022/hash/b1efde-53be364a73914f58805a001731-Abstract-Conference.html.

Parente, S., and E. Prescott. 1994. "Barriers to Technology Adoption and Development." *Journal of Political Economy* 102, no. 2: 298–321. https://doi.org/10.1086/261933.

Peng, S., E. Kalliamvakou, P. Cihon, and M. Demirer. 2023. *The Impact of AI on Developer Productivity: Evidence from GitHub Copilot.* ArXiv Preprint ArXiv:2302.06590. Ithaca, NY: Cornell University. https://doi.org/10.48550/arXiv.2302.06590.

Perrigo, B. 2023. "Exclusive: OpenAI Used Kenyan Workers on Less Than $2 Per Hour to Make ChatGPT Less Toxic." *Time*, January 18. https://time.com/6247678/openai-chatgpt-kenya-workers/.

Perault, M. 2023. "Section 230 Won't Protect ChatGPT." *Journal of Free Speech Law* 3: 363–73. https://heinonline.org/HOL/P?h=hein.journals/jfspl3&i=363.

Peterson, N., M. Mumford, W. Borman, P. Jeanneret, and E. Fleishman. 1995. "Development of Prototype Occupational Information Network (O*NET) Content Model." O*Net: Occupational Information Network. https://www.onetcenter.org/dl_files/Prototype_Vol1.pdf.

Philippon, T. 2022. *Additive Growth.* NBER Working Paper 29950. Cambridge, MA: National Bureau for Economic Research. https://doi.org/10.3386/w29950.

Pizzinelli, C., A. Panton, M. Mendes Tavares, M. Cazzaniga, and L. Li. 2023. "Labor Market Exposure to AI: Cross-Country Differences and Distributional Implications." https://papers.ssrn.com/sol3/papers.cfm?abstract_id=4612697.

Post, C., E. De Lia, N. DiTomaso, T. Tirpak, and R. Borwankar, 2009. "Capitalizing on Thought Diversity for Innovation." *Research-Technology Management* 52: 14–25. https://doi.org/10.1080/08956308.2009.11657596.

Price, D. 2019. "Goodbye, Operator." Federal Reserve Bank of Richmond, Econ Focus. https://www.richmondfed.org/publications/research/econ_focus/2019/q4/economic_history.

Quartz. 2017. "Bill Gates: The Robot That Takes Your Job Should Pay Taxes." https://qz.com/911968/bill-gates-the-robot-that-takes-your-job-should-pay-taxes.

Raji, I., T. Gebru, M. Mitchell, J. Buolamwini, J. Lee, and E. Denton. 2020a. "Saving Face: Investigating the Ethical Concerns of Facial Recognition Auditing." *Proceedings of the AAAI/ACM Conference on AI, Ethics, and Society*: 145-51. https://doi.org/10.1145/3375627.3375820.

Raji, I., A. Smart, R. White, M. Mitchell, T. Gebru, B. Hutchinson, J. Smith-Loud, D. Theron, and P. Barnes. 2020b. "Closing the AI Accountability Gap: Defining an End-to-End Framework for Internal Algorithmic Auditing." In *Proceedings of the 2020 Conference on Fairness, Accountability, and Transparency*, 33–44. FAT* '20. New York: Association for Computing Machinery. https://doi.org/10.1145/3351095.3372873.

Rees, T. 2023. "AI Could Enable Humans to Work 4 Days a Week, Says Nobel Prize-Winning Economist." *Time*. https://time.com/6268804/artificial-intelligence-pissarides-productivity/.

Ricardo, D. 1817. *On The Principles of Political Economy and Taxation.* Kitchener, Canada: Batoche Books. https://socialsciences.mcmaster.ca/econ/ugcm/3ll3/ricardo/Principles.pdf.

Roosen, J., and D. Hennessy. 2003. "Tests for the Role of Risk Aversion on Input Use." *American Journal of Agricultural Economics* 85, no. 1: 30–43. https://doi.org/10.1111/1467-8276.00101.

Roser, M., H. Richie, and E. Mathieu. 2023. "Technological Change." *Our World in Data.* https://ourworldindata.org/technological-change?ref=bitcoinalpha.nl.

Roziere, B., M. Lachaux, L. Chanussot, and G. Lample. 2020. "Unsupervised Translation of Programming Languages." *Advances in Neural Information Processing Systems* 33: 20601–11. https://proceedings.neurips.cc/paper/2020/hash/ed23fbf-18c2cd35f8c7f8de44f85c08d-Abstract.html.

Ryman-Tubb, N., P. Krause, and W. Garn. 2018. "How Artificial Intelligence and Machine Learning Research Impacts Payment Card Fraud Detection: A Survey and Industry Benchmark." *Engineering Applications of Artificial Intelligence* 76: 130–57. https://doi.org/10.1016/j.engappai.2018.07.008.

Saez, E., and S. Stantcheva. 2018. "A Simpler Theory of Optimal Capital Taxation." *Journal of Public Economics* 162: 120–42. https://doi.org/10.1016/j.jpubeco.2017.10.004.

Sag, M. 2023. "Fairness and Fair Use in Generative AI." *Fordham Law Review.* https://ssrn.com/abstract=4654875.

SAG-AFTRA (Screen Actors Guild–American Federation of Television and Radio Artists). 2023. "TV/Theatrical Contracts 2023: Summary of Tentative Agreement." https://www.sagaftra.org/files/sa_documents/TV-Theatrical_23_Summary_Agreement_Final.pdf.

Sampat, B., and H. Williams. 2019. "How Do Patents Affect Follow-On Innovation? Evidence from the Human Genome." *American Economic Review* 109, no. 1: 203–36. https://doi.org/10.1257/aer.20151398.

Samuelson, P. 2023. "Generative AI Meets Copyright." *Science* 381, no. 6654: 158–61. https://doi.org/10.1126/science.adi0656.

Schaeffer, R., B. Miranda, and S. Koyejo. 2023. "Are Emergent Abilities of Large Language Models a Mirage?" *Advances in Neural Information Processing Systems* 36. https://proceedings.neurips.cc/paper_files/paper/2023/hash/adc98a266f45005c403b8311ca7e8bd7-Abstract-Conference.html.

Schmieder, J., T. von Wachter, and S. Bender. 2012. "The Effects of Extended Unemployment Insurance Over the Business Cycle: Evidence from Regression Discontinuity Estimates Over 20 Years." *Quarterly Journal of Economics* 127, no. 2: 701–52. https://doi.org/10.1093/qje/qjs010.

Schneider, P., W. Walters, A. Plowright, N. Sieroka, J. Listgarten, R. Goodnow Jr., J. Fisher, J. Jansen, J. Duca, T. Rush, M. Zentgraf, J. Hill, E. Krutoholow, M. Kohler, J. Blaney, K. Funatsu, C. Luebkemann, and G. Schneider. 2020. "Rethinking Drug Design in the Artificial Intelligence Era." *Nature Reviews Drug Discovery* 19: 353–64. https://doi.org/10.1038/s41573-019-0050-3.

Scotchmer, S. 1991. "Standing on the Shoulders of Giants: Cumulative Research and the Patent Law." *Journal of Economic Perspectives* 5, no. 1: 29–41. https://doi.org/10.1257/jep.5.1.29.

Setty, R. 2023. "Getty Images Sues Stability AI Over Art Generator IP Violations." Bloomberg Law. https://news.bloomberglaw.com/ip-law/getty-images-sues-stability-ai-over-art-generator-ip-violations.

Shan, S., W. Ding, J. Passananti, S. Wu, H. Zheng, and B. Zhao. 2023. *Prompt-Specific Poisoning Attacks on Text-to-Image Generative Models.* ArXiv Preprint ArXiv:2310.13828. Ithaca, NY: Cornell University. https://doi.org/10.48550/arXiv.2310.13828.

Sharifani, K., and M. Amini. 2023. "Machine Learning and Deep Learning: A Review of Methods and Applications." *World Information Technology and Engineering Journal* 10, no. 7: 3897–904. https://ssrn.com/abstract=4458723.

Sharkey, C. 2022. "Products Liability in the Digital Age: Online Platforms as 'Cheapest Cost Avoiders.'" *Hastings Law Journal* 73: 1327–51. https://heinonline.org/HOL/P?h=hein.journals/hastlj73&i=1329.

Shavell, S. 2004. *Foundations of Economic Analysis of Law.* Cambridge, MA: Harvard University Press. https://www.jstor.org/stable/j.ctv1m0kjr4.

Sintchenko, V., and E. Coiera. 2003. "Which Clinical Decisions Benefit from Automation? A Task Complexity Approach." *International Journal of Medical Informatics* 70, nos. 2–3: 309–16. https://doi.org/10.1016/S1386-5056(03)00040-6.

Smith, A. 1776. *An Inquiry into the Nature and Causes of the Wealth of Nations.* Oxford: Oxford University Press. https://doi.org/10.1093/oseo/instance.00043218.

Smith, H. 2012. "Property as the Law of Things." *Harvard Law Review* 125, no. 7: 1691–1726. https://www.jstor.org/stable/23214445.

Sobel, B. 2017. "Artificial Intelligence's Fair Use Crisis." *Columbia Journal of Law & the Arts* 41, no. 1: 45–98. https://doi.org/10.7916/jla.v41i1.2036.

Solow, R. 1956. "A Contribution to the Theory of Economic Growth." *Quarterly Journal of Economics* 70, no. 1: 65–94. https://doi.org/10.2307/1884513.

Sorscher, B., R. Geirhos, S. Shekhar, S. Ganguli, and A. Morcos. 2022. "Beyond Neural Scaling Laws: Beating Power Law Scaling via Data Pruning." *Advances in Neural Information Processing Systems* 35: 19523–36. https://proceedings.neurips.cc/paper_files/paper/2022/file/7b75da9b61eda40fa35453ee5d077df6-Paper-Conference.pdf.

Svanberg, M., W. Li, M. Fleming, B. Goehring, and N. Thompson, 2024. "Beyond AI Exposure: Which Tasks Are Cost-Effective to Automate with Computer Vision?" SSRN 4700751. https://futuretech-site.s3.us-east-2.amazonaws.com/2024-01-18+Beyond_AI_Exposure.pdf.

Taddy, M. 2019. "The Technological Elements of Artificial Intelligence." In *The Economics of Artificial Intelligence: An Agenda*, ed. A. Agrawal, J. Gans, and A. Goldfarb, 61–89. Chicago: University of Chicago Press. https://www.nber.org/papers/w24301.

Taub, D., and H. Levitt. 2023. "JPMorgan's Dimon Predicts 3.5-Day Work Week for Next Generation Thanks to AI." Bloomberg. https://www.bloomberg.com/news/articles/2023-10-02/dimon-sees-ai-giving-a-3-1-2-day-workweek-to-the-next-generation.

Thaler v. Perlmutter. 2023. U.S. District Court for the District of Columbia. https://ecf.dcd.uscourts.gov/cgi-bin/show_public_doc?2022cv1564-24.

Thaler v. Vidal. 2022. U.S. District Court for the Eastern District of Virginia. https://cafc.uscourts.gov/opinions-orders/21-2347.OPINION.8-5-2022_1988142.pdf.

Thompson, P. 2010. "Chapter 10: Learning by Doing." In *Handbook of the Economics of Innovation* 1, ed. B. Hall and N. Rosenberg, 429–76. Amsterdam: Elsevier. https://doi.org/10.1016/S0169-7218(10)01010-5.

Thuemmel, U. 2022. "Optimal Taxation of Robots." *Journal of the European Economic Association* 21, no. 3: 1154–90. https://doi.org/10.1093/jeea/jvac062.

Tirole, J. 1988. *The Theory of Industrial Organization.* Cambridge, MA: MIT Press. https://mitpress.mit.edu/9780262200714/the-theory-of-industrial-organization/.

———. 2023. "Competition and the Industrial Challenge for the Digital Age." *Annual Review of Economics* 15: 573–605. https://www.annualreviews.org/doi/10.1146/annurev-economics-090622-024222.

U.S. Department of the Treasury. 2023. "Labor Unions and the Middle Class." https://home.treasury.gov/system/files/136/Labor-Unions-And-The-Middle-Class.pdf.

Vaswani, A., N. Shazeer, N. Parmar, J. Uszkoreit, L. Jones, A. Gomez, L. Kaiser, and I. Polosukhin, 2017. "Attention Is All You Need." Advances in Neural Information Processing Systems. https://doi.org/10.48550/arXiv.1706.03762.

Verhoef, P., T. Broekhuizen, Y. Bart, A. Bhattacharya, J. Dong, N. Fabian, and M. Haenlein. 2021. "Digital Transformation: A Multidisciplinary Reflection and Research Agenda." *Journal of Business Research* 122: 889–901. https://doi.org/10.1016/j.jbusres.2019.09.022.

Vipra, J., and A. Korinek. 2023. "Market Concentration Implications of Foundation Models: The Invisible Hand of ChatGPT." Working paper, Brookings Center on Regulation and Markets. https://www.brookings.edu/wp-content/uploads/2023/09/Market-concentration-implications-of-foundation-models-FINAL-1.pdf.

Volokh, E. 2023. "Large Libel Models? Liability for AI Output." *Journal of Free Speech* 3: 489–558. https://heinonline.org/HOL/P?h=hein.journals/jfspl3&i=489.

Webb, G., and Z. Zheng. 2004. "Multistrategy Ensemble Learning: Reducing Error by Combining Ensemble Learning Techniques." *IEEE Transactions on Knowledge and Data Engineering* 16: 980–91. https://ieeexplore.ieee.org/abstract/document/1318582.

Weisz, J., M. Muller, S. Ross, F. Martinez, S. Houde, M. Agarwal, K. Talamadupula, and J. Richards. 2022. *Better Together? An Evaluation of AI-Supported Code Translation.* 27th International Conference on Intelligent User Interfaces, 369–91. New York: Association for Computing Machinery. https://doi.org/10.1145/3490099.3511157.

Werden, G. 2001. "Network Effects and Conditions of Entry: Lessons from the Microsoft Case." *Antitrust Law Journal* 69, no. 1: 87–112. https://heinonline.org/HOL/Page?collection=journals&handle=hein.journals/antil69&id=99&men_tab=srchresults.

WGAW (Writers Guild of America West). 2023. "Summary of the 2023 WGA MBA." https://www.wga.org/contracts/contracts/mba/summary-of-the-2023-wga-mba.

Whalley, A. 2011. "Optimal R&D Investment for a Risk-Averse Entrepreneur." *Journal of Economic Dynamics and Control* 35, no. 4: 413–29. https://doi.org/10.1016/j.jedc.2009.11.009.

White House. 2022. "Blueprint for an AI Bill of Rights: Making Automated Systems Work for the American People." https://www.whitehouse.gov/wp-content/uploads/2022/10/Blueprint-for-an-AI-Bill-of-Rights.pdf.

———. 2023a. "Executive Order on the Safe, Secure, and Trustworthy Development and Use of Artificial Intelligence." https://www.whitehouse.gov/briefing-room/presidential-actions/2023/10/30/executive-order-on-the-safe-secure-and-trustworthy-development-and-use-of-artificial-intelligence/.

———. 2023b. "Biden-Harris Administration Secures Voluntary Commitments from Eight Additional Intelligence Companies to Manage the Risks Posed by AI." https://www.whitehouse.gov/briefing-room/statements-releases/2023/09/12/fact-sheet-biden-harris-administration-secures-voluntary-commitments-from-eight-additional-artificial-intelligence-companies-to-manage-the-risks-posed--by-ai.

———. 2023c. "Biden-Harris Administration Roadmap to Support Good Jobs." https://www.whitehouse.gov/briefing-room/statements-releases/2023/05/16/biden-harris-administration-roadmap-to-support-good-jobs/.

Williamson, O. 1971. "The Vertical Integration of Production: Market Failure Considerations." *American Economic Review* 61, no. 2: 112–23. http://dx.doi.org/10.1179/102452907X166845.

Xiong, W., J. Droppo, X. Huang, F. Seide, M. Seltzer, A. Stolcke, D. Yu, and G, Zweig. 2016. *Achieving Human Parity in Conversational Speech Recognition.* Microsoft Research Technical Report MSR-TR-2016-71. Redmond, WA: Microsoft Research. https://doi.org/10.48550/arXiv.1610.05256.

Xu, Y., C. Shieh, P. van Esch, and I. Ling. 2020. "AI Customer Service: Task Complexity, Problem-Solving Ability, and Usage Intention." *Australian Marketing Journal* 28, no. 4: 189–99. https://doi.org/10.1016/j.ausmj.2020.03.005.

Zeira, J. 1998. "Workers, Machines, and Economic Growth." *Quarterly Journal of Economics* 113, no. 4: 1091–117. https://doi.org/10.1162/003355398555847.

Zhai, X., A. Kolesnikov, N. Houlsby, and L. Beyer. 2022. "Scaling Vision Transformers." *Proceedings of the IEEE/CVF Conference on Computer Vision and Pattern Recognition (CVPR)*: 12104–113. https://doi.org/10.48550/arXiv.2106.04560.

Zhang, N., Y. Yao, B. Tian, P. Wang, S. Deng, M. Wang, Z. Xi, S. Mao, J. Zhang, Y. Ni, S. Cheng, Z. Xu, X. Xu, J. Gu, Y. Jiang, P. Xie, F. Huang, L. Liang, Z. Zhang, X. Zhu, J. Zhou, and H. Chen. 2024. *A Comprehensive Study of Knowledge Editing for Large Language Models.* ArXiv Preprint ArXiv:2401.01286. Ithaca, NY: Cornell University. https://doi.org/10.48550/arXiv.2401.01286.

Zhou, H., X. Wang, W. Au, H. Kang, and C. Chen. 2022. "Intelligent Robots for Fruit Harvesting: Recent Developments and Future Challenges." *Precision Agriculture* 23: 1856–907. https://doi.org/10.1007/s11119-022-09913-3.

Zilibotti, F. 2007. "Economic Possibilities for Our Grandchildren 75 Years After: A Global Perspective." In *Revisiting Keynes: Economic Possibilities for Our*

Grandchildren, ed. L. Pecchi, and G. Piga, 27–39. Scholarship Online. Cambridge, MA: MIT Press. https://doi.org/10.7551/mitp ress/9780262162494.003.0003.

Zirar, A., S. Ali, and N. Islam, 2023. "Worker and Workplace Artificial Intelligence (AI) Coexistence: Emerging Themes and Research Agenda." *Technovation* 124: 102747. https://doi.org/10.1016/j.technovation.2023.102747.

Zolas, N., Z. Kroff, E. Brynjolfsson, K. McElheran, D. Beede, C. Buffington, N. Gold-schlag, L. Foster, and E. Dinlersoz. 2020. "Advanced Technologies Adoption and Use by U.S. Firms: Evidence from the Annual Business Survey." *NBER Working Paper 28290*. Cambridge, MA: National Bureau for Economic Research. https://doi.org/10.3386/w28290.

★ ★ ★ ★ ★ ★

Appendix A

Report to the President on the Activities of the Council of Economic Advisers during 2023

$\star\ \star\ \star\ \star\ \star\ \star$

Letter of Transmittal

Council of Economic Advisers
Washington, December 31, 2023

Mr. President:

The Council of Economic Advisers submits this report on its activities during calendar year 2023 in accordance with the requirements of Congress, as set forth by Section 10(d) of the Employment Act of 1946, as amended by the Full Employment and Balanced Growth Act of 1978.

Sincerely yours,

Jared Bernstein
Chair

Heather Boushey
Member

C. Kirabo Jackson
Member

Council Members and Their Dates of Service

Name	Position	Oath of office date	Separation date
Edwin G. Nourse	Chairman	August 9, 1946	November 1, 1949
Leon H. Keyserling	Vice Chairman	August 9, 1946	
	Acting Chairman	November 2, 1949	
	Chairman	May 10, 1950	January 20, 1953
John D. Clark	Member	August 9, 1946	
	Vice Chairman	May 10, 1950	February 11, 1953
Roy Blough	Member	June 29, 1950	August 20, 1952
Robert C. Turner	Member	September 8, 1952	January 20, 1953
Arthur F. Burns	Chairman	March 19, 1953	December 1, 1956
Neil H. Jacoby	Member	September 15, 1953	February 9, 1955
Walter W. Stewart	Member	December 2, 1953	April 29, 1955
Raymond J. Saulnier	Member	April 4, 1955	
	Chairman	December 3, 1956	January 20, 1961
Joseph S. Davis	Member	May 2, 1955	October 31, 1958
Paul W. McCracken	Member	December 3, 1956	January 31, 1959
Karl Brandt	Member	November 1, 1958	January 20, 1961
Henry C. Wallich	Member	May 7, 1959	January 20, 1961
Walter W. Heller	Chairman	January 29, 1961	November 15, 1964
James Tobin	Member	January 29, 1961	July 31, 1962
Kermit Gordon	Member	January 29, 1961	December 27, 1962
Gardner Ackley	Member	August 3, 1962	
	Chairman	November 16, 1964	February 15, 1968
John P. Lewis	Member	May 17, 1963	August 31, 1964
Otto Eckstein	Member	September 2, 1964	February 1, 1966
Arthur M. Okun	Member	November 16, 1964	
	Chairman	February 15, 1968	January 20, 1969
James S. Duesenberry	Member	February 2, 1966	June 30, 1968
Merton J. Peck	Member	February 15, 1968	January 20, 1969
Warren L. Smith	Member	July 1, 1968	January 20, 1969
Paul W. McCracken	Chairman	February 4, 1969	December 31, 1971
Hendrik S. Houthakker	Member	February 4, 1969	July 15, 1971
Herbert Stein	Member	February 4, 1969	
	Chairman	January 1, 1972	August 31, 1974
Ezra Solomon	Member	September 9, 1971	March 26, 1973
Marina v.N. Whitman	Member	March 13, 1972	August 15, 1973
Gary L. Seevers	Member	July 23, 1973	April 15, 1975
William J. Fellner	Member	October 31, 1973	February 25, 1975
Alan Greenspan	Chairman	September 4, 1974	January 20, 1977
Paul W. MacAvoy	Member	June 13, 1975	November 15, 1976
Burton G. Malkiel	Member	July 22, 1975	January 20, 1977
Charles L. Schultze	Chairman	January 22, 1977	January 20, 1981
William D. Nordhaus	Member	March 18, 1977	February 4, 1979
Lyle E. Gramley	Member	March 18, 1977	May 27, 1980
George C. Eads	Member	June 6, 1979	January 20, 1981
Stephen M. Goldfeld	Member	August 20, 1980	January 20, 1981
Murray L. Weidenbaum	Chairman	February 27, 1981	August 25, 1982
William A. Niskanen	Member	June 12, 1981	March 30, 1985
Jerry L. Jordan	Member	July 14, 1981	July 31, 1982

Council Members and Their Dates of Service

Name	Position	Oath of office date	Separation date
Martin Feldstein	Chairman	October 14, 1982	July 10, 1984
William Poole	Member	December 10, 1982	January 20, 1985
Beryl W. Sprinkel	Chairman	April 18, 1985	January 20, 1989
Thomas Gale Moore	Member	July 1, 1985	May 1, 1989
Michael L. Mussa	Member	August 18, 1986	September 19, 1988
Michael J. Boskin	Chairman	February 2, 1989	January 12, 1993
John B. Taylor	Member	June 9, 1989	August 2, 1991
Richard L. Schmalensee	Member	October 3, 1989	June 21, 1991
David F. Bradford	Member	November 13, 1991	January 20, 1993
Paul Wonnacott	Member	November 13, 1991	January 20, 1993
Laura D'Andrea Tyson	Chair	February 5, 1993	April 22, 1995
Alan S. Blinder	Member	July 27, 1993	June 26, 1994
Joseph E. Stiglitz	Member	July 27, 1993	
	Chairman	June 28, 1995	February 10, 1997
Martin N. Baily	Member	June 30, 1995	August 30, 1996
Alicia H. Munnell	Member	January 29, 1996	August 1, 1997
Janet L. Yellen	Chair	February 18, 1997	August 3, 1999
Jeffrey A. Frankel	Member	April 23, 1997	March 2, 1999
Rebecca M. Blank	Member	October 22, 1998	July 9, 1999
Martin N. Baily	Chairman	August 12, 1999	January 19, 2001
Robert Z. Lawrence	Member	August 12, 1999	January 12, 2001
Kathryn L. Shaw	Member	May 31, 2000	January 19, 2001
R. Glenn Hubbard	Chairman	May 11, 2001	February 28, 2003
Mark B. McClellan	Member	July 25, 2001	November 13, 2002
Randall S. Kroszner	Member	November 30, 2001	July 1, 2003
N. Gregory Mankiw	Chairman	May 29, 2003	February 18, 2005
Kristin J. Forbes	Member	November 21, 2003	June 3, 2005
Harvey S. Rosen	Member	November 21, 2003	
	Chairman	February 23, 2005	June 10, 2005
Ben S. Bernanke	Chairman	June 21, 2005	January 31, 2006
Katherine Baicker	Member	November 18, 2005	July 11, 2007
Matthew J. Slaughter	Member	November 18, 2005	March 1, 2007
Edward P. Lazear	Chairman	February 27, 2006	January 20, 2009
Donald B. Marron	Member	July 17, 2008	January 20, 2009
Christina D. Romer	Chair	January 29, 2009	September 3, 2010
Austan D. Goolsbee	Member	March 11, 2009	
	Chairman	September 10, 2010	August 5, 2011
Cecilia Elena Rouse	Member	March 11, 2009	February 28, 2011
Katharine G. Abraham	Member	April 19, 2011	April 19, 2013
Carl Shapiro	Member	April 19, 2011	May 4, 2012
Alan B. Krueger	Chairman	November 7, 2011	August 2, 2013
James H. Stock	Member	February 7, 2013	May 19, 2014
Jason Furman	Chairman	August 4, 2013	January 20, 2017
Betsey Stevenson	Member	August 6, 2013	August 7, 2015
Maurice Obstfeld	Member	July 21, 2014	August 28, 2015
Sandra E. Black	Member	August 10, 2015	January 20, 2017
Jay C. Shambaugh	Member	August 31, 2015	January 20, 2017

Council Members and Their Dates of Service

Name	Position	Oath of office date	Separation date
Kevin A. Hassett	Chairman	September 13, 2017	June 30, 2019
Richard V. Burkhauser	Member	September 28, 2017	May 18, 2019
Tomas J. Philipson	Member	August 31, 2017	
	Acting Chairman	July 1, 2019	
	Vice Chairman	July 24, 2019	June 22, 2020
Tyler B. Goodspeed	Member	May 22, 2019	
	Acting Chairman	June 23, 2020	
	Vice Chairman	June 23, 2020	January 6, 2021
Cecilia Elena Rouse	Chair	March 2, 2021	April 1, 2023
Jared Bernstein	Member	January 20, 2021	
	Chair	June 13, 2023	
Heather Boushey	Member	January 20, 2021	
C. Kirabo Jackson	Member	August 28, 2023	

Report to the President on the Activities of the Council of Economic Advisers during 2023

Established by the Employment Act of 1946, the Council of Economic Advisers is charged with advising the President on economic policy based on data, research, and evidence. The Council is composed of three members: a Chair, who is appointed by the President with the advice and consent of the Senate; and two members, who are appointed by the President. Along with a team of economists, they analyze and interpret economic developments and formulate and recommend economic policies that advance the interests of the American people.

The Chair of the Council

Jared Bernstein was confirmed by the Senate on June 13, 2023, as the 31st Chair of the Council of Economic Advisers. In this role, he serves as President Biden's Chief Economist and as a Member of the Cabinet. Before his appointment as Chair, Dr. Bernstein served as a CEA Member from the beginning of the Biden-Harris Administration.

Chair Bernstein has held a variety of posts in economic policy and research. In policy, he was Chief Economist and Economic Adviser to then–Vice President Biden from 2009 to 2011 and served as Deputy Chief Economist at the Department of Labor during the Clinton Administration. In research, Dr. Bernstein was a Senior Fellow at the Center on Budget and Policy Priorities from 2011 to 2020 and spent 16 years in senior roles at the Economic Policy Institute. An expert on labor markets and macroeconomics, Dr. Bernstein's research focuses on income inequality, mobility, employment and earnings, international trade, and the living standards of the middle class. He received a BA from the Manhattan School of Music; an MA from the Hunter School of Social Work; and an MA and PhD from Columbia University.

The Members of the Council

Heather Boushey was appointed to the Council by the President on January 20, 2021. Before assuming this position, Dr. Boushey cofounded the Washington Center for Equitable Growth, where she was President and CEO from 2013 to 2020. She previously served as Chief Economist for Secretary of State Hillary Clinton's 2016 transition team and as an economist at the Center for American Progress, the Joint Economic Committee of the U.S. Congress, the Center for Economic and Policy Research, and the Economic Policy Institute. She received a BA from Hampshire College and a PhD in economics from The New School for Social Research.

C. Kirabo Jackson was appointed to the Council by the President on August 28, 2023. Dr. Jackson is on leave from Northwestern University, where he is the Abraham Harris Professor of Education and Social Policy, a Professor of Economics, and a Faculty Fellow at the Institute for Policy Research. Dr. Jackson is also on leave as editor-in-chief for the American Economic Journal: Economic Policy. Dr. Jackson's research focuses on the economics of education, labor economics, and social policy issues. He received a BA from Yale University, an MA from Harvard University, and a PhD in economics from Harvard University.

Areas of Activity

A central function of the Council is to advise the President on all economic issues and developments, including preparing frequent memos for the President, the Vice President, and White House senior staff on key economic data releases and policy issues. The Council works closely with officials at various government entities—including the National Economic Council, the Domestic Policy Council, the Office of Management and Budget, and administrative agencies—to engage in discussions on numerous policy matters. The Council, the Department of the Treasury, and the Office of Management and Budget are responsible for producing the economic forecasts that underlie the Administration's Budget proposals. Finally, the Council is a leading participant in the Organization for Economic Cooperation and Development (OECD), historically chairing the Economic Policy Committee and participating in OECD working meetings. The Council produces economic analysis that is presented in blog posts, issue briefs, white papers, and public speeches. Under Chair Bernstein's leadership, the CEA has increased the frequency of its blog posts, with a particular focus on the analysis and interpretation of economic data releases.

Blog Posts

- "A New Wage Measure for Core Non-Housing Services," a blog presenting a CEA-constructed wage measure specific to NHS industries that can address limitations of other prominent wage measures (February 2023).

- "The Employment Situation in [Month]" a series of blogs analyzing the monthly Employment Report from the Bureau of Labor Statistics (February, March, June, July, August, September, October 2023).

- "How Junk Fees Distort Competition," a blog identifying specific junk fees and the challenges they pose to consumers and competition broadly (March 2023).

- "The Labor Supply Rebound from the Pandemic," a blog on the return of "missing workers" to the labor market following the pandemic and the rebound in immigration flows (April 2023).

- "An Update on Housing Inflation in the Consumer Price Index," a blog analyzing the rise in housing inflation and its contribution to CPI inflation (April 2023).

- "Investing in America Means Investing in America's Small Businesses," a blog on how the Administration's policies support small businesses (May 2023).

- "The DAME Tax: Making Cryptominers Pay for Costs They Impose on Others," a blog on how the proposed DAME tax can make cryptominers pay for costs imposed on local communities and the environment (May 2023).

- "The Potential Economic Impacts of Various Debt Ceiling Scenarios," a blog outlining the potential economic consequences if the U.S. government were to default on its obligations (May 2023).

- "The Signal and the Noise: Trend Job Gains Reveal Transition to Steady Growth," a blog highlighting robust but decelerating job gains and a normalization of labor supply back to prepandemic levels (May 2023).

- "The Signal and the Noise, Part II: CPI Inflation," a blog analyzing total and core CPI inflation based on 3-month annualized changes (May 2023).

- "This Mother's Day, More Moms Back at Work, but Care Challenges Remain," a blog on postpandemic maternal employment recovery and how the Administration's policies supporting parents and caregivers can boost mothers' labor supply (May 2023).

- "Wage Sensitivity in Non-Housing Services Inflation," a blog presenting a more disaggregated analysis of wage sensitivity in NHS inflation (May 2023).

- "Unsnarled Supply Chains Appear to Help Ease Goods Inflation," a blog analyzing the normalization of supply chains and cooling of core goods inflation (June 2023).

- "Comments on the May 2023 Consumer Price Index Report," a blog analyzing total and core CPI inflation in May 2023 (June 2023).

- "Grocery Inflation is Finally Showing Signs of Cooling," a blog outlining facts about grocery prices and inflation (June 2023).

- "On Anniversary of Equal Pay Act, Signs of Progress and Remaining Challenges for Women in the Labor Market," a blog on the progress in educational attainment, employment, and pay since the enactment of the Equal Pay Act and remaining gender gaps in employment (June 2023).

- "Apples to Äpfel: Recent Inflation Trends in the G7," a blog analyzing harmonized inflation data for G7 countries (June 2023).

- "The June Consumer Price Index: Disinflation, Deflation, and Buying Power in the U.S. Economy," a blog on how the U.S. economy experienced falling inflation and real wage growth in June 2023 (July 2023).

- "Improving Access, Affordability, and Quality in the Early Care and Education (ECE) Market," a blog on the lack of affordable quality care for young children and policy solutions that can expand the availability and affordability of high-quality early childhood education (July 2023).

- "Labor Market Indicators Are Historically Strong After Adjusting for Population Aging," a blog outlining facts about the strength of labor supply and demand after accounting for the effects of aging (July 2023).

- "The Advance Estimate of Second Quarter Real GDP," a blog analyzing the advance estimate of second-quarter real GDP (July 2023).

- "The July Consumer Price Index: It's All About That Base (Effect)," a blog about measuring CPI inflation over various timespans (August 2023).

- "Chain Reaction: 'Immaculate' Disinflation and the Role of Easing Supply Chains," a blog on how supply chain normalization contributed to falling inflation despite low unemployment (August 2023).

- "New Student Loan Repayment Plan Benefits Borrowers Beyond Lower Monthly Payments," a blog on the benefits of SAVE over previous income-driven repayment plans for Federal student loan borrowers (August 2023).

- "Early Signs That Bidenomics is Attracting New Foreign Investment in U.S. Manufacturing," a blog on increases in foreign direct investment in U.S. manufacturing (August 2023).

- "What to Expect: The 2022 Census Poverty, Income, and Health Insurance Reports," a blog outlining the CEA's expectations and important context for the Census Bureau's release of the 2022 income, poverty, and health insurance reports (September 2023).

- "The 2022 Income, Poverty, and Health Insurance Reports," a blog on key findings from the Census Bureau's reports on poverty, income, and health insurance for 2022 (September 2023).

- "Chronic Absenteeism and Disrupted Learning Require an All-Hands-on-Deck Approach," a blog on the importance of improving student engagement and addressing chronic absenteeism exacerbated by the COVID-19 pandemic (September 2023).

- "The August 2023 Consumer Price Index," a blog analyzing CPI inflation in August 2023 (September 2023).

- "Crosswalk Talk: What's the difference between the PCE and the CPI?," a blog on how and why the PCE and CPI differ (September 2023).

- "An Update on Non-Housing Services Inflation: Progress in Wage-Sensitive Prices," a blog on easing in the wage-sensitive part of NHS inflation and an update on housing inflation (September 2023).

- "Federal Revenues After the 2017 Tax Cuts," a blog on the effect of lower tax revenues on the 2023 deficit and deficits dating back to the enactment of the 2017 Tax Cuts and Jobs Act (October 2023).

- "Union Deterrence and Recent NLRB Action," a blog on the NLRB's decision in Cemex Construction Materials Pacific, LLC, and its relation to economic forces influencing unionization (October 2023).

- "Four Facts About Hispanic Achievements in the U.S. Economy," a blog highlighting recent economic achievements of the Hispanic community in the United States in celebration of Hispanic Heritage Month (October 2023).

- "Commercial-to-residential Conversion: Addressing Office Vacancies," a blog assessing the benefits and challenges of transforming excess office space into housing in high-demand markets (October 2023).

- "As the U.S. Consumer Goes, So Goes the U.S. Economy," a blog highlighting the importance of consumption and the strong labor market for economic growth (October 2023).

- "The Retirement Security Rule—Strengthening Protections for Americans Saving for Retirement," a blog outlining a new rule proposed by the Department of Labor to close loopholes and ensure the financial advice Americans get for retirement is in their best interest (October 2023).

- "The Power of Empowering Workers: Reducing Racial Employment and Unemployment Gaps," a blog on the role of tight labor markets in reducing racial labor market inequality (November 2023).

- "American Rescue Plan's Child Care Stabilization Funds Stabilized the Industry While Helping Mothers Return to Work," a blog outlining the effect of the ARP stabilization funds on child care prices, child care worker employment and wages, and maternal labor force participation (November 2023).

- "The Anti-Poverty and Income-Boosting Impacts of the Enhanced CTC," a blog on the effects of the 2021 expansion of the Child Tax Credit and subsequent expiration (November 2023).

- "The Global Clean Energy Manufacturing Gap," a blog on how the Bipartisan Infrastructure Law and Inflation Reduction Act will support global manufacturing of clean energy technologies (November 2023).

- "Disinflation Explanation: Supply, Demand, and their Interaction," a blog decomposing inflation to highlight the central role of unsnarled supply chains (November 2023).

- "Go with the Flow: Getting Beneath the Surface of the Jobs Report," a blog about some of the dynamics underlying the topline numbers of the November jobs report (December 2023).

- "Disinflation Explanation, Part 2: Contribution Analysis," a blog decomposing core inflation into goods, housing, and non-housing services (December 2023).

- "Ten Charts That Explain the U.S. Economy in 2023," a blog on how the performance of the U.S. economy exceeded expectations in 2023 (December 2023).

- "A Progress Report on Climate-Energy-Macro Modeling," a blog on how the CEA has worked with other Federal agencies to make progress on quantifying climate risk within the President's Budget (December 2023).

Issue Briefs, Speeches, and White Papers

- "The U.S. Economy: Where It's Been and Where It's Going," a speech given by Chair Jared Bernstein at the Brookings Institution (February 8, 2023).

- "Methodologies and Considerations for Integrating the Physical and Transition Risks of Climate Change into Macroeconomic Forecasting for the President's Budget," a white paper, cowritten with OMB, outlining considerations for quantifying the macroeconomic effects of climate change and more fully integrating them into future Budget forecasts (March 2023).

- "How President Biden's Invest in America Agenda Has Laid the Foundation for Decades of Strong, Stable, and Sustained, Equitable Growth," a speech given by CEA Member Heather Boushey at the Peterson Institute for International Economics (May 31, 2023).

- "The Economics of Demand-Side Support for the Department of Energy's Clean Hydrogen Hubs," an issue brief on the importance of demand-side support for expanding clean hydrogen capacity (July 2023).

- "Protecting Competition Through Updated Merger Guidelines," an issue brief on how the draft of the updated Merger Guidelines from the United States' primary antitrust enforcement authorities reflects the current economic evidence and the realities of the market (July 2023).

- "Remarks by Chair Jared Bernstein at the Economic Policy Institute," a speech about the Biden-Harris Administration's approach to international trade (September 28, 2023), a white paper.

- "Did Stabilization Funds Help Mothers Get Back to Work After the COVID-19 Recession?" a white paper on the effect of the American Rescue Plan child care funding on maternal labor supply, cost growth for families, and wages for child care workers (November 2023).

- "Supply Chain Resilience," an issue brief on progress making supply chains more resilient and ongoing efforts to prepare for future economic shocks (November 2023).

- "'Weathering the Storm': Federal Efforts Helped Bolster U.S. Education Standing Among Peer Nations," an issue brief on the Federal government's policy response to test score declines due to COVID-19, successful interventions, and remaining challenges (December 2023).

Public Information

The Economic Report of the President, together with the Annual Report of the Council of Economic Advisers, is an important vehicle for presenting the Administration's domestic and international economic policies. It is available for purchase through the Government Publishing Office, and is viewable at no cost at www.gpo.gov/erp. All the Council's written materials noted above, including this *Report*, can be found at www.whitehouse.gov/cea. All links provided in this *Report* are active as of the date of publication.

The Staff of the Council of Economic Advisers

Front Office

Amy Ganz	Chief of Staff
Ernie Tedeschi	Chief Economist
Molly Opinsky	Special Assistant to the Chair
Kaleb Snider	Special Assistant to a Member
Reid Fauble	Special Adviser to a Member

Senior Economists

Alessandro Barbarino	Macroeconomics, Labor, Econometrics
Jacob Bastian	Public Finance, Social Insurance
Steven Braun	Director of Macroeconomic Forecasting
Evan Gee	Technology, Industrial Organization
Michael Geruso	Health and Demography, Public Finance
Sandile Hlatshwayo	International Trade
Fariha Kamal	International Trade
Kyle Meng	Climate, Energy, Environment
Jonas Nahm	Industrial Strategy
Elena Patel	Public Finance and Tax, Housing
David Ratner	Labor, Macroeconomics
Krista Schwarz	Finance
Elizabeth Tucker	Senior Adviser for National Security
Lee Tucker	Labor

Staff Economists

Will Nober	Industrial Organization, Climate
Chinemelu Okafor	International
Aastha Rajan	Labor, Public Finance
Lea Rendell	Labor
Sam Slocum	Finance, Macroeconomics, Energy

Julia Turner . . . . Labor, Education, Care

Research Assistants

Erin Deal . . . . Macroeconomics
Aiden Lee . . . . Industrial Strategy
Shawdi Mehrvarzan . . . . Labor, International, OECD
Asha Reddy Patt . . . . Education, Health, International
Naomi Shimberg . . . . Climate, Energy, Environment
Natalie Tomeh . . . . Housing, Public Finance

Special Adviser

Anna Katherine Pasnau . . . . Clean Energy, Infrastructure, Labor

Statistical Office

Brian Amorosi . . . . Director of the Statistical Office
Madison Fox . . . . Statistical Office Associate

Administrative Office

Megan Packer . . . . Manager of Finance and
Administration

Interns

Ayumi Akiyama, Karthick Arunachalam, Katherine Ashby, Steven Berit,
Atreya Bhamidi, Nissi Cantu, Andrew Gasparini, Cameron Greene, Simon
Hodson, Aarjav Joshi, Devansh Jotsinghani, Victoria Kidder, Margaret
Lin, Nour Ben Ltaifa, Rebecca Mann, Andrew Morin, Julian Ching Wang,
Griffin Young.

ERP Production

Alfred Imhoff . . . . Editor
Shea Gibbs . . . . Editor
Michael Sarinsky . . . . Editor

Appendix B

Statistical Tables Relating to Income, Employment, and Production

Contents

Labor Market Indicators

Production and Business Activity

Prices

General Notes

Detail in these tables may not add to totals due to rounding.

Because of the formula used for calculating real gross domestic product (GDP), the chained (2017) dollar estimates for the detailed components do not add to the chained-dollar value of GDP or to any intermediate aggregate. The Department of Commerce (Bureau of Economic Analysis) no longer publishes chained-dollar estimates prior to 2007, except for selected series.

Because of the method used for seasonal adjustment, the sum or average of seasonally adjusted monthly values generally will not equal annual totals based on unadjusted values.

Unless otherwise noted, all dollar figures are in current dollars.

Symbols used:
    p Preliminary.
    ... Not available (also, not applicable).
    NSA Not seasonally adjusted.

Data in these tables reflect revisions made by source agencies through February 8, 2024.

Excel versions of these tables are available at www.gpo.gov/erp.

National Income or Expenditure

TABLE B–1. Percent changes in real gross domestic product, 1973–2023

[Percent change, fourth quarter over fourth quarter; quarterly changes at seasonally adjusted annual rates]

Year or quarter	Gross domestic product	Personal consumption expenditures			Gross private domestic investment							
		Total	Goods	Services	Total	Fixed investment						Change in private inventories
						Total	Nonresidential				Residential	
							Total	Structures	Equipment	Intellectual property products		
1973	4.0	1.8	0.4	3.2	10.2	3.5	10.6	7.9	13.5	5.1	-10.5	
1974	-1.9	-1.6	-5.6	2.4	-10.4	-9.9	-3.9	-6.4	-3.7	1.6	-24.6	
1975	2.6	5.1	6.1	4.1	-9.8	-2.6	-5.9	-8.1	-6.7	2.8	7.8	
1976	4.3	5.4	6.4	4.5	15.2	12.1	7.8	3.8	9.0	11.8	23.8	
1977	5.0	4.2	4.9	3.7	14.9	12.1	11.9	5.7	17.2	4.8	12.6	
1978	6.7	4.0	3.5	4.4	14.3	13.1	16.0	21.7	14.5	10.3	6.8	
1979	1.3	1.7	.3	2.9	-3.4	1.1	5.5	8.8	2.7	9.4	-9.1	
1980	.0	.0	-2.5	2.2	-7.2	-4.8	-.9	2.7	-4.4	4.7	-15.3	
1981	1.3	.1	-.2	.3	6.7	1.5	9.0	14.1	4.6	12.1	-22.0	
1982	-1.4	3.5	3.6	3.4	-17.3	-8.0	-9.5	-13.5	-10.0	3.4	-1.7	
1983	7.9	6.6	8.3	5.3	31.3	18.3	10.4	-3.9	19.9	13.0	49.7	
1984	5.6	4.3	5.3	3.6	14.2	11.3	13.9	15.7	13.4	12.6	3.7	
1985	4.2	4.8	4.6	5.0	1.9	3.7	3.2	3.3	1.7	7.7	5.2	
1986	2.9	4.4	6.5	3.0	-4.1	.6	-3.2	-14.3	.8	5.4	11.8	
1987	4.5	2.8	.4	4.5	9.8	1.5	2.2	4.9	.1	4.2	-.5	
1988	3.8	4.6	4.5	4.7	-.5	3.7	5.1	-3.3	8.2	9.8	.1	
1989	2.7	2.4	1.8	2.7	.7	1.5	4.5	3.3	2.5	11.3	-6.5	
1990	.6	.8	-1.6	2.3	-6.5	-4.2	-.9	-3.2	-2.7	6.2	-13.6	
1991	1.2	.9	-.8	2.0	2.1	-1.9	-3.4	-12.8	-3.2	7.2	2.9	
1992	4.4	4.9	5.3	4.7	7.7	8.7	7.1	1.0	11.3	4.8	13.6	
1993	2.6	3.3	4.4	2.7	7.6	8.4	7.6	.2	13.1	2.9	10.6	
1994	4.1	3.8	5.5	2.8	11.5	6.6	8.5	1.6	12.5	5.8	1.6	
1995	2.2	2.8	2.3	3.0	.8	5.5	7.4	4.7	8.1	8.3	.1	
1996	4.4	3.4	4.8	2.7	11.2	9.9	11.3	10.9	11.1	12.1	5.6	
1997	4.5	4.5	5.3	4.0	11.4	8.3	9.7	4.4	10.7	12.4	4.0	
1998	4.9	5.6	8.1	4.3	9.7	11.5	11.6	4.3	14.8	11.5	11.3	
1999	4.8	5.2	6.6	4.5	8.5	7.2	8.4	-.1	9.5	13.3	3.5	
2000	2.9	4.3	4.0	4.5	4.4	5.9	8.5	10.8	8.5	6.6	-1.5	
2001	.2	2.5	4.9	1.3	-11.1	-4.7	-6.8	-10.6	-7.7	-2.1	2.0	
2002	2.0	2.0	1.7	2.1	4.4	-1.5	-5.1	-15.7	-3.7	.9	8.1	
2003	4.3	3.8	6.6	2.3	8.7	8.6	6.8	1.9	9.6	5.8	12.7	
2004	3.4	3.8	4.3	3.6	8.0	6.5	6.5	.3	9.8	5.7	6.6	
2005	3.0	2.8	3.0	2.7	6.1	5.8	6.1	1.5	8.7	5.1	5.2	
2006	2.6	3.2	4.6	2.5	-1.4	0	8.1	9.0	7.1	9.3	-15.2	
2007	2.1	2.0	1.8	2.0	-2.0	-1.1	7.3	17.7	3.9	4.0	-21.2	
2008	-2.5	-1.5	-6.8	1.2	-15.3	-11.1	-7.0	-.9	-15.9	.9	-24.7	
2009	.1	-.2	.6	-.6	-9.0	-10.5	-10.3	-27.1	-8.4	3.8	-11.5	
2010	2.8	2.8	4.3	2.1	12.0	6.2	9.0	-3.4	22.6	1.6	-5.7	
2011	1.5	1.0	.9	1.0	10.5	9.2	10.1	9.0	12.7	7.2	5.3	
2012	1.6	1.5	2.4	1.1	3.9	7.3	5.7	4.1	7.8	3.7	15.4	
2013	3.0	2.2	3.9	1.4	10.6	6.6	6.4	6.4	6.7	6.1	7.5	
2014	2.7	3.5	5.3	2.6	5.8	7.8	7.7	9.6	6.4	8.2	8.1	
2015	2.1	2.6	4.0	1.9	3.5	2.6	.9	-5.6	2.0	4.3	9.7	
2016	2.2	2.5	3.7	1.9	2.3	3.5	3.3	3.7	-.9	9.0	4.5	
2017	3.0	3.1	5.4	2.0	4.9	5.5	5.6	-.4	7.5	7.2	5.1	
2018	2.1	2.0	2.1	2.0	4.7	3.3	5.6	3.5	3.3	9.9	-4.1	
2019	3.2	2.6	3.8	2.0	1.3	2.9	3.1	6.4	-2.1	7.3	2.2	
2020	-1.1	-.8	8.8	-5.1	2.1	.7	-3.7	-14.9	-3.7	3.4	15.9	
2021	5.4	7.2	6.6	7.6	7.9	3.8	4.9	-.9	1.4	11.6	.4	
2022	.7	1.2	-.6	2.1	-2.4	-.8	5.6	.8	5.3	8.3	-17.4	
2023 ᴾ	3.1	2.6	3.5	2.2	1.8	3.1	4.1	14.8	-.1	2.6	.0	
2020: I	-5.3	-6.4	-2.1	-8.4	-9.9	-3.3	-7.7	-5.2	-20.5	6.2	14.1	
II	-28.0	-30.2	-8.6	-38.7	-46.4	-28.2	-28.6	-40.0	-38.0	-9.5	-26.7	
III	34.8	40.5	51.7	35.1	98.9	28.3	18.3	-8.9	50.8	7.9	66.1	
IV	4.2	5.6	3.2	6.8	13.2	15.2	10.5	1.5	15.6	10.4	30.1	
2021: I	5.2	8.9	16.5	5.1	-3.3	9.3	8.9	7.8	2.0	16.9	9.8	
II	6.2	13.6	14.7	13.0	-5.4	5.9	9.7	1.0	10.5	13.6	-4.4	
III	3.3	2.8	-8.5	9.3	16.1	-1.6	-1.3	-4.1	-8.0	7.1	-2.7	
IV	7.0	4.0	5.6	3.2	27.9	1.9	2.7	-7.7	1.9	9.1	-.5	
2022: I	-2.0	.0	-1.2	.6	6.2	7.2	10.7	-1.2	16.8	11.4	-1.8	
II	-.6	2.0	-.3	3.2	-10.6	-.2	5.3	-.5	4.9	8.7	-14.1	
III	2.7	1.6	-.7	2.8	-7.6	-4.3	4.7	-1.3	5.6	7.1	-26.4	
IV	2.6	1.2	.0	1.8	3.4	-5.4	1.7	6.5	-5.0	6.1	-24.9	
2023: I	2.2	3.8	5.1	3.1	-9.0	3.1	5.7	30.3	-4.1	3.8	-5.3	
II	2.1	.8	.5	1.0	5.2	5.2	7.4	16.1	7.7	2.7	-2.2	
III	4.9	3.1	4.9	2.2	10.0	2.6	1.4	11.2	-4.4	1.8	6.7	
IV ᴾ	3.3	2.8	3.8	2.4	2.1	1.7	1.9	3.2	1.0	2.1	1.1	

See next page for continuation of table.

TABLE B–1. Percent changes in real gross domestic product, 1973–2023—*Continued*

[Percent change, fourth quarter over fourth quarter; quarterly changes at seasonally adjusted annual rates]

Year or quarter	Net exports of goods and services — Net exports	Exports	Imports	Government — Total	Federal — Total	Federal — National defense	Federal — Non-defense	State and local	Final sales of domestic product	Gross domestic purchases [1]	Final sales to private domestic purchasers [2]	Gross domestic income (GDI) [3]	Average of GDP and GDI
1973		18.4	-0.5	-0.3	-3.6	-5.0	-0.3	2.9	2.8	2.9	2.2	3.8	3.9
1974		3.1	-1.0	3.0	3.7	1.2	9.5	2.4	-1.7	-2.3	-3.5	-2.9	-2.4
1975		1.5	-5.6	3.0	.8	.5	1.4	4.9	3.9	2.0	3.4	2.7	2.6
1976		4.3	19.2	-1.3	-1.0	-2.1	1.3	-1.6	3.8	5.4	6.7	3.8	4.1
1977		-1.4	5.7	1.9	2.3	.1	6.8	1.7	4.5	5.6	5.9	6.0	5.5
1978		18.8	9.9	4.4	3.5	2.9	4.8	5.2	6.4	6.0	6.1	5.4	6.0
1979		10.5	.9	.9	1.2	2.4	-1.1	.7	2.2	.5	1.5	.8	1.0
1980		3.9	-9.3	.3	4.0	3.7	4.6	-2.9	.5	-1.4	-1.2	1.3	.6
1981		.7	6.2	2.5	6.0	7.9	2.0	-.7	.3	1.8	.4	1.2	1.2
1982		-12.2	-3.9	2.6	4.5	7.3	-1.6	.8	.4	-.7	.8	-1.2	-1.3
1983		5.5	24.6	1.9	2.7	6.5	-6.6	1.1	6.0	9.5	9.1	6.6	7.3
1984		9.1	18.9	6.3	7.1	5.6	11.5	5.4	5.0	6.5	5.9	6.7	6.1
1985		1.5	5.6	6.1	6.7	8.2	2.8	5.5	4.6	4.5	4.6	3.4	3.8
1986		10.6	7.9	4.7	5.3	4.7	6.8	4.1	3.9	2.9	3.5	2.7	2.8
1987		12.8	6.3	3.0	3.6	5.3	-1.0	2.4	3.0	4.1	2.5	5.5	5.0
1988		14.0	3.8	1.4	-1.4	-.8	-3.0	4.1	4.6	3.0	4.4	4.7	4.2
1989		10.2	2.6	2.5	.5	-1.3	5.8	4.3	2.9	2.1	2.2	1.0	1.9
1990		7.4	-.2	2.6	1.5	.0	5.4	3.6	1.0	-.1	-.3	1.0	.8
1991		9.2	5.7	.0	-2.3	-4.9	4.3	1.9	.5	.9	.3	.7	.9
1992		4.5	6.5	1.3	1.6	-.4	6.2	1.1	4.5	4.6	5.6	3.9	4.1
1993		4.4	9.9	-.7	-4.5	-5.4	-2.5	2.2	2.7	3.2	4.3	3.0	2.8
1994		10.8	12.2	.0	-4.2	-6.7	1.1	3.1	3.3	4.3	4.4	4.3	4.2
1995		9.4	4.8	-.6	-4.8	-5.0	-4.3	2.2	3.0	1.8	3.3	2.9	2.6
1996		10.1	11.1	2.6	1.1	.3	2.6	3.6	4.2	4.6	4.8	4.8	4.6
1997		8.3	14.2	1.7	.2	-.8	1.9	2.7	3.9	5.2	5.3	5.5	5.0
1998		2.6	11.0	2.8	-.3	-2.4	3.3	4.6	5.2	5.9	6.9	4.9	4.9
1999		6.2	12.4	3.9	3.3	3.8	2.4	4.2	4.6	5.6	5.7	4.4	4.6
2000		6.0	11.1	.5	-1.9	-3.3	.4	1.8	3.2	3.7	4.7	3.6	3.3
2001		-12.2	-7.6	4.9	5.5	4.7	6.8	4.6	1.5	.4	.9	-.4	-.1
2002		4.0	9.6	3.8	8.1	8.1	8.2	1.5	.9	2.7	1.3	3.2	2.6
2003		7.2	5.9	1.8	6.6	9.0	2.6	-.8	4.3	4.2	4.8	2.7	3.5
2004		7.2	10.9	.8	2.6	2.8	2.3	-.2	3.1	4.0	4.4	3.8	3.6
2005		7.4	6.1	.8	1.8	1.8	1.9	.2	2.9	3.0	3.4	4.1	3.6
2006		9.9	4.0	1.9	2.4	3.1	1.3	1.6	2.9	2.1	2.5	2.6	2.6
2007		9.2	1.6	2.3	3.6	3.9	3.1	1.5	2.3	1.3	1.3	-.3	.9
2008		-2.0	-5.4	2.6	6.4	7.4	4.5	.3	-1.8	-3.1	-3.5	-2.6	-2.6
2009		1.3	-5.2	3.1	6.2	4.9	8.9	1.0	-.2	-.8	-2.1	.6	.4
2010		10.4	11.3	-1.5	1.8	1.3	2.7	-3.7	2.0	3.1	3.4	3.3	3.0
2011		4.8	3.3	-3.4	-3.6	-3.6	-3.5	-3.2	1.3	1.4	2.4	2.0	1.8
2012		2.9	.5	-2.1	-2.6	-4.7	1.2	-1.7	2.0	1.2	2.6	2.8	2.2
2013		5.2	2.9	-2.3	-6.0	-6.4	-5.4	.2	2.4	2.7	3.1	1.3	2.1
2014		2.4	6.5	.3	-1.0	-3.4	2.8	1.1	3.0	3.3	4.3	4.1	3.4
2015		-1.5	3.3	2.6	1.4	-.2	3.8	3.3	2.0	2.7	2.6	1.4	1.8
2016		1.4	2.2	1.5	.2	-.5	1.2	2.2	2.4	2.3	2.7	1.3	1.7
2017		6.1	5.8	1.0	1.4	2.1	.4	.8	3.1	3.0	3.6	3.0	3.0
2018		.3	3.0	1.9	3.5	4.5	2.1	.9	1.9	2.5	2.3	2.8	2.4
2019		.8	-1.9	4.7	3.9	4.3	3.2	5.2	3.5	2.7	2.7	2.6	2.9
2020		-9.7	.1	1.1	4.5	3.2	6.4	-.9	-1.3	.0	-.5	.2	-.4
2021		6.7	11.1	-.2	.6	-5.0	8.6	-.6	4.7	6.1	6.5	4.4	4.9
2022		4.3	2.1	.8	-.1	.2	-.6	1.3	1.0	.5	.8	.0	.3
2023 *p*		2.1	-.2	4.3	4.0	3.3	4.7	4.5	3.4	2.8	2.7		
2020: I		-15.4	-13.0	4.4	5.2	3.9	7.1	4.0	-4.2	-5.2	-5.8	-2.4	-3.9
II		-61.5	-53.6	8.6	31.8	.9	90.1	-3.6	-24.4	-27.5	-29.8	-30.5	-29.3
III		62.0	88.6	-6.1	-12.3	-.4	-25.8	-2.0	25.1	38.1	37.9	28.9	31.8
IV		25.8	32.0	-1.9	-1.9	8.7	-15.1	-1.9	4.5	5.5	7.5	15.3	9.6
2021: I		.9	8.0	5.7	18.1	-7.1	63.4	-1.3	7.6	6.1	8.9	3.1	4.2
II		2.0	7.7	-4.3	-8.9	-4.7	-13.9	-1.4	8.3	6.9	11.9	4.6	5.4
III		1.5	8.5	-1.5	-6.8	-3.2	-11.4	2.0	.3	4.2	1.9	3.6	3.4
IV		24.2	20.6	-.3	2.1	-4.8	11.8	-1.6	2.6	7.1	3.6	6.2	6.6
2022: I		-4.6	14.7	-2.9	-6.9	-6.9	-6.9	-.4	-1.9	.6	1.5	.5	-.8
II		10.6	4.1	-1.9	-3.9	.9	-9.8	-.8	1.5	-1.1	1.5	.0	-.3
III		16.2	-4.8	2.9	1.2	-.3	3.3	3.8	3.4	.1	.3	2.7	2.7
IV		-3.5	-4.3	5.3	9.8	7.7	12.6	2.8	1.0	2.2	-.2	-3.0	-.3
2023: I		6.8	1.3	4.8	5.2	1.9	9.5	4.6	4.6	1.6	3.6	.5	1.4
II		-9.3	-7.6	3.3	1.1	2.3	-.4	4.7	2.1	2.0	1.7	.5	1.3
III		5.4		5.8	7.1	8.4	5.5	5.0	3.6	4.7	3.0	1.5	3.2
IV *p*		6.3	1.9	3.3	2.5	.9	4.6	3.7	3.2	2.8	2.6		

[1] Gross domestic product (GDP) less exports of goods and services plus imports of goods and services.
[2] Personal consumption expenditures plus gross private fixed investment.
[3] Gross domestic income is deflated by the implicit price deflator for GDP.

Note: Percent changes based on unrounded GDP quantity indexes.

Source: Department of Commerce (Bureau of Economic Analysis).

TABLE B–2. Contributions to percent change in real gross domestic product, 1973–2023

[Percentage points, except as noted; annual average to annual average, quarterly data at seasonally adjusted annual rates]

Year or quarter	Gross domestic product (percent change)	Personal consumption expenditures			Gross private domestic investment							
		Total	Goods	Services	Total	Fixed investment						Change in private inventories
						Total	Nonresidential				Residential	
							Total	Structures	Equipment	Intellectual property products		
1973	5.6	2.97	1.52	1.45	1.95	1.47	1.51	0.30	1.12	0.08	-0.04	0.48
1974	-.5	-.50	-1.08	.58	-1.24	-.98	.10	-.08	.14	.05	-1.08	-.26
1975	-.2	1.36	.20	1.16	-2.91	-1.68	-1.13	-.42	-.73	.01	-.54	-1.24
1976	5.4	3.41	2.03	1.38	2.91	1.54	.66	.09	.39	.18	.88	1.37
1977	4.6	2.59	1.26	1.33	2.47	2.23	1.26	.15	1.01	.11	.97	.24
1978	5.5	2.68	1.19	1.49	2.22	2.10	1.72	.52	1.08	.12	.38	.12
1979	3.2	1.44	.45	.99	.72	1.11	1.34	.51	.62	.20	-.22	-.40
1980	-.3	-.19	-.72	.53	-2.07	-1.18	.00	.26	-.35	.09	-1.19	-.89
1981	2.5	.85	.33	.52	1.64	.50	.87	.39	.28	.21	-.37	1.13
1982	-1.8	.88	.19	.69	-2.46	-1.16	-.43	-.09	-.47	.12	-.72	-1.31
1983	4.6	3.51	1.69	1.82	1.60	1.32	-.06	-.56	.32	.17	1.38	.28
1984	7.2	3.30	1.91	1.39	4.73	2.83	2.18	.58	1.29	.30	.65	1.90
1985	4.2	3.20	1.38	1.83	-.01	1.02	.91	.31	.39	.21	.11	-1.03
1986	3.5	2.58	1.45	1.13	.03	.34	-.24	-.49	.08	.17	.58	-.31
1987	3.5	2.14	.47	1.67	.53	.11	.01	-.11	.03	.10	.10	.41
1988	4.2	2.65	.96	1.69	.45	.59	.63	.02	.43	.18	-.05	-.13
1989	3.7	1.86	.64	1.21	.72	.55	.71	.07	.35	.29	-.16	.17
1990	1.9	1.28	.16	1.12	-.45	-.25	.14	.05	-.14	.22	-.38	-.21
1991	-.1	.12	-.49	.61	-1.09	-.84	-.48	-.38	-.28	.18	-.35	-.26
1992	3.5	2.36	.76	1.60	1.11	.83	.33	-.18	.34	.17	.49	.28
1993	2.7	2.24	.99	1.26	1.24	1.17	.84	-.01	.73	.12	.32	.07
1994	4.0	2.51	1.26	1.26	1.90	1.29	.91	.05	.75	.11	.38	.61
1995	2.7	1.91	.71	1.20	.55	.99	1.15	.16	.78	.20	-.15	-.44
1996	3.8	2.26	1.06	1.20	1.49	1.48	1.13	.15	.65	.33	.35	.02
1997	4.4	2.45	1.12	1.33	2.01	1.49	1.38	.21	.76	.41	.11	.52
1998	4.5	3.42	1.54	1.88	1.76	1.82	1.44	.16	.91	.37	.38	-.07
1999	4.8	3.49	1.83	1.66	1.62	1.65	1.36	.01	.89	.45	.29	-.03
2000	4.1	3.29	1.23	2.06	1.31	1.34	1.31	.24	.71	.36	.03	-.03
2001	1.0	1.63	.72	.92	-1.11	-.27	-.31	-.04	-.31	.04	.04	-.84
2002	1.7	1.70	.92	.78	-.16	-.64	-.94	-.56	-.35	-.03	.29	.49
2003	2.8	2.13	1.15	.98	.76	.77	.30	-.09	.26	.14	.47	-.02
2004	3.8	2.54	1.21	1.34	1.64	1.23	.67	.00	.49	.18	.57	.40
2005	3.5	2.38	.98	1.40	1.26	1.33	.92	.06	.60	.26	.41	-.07
2006	2.8	1.95	.87	1.08	.60	.50	1.00	.22	.57	.21	-.50	.10
2007	2.0	1.63	.65	.98	-.49	-.24	.89	.42	.25	.23	-1.13	-.25
2008	.1	.10	-.71	.81	-1.52	-1.05	.08	.23	-.29	.14	-1.14	-.47
2009	-2.6	-.88	-.70	-.18	-3.49	-2.69	-1.95	-.71	-1.21	-.02	-.74	-.80
2010	2.7	1.31	.62	.68	1.84	.44	.52	-.50	.91	.11	-.08	1.40
2011	1.6	1.16	.49	.68	.95	1.00	1.00	.08	.69	.24	.00	-.05
2012	2.3	.94	.48	.46	1.65	1.48	1.16	.35	.62	.20	.31	.17
2013	2.1	1.18	.76	.42	1.19	.96	.61	.03	.33	.25	.34	.24
2014	2.5	1.91	.96	.95	1.09	1.20	1.07	.33	.48	.26	.13	-.11
2015	2.9	2.27	1.08	1.19	1.08	.78	.44	.01	.24	.20	.34	.30
2016	1.8	1.65	.78	.87	-.02	.50	.25	-.10	-.05	.40	.25	-.52
2017	2.5	1.79	.88	.90	.77	.77	.61	.08	.22	.31	.16	.00
2018	3.0	1.86	.84	1.01	1.02	.90	.93	.17	.35	.41	-.03	.12
2019	2.5	1.35	.63	.71	.55	.48	.51	.08	.06	.37	-.04	.08
2020	-2.2	-1.69	1.02	-2.70	-.85	-.37	-.66	-.30	-.58	.22	.28	-.48
2021	5.8	5.59	2.51	3.08	1.52	1.25	.78	-.09	.33	.54	.47	.26
2022	1.9	1.72	.07	1.65	.86	.24	.68	-.06	.26	.48	-.44	.62
2023 ᵖ	2.5	1.49	.47	1.02	-.21	.09	.58	.36	-.01	.23	-.49	-.31
2020: I	-5.3	-4.34	-.44	-3.90	-1.87	-.57	-1.09	-.16	-1.23	.31	.52	-1.30
II	-28.0	-21.51	-1.59	-19.92	-9.29	-5.28	-4.12	-1.47	-2.16	-.49	-1.16	-4.01
III	34.8	24.93	10.23	14.70	13.52	5.04	2.69	-.27	2.50	.46	2.35	8.48
IV	4.2	3.63	.71	2.92	2.36	2.55	1.35	.03	.79	.53	1.20	-.18
2021: I	5.2	5.70	3.52	2.18	-.46	1.63	1.18	.19	.15	.85	.44	-2.08
II	6.2	8.73	3.24	5.49	-.84	1.05	1.27	.02	.55	.70	-.22	-1.89
III	3.3	1.89	-2.10	3.99	2.71	-.28	-.15	-.12	-.40	.37	-.13	2.99
IV	7.0	2.71	1.26	1.45	4.63	.35	.37	-.21	.11	.47	-.02	4.28
2022: I	-2.0	-.03	-.30	.27	1.16	1.23	1.32	-.03	.77	.58	-.09	-.07
II	-.6	1.32	-.09	1.41	-2.10	-.05	.68	-.01	.25	.45	-.73	-2.05
III	2.7	1.05	-.18	1.23	-1.45	-.79	.62	-.03	.28	.37	-1.41	-.66
IV	2.6	.79	-.01	.80	.62	-.99	-.24	.17	-.26	.32	-1.23	1.61
2023: I	2.2	2.54	1.14	1.40	-1.69	.53	.76	.77	-.21	.20	-.22	-2.22
II	2.1	.55	.11	.44	.90	.90	.98	.46	.38	.15	-.09	.00
III	4.9	2.11	1.09	1.02	1.74	.46	.21	.33	-.22	.10	.26	1.27
IV ᵖ	3.3	1.91	.85	1.06	.38	.31	.26	.10	.05	.11	.04	.07

See next page for continuation of table.

TABLE B–2. Contributions to percent change in real gross domestic product, 1973–2023—*Continued*

[Percentage points, except as noted; annual average to annual average, quarterly data at seasonally adjusted annual rates]

Year or quarter	Net exports of goods and services							Government consumption expenditures and gross investment					Final sales of domestic product
	Net exports	Exports			Imports			Total	Federal			State and local	
		Total	Goods	Services	Total	Goods	Services		Total	National defense	Non-defense		
1973	0.80	1.08	1.05	0.02	−0.28	−0.33	0.05	−0.07	−0.39	−0.40	0.01	0.32	5.16
1974	.73	.56	.49	.08	.17	.17	.00	.47	.06	−.07	.14	.41	−.28
1975	.86	−.05	−.14	.09	.91	.85	.06	.49	.05	−.07	.13	.43	1.03
1976	−1.05	.36	.34	.02	−1.41	−1.31	−.10	.12	.01	−.04	.06	.10	4.01
1977	−.70	.19	.12	.07	−.89	−.82	−.07	.26	.21	.06	.15	.05	4.38
1978	.05	.80	.64	.17	−.76	−.66	−.10	.60	.23	.04	.19	.37	5.42
1979	.64	.80	.69	.11	−.16	−.13	−.02	.36	.20	.15	.05	.16	3.56
1980	1.64	.95	.88	.07	.69	.66	.03	.36	.38	.22	.16	−.02	.63
1981	−.15	.12	−.05	.17	−.26	−.18	−.09	.20	.43	.40	.03	−.23	1.41
1982	−.59	−.71	−.63	−.08	.12	.20	−.08	.37	.35	.47	−.11	.01	−.50
1983	−1.32	−.22	−.21	.00	−1.10	−.98	−.12	.79	.65	.51	.14	.14	4.31
1984	−1.54	.61	.41	.20	−2.16	−1.78	−.38	.74	.33	.38	−.04	.41	5.34
1985	−.39	.24	.20	.05	−.63	−.50	−.13	1.37	.78	.62	.16	.59	5.20
1986	−.29	.53	.27	.25	−.82	−.80	−.02	1.14	.61	.52	.09	.53	3.77
1987	.17	.77	.62	.15	−.60	−.39	−.21	.62	.38	.38	.01	.24	3.04
1988	.81	1.23	.99	.24	−.41	−.35	−.07	.26	−.15	−.04	−.12	.42	4.31
1989	.51	.97	.72	.26	−.46	−.37	−.09	.58	.15	−.02	.18	.43	3.50
1990	.40	.78	.56	.22	−.37	−.25	−.13	.65	.20	.02	.18	.45	2.09
1991	.62	.61	.45	.16	.01	−.04	.05	.25	.01	−.06	.10	.24	.15
1992	−.04	.66	.52	.14	−.70	−.76	.05	.10	−.15	−.31	.16	.25	3.24
1993	−.56	.31	.22	.09	−.87	−.82	−.05	−.17	−.32	−.32	.00	.15	2.68
1994	−.41	.84	.65	.19	−1.25	−1.15	−.10	.02	−.31	−.28	−.02	.32	3.41
1995	.12	1.02	.83	.19	−.90	−.84	−.06	.10	−.21	−.21	.00	.31	3.13
1996	−.15	.86	.68	.18	−1.01	−.91	−.10	.18	−.09	−.08	−.01	.27	3.76
1997	−.31	1.26	1.10	.16	−1.57	−1.40	−.17	.30	−.06	−.13	.07	.36	3.92
1998	−1.14	.26	.17	.08	−1.39	−1.18	−.21	.44	−.06	−.09	.03	.50	4.55
1999	−.90	.52	.32	.20	−1.42	−1.31	−.11	.59	.12	.06	.06	.47	4.82
2000	−.85	.86	.72	.13	−1.71	−1.45	−.26	.33	.02	−.04	.06	.31	4.11
2001	−.24	−.59	−.49	−.10	.35	.39	−.04	.67	.24	.13	.12	.43	1.80
2002	−.67	−.19	−.24	.05	−.48	−.41	−.07	.83	.47	.30	.18	.35	1.21
2003	−.49	.19	.19	.01	−.68	−.67	−.01	.40	.45	.35	.10	−.06	2.81
2004	−.63	.88	.58	.30	−1.51	−1.28	−.22	.30	.31	.26	.05	−.02	3.45
2005	−.30	.67	.52	.15	−.98	−.88	−.09	.14	.15	.11	.04	.00	3.55
2006	−.06	.95	.71	.24	−1.01	−.81	−.20	.30	.17	.07	.10	.13	2.68
2007	.52	.94	.53	.41	−.42	−.27	−.15	.34	.14	.13	.01	.20	2.26
2008	1.04	.67	.48	.19	.37	.47	−.10	.49	.46	.33	.14	.03	.58
2009	1.07	−1.00	−1.00	.00	2.07	2.10	−.03	.72	.48	.29	.20	.24	−1.78
2010	−.43	1.40	1.13	.28	−1.83	−1.73	−.10	−.02	.34	.16	.18	−.36	1.30
2011	.12	.90	.65	.26	−.79	−.74	−.05	−.67	−.23	−.12	−.12	−.44	1.61
2012	.12	.54	.37	.17	−.42	−.38	−.04	−.42	−.16	−.18	.02	−.26	2.12
2013	.20	.41	.27	.13	−.20	−.28	.07	−.46	−.43	−.33	−.10	−.03	1.88
2014	−.31	.52	.41	.12	−.84	−.75	−.09	−.16	−.18	−.18	.00	.02	2.64
2015	−.77	.04	−.03	.07	−.81	−.74	−.07	.37	.00	−.09	.09	.36	2.65
2016	−.16	.06	.05	.01	−.22	−.14	−.08	.35	.04	−.02	.06	.31	2.34
2017	−.20	.49	.32	.17	−.69	−.53	−.16	.10	.03	.04	−.01	.07	2.46
2018	−.26	.35	.34	.01	−.60	−.62	.02	.35	.22	.13	.09	.12	2.85
2019	−.12	.06	.01	.05	−.18	−.07	−.11	.68	.25	.21	.04	.43	2.39
2020	−.24	−1.52	−.75	−.77	1.28	.67	.61	.56	.40	.11	.29	.16	−1.74
2021	−1.25	.66	.53	.13	−1.91	−1.60	−.31	−.05	.10	−.08	.17	−.15	5.54
2022	−.48	.76	.44	.33	−1.24	−.82	−.42	−.16	−.19	−.11	−.08	.03	1.31
2023 ᴾ	.58	.32	.21	.11	.26	.21	.05	.68	.27	.12	.14	.42	2.84
2020: I	.09	−1.81	−.27	−1.53	1.89	1.10	.79	.78	.34	.15	.19	.44	−4.04
II	1.00	−8.78	−6.58	−2.20	9.78	7.07	2.71	1.78	2.07	.07	2.00	−.29	−24.01
III	−2.58	5.06	4.90	.16	−7.65	−7.21	−.44	−1.03	−.89	.01	−.90	−.14	26.36
IV	−1.44	2.31	1.65	.65	−3.74	−3.06	−.68	−.35	−.13	.34	−.47	−.22	4.39
2021: I	−1.04	.06	−.02	.08	−1.10	−1.02	−.08	1.04	1.19	−.30	1.49	−.15	7.33
II	−.87	.20	−.03	.24	−1.07	−.51	−.56	−.80	−.65	−.19	−.46	−.15	8.11
III	−1.03	.16	−.13	.29	−1.19	−.20	−.99	−.26	−.48	−.12	−.36	.22	.31
IV	−.34	2.42	1.83	.59	−2.76	−2.38	−.38	−.04	.13	−.18	.31	−.17	2.68
2022: I	−2.59	−.50	−.69	.18	−2.08	−1.72	−.36	−.52	−.47	−.26	−.21	−.04	−1.90
II	.56	1.19	.73	.46	−.63	−.28	−.35	−.34	−.26	.03	−.29	−.08	1.49
III	2.58	1.80	1.63	.17	.77	.98	−.21	.49	.07	−.01	.08	.41	3.32
IV	.26	−.41	−.52	.11	.66	.55	.11	.90	.59	.27	.32	.31	.95
2023: I	.58	.76	.89	−.13	−.18	−.22	.04	.82	.33	.07	.26	.49	4.47
II	.04	−1.09	−1.31	.22	1.13	.78	.35	.57	.07	.08	−.01	.50	2.06
III	.03	.59	.55	.04	−.56	−.64	.08	.99	.45	.30	.15	.53	3.59
IV ᴾ	.43	.68	.34	.34	−.25	−.08	−.17	.56	.16	.03	.13	.40	3.21

Source: Department of Commerce (Bureau of Economic Analysis).

TABLE B–3. Gross domestic product, 2008–2023

[Quarterly data at seasonally adjusted annual rates]

Year or quarter	Gross domestic product	Personal consumption expenditures			Gross private domestic investment							
						Fixed investment						Change in private inventories
							Nonresidential					
		Total	Goods	Services	Total	Total	Total	Structures	Equipment	Intellectual property products	Residential	

Billions of dollars

2008	14,769.9	10,050.1	3,363.2	6,686.9	2,477.6	2,506.9	1,990.9	571.1	845.4	574.4	516.0	–29.2
2009	14,478.1	9,891.2	3,180.0	6,711.2	1,929.7	2,080.4	1,690.4	455.8	670.3	564.4	390.0	–150.8
2010	15,049.0	10,260.3	3,317.8	6,942.4	2,165.5	2,111.6	1,735.0	379.8	777.0	578.2	376.6	53.9
2011	15,599.7	10,698.9	3,518.1	7,180.7	2,332.6	2,286.3	1,907.5	404.5	881.3	621.7	378.8	46.3
2012	16,254.0	11,047.4	3,637.7	7,409.6	2,621.8	2,550.5	2,118.5	479.4	983.4	655.7	432.0	71.2
2013	16,880.7	11,388.2	3,742.2	7,646.1	2,838.3	2,732.9	2,221.3	491.5	1,035.3	694.6	511.5	105.5
2014	17,608.1	11,874.5	3,886.6	7,987.9	3,074.0	2,989.2	2,425.2	574.6	1,109.1	741.5	564.0	84.8
2015	18,295.0	12,297.4	3,955.1	8,342.3	3,288.5	3,148.4	2,507.5	584.5	1,144.1	778.9	640.9	140.1
2016	18,804.9	12,726.8	4,033.0	8,693.8	3,278.3	3,239.2	2,529.0	566.2	1,119.8	843.0	710.2	39.1
2017	19,612.1	13,290.6	4,212.2	9,078.4	3,467.7	3,435.0	2,661.1	594.9	1,160.0	906.2	773.9	32.7
2018	20,656.5	13,934.4	4,414.2	9,520.2	3,724.8	3,668.4	2,856.5	636.6	1,227.6	992.2	811.9	56.4
2019	21,521.4	14,417.6	4,529.2	9,888.5	3,892.4	3,820.2	2,993.1	678.7	1,241.5	1,072.9	827.2	72.2
2020	21,323.0	14,206.2	4,713.1	9,493.1	3,748.4	3,785.9	2,869.4	623.2	1,110.8	1,135.5	916.5	–37.6
2021	23,594.0	16,043.0	5,506.6	10,536.3	4,216.3	4,204.6	3,078.4	623.9	1,188.2	1,266.3	1,126.2	11.7
2022 [p]	25,744.1	17,511.7	5,997.0	11,514.7	4,756.6	4,599.3	3,433.0	700.5	1,327.2	1,405.4	1,166.4	157.3
2023 [p]	27,356.4	18,564.0	6,192.7	12,371.4	4,849.0	4,786.2	3,712.3	836.1	1,383.4	1,492.8	1,073.9	62.8
2020: I	21,706.5	14,473.1	4,559.5	9,913.6	3,807.8	3,840.7	2,962.2	694.7	1,145.2	1,122.3	878.5	–33.0
II	19,913.1	13,168.9	4,391.9	8,777.1	3,254.3	3,549.2	2,734.4	609.1	1,016.6	1,108.8	814.8	–295.0
III	21,647.6	14,456.2	4,923.3	9,532.8	3,891.2	3,796.4	2,850.5	594.3	1,122.3	1,133.9	945.9	94.9
IV	22,024.5	14,726.7	4,977.8	9,748.8	4,040.2	3,957.4	2,930.7	594.6	1,158.9	1,177.1	1,026.7	82.8
2021: I	22,600.2	15,217.7	5,241.5	9,976.2	4,031.1	4,075.4	2,993.4	607.2	1,173.3	1,212.9	1,082.1	–44.4
II	23,292.4	15,950.9	5,536.4	10,414.5	4,013.3	4,174.5	3,065.2	618.0	1,192.9	1,254.3	1,109.4	–161.2
III	23,829.0	16,285.1	5,515.9	10,769.2	4,226.6	4,229.9	3,088.9	625.0	1,182.1	1,281.8	1,141.0	–3.3
IV	24,654.6	16,718.2	5,732.8	10,985.4	4,594.0	4,338.5	3,166.0	645.2	1,204.6	1,316.3	1,172.5	255.5
2022: I	25,029.1	17,030.6	5,879.3	11,151.4	4,766.8	4,517.8	3,299.8	664.5	1,277.7	1,357.6	1,218.0	249.0
II	25,544.3	17,415.1	6,014.4	11,400.7	4,739.0	4,618.9	3,403.0	688.7	1,318.9	1,395.4	1,215.8	120.2
III	25,994.6	17,684.2	6,046.8	11,637.4	4,724.6	4,642.3	3,493.1	712.6	1,355.0	1,425.6	1,149.1	82.3
IV	26,408.4	17,917.0	6,047.6	11,869.4	4,796.2	4,618.4	3,536.0	736.1	1,357.1	1,442.8	1,082.5	177.7
2023: I	26,813.6	18,269.6	6,133.8	12,135.7	4,725.8	4,702.1	3,641.3	800.2	1,368.7	1,472.5	1,060.8	23.7
II	27,063.0	18,419.0	6,144.7	12,274.4	4,780.3	4,761.7	3,709.1	832.5	1,390.4	1,486.2	1,052.6	18.6
III	27,610.1	18,679.5	6,231.8	12,447.7	4,915.0	4,813.0	3,730.6	849.8	1,382.6	1,498.2	1,082.4	102.0
IV [p]	27,938.8	18,888.1	6,260.4	12,627.7	4,975.0	4,868.1	3,768.2	862.0	1,391.7	1,514.5	1,099.9	106.9

Billions of chained (2017) dollars

2008	16,781.5	11,270.7	3,312.7	7,981.2	2,564.3	2,620.6	2,008.3	666.0	799.7	573.7	623.0	–32.3
2009	16,349.1	11,123.6	3,209.4	7,948.6	2,025.3	2,201.6	1,716.4	541.4	630.2	570.8	487.9	–170.3
2010	16,789.8	11,335.6	3,300.2	8,065.3	2,309.0	2,269.9	1,794.3	454.8	757.8	586.4	472.8	54.4
2011	17,052.4	11,528.5	3,372.3	8,183.9	2,463.1	2,432.5	1,951.3	469.0	859.6	622.9	472.2	44.4
2012	17,442.8	11,686.1	3,444.2	8,265.3	2,735.3	2,678.0	2,137.1	531.5	953.9	653.8	533.3	69.2
2013	17,812.2	11,889.9	3,562.3	8,341.9	2,938.7	2,842.0	2,238.6	537.3	1,006.5	695.0	601.1	103.5
2014	18,261.7	12,226.4	3,717.7	8,516.3	3,129.0	3,052.6	2,421.1	597.2	1,086.0	739.1	626.8	85.1
2015	18,799.6	12,638.8	3,902.5	8,738.9	3,323.4	3,193.6	2,498.9	598.2	1,127.2	774.0	693.2	133.6
2016	19,141.7	12,949.0	4,044.7	8,904.9	3,320.2	3,286.9	2,544.8	579.7	1,117.5	847.6	742.2	33.4
2017	19,612.1	13,290.6	4,212.2	9,078.4	3,467.7	3,435.0	2,661.1	594.9	1,160.0	906.2	773.9	32.7
2018	20,193.9	13,654.9	4,378.7	9,276.6	3,668.1	3,611.7	2,844.3	629.2	1,228.6	986.5	768.5	54.3
2019	20,692.1	13,928.3	4,509.9	9,420.1	3,780.3	3,708.5	2,950.1	644.8	1,241.7	1,063.5	761.3	71.3
2020	20,234.1	13,570.0	4,729.9	8,867.6	3,602.5	3,630.1	2,810.6	583.4	1,116.3	1,111.0	816.2	–29.9
2021	21,407.7	14,718.2	5,265.9	9,483.4	3,914.4	3,887.3	2,975.5	564.8	1,187.4	1,226.6	903.8	12.5
2022 [p]	21,822.0	15,090.8	5,281.5	9,836.1	4,102.8	3,939.3	3,131.6	552.9	1,249.2	1,338.7	822.6	128.1
2023 [p]	22,375.3	15,421.9	5,390.4	10,059.5	4,055.2	3,960.4	3,268.0	623.2	1,247.5	1,396.7	734.5	50.6
2020: I	20,665.6	13,862.3	4,551.8	9,313.6	3,676.6	3,708.2	2,912.0	647.7	1,147.7	1,114.3	796.8	–36.8
II	19,034.8	12,668.7	4,450.2	8,240.0	3,145.2	3,414.0	2,676.9	570.1	1,018.5	1,086.8	737.3	–274.1
III	20,511.8	13,793.9	4,939.2	8,884.4	3,735.1	3,633.6	2,791.6	556.9	1,128.7	1,107.6	837.0	105.7
IV	20,724.1	13,982.9	4,978.3	9,032.2	3,853.1	3,764.7	2,862.0	559.0	1,170.4	1,135.2	893.9	85.7
2021: I	20,990.5	14,282.6	5,171.7	9,144.9	3,820.4	3,849.1	2,923.9	569.5	1,176.2	1,180.5	915.0	–25.8
II	21,309.5	14,745.6	5,351.8	9,429.6	3,767.3	3,904.3	2,992.4	570.9	1,205.9	1,218.9	904.7	–138.4
III	21,483.1	14,848.8	5,234.3	9,641.1	3,910.8	3,888.8	2,982.8	565.0	1,181.0	1,239.9	898.4	7.3
IV	21,847.6	14,995.6	5,305.6	9,717.9	4,159.1	3,907.1	3,002.7	553.8	1,186.5	1,267.1	897.3	207.1
2022: I	21,738.9	14,995.2	5,289.7	9,733.0	4,222.4	3,976.0	3,080.0	552.1	1,233.5	1,301.8	893.1	197.0
II	21,708.2	15,069.2	5,285.3	9,810.8	4,105.5	3,974.0	3,120.0	551.4	1,248.5	1,329.1	859.9	92.7
III	21,851.1	15,127.4	5,275.7	9,878.2	4,024.8	3,930.9	3,156.3	549.7	1,265.5	1,351.9	796.3	70.7
IV	21,990.0	15,171.4	5,275.2	9,922.3	4,058.5	3,876.5	3,170.0	558.4	1,249.5	1,372.1	741.2	151.9
2023: I	22,112.3	15,312.9	5,341.0	9,998.9	3,963.7	3,905.9	3,214.5	596.6	1,236.4	1,384.9	731.1	27.2
II	22,225.4	15,343.6	5,347.3	10,023.1	4,014.1	3,955.9	3,272.7	619.3	1,259.6	1,394.0	727.1	14.9
III	22,490.7	15,461.4	5,411.3	10,078.7	4,111.1	3,981.3	3,284.5	635.9	1,245.5	1,400.4	738.9	77.8
IV [p]	22,672.9	15,569.8	5,462.1	10,137.4	4,132.1	3,998.5	3,300.3	641.0	1,248.5	1,407.7	740.8	82.7

See next page for continuation of table.

[Quarterly data at seasonally adjusted annual rates]

Year or quarter	Net exports of goods and services			Government consumption expenditures and gross investment					Final sales of domestic product	Gross domestic purchases [1]	Final sales to private domestic purchasers [2]	Gross domestic income (GDI) [3]	Average of GDP and GDI
	Net exports	Exports	Imports	Total	Federal			State and local					
					Total	National defense	Non-defense						
									Billions of dollars				
2008	−740.9	1,835.3	2,576.2	2,983.0	1,152.0	750.3	401.6	1,831.1	14,799.1	15,510.7	12,556.9	14,578.7	14,674.3
2009	−419.2	1,582.8	2,001.9	3,076.3	1,220.8	787.6	433.2	1,855.6	14,628.8	14,897.2	11,971.7	14,286.3	14,382.2
2010	−532.3	1,857.2	2,389.6	3,155.6	1,300.2	828.0	472.2	1,855.4	14,995.1	15,581.3	12,371.8	14,979.5	15,014.2
2011	−579.6	2,115.9	2,695.5	3,147.9	1,299.8	834.0	465.8	1,848.2	15,553.5	16,179.3	12,985.2	15,624.0	15,611.9
2012	−551.6	2,217.7	2,769.3	3,136.5	1,287.0	814.2	472.8	1,849.5	16,182.8	16,805.6	13,597.9	16,407.6	16,330.8
2013	−478.5	2,287.9	2,766.4	3,132.6	1,227.4	764.3	463.1	1,905.2	16,775.2	17,359.1	14,121.1	16,910.5	16,895.6
2014	−508.9	2,378.5	2,887.4	3,168.6	1,217.1	744.1	473.0	1,951.5	17,523.3	18,117.0	14,863.6	17,749.1	17,678.6
2015	−524.3	2,270.6	2,794.9	3,233.4	1,222.8	730.4	492.4	2,010.6	18,154.9	18,819.3	15,445.8	18,388.0	18,341.5
2016	−503.3	2,235.6	2,738.8	3,303.0	1,237.4	729.4	507.9	2,065.7	18,765.8	19,308.2	15,966.1	18,752.0	18,778.5
2017	−543.3	2,388.3	2,931.6	3,397.1	1,266.1	748.3	517.8	2,131.1	19,579.4	20,155.4	16,725.6	19,544.2	19,578.2
2018	−593.1	2,538.1	3,131.2	3,590.4	1,346.3	795.1	551.2	2,244.1	20,600.1	21,249.6	17,602.8	20,593.1	20,624.8
2019	−578.5	2,538.5	3,117.0	3,789.9	1,422.2	851.1	571.1	2,367.7	21,449.2	22,099.9	18,237.8	21,479.0	21,500.2
2020	−626.4	2,150.1	2,776.5	3,994.8	1,523.4	884.6	638.8	2,471.3	21,360.5	21,949.3	17,992.2	21,264.7	21,293.8
2021	−858.2	2,550.0	3,408.3	4,193.1	1,594.3	898.6	695.7	2,598.7	23,582.4	24,452.3	20,247.5	23,599.5	23,596.8
2022	−971.1	2,995.0	3,966.2	4,446.8	1,635.5	928.4	707.1	2,811.3	25,586.8	26,715.2	22,111.1	25,796.4	25,770.3
2023 *P*	−798.0	3,027.8	3,825.9	4,741.3	1,771.7	994.6	777.0	2,969.6	27,293.6	28,154.4	23,350.3	....	....
2020: I	−518.0	2,416.1	2,934.1	3,943.7	1,464.7	876.0	588.7	2,478.9	21,739.5	22,224.5	18,313.8	21,769.7	21,738.1
II	−531.1	1,811.4	2,342.5	4,021.1	1,569.8	875.6	694.2	2,451.3	20,208.1	20,444.3	16,718.2	19,799.4	19,856.3
III	−695.7	2,106.6	2,802.3	3,996.0	1,527.7	881.1	646.6	2,468.3	21,552.8	22,343.4	18,252.5	21,282.1	21,464.9
IV	−760.7	2,266.4	3,027.1	4,018.3	1,531.4	905.8	625.7	2,486.9	21,941.7	22,785.2	18,684.1	22,207.8	22,116.1
2021: I	−792.4	2,382.8	3,175.2	4,143.9	1,609.9	898.6	711.3	2,533.9	22,644.5	23,392.6	19,293.1	22,672.5	22,636.3
II	−832.0	2,498.3	3,330.2	4,160.2	1,588.5	897.2	691.2	2,571.7	23,453.6	24,124.3	20,125.4	23,279.2	23,285.8
III	−884.3	2,566.0	3,450.2	4,201.5	1,576.4	899.3	677.2	2,625.1	23,832.2	24,713.3	20,515.0	23,832.8	23,830.9
IV	−924.3	2,753.1	3,677.4	4,266.6	1,602.5	899.2	703.2	2,664.2	24,399.1	25,578.9	21,056.7	24,613.6	24,634.1
2022: I	−1,089.7	2,837.6	3,927.3	4,321.4	1,601.7	902.6	699.1	2,719.7	24,780.1	26,118.8	21,548.4	25,142.0	25,085.6
II	−1,025.6	3,044.3	4,069.8	4,415.7	1,612.3	924.5	687.7	2,803.4	25,424.1	26,569.8	22,034.0	25,695.8	25,620.0
III	−892.0	3,084.5	3,976.5	4,477.9	1,636.3	930.4	705.9	2,841.5	25,912.3	26,886.7	22,326.5	26,149.7	26,072.2
IV	−877.2	3,013.8	3,891.0	4,572.4	1,691.8	956.2	735.5	2,880.6	26,230.7	27,285.6	22,535.5	26,198.2	26,303.3
2023: I	−825.7	3,064.8	3,890.5	4,643.9	1,730.6	968.7	761.9	2,913.2	26,789.9	27,639.3	22,971.7	26,485.4	26,649.5
II	−806.1	2,961.8	3,767.9	4,669.8	1,744.3	978.9	765.5	2,925.5	27,044.5	27,869.1	23,180.7	26,625.7	26,844.4
III	−779.2	3,030.8	3,810.0	4,794.8	1,791.9	1,009.1	782.8	3,002.9	27,508.1	28,389.4	23,492.5	26,945.1	27,277.6
IV *P*	−781.1	3,054.0	3,835.1	4,856.8	1,819.8	1,021.8	798.0	3,036.9	27,831.9	28,719.9	23,756.2	....	....
									Billions of chained (2017) dollars				
2008	−478.8	1,846.6	2,325.4	3,420.1	1,287.2	824.6	461.2	2,136.8	16,841.4	17,268.4	13,906.8	16,564.3	16,672.9
2009	−338.7	1,693.1	2,031.8	3,542.7	1,367.4	871.7	494.3	2,177.9	16,542.9	16,664.4	13,319.2	16,132.6	16,240.9
2010	−388.0	1,907.3	2,295.3	3,539.7	1,422.6	897.3	524.1	2,117.0	16,755.0	17,169.9	13,600.3	16,712.3	16,751.0
2011	−361.6	2,044.2	2,405.8	3,426.9	1,384.2	878.1	504.9	2,042.3	17,025.8	17,409.2	13,957.7	17,079.0	17,065.7
2012	−338.4	2,126.3	2,464.7	3,356.0	1,357.9	848.2	508.8	1,997.7	17,387.5	17,773.1	14,362.5	17,607.6	17,525.2
2013	−304.3	2,190.3	2,494.6	3,275.6	1,283.9	792.4	491.0	1,991.8	17,715.9	18,102.6	14,730.8	17,843.6	17,827.9
2014	−347.6	2,275.8	2,623.4	3,247.3	1,251.9	760.4	491.3	1,995.3	18,185.6	18,602.0	15,278.6	18,407.9	18,334.8
2015	−476.5	2,283.1	2,759.5	3,313.6	1,252.7	744.9	507.8	2,060.8	18,669.0	19,276.0	15,832.3	18,895.2	18,847.4
2016	−505.8	2,293.9	2,799.7	3,378.5	1,260.0	741.1	518.8	2,118.5	19,108.4	19,647.5	16,235.9	19,087.8	19,114.7
2017	−543.3	2,388.3	2,931.6	3,397.1	1,266.1	748.3	517.8	2,131.1	19,579.4	20,155.4	16,725.6	19,544.2	19,578.2
2018	−593.5	2,456.4	3,050.0	3,465.0	1,309.9	774.6	535.3	2,155.2	20,137.6	20,787.5	17,266.5	20,131.9	20,162.9
2019	−617.5	2,469.0	3,086.5	3,601.4	1,360.1	815.9	544.3	2,241.3	20,620.5	21,310.1	17,636.5	20,651.3	20,671.7
2020	−663.4	2,144.8	2,808.3	3,715.5	1,442.6	838.8	603.7	2,273.8	20,260.8	20,899.8	17,206.8	20,178.8	20,206.5
2021	−933.8	2,280.9	3,214.7	3,704.7	1,462.4	823.0	639.3	2,244.3	21,380.6	22,333.3	18,605.4	21,412.7	21,410.2
2022	−1,051.0	2,439.6	3,490.6	3,670.4	1,420.9	800.1	620.6	2,249.6	21,661.2	22,854.4	19,030.0	21,866.4	21,844.2
2023 *P*	−925.5	2,505.7	3,431.3	3,816.6	1,480.9	827.7	653.1	2,336.0	22,281.2	23,287.0	19,381.7	....	....
2020: I	−562.0	2,371.4	2,933.5	3,691.9	1,393.8	833.5	560.3	2,298.0	20,696.1	21,233.8	17,570.3	20,725.7	20,695.6
II	−553.0	1,868.2	2,421.1	3,768.9	1,493.5	835.3	657.9	2,277.1	19,300.0	19,595.9	16,082.4	18,926.1	18,980.4
III	−729.6	2,107.6	2,837.2	3,709.7	1,445.2	834.5	610.6	2,265.5	20,410.8	21,241.5	17,427.3	20,165.5	20,338.6
IV	−809.1	2,232.1	3,041.2	3,691.5	1,438.1	852.0	586.1	2,254.5	20,636.4	21,527.9	17,747.3	20,896.6	20,810.4
2021: I	−863.1	2,237.0	3,100.0	3,743.1	1,499.1	836.3	662.7	2,247.0	21,017.9	21,846.9	18,131.1	21,057.7	21,024.1
II	−910.0	2,248.1	3,158.1	3,701.8	1,464.8	826.3	638.3	2,239.2	21,442.8	22,212.9	18,649.8	21,297.5	21,303.5
III	−966.5	2,256.4	3,223.0	3,688.2	1,439.1	819.7	619.3	2,250.1	21,461.1	22,442.5	18,737.7	21,486.5	21,484.8
IV	−995.6	2,382.0	3,377.6	3,685.8	1,446.5	809.7	636.8	2,240.9	21,600.6	22,830.9	18,903.0	21,811.3	21,829.4
2022: I	−1,141.1	2,354.1	3,495.2	3,658.8	1,420.9	795.3	625.6	2,238.4	21,497.3	22,865.7	18,971.4	21,836.9	21,787.9
II	−1,116.2	2,414.1	3,530.3	3,641.2	1,406.9	797.1	609.6	2,234.1	21,579.0	22,805.4	19,043.3	21,836.9	21,772.5
III	−981.0	2,506.2	3,487.4	3,667.0	1,411.2	796.6	614.5	2,255.1	21,758.5	22,809.8	19,058.1	21,981.4	21,916.3
IV	−965.6	2,484.1	3,449.6	3,714.8	1,444.5	811.5	633.0	2,270.8	21,809.9	22,936.7	19,047.2	21,814.9	21,902.4
2023: I	−335.1	2,525.4	3,460.5	3,758.8	1,462.8	815.4	647.4	2,296.5	22,054.3	23,028.5	19,218.1	21,841.7	21,977.0
II	−928.2	2,464.7	3,392.9	3,789.8	1,466.9	820.1	646.7	2,323.0	22,167.1	23,140.9	19,298.9	21,866.2	22,045.8
III	−930.7	2,497.3	3,428.0	3,843.4	1,492.3	836.8	655.5	2,351.4	22,362.5	23,409.0	19,442.1	21,949.0	22,219.8
IV *P*	−908.2	2,535.6	3,443.8	3,874.4	1,501.6	836.6	662.9	2,373.0	22,540.8	23,569.7	19,567.8	....	....

[1] Gross domestic product (GDP) less exports of goods and services plus imports of goods and services.
[2] Personal consumption expenditures plus gross private fixed investment.
[3] For chained dollar measures, gross domestic income is deflated by the implicit price deflator for GDP.

Source: Department of Commerce (Bureau of Economic Analysis).

[Percent of nominal GDP]

Year or quarter	Gross domestic product (percent)	Personal consumption expenditures			Gross private domestic investment							
		Total	Goods	Services	Total	Fixed investment						Change in private inventories
						Total	Nonresidential				Residential	
							Total	Structures	Equipment	Intellectual property products		
1973	100.0	59.6	29.2	30.4	18.7	17.6	12.1	3.9	6.7	1.6	5.5	1.1
1974	100.0	60.2	29.2	31.0	17.8	16.9	12.4	4.0	6.8	1.7	4.5	.9
1975	100.0	61.2	29.2	32.0	15.3	15.6	11.7	3.6	6.4	1.7	4.0	-.4
1976	100.0	61.3	29.2	32.1	17.3	16.3	11.7	3.5	6.5	1.7	4.6	.9
1977	100.0	61.2	28.8	32.4	19.1	18.0	12.4	3.6	7.1	1.7	5.5	1.1
1978	100.0	60.5	28.2	32.3	20.3	19.2	13.4	4.0	7.7	1.7	5.9	1.1
1979	100.0	60.3	28.1	32.3	20.5	19.9	14.2	4.5	7.9	1.8	5.6	.7
1980	100.0	61.3	28.0	33.3	18.6	18.8	14.2	4.8	7.6	1.9	4.5	-.2
1981	100.0	60.3	27.1	33.2	19.7	18.8	14.7	5.2	7.5	2.0	4.0	.9
1982	100.0	61.9	26.9	35.0	17.4	17.8	14.5	5.3	7.0	2.2	3.3	-.4
1983	100.0	62.8	26.8	36.0	17.5	17.7	13.3	4.2	6.8	2.2	4.4	-.2
1984	100.0	61.7	26.3	35.4	20.3	18.7	14.0	4.4	7.2	2.4	4.7	1.6
1985	100.0	62.5	26.2	36.3	19.1	18.6	14.0	4.5	7.1	2.4	4.6	.5
1986	100.0	63.0	26.1	36.9	18.5	18.4	13.3	3.9	6.9	2.5	5.1	.1
1987	100.0	63.4	25.9	37.5	18.4	17.8	12.7	3.6	6.6	2.5	5.1	.6
1988	100.0	63.6	25.5	38.1	17.9	17.5	12.6	3.5	6.6	2.5	4.9	.4
1989	100.0	63.4	25.2	38.2	17.7	17.2	12.7	3.4	6.6	2.7	4.5	.5
1990	100.0	63.9	25.0	38.9	16.7	16.4	12.4	3.4	6.2	2.8	4.0	.2
1991	100.0	64.0	24.3	39.7	15.3	15.3	11.8	3.0	5.9	2.9	3.6	.0
1992	100.0	64.4	24.0	40.4	15.5	15.3	11.4	2.6	5.9	2.9	3.9	.3
1993	100.0	64.9	23.9	41.0	16.1	15.8	11.7	2.6	6.2	2.9	4.2	.3
1994	100.0	64.8	24.0	40.8	17.2	16.4	11.9	2.6	6.5	2.8	4.4	.9
1995	100.0	65.0	23.8	41.2	17.2	16.8	12.6	2.7	6.9	3.0	4.2	.4
1996	100.0	65.0	23.8	41.2	17.7	17.4	12.9	2.8	7.0	3.1	4.4	.4
1997	100.0	64.5	23.4	41.2	18.6	17.8	13.4	2.9	7.1	3.4	4.4	.8
1998	100.0	64.9	23.3	41.6	19.2	18.5	13.8	3.0	7.3	3.5	4.6	.7
1999	100.0	65.2	23.7	41.5	19.6	19.0	14.2	3.0	7.4	3.8	4.8	.6
2000	100.0	66.0	23.9	42.1	19.9	19.4	14.6	3.1	7.5	4.0	4.7	.5
2001	100.0	66.8	23.9	43.0	18.3	18.6	13.8	3.2	6.7	3.9	4.8	-.4
2002	100.0	67.2	23.8	43.5	17.7	17.5	12.4	2.6	6.0	3.7	5.1	.2
2003	100.0	67.6	23.8	43.8	17.7	17.6	12.0	2.5	5.9	3.7	5.6	.1
2004	100.0	67.4	23.8	43.6	18.7	18.1	12.0	2.5	5.9	3.6	6.1	.5
2005	100.0	67.3	23.6	43.6	19.4	19.0	12.4	2.7	6.1	3.6	6.6	.4
2006	100.0	67.2	23.4	43.7	19.6	19.1	13.0	3.1	6.2	3.7	6.1	.5
2007	100.0	67.3	23.3	44.1	18.5	18.2	13.5	3.5	6.2	3.8	4.8	.2
2008	100.0	68.0	22.8	45.3	16.8	17.0	13.5	3.9	5.7	3.9	3.5	-.2
2009	100.0	68.3	22.0	46.4	13.3	14.4	11.7	3.1	4.6	3.9	2.7	-1.0
2010	100.0	68.2	22.0	46.1	14.4	14.0	11.5	2.5	5.2	3.8	2.5	.4
2011	100.0	68.6	22.6	46.0	15.0	14.7	12.2	2.6	5.6	4.0	2.4	.3
2012	100.0	68.0	22.4	45.6	16.1	15.7	13.0	2.9	6.1	4.0	2.7	.4
2013	100.0	67.5	22.2	45.3	16.8	16.2	13.2	2.9	6.1	4.1	3.0	.6
2014	100.0	67.4	22.1	45.4	17.5	17.0	13.8	3.3	6.3	4.2	3.2	.5
2015	100.0	67.2	21.6	45.6	18.0	17.2	13.7	3.2	6.3	4.3	3.5	.8
2016	100.0	67.7	21.4	46.2	17.4	17.2	13.4	3.0	6.0	4.5	3.8	.2
2017	100.0	67.8	21.5	46.3	17.7	17.5	13.6	3.0	5.9	4.6	3.9	.2
2018	100.0	67.5	21.4	46.1	18.0	17.8	13.8	3.1	5.9	4.8	3.9	.3
2019	100.0	67.0	21.0	45.9	18.1	17.8	13.9	3.2	5.8	5.0	3.8	.3
2020	100.0	66.6	22.1	44.5	17.6	17.8	13.5	2.9	5.2	5.3	4.3	-.2
2021	100.0	68.0	23.3	44.7	17.9	17.8	13.0	2.6	5.0	5.4	4.8	.0
2022	100.0	68.0	23.3	44.7	18.5	17.9	13.3	2.7	5.2	5.5	4.5	.6
2023 ᵖ	100.0	67.9	22.6	45.2	17.7	17.5	13.6	3.1	5.1	5.5	3.9	.2
2020: I	100.0	66.7	21.0	45.7	17.5	17.7	13.6	3.2	5.3	5.2	4.0	-.2
II	100.0	66.1	22.1	44.1	16.3	17.8	13.7	3.1	5.1	5.6	4.1	-1.5
III	100.0	66.8	22.7	44.0	18.0	17.5	13.2	2.7	5.2	5.2	4.4	.4
IV	100.0	66.9	22.6	44.3	18.3	18.0	13.3	2.7	5.3	5.3	4.7	.4
2021: I	100.0	67.3	23.2	44.1	17.8	18.0	13.2	2.7	5.2	5.4	4.8	-.2
II	100.0	68.5	23.8	44.7	17.2	17.9	13.2	2.7	5.1	5.4	4.8	-.7
III	100.0	68.3	23.1	45.2	17.7	17.8	13.0	2.6	5.0	5.4	4.8	.0
IV	100.0	67.8	23.3	44.6	18.6	17.6	12.8	2.6	4.9	5.3	4.8	1.0
2022: I	100.0	68.0	23.5	44.6	19.0	18.1	13.2	2.7	5.1	5.4	4.9	1.0
II	100.0	68.2	23.5	44.6	18.6	18.1	13.3	2.7	5.2	5.5	4.8	.5
III	100.0	68.0	23.3	44.8	18.2	17.9	13.4	2.7	5.2	5.5	4.4	.3
IV	100.0	67.8	22.9	44.9	18.2	17.5	13.4	2.8	5.1	5.5	4.1	.7
2023: I	100.0	68.1	22.9	45.3	17.6	17.5	13.6	3.0	5.1	5.5	4.0	.1
II	100.0	68.1	22.7	45.4	17.7	17.6	13.7	3.1	5.1	5.5	3.9	.1
III	100.0	67.7	22.6	45.1	17.8	17.4	13.5	3.1	5.0	5.4	3.9	.4
IV ᵖ	100.0	67.6	22.4	45.2	17.8	17.4	13.5	3.1	5.0	5.4	3.9	.4

See next page for continuation of table.

[Percent of nominal GDP]

Year or quarter	Net exports of goods and services							Government consumption expenditures and gross investment				
	Net exports	Exports			Imports			Total	Federal			State and local
		Total	Goods	Services	Total	Goods	Services		Total	National defense	Non-defense	
1973	0.3	6.7	5.3	1.4	6.4	5.0	1.4	21.4	10.3	7.2	3.1	11.1
1974	−.1	8.2	6.7	1.5	8.2	6.8	1.5	22.1	10.3	7.1	3.2	11.8
1975	.9	8.2	6.7	1.6	7.3	5.9	1.4	22.6	10.3	7.0	3.3	12.3
1976	−.1	8.0	6.5	1.5	8.1	6.7	1.4	21.6	9.9	6.7	3.2	11.7
1977	−1.1	7.7	6.2	1.5	8.8	7.3	1.4	20.9	9.6	6.5	3.2	11.2
1978	−1.1	7.9	6.4	1.6	9.0	7.5	1.5	20.3	9.3	6.2	3.1	10.9
1979	−.9	8.8	7.1	1.6	9.6	8.1	1.5	20.0	9.2	6.1	3.0	10.8
1980	−.5	9.8	8.1	1.8	10.3	8.7	1.6	20.6	9.6	6.4	3.2	11.0
1981	−.4	9.5	7.6	1.9	9.9	8.4	1.6	20.4	9.8	6.7	3.1	10.6
1982	−.6	8.5	6.7	1.8	9.1	7.5	1.6	21.3	10.4	7.3	3.1	10.9
1983	−1.4	7.6	5.9	1.7	9.0	7.5	1.5	21.1	10.5	7.5	3.0	10.6
1984	−2.5	7.5	5.7	1.8	10.0	8.3	1.7	20.5	10.2	7.4	2.8	10.3
1985	−2.6	7.0	5.2	1.7	9.6	7.9	1.7	21.0	10.4	7.6	2.8	10.5
1986	−2.9	7.0	5.1	2.0	9.9	8.1	1.8	21.3	10.5	7.7	2.8	10.8
1987	−3.0	7.5	5.5	2.0	10.5	8.5	1.9	21.2	10.4	7.7	2.7	10.9
1988	−2.1	8.5	6.3	2.1	10.6	8.6	1.9	20.6	9.8	7.3	2.5	10.8
1989	−1.5	8.9	6.6	2.3	10.5	8.6	1.9	20.4	9.5	6.9	2.5	11.0
1990	−1.3	9.3	6.8	2.5	10.6	8.5	2.0	20.8	9.4	6.8	2.6	11.3
1991	−.5	9.7	7.0	2.7	10.1	8.1	2.0	21.1	9.5	6.7	2.7	11.6
1992	−.5	9.7	7.0	2.7	10.2	8.4	1.9	20.6	9.0	6.2	2.8	11.6
1993	−1.0	9.5	6.8	2.7	10.5	8.6	1.9	19.9	8.5	5.7	2.7	11.4
1994	−1.3	9.9	7.1	2.8	11.2	9.3	1.9	19.2	7.9	5.2	2.6	11.4
1995	−1.2	10.6	7.8	2.9	11.8	9.9	1.9	19.0	7.5	4.9	2.6	11.4
1996	−1.2	10.7	7.8	3.0	11.9	10.0	1.9	18.5	7.2	4.7	2.5	11.3
1997	−1.2	11.1	8.2	3.0	12.3	10.3	2.0	18.0	6.8	4.3	2.5	11.2
1998	−1.8	10.5	7.6	2.9	12.3	10.3	2.0	17.8	6.5	4.1	2.4	11.3
1999	−2.7	10.3	7.4	2.9	13.0	10.9	2.1	17.9	6.3	4.0	2.4	11.5
2000	−3.7	10.7	7.8	2.9	14.4	12.2	2.2	17.8	6.2	3.8	2.3	11.6
2001	−3.6	9.7	7.0	2.7	13.3	11.1	2.1	18.4	6.3	3.9	2.4	12.1
2002	−4.0	9.1	6.5	2.7	13.2	11.0	2.2	19.1	6.8	4.2	2.6	12.3
2003	−4.6	9.0	6.4	2.6	13.6	11.3	2.3	19.3	7.2	4.5	2.7	12.1
2004	−5.2	9.6	6.8	2.9	14.8	12.4	2.4	19.1	7.3	4.7	2.6	11.8
2005	−5.7	10.0	7.1	2.9	15.7	13.2	2.4	19.0	7.3	4.7	2.6	11.7
2006	−5.7	10.6	7.6	3.1	16.3	13.8	2.6	19.0	7.2	4.6	2.6	11.7
2007	−5.1	11.5	8.0	3.5	16.5	13.8	2.7	19.3	7.3	4.7	2.6	12.0
2008	−5.0	12.4	8.7	3.7	17.4	14.5	2.9	20.2	7.8	5.1	2.7	12.4
2009	−2.9	10.9	7.3	3.6	13.8	11.0	2.9	21.2	8.4	5.4	3.0	12.8
2010	−3.5	12.3	8.5	3.9	15.9	12.9	2.9	21.0	8.6	5.5	3.1	12.3
2011	−3.7	13.6	9.4	4.2	17.3	14.3	3.0	20.2	8.3	5.3	3.0	11.8
2012	−3.4	13.6	9.4	4.2	17.0	14.1	2.9	19.3	7.9	5.0	2.9	11.4
2013	−2.8	13.6	9.3	4.3	16.4	13.6	2.8	18.6	7.3	4.5	2.7	11.3
2014	−2.9	13.5	9.2	4.3	16.4	13.6	2.8	18.0	6.9	4.2	2.7	11.1
2015	−2.9	12.4	8.2	4.2	15.3	12.5	2.8	17.7	6.7	4.0	2.7	11.0
2016	−2.7	11.9	7.7	4.2	14.6	11.8	2.8	17.6	6.6	3.9	2.7	11.0
2017	−2.8	12.2	7.9	4.3	14.9	12.1	2.9	17.3	6.5	3.8	2.6	10.9
2018	−2.9	12.3	8.1	4.2	15.2	12.4	2.8	17.4	6.5	3.8	2.7	10.9
2019	−2.7	11.8	7.6	4.2	14.5	11.7	2.8	17.6	6.6	4.0	2.7	11.0
2020	−2.9	10.1	6.7	3.4	13.0	10.8	2.2	18.7	7.1	4.1	3.0	11.6
2021	−3.6	10.8	7.4	3.4	14.4	12.0	2.4	17.8	6.8	3.8	2.9	11.0
2022	−3.8	11.6	8.0	3.6	15.4	12.7	2.7	17.3	6.4	3.6	2.7	10.9
2023 ᵖ	−2.9	11.1	7.4	3.7	14.0	11.4	2.6	17.3	6.5	3.6	2.8	10.9
2020: I	−2.4	11.1	7.4	3.8	13.5	11.0	2.6	18.2	6.7	4.0	2.7	11.4
II	−2.7	9.1	5.7	3.4	11.8	9.7	2.1	20.2	7.9	4.4	3.5	12.3
III	−3.2	9.7	6.5	3.2	12.9	10.9	2.0	18.5	7.1	4.1	3.0	11.4
IV	−3.5	10.3	7.0	3.3	13.7	11.6	2.2	18.2	7.0	4.1	2.8	11.3
2021: I	−3.5	10.5	7.2	3.4	14.0	11.9	2.2	18.3	7.1	4.0	3.1	11.2
II	−3.6	10.7	7.4	3.4	14.3	12.0	2.3	17.9	6.8	3.9	3.0	11.0
III	−3.7	10.8	7.4	3.4	14.5	12.0	2.5	17.6	6.6	3.8	2.8	11.0
IV	−3.7	11.2	7.7	3.5	14.9	12.3	2.6	17.3	6.5	3.6	2.9	10.8
2022: I	−4.4	11.3	7.8	3.5	15.7	13.0	2.7	17.3	6.4	3.6	2.8	10.9
II	−4.0	11.9	8.3	3.6	15.9	13.2	2.7	17.3	6.3	3.6	2.7	11.0
III	−3.4	11.9	8.2	3.6	15.3	12.5	2.8	17.2	6.3	3.6	2.7	10.9
IV	−3.3	11.4	7.8	3.7	14.7	12.0	2.8	17.3	6.4	3.6	2.8	10.9
2023: I	−3.1	11.4	7.8	3.6	14.5	11.8	2.7	17.3	6.5	3.6	2.8	10.9
II	−3.0	10.9	7.3	3.7	13.9	11.3	2.6	17.3	6.4	3.6	2.8	10.8
III	−2.8	11.0	7.3	3.6	13.8	11.3	2.5	17.4	6.5	3.7	2.8	10.9
IV ᵖ	−2.8	10.9	7.3	3.7	13.7	11.2	2.6	17.4	6.5	3.7	2.9	10.9

Source: Department of Commerce (Bureau of Economic Analysis).

TABLE B–5. Chain-type price indexes for gross domestic product, 1973–2023

[Index numbers, 2017=100, except as noted; quarterly data seasonally adjusted]

Year or quarter	Gross domestic product	Personal consumption expenditures			Gross private domestic investment						
						Fixed investment					
							Nonresidential				
		Total	Goods	Services	Total	Total	Total	Structures	Equipment	Intellectual property products	Residential
1973	23.340	22.455	37.970	16.389	32.770	31.635	40.595	13.393	67.811	42.618	15.854
1974	25.434	24.793	42.709	17.778	36.038	34.764	44.542	15.244	72.897	46.596	17.492
1975	27.796	26.860	46.159	19.302	40.356	38.984	50.410	17.065	84.000	50.336	19.109
1976	29.327	28.333	47.966	20.641	42.587	41.233	53.187	17.901	89.157	52.561	20.347
1977	31.148	30.176	50.526	22.203	45.725	44.397	56.710	19.454	94.635	54.868	22.425
1978	33.339	32.276	53.626	23.910	49.431	48.111	60.502	21.332	99.891	57.725	25.179
1979	36.104	35.143	58.698	25.915	53.867	52.434	65.368	23.811	106.353	61.562	28.023
1980	39.375	38.928	65.271	28.610	58.908	57.325	71.138	26.024	115.715	66.316	31.045
1981	43.092	42.415	70.120	31.541	64.404	62.589	77.902	29.603	124.182	71.265	33.557
1982	45.756	44.771	72.031	34.017	67.817	66.105	82.329	31.939	129.288	75.312	35.356
1983	47.545	46.676	73.331	36.106	68.025	66.357	82.193	31.125	129.659	78.125	36.193
1984	49.262	48.439	74.718	37.985	68.758	67.004	82.453	31.397	128.600	80.315	37.265
1985	50.820	50.128	75.917	39.843	69.609	67.980	83.305	32.144	128.600	81.651	38.289
1986	51.850	51.219	75.562	41.480	71.174	69.644	84.766	32.760	131.183	82.286	39.978
1987	53.126	52.802	77.992	42.726	72.656	71.061	85.734	33.286	132.038	83.761	41.707
1988	55.002	54.865	80.048	44.769	74.483	73.044	87.893	34.698	133.864	86.381	43.159
1989	57.159	57.261	83.128	46.880	76.382	74.928	89.937	36.057	136.423	87.494	44.570
1990	59.307	59.775	86.532	49.029	77.978	76.565	91.867	37.222	139.212	88.404	45.597
1991	61.303	61.774	88.647	50.946	79.300	77.906	93.606	37.896	141.570	90.535	46.190
1992	62.701	63.420	89.717	52.758	79.300	77.949	93.300	37.905	141.355	89.634	46.759
1993	64.189	65.000	90.496	54.582	80.240	78.886	93.500	39.016	139.703	90.261	48.663
1994	65.557	66.356	91.417	56.066	81.437	80.099	94.238	40.394	139.454	90.732	50.424
1995	66.933	67.754	92.271	57.632	82.748	81.430	95.176	42.143	137.927	93.406	52.227
1996	68.156	69.203	93.285	59.214	82.700	81.498	94.599	43.214	134.799	93.818	53.348
1997	69.337	70.407	93.177	60.883	82.748	81.640	94.070	44.864	131.083	94.326	54.634
1998	70.102	70.967	91.777	62.172	82.140	81.196	92.594	46.915	125.201	93.868	56.075
1999	71.084	72.001	92.258	63.409	82.218	81.333	91.666	48.357	120.368	95.383	58.176
2000	72.709	73.822	94.089	65.210	83.296	82.486	92.068	50.252	117.751	98.100	60.758
2001	74.385	75.302	94.018	67.292	84.006	83.206	91.698	52.884	114.281	97.969	63.642
2002	75.500	76.291	93.122	69.033	84.281	83.453	91.219	55.089	111.883	96.657	65.218
2003	77.012	77.894	93.003	71.336	84.973	84.183	90.517	57.057	108.990	95.926	68.308
2004	79.069	79.827	94.311	73.528	87.455	86.642	91.409	61.282	108.078	95.613	73.102
2005	81.537	82.127	96.203	75.998	90.993	90.223	93.780	68.841	107.827	96.232	78.338
2006	84.074	84.440	97.494	78.750	94.194	93.428	96.066	77.037	106.758	97.372	82.914
2007	86.352	86.607	98.576	81.388	95.615	94.857	97.621	81.581	106.377	98.571	84.010
2008	87.977	89.170	101.524	83.783	96.400	95.658	99.131	85.751	105.708	100.125	82.828
2009	88.557	88.921	99.084	84.432	95.297	94.494	98.488	84.186	106.354	98.877	79.930
2010	89.618	90.514	100.533	86.077	93.688	93.026	96.695	83.502	102.543	98.593	79.643
2011	91.466	92.804	104.325	87.742	94.598	93.991	97.756	86.244	102.518	99.807	80.236
2012	93.176	94.534	105.620	89.648	95.797	95.241	99.130	90.209	103.088	100.292	81.006
2013	94.786	95.781	105.049	91.659	96.678	96.160	99.229	91.474	102.857	99.948	85.095
2014	96.436	97.121	104.542	93.795	98.331	97.922	100.170	96.213	102.124	100.326	89.986
2015	97.277	97.299	101.350	95.462	98.728	98.582	100.345	97.719	101.498	100.626	92.454
2016	98.208	98.284	99.710	97.629	98.549	98.550	99.380	97.668	100.206	99.453	95.699
2017	100.000	100.000	100.000	100.000	100.000	100.000	100.000	100.000	100.000	100.000	100.000
2018	102.290	102.047	100.811	102.626	101.539	101.568	100.427	101.174	99.921	100.582	105.640
2019	104.008	103.513	100.427	104.972	102.966	103.014	101.457	105.258	99.980	100.882	108.656
2020	105.407	104.635	99.646	107.054	104.190	104.292	102.092	106.811	99.502	102.208	112.280
2021	110.220	109.001	104.572	111.103	107.750	108.162	103.458	110.459	100.066	103.235	124.606
2022	117.996	116.043	113.548	117.066	116.056	116.754	109.624	126.692	106.238	104.977	141.785
2023 ᵖ	122.272	120.370	114.877	122.982	119.593	120.822	113.614	134.201	110.905	106.884	145.916
2020: I	105.042	104.416	100.178	106.443	103.550	103.580	101.723	107.281	99.778	100.723	110.354
II	104.661	103.962	98.701	106.520	103.676	103.970	102.143	106.864	99.798	102.032	110.646
III	105.593	104.819	99.694	107.306	104.435	104.490	102.104	106.723	99.425	102.377	113.152
IV	106.330	105.343	100.009	107.949	105.098	105.128	102.399	106.378	99.007	103.701	114.967
2021: I	107.731	106.578	101.367	109.118	105.784	105.893	102.380	106.584	99.744	102.756	118.315
II	109.332	108.208	103.467	110.468	106.596	106.931	102.436	108.207	98.909	102.913	122.618
III	110.957	109.705	105.394	111.738	108.192	108.780	103.564	110.578	100.088	103.385	126.940
IV	112.858	111.514	108.062	113.076	110.429	111.043	105.451	116.466	101.525	103.885	130.551
2022: I	115.182	113.590	111.150	114.595	113.058	113.617	107.151	120.339	103.590	104.294	136.190
II	117.704	115.577	113.794	116.220	115.531	116.210	109.088	124.904	105.650	104.999	141.165
III	118.980	116.905	114.613	117.818	117.412	118.075	110.693	129.662	107.087	105.453	144.034
IV	120.115	118.098	114.637	119.631	118.225	119.114	111.566	131.864	108.625	105.164	145.752
2023: I	121.264	119.309	114.838	121.377	119.168	120.358	113.299	134.161	110.715	106.332	144.813
II	121.789	120.044	114.905	122.468	119.135	120.344	113.355	134.464	110.396	106.616	144.490
III	122.792	120.814	115.157	123.513	119.643	120.864	113.602	133.668	111.025	106.991	146.195
IV ᵖ	123.244	121.312	114.609	124.572	120.424	121.722	114.199	134.512	111.485	107.596	148.167

See next page for continuation of table.

[Index numbers, 2017=100, except as noted; quarterly data seasonally adjusted]

Year or quarter	Exports and imports of goods and services			Government consumption expenditures and gross investment					Final sales of domestic product	Personal consumption expenditures excluding food and energy	Gross domestic purchases [1]	Percent change [2]			
					Federal							Gross domestic product	Personal consumption expenditures		Gross domestic purchases [1]
	Exports	Imports	Total	Total	Total	National defense	Non-defense	State and local					Total	Excluding food and energy	
1973	37.931	29.738	18.623	22.800	22.543	23.259	15.949	23.184	23.003	23.137	5.5	5.4	3.8	5.7
1974	46.714	42.545	20.412	24.620	24.387	25.013	17.717	25.259	24.825	25.486	9.0	10.4	7.9	10.2
1975	51.491	46.087	22.297	26.785	26.442	27.411	19.421	27.609	26.899	27.815	9.3	8.3	8.4	9.1
1976	53.181	47.475	23.522	28.451	28.170	28.935	20.369	29.140	28.534	29.343	5.5	5.5	6.1	5.5
1977	55.348	51.658	24.977	30.201	30.015	30.477	21.636	30.962	30.369	31.278	6.2	6.5	6.4	6.6
1978	58.715	55.299	26.629	32.239	32.216	32.179	23.042	33.151	32.382	33.501	7.0	7.0	6.6	7.1
1979	65.787	64.761	28.820	34.664	34.765	34.353	25.077	35.899	34.743	36.440	8.3	8.9	7.3	8.8
1980	72.462	80.674	31.802	38.013	38.319	37.286	27.821	39.148	37.936	40.234	9.1	10.8	9.2	10.4
1981	77.828	85.035	34.959	41.563	41.995	40.574	30.731	42.834	41.260	43.945	9.4	9.0	8.8	9.2
1982	78.199	82.173	37.336	44.501	45.155	43.034	32.742	45.508	43.942	46.478	6.2	5.6	6.5	5.8
1983	78.518	79.093	38.781	45.977	46.824	44.065	34.189	47.289	46.191	48.095	3.9	4.3	5.1	3.5
1984	79.252	78.409	40.464	48.003	48.969	45.814	35.650	48.997	48.106	49.722	3.6	3.8	4.1	3.4
1985	76.893	75.834	41.718	49.022	49.794	47.327	37.102	50.578	50.060	51.200	3.2	3.5	4.1	3.0
1986	75.610	75.832	42.418	49.255	49.815	48.109	38.171	51.621	51.788	52.268	2.0	2.2	3.5	2.1
1987	77.280	80.416	43.564	49.597	50.173	48.415	39.953	52.888	53.460	53.747	2.5	3.1	3.2	2.8
1988	81.237	84.264	45.004	51.215	51.745	50.179	41.289	54.784	55.732	55.648	3.5	3.9	4.2	3.5
1989	82.583	86.106	46.723	52.646	53.147	51.695	43.244	56.938	58.045	57.838	3.9	4.4	4.2	3.9
1990	83.048	88.575	48.682	54.272	54.872	53.079	45.465	59.091	60.397	60.127	3.8	4.4	4.1	4.0
1991	83.974	87.837	50.450	56.224	56.601	55.584	47.130	61.086	62.554	62.015	3.4	3.3	3.6	3.1
1992	83.566	87.907	51.978	57.660	58.247	56.548	48.736	62.486	64.456	63.457	2.3	2.7	3.0	2.3
1993	83.704	87.234	53.203	58.918	59.147	58.565	49.950	63.972	66.206	64.890	2.4	2.5	2.7	2.3
1994	84.676	88.053	54.613	60.539	60.696	60.335	51.237	65.343	67.688	66.251	2.1	2.1	2.2	2.1
1995	86.569	90.466	56.163	62.413	62.422	62.496	52.602	66.722	69.163	67.680	2.1	2.1	2.2	2.2
1996	85.419	88.889	57.314	63.455	63.465	63.538	53.809	67.963	70.474	68.857	1.8	2.1	1.9	1.7
1997	83.914	85.800	58.439	64.436	64.350	64.698	55.006	69.162	71.718	69.873	1.7	1.7	1.8	1.5
1998	81.927	81.180	59.433	65.260	65.152	65.560	56.078	69.958	72.630	70.339	1.1	.8	1.3	.7
1999	81.311	81.664	61.422	66.872	66.801	67.112	58.231	70.955	73.583	71.410	1.4	1.5	1.3	1.5
2000	82.873	85.236	64.059	69.115	69.056	69.339	61.030	72.595	74.898	73.265	2.3	2.5	1.8	2.6
2001	82.223	83.031	65.909	70.395	70.365	70.576	63.128	74.272	76.317	74.690	2.3	2.0	1.9	1.9
2002	81.507	82.042	67.610	72.669	72.712	72.735	64.538	75.380	77.593	75.713	1.5	1.3	1.7	1.4
2003	82.800	84.523	70.091	75.849	76.317	75.221	66.646	76.898	78.845	77.355	2.0	2.1	1.6	2.2
2004	85.818	88.553	73.016	78.458	78.965	77.770	69.726	78.952	80.396	79.572	2.7	2.5	2.0	2.9
2005	88.784	93.764	76.726	81.723	82.562	80.461	73.667	81.426	82.158	82.346	3.1	2.9	2.2	3.5
2006	91.604	97.393	80.063	84.327	85.452	82.573	77.406	83.963	84.126	84.997	3.1	2.8	2.4	3.2
2007	95.059	100.794	83.653	86.829	88.071	84.879	81.603	86.244	86.001	87.308	2.7	2.6	2.2	2.7
2008	99.387	110.783	87.213	89.472	90.999	87.023	85.692	87.871	87.688	89.787	1.9	3.0	2.0	2.8
2009	93.484	98.534	86.836	89.279	90.352	87.637	85.201	88.429	88.503	89.397	.7	–.3	.9	–.4
2010	97.378	104.107	89.149	91.394	92.273	90.094	87.642	89.496	89.785	90.734	1.2	1.8	1.4	1.5
2011	103.508	112.040	91.861	93.900	94.979	92.262	90.494	91.352	91.209	92.921	2.1	2.5	1.6	2.4
2012	104.298	112.359	93.460	94.783	95.990	92.927	92.579	93.071	92.897	94.548	1.9	1.9	1.9	1.8
2013	104.457	110.894	95.634	95.597	96.459	94.308	95.654	94.690	94.285	95.908	1.7	1.3	1.5	1.4
2014	104.515	110.067	97.578	97.215	97.850	96.287	97.804	96.358	95.697	97.408	1.7	1.4	1.5	1.6
2015	99.455	101.283	97.581	97.609	98.053	96.968	97.567	97.246	96.874	97.593	.9	.2	1.2	.2
2016	97.457	97.825	97.766	98.205	98.419	97.897	97.505	98.207	98.426	98.241	1.0	1.0	1.6	.7
2017	100.000	100.000	100.000	100.000	100.000	100.000	100.000	100.000	100.000	100.000	1.8	1.7	1.6	1.8
2018	103.325	102.662	103.619	102.775	102.642	102.968	104.126	102.297	101.897	102.222	2.3	2.0	1.9	2.2
2019	102.814	100.987	105.235	104.560	104.312	104.923	105.640	104.019	103.577	103.706	1.7	1.4	1.6	1.5
2020	100.247	98.870	107.516	105.599	105.458	105.806	108.689	105.428	104.942	105.046	1.3	1.1	1.3	1.3
2021	111.801	106.025	113.181	109.024	109.181	108.835	115.792	110.298	108.736	109.495	4.6	4.2	3.6	4.2
2022	122.767	113.623	121.153	115.108	116.038	113.924	124.970	118.123	114.437	116.915	7.1	6.5	5.2	6.8
2023 *p*	120.834	111.489	124.233	119.642	120.169	118.978	127.130	122.498	119.121	120.904	3.6	3.7	4.1	3.4
2020: I	102.016	100.097	106.818	105.088	105.104	105.067	107.871	105.050	104.575	104.670	1.8	1.3	1.7	1.8
II	97.129	96.850	106.688	105.113	104.826	105.516	107.643	104.715	104.376	104.375	–1.4	–1.7	–.8	–1.1
III	100.138	98.883	107.712	105.713	105.594	105.899	108.940	105.607	105.178	105.243	3.6	3.3	3.1	3.4
IV	101.704	99.648	108.845	106.481	106.308	106.742	110.302	106.339	105.640	105.896	2.8	2.0	1.8	2.5
2021: I	106.637	102.524	110.695	107.378	107.430	107.329	112.765	107.756	106.570	107.140	5.4	4.8	3.6	4.8
II	111.204	105.536	112.369	108.424	108.563	108.259	114.846	109.396	108.139	108.636	6.1	6.3	6.0	5.7
III	113.760	107.118	113.907	109.523	109.686	109.325	116.664	111.067	109.420	110.157	6.1	5.6	4.8	5.7
IV	115.602	108.923	115.753	110.771	111.046	110.425	118.892	112.972	110.814	112.047	7.0	6.8	5.2	7.0
2022: I	120.553	112.390	118.110	112.724	113.492	111.748	121.509	115.284	112.430	114.269	8.5	7.7	6.0	8.2
II	126.113	115.293	121.278	114.607	115.990	112.835	125.490	117.830	113.734	116.533	9.1	7.2	4.7	8.2
III	123.078	114.023	122.123	115.966	116.814	114.890	126.015	119.100	115.126	117.883	4.4	4.7	5.0	4.7
IV	121.326	112.788	123.099	117.135	117.855	116.225	126.868	120.278	116.457	118.973	3.9	4.1	4.7	3.8
2023: I	121.359	112.419	123.561	118.327	118.823	117.702	126.866	121.481	117.874	120.016	3.9	4.2	5.0	3.6
II	120.169	111.045	123.234	118.933	119.373	118.377	125.947	122.011	118.938	120.445	1.7	2.5	3.7	1.4
III	121.362	111.137	124.769	120.097	120.614	119.446	127.717	123.019	119.541	121.295	3.3	2.6	2.0	2.9
IV *p*	120.447	111.356	125.368	121.211	121.864	120.387	127.990	123.482	120.131	121.860	1.5	1.7	2.0	1.9

[1] Gross domestic product (GDP) less exports of goods and services plus imports of goods and services.
[2] Quarterly percent changes are at annual rates.

Source: Department of Commerce (Bureau of Economic Analysis).

TABLE B–6. Gross value added by sector, 1973–2023

[Billions of dollars; quarterly data at seasonally adjusted annual rates]

Year or quarter	Gross domestic product	Business[1] Total	Nonfarm[1]	Farm	Households and institutions Total	Households	Nonprofit institutions serving households[2]	General government[3] Total	Federal	State and local	Addendum: Gross housing value added
1973	1,425.4	1,094.0	1,047.2	46.8	124.6	78.5	46.1	206.8	96.4	110.4	101.4
1974	1,545.2	1,182.8	1,138.5	44.2	137.2	85.5	51.7	225.3	102.5	122.8	110.4
1975	1,684.9	1,284.8	1,239.2	45.6	151.6	93.7	58.0	248.4	110.5	138.0	121.3
1976	1,873.4	1,443.3	1,400.2	43.0	164.9	101.7	63.2	265.3	117.3	148.0	130.9
1977	2,081.8	1,616.2	1,572.7	43.5	179.9	110.7	69.2	285.7	125.2	160.6	144.2
1978	2,351.6	1,838.2	1,787.5	50.7	202.1	124.8	77.3	311.3	135.8	175.5	160.2
1979	2,627.3	2,062.8	2,002.7	60.1	226.3	139.5	86.9	338.2	145.4	192.8	177.7
1980	2,857.3	2,225.8	2,174.4	51.4	258.2	158.8	99.3	373.4	159.8	213.5	204.0
1981	3,207.0	2,502.0	2,437.0	65.0	291.6	179.2	112.4	413.5	178.3	235.2	231.6
1982	3,343.8	2,568.6	2,508.2	60.4	323.8	198.2	125.6	451.4	195.7	255.6	258.6
1983	3,634.0	2,801.9	2,757.0	44.9	352.5	213.6	138.9	479.7	207.1	272.6	280.6
1984	4,037.6	3,136.7	3,072.6	64.2	383.8	230.9	152.8	517.1	225.3	291.9	303.1
1985	4,339.0	3,369.6	3,305.9	63.7	411.8	248.2	163.6	557.5	240.0	317.6	333.8
1986	4,579.6	3,539.3	3,479.4	59.9	447.0	268.4	178.6	593.3	250.6	342.7	364.5
1987	4,855.2	3,735.2	3,673.2	62.0	489.5	289.8	199.7	630.4	261.0	369.4	392.1
1988	5,236.4	4,019.3	3,957.9	61.4	539.8	316.4	223.4	677.4	278.5	398.8	424.2
1989	5,641.6	4,326.7	4,252.8	73.9	586.0	341.4	244.6	728.8	292.8	436.1	452.7
1990	5,963.1	4,542.0	4,464.2	77.8	636.3	367.6	268.8	784.9	306.7	478.2	487.0
1991	6,158.1	4,645.0	4,574.7	70.4	677.3	386.6	290.7	835.8	323.5	512.2	515.3
1992	6,520.3	4,920.2	4,840.4	79.9	720.3	407.1	313.2	879.8	329.6	550.2	545.2
1993	6,858.6	5,177.4	5,106.2	71.3	772.8	437.6	335.1	908.3	331.5	576.9	578.4
1994	7,287.2	5,523.7	5,440.1	83.6	824.7	472.7	352.0	938.8	332.6	606.2	619.6
1995	7,639.7	5,795.1	5,726.7	68.4	877.8	506.9	370.9	966.9	333.0	633.9	662.6
1996	8,073.1	6,159.5	6,066.9	92.6	923.2	534.6	388.7	990.3	331.8	658.6	695.0
1997	8,577.6	6,578.8	6,490.6	88.1	975.9	565.7	410.2	1,022.9	333.5	689.3	731.9
1998	9,062.8	6,959.2	6,879.2	80.0	1,040.6	601.6	439.0	1,063.0	336.8	726.2	774.8
1999	9,631.2	7,401.8	7,330.2	71.7	1,111.2	644.0	467.2	1,118.1	345.0	773.1	825.1
2000	10,251.0	7,875.9	7,799.3	76.7	1,190.7	692.3	498.4	1,184.3	360.3	824.0	880.6
2001	10,581.9	8,057.7	7,978.6	79.0	1,271.7	748.9	522.8	1,252.6	370.3	882.3	947.7
2002	10,929.1	8,256.0	8,181.0	75.1	1,344.7	781.6	563.0	1,328.4	397.8	930.6	983.5
2003	11,456.5	8,642.9	8,550.4	92.4	1,408.8	814.1	594.6	1,404.8	434.7	970.1	1,014.8
2004	12,217.2	9,249.3	9,128.4	120.9	1,489.2	862.6	626.6	1,478.7	459.4	1,019.3	1,074.1
2005	13,039.2	9,911.0	9,804.7	106.3	1,572.6	922.3	650.5	1,555.4	488.4	1,067.0	1,149.7
2006	13,815.6	10,524.7	10,426.4	98.3	1,658.9	976.2	682.8	1,631.9	509.9	1,122.1	1,209.4
2007	14,474.2	10,997.8	10,880.0	117.9	1,749.5	1,035.9	713.6	1,726.9	535.7	1,191.2	1,279.3
2008	14,769.9	11,061.8	10,943.0	118.8	1,886.9	1,125.2	761.7	1,821.2	569.1	1,252.1	1,388.7
2009	14,478.1	10,659.6	10,557.1	102.5	1,934.9	1,136.8	798.2	1,883.5	603.0	1,280.5	1,415.5
2010	15,049.0	11,137.8	11,020.8	117.0	1,965.0	1,150.7	814.3	1,946.1	640.0	1,306.1	1,443.9
2011	15,599.7	11,614.9	11,463.7	151.1	2,012.0	1,164.0	848.0	1,972.9	659.8	1,313.1	1,471.0
2012	16,254.0	12,206.4	12,057.7	148.8	2,058.4	1,168.8	889.6	1,989.1	663.7	1,325.5	1,493.6
2013	16,880.7	12,723.8	12,539.3	184.5	2,117.2	1,203.0	914.2	2,039.7	658.6	1,381.1	1,534.5
2014	17,608.1	13,340.5	13,173.5	167.1	2,177.9	1,230.6	947.3	2,089.7	667.9	1,421.8	1,574.4
2015	18,295.0	13,900.9	13,754.7	146.3	2,251.0	1,260.3	990.6	2,143.1	674.6	1,468.5	1,618.6
2016	18,804.9	14,282.7	14,152.4	130.3	2,334.3	1,304.1	1,030.3	2,187.9	686.8	1,501.1	1,675.4
2017	19,612.1	14,941.9	14,803.1	138.7	2,423.2	1,359.3	1,063.9	2,247.0	702.1	1,544.9	1,734.0
2018	20,656.5	15,776.7	15,639.9	136.8	2,539.1	1,423.3	1,115.7	2,340.8	729.7	1,611.0	1,814.9
2019	21,521.4	16,450.1	16,329.6	120.5	2,655.9	1,484.4	1,171.5	2,415.4	753.4	1,662.0	1,900.4
2020	21,323.0	16,047.6	15,930.6	117.0	2,778.3	1,560.8	1,217.5	2,497.0	787.4	1,709.6	1,981.0
2021	23,594.0	18,088.8	17,907.8	180.9	2,916.0	1,643.8	1,272.2	2,589.3	823.0	1,766.3	2,089.9
2022	25,744.1	19,875.2	19,651.7	223.5	3,165.8	1,793.5	1,372.3	2,703.1	864.5	1,838.6	2,262.7
2023 [p]	27,356.4	21,048.6	20,844.0	204.7	3,446.9	1,975.9	1,470.9	2,860.9	915.1	1,945.8	2,487.3
2020: I	21,706.5	16,447.2	16,319.0	128.3	2,761.7	1,537.1	1,224.6	2,497.6	770.5	1,727.1	1,954.1
II	19,913.1	14,709.3	14,620.9	88.4	2,737.1	1,553.6	1,183.6	2,466.7	782.2	1,684.5	1,970.8
III	21,647.6	16,352.6	16,238.0	114.5	2,786.3	1,570.4	1,215.9	2,508.8	796.7	1,712.1	1,990.6
IV	22,024.5	16,681.2	16,544.5	136.7	2,828.2	1,582.2	1,246.0	2,515.1	800.4	1,714.8	2,008.6
2021: I	22,600.2	17,226.5	17,074.1	152.4	2,835.2	1,595.4	1,239.8	2,538.5	809.4	1,729.1	2,031.3
II	23,292.4	17,836.8	17,645.4	191.4	2,884.5	1,632.2	1,252.4	2,571.0	819.8	1,751.2	2,076.5
III	23,829.0	18,270.3	18,073.9	196.4	2,943.6	1,657.8	1,285.8	2,615.1	826.7	1,788.4	2,107.9
IV	24,654.6	19,021.5	18,838.0	183.5	3,000.6	1,689.7	1,311.0	2,632.4	835.9	1,796.5	2,144.1
2022: I	25,029.1	19,313.5	19,108.7	204.8	3,057.2	1,726.8	1,330.4	2,658.4	849.2	1,809.2	2,184.4
II	25,544.3	19,737.3	19,509.9	227.4	3,124.5	1,770.0	1,354.5	2,682.5	858.6	1,823.9	2,232.9
III	25,994.6	20,065.4	19,837.0	228.4	3,210.7	1,816.7	1,394.0	2,718.5	870.0	1,848.5	2,289.0
IV	26,408.4	20,384.7	20,151.2	233.5	3,270.6	1,860.3	1,410.3	2,753.1	880.4	1,872.7	2,344.4
2023: I	26,813.6	20,658.0	20,435.6	222.3	3,357.2	1,916.7	1,440.5	2,798.5	893.4	1,905.0	2,414.1
II	27,063.0	20,813.7	20,606.1	207.6	3,419.6	1,958.9	1,460.7	2,829.7	905.5	1,924.2	2,466.3
III	27,610.1	21,248.6	21,049.3	199.3	3,477.4	1,997.6	1,479.8	2,884.1	922.5	1,961.6	2,513.5
IV [p]	27,938.8	21,474.2	21,284.9	189.3	3,533.2	2,030.5	1,502.7	2,931.4	938.9	1,992.5	2,555.3

[1] Gross domestic business value added equals gross domestic product excluding gross value added of households and institutions and of general government. Nonfarm value added equals gross domestic business value added excluding gross farm value added.
[2] Equals compensation of employees of nonprofit institutions, the rental value of nonresidential fixed assets owned and used by nonprofit institutions serving households, and rental income of persons for tenant-occupied housing owned by nonprofit institutions.
[3] Equals compensation of general government employees plus general government consumption of fixed capital.

Source: Department of Commerce (Bureau of Economic Analysis).

TABLE B–7. Real gross value added by sector, 1973–2023

[Billions of chained (2017) dollars; quarterly data at seasonally adjusted annual rates]

Year or quarter	Gross domestic product	Business [1]			Households and institutions			General government [3]			Addendum: Gross housing value added
		Total	Nonfarm [1]	Farm	Total	Households	Nonprofit institutions serving households [2]	Total	Federal	State and local	
1973	6,106.4	4,093.6	4,072.1	36.6	839.7	494.6	341.5	1,373.1	511.0	848.3	643.1
1974	6,073.4	4,031.2	4,011.2	35.8	873.9	516.7	353.2	1,400.0	511.1	879.2	674.6
1975	6,060.9	3,992.9	3,945.4	42.6	904.3	531.5	369.0	1,421.0	509.4	905.9	696.2
1976	6,387.4	4,262.7	4,227.8	40.7	916.0	538.4	373.8	1,433.1	510.6	917.9	703.1
1977	6,682.8	4,506.8	4,470.2	42.9	923.2	538.3	381.6	1,448.1	512.7	932.2	713.2
1978	7,052.7	4,794.2	4,770.3	40.8	957.8	564.2	389.4	1,475.7	519.5	954.1	738.8
1979	7,276.0	4,964.5	4,932.3	44.5	984.4	575.7	404.9	1,492.2	520.6	971.5	753.1
1980	7,257.3	4,919.7	4,890.7	43.1	1,014.0	592.1	418.2	1,514.4	529.0	985.1	779.7
1981	7,441.5	5,063.2	5,002.0	57.1	1,033.5	598.6	431.7	1,525.1	537.9	984.9	795.0
1982	7,307.3	4,917.8	4,848.9	59.8	1,064.8	606.7	456.5	1,543.2	547.8	991.6	813.5
1983	7,642.3	5,178.5	5,150.1	41.0	1,108.7	630.4	476.9	1,556.5	561.6	987.7	845.0
1984	8,195.3	5,637.8	5,585.3	55.1	1,134.2	642.3	491.0	1,579.4	576.2	993.9	861.2
1985	8,537.0	5,900.7	5,831.8	65.0	1,153.9	656.9	495.5	1,627.1	594.6	1,022.5	896.8
1986	8,832.6	6,115.1	6,051.8	62.5	1,190.0	670.0	519.6	1,670.9	608.9	1,052.3	921.2
1987	9,137.7	6,334.2	6,271.3	63.1	1,234.6	687.0	548.5	1,712.2	628.1	1,073.2	942.6
1988	9,519.4	6,605.5	6,556.6	56.3	1,298.0	715.5	584.6	1,760.2	640.2	1,110.0	973.7
1989	9,869.0	6,858.3	6,796.9	64.4	1,350.7	737.7	616.2	1,803.3	650.0	1,144.2	994.1
1990	10,055.1	6,968.2	6,899.1	69.1	1,394.0	752.0	646.9	1,848.3	661.3	1,178.4	1,014.0
1991	10,044.2	6,925.7	6,856.1	69.3	1,422.6	763.6	664.6	1,867.1	665.0	1,193.9	1,034.7
1992	10,398.0	7,218.9	7,134.5	80.2	1,458.6	780.9	683.8	1,875.1	654.2	1,214.3	1,059.9
1993	10,684.2	7,424.8	7,354.4	71.2	1,533.7	818.8	721.6	1,879.6	643.3	1,231.0	1,097.9
1994	11,114.6	7,782.8	7,693.2	85.9	1,585.5	860.3	730.1	1,881.4	625.5	1,252.5	1,144.8
1995	11,413.0	8,022.0	7,957.5	68.4	1,632.7	890.1	747.0	1,884.2	605.5	1,277.3	1,185.6
1996	11,843.6	8,394.4	8,315.0	79.5	1,665.2	908.3	761.4	1,887.8	591.1	1,297.1	1,206.1
1997	12,370.3	8,835.1	8,744.4	88.6	1,716.4	934.1	787.4	1,902.2	581.4	1,322.7	1,235.1
1998	12,924.9	9,321.2	9,234.3	86.7	1,738.7	958.3	783.9	1,923.0	575.1	1,350.9	1,264.0
1999	13,543.8	9,859.2	9,771.4	88.2	1,779.1	989.0	792.6	1,939.8	570.4	1,373.2	1,299.7
2000	14,096.0	10,301.6	10,198.8	103.0	1,847.6	1,032.8	816.8	1,971.2	573.4	1,402.2	1,344.3
2001	14,230.7	10,363.5	10,266.6	97.2	1,893.5	1,070.7	823.7	2,005.7	575.0	1,435.6	1,386.9
2002	14,472.7	10,540.7	10,439.8	101.1	1,920.8	1,076.3	846.3	2,043.9	585.2	1,463.8	1,385.5
2003	14,877.3	10,873.0	10,763.5	109.7	1,961.9	1,107.7	855.5	2,069.7	601.0	1,473.2	1,409.2
2004	15,449.8	11,350.4	11,228.2	121.5	2,034.1	1,148.5	887.0	2,084.2	609.7	1,478.6	1,459.1
2005	15,988.0	11,796.2	11,667.5	127.9	2,101.3	1,202.8	898.9	2,103.0	617.5	1,489.3	1,528.8
2006	16,433.1	12,182.9	12,056.6	125.1	2,135.6	1,234.6	900.8	2,120.3	622.2	1,502.0	1,558.9
2007	16,762.4	12,441.8	12,330.8	110.3	2,174.4	1,264.1	909.8	2,150.3	630.8	1,523.5	1,589.1
2008	16,781.5	12,332.0	12,221.0	110.1	2,269.8	1,333.7	935.0	2,194.9	654.2	1,543.9	1,672.1
2009	16,349.1	11,882.3	11,754.4	126.8	2,256.0	1,307.7	947.8	2,234.8	686.9	1,549.8	1,655.4
2010	16,789.8	12,264.0	12,139.2	123.3	2,301.5	1,335.3	965.6	2,245.5	710.0	1,536.1	1,700.6
2011	17,052.4	12,507.6	12,389.8	118.0	2,328.3	1,335.3	992.8	2,235.3	716.7	1,518.6	1,710.8
2012	17,442.8	12,911.8	12,803.2	112.4	2,327.9	1,315.4	1,012.5	2,215.2	716.1	1,498.8	1,702.4
2013	17,812.2	13,267.3	13,139.5	126.5	2,351.5	1,330.7	1,020.8	2,201.6	704.6	1,497.0	1,715.7
2014	18,261.7	13,709.7	13,586.7	124.5	2,356.9	1,333.2	1,023.8	2,198.7	699.9	1,498.8	1,719.5
2015	18,799.6	14,222.0	14,087.6	134.8	2,371.9	1,330.9	1,041.0	2,206.4	695.9	1,510.4	1,718.4
2016	19,141.7	14,515.7	14,372.3	143.9	2,397.3	1,341.3	1,056.0	2,228.8	700.1	1,528.7	1,727.4
2017	19,612.1	14,941.9	14,803.1	138.7	2,423.2	1,359.3	1,063.9	2,247.0	702.1	1,544.9	1,734.0
2018	20,193.9	15,456.6	15,312.5	144.1	2,472.1	1,379.5	1,092.6	2,265.6	706.9	1,558.7	1,756.9
2019	20,692.1	15,896.1	15,764.5	130.0	2,504.6	1,393.0	1,111.7	2,292.7	715.3	1,577.4	1,776.6
2020	20,234.1	15,455.1	15,323.9	130.2	2,506.8	1,422.4	1,084.6	2,269.6	735.9	1,534.3	1,799.6
2021	21,407.7	16,574.7	16,432.7	141.1	2,561.6	1,468.1	1,094.2	2,279.7	744.8	1,535.7	1,861.4
2022	21,822.0	16,894.7	16,770.0	128.6	2,629.3	1,519.5	1,111.0	2,306.3	743.5	1,563.3	1,907.5
2023 ᵖ	22,375.3	17,336.2	17,202.0	136.0	2,692.8	1,554.8	1,139.2	2,355.0	753.5	1,602.0	1,944.8
2020: I	20,665.6	15,817.8	15,685.3	131.2	2,537.0	1,411.0	1,125.9	2,309.3	726.8	1,582.4	1,787.7
II	19,034.8	14,318.0	14,199.5	117.0	2,460.7	1,417.9	1,043.5	2,240.0	733.8	1,507.1	1,792.7
III	20,511.8	15,737.5	15,602.3	134.6	2,504.1	1,426.5	1,077.9	2,272.9	742.9	1,530.7	1,802.7
IV	20,724.1	15,947.3	15,808.5	138.1	2,525.3	1,434.2	1,091.2	2,256.4	740.3	1,516.9	1,815.2
2021: I	20,990.5	16,206.9	16,061.2	144.3	2,531.2	1,441.4	1,090.2	2,259.6	742.8	1,517.7	1,829.9
II	21,309.5	16,489.6	16,346.9	141.4	2,558.1	1,465.5	1,093.3	2,270.1	745.4	1,525.7	1,859.7
III	21,483.1	16,623.9	16,484.4	138.8	2,571.8	1,477.5	1,095.1	2,295.1	745.3	1,550.4	1,873.5
IV	21,847.6	16,978.5	16,838.6	139.7	2,585.1	1,487.9	1,098.2	2,294.0	745.8	1,548.9	1,882.4
2022: I	21,738.9	16,848.4	16,717.1	132.8	2,601.6	1,501.2	1,101.5	2,297.5	744.2	1,553.9	1,892.4
II	21,708.2	16,794.5	16,670.3	127.9	2,622.9	1,516.5	1,107.7	2,298.8	741.6	1,557.8	1,904.5
III	21,851.1	16,907.8	16,787.1	126.1	2,641.5	1,527.7	1,115.0	2,309.8	743.3	1,567.1	1,914.4
IV	21,990.0	17,028.0	16,905.3	127.7	2,651.1	1,532.6	1,119.8	2,319.0	744.9	1,574.6	1,918.8
2023: I	22,112.3	17,116.3	16,980.8	136.9	2,669.0	1,540.8	1,129.4	2,335.0	747.5	1,588.0	1,928.1
II	22,225.4	17,200.5	17,063.6	138.1	2,686.7	1,552.1	1,135.8	2,346.1	751.0	1,595.6	1,941.9
III	22,490.7	17,437.7	17,303.9	135.9	2,700.2	1,560.8	1,140.7	2,361.8	755.7	1,606.6	1,951.7
IVᵖ	22,672.9	17,590.2	17,459.9	133.2	2,715.1	1,565.7	1,150.7	2,377.1	759.9	1,617.7	1,957.5

[1] Gross domestic business value added equals gross domestic product excluding gross value added of households and institutions and of general government. Nonfarm value added equals gross domestic business value added excluding gross farm value added.
[2] Equals compensation of employees of nonprofit institutions, the rental value of nonresidential fixed assets owned and used by nonprofit institutions serving households, and rental income of persons for tenant-occupied housing owned by nonprofit institutions.
[3] Equals compensation of general government employees plus general government consumption of fixed capital.

Source: Department of Commerce (Bureau of Economic Analysis).

TABLE B–8. Gross domestic product (GDP) by industry, value added, in current dollars and as a percentage of GDP, 2017–2023

[Billions of dollars; except as noted]

Year	Gross domestic product	Total private industries	Private industries								
			Agriculture, forestry, fishing, and hunting	Mining	Construction	Manufacturing			Utilities	Wholesale trade	Retail trade
						Total manufacturing	Durable goods	Nondurable goods			
						Value added					
2017	19,612.1	17,156.3	176.8	267.3	840.2	2,109.7	1,178.3	931.4	313.7	1,176.1	1,178.9
2018	20,656.5	18,097.8	177.1	313.5	889.1	2,261.8	1,232.5	1,029.3	320.4	1,222.1	1,223.6
2019	21,521.4	18,889.1	162.0	293.9	952.8	2,267.7	1,262.2	1,005.5	331.2	1,295.9	1,277.3
2020	21,323.0	18,612.2	160.8	201.6	951.8	2,148.1	1,199.7	948.5	344.8	1,299.9	1,335.6
2021	23,594.0	20,784.8	225.7	332.0	1,014.3	2,366.5	1,270.3	1,096.2	386.7	1,415.6	1,534.9
2022	25,744.1	22,807.5	270.8	457.4	1,090.1	2,649.7	1,406.9	1,242.8	438.2	1,546.8	1,621.0
2020: I	21,706.5	18,978.7	172.3	241.1	962.7	2,215.7	1,238.3	977.4	327.7	1,321.4	1,289.1
II	19,913.1	17,244.5	128.5	146.5	910.5	1,972.4	1,081.6	890.8	339.9	1,188.2	1,232.7
III	21,647.6	18,935.3	159.0	195.0	959.2	2,190.4	1,235.1	955.3	356.3	1,343.8	1,427.8
IV	22,024.5	19,290.4	183.3	223.6	974.8	2,214.1	1,243.7	970.4	355.2	1,346.3	1,392.8
2021: I	22,600.2	19,844.5	196.8	278.9	997.3	2,265.4	1,247.9	1,017.5	382.7	1,368.7	1,481.1
II	23,292.4	20,503.0	234.6	309.1	1,006.9	2,320.7	1,260.0	1,060.7	371.5	1,404.0	1,549.3
III	23,829.0	20,992.3	241.1	340.7	1,011.7	2,369.1	1,253.4	1,115.7	387.1	1,424.0	1,522.2
IV	24,654.6	21,799.6	230.2	399.4	1,041.4	2,510.7	1,319.7	1,190.9	405.6	1,465.8	1,587.1
2022: I	25,029.1	22,141.8	251.8	419.5	1,062.8	2,564.8	1,356.7	1,208.2	392.3	1,519.3	1,577.4
II	25,544.3	22,630.1	273.2	504.0	1,066.2	2,635.3	1,385.1	1,250.2	451.3	1,537.9	1,600.9
III	25,994.6	23,041.1	276.0	484.4	1,093.1	2,658.5	1,422.2	1,236.3	462.0	1,554.4	1,629.6
IV	26,408.4	23,417.0	282.2	421.9	1,138.4	2,740.1	1,463.5	1,276.7	447.2	1,575.7	1,676.2
2023: I	26,813.6	23,772.8	271.1	382.5	1,161.2	2,729.0	1,470.9	1,258.1	442.2	1,592.9	1,704.5
II	27,063.0	23,988.8	256.4	357.7	1,180.7	2,750.8	1,513.7	1,237.1	437.7	1,596.6	1,715.1
III	27,610.1	24,477.4	247.4	389.4	1,219.7	2,853.1	1,547.1	1,306.0	437.6	1,624.4	1,759.2
	Percent		Industry value added as a percentage of GDP (percent)								
2017	100.0	87.5	0.9	1.4	4.3	10.8	6.0	4.7	1.6	6.0	6.0
2018	100.0	87.6	.9	1.5	4.3	10.9	6.0	5.0	1.6	5.9	5.9
2019	100.0	87.8	.8	1.4	4.4	10.5	5.9	4.7	1.5	6.0	5.9
2020	100.0	87.3	.8	.9	4.5	10.1	5.6	4.4	1.6	6.1	6.3
2021	100.0	88.1	1.0	1.4	4.3	10.0	5.4	4.6	1.6	6.0	6.5
2022	100.0	88.6	1.1	1.8	4.2	10.3	5.5	4.8	1.7	6.0	6.3
2020: I	100.0	87.4	.8	1.1	4.4	10.2	5.7	4.5	1.5	6.1	5.9
II	100.0	86.6	.6	.7	4.6	9.9	5.4	4.5	1.7	6.0	6.2
III	100.0	87.5	.7	.9	4.4	10.1	5.7	4.4	1.6	6.2	6.6
IV	100.0	87.6	.8	1.0	4.4	10.1	5.6	4.4	1.6	6.1	6.3
2021: I	100.0	87.8	.9	1.2	4.4	10.0	5.5	4.5	1.7	6.1	6.6
II	100.0	88.0	1.0	1.3	4.3	10.0	5.4	4.6	1.6	6.0	6.7
III	100.0	88.1	1.0	1.4	4.2	9.9	5.3	4.7	1.6	6.0	6.4
IV	100.0	88.4	.9	1.6	4.2	10.2	5.4	4.8	1.6	5.9	6.4
2022: I	100.0	88.5	1.0	1.7	4.2	10.2	5.4	4.8	1.6	6.1	6.3
II	100.0	88.6	1.1	2.0	4.2	10.3	5.4	4.9	1.8	6.0	6.3
III	100.0	88.6	1.1	1.9	4.2	10.2	5.5	4.8	1.8	6.0	6.3
IV	100.0	88.7	1.1	1.6	4.3	10.4	5.5	4.8	1.7	6.0	6.3
2023: I	100.0	88.7	1.0	1.4	4.3	10.2	5.5	4.7	1.6	5.9	6.4
II	100.0	88.6	.9	1.3	4.4	10.2	5.6	4.6	1.6	5.9	6.3
III	100.0	88.7	.9	1.4	4.4	10.3	5.6	4.7	1.6	5.9	6.4

[1] Consists of agriculture, forestry, fishing, and hunting; mining; construction; and manufacturing.
[2] Consists of utilities; wholesale trade; retail trade; transportation and warehousing; information; finance, insurance, real estate, rental, and leasing; professional and business services; educational services, health care, and social assistance; arts, entertainment, recreation, accommodation, and food services; and other services, except government.

Note: Data shown in shown in Tables B–8 and B–9 are consistent with the 2023 annual revision of the industry accounts released in September 2023. For details see *Survey of Current Business*, November 2023. Data for earlier years will be released in 2024.

See next page for continuation of table.

TABLE B–8. Gross domestic product (GDP) by industry, value added, in current dollars and as a percentage of GDP, 2017–2023—*Continued*

[Billions of dollars; except as noted]

Year	Transportation and warehousing	Information	Finance, insurance, real estate, rental, and leasing	Professional and business services	Educational services, health care, and social assistance	Arts, entertainment, recreation, accommodation, and food services	Other services, except government	Government	Private goods-producing industries [1]	Private services-producing industries [2]
						Private industries—Continued				
					Value added					
2017	635.5	1,010.0	4,033.0	2,433.6	1,716.9	831.2	433.2	2,455.8	3,394.1	13,762.2
2018	677.3	1,041.5	4,258.2	2,589.1	1,792.0	874.6	457.7	2,558.8	3,641.5	14,456.3
2019	708.5	1,141.5	4,446.5	2,727.9	1,883.8	922.2	477.7	2,632.3	3,676.4	15,212.7
2020	637.4	1,177.7	4,606.5	2,725.8	1,875.2	694.2	452.9	2,710.7	3,462.3	15,149.9
2021	776.2	1,318.7	4,972.4	3,030.6	2,019.3	904.2	487.8	2,809.2	3,938.4	16,846.4
2022	920.5	1,392.8	5,329.9	3,314.3	2,149.8	1,081.6	544.4	2,936.6	4,468.1	18,339.4
2020: I	708.6	1,160.1	4,544.2	2,766.0	1,917.2	871.0	481.5	2,727.8	3,591.8	15,386.9
II	566.9	1,130.9	4,498.1	2,574.3	1,678.1	481.3	396.1	2,668.7	3,158.0	14,086.5
III	625.7	1,194.8	4,640.6	2,737.5	1,937.6	701.3	466.3	2,712.3	3,503.6	15,431.7
IV	648.6	1,224.9	4,743.1	2,825.3	1,968.0	723.2	467.5	2,734.1	3,595.8	15,694.7
2021: I	698.3	1,259.5	4,798.9	2,909.1	1,977.0	767.5	463.5	2,755.7	3,738.4	16,106.1
II	751.6	1,306.8	4,916.1	2,975.5	1,994.8	880.2	482.0	2,789.4	3,871.2	16,631.7
III	801.3	1,331.6	5,011.4	3,064.6	2,029.7	960.3	497.6	2,836.7	3,962.6	17,029.7
IV	853.8	1,377.2	5,163.3	3,173.0	2,075.6	1,008.6	508.0	2,855.0	4,181.6	17,617.9
2022: I	880.5	1,365.1	5,239.1	3,242.0	2,096.9	1,010.1	520.1	2,887.3	4,299.1	17,842.7
II	910.6	1,376.7	5,291.6	3,275.5	2,114.8	1,061.3	530.7	2,914.2	4,478.7	18,151.4
III	940.4	1,400.7	5,361.6	3,346.9	2,171.4	1,109.8	552.5	2,953.5	4,511.9	18,529.1
IV	950.6	1,428.6	5,427.2	3,393.0	2,216.1	1,145.3	574.5	2,991.4	4,582.6	18,834.4
2023: I	967.6	1,440.2	5,537.9	3,462.5	2,290.5	1,205.9	585.0	3,040.8	4,543.8	19,229.1
II	976.7	1,456.6	5,588.6	3,526.5	2,330.7	1,222.0	592.7	3,074.2	4,545.6	19,443.3
III	962.7	1,496.5	5,711.1	3,570.2	2,368.7	1,238.2	599.3	3,132.7	4,709.6	19,767.8
					Industry value added as a percentage of GDP (percent)					
2017	3.2	5.1	20.6	12.4	8.8	4.2	2.2	12.5	17.3	70.2
2018	3.3	5.0	20.6	12.5	8.7	4.2	2.2	12.4	17.6	70.0
2019	3.3	5.3	20.7	12.7	8.8	4.3	2.2	12.2	17.1	70.7
2020	3.0	5.5	21.6	12.8	8.8	3.3	2.1	12.7	16.2	71.0
2021	3.3	5.6	21.1	12.8	8.6	3.8	2.1	11.9	16.7	71.4
2022	3.6	5.4	20.7	12.9	8.4	4.2	2.1	11.4	17.4	71.2
2020: I	3.3	5.3	20.9	12.7	8.8	4.0	2.2	12.6	16.5	70.9
II	2.8	5.7	22.6	12.9	8.4	2.4	2.0	13.4	15.9	70.7
III	2.9	5.5	21.4	12.6	9.0	3.2	2.2	12.5	16.2	71.3
IV	2.9	5.6	21.5	12.8	8.9	3.3	2.1	12.4	16.3	71.3
2021: I	3.1	5.6	21.2	12.9	8.7	3.4	2.1	12.2	16.5	71.3
II	3.2	5.6	21.1	12.8	8.6	3.8	2.1	12.0	16.6	71.4
III	3.4	5.6	21.0	12.9	8.5	4.0	2.1	11.9	16.6	71.5
IV	3.5	5.6	20.9	12.9	8.4	4.1	2.1	11.6	17.0	71.5
2022: I	3.5	5.5	20.9	13.0	8.4	4.0	2.1	11.5	17.2	71.3
II	3.6	5.4	20.7	12.8	8.3	4.2	2.1	11.4	17.5	71.1
III	3.6	5.4	20.6	12.9	8.4	4.3	2.1	11.4	17.4	71.3
IV	3.6	5.4	20.6	12.8	8.4	4.3	2.2	11.3	17.4	71.3
2023: I	3.6	5.4	20.7	12.9	8.5	4.5	2.2	11.3	16.9	71.7
II	3.6	5.4	20.7	13.0	8.6	4.5	2.2	11.4	16.8	71.8
III	3.5	5.4	20.7	12.9	8.6	4.5	2.2	11.3	17.1	71.6

Note (cont'd): Value added is the contribution of each private industry and of government to GDP. Value added is equal to an industry's gross output minus its intermediate inputs. Current-dollar value added is calculated as the sum of distributions by an industry to its labor and capital, which are derived from the components of gross domestic income.

Value added industry data shown in Tables B–8 and B–9 are based on the 2017 North American Industry Classification System (NAICS).

Source: Department of Commerce (Bureau of Economic Analysis).

National Income or Expenditure | 421

TABLE B–9. Real gross domestic product by industry, value added, and percent changes, 2017–2023

Year	Gross domestic product	Total private industries	Agriculture, forestry, fishing, and hunting	Mining	Construction	Manufacturing			Utilities	Wholesale trade	Retail trade
						Total manufacturing	Durable goods	Non-durable goods			
				Chain-type quantity indexes for value added (2017=100)							
2017	100.000	100.000	100.000	100.000	100.000	100.000	100.000	100.000	100.000	100.000	100.000
2018	102.967	103.238	104.108	103.633	102.801	104.897	104.189	105.774	98.584	100.829	103.490
2019	105.507	106.059	96.782	117.696	104.978	105.385	105.355	105.423	99.748	101.300	106.306
2020	103.171	103.530	98.201	114.323	101.936	100.822	99.444	102.602	105.937	102.041	104.759
2021	109.156	110.219	103.903	100.814	105.699	106.557	106.046	107.322	100.922	101.418	105.281
2022	111.268	112.397	96.165	91.765	98.518	107.965	110.074	105.793	101.492	97.507	100.283
2020: I	105.371	105.727	98.851	121.961	103.170	103.001	102.881	103.114	104.142	103.737	105.201
II	97.057	96.779	88.888	113.727	97.103	92.551	89.329	96.742	105.378	95.431	98.341
III	104.587	105.197	101.101	112.018	102.884	103.218	102.074	104.675	108.021	104.780	108.981
IV	105.670	106.417	103.965	109.586	104.589	104.520	103.492	105.878	106.207	104.218	106.513
2021: I	107.029	107.955	105.952	107.578	106.163	105.041	104.781	105.488	99.100	103.372	111.335
II	108.655	109.727	103.685	101.234	108.064	105.757	105.656	106.052	100.426	102.735	105.850
III	109.540	110.533	102.511	99.126	105.708	105.708	104.932	106.886	101.931	99.493	101.284
IV	111.399	112.664	103.462	95.317	102.861	109.683	108.814	110.862	102.233	100.073	102.656
2022: I	110.844	111.969	98.964	89.840	103.714	109.065	109.314	108.943	99.315	98.730	97.952
II	110.688	111.741	95.267	85.885	99.212	107.232	109.908	104.449	103.354	96.459	98.384
III	111.417	112.558	94.458	91.422	95.583	107.450	110.027	104.756	99.476	97.246	100.785
IV	112.125	113.320	95.971	99.915	95.563	108.113	111.048	105.023	103.824	97.592	104.011
2023: I	112.748	113.983	102.048	102.758	96.332	105.565	109.726	101.145	103.019	97.018	106.870
II	113.325	114.607	102.954	109.533	97.630	107.234	111.435	102.772	116.033	95.721	106.119
III	114.677	116.079	101.389	112.715	101.272	109.630	112.531	106.637	107.194	95.120	111.841
				Percent change from year earlier; quarterly changes at seasonally adjusted annual rates							
2018	3.0	3.2	4.1	3.6	2.8	4.9	4.2	5.8	−1.4	0.8	3.5
2019	2.5	2.7	−7.0	13.6	2.1	.5	1.1	−.3	1.2	.5	2.7
2020	−2.2	−2.4	1.5	−2.9	−2.9	−4.3	−5.6	−2.7	6.2	.7	−1.5
2021	5.8	6.5	5.8	−11.8	3.7	5.7	6.6	4.6	−4.7	−.6	.5
2022	1.9	2.0	−7.4	−9.0	−6.8	1.3	3.8	−1.4	.6	−3.9	−4.7
2020: I	−5.3	−6.0	9.4	15.6	−6.7	−9.7	−8.6	−11.2	−7.3	5.9	−8.5
II	−28.0	−29.8	−34.6	−24.4	−21.5	−34.8	−43.2	−22.5	4.8	−28.4	−23.6
III	34.8	39.6	67.4	−5.9	26.0	54.7	70.5	37.1	10.4	45.3	50.8
IV	4.2	4.7	11.8	−8.4	6.8	5.1	5.7	4.7	−6.5	−2.1	−8.8
2021: I	5.2	5.9	7.9	−7.1	6.2	2.0	5.1	−1.5	−24.2	−3.2	19.4
II	6.2	6.7	−8.3	−21.6	7.4	2.8	3.4	2.2	5.5	−2.4	−18.3
III	3.3	3.0	−4.5	−8.1	−8.4	.0	−2.7	3.2	6.1	−12.0	−16.2
IV	7.0	7.9	3.8	−14.5	−10.3	15.7	15.6	15.7	1.2	2.4	5.5
2022: I	−2.0	−2.4	−16.3	−21.1	3.4	−2.2	1.9	−6.7	−10.9	−5.3	−17.1
II	−.6	−.8	−14.1	−16.5	−16.3	−6.6	2.2	−15.5	17.3	−8.9	1.8
III	2.7	3.0	−3.4	28.4	−13.8	.8	.4	1.2	−14.2	3.3	10.1
IV	2.6	2.7	6.6	42.7	−.1	2.5	3.8	1.0	18.7	1.4	13.4
2023: I	2.2	2.4	27.8	11.9	3.3	−9.1	−4.7	−14.0	−3.1	−2.3	11.5
II	2.1	2.2	3.6	29.1	5.5	6.5	6.4	6.6	60.9	−5.2	−2.8
III	4.9	5.2	−5.9	12.1	15.8	9.2	9.2	4.0	15.9	−27.2	23.4

¹ Consists of agriculture, forestry, fishing, and hunting; mining; construction; and manufacturing.
² Consists of utilities; wholesale trade; retail trade; transportation and warehousing; information; finance, insurance, real estate, rental, and leasing; professional and business services; educational services; health care, and social assistance; arts, entertainment, recreation, accommodation, and food services; and other services, except government.

See next page for continuation of table.

TABLE B–9. Real gross domestic product by industry, value added, and percent changes, 2017–2023—*Continued*

Year	Private industries—Continued								Government	Private goods-producing industries [1]	Private services-producing industries [2]
	Transportation and warehousing	Information	Finance, insurance, real estate, rental, and leasing	Professional and business services	Educational services, health care, and social assistance	Arts, entertainment, recreation, accommodation, and food services	Other services, except government				
	Chain-type quantity indexes for value added (2017=100)										
2017	100.000	100.000	100.000	100.000	100.000	100.000	100.000	100.000	100.000	100.000	
2018	103.487	105.547	101.493	106.203	102.806	101.915	103.209	101.110	104.232	102.991
2019	103.640	116.516	103.512	111.370	106.047	104.086	103.659	101.762	105.851	106.107
2020	95.067	120.902	104.578	110.728	102.947	76.533	93.998	100.356	102.044	103.883
2021	107.887	138.662	110.326	123.294	107.877	96.004	97.166	101.193	106.006	111.223
2022	110.040	149.058	112.816	132.503	112.014	106.369	100.245	102.842	103.622	114.566
2020: I	103.686	117.862	103.500	112.607	106.215	96.381	101.202	102.741	104.212	106.087
II	84.533	116.503	102.651	104.691	92.320	53.287	82.470	98.532	95.031	97.192
III	95.098	123.601	105.199	111.245	105.967	77.530	96.473	100.044	103.846	105.519
IV	96.951	125.641	106.964	114.368	107.288	78.932	95.847	100.107	105.087	106.733
2021: I	104.058	130.233	107.796	117.718	106.083	83.885	93.590	100.115	105.821	108.459
II	106.615	136.943	109.524	121.308	107.153	95.743	97.063	100.679	106.185	110.566
III	109.413	140.722	110.765	125.159	108.327	101.187	98.895	101.981	105.370	111.765
IV	111.461	146.750	113.219	128.993	109.944	103.201	99.114	101.999	106.649	114.104
2022: I	109.287	145.890	113.368	130.262	110.579	101.932	99.377	102.453	105.562	113.508
II	109.150	147.130	113.198	131.335	111.155	106.652	99.896	102.790	102.628	113.998
III	110.744	150.183	112.852	133.506	112.839	108.882	100.811	102.884	102.466	115.081
IV	110.981	153.027	111.847	134.908	113.482	108.011	100.896	103.243	103.831	115.676
2023: I	112.599	154.669	111.931	135.306	116.463	111.192	100.258	103.596	103.201	116.685
II	114.716	155.531	111.895	136.015	116.880	109.882	98.762	103.854	105.135	116.963
III	115.844	160.923	113.009	136.999	117.793	109.752	97.446	104.379	107.727	118.142
	Percent change from year earlier; quarterly changes at seasonally adjusted annual rates										
2018	3.5	5.5	1.5	6.2	2.8	1.9	3.2	1.1	4.2	3.0
2019	.1	10.4	2.0	4.9	3.2	2.1	.4	.6	1.6	3.0
2020	-8.3	3.8	1.0	-.6	-2.9	-26.5	-9.3	-1.4	-3.6	-2.1
2021	13.5	14.7	5.5	11.3	4.8	25.4	3.4	.8	3.9	7.1
2022	2.0	7.5	2.3	7.5	3.8	10.8	3.2	1.6	-2.2	3.0
2020: I	-2.5	-6.1	-6.6	-.5	-3.1	-30.4	-14.3	-.5	-6.6	-5.9
II	-55.8	-4.5	-3.2	-25.3	-42.9	-90.7	-55.9	-15.4	-30.9	-29.6
III	60.2	26.7	10.3	27.5	73.6	348.1	87.3	6.3	42.6	38.9
IV	8.0	6.8	6.9	11.7	5.1	7.4	-2.6	.3	4.9	4.7
2021: I	32.7	15.4	3.1	12.2	-4.4	27.6	-9.1	.0	2.8	6.6
II	10.2	22.3	6.6	12.8	4.1	69.7	15.7	2.3	1.4	8.0
III	10.9	11.5	4.6	13.3	4.5	24.8	7.8	5.3	-3.0	4.4
IV	7.7	18.3	9.2	12.8	6.1	8.2	.9	.1	4.9	8.6
2022: I	-7.6	-2.3	.5	4.0	2.3	-4.8	1.1	1.8	-4.0	-2.1
II	-.5	3.4	-.6	3.3	2.1	19.8	2.1	1.3	-10.7	1.7
III	6.0	8.6	-1.2	6.8	6.2	8.6	3.7	.4	-.6	3.9
IV	.9	7.8	-3.5	4.3	2.3	-3.2	.3	1.4	5.4	2.1
2023: I	6.0	4.4	.3	1.2	10.9	12.3	-2.5	1.4	-2.4	3.5
II	7.7	2.2	-.1	2.1	1.4	-4.6	-5.8	1.0	7.7	1.0
III	4.0	14.6	4.0	2.9	3.2	-.5	-5.2	2.0	10.2	4.1

Note: Data are based on the 2017 North American Industry Classification System (NAICS).
See Note, Table B–8.
Source: Department of Commerce (Bureau of Economic Analysis).

TABLE B–10. Personal consumption expenditures, 1973–2023

[Billions of dollars; quarterly data at seasonally adjusted annual rates]

Year or quarter	Personal consumption expenditures	Goods						Services					Addendum: Personal consumption expenditures excluding food and energy [2]
		Total	Durable		Nondurable			Total	Household consumption expenditures				
			Total [1]	Motor vehicles and parts	Total [1]	Food and beverages purchased for off-premises consumption	Gasoline and other energy goods		Total [1]	Housing and utilities	Health care	Financial services and insurance	
1973	849.6	416.6	130.5	54.4	286.1	126.7	34.3	432.9	419.2	143.5	67.2	39.9	668.5
1974	930.2	451.5	130.2	48.2	321.4	143.0	43.8	478.6	463.1	158.6	76.1	44.1	719.7
1975	1,030.5	491.3	142.2	52.6	349.2	156.6	48.0	539.2	522.2	176.5	89.0	51.8	797.3
1976	1,147.7	546.3	168.6	68.2	377.7	167.3	53.0	601.4	582.4	194.7	101.8	56.8	894.7
1977	1,274.0	600.4	192.0	79.8	408.4	179.8	57.8	673.6	653.0	217.8	115.7	65.1	998.6
1978	1,422.3	663.6	213.3	89.2	450.2	196.1	61.5	758.7	735.7	244.3	131.2	76.7	1,122.4
1979	1,585.4	737.9	226.3	90.2	511.6	218.4	80.4	847.5	821.4	273.4	148.8	83.6	1,239.7
1980	1,750.7	799.8	226.4	84.4	573.4	239.2	101.9	950.9	920.8	312.5	171.7	91.7	1,353.1
1981	1,934.0	869.4	243.9	93.0	625.4	255.3	113.4	1,064.6	1,030.4	352.1	201.9	98.5	1,501.5
1982	2,071.3	899.3	253.0	100.0	646.3	267.1	108.4	1,172.0	1,134.0	387.5	225.2	113.7	1,622.9
1983	2,281.6	973.8	295.0	122.9	678.8	277.0	106.5	1,307.8	1,267.1	421.2	253.1	141.0	1,817.2
1984	2,492.3	1,063.7	342.2	147.2	721.5	291.1	108.2	1,428.6	1,383.3	457.5	276.5	150.8	2,008.1
1985	2,712.8	1,137.6	380.4	170.1	757.2	303.0	110.5	1,575.2	1,527.3	500.6	302.2	178.2	2,210.3
1986	2,886.3	1,195.6	421.4	187.5	774.2	316.4	91.2	1,690.7	1,638.0	537.0	330.2	187.7	2,391.3
1987	3,076.3	1,256.3	442.0	188.2	814.3	324.3	96.4	1,820.0	1,764.3	571.6	366.0	189.5	2,566.6
1988	3,330.0	1,337.3	475.1	202.2	862.3	342.8	99.9	1,992.7	1,929.4	614.4	410.1	202.9	2,793.1
1989	3,576.8	1,423.8	494.3	207.8	929.5	365.4	110.4	2,153.0	2,084.9	655.2	451.2	222.3	3,002.1
1990	3,809.0	1,491.3	497.1	205.1	994.2	391.2	124.2	2,317.7	2,241.8	696.5	506.2	230.8	3,194.9
1991	3,943.4	1,497.4	477.2	185.7	1,020.3	403.0	121.1	2,446.0	2,365.9	735.2	555.8	250.1	3,314.4
1992	4,197.6	1,563.3	508.1	204.8	1,055.2	404.5	125.0	2,634.3	2,546.4	771.1	612.8	277.0	3,561.7
1993	4,452.0	1,642.3	551.5	224.7	1,090.8	413.5	126.9	2,809.6	2,719.6	814.9	648.8	314.0	3,796.6
1994	4,721.0	1,746.6	607.2	249.8	1,139.4	432.1	129.2	2,974.4	2,876.6	863.3	680.5	327.9	4,042.5
1995	4,962.6	1,815.5	635.7	255.7	1,179.8	443.7	133.4	3,147.1	3,044.7	913.7	719.9	347.0	4,267.2
1996	5,244.6	1,917.7	676.3	273.5	1,241.4	461.9	144.7	3,326.9	3,216.9	962.4	752.1	372.1	4,513.0
1997	5,536.8	2,006.5	715.5	293.1	1,291.0	474.8	147.7	3,530.3	3,424.7	1,009.8	790.9	408.9	4,787.8
1998	5,877.2	2,108.4	779.3	320.2	1,329.1	487.4	132.4	3,768.8	3,645.0	1,065.5	832.0	446.1	5,132.4
1999	6,283.8	2,287.1	855.6	350.7	1,431.5	515.5	146.5	3,996.7	3,858.5	1,123.1	863.6	484.6	5,495.9
2000	6,767.2	2,453.2	912.6	363.2	1,540.6	540.6	184.5	4,314.0	4,156.0	1,198.6	918.4	541.9	5,904.5
2001	7,073.8	2,525.6	941.5	383.3	1,584.1	564.0	178.0	4,548.2	4,369.1	1,287.5	996.6	529.3	6,182.2
2002	7,348.9	2,598.8	985.4	401.3	1,613.4	575.1	167.9	4,750.1	4,551.8	1,329.5	1,082.9	539.0	6,460.4
2003	7,740.7	2,722.6	1,017.8	401.5	1,704.8	599.6	196.4	5,018.2	4,812.6	1,391.1	1,154.0	574.2	6,784.4
2004	8,232.0	2,902.0	1,080.6	409.3	1,821.4	632.6	232.7	5,329.9	5,123.6	1,466.6	1,238.9	619.3	7,198.5
2005	8,769.1	3,082.9	1,128.6	410.0	1,954.3	668.2	283.8	5,686.1	5,475.9	1,580.1	1,320.5	676.8	7,627.2
2006	9,277.2	3,239.7	1,158.3	394.9	2,081.3	700.3	319.7	6,037.6	5,798.4	1,665.7	1,391.9	719.5	8,056.6
2007	9,746.6	3,367.0	1,188.0	400.6	2,179.0	737.3	345.5	6,379.6	6,130.8	1,759.6	1,478.2	762.7	8,453.5
2008	10,050.1	3,363.2	1,098.8	343.3	2,264.5	769.1	391.1	6,686.9	6,399.6	1,872.7	1,555.3	777.5	8,666.3
2009	9,891.2	3,180.0	1,012.1	318.6	2,167.9	772.9	287.0	6,711.2	6,422.0	1,900.0	1,632.7	720.5	8,616.1
2010	10,260.3	3,317.8	1,049.0	344.5	2,268.9	786.9	336.7	6,942.4	6,648.0	1,947.9	1,699.6	768.0	8,915.3
2011	10,698.9	3,518.1	1,093.5	365.2	2,424.6	819.5	413.8	7,180.7	6,868.9	1,983.3	1,757.1	811.1	9,246.6
2012	11,047.4	3,637.7	1,144.2	396.6	2,493.5	846.2	421.9	7,409.6	7,068.1	2,014.7	1,821.3	830.9	9,571.6
2013	11,388.2	3,742.2	1,191.8	422.1	2,550.4	870.5	421.6	7,646.1	7,298.7	2,085.7	1,863.8	870.8	9,876.2
2014	11,874.5	3,886.6	1,247.3	451.6	2,639.3	910.4	410.9	7,987.9	7,634.6	2,146.0	1,945.5	925.6	10,321.0
2015	12,297.4	3,955.1	1,315.8	490.7	2,639.3	942.0	318.8	8,342.3	7,978.5	2,196.1	2,059.8	976.8	10,811.0
2016	12,726.8	4,033.0	1,356.5	504.6	2,676.5	969.6	287.0	8,693.8	8,305.5	2,269.0	2,164.6	996.1	11,249.4
2017	13,290.6	4,212.2	1,415.9	529.4	2,796.3	1,010.4	324.0	9,078.4	8,682.0	2,350.2	2,245.3	1,073.2	11,730.3
2018	13,934.4	4,414.2	1,488.8	550.0	2,925.4	1,044.4	366.7	9,520.2	9,099.3	2,459.3	2,344.7	1,130.9	12,278.0
2019	14,417.6	4,529.2	1,522.7	545.1	3,006.5	1,082.0	352.5	9,888.5	9,470.6	2,554.9	2,469.1	1,132.8	12,741.8
2020	14,206.2	4,713.1	1,628.9	547.0	3,084.2	1,196.5	258.3	9,493.1	9,008.6	2,676.0	2,354.8	1,148.9	12,509.3
2021	16,043.0	5,506.6	2,006.4	700.8	3,500.2	1,287.7	385.7	10,536.3	10,078.5	2,831.0	2,630.5	1,224.1	14,109.5
2022	17,511.7	5,997.0	2,128.9	730.8	3,868.1	1,393.5	510.1	11,514.7	10,982.6	3,053.3	2,776.7	1,252.5	15,294.2
2023 ᵖ	18,564.0	6,192.7	2,200.7	768.0	3,992.0	1,443.1	468.4	12,371.4	11,821.0	3,280.1	2,991.2	1,320.5	16,343.4
2020: I	14,473.1	4,559.5	1,479.8	493.1	3,079.7	1,170.4	317.3	9,913.6	9,425.3	2,615.7	2,436.6	1,149.4	12,757.7
II	13,168.9	4,391.9	1,467.6	484.3	2,924.3	1,201.9	196.9	8,777.1	8,247.3	2,665.4	2,073.7	1,120.2	11,523.3
III	14,456.2	4,923.3	1,766.0	597.6	3,157.4	1,208.0	259.7	9,532.8	9,071.0	2,695.1	2,406.6	1,150.6	12,742.4
IV	14,726.7	4,977.8	1,802.2	613.0	3,175.6	1,205.9	259.4	9,748.8	9,290.7	2,727.9	2,502.1	1,175.3	13,013.9
2021: I	15,217.7	5,241.5	1,924.3	671.5	3,317.1	1,247.4	318.5	9,976.2	9,526.1	2,774.9	2,530.0	1,202.6	13,393.0
II	15,950.9	5,536.4	2,058.4	745.1	3,478.0	1,276.7	368.3	10,414.5	9,976.1	2,808.1	2,617.8	1,218.9	14,050.9
III	16,285.1	5,515.9	1,972.7	671.0	3,543.2	1,297.3	405.5	10,769.2	10,312.3	2,851.7	2,667.8	1,231.0	14,319.0
IV	16,718.2	5,732.8	2,070.2	715.4	3,662.6	1,329.3	450.4	10,985.4	10,499.6	2,889.1	2,706.4	1,243.9	14,675.0
2022: I	17,030.6	5,879.3	2,120.7	735.3	3,758.5	1,353.9	488.6	11,151.4	10,644.9	2,959.1	2,726.5	1,243.1	14,890.9
II	17,415.1	6,014.4	2,122.9	725.9	3,891.5	1,382.0	557.4	11,400.7	10,868.5	3,017.8	2,735.9	1,239.6	15,163.4
III	17,684.2	6,046.8	2,143.1	728.2	3,903.7	1,409.2	509.0	11,637.4	11,092.8	3,081.1	2,792.8	1,254.3	15,448.4
IV	17,917.0	6,047.6	2,129.0	733.9	3,918.6	1,428.9	485.5	11,869.4	11,324.1	3,155.0	2,851.7	1,273.0	15,674.0
2023: I	18,269.6	6,133.8	2,194.9	776.2	3,939.0	1,430.6	465.3	12,135.7	11,595.2	3,206.1	2,929.5	1,298.0	16,060.6
II	18,419.0	6,144.7	2,193.6	772.7	3,951.1	1,434.1	456.7	12,274.4	11,730.1	3,243.8	2,972.9	1,316.7	16,231.8
III	18,679.5	6,231.8	2,204.5	764.6	4,027.3	1,447.8	484.5	12,447.7	11,890.7	3,309.0	3,009.1	1,336.0	16,434.7
IV ᵖ	18,888.1	6,260.4	2,209.9	758.7	4,050.5	1,460.1	467.1	12,627.7	12,068.0	3,361.4	3,053.5	1,331.1	16,646.3

[1] Includes other items not shown separately.
[2] Food consists of food and beverages purchased for off-premises consumption; food services, which include purchased meals and beverages, are not classified as food.

Source: Department of Commerce (Bureau of Economic Analysis).

TABLE B–11. Real personal consumption expenditures, 2007–2023

[Billions of chained (2017) dollars; quarterly data at seasonally adjusted annual rates]

Year or quarter	Personal consumption expenditures	Goods Total	Durable Total [1]	Durable Motor vehicles and parts	Nondurable Total [1]	Nondurable Food and beverages purchased for off-premises consumption	Gasoline and other energy goods	Services Total	Household consumption expenditures Total [1]	Housing and utilities	Health care	Financial services and insurance	Addendum: Personal consumption expenditures excluding food and energy [2]
2007	11,253.9	3,415.7	985.4	424.3	2,434.5	869.7	314.1	7,838.5	7,571.1	2,193.9	1,754.0	1,013.6	9,829.5
2008	11,270.7	3,312.7	928.8	370.4	2,396.1	855.1	301.7	7,981.2	7,669.9	2,255.7	1,797.0	1,038.2	9,883.2
2009	11,123.6	3,209.4	871.9	344.2	2,356.4	849.3	303.5	7,948.6	7,624.8	2,263.0	1,836.4	1,028.0	9,735.4
2010	11,335.6	3,300.2	920.6	357.5	2,393.5	862.0	302.0	8,065.3	7,730.8	2,314.8	1,864.5	1,026.5	9,929.6
2011	11,528.5	3,372.3	967.5	367.5	2,414.6	863.3	295.0	8,183.9	7,833.3	2,323.8	1,893.1	1,053.2	10,137.8
2012	11,686.1	3,444.2	1,025.3	393.8	2,424.9	870.7	291.0	8,265.3	7,882.6	2,318.8	1,927.6	1,040.2	10,303.5
2013	11,889.9	3,562.3	1,087.9	415.2	2,478.6	887.0	298.8	8,341.9	7,956.1	2,343.2	1,945.6	1,037.2	10,474.9
2014	12,226.4	3,717.7	1,168.2	443.6	2,552.3	910.3	302.0	8,516.3	8,131.1	2,341.5	2,008.2	1,047.9	10,785.1
2015	12,638.8	3,902.5	1,257.7	481.3	2,646.3	931.4	318.8	8,738.9	8,355.1	2,336.7	2,114.2	1,073.6	11,159.9
2016	12,949.0	4,044.7	1,325.5	498.1	2,719.9	968.3	323.8	8,904.9	8,507.0	2,347.0	2,196.3	1,046.5	11,429.3
2017	13,290.6	4,212.2	1,415.9	529.4	2,796.3	1,010.4	324.0	9,078.4	8,682.0	2,350.2	2,245.3	1,073.2	11,730.3
2018	13,654.9	4,378.7	1,509.5	549.9	2,869.8	1,039.0	323.0	9,276.6	8,861.3	2,385.0	2,301.8	1,073.4	12,049.5
2019	13,928.3	4,509.9	1,558.9	540.6	2,951.8	1,065.7	321.6	9,420.1	9,018.3	2,404.6	2,381.9	1,048.4	12,301.7
2020	13,577.0	4,729.9	1,683.1	533.5	3,049.6	1,140.7	277.5	8,867.6	8,406.7	2,454.1	2,215.6	1,050.4	11,920.2
2021	14,718.2	5,265.9	1,964.9	613.4	3,307.5	1,190.5	311.1	9,483.4	9,079.0	2,521.4	2,405.2	1,049.7	12,975.9
2022	15,090.8	5,281.5	1,960.0	572.6	3,327.5	1,167.8	311.1	9,836.1	9,413.1	2,549.1	2,479.3	1,031.4	13,364.8
2023 ᵖ	15,421.9	5,390.4	2,043.6	601.9	3,356.5	1,151.6	317.9	10,059.5	9,657.7	2,559.0	2,610.2	1,045.6	13,719.8
2020: I	13,862.3	4,551.8	1,531.7	488.7	3,019.0	1,140.5	296.5	9,313.6	8,849.4	2,417.4	2,321.2	1,050.8	12,200.6
II	12,668.7	4,450.2	1,530.9	481.1	2,919.8	1,135.0	245.4	8,240.0	7,735.6	2,450.2	1,956.5	1,039.9	11,041.5
III	13,793.9	4,939.2	1,822.1	581.0	3,122.8	1,145.7	288.7	8,884.4	8,444.0	2,466.6	2,252.5	1,048.6	12,117.0
IV	13,982.9	4,978.3	1,847.5	583.2	3,136.7	1,141.8	279.4	9,032.2	8,597.8	2,482.3	2,332.0	1,062.1	12,321.6
2021: I	14,282.6	5,171.7	1,966.7	641.0	3,212.9	1,176.9	287.7	9,144.9	8,727.4	2,509.8	2,327.2	1,059.1	12,570.6
II	14,745.6	5,351.8	2,033.6	664.0	3,325.9	1,195.1	313.8	9,429.6	9,035.3	2,517.6	2,398.8	1,048.8	12,997.2
III	14,848.8	5,234.3	1,904.3	568.5	3,335.0	1,194.3	321.4	9,641.1	9,243.1	2,531.5	2,435.5	1,044.7	13,089.8
IV	14,995.6	5,305.6	1,955.0	580.1	3,356.3	1,195.8	321.6	9,717.9	9,310.4	2,526.6	2,459.3	1,045.9	13,246.1
2022: I	14,995.2	5,289.7	1,962.3	580.3	3,333.4	1,185.9	311.5	9,733.0	9,314.8	2,547.9	2,454.9	1,033.2	13,246.6
II	15,069.2	5,285.3	1,957.8	571.2	3,333.4	1,171.5	313.1	9,810.8	9,382.4	2,549.4	2,455.0	1,026.4	13,333.6
III	15,127.4	5,275.7	1,962.3	566.5	3,319.7	1,158.8	309.3	9,878.2	9,449.4	2,544.5	2,484.4	1,033.2	13,419.3
IV	15,171.4	5,275.2	1,957.5	572.5	3,323.7	1,155.0	310.6	9,922.3	9,505.9	2,554.7	2,523.0	1,032.8	13,459.4
2023: I	15,312.9	5,341.0	2,022.5	614.1	3,327.8	1,145.8	313.0	9,998.9	9,597.0	2,545.8	2,584.0	1,037.3	13,625.6
II	15,343.6	5,347.3	2,020.9	599.6	3,335.4	1,148.5	319.8	10,023.1	9,622.9	2,550.0	2,600.0	1,048.7	13,647.6
III	15,461.4	5,411.3	2,053.9	597.8	3,367.3	1,153.9	319.0	10,078.7	9,675.8	2,568.7	2,617.5	1,052.2	13,748.5
IV ᵖ	15,569.8	5,462.1	2,077.1	596.1	3,395.4	1,158.3	319.6	10,137.4	9,735.2	2,571.3	2,639.3	1,044.3	13,857.2

[1] Includes other items not shown separately.
[2] Food consists of food and beverages purchased for off-premises consumption; food services, which include purchased meals and beverages, are not classified as food.

Source: Department of Commerce (Bureau of Economic Analysis).

TABLE B–12. Private fixed investment by type, 1973–2023

[Billions of dollars; quarterly data at seasonally adjusted annual rates]

Year or quarter	Private fixed investment	Nonresidential Total nonresidential	Structures	Equipment Total[1]	Information processing equipment Total	Computers and peripheral equipment	Other	Industrial equipment	Transportation equipment	Intellectual property products Total[1]	Software	Research and development[2]	Residential Total residential[1]	Structures Total[1]	Single family
1973	251.0	172.7	55.0	95.1	19.9	3.5	16.3	26.0	26.6	22.7	3.2	14.6	78.3	76.6	35.2
1974	260.5	191.1	61.2	104.3	23.1	3.9	19.2	30.7	26.3	25.5	3.9	16.4	69.5	67.6	29.7
1975	263.5	196.8	61.4	107.6	23.8	3.6	20.2	31.3	25.2	27.8	4.8	17.5	66.7	64.8	29.6
1976	306.1	219.3	65.9	121.2	27.5	4.4	23.1	34.1	30.0	32.2	5.2	19.6	86.8	84.6	43.9
1977	374.3	259.1	74.6	148.7	33.7	5.7	28.0	39.4	39.3	35.8	5.5	21.8	115.2	112.8	62.2
1978	452.6	314.6	93.6	180.6	42.3	7.6	34.8	47.7	47.3	40.4	6.3	24.9	138.0	135.3	72.8
1979	521.7	373.8	117.7	208.1	50.3	10.2	40.2	56.2	53.6	48.1	8.1	29.1	147.8	144.7	72.3
1980	536.4	406.9	136.2	216.4	58.9	12.5	46.4	60.7	48.4	54.4	9.8	34.2	129.5	126.1	52.9
1981	601.4	472.9	167.3	240.9	69.6	17.1	52.5	65.5	50.6	64.8	11.8	39.7	128.5	124.9	52.0
1982	595.9	485.1	177.6	234.9	74.2	18.9	55.3	62.7	46.8	72.7	14.0	44.8	110.8	107.2	41.5
1983	643.3	482.2	154.3	246.5	83.7	23.9	59.8	58.9	53.5	81.3	16.4	49.6	161.1	156.9	72.5
1984	754.7	564.3	177.4	291.9	101.2	31.6	69.6	68.1	64.4	95.0	20.4	56.9	190.4	185.6	86.4
1985	807.8	607.8	194.5	307.9	106.6	33.7	72.9	72.5	69.0	105.3	23.8	63.0	200.1	195.0	87.4
1986	842.6	607.8	176.5	317.7	111.1	33.4	77.7	75.4	70.5	113.5	25.6	66.5	234.8	229.3	104.1
1987	865.0	615.2	174.2	320.9	112.2	35.8	76.4	76.7	68.1	120.1	29.0	69.2	249.8	244.0	117.2
1988	918.5	662.3	182.8	346.8	120.8	38.0	82.8	84.2	72.9	132.7	33.3	76.4	256.2	250.1	120.1
1989	972.0	716.0	193.7	372.2	130.7	43.1	87.6	93.3	67.9	150.1	40.6	84.1	256.0	249.9	120.9
1990	978.9	739.2	202.9	371.9	129.6	38.6	90.9	92.1	70.0	164.4	45.4	91.5	239.7	233.7	112.9
1991	944.7	723.6	183.6	360.8	129.2	37.7	91.5	89.3	71.5	179.1	48.7	101.0	221.2	215.4	99.4
1992	996.7	741.9	172.6	381.7	142.1	44.0	98.1	93.0	74.7	187.7	51.1	105.4	254.7	248.8	122.0
1993	1,086.0	799.2	177.2	425.1	153.3	47.9	105.4	102.2	89.4	196.9	57.2	106.3	286.8	280.7	140.1
1994	1,192.7	868.9	186.8	476.4	167.0	52.4	114.6	113.6	107.7	205.7	60.4	109.2	323.8	317.6	162.3
1995	1,286.3	962.2	207.3	528.1	188.4	66.1	122.3	129.0	116.1	226.8	65.5	121.2	324.1	317.7	153.5
1996	1,401.3	1,043.2	224.6	565.3	204.7	72.8	131.9	136.5	123.2	253.3	74.5	134.5	358.1	351.7	170.8
1997	1,524.7	1,149.1	250.3	610.9	222.8	81.4	141.4	140.4	135.5	288.0	93.8	148.1	375.6	369.3	175.2
1998	1,673.0	1,254.1	276.0	660.0	240.1	87.9	152.2	147.4	147.1	318.1	109.2	160.6	418.8	412.1	199.4
1999	1,826.2	1,364.5	285.7	713.6	259.8	97.2	162.5	149.1	174.4	365.1	136.6	177.5	461.8	454.5	223.8
2000	1,983.9	1,498.4	321.0	766.1	293.8	103.2	190.6	162.9	170.8	411.3	156.8	199.0	485.4	477.7	236.8
2001	1,973.1	1,460.1	333.5	711.5	265.9	87.6	178.4	151.9	154.2	415.0	157.7	202.7	513.1	505.2	249.1
2002	1,910.4	1,352.8	287.0	659.6	236.7	79.7	157.0	141.7	141.6	406.2	152.5	196.1	557.6	549.6	265.9
2003	2,013.0	1,375.9	286.6	670.6	242.7	79.9	162.8	143.4	134.1	418.7	155.0	201.0	637.1	628.8	310.6
2004	2,217.2	1,467.4	307.7	721.9	255.8	84.2	171.6	144.2	159.2	437.8	166.3	207.4	749.8	740.8	377.6
2005	2,477.2	1,621.0	353.0	794.9	267.0	84.2	182.8	162.4	179.6	473.1	178.6	224.7	856.2	846.6	433.5
2006	2,632.0	1,793.8	425.2	862.3	288.5	92.6	195.9	181.6	194.3	506.3	189.5	245.6	838.2	828.1	416.0
2007	2,639.1	1,948.6	510.3	893.4	310.9	95.4	215.5	194.1	188.8	544.8	206.4	268.0	690.5	680.6	305.2
2008	2,506.9	1,990.9	571.1	845.4	306.3	93.9	212.4	194.3	148.7	574.4	223.8	284.2	516.0	506.4	185.8
2009	2,080.4	1,690.4	455.8	670.3	275.6	88.9	186.7	153.7	74.9	564.4	226.0	274.6	390.0	381.2	105.3
2010	2,111.6	1,735.0	379.8	777.0	307.5	99.6	207.9	155.2	135.8	578.2	226.4	282.4	376.6	367.4	112.6
2011	2,286.3	1,907.5	404.5	881.3	313.3	95.6	217.7	191.5	177.8	621.7	249.8	303.4	378.8	369.1	108.2
2012	2,550.5	2,118.5	479.4	983.4	331.2	103.5	227.7	211.2	215.3	655.7	272.1	313.4	432.0	421.5	132.0
2013	2,732.9	2,221.3	491.5	1,035.3	344.8	102.1	242.6	211.4	243.4	694.6	285.6	338.7	511.5	500.0	170.8
2014	2,989.2	2,425.2	574.6	1,109.1	352.2	101.9	250.2	223.4	274.9	741.5	303.7	364.4	564.0	551.7	193.6
2015	3,148.4	2,507.5	584.5	1,144.1	362.2	101.3	260.9	224.7	309.8	778.9	316.3	385.3	640.9	627.6	221.1
2016	3,239.2	2,529.0	566.2	1,119.8	365.2	99.5	265.8	222.9	297.8	843.0	347.9	413.2	710.2	696.0	242.5
2017	3,435.0	2,661.1	594.9	1,160.0	386.0	105.8	280.2	237.3	299.9	906.2	382.9	437.5	773.9	758.9	270.2
2018	3,668.4	2,856.5	636.6	1,227.6	406.6	120.4	286.2	253.6	319.3	992.2	422.8	479.5	811.9	796.2	289.6
2019	3,820.2	2,993.1	678.7	1,241.5	405.6	119.2	286.5	262.2	308.1	1,072.9	447.8	533.2	827.2	811.3	280.0
2020	3,785.9	2,869.4	623.2	1,110.8	400.7	127.2	273.5	241.0	221.0	1,135.5	479.2	567.0	916.5	899.4	309.4
2021	4,204.6	3,078.4	623.9	1,188.2	438.2	143.8	294.3	267.9	215.1	1,266.3	533.8	642.1	1,126.2	1,106.0	423.9
2022	4,599.3	3,433.0	700.5	1,327.2	479.3	158.6	320.7	300.0	232.0	1,405.4	598.1	703.1	1,166.4	1,145.3	453.2
2023 ᵖ	4,786.2	3,712.3	836.1	1,383.4	460.7	145.4	315.3	308.5	293.2	1,492.8	638.7	742.1	1,073.9	1,053.2	389.8
2020: I	3,840.7	2,962.2	694.7	1,145.2	373.1	109.6	263.5	247.6	269.3	1,122.3	473.4	554.9	878.5	862.7	303.7
II	3,549.2	2,734.4	609.1	1,016.6	389.1	128.0	261.0	228.5	172.4	1,108.8	471.7	546.8	814.8	798.9	276.8
III	3,796.4	2,850.5	594.3	1,122.3	416.6	133.2	283.4	239.2	214.2	1,133.9	477.2	570.6	945.9	927.7	300.3
IV	3,957.4	2,930.7	594.6	1,158.9	424.0	137.9	286.1	248.2	228.1	1,177.1	494.5	595.9	1,026.7	1,008.4	356.8
2021: I	4,075.4	2,993.4	607.2	1,173.4	433.0	144.5	288.5	249.4	230.3	1,212.9	512.2	614.8	1,082.1	1,062.3	394.1
II	4,174.5	3,065.2	618.0	1,192.9	432.8	139.9	292.9	264.6	234.4	1,254.3	530.6	635.8	1,109.4	1,088.8	416.2
III	4,229.9	3,088.9	625.0	1,182.1	428.5	139.8	288.7	274.1	211.5	1,281.8	540.4	649.8	1,141.0	1,120.9	437.5
IV	4,338.5	3,166.0	645.2	1,204.6	458.3	151.1	307.2	283.5	184.2	1,316.3	552.1	668.2	1,172.5	1,152.1	447.7
2022: I	4,517.8	3,299.8	664.5	1,277.7	487.7	165.0	322.7	297.6	188.4	1,357.6	576.5	683.6	1,218.0	1,196.9	479.5
II	4,618.9	3,403.0	688.7	1,318.9	480.2	157.3	322.8	300.1	221.9	1,395.4	590.4	701.3	1,215.8	1,194.6	490.6
III	4,642.3	3,493.1	712.6	1,355.0	486.7	162.9	323.8	299.0	247.8	1,425.6	609.1	708.8	1,149.1	1,128.0	442.6
IV	4,618.4	3,536.0	736.1	1,357.1	462.6	149.0	313.6	303.2	269.9	1,442.8	616.3	718.8	1,082.5	1,061.8	400.2
2023: I	4,702.1	3,641.3	800.2	1,368.7	465.2	146.4	318.8	310.6	273.8	1,472.5	632.4	730.2	1,060.8	1,039.8	374.4
II	4,761.7	3,709.1	832.5	1,390.4	457.8	146.3	311.4	308.6	302.7	1,486.2	633.6	740.2	1,052.6	1,032.1	371.0
III	4,813.0	3,730.6	849.8	1,382.6	450.0	138.4	311.7	305.9	298.9	1,498.2	640.9	745.5	1,082.4	1,061.7	396.5
IV ᵖ	4,868.1	3,768.2	862.0	1,391.7	469.6	150.4	319.2	309.0	290.2	1,514.5	648.0	752.7	1,099.9	1,079.2	417.2

[1] Includes other items not shown separately.
[2] Research and development investment includes expenditures for software.

Source: Department of Commerce (Bureau of Economic Analysis).

TABLE B–13. Real private fixed investment by type, 2007–2023

[Billions of chained (2017) dollars; quarterly data at seasonally adjusted annual rates]

Year or quarter	Private fixed investment	Nonresidential												Residential		
		Total nonresidential	Structures	Equipment						Intellectual property products			Total residential²	Structures	
				Total²	Information processing equipment			Industrial equipment	Transportation equipment	Total²	Software	Research and development³		Total²	Single family
					Total	Computers and peripheral equipment¹	Other								
2007	2,782.2	1,996.1	625.5	839.9	204.5	72.2	134.2	219.6	212.9	552.7	173.3	316.0	821.9	818.3	356.6
2008	2,620.6	2,008.3	666.0	799.7	215.6	77.9	140.1	210.5	166.9	573.7	187.4	325.3	623.0	617.7	224.0
2009	2,201.6	1,716.4	541.4	630.2	204.8	79.2	128.9	164.4	78.1	570.8	193.1	317.3	487.9	482.1	132.4
2010	2,269.9	1,794.3	454.8	757.8	239.2	91.9	151.1	164.2	152.4	586.4	200.4	318.5	472.8	465.8	143.8
2011	2,432.5	1,951.3	469.0	859.6	250.8	91.8	162.1	197.0	195.8	622.9	222.3	331.8	472.2	464.1	137.2
2012	2,678.0	2,137.1	531.5	953.9	274.0	101.1	176.4	213.5	231.8	653.8	246.7	334.5	533.3	525.3	166.0
2013	2,842.0	2,238.6	537.3	1,006.5	293.9	100.6	195.5	212.8	257.7	695.0	264.3	357.7	601.1	592.1	203.6
2014	3,052.6	2,421.1	597.2	1,086.0	312.9	100.4	213.7	223.5	287.4	739.1	286.1	377.0	626.8	616.2	216.1
2015	3,193.6	2,498.9	598.2	1,127.2	336.7	100.4	236.7	225.7	318.7	774.0	304.6	390.3	693.2	681.1	240.8
2016	3,286.9	2,544.8	579.7	1,117.5	356.1	99.7	256.5	224.9	302.6	847.6	340.5	424.5	742.2	728.6	253.2
2017	3,435.0	2,661.1	594.9	1,160.0	386.0	105.8	280.2	237.3	299.9	906.2	382.9	437.5	773.9	758.9	270.2
2018	3,611.7	2,844.3	629.2	1,228.6	416.8	119.6	297.1	248.7	318.3	986.5	433.9	464.3	768.5	753.4	277.7
2019	3,708.5	2,950.1	644.8	1,241.7	429.2	121.3	307.8	253.2	304.6	1,063.5	466.5	507.4	761.3	746.1	260.1
2020	3,630.1	2,810.6	583.4	1,116.3	432.2	132.1	299.5	230.8	220.0	1,111.0	509.8	517.6	816.2	800.4	276.1
2021	3,887.3	2,975.5	564.8	1,187.4	473.8	147.2	325.8	245.9	225.7	1,226.6	581.9	565.5	903.8	886.6	338.3
2022	3,939.3	3,131.6	552.9	1,249.2	509.9	156.5	352.7	254.8	228.2	1,338.7	660.2	597.7	822.6	805.9	310.6
2023 ᵖ	3,960.4	3,268.0	623.2	1,247.5	484.4	143.1	341.3	252.4	263.5	1,396.7	718.9	602.9	734.5	717.3	258.9
2020: I	3,708.2	2,912.0	647.7	1,147.7	401.2	114.1	287.0	237.5	264.7	1,114.3	502.2	522.6	796.8	781.4	276.5
II	3,414.0	2,676.9	570.1	1,018.5	419.9	132.9	286.2	219.3	168.1	1,086.8	501.0	502.5	737.3	722.1	250.4
III	3,633.6	2,791.6	556.9	1,128.7	449.4	138.1	310.7	229.7	214.2	1,107.6	509.1	517.5	837.0	820.3	265.8
IV	3,764.7	2,862.0	559.0	1,170.4	458.4	143.4	314.2	236.6	233.2	1,135.2	527.1	527.7	893.9	877.8	311.7
2021: I	3,849.1	2,923.9	569.5	1,176.2	468.6	149.4	318.2	235.2	229.8	1,180.5	558.2	545.2	915.0	897.5	333.9
II	3,904.3	2,992.4	570.9	1,205.9	468.7	143.9	324.1	245.4	253.1	1,218.9	577.8	563.5	904.7	886.9	339.5
III	3,888.8	2,982.8	565.0	1,181.0	463.0	142.3	320.1	249.5	226.3	1,239.9	589.3	571.0	898.4	881.6	342.4
IV	3,907.1	3,002.7	553.8	1,186.5	494.8	153.0	341.0	253.5	193.8	1,267.1	602.3	582.2	897.3	880.5	337.3
2022: I	3,976.0	3,080.0	552.1	1,233.5	520.2	163.9	355.1	259.0	196.0	1,301.8	634.0	588.5	893.1	876.3	345.5
II	3,974.0	3,120.0	551.4	1,248.5	511.1	155.1	355.5	255.3	222.5	1,329.1	648.4	598.3	859.9	843.0	337.5
III	3,930.9	3,156.3	549.7	1,265.5	517.4	160.8	355.8	251.4	242.1	1,351.9	668.1	601.0	796.3	779.5	296.8
IV	3,876.5	3,170.0	558.4	1,249.5	490.7	146.1	344.6	253.6	252.1	1,372.1	690.4	602.8	741.2	724.8	262.7
2023: I	3,905.9	3,214.5	596.6	1,236.4	489.6	142.7	347.1	256.0	243.8	1,384.9	702.2	604.9	731.1	714.2	248.7
II	3,955.9	3,272.7	619.3	1,259.6	482.0	144.3	337.5	252.7	276.7	1,394.0	712.1	605.1	727.1	710.0	249.5
III	3,981.3	3,284.5	635.9	1,245.5	473.3	136.8	336.8	249.2	275.5	1,400.4	724.9	601.7	738.9	721.5	265.0
IV ᵖ	3,998.5	3,300.3	641.0	1,248.5	492.7	148.6	343.9	251.5	257.9	1,407.7	736.2	599.9	740.8	723.2	272.4

[1] Because computers exhibit rapid changes in prices relative to other prices in the economy, the chained-dollar estimates should not be used to measure the component's relative importance or its contribution to the growth rate of more aggregate series. The quantity index for computers can be used to accurately measure the real growth rate of this series. For information on this component, see *Survey of Current Business* Table 5.3.1 (for growth rates), Table 5.3.2 (for contributions), and Table 5.3.3 (for quantity indexes).

[2] Includes other items not shown separately.

[3] Research and development investment includes expenditures for software.

Source: Department of Commerce (Bureau of Economic Analysis).

Foreign transactions in the national income and product accounts, 1973–2023

[Billions of dollars; quarterly data at seasonally adjusted annual rates]

	Current receipts from rest of the world					Current payments to rest of the world									
		Exports of goods and services			Income receipts		Imports of goods and services			Income payments	Current taxes and transfer payments to rest of the world (net)				Balance on current account, NIPA[2]
Year or quarter	Total	Total	Goods[1]	Services[1]		Total	Total	Goods[1]	Services[1]		Total	From persons (net)	From government (net)	From business (net)	
1973	118.8	95.3	75.8	19.5	23.5	109.9	91.2	71.8	19.3	10.9	7.9	1.6	5.6	0.7	8.9
1974	156.5	126.7	103.5	23.2	29.8	150.5	127.5	104.5	22.9	14.3	8.7	1.4	6.4	1.0	6.0
1975	166.7	138.7	112.5	26.2	28.0	146.9	122.7	99.0	23.7	15.0	9.1	1.3	7.1	.7	19.8
1976	181.9	149.5	121.5	28.0	32.4	174.8	151.1	124.6	26.5	15.5	8.1	1.4	5.7	1.1	7.1
1977	196.5	159.3	128.4	30.9	37.2	207.5	182.4	152.6	29.8	16.9	8.1	1.4	5.3	1.4	−10.9
1978	233.1	186.9	149.9	37.0	46.3	245.8	212.3	177.4	34.8	24.7	8.8	1.6	5.9	1.4	−12.6
1979	298.5	230.1	187.3	42.9	68.3	299.6	252.7	212.8	39.9	36.4	10.6	1.7	6.8	2.0	−1.2
1980	359.9	280.8	230.4	50.3	79.1	351.4	293.8	248.6	45.3	44.9	12.6	2.0	8.3	2.4	8.5
1981	397.3	305.2	245.2	60.0	92.0	393.9	317.8	267.8	49.9	59.1	17.0	5.6	8.3	3.2	3.4
1982	384.2	283.2	222.6	60.7	101.0	387.5	303.2	250.5	52.6	64.5	19.8	6.7	9.7	3.4	−3.3
1983	378.9	277.0	214.0	62.9	101.9	413.9	328.6	272.7	56.0	64.8	20.5	7.0	10.1	3.4	−35.1
1984	424.2	302.4	231.3	71.1	121.9	514.3	405.1	336.3	68.8	85.6	23.6	7.9	12.2	3.5	−90.1
1985	415.9	303.2	227.5	75.7	112.7	530.2	417.2	343.3	73.9	87.3	25.7	8.3	14.4	2.9	−114.3
1986	432.3	321.0	231.4	89.6	111.3	575.0	452.9	370.0	82.9	94.4	27.8	9.1	15.4	3.2	−142.7
1987	487.2	363.9	265.6	98.4	123.3	641.3	508.7	414.8	93.9	105.8	26.8	10.0	13.4	3.4	−154.1
1988	596.7	444.6	332.1	112.5	152.1	712.4	554.0	452.1	101.9	129.5	29.0	10.8	13.7	4.5	−115.7
1989	682.0	504.3	374.8	129.5	177.7	774.3	591.0	484.8	106.2	152.9	30.4	11.6	14.2	4.6	−92.4
1990	740.7	551.9	403.3	148.6	188.8	815.6	629.7	508.1	121.7	154.2	31.7	12.2	14.7	4.8	−74.9
1991	763.3	594.9	430.1	164.8	168.4	755.4	623.5	500.7	122.8	136.8	−4.9	14.1	−24.0	5.0	7.9
1992	785.1	633.1	455.3	177.7	152.1	830.7	667.8	544.9	122.9	121.0	41.9	14.5	22.0	5.4	−45.6
1993	810.4	654.8	467.7	187.1	155.6	889.8	720.0	592.8	127.2	124.4	45.4	17.1	22.9	5.4	−79.4
1994	905.5	720.9	518.4	202.6	184.5	1,021.1	813.4	676.8	136.6	161.6	46.1	18.9	21.1	6.0	−115.6
1995	1,042.6	812.8	592.4	220.4	229.8	1,148.5	902.6	757.4	145.1	201.9	44.1	20.3	15.6	8.2	−105.9
1996	1,114.0	867.6	628.8	238.8	246.4	1,229.0	964.0	807.4	156.5	215.5	49.5	22.6	20.0	6.9	−115.0
1997	1,233.9	953.8	699.9	253.9	280.1	1,364.0	1,055.8	885.7	170.1	256.8	51.4	25.7	16.7	9.1	−130.1
1998	1,239.8	953.0	692.6	260.4	286.8	1,445.1	1,115.7	930.8	184.9	269.4	60.0	29.7	17.4	13.0	−205.3
1999	1,355.2	992.9	711.7	281.2	324.6	1,631.9	1,252.5	1,051.2	201.3	293.7	85.7	36.3	25.0	24.4	−276.6
2000	1,527.8	1,096.1	795.1	301.1	390.6	1,924.7	1,477.2	1,251.2	226.0	352.2	95.4	38.6	26.8	29.9	−396.9
2001	1,411.6	1,026.8	739.6	287.2	339.6	1,803.0	1,403.6	1,176.2	227.4	289.3	110.2	42.5	26.7	41.1	−391.4
2002	1,390.6	998.0	706.6	291.4	335.8	1,846.0	1,437.7	1,198.9	238.9	290.0	118.3	44.4	29.3	44.6	−455.4
2003	1,478.5	1,035.2	733.9	301.3	377.4	2,006.2	1,557.1	1,299.0	258.1	318.9	130.1	46.1	32.0	52.0	−527.6
2004	1,705.6	1,176.4	828.0	348.4	464.7	2,343.4	1,810.5	1,513.6	296.9	388.0	144.9	49.5	34.0	61.4	−637.8
2005	1,940.9	1,301.6	919.3	382.2	569.3	2,692.0	2,041.5	1,722.8	318.7	494.5	156.1	54.4	39.9	61.8	−751.2
2006	2,247.7	1,470.2	1,043.1	427.1	702.6	3,067.0	2,256.6	1,900.6	356.0	656.2	154.2	57.1	41.7	55.3	−819.3
2007	2,584.4	1,659.3	1,159.7	499.6	850.2	3,325.2	2,395.2	2,002.7	392.5	754.5	175.5	65.3	49.1	61.0	−740.9
2008	2,779.9	1,835.3	1,291.0	544.3	855.2	3,484.1	2,576.2	2,148.7	427.5	710.0	198.0	71.1	54.3	72.5	−704.2
2009	2,362.1	1,582.8	1,057.4	525.4	689.3	2,745.3	2,001.9	1,588.1	413.8	539.0	204.3	69.8	62.9	71.6	−383.1
2010	2,714.1	1,857.2	1,272.9	584.3	760.0	3,153.8	2,389.6	1,947.0	442.5	554.3	209.9	72.1	63.3	74.6	−439.8
2011	3,049.8	2,115.9	1,468.5	647.4	827.9	3,510.1	2,695.5	2,231.1	464.3	589.9	224.7	74.7	66.8	83.2	−460.3
2012	3,161.8	2,217.7	1,529.6	688.1	827.4	3,585.8	2,769.3	2,293.3	476.1	594.7	221.8	75.7	67.3	78.7	−424.0
2013	3,266.0	2,287.9	1,563.9	724.1	847.2	3,617.2	2,766.4	2,293.9	472.5	616.9	233.9	77.8	66.6	89.6	−351.2
2014	3,405.9	2,378.5	1,617.0	761.6	881.5	3,781.0	2,887.4	2,389.3	498.1	646.4	247.2	83.7	65.3	98.1	−375.1
2015	3,269.3	2,270.6	1,496.7	773.9	860.6	3,692.4	2,794.9	2,289.6	505.4	640.5	257.0	89.5	65.2	102.4	−423.1
2016	3,275.1	2,235.6	1,447.6	788.0	892.9	3,676.5	2,738.8	2,218.7	520.1	661.5	276.1	90.6	69.2	116.3	−401.4
2017	3,585.1	2,388.3	1,546.7	841.6	1,031.1	3,963.1	2,931.6	2,369.9	561.7	738.2	293.4	95.7	67.8	129.8	−378.0
2018	3,830.7	2,538.1	1,669.3	868.8	1,138.7	4,271.8	3,131.2	2,559.1	572.1	848.4	292.3	98.7	74.3	119.3	−441.2
2019	3,875.2	2,538.5	1,644.8	893.7	1,174.7	4,323.6	3,117.0	2,516.7	600.3	892.8	313.8	102.3	74.3	137.2	−448.4
2020	3,315.6	2,150.1	1,421.6	728.5	993.0	3,885.3	2,776.5	2,305.1	471.4	778.1	330.7	102.3	87.6	140.8	−569.7
2021	3,842.5	2,550.0	1,746.0	804.1	1,112.1	4,690.3	3,408.3	2,842.4	565.9	928.6	353.4	114.4	94.3	144.8	−847.8
2022	4,441.7	2,995.0	2,063.2	931.8	1,252.6	5,427.5	3,966.2	3,262.4	703.8	1,070.7	390.6	121.5	117.5	151.6	−985.8
2023 *p*	....	3,027.8	2,028.2	999.7	....	....	3,825.9	3,111.7	714.2	....	389.2	121.5	120.3	147.5	....
2020: I	3,661.5	2,416.1	1,598.7	817.4	1,074.5	4,055.5	2,934.1	2,377.1	557.0	802.3	319.1	101.8	79.8	137.5	−394.0
II	2,863.9	1,811.4	1,139.0	672.3	884.9	3,374.8	2,342.5	1,932.8	409.6	704.8	327.5	102.2	94.1	131.3	−511.0
III	3,275.2	2,106.6	1,416.7	689.9	991.7	3,924.2	2,802.3	2,364.1	438.3	775.8	346.0	101.5	94.6	149.9	−649.0
IV	3,461.8	2,266.4	1,532.2	734.2	1,020.7	4,186.7	3,027.1	2,546.4	480.7	829.5	330.1	103.9	82.0	144.3	−725.0
2021: I	3,657.8	2,382.8	1,625.0	757.8	1,092.3	4,386.9	3,175.2	2,683.0	492.2	861.8	349.9	109.0	100.6	140.4	−729.1
II	3,764.6	2,498.3	1,713.5	784.8	1,091.5	4,585.8	3,330.2	2,794.7	535.6	921.1	334.5	112.2	83.7	138.7	−821.3
III	3,871.1	2,566.0	1,751.9	814.0	1,124.9	4,787.9	3,450.2	2,847.6	602.6	963.8	373.9	117.0	108.4	148.4	−916.8
IV	4,076.5	2,753.1	1,893.4	859.7	1,139.8	5,000.6	3,677.4	3,044.4	633.0	967.8	355.4	119.4	84.4	151.6	−924.1
2022: I	4,176.7	2,837.6	1,951.0	886.6	1,154.8	5,291.8	3,927.3	3,263.9	663.4	1,006.2	358.3	121.2	94.6	142.6	−1,115.1
II	4,460.6	3,044.3	2,115.1	929.1	1,229.4	5,471.7	4,069.8	3,368.7	701.1	1,027.4	374.5	122.4	105.8	146.2	−1,011.1
III	4,557.4	3,084.5	2,139.9	944.6	1,285.5	5,492.0	3,976.5	3,254.0	722.5	1,094.3	421.2	121.8	142.9	156.4	−934.6
IV	4,572.1	3,013.8	2,046.9	966.9	1,340.7	5,454.6	3,891.0	3,163.0	728.0	1,155.2	408.4	120.7	126.7	161.1	−882.5
2023: I	4,641.3	3,064.8	2,090.4	974.4	1,390.7	5,513.8	3,890.5	3,158.5	731.9	1,231.8	391.6	120.0	126.9	144.7	−872.6
II	4,604.2	2,961.8	1,968.6	993.2	1,452.7	5,441.4	3,767.9	3,058.0	709.8	1,279.7	393.9	119.9	126.5	147.4	−837.2
III	4,717.8	3,030.8	2,026.7	1,004.0	1,499.9	5,538.7	3,810.0	3,107.5	702.4	1,335.8	392.8	122.1	121.8	148.9	−820.9
IV *p*	....	3,054.0	2,026.9	1,027.2	....	....	3,835.1	3,122.5	712.6	....	378.7	123.9	105.8	148.9	....

[1] Certain goods, primarily military equipment purchased and sold by the Federal Government, are included in services. Beginning with 1986, repairs and alterations of equipment were reclassified from goods to services.

[2] National income and product accounts (NIPA).

Source: Department of Commerce (Bureau of Economic Analysis).

TABLE B–15. Real exports and imports of goods and services, 2007–2023

[Billions of chained (2017) dollars; quarterly data at seasonally adjusted annual rates]

Year or quarter	Exports of goods and services						Imports of goods and services					
	Total	Goods [1]				Services [1]	Total	Goods [1]				Services [1]
		Total	Durable goods	Non-durable goods	Non-agricultural goods			Total	Durable goods	Non-durable goods	Non-petroleum goods	
2007	1,745.5	1,146.7	764.1	382.9	1,040.1	595.2	2,376.4	1,927.5	1,050.8	866.7	1,602.4	446.7
2008	1,846.6	1,214.0	801.1	413.0	1,101.0	628.5	2,325.4	1,864.5	1,017.4	837.3	1,550.6	463.5
2009	1,693.1	1,070.0	666.5	402.6	960.6	628.3	2,031.8	1,576.0	811.2	760.6	1,284.3	468.2
2010	1,907.3	1,232.4	786.3	445.1	1,111.0	675.6	2,295.3	1,818.3	1,002.3	802.9	1,526.0	485.1
2011	2,044.2	1,324.5	861.8	463.3	1,204.9	719.7	2,405.8	1,918.6	1,096.9	808.8	1,638.7	493.1
2012	2,126.3	1,376.9	905.0	474.0	1,256.4	749.6	2,464.7	1,969.5	1,186.2	776.0	1,729.5	500.4
2013	2,190.3	1,417.3	924.9	493.5	1,295.3	773.5	2,494.6	2,009.0	1,242.0	763.1	1,795.5	487.7
2014	2,275.8	1,480.6	963.5	517.9	1,348.8	794.3	2,623.4	2,120.8	1,352.1	769.3	1,929.5	503.4
2015	2,283.1	1,475.7	942.5	532.6	1,341.3	807.5	2,759.5	2,243.5	1,442.2	802.7	2,052.5	515.8
2016	2,293.9	1,485.2	932.7	552.3	1,343.6	808.7	2,799.7	2,268.4	1,459.7	810.0	2,069.6	531.4
2017	2,388.3	1,546.7	962.5	584.1	1,402.8	841.6	2,931.6	2,369.9	1,562.3	807.6	2,172.5	561.7
2018	2,456.4	1,612.1	996.5	615.4	1,467.7	844.2	3,050.0	2,491.6	1,650.9	841.0	2,305.0	558.4
2019	2,469.0	1,614.9	974.2	639.5	1,471.6	854.0	3,086.5	2,505.4	1,656.3	849.1	2,332.2	580.9
2020	2,144.8	1,452.6	819.7	633.6	1,301.9	694.3	2,808.3	2,358.0	1,534.6	822.9	2,209.7	453.4
2021	2,280.9	1,563.2	917.3	647.9	1,421.8	720.6	3,214.7	2,701.8	1,808.4	895.2	2,542.5	516.6
2022	2,439.6	1,653.3	963.0	691.1	1,517.6	790.0	3,490.6	2,886.2	1,954.8	936.7	2,735.4	607.0
2023 ᵖ	2,505.7	1,695.6	991.4	704.5	1,570.6	813.4	3,431.3	2,837.7	1,931.1	912.2	2,677.3	597.1
2020: I	2,371.4	1,598.4	933.7	663.0	1,456.0	774.9	2,933.5	2,397.6	1,558.5	838.7	2,232.2	535.6
II	1,868.2	1,212.8	637.6	581.1	1,072.9	653.4	2,421.1	2,024.4	1,239.8	785.4	1,890.4	398.9
III	2,107.6	1,454.0	828.1	624.7	1,296.0	657.8	2,837.2	2,420.9	1,598.8	820.5	2,276.7	421.8
IV	2,232.1	1,545.1	879.3	665.5	1,382.6	691.3	3,041.2	2,589.2	1,741.6	847.0	2,439.3	457.3
2021: I	2,237.0	1,544.5	898.6	646.7	1,391.2	695.9	3,100.0	2,643.5	1,773.7	870.7	2,491.2	462.0
II	2,248.1	1,542.7	920.3	626.1	1,407.0	708.2	3,158.1	2,670.2	1,792.9	879.4	2,511.0	492.2
III	2,256.4	1,535.7	912.3	627.2	1,406.7	723.5	3,223.0	2,680.1	1,783.8	897.6	2,515.0	545.4
IV	2,382.0	1,629.9	937.8	691.7	1,482.1	754.8	3,377.6	2,813.7	1,883.4	933.0	2,652.7	566.7
2022: I	2,354.1	1,593.0	939.0	657.9	1,454.6	764.8	3,495.2	2,910.4	1,971.3	944.9	2,762.1	587.6
II	2,414.1	1,628.4	952.0	678.3	1,483.3	790.0	3,530.3	2,925.6	1,983.8	947.6	2,782.9	607.5
III	2,506.2	1,709.7	983.8	723.7	1,576.0	799.6	3,487.4	2,870.3	1,957.2	920.8	2,715.4	619.5
IV	2,484.1	1,682.0	977.4	704.5	1,556.8	805.6	3,449.6	2,838.6	1,907.0	933.7	2,681.3	613.4
2023: I	2,525.4	1,730.5	995.4	733.2	1,600.4	798.5	3,460.5	2,851.6	1,924.4	930.7	2,686.9	611.5
II	2,464.7	1,656.8	978.1	680.3	1,537.5	810.7	3,392.9	2,804.3	1,916.8	894.2	2,651.5	591.8
III	2,497.3	1,687.7	1,005.5	685.0	1,567.0	812.8	3,428.0	2,844.7	1,939.6	911.2	2,685.0	587.6
IV ᵖ	2,535.6	1,707.2	986.4	719.7	1,577.3	831.5	3,443.8	2,850.1	1,943.5	912.8	2,686.0	597.4

[1] Certain goods, primarily military equipment purchased and sold by the Federal Government, are included in services. Repairs and alterations of equipment are also included in services.

Source: Department of Commerce (Bureau of Economic Analysis).

TABLE B–16. Sources of personal income, 1973–2023

[Billions of dollars; quarterly data at seasonally adjusted annual rates]

Year or quarter	Personal income	Compensation of employees							Proprietors' income with inventory valuation and capital consumption adjustments			Rental income of persons with capital consumption adjustment
		Total	Wages and salaries			Supplements to wages and salaries			Total	Farm	Nonfarm	
			Total	Private industries	Government	Total	Employer contributions for employee pension and insurance funds	Employer contributions for government social insurance				
1973	1,140.8	812.7	708.8	560.0	148.8	103.9	64.1	39.8	112.5	29.1	83.4	23.1
1974	1,251.8	887.7	772.3	611.8	160.5	115.4	70.7	44.7	112.2	23.5	88.7	23.2
1975	1,369.4	947.2	814.8	638.6	176.2	132.4	85.7	46.7	118.2	22.0	96.2	22.3
1976	1,502.6	1,048.3	899.7	710.8	188.9	148.6	94.2	54.4	131.0	17.2	113.8	20.3
1977	1,659.2	1,165.8	994.2	791.6	202.6	171.7	110.6	61.1	144.5	16.0	128.5	15.9
1978	1,863.7	1,316.8	1,120.6	900.6	220.0	196.2	124.7	71.5	166.0	19.9	146.1	16.5
1979	2,082.7	1,477.2	1,253.3	1,016.2	237.1	223.9	141.3	82.6	179.4	22.2	157.3	16.1
1980	2,324.5	1,622.2	1,373.4	1,112.0	261.5	248.8	159.9	88.9	171.6	11.7	159.9	19.0
1981	2,603.2	1,792.5	1,511.4	1,225.5	285.8	281.2	177.5	103.6	179.7	19.0	160.7	23.8
1982	2,789.5	1,893.0	1,587.5	1,280.0	307.5	305.5	195.7	109.8	171.2	13.3	157.9	23.8
1983	2,961.7	2,012.5	1,677.5	1,352.7	324.8	335.0	215.1	119.9	186.3	6.2	180.1	24.4
1984	3,288.7	2,215.9	1,844.9	1,496.8	348.1	371.0	231.9	139.0	228.2	20.9	207.3	24.7
1985	3,522.9	2,387.3	1,982.6	1,608.7	373.9	404.8	257.0	147.7	241.1	21.0	220.1	26.2
1986	3,731.2	2,542.1	2,102.3	1,705.1	397.2	439.7	281.9	157.9	256.5	22.8	233.7	18.3
1987	3,946.8	2,722.4	2,256.3	1,833.2	423.1	466.1	299.9	166.3	286.5	28.9	257.6	16.6
1988	4,280.0	2,948.0	2,439.8	1,987.7	452.0	508.2	323.6	184.6	325.5	26.8	298.7	22.5
1989	4,621.0	3,139.6	2,583.1	2,101.9	481.1	556.6	362.9	193.7	341.1	33.0	308.1	21.5
1990	4,913.3	3,340.4	2,741.2	2,222.2	519.0	599.2	392.7	206.5	353.2	32.2	321.0	28.2
1991	5,089.9	3,450.5	2,814.5	2,265.7	548.8	636.0	420.9	215.1	354.2	26.8	327.4	38.6
1992	5,417.5	3,668.2	2,965.5	2,393.5	572.0	702.7	474.3	228.4	400.2	34.8	365.4	60.6
1993	5,652.9	3,817.3	3,079.3	2,490.3	589.0	737.9	498.3	239.7	428.0	31.4	396.6	90.1
1994	5,940.9	4,006.2	3,236.6	2,627.1	609.5	769.6	515.5	254.1	456.6	34.7	422.0	113.7
1995	6,283.4	4,198.1	3,418.0	2,789.0	629.0	780.1	515.9	264.1	481.2	22.0	459.2	124.9
1996	6,666.2	4,416.9	3,616.5	2,968.4	648.1	800.5	525.7	274.8	543.8	37.3	506.4	142.5
1997	7,074.0	4,708.8	3,876.8	3,205.0	671.9	832.0	542.4	289.6	584.0	32.4	551.6	147.1
1998	7,588.4	5,071.1	4,181.6	3,480.3	701.3	889.5	582.3	307.2	640.3	28.6	611.7	165.2
1999	7,978.6	5,402.7	4,457.9	3,724.2	733.8	944.8	621.4	323.3	696.4	28.0	668.3	178.5
2000	8,621.3	5,847.1	4,824.9	4,045.2	779.8	1,022.2	677.0	345.2	753.6	31.2	722.4	183.5
2001	8,993.1	6,038.3	4,953.6	4,131.6	822.0	1,084.7	726.7	358.0	831.1	32.1	798.9	202.4
2002	9,150.0	6,135.1	4,995.8	4,123.0	872.9	1,139.3	773.2	366.0	870.1	20.3	849.8	208.4
2003	9,481.8	6,353.6	5,138.3	4,224.3	914.0	1,215.3	832.8	382.5	897.5	37.1	860.4	227.1
2004	10,015.9	6,719.5	5,421.0	4,468.7	952.3	1,298.5	889.7	408.8	962.9	52.4	910.5	242.8
2005	10,546.1	7,066.1	5,691.4	4,700.1	991.3	1,374.7	946.7	428.1	979.1	47.9	931.2	221.1
2006	11,302.0	7,479.7	6,056.7	5,022.2	1,034.5	1,422.9	975.6	447.3	1,050.9	34.3	1,016.6	181.1
2007	11,932.1	7,878.5	6,396.4	5,307.8	1,088.5	1,482.1	1,020.4	461.7	995.4	41.5	953.9	186.3
2008	12,425.7	8,056.8	6,534.1	5,390.2	1,143.9	1,522.7	1,051.3	471.4	960.3	39.5	920.8	290.3
2009	12,065.7	7,759.0	6,249.1	5,073.9	1,175.2	1,509.9	1,051.8	458.1	938.1	27.6	910.5	347.6
2010	12,556.6	7,925.4	6,372.5	5,181.3	1,191.2	1,552.9	1,083.9	469.0	1,108.5	38.7	1,069.8	433.7
2011	13,309.6	8,226.2	6,626.2	5,431.3	1,194.9	1,600.0	1,107.3	492.7	1,228.3	63.9	1,164.4	506.5
2012	13,917.8	8,567.4	6,928.1	5,729.8	1,198.3	1,639.2	1,125.9	513.3	1,299.9	61.0	1,238.9	534.5
2013	14,068.8	8,835.0	7,114.0	5,906.0	1,208.0	1,721.0	1,194.7	526.3	1,351.7	87.5	1,264.2	578.7
2014	14,784.1	9,250.2	7,476.3	6,239.4	1,236.9	1,773.9	1,227.5	546.4	1,370.0	68.5	1,301.5	598.5
2015	15,473.7	9,699.4	7,859.5	6,583.7	1,275.8	1,839.9	1,270.6	569.4	1,347.7	55.5	1,292.3	601.4
2016	15,887.7	9,966.1	8,091.2	6,783.2	1,308.0	1,874.9	1,293.9	580.9	1,349.2	36.0	1,313.2	618.7
2017	16,662.8	10,424.4	8,474.4	7,126.2	1,348.2	1,950.0	1,345.3	604.7	1,428.6	41.0	1,387.6	642.0
2018	17,528.2	10,957.4	8,899.8	7,498.0	1,401.9	2,057.6	1,432.8	624.8	1,495.3	32.1	1,463.2	671.5
2019	18,356.2	11,447.9	9,325.0	7,874.3	1,450.7	2,123.0	1,472.4	650.6	1,554.1	32.1	1,522.1	684.5
2020	19,629.0	11,594.7	9,464.6	7,970.3	1,494.3	2,130.0	1,471.5	658.6	1,583.8	44.4	1,539.4	756.1
2021	21,407.7	12,545.9	10,312.6	8,766.4	1,546.3	2,233.2	1,526.8	706.4	1,749.1	72.2	1,676.8	814.2
2022	21,840.8	13,439.2	11,116.0	9,493.6	1,622.5	2,323.2	1,559.1	764.0	1,790.9	81.7	1,709.1	878.3
2023 ᵖ	22,966.3	14,241.8	11,805.3	10,070.4	1,734.8	2,436.5	1,620.7	815.8	1,849.4	55.6	1,793.9	967.0
2020: I	18,774.8	11,780.7	9,627.0	8,113.8	1,513.2	2,153.7	1,487.7	666.1	1,577.7	35.3	1,542.4	740.9
II	20,183.0	11,051.0	8,998.0	7,531.8	1,466.2	2,053.0	1,417.6	635.4	1,411.5	23.3	1,388.2	738.2
III	19,843.5	11,565.7	9,433.7	7,934.9	1,498.8	2,132.0	1,473.4	658.6	1,691.6	42.5	1,649.1	765.2
IV	19,714.7	11,981.3	9,799.8	8,300.7	1,499.2	2,181.5	1,507.3	674.2	1,654.4	76.4	1,578.0	780.3
2021: I	22,162.2	12,078.0	9,878.7	8,368.1	1,510.6	2,199.3	1,519.9	679.4	1,650.2	48.4	1,601.9	791.6
II	21,046.1	12,390.2	10,170.0	8,639.2	1,530.7	2,220.3	1,523.8	696.5	1,784.1	93.7	1,690.4	807.2
III	21,138.3	12,689.9	10,447.7	8,880.9	1,566.8	2,242.2	1,528.3	713.9	1,792.8	85.6	1,707.2	822.4
IV	21,284.0	13,025.3	10,754.1	9,177.2	1,577.0	2,271.2	1,535.4	735.8	1,769.2	61.3	1,707.9	835.5
2022: I	21,410.5	13,177.4	10,886.7	9,292.4	1,594.3	2,290.7	1,544.0	746.6	1,756.4	73.0	1,683.4	837.2
II	21,659.7	13,295.2	10,988.9	9,381.7	1,607.2	2,306.2	1,550.6	755.6	1,774.4	86.0	1,688.4	875.3
III	22,018.8	13,609.2	11,271.4	9,639.2	1,632.2	2,337.8	1,562.2	775.6	1,807.4	84.0	1,723.4	893.1
IV	22,274.1	13,675.0	11,317.0	9,660.8	1,656.2	2,357.9	1,579.6	778.3	1,825.3	84.0	1,741.4	907.5
2023: I	22,643.9	13,965.2	11,565.4	9,879.6	1,685.8	2,399.8	1,598.8	800.9	1,827.4	71.2	1,756.2	945.8
II	22,868.0	14,154.1	11,733.3	10,022.3	1,710.9	2,420.9	1,609.7	811.2	1,824.1	58.2	1,765.9	961.1
III	23,064.2	14,344.2	11,894.5	10,141.2	1,753.3	2,449.6	1,628.5	821.1	1,859.6	49.9	1,809.6	974.4
IV ᵖ	23,289.0	14,503.7	12,027.9	10,238.6	1,789.3	2,475.8	1,645.9	829.9	1,886.7	42.9	1,843.8	986.9

See next page for continuation of table.

TABLE B–16. Sources of personal income, 1973–2023—*Continued*

[Billions of dollars; quarterly data at seasonally adjusted annual rates]

Year or quarter	Personal income receipts on assets			Personal current transfer receipts								Less: Contributions for government social insurance, domestic
	Total	Personal interest income	Personal dividend income	Total	Government social benefits to persons						Other current transfer receipts, from business (net)	
					Total [1]	Social security [2]	Medicare [3]	Medicaid	Unemployment insurance	Other		
1973	155.4	125.5	29.9	112.6	108.6	50.7	10.2	9.6	4.6	23.3	3.9	75.5
1974	180.6	147.4	33.2	133.3	128.6	57.6	12.7	11.2	7.0	28.4	4.7	85.2
1975	201.0	168.0	32.9	170.0	163.1	65.9	15.6	13.9	18.1	35.7	6.8	89.3
1976	220.0	181.0	39.0	184.3	177.6	74.5	18.8	15.5	16.4	38.7	6.7	101.3
1977	251.6	206.9	44.7	194.6	189.5	83.2	22.1	16.7	13.1	40.9	5.1	113.1
1978	285.8	235.1	50.7	209.9	203.4	91.4	25.5	18.6	9.4	44.9	6.5	131.3
1979	327.1	269.5	57.7	235.6	227.3	102.6	29.9	21.1	9.7	49.9	8.2	152.7
1980	397.7	333.5	64.2	280.1	271.5	118.6	36.2	23.9	16.1	62.1	8.6	166.2
1981	483.9	414.2	69.7	319.0	307.8	138.6	43.5	27.7	15.9	66.3	11.2	195.7
1982	554.9	481.8	73.1	355.5	343.1	153.7	50.9	30.2	25.2	66.8	12.4	208.9
1983	600.2	518.2	82.0	384.3	370.5	164.4	57.8	33.9	26.4	71.5	13.8	226.0
1984	676.7	590.9	85.8	400.6	380.9	173.0	64.7	36.6	16.0	74.3	19.7	257.5
1985	724.3	630.5	93.8	425.4	403.1	183.3	69.7	39.7	15.9	78.0	22.3	281.4
1986	766.3	663.1	103.1	451.6	428.6	193.6	75.3	43.6	16.5	83.0	22.9	303.4
1987	776.3	674.3	102.0	468.1	447.9	201.0	81.6	47.8	14.6	86.4	20.2	323.1
1988	848.0	720.1	128.0	497.5	476.9	213.9	86.3	53.0	13.3	93.6	20.6	361.5
1989	959.7	802.3	157.5	524.2	521.1	227.4	98.2	60.8	14.4	103.1	23.2	385.2
1990	1,004.8	835.1	169.7	596.9	574.7	244.1	107.6	73.1	18.2	113.9	22.2	410.1
1991	1,008.7	827.7	181.0	668.1	650.5	264.2	117.5	96.9	26.8	127.0	17.6	430.2
1992	995.4	806.2	189.3	748.0	731.8	281.8	132.6	116.2	39.6	142.9	16.3	455.0
1993	1,001.9	796.8	205.1	793.0	778.9	297.9	146.8	130.1	34.8	150.0	14.1	477.4
1994	1,043.6	806.3	237.3	829.0	815.7	312.2	164.4	139.4	23.9	156.1	13.3	508.2
1995	1,128.5	869.4	259.2	883.5	864.7	327.7	181.2	149.6	21.7	164.0	18.7	532.8
1996	1,188.8	886.4	302.4	929.2	906.3	342.0	194.9	158.2	22.3	167.6	22.9	555.1
1997	1,266.5	928.8	337.8	954.9	935.4	356.6	206.9	163.1	20.1	166.4	19.4	587.2
1998	1,352.5	994.0	358.4	983.9	957.9	369.2	205.6	170.2	19.7	170.0	26.0	624.7
1999	1,336.2	987.7	348.5	1,026.2	992.2	379.9	208.7	184.6	20.5	174.4	34.0	661.3
2000	1,455.6	1,069.3	386.4	1,087.3	1,044.9	401.4	219.1	199.5	20.7	179.1	42.4	705.8
2001	1,461.9	1,087.5	374.4	1,192.6	1,145.8	425.1	242.6	227.3	31.9	192.4	46.8	733.2
2002	1,402.6	1,001.2	401.5	1,285.2	1,251.0	446.9	259.7	250.0	53.5	211.3	34.2	751.5
2003	1,435.6	1,004.4	431.2	1,347.3	1,321.0	463.5	276.7	264.5	53.2	231.2	26.3	779.3
2004	1,498.7	939.3	559.4	1,421.2	1,404.5	485.5	304.4	289.8	36.4	254.3	16.8	829.2
2005	1,636.4	1,081.3	555.0	1,516.7	1,490.9	512.7	332.1	304.4	31.8	273.5	25.8	873.3
2006	1,899.0	1,215.4	683.6	1,613.8	1,593.0	544.1	399.1	299.1	30.4	281.5	20.8	922.5
2007	2,105.3	1,325.2	780.1	1,728.1	1,697.3	575.7	428.2	324.2	32.7	294.9	30.8	961.4
2008	2,151.5	1,345.8	805.7	1,955.1	1,919.3	605.5	461.6	338.3	51.1	417.7	35.8	988.4
2009	1,838.5	1,272.8	565.6	2,146.7	2,107.7	664.5	493.0	369.6	131.2	398.0	39.0	964.3
2010	1,747.7	1,211.1	536.6	2,325.2	2,281.4	690.2	513.4	396.9	138.9	484.2	43.7	983.7
2011	1,906.5	1,216.1	690.4	2,358.7	2,310.1	713.3	535.6	406.0	107.2	484.8	48.5	916.7
2012	2,103.6	1,271.8	831.7	2,363.0	2,322.6	762.1	554.7	417.5	83.6	434.4	40.4	950.5
2013	1,983.2	1,201.6	781.6	2,424.3	2,385.9	799.0	572.8	440.0	62.5	432.5	38.4	1,104.3
2014	2,177.4	1,260.4	917.0	2,541.6	2,498.6	834.6	600.0	490.9	35.5	453.5	42.9	1,153.6
2015	2,344.6	1,347.7	996.9	2,685.4	2,635.1	871.8	634.9	535.9	32.5	467.4	50.3	1,204.7
2016	2,415.4	1,388.0	1,027.4	2,777.0	2,717.3	895.5	662.1	562.8	32.0	467.1	59.7	1,238.8
2017	2,611.0	1,466.7	1,144.3	2,855.7	2,807.4	926.1	691.8	573.7	30.2	474.2	48.3	1,298.9
2018	2,789.4	1,554.5	1,234.9	2,976.3	2,926.0	972.4	733.6	589.8	27.6	482.9	50.3	1,361.7
2019	2,949.9	1,603.4	1,346.5	3,144.3	3,088.5	1,030.7	787.2	614.0	27.5	498.1	55.8	1,424.6
2020	2,913.7	1,510.3	1,403.5	4,229.9	4,182.7	1,077.9	816.8	657.6	529.5	955.5	47.2	1,449.3
2021	3,214.7	1,515.5	1,699.2	4,641.9	4,554.1	1,114.6	874.5	736.5	324.0	1,350.5	87.7	1,558.0
2022 ᵖ	3,432.0	1,627.5	1,804.5	4,002.1	3,903.0	1,211.5	926.1	814.4	22.3	758.2	99.1	1,701.7
2023 ᵖ	3,613.8	1,772.7	1,841.1	4,097.8	3,993.5	1,357.4	944.4	881.7	22.0	615.1	104.3	1,803.6
2020: I	2,926.1	1,547.9	1,378.2	3,217.5	3,174.3	1,068.2	798.4	606.4	40.9	519.3	43.2	1,468.1
II	2,869.8	1,505.9	1,363.9	5,510.1	5,464.2	1,075.1	811.1	654.6	951.4	1,827.4	46.0	1,397.6
III	2,865.0	1,493.0	1,372.0	4,403.2	4,358.2	1,080.3	823.1	690.8	802.3	814.5	45.0	1,447.1
IV	2,994.0	1,494.2	1,499.8	3,788.9	3,734.2	1,088.2	834.5	678.6	323.5	660.7	54.8	1,484.3
2021: I	3,079.2	1,506.5	1,572.7	6,063.8	5,993.5	1,105.7	849.4	705.0	583.5	2,600.1	70.4	1,500.6
II	3,198.3	1,518.9	1,679.4	4,402.7	4,311.8	1,109.6	865.6	745.7	451.8	987.6	90.9	1,536.5
III	3,262.6	1,514.0	1,748.7	4,144.6	4,050.6	1,116.8	882.6	749.2	226.8	920.1	94.0	1,574.0
IV	3,318.6	1,522.6	1,795.9	3,956.3	3,860.6	1,126.3	900.3	746.1	33.9	894.2	95.7	1,620.9
2022: I	3,342.2	1,550.9	1,791.3	3,960.6	3,863.6	1,198.7	918.2	791.4	26.2	763.6	96.9	1,663.2
II	3,407.0	1,604.7	1,802.4	3,992.4	3,890.5	1,207.0	924.7	818.7	21.4	748.6	101.9	1,684.7
III	3,453.4	1,647.6	1,805.8	3,981.8	3,882.9	1,214.5	927.2	819.0	19.6	729.9	98.9	1,726.1
IV	3,525.4	1,706.7	1,818.7	4,073.7	3,974.9	1,225.8	934.2	828.4	22.1	790.7	98.8	1,732.8
2023: I	3,577.0	1,744.3	1,832.7	4,102.4	4,001.5	1,340.0	938.1	871.5	22.0	657.1	100.9	1,773.9
II	3,602.6	1,754.8	1,847.8	4,120.1	4,017.3	1,353.8	941.9	911.4	22.3	615.4	102.8	1,794.0
III	3,606.5	1,776.4	1,830.2	4,093.7	3,987.8	1,361.3	946.3	880.6	21.0	605.7	105.9	1,814.1
IV ᵖ	3,669.1	1,815.5	1,853.6	4,074.9	3,967.3	1,374.4	951.3	863.3	22.7	582.0	107.5	1,832.3

[1] Includes Veterans' benefits, not shown seperately.
[2] Includes old-age, survivors, and disability insurance benefits that are distributed from the federal old-age and survivors insurance trust fund and the disability insurance trust fund.
[3] Includes hospital and supplementary medical insurance benefits that are distributed from the federal hospital insurance trust fund and the supplementary medical insurance trust fund.

Source: Department of Commerce (Bureau of Economic Analysis).

TABLE B–17. Disposition of personal income, 1973–2023

[Billions of dollars, except as noted; quarterly data at seasonally adjusted annual rates]

Year or quarter	Personal income	Less: Personal current taxes	Equals: Disposable personal income	Less: Personal outlays				Equals: Personal saving	Percent of disposable personal income [2]		
				Total	Personal consumption expenditures	Personal interest payments [1]	Personal current transfer payments		Personal outlays		Personal saving
									Total	Personal consumption expenditures	
1973	1,140.8	132.4	1,008.4	872.6	849.6	19.6	3.4	135.8	86.5	84.3	13.5
1974	1,251.8	151.0	1,100.8	954.5	930.2	20.9	3.4	146.3	86.7	84.5	13.3
1975	1,369.4	147.6	1,221.8	1,057.8	1,030.5	23.4	3.8	164.0	86.6	84.3	13.4
1976	1,502.6	172.7	1,330.0	1,175.6	1,147.7	23.5	4.4	154.4	88.4	86.3	11.6
1977	1,659.2	197.9	1,461.4	1,305.4	1,274.0	26.6	4.8	155.9	89.3	87.2	10.7
1978	1,863.7	229.6	1,634.1	1,459.0	1,422.3	31.3	5.4	175.1	89.3	87.0	10.7
1979	2,082.7	268.9	1,813.8	1,627.0	1,585.4	35.5	6.0	186.8	89.7	87.4	10.3
1980	2,324.5	299.5	2,024.9	1,800.1	1,750.7	42.5	6.9	224.9	88.9	86.5	11.1
1981	2,603.2	345.8	2,257.4	1,993.9	1,934.0	48.4	11.5	263.6	88.3	85.7	11.7
1982	2,789.5	354.7	2,434.7	2,143.5	2,071.3	58.5	13.8	291.2	88.0	85.1	12.0
1983	2,981.7	352.9	2,628.8	2,364.2	2,281.6	67.4	15.1	264.7	89.9	86.8	10.1
1984	3,288.7	377.9	2,910.8	2,584.5	2,492.3	75.0	17.1	326.3	88.8	85.6	11.2
1985	3,522.9	417.8	3,105.1	2,822.1	2,712.8	90.6	18.8	282.9	90.9	87.4	9.1
1986	3,731.2	437.8	3,293.4	3,004.7	2,886.3	97.3	21.1	288.7	91.2	87.6	8.8
1987	3,946.8	489.6	3,457.2	3,196.6	3,076.3	97.1	23.2	260.6	92.5	89.0	7.5
1988	4,280.0	505.9	3,774.1	3,457.0	3,330.0	101.3	25.6	317.1	91.6	88.2	8.4
1989	4,621.0	567.7	4,053.3	3,717.9	3,576.8	113.1	28.0	335.4	91.7	88.2	8.3
1990	4,913.3	594.7	4,318.6	3,958.0	3,809.0	118.4	30.6	360.6	91.7	88.2	8.4
1991	5,089.9	588.9	4,501.0	4,100.0	3,943.4	119.9	36.7	401.0	91.1	87.6	8.9
1992	5,417.5	612.8	4,804.7	4,354.2	4,197.6	116.1	40.5	450.5	90.6	87.4	9.4
1993	5,652.9	648.8	5,004.1	4,611.5	4,452.0	113.9	45.6	392.6	92.2	89.0	7.8
1994	5,940.9	693.1	5,247.8	4,890.6	4,721.0	119.9	49.8	357.2	93.2	90.0	6.8
1995	6,283.4	748.4	5,535.0	5,155.9	4,962.6	140.4	52.9	379.0	93.2	89.7	6.8
1996	6,666.2	837.1	5,829.1	5,459.2	5,244.6	157.0	57.6	369.9	93.7	90.0	6.3
1997	7,074.0	931.8	6,142.2	5,770.4	5,536.8	169.7	63.9	371.8	93.9	90.1	6.1
1998	7,588.4	1,032.4	6,555.9	6,131.3	5,877.2	184.6	69.5	424.6	93.5	89.6	6.5
1999	7,978.6	1,111.9	6,866.7	6,550.9	6,283.8	190.8	76.3	315.8	95.4	91.5	4.6
2000	8,621.3	1,236.3	7,385.0	7,068.1	6,767.2	217.7	83.2	316.8	95.7	91.6	4.3
2001	8,993.1	1,239.0	7,754.1	7,390.9	7,073.8	225.6	91.5	363.2	95.3	91.2	4.7
2002	9,150.0	1,052.2	8,097.9	7,646.3	7,348.9	200.6	96.7	451.6	94.4	90.8	5.6
2003	9,481.8	1,003.5	8,478.2	8,038.3	7,740.7	196.5	101.1	439.9	94.8	91.3	5.2
2004	10,015.9	1,048.7	8,967.1	8,550.1	8,232.0	207.3	110.9	417.0	95.3	91.8	4.7
2005	10,546.1	1,212.5	9,333.6	9,124.5	8,769.1	237.3	118.1	209.2	97.8	94.0	2.2
2006	11,302.0	1,357.0	9,945.0	9,669.1	9,277.2	266.9	124.9	276.0	97.2	93.3	2.8
2007	11,932.1	1,492.5	10,439.6	10,176.2	9,746.6	291.2	138.4	263.4	97.5	93.4	2.5
2008	12,425.7	1,507.5	10,918.2	10,466.7	10,050.1	272.0	144.6	451.5	95.9	92.0	4.1
2009	12,065.7	1,152.4	10,913.3	10,288.4	9,891.2	252.8	144.3	624.9	94.3	90.6	5.7
2010	12,556.6	1,237.6	11,319.0	10,647.6	10,260.3	242.3	145.0	671.4	94.1	90.6	5.9
2011	13,309.6	1,453.7	11,855.9	11,079.6	10,698.9	229.9	150.8	776.3	93.5	90.2	6.5
2012	13,917.8	1,509.5	12,408.3	11,431.8	11,047.4	229.6	154.8	976.5	92.1	89.0	7.9
2013	14,068.8	1,677.5	12,391.2	11,775.5	11,388.2	229.5	157.8	615.7	95.0	91.9	5.0
2014	14,784.1	1,785.7	12,998.4	12,286.4	11,874.5	243.7	168.2	712.0	94.5	91.4	5.5
2015	15,473.7	1,940.9	13,532.9	12,742.3	12,297.4	263.5	181.4	790.6	94.2	90.9	5.8
2016	15,887.7	1,958.8	13,928.9	13,182.7	12,726.8	272.8	183.1	746.2	94.6	91.4	5.4
2017	16,662.8	2,048.8	14,613.9	13,772.3	13,290.6	290.4	191.3	841.6	94.2	90.9	5.8
2018	17,528.2	2,074.2	15,454.0	14,457.4	13,934.4	321.3	201.6	996.7	93.6	90.2	6.4
2019	18,356.2	2,199.3	16,157.0	14,966.1	14,417.6	340.8	207.6	1,190.9	92.6	89.2	7.4
2020	19,629.0	2,256.5	17,372.5	14,694.0	14,206.2	285.8	202.0	2,678.6	84.6	81.8	15.4
2021	21,407.7	2,743.3	18,664.4	16,543.9	16,043.0	273.6	227.3	2,120.5	88.6	86.0	11.4
2022 ᵖ	21,840.8	3,138.3	18,702.5	18,079.7	17,511.7	326.1	241.8	622.8	96.7	93.6	3.3
2023 ᵖ	22,966.3	2,748.4	20,217.9	19,306.4	18,564.0	497.2	245.1	911.5	95.5	91.8	4.5
2020: I	18,774.8	2,255.9	16,518.9	15,014.5	14,473.1	341.2	200.2	1,504.4	90.9	87.6	9.1
II	20,183.0	2,111.9	18,071.1	13,647.4	13,168.9	275.8	202.7	4,423.7	75.5	72.9	24.5
III	19,843.5	2,263.3	17,580.2	14,925.8	14,456.2	273.0	196.6	2,654.4	84.9	82.2	15.1
IV	19,714.7	2,394.7	17,320.0	15,188.1	14,726.7	253.1	208.3	2,131.9	87.7	85.0	12.3
2021: I	22,162.2	2,577.6	19,584.6	15,694.9	15,217.7	259.7	217.5	3,889.7	80.1	77.7	19.9
II	21,046.1	2,703.9	18,342.2	16,453.5	15,950.9	278.6	224.0	1,888.6	89.7	87.0	10.3
III	21,138.3	2,789.9	18,348.5	16,796.3	16,285.1	280.1	231.1	1,552.1	91.5	88.8	8.5
IV	21,284.0	2,901.6	18,382.4	17,230.8	16,718.2	275.9	236.7	1,151.6	93.7	90.9	6.3
2022: I	21,410.5	3,162.8	18,247.8	17,544.0	17,030.6	275.0	238.4	703.7	96.1	93.3	3.9
II	21,659.7	3,157.8	18,501.9	17,949.5	17,415.1	291.8	242.6	552.4	97.0	94.1	3.0
III	22,018.8	3,137.0	18,881.7	18,269.1	17,684.2	342.4	242.5	612.6	96.8	93.7	3.2
IV	22,274.1	3,095.7	19,178.4	18,556.0	17,917.0	395.3	243.7	622.4	96.8	93.4	3.2
2023: I	22,643.9	2,763.7	19,880.2	18,932.0	18,269.6	419.8	242.6	948.2	95.2	91.9	4.8
II	22,868.0	2,703.8	20,164.2	19,136.6	18,419.0	474.7	242.9	1,027.6	94.9	91.3	5.1
III	23,064.2	2,756.5	20,307.7	19,456.5	18,679.5	530.6	246.4	851.2	95.8	92.0	4.2
IV ᵖ	23,289.0	2,769.6	20,519.4	19,700.5	18,888.1	563.8	248.6	818.9	96.0	92.0	4.0

[1] Consists of nonmortgage interest paid by households.
[2] Percents based on data in millions of dollars.

Source: Department of Commerce (Bureau of Economic Analysis).

TABLE B–18. Total and per capita disposable personal income and personal consumption expenditures, and per capita gross domestic product, in current and real dollars, 1973–2023

[Quarterly data at seasonally adjusted annual rates, except as noted]

Year or quarter	Disposable personal income				Personal consumption expenditures				Gross domestic product per capita (dollars)		Population (thou- sands)[1]
	Total (billions of dollars)		Per capita (dollars)		Total (billions of dollars)		Per capita (dollars)				
	Current dollars	Chained (2017) dollars	Current dollars	Chained (2017) dollars	Current dollars	Chained (2017) dollars	Current dollars	Chained (2017) dollars	Current dollars	Chained (2017) dollars	
1973	1,008.4	4,490.5	4,758	21,188	849.6	3,783.4	4,009	17,851	6,725	28,812	211,939
1974	1,100.8	4,439.8	5,146	20,757	930.2	3,751.7	4,349	17,540	7,224	28,394	213,898
1975	1,221.8	4,548.7	5,657	21,061	1,030.5	3,836.7	4,771	17,764	7,801	28,062	215,981
1976	1,330.0	4,694.0	6,098	21,524	1,147.7	4,050.6	5,262	18,573	8,590	29,289	218,086
1977	1,461.4	4,842.7	6,634	21,984	1,274.0	4,221.8	5,783	19,165	9,450	30,337	220,289
1978	1,634.1	5,062.8	7,340	22,741	1,422.3	4,406.5	6,388	19,793	10,563	31,679	222,629
1979	1,813.8	5,161.1	8,058	22,928	1,585.4	4,511.3	7,043	20,041	11,672	32,323	225,106
1980	2,024.9	5,201.8	8,892	22,842	1,750.7	4,497.2	7,688	19,748	12,547	31,869	227,726
1981	2,257.4	5,322.2	9,815	23,139	1,934.0	4,559.6	8,408	19,823	13,943	32,353	230,008
1982	2,434.7	5,438.1	10,485	23,418	2,071.3	4,626.3	8,919	19,922	14,399	31,467	232,218
1983	2,628.8	5,632.1	11,218	24,035	2,281.6	4,888.2	9,737	20,860	15,508	32,613	234,333
1984	2,910.8	6,009.2	12,313	25,420	2,492.3	5,145.4	10,543	21,766	17,080	34,668	236,394
1985	3,105.1	6,194.3	13,019	25,971	2,712.8	5,411.8	11,374	22,690	18,192	35,794	238,506
1986	3,293.4	6,430.0	13,684	26,716	2,886.3	5,635.2	11,992	23,413	19,028	36,698	240,683
1987	3,457.2	6,547.5	14,236	26,962	3,076.3	5,826.1	12,668	23,991	19,993	37,628	242,843
1988	3,774.1	6,878.8	15,401	28,070	3,330.0	6,069.4	13,589	24,767	21,368	38,845	245,061
1989	4,053.3	7,078.6	16,384	28,613	3,576.8	6,246.4	14,458	25,249	22,805	39,893	247,387
1990	4,318.6	7,224.8	17,262	28,878	3,809.0	6,372.2	15,225	25,470	23,835	40,191	250,181
1991	4,501.0	7,286.3	17,753	28,739	3,943.4	6,383.7	15,554	25,179	24,290	39,618	253,530
1992	4,804.7	7,575.9	18,701	29,487	4,197.6	6,618.6	16,338	25,761	25,379	40,472	256,922
1993	5,004.1	7,698.6	19,226	29,578	4,452.0	6,849.2	17,104	26,314	26,350	41,048	260,282
1994	5,247.8	7,908.6	19,919	30,019	4,721.0	7,114.5	17,919	27,005	27,660	42,188	263,455
1995	5,535.0	8,169.2	20,762	30,644	4,962.6	7,324.5	18,615	27,475	28,658	42,811	266,588
1996	5,829.1	8,423.3	21,612	31,230	5,244.6	7,578.6	19,445	28,099	29,932	43,912	269,714
1997	6,142.2	8,723.8	22,502	31,960	5,536.8	7,864.0	20,284	28,810	31,424	45,319	272,958
1998	6,555.9	9,238.0	23,740	33,452	5,877.2	8,281.7	21,283	29,989	32,818	46,803	276,154
1999	6,866.7	9,536.9	24,583	34,142	6,283.8	8,727.3	22,496	31,244	34,480	48,487	279,328
2000	7,385.0	10,003.7	26,151	35,424	6,767.2	9,166.9	23,963	32,461	36,300	49,915	282,398
2001	7,754.1	10,297.3	27,186	36,102	7,073.8	9,393.9	24,801	32,935	37,100	49,893	285,225
2002	8,097.9	10,614.4	28,122	36,861	7,348.9	9,632.8	25,521	33,452	37,954	50,260	287,955
2003	8,478.2	10,884.3	29,172	37,451	7,740.7	9,937.6	26,635	34,194	39,420	51,191	290,626
2004	8,967.1	11,233.2	30,577	38,304	8,232.0	10,312.2	28,070	35,164	41,660	52,682	293,262
2005	9,333.6	11,364.9	31,533	38,396	8,769.1	10,677.4	29,626	36,073	44,052	54,015	295,993
2006	9,945.0	11,777.6	33,281	39,414	9,277.2	10,986.8	31,046	36,767	46,234	54,994	298,818
2007	10,439.6	12,054.1	34,603	39,954	9,746.6	11,253.9	32,306	37,302	47,976	55,561	301,696
2008	10,918.2	12,244.3	35,851	40,205	10,050.1	11,270.7	33,001	37,009	48,498	55,104	304,543
2009	10,913.3	12,273.0	35,520	39,946	9,891.2	11,123.6	32,194	36,205	47,123	53,213	307,240
2010	11,319.0	12,505.3	36,532	40,361	10,260.3	11,335.6	33,115	36,586	48,570	54,189	309,839
2011	11,855.9	12,775.2	37,964	40,908	10,698.9	11,528.5	34,259	36,915	49,952	54,604	312,295
2012	12,408.3	13,125.7	39,426	41,705	11,047.4	11,686.1	35,102	37,131	51,645	55,422	314,725
2013	12,391.2	12,937.1	39,077	40,798	11,388.2	11,889.9	35,914	37,496	53,235	56,172	317,099
2014	12,998.4	13,383.7	40,671	41,876	11,874.5	12,226.4	37,154	38,255	55,094	57,139	319,601
2015	13,532.9	13,908.5	42,013	43,179	12,297.4	12,638.8	38,177	39,237	56,797	58,364	322,113
2016	13,928.9	14,172.0	42,910	43,659	12,726.8	12,949.0	39,207	39,891	57,931	58,968	324,609
2017	14,613.9	14,613.9	44,710	44,710	13,290.6	13,290.6	40,662	40,662	60,002	60,002	326,860
2018	15,454.0	15,144.0	47,002	46,059	13,934.4	13,654.9	42,380	41,530	62,825	61,418	328,794
2019	16,157.0	15,608.6	48,885	47,225	14,417.6	13,928.3	43,622	42,141	65,115	62,606	330,513
2020	17,372.5	16,603.0	52,359	50,039	14,206.2	13,577.0	42,816	40,919	64,265	60,983	331,800
2021	18,664.4	17,123.1	56,156	51,519	16,043.0	14,718.2	48,269	44,283	70,988	64,410	332,367
2022	18,702.5	16,116.9	56,068	48,317	17,511.7	15,090.8	52,498	45,240	77,178	66,510	333,568
2023 ᵖ	20,217.9	16,795.8	60,314	50,106	18,564.0	15,421.9	55,381	46,007	81,610	66,750	335,208
2020: I	16,518.9	15,821.7	49,825	47,722	14,473.1	13,862.3	43,655	41,812	65,472	62,333	331,537
II	18,071.1	17,384.6	54,478	52,408	13,168.9	12,668.7	39,700	38,192	60,031	57,383	331,715
III	17,580.2	16,774.8	52,970	50,544	14,456.2	13,793.9	43,557	41,562	65,226	61,803	331,887
IV	17,320.0	16,445.2	52,159	49,525	14,726.7	13,982.9	44,349	42,110	66,327	62,411	332,060
2021: I	19,584.6	18,381.1	58,989	55,364	15,217.7	14,282.6	45,836	43,019	68,072	63,224	332,005
II	18,342.2	16,956.2	55,220	51,047	15,950.9	14,745.6	48,021	44,392	70,123	64,153	332,166
III	18,348.5	16,740.2	55,184	50,317	16,285.1	14,848.8	48,978	44,659	71,667	64,611	332,497
IV	18,382.4	16,488.4	55,235	49,544	16,718.2	14,995.6	50,235	45,059	74,082	65,648	332,802
2022: I	18,247.8	16,066.9	54,800	48,250	17,030.6	14,995.2	51,144	45,032	75,165	65,284	332,991
II	18,501.9	16,009.6	55,508	48,031	17,415.1	15,069.2	52,247	45,209	76,636	65,127	333,320
III	18,881.7	16,151.8	56,572	48,393	17,684.2	15,127.4	52,984	45,324	77,884	65,469	333,762
IV	19,178.4	16,239.5	57,386	48,592	17,917.0	15,171.4	53,612	45,396	79,019	65,799	334,201
2023: I	19,880.2	16,662.8	59,424	49,807	18,269.6	15,312.9	54,610	45,772	80,149	66,096	334,547
II	20,164.2	16,797.3	60,203	50,151	18,419.0	15,343.6	54,993	45,811	80,801	66,357	334,934
III	20,307.7	16,809.1	60,542	50,112	18,679.5	15,461.4	55,688	46,094	82,313	67,050	335,430
IV ᵖ	20,519.4	16,914.6	61,084	50,353	18,888.1	15,569.8	56,228	46,350	83,170	67,494	335,923

[1] Population of the United States including Armed Forces overseas. Annual data are averages of quarterly data. Quarterly data are averages for the period.

Source: Department of Commerce (Bureau of Economic Analysis and Bureau of the Census).

TABLE B–19. Gross saving and investment, 1973–2023

[Billions of dollars, except as noted; quarterly data at seasonally adjusted annual rates]

Year or quarter	Total gross saving	Gross saving									
		Net saving							Consumption of fixed capital		
		Total net saving	Net private saving			Net government saving			Total	Private	Government
			Total	Personal saving	Undis-tributed corporate profits [1]	Total	Federal	State and local			
1973	335.3	156.6	189.3	135.8	53.5	−32.7	−38.3	5.6	178.7	131.5	47.2
1974	349.2	142.3	186.0	146.3	39.7	−43.7	−41.3	−2.3	206.9	153.2	53.7
1975	348.1	109.6	218.3	164.0	54.3	−108.6	−97.9	−10.7	238.5	178.8	59.7
1976	399.3	139.1	224.4	154.4	70.0	−85.3	−80.9	−4.4	260.2	196.5	63.7
1977	459.4	169.6	242.5	155.9	86.6	−72.9	−73.4	.5	289.8	221.1	68.7
1978	548.0	220.8	278.0	175.1	102.9	−57.2	−62.0	4.9	327.2	252.1	75.1
1979	613.6	239.7	288.3	186.8	101.5	−48.6	−47.4	−1.2	373.9	290.7	83.1
1980	630.3	201.9	296.5	224.9	71.6	−94.7	−88.8	−5.9	428.4	335.0	93.5
1981	744.2	257.0	355.3	263.6	91.7	−98.2	−88.1	−10.2	487.2	381.9	105.3
1982	726.0	189.1	379.2	291.2	88.0	−190.1	−167.4	−22.8	537.0	420.4	116.6
1983	716.8	154.2	379.8	264.7	115.1	−225.6	−207.2	−18.4	562.6	438.8	123.8
1984	881.8	283.4	480.1	326.3	153.8	−196.7	−196.5	−.2	598.4	463.5	134.9
1985	881.2	241.0	442.7	282.9	159.7	−201.7	−199.2	−2.4	640.1	496.4	143.7
1986	864.7	179.4	399.3	288.7	110.6	−219.9	−215.9	−4.0	685.3	531.6	153.7
1987	949.1	218.7	398.8	260.6	138.2	−180.1	−165.7	−14.4	730.4	566.3	164.1
1988	1,076.8	292.3	463.6	317.1	146.5	−171.3	−160.0	−11.3	784.5	607.9	176.6
1989	1,110.0	271.7	450.4	335.4	115.0	−178.7	−159.4	−19.3	838.3	649.6	188.6
1990	1,113.6	225.0	464.6	360.6	104.0	−239.5	−203.3	−36.3	888.5	688.4	200.1
1991	1,153.6	221.2	529.8	401.0	128.8	−308.5	−248.4	−60.1	932.4	721.5	210.9
1992	1,148.0	187.8	593.4	450.5	142.9	−405.6	−334.5	−71.1	960.2	742.9	217.4
1993	1,163.9	160.4	546.6	392.6	154.0	−386.2	−313.5	−72.6	1,003.5	778.2	225.3
1994	1,295.8	240.2	560.1	357.2	202.9	−319.9	−255.6	−64.2	1,055.6	822.5	233.1
1995	1,427.2	304.8	617.7	379.0	238.7	−312.9	−242.1	−70.8	1,122.4	880.7	241.7
1996	1,580.0	404.7	638.3	369.9	268.3	−233.6	−179.4	−54.2	1,175.3	929.1	246.2
1997	1,781.9	542.5	676.9	371.8	305.2	−134.4	−92.0	−42.4	1,239.3	987.8	251.6
1998	1,931.7	622.0	651.3	424.6	226.7	−29.3	1.4	−30.7	1,309.7	1,052.2	257.6
1999	2,008.2	609.3	579.8	315.8	264.0	29.5	69.1	−39.7	1,398.9	1,132.2	266.7
2000	2,126.2	614.9	496.7	316.8	179.9	118.2	159.7	−41.5	1,511.2	1,231.5	279.7
2001	2,072.0	472.5	577.3	363.2	214.1	−104.7	15.0	−119.8	1,599.5	1,311.7	287.8
2002	2,000.3	342.3	793.8	451.6	342.2	−451.4	−267.8	−183.6	1,658.0	1,361.8	296.2
2003	1,987.8	268.7	848.2	439.9	408.3	−579.4	−397.4	−182.0	1,719.1	1,412.0	307.1
2004	2,157.8	336.0	879.2	417.0	462.2	−543.3	−393.5	−149.8	1,821.8	1,497.1	324.7
2005	2,353.8	382.8	780.2	209.2	571.0	−397.4	−293.8	−103.7	1,971.1	1,622.6	348.4
2006	2,642.3	518.2	826.1	276.0	550.1	−307.9	−221.9	−86.0	2,124.2	1,751.8	372.3
2007	2,511.9	259.1	649.2	263.4	385.7	−390.0	−259.7	−130.4	2,252.8	1,852.4	400.3
2008	2,211.8	−147.2	699.8	451.5	248.3	−847.0	−624.9	−222.1	2,359.0	1,931.9	427.0
2009	1,997.7	−373.5	1,211.9	624.9	587.0	−1,585.5	−1,243.2	−342.3	2,371.3	1,928.5	442.8
2010	2,300.7	−89.6	1,537.7	671.4	866.2	−1,627.3	−1,318.4	−309.0	2,390.4	1,933.2	457.2
2011	2,533.1	58.8	1,570.6	776.3	793.7	−1,511.2	−1,234.1	−277.0	2,474.4	1,997.2	477.2
2012	2,972.4	396.9	1,754.4	976.5	777.8	−1,357.5	−1,072.7	−284.8	2,575.5	2,081.9	493.6
2013	3,118.8	437.2	1,337.1	615.7	721.4	−899.9	−633.9	−266.0	2,681.6	2,176.6	505.0
2014	3,446.2	626.5	1,458.0	712.0	746.0	−831.6	−594.0	−237.6	2,819.7	2,301.4	518.3
2015	3,587.8	664.9	1,438.9	790.6	648.3	−774.0	−557.4	−216.6	2,922.9	2,397.9	525.1
2016	3,473.7	465.6	1,375.1	746.2	628.9	−909.5	−667.3	−242.2	3,008.1	2,475.6	532.5
2017	3,703.2	554.2	1,515.9	841.6	674.2	−961.6	−736.8	−224.8	3,149.0	2,599.1	549.9
2018	3,950.8	638.2	1,744.5	996.7	747.8	−1,106.2	−906.4	−199.9	3,312.6	2,737.3	575.3
2019	4,176.5	696.7	1,947.0	1,190.9	756.1	−1,250.3	−1,044.4	−205.9	3,479.8	2,881.8	598.0
2020	3,936.9	311.3	3,257.6	2,678.6	579.1	−2,946.3	−2,894.4	−51.9	3,625.5	3,007.7	617.8
2021	4,200.7	327.4	2,823.9	2,120.5	703.4	−2,496.6	−2,739.9	243.4	3,873.3	3,214.3	659.0
2022	4,699.9	400.0	1,401.8	622.8	779.0	−1,001.9	−1,062.2	60.4	4,299.9	3,577.6	722.3
2023 [p]					911.5				4,584.5	3,820.8	763.7
2020: I	4,281.4	711.3	2,038.1	1,504.4	533.7	−1,326.8	−1,070.4	−256.5	3,570.1	2,961.3	608.8
II	3,443.6	−159.6	4,755.2	4,423.7	331.6	−4,914.8	−5,286.3	371.5	3,603.2	2,989.8	613.3
III	3,693.1	52.7	3,561.7	2,654.4	907.3	−3,508.9	−3,316.9	−192.1	3,640.3	3,019.7	620.7
IV	4,329.5	640.9	2,675.6	2,131.9	543.7	−2,034.7	−1,904.3	−130.4	3,688.6	3,060.0	628.5
2021: I	4,198.1	461.7	4,631.9	3,889.7	742.2	−4,170.2	−4,048.0	−122.2	3,736.4	3,097.9	638.4
II	4,001.9	182.9	2,695.3	1,888.6	806.7	−2,512.4	−3,270.7	758.3	3,819.0	3,166.8	652.2
III	4,137.0	220.3	2,226.8	1,552.1	674.7	−2,006.5	−2,189.4	182.9	3,916.6	3,251.9	664.8
IV	4,465.8	444.5	1,741.6	1,151.6	590.0	−1,297.2	−1,451.6	154.4	4,021.4	3,340.8	680.6
2022: I	4,612.7	471.8	1,268.8	703.7	565.1	−797.0	−974.4	177.4	4,140.9	3,442.9	698.0
II	4,738.0	477.8	1,344.3	552.4	791.9	−866.5	−960.5	93.9	4,260.2	3,542.8	717.4
III	4,827.4	459.2	1,511.6	612.6	899.0	−1,052.3	−1,072.7	20.4	4,368.2	3,636.4	731.8
IV	4,621.4	191.1	1,482.7	622.4	860.2	−1,291.6	−1,241.2	−50.4	4,430.3	3,688.2	742.1
2023: I	4,466.9	−40.5	1,696.6	948.2	748.4	−1,737.1	−1,673.7	−63.4	4,507.4	3,753.3	754.1
II	4,480.2	−76.9	1,773.6	1,027.6	746.0	−1,850.4	−1,665.7	−184.7	4,557.0	3,797.3	759.7
III	4,433.8	−177.7	1,711.6	851.2	860.3	−1,889.2	−1,676.0	−213.2	4,611.5	3,844.5	766.9
IV [p]				818.9					4,662.3	3,888.2	774.1

[1] With inventory valuation and capital consumption adjustments.

See next page for continuation of table.

[Billions of dollars, except as noted; quarterly data at seasonally adjusted annual rates]

Year or quarter	Gross domestic investment, capital account transactions, and net lending, NIPA [2]							Addenda:						
	Gross domestic investment				Capital account trans-actions (net) [3]	Net lending or net borrow-ing (–), NIPA [2,4]	Statis-tical discrep-ancy	Gross private saving	Gross government saving			Net domestic invest-ment	Gross saving as a percent of gross national income	Net saving as a percent of gross national income
	Total	Total	Gross private domes-tic invest-ment	Gross govern-ment invest-ment					Total	Federal	State and local			
1973	341.4	332.6	266.9	65.6	0.0	8.8	6.1	320.8	14.5	−6.0	20.4	153.9	23.4	10.9
1974	356.6	350.7	274.5	76.2	.0	5.9	7.5	339.1	10.1	−6.0	16.0	143.8	22.5	9.2
1975	361.5	341.7	257.3	84.4	.1	19.8	13.3	397.1	−48.9	−59.2	10.3	103.1	20.7	6.5
1976	420.0	412.9	323.2	89.6	.1	7.0	20.7	420.9	−21.6	−39.2	17.6	152.6	21.4	7.4
1977	478.9	489.8	396.6	93.2	.1	−11.0	19.4	463.6	−4.2	−28.2	24.0	199.9	22.1	8.1
1978	571.3	583.9	478.4	105.6	.1	−12.7	23.3	530.1	17.9	−12.4	30.3	256.7	23.3	9.4
1979	658.6	659.8	539.7	120.1	.1	−1.3	45.0	579.0	34.6	7.2	27.3	285.9	23.5	9.2
1980	674.6	666.0	530.1	135.9	.1	8.4	44.3	631.5	−1.2	−28.4	27.1	237.6	22.1	7.1
1981	781.9	778.6	631.2	147.3	.1	3.3	37.7	737.2	7.1	−20.6	27.6	291.3	23.2	8.0
1982	734.7	738.0	581.0	156.9	.1	−3.4	8.6	799.6	−73.5	−92.0	18.4	201.0	21.5	5.6
1983	773.6	808.7	637.5	171.2	.1	−35.2	56.9	818.6	−101.8	−126.1	24.3	246.1	19.8	4.3
1984	923.2	1,013.3	820.1	193.2	.1	−90.2	41.4	943.6	−61.8	−105.9	44.1	414.9	21.9	7.0
1985	935.2	1,049.5	829.7	219.9	.1	−114.4	54.1	939.1	−57.9	−102.3	44.4	409.4	20.4	5.6
1986	944.6	1,087.2	849.1	238.1	.1	−142.8	79.8	930.9	−66.2	−112.4	46.2	401.9	19.1	4.0
1987	992.7	1,146.8	892.2	254.6	.1	−154.2	43.6	965.1	−16.0	−55.6	39.6	416.4	19.7	4.5
1988	1,079.6	1,195.4	937.0	258.4	.1	−115.9	2.8	1,071.5	5.3	−41.0	46.4	410.9	20.5	5.6
1989	1,177.8	1,270.1	999.7	270.4	.3	−92.7	67.8	1,100.0	9.9	−32.5	42.4	431.9	19.8	4.9
1990	1,208.9	1,283.8	993.4	290.4	7.4	−82.3	95.4	1,153.0	−39.4	−69.8	30.4	395.3	18.9	3.8
1991	1,246.3	1,238.4	944.3	294.1	5.3	2.6	92.7	1,251.2	−97.6	−108.3	10.7	306.0	18.9	3.6
1992	1,263.6	1,309.1	1,013.0	296.1	−1.3	−44.3	115.5	1,336.3	−188.2	−191.2	3.0	348.9	17.8	2.9
1993	1,319.3	1,398.7	1,106.8	291.9	.9	−80.2	155.4	1,324.8	−160.9	−166.5	5.6	395.2	17.3	2.4
1994	1,435.1	1,550.7	1,256.5	294.2	1.3	−116.9	139.2	1,382.6	−86.8	−105.3	18.5	495.0	18.1	3.3
1995	1,519.3	1,625.2	1,317.5	307.7	.4	−106.3	92.2	1,498.5	−71.3	−88.6	17.3	502.8	18.8	4.0
1996	1,637.0	1,752.0	1,432.1	320.0	.2	−115.2	57.0	1,567.4	12.6	−25.7	38.3	576.7	19.6	5.0
1997	1,792.1	1,922.2	1,595.6	326.6	.5	−130.6	10.3	1,664.7	117.2	62.3	54.8	682.9	20.7	6.3
1998	1,875.3	2,080.7	1,736.7	344.0	.2	−205.6	−56.4	1,703.5	228.2	156.8	71.4	770.9	21.1	6.8
1999	1,978.9	2,255.5	1,887.1	368.5	6.7	−283.3	−29.3	1,712.0	296.2	227.3	68.9	856.6	20.7	6.3
2000	2,030.4	2,427.3	2,038.4	388.9	4.6	−401.4	−95.8	1,728.2	397.9	322.8	75.1	916.0	20.5	5.9
2001	1,955.3	2,346.7	1,934.8	411.9	−11.9	−379.5	−116.7	1,889.0	183.1	179.5	3.6	747.2	19.3	4.4
2002	1,918.7	2,374.1	1,930.4	443.7	4.2	−459.6	−81.7	2,155.6	−155.3	−101.0	−54.3	716.1	18.1	3.1
2003	1,963.6	2,491.3	2,027.1	464.2	8.8	−536.4	−24.2	2,260.1	−272.3	−225.1	−47.1	772.2	17.2	2.3
2004	2,129.7	2,767.5	2,281.3	486.2	4.6	−642.4	−28.1	2,376.4	−218.6	−213.0	−5.6	945.6	17.5	2.7
2005	2,296.8	3,048.0	2,534.7	513.3	−.7	−750.5	−57.0	2,402.8	−49.0	−103.2	54.2	1,077.0	17.9	2.9
2006	2,432.5	3,251.8	2,701.0	550.9	7.7	−827.0	−209.8	2,577.9	64.4	−20.7	85.1	1,127.7	18.8	3.7
2007	2,524.2	3,265.0	2,673.0	592.0	6.4	−747.2	12.3	2,501.6	10.3	−46.9	57.2	1,012.3	17.3	1.8
2008	2,403.0	3,107.2	2,477.6	629.6	.8	−705.0	191.2	2,631.8	−420.0	−399.1	−20.9	748.2	15.0	−1.0
2009	2,189.5	2,572.6	1,929.7	642.9	6.3	−389.4	191.7	3,140.4	−1,142.7	−1,009.5	−133.2	201.3	13.8	−2.6
2010	2,370.2	2,810.0	2,165.5	644.5	7.4	−447.2	69.4	3,470.9	−1,170.2	−1,074.6	−95.5	419.6	15.2	−.6
2011	2,508.8	2,969.2	2,332.6	636.6	9.5	−469.8	−24.3	3,567.2	−1,034.0	−979.2	−54.8	494.8	16.0	.4
2012	2,818.8	3,242.8	2,621.8	621.0	−.5	−423.5	−153.6	3,836.3	−863.9	−811.0	−52.8	667.2	17.9	2.4
2013	3,089.0	3,440.2	2,838.3	601.8	7.0	−358.2	−29.8	3,513.7	−394.9	−367.9	−27.1	758.6	18.2	2.6
2014	3,305.2	3,680.3	3,074.0	606.3	6.9	−382.0	−140.9	3,759.4	−313.2	−322.7	9.5	860.6	19.2	3.5
2015	3,494.8	3,917.9	3,288.5	629.4	8.3	−431.4	−93.0	3,836.7	−248.9	−285.0	36.1	995.0	19.3	3.6
2016	3,526.6	3,928.0	3,278.3	649.7	7.0	−408.4	52.9	3,850.6	−376.9	−393.6	16.7	919.9	18.3	2.5
2017	3,771.1	4,149.1	3,467.7	681.4	16.0	−394.0	67.9	4,114.9	−411.8	−456.6	44.9	1,000.1	18.7	2.8
2018	4,014.3	4,455.4	3,724.8	730.6	4.7	−445.8	63.4	4,481.8	−530.9	−616.2	85.3	1,142.8	18.9	3.1
2019	4,219.0	4,667.4	3,892.4	775.0	6.9	−455.3	42.4	4,828.8	−652.2	−745.2	93.0	1,187.5	19.2	3.2
2020	3,995.1	4,564.8	3,748.4	816.5	6.1	−575.8	58.2	6,265.3	−2,328.5	−2,585.0	256.5	939.3	18.3	1.4
2021	4,195.2	5,043.0	4,216.3	826.8	3.7	−851.5	−5.5	6,038.3	−1,837.6	−2,413.9	576.3	1,169.7	17.7	1.4
2022	4,647.6	5,633.4	4,756.6	876.8	5.3	−991.1	−52.3	4,979.4	−279.5	−711.4	431.9	1,333.5	18.1	1.5
2023 *p*	....	5,836.9	4,849.0	987.8	....	....	....	....	....	....	....	1,252.3	....	....
2020: I	4,218.2	4,612.2	3,807.8	804.4	12.1	−406.0	−63.2	4,999.4	−718.0	−766.2	48.2	1,042.1	19.4	3.2
II	3,557.4	4,068.3	3,254.3	814.1	4.4	−515.4	113.8	7,745.0	−4,301.5	−4,978.5	677.0	465.2	17.2	−.8
III	4,058.6	4,707.5	3,891.2	816.3	2.8	−651.8	365.5	6,581.4	−2,888.3	−3,006.2	117.9	1,067.2	17.2	.2
IV	4,146.2	4,871.2	4,040.2	831.1	5.0	−730.0	−183.3	5,735.6	−1,406.1	−1,589.1	183.0	1,182.6	19.3	2.9
2021: I	4,125.8	4,854.9	4,031.1	823.8	14.1	−743.2	−72.3	7,729.8	−3,531.7	−3,729.4	197.6	1,118.5	18.3	2.0
II	4,015.1	4,836.4	4,013.3	823.1	4.0	−825.2	13.2	5,862.1	−1,860.1	−2,947.1	1,087.0	1,017.4	17.1	.8
III	4,133.2	5,050.0	4,226.6	823.4	−11.5	−905.3	−3.8	5,478.7	−1,341.7	−1,861.5	519.8	1,133.4	17.2	.9
IV	4,506.8	5,430.9	4,594.0	836.9	8.1	−932.2	41.0	5,082.4	−616.6	−1,117.5	500.9	1,409.5	18.0	1.8
2022: I	4,499.8	5,615.0	4,766.8	848.2	8.6	−1,123.8	−112.9	4,711.7	−99.0	−633.3	534.2	1,474.1	18.2	1.9
II	4,586.5	5,597.6	4,739.0	858.5	14.1	−1,025.2	−151.5	4,887.1	−149.1	−611.8	462.7	1,337.4	18.3	1.8
III	4,672.4	5,607.0	4,724.6	882.3	−16.2	−918.4	−155.0	5,147.9	−320.5	−718.3	397.8	1,238.8	18.3	1.7
IV	4,831.6	5,714.1	4,796.2	918.0	14.6	−897.1	210.2	5,170.9	−549.5	−882.2	332.7	1,283.8	17.5	.7
2023: I	4,795.1	5,667.6	4,725.8	941.8	24.1	−896.7	328.2	5,449.9	−983.0	−1,309.4	326.4	1,160.2	16.8	−.2
II	4,917.4	5,754.6	4,780.3	974.4	11.5	−848.7	437.3	5,570.9	−1,090.7	−1,297.7	206.9	1,197.6	16.7	−.3
III	5,098.8	5,919.7	4,915.0	1,004.7	9.0	−829.9	665.0	5,556.1	−1,122.3	−1,303.5	181.2	1,308.2	16.4	−.7
IV *p*	....	6,005.6	4,975.0	1,030.5	....	....	....	....	....	....	....	1,343.3	....	....

[2] National income and product accounts (NIPA).
[3] Consists of capital transfers and the acquisition and disposal of nonproduced nonfinancial assets.
[4] Prior to 1982, equals the balance on current account, NIPA.

Source: Department of Commerce (Bureau of Economic Analysis).

Table B–20. Median money income (in 2022 dollars) and poverty status of families and people, by race, 2014–2022

Race, Hispanic origin, and year	Families[1] Number (millions)	Median money income (in 2022 dollars)[3]	Below poverty level[2] Total Number (millions)	Total Percent	Female householder, no husband present Number (millions)	Female householder Percent	People below poverty level[2] Number (millions)	Percent	Median money income (in 2022 dollars) of people 15 years old and over with income[3] Males All people	Males Year-round full-time workers	Females All people	Females Year-round full-time workers
TOTAL (all races)[4]												
2014	81.7	$80,600	9.5	11.6	4.8	30.6	46.7	14.8	$43,910	$62,240	$26,900	$49,350
2015	82.2	85,580	8.6	10.4	4.4	28.2	43.1	13.5	44,960	63,240	28,770	50,540
2016	82.9	87,240	8.1	9.8	4.1	26.6	40.6	12.7	46,640	64,160	29,870	51,830
2017	83.1	89,540	7.8	9.3	4.0	25.7	39.7	12.3	47,630	65,840	30,050	52,330
2017[5]	83.5	89,770	7.8	9.3	4.0	26.2	39.6	12.3	47,630	65,440	30,540	54,040
2018	83.5	90,900	7.5	9.0	3.7	24.9	38.2	11.8	48,100	66,140	31,300	53,780
2019[6]	83.7	97,970	6.6	7.8	3.3	22.2	34.0	10.5	50,470	69,340	33,490	57,100
2020[6]	83.7	95,080	7.3	8.7	3.6	23.5	37.6	11.5	48,130	73,200	33,150	59,300
2021	84.3	95,530	7.4	8.8	3.6	23.0	37.9	11.6	49,520	68,730	33,360	57,130
2022	84.4	92,750	7.4	8.8	3.5	23.0	37.9	11.5	48,450	66,180	32,790	55,560
WHITE, non-Hispanic[7]												
2014	53.8	92,730	3.9	7.3	1.7	23.7	19.7	10.1	49,680	71,020	29,040	53,510
2015	53.8	97,480	3.5	6.4	1.6	21.7	17.8	9.1	51,090	73,540	31,020	55,310
2016	54.1	98,470	3.4	6.3	1.6	21.1	17.3	8.8	52,070	73,430	31,790	56,770
2017	53.9	101,200	3.2	6.0	1.4	19.8	17.0	8.7	54,050	73,600	31,970	57,730
2017[5]	54.2	102,500	3.2	5.9	1.4	20.2	16.6	8.5	54,470	73,480	32,790	59,620
2018	54.2	103,400	3.2	5.8	1.4	19.7	15.7	8.1	55,270	75,460	34,060	58,600
2019[6]	54.3	110,600	2.7	5.0	1.1	17.1	14.2	7.3	57,590	80,070	35,690	61,200
2020[6]	53.5	108,900	3.1	5.8	1.3	18.8	16.0	8.2	56,570	81,480	35,500	64,560
2021	53.5	108,900	3.0	5.6	1.2	17.3	15.8	8.1	55,470	78,340	35,200	62,330
2022	53.0	103,400	3.2	6.1	1.3	18.9	16.7	8.6	52,720	75,640	35,180	60,550
BLACK[7]												
2014	9.9	52,200	2.3	22.9	1.6	37.2	10.8	26.2	32,140	49,950	25,360	42,730
2015	9.8	55,420	2.1	21.1	1.5	33.9	10.0	24.1	33,170	50,490	26,160	44,920
2016	10.0	59,230	1.9	19.0	1.3	31.6	9.2	22.0	35,560	50,370	27,400	44,800
2017	10.0	59,660	1.8	18.2	1.3	30.8	9.0	21.2	35,510	51,530	27,870	44,280
2017[5]	10.0	59,720	1.9	18.9	1.4	31.9	9.2	21.7	34,640	50,020	28,210	45,470
2018	9.8	61,380	1.7	17.7	1.2	29.4	8.9	20.8	35,970	52,700	29,430	46,480
2019[6]	10.0	66,650	1.6	16.3	1.1	27.3	8.1	18.8	35,610	53,240	30,780	47,830
2020[6]	10.2	64,900	1.7	16.8	1.2	28.2	8.6	19.6	35,250	58,000	30,130	51,910
2021	10.3	64,200	1.8	17.4	1.3	29.3	8.6	19.5	36,550	55,140	30,710	51,950
2022	10.4	66,760	1.5	14.3	1.0	24.5	7.6	17.1	37,300	52,400	32,370	50,520
ASIAN[7]												
2014	4.5	100,100	.4	8.9	.1	18.9	2.1	12.0	49,470	72,940	30,710	58,720
2015	4.7	110,000	.4	8.0	.1	16.2	2.1	11.4	52,900	78,370	32,120	60,670
2016	4.7	112,200	.3	7.2	.1	19.4	1.9	10.1	55,900	80,670	32,120	61,650
2017	4.9	109,400	.4	7.8	.1	15.5	2.0	10.0	57,590	83,500	33,320	61,580
2017[5]	4.9	111,700	.4	7.4	.1	16.3	1.9	9.7	58,000	83,260	32,550	63,260
2018	5.1	117,000	.4	7.6	.1	19.6	2.0	10.1	59,660	82,940	36,050	67,100
2019[6]	5.1	127,800	.3	5.7	.1	14.4	1.5	7.3	61,140	89,240	36,560	68,650
2020[6]	5.2	123,600	.3	6.4	.1	15.4	1.6	8.1	58,410	100,200	36,350	81,060
2021	5.3	127,700	.4	7.1	.1	14.7	1.9	9.3	61,120	92,950	36,950	74,220
2022	5.5	126,200	.3	6.3	.1	15.0	1.9	8.6	61,120	90,800	40,640	71,430
HISPANIC (any race)[7]												
2014	12.5	54,570	2.7	21.5	1.3	37.9	13.1	23.6	32,270	42,470	21,270	37,290
2015	12.8	57,290	2.5	19.6	1.2	35.5	12.1	21.4	34,030	43,550	22,880	38,320
2016	13.0	61,320	2.3	17.8	1.1	32.7	11.1	19.4	36,610	45,810	23,880	38,440
2017	13.2	63,220	2.2	16.3	1.1	32.7	10.8	18.3	36,190	47,050	23,950	38,250
2017[5]	13.3	63,200	2.2	16.4	1.1	33.4	10.8	18.3	35,950	45,450	24,190	38,740
2018	13.3	63,680	2.1	15.5	1.0	30.8	10.5	17.6	36,310	46,650	25,070	40,650
2019[6]	13.2	69,400	1.8	13.9	.9	26.8	9.5	15.7	36,770	47,830	26,680	42,030
2020[6]	13.7	67,700	2.0	14.8	1.0	28.6	10.5	17.0	36,160	51,680	25,820	45,440
2021	14.1	67,180	2.1	15.0	1.0	28.2	10.7	17.1	39,180	50,000	27,310	43,750
2022	14.2	67,880	2.2	15.2	1.0	29.6	10.8	16.9	37,260	48,430	26,800	41,810

[1] The term "family" refers to a group of two or more persons related by birth, marriage, or adoption and residing together. Every family must include a reference person.
[2] Poverty thresholds are updated each year to reflect changes in the consumer price index for all urban consumers (CPI-U).
[3] Adjusted by the chained consumer price index for all urban consumers (C-CPI-U).
[4] Data for American Indians and Alaska natives, native Hawaiians and other Pacific Islanders, and those reporting two or more races are included in the total but not shown separately.
[5] Reflects implementation of an updated data processing system.
[6] Reflects implementation of Census 2020-based population controls comparable to succeeding years.
[7] The CPS allows respondents to choose more than one race. Data shown are for "white alone, non-Hispanic," "black alone," and "Asian alone" race categories. ("Black" is also "black or African American.") Family race and Hispanic origin are based on the reference person.

Note: For details see *Income and Poverty in the United States* in publication Series P–60 on the CPS ASEC.

Source: Department of Commerce (Bureau of the Census).

TABLE B–21. Real farm income, 1957–2024

[Billions of chained (2024) dollars]

Year	Income of farm operators from farming [1]							
	Gross farm income						Production expenses	Net farm income
	Total	Value of agricultural sector production			Farm-related income [4]	Direct Federal Government payments		
		Total	Crops [2,3]	Animals and animal products [3]				
1957	294.8	286.1	115.7	153.9	16.6	8.6	200.8	93.9
1958	322.6	313.6	124.3	172.0	17.2	9.0	213.5	109.0
1959	309.6	304.1	120.7	164.9	18.5	5.6	222.1	87.5
1960	311.1	305.4	126.3	160.2	18.9	5.7	220.7	90.4
1961	323.4	311.5	126.2	165.8	19.5	11.9	228.1	95.4
1962	333.7	320.0	131.3	168.8	19.8	13.8	238.6	95.1
1963	337.9	324.7	139.7	164.4	20.6	13.2	246.2	91.7
1964	324.7	308.0	129.5	157.1	21.3	16.7	244.2	80.5
1965	350.9	332.3	143.4	167.3	21.6	18.6	253.6	97.2
1966	370.0	346.0	134.3	189.6	22.1	24.0	267.7	102.4
1967	360.0	338.0	136.9	178.1	23.0	21.9	272.0	87.9
1968	354.3	330.7	129.3	178.4	23.0	23.7	270.1	84.2
1969	367.5	342.7	128.2	191.0	23.5	24.7	274.3	93.1
1970	364.0	341.0	127.0	190.4	23.6	23.0	275.1	88.9
1971	365.8	347.3	138.0	185.3	24.1	18.5	277.4	88.4
1972	401.6	379.2	146.5	208.3	24.4	22.4	291.8	109.8
1973	529.4	515.4	230.4	258.8	26.2	14.0	345.5	183.9
1974	482.5	479.9	241.4	210.3	28.2	2.6	348.6	133.9
1975	451.9	448.3	226.5	193.2	28.6	3.6	337.2	114.6
1976	438.4	435.2	206.0	198.6	30.6	3.1	352.4	85.9
1977	436.2	428.9	205.1	189.8	34.0	7.3	356.5	79.7
1978	481.3	469.9	212.1	220.5	37.3	11.4	386.8	94.4
1979	521.5	516.7	230.6	246.3	39.8	4.8	426.6	94.9
1980	473.6	469.5	204.2	223.1	42.2	4.1	422.4	51.2
1981	482.1	476.5	228.7	204.1	43.7	5.6	404.2	77.9
1982	448.1	438.6	196.0	192.5	50.1	9.5	383.0	65.1
1983	404.2	379.8	149.4	184.0	46.4	24.4	366.7	37.5
1984	425.9	404.6	197.1	182.6	24.8	21.4	360.1	65.9
1985	395.9	377.0	181.0	169.6	26.4	18.9	325.8	70.1
1986	376.1	347.7	152.5	170.4	24.7	28.5	301.2	75.0
1987	396.0	356.6	151.6	178.1	26.9	39.4	306.6	89.4
1988	404.1	371.2	157.3	178.6	35.3	32.9	314.1	90.0
1989	418.7	394.9	178.1	182.4	34.4	23.8	317.1	101.6
1990	416.6	397.0	175.2	189.6	32.1	19.6	319.2	97.4
1991	391.3	374.6	165.4	177.8	31.4	16.7	309.3	82.0
1992	399.5	381.3	177.4	173.6	30.3	18.3	299.6	100.0
1993	399.0	372.9	160.9	179.0	33.0	26.1	308.0	90.9
1994	411.8	396.8	191.5	171.0	34.3	15.0	311.6	100.2
1995	393.5	379.9	179.0	163.8	37.1	13.6	319.2	74.2
1996	432.2	418.7	212.0	168.7	38.0	13.5	324.2	108.0
1997	428.8	415.3	202.7	173.5	39.1	13.5	336.4	92.4
1998	414.4	392.4	182.0	167.8	42.6	22.1	330.5	84.0
1999	412.8	375.0	163.0	167.3	44.7	37.8	329.0	83.8
2000	415.2	375.3	163.1	170.2	42.0	39.9	328.1	87.1
2001	419.6	382.0	159.6	178.6	43.8	37.7	327.5	92.2
2002	381.5	360.9	162.0	154.6	44.3	20.5	316.7	64.8
2003	419.6	392.8	176.1	170.3	46.4	26.8	320.7	98.9
2004	465.8	445.3	197.7	196.3	51.3	20.5	327.7	138.1
2005	457.3	419.9	175.2	193.8	50.9	37.4	336.6	120.7
2006	431.1	407.7	176.4	177.3	54.0	23.5	345.8	85.3
2007	491.2	474.0	218.6	200.2	55.2	17.2	389.9	101.3
2008	517.5	500.1	246.7	197.9	55.5	17.4	406.8	110.7
2009	474.7	457.6	232.2	168.7	56.7	17.2	387.0	87.7
2010	496.9	479.6	234.3	195.5	49.9	17.3	389.4	107.5
2011	574.1	559.9	272.2	223.6	64.1	14.2	419.1	155.1
2012	602.9	588.7	285.4	226.7	76.6	14.3	473.7	129.2
2013	637.9	623.4	308.1	238.7	76.7	14.5	474.9	163.0
2014	626.0	613.3	267.2	277.6	68.5	12.7	506.5	119.5
2015	566.0	552.1	236.7	249.3	66.2	13.9	461.2	104.9
2016	524.4	507.8	240.8	210.4	56.7	16.5	445.1	79.3
2017	531.4	517.0	234.7	221.0	61.3	14.4	437.6	93.8
2018	518.9	502.2	227.2	216.6	58.4	16.7	419.0	100.0
2019	514.5	487.6	214.0	210.4	63.2	27.0	417.7	96.8
2020	537.2	483.2	226.1	195.2	61.9	54.0	423.4	113.8
2021	582.9	553.5	274.0	220.1	59.4	29.4	421.6	161.3
2022	650.0	633.5	283.6	270.6	79.3	16.5	453.6	196.4
2023 _p_	607.1	594.6	266.9	248.2	79.6	12.4	447.8	159.2
2024 _p_	571.2	560.9	242.6	239.7	78.6	10.2	455.1	116.1

[1] The GDP chain-type price index is used to convert the current-dollar statistics to 2024=100 equivalents.
[2] Crop receipts include proceeds received from commodities placed under Commodity Credit Corporation loans.
[3] The value of production equates to the sum of cash receipts, home consumption, and the value of the change in inventories.
[4] Includes income from forest products sold, the gross imputed rental value of farm dwellings, machine hire and custom work, and other sources of farm income such as commodity insurance indemnities.

Note: Data for 2023 and 2024 are forecasts.

Source: Department of Agriculture (Economic Research Service).

Labor Market Indicators

TABLE B–22. Civilian labor force, 1929–2023

[Monthly data seasonally adjusted, except as noted]

Year or month	Civilian noninstitutional population [1]	Civilian labor force Total	Employment Total	Employment Agricultural	Employment Non-agricultural	Unemployment	Not in labor force	Civilian labor force participation rate [2]	Civilian employment/population ratio [3]	Unemployment rate, civilian workers [4]
		Thousands of persons 14 years of age and over							Percent	
1929		49,180	47,630	10,450	37,180	1,550				3.2
1930		49,820	45,480	10,340	35,140	4,340				8.7
1931		50,420	42,400	10,290	32,110	8,020				15.9
1932		51,000	38,940	10,170	28,770	12,060				23.6
1933		51,590	38,760	10,090	28,670	12,830				24.9
1934		52,230	40,890	9,900	30,990	11,340				21.7
1935		52,870	42,260	10,110	32,150	10,610				20.1
1936		53,440	44,410	10,000	34,410	9,030				16.9
1937		54,000	46,300	9,820	36,480	7,700				14.3
1938		54,610	44,220	9,690	34,530	10,390				19.0
1939		55,230	45,750	9,610	36,140	9,480				17.2
1940	99,840	55,640	47,520	9,540	37,980	8,120	44,200	55.7	47.6	14.6
1941	99,900	55,910	50,350	9,100	41,250	5,560	43,990	56.0	50.4	9.9
1942	98,640	56,410	53,750	9,250	44,500	2,660	42,230	57.2	54.5	4.7
1943	94,640	55,540	54,470	9,080	45,390	1,070	39,100	58.7	57.6	1.9
1944	93,220	54,630	53,960	8,950	45,010	670	38,590	58.6	57.9	1.2
1945	94,090	53,860	52,820	8,580	44,240	1,040	40,230	57.2	56.1	1.9
1946	103,070	57,520	55,250	8,320	46,930	2,270	45,550	55.8	53.6	3.9
1947	106,018	60,168	57,812	8,256	49,557	2,356	45,850	56.8	54.5	3.9
		Thousands of persons 16 years of age and over								
1947	101,827	59,350	57,038	7,890	49,148	2,311	42,477	58.3	56.0	3.9
1948	103,068	60,621	58,343	7,629	50,714	2,276	42,447	58.8	56.6	3.8
1949	103,994	61,286	57,651	7,658	49,993	3,637	42,708	58.9	55.4	5.9
1950	104,995	62,208	58,918	7,160	51,758	3,288	42,787	59.2	56.1	5.3
1951	104,621	62,017	59,961	6,726	53,235	2,055	42,604	59.2	57.3	3.3
1952	105,231	62,138	60,250	6,500	53,749	1,883	43,093	59.0	57.3	3.0
1953	107,056	63,015	61,179	6,260	54,919	1,834	44,041	58.9	57.1	2.9
1954	108,321	63,643	60,109	6,205	53,904	3,532	44,678	58.8	55.5	5.5
1955	109,683	65,023	62,170	6,450	55,722	2,852	44,660	59.3	56.7	4.4
1956	110,954	66,552	63,799	6,283	57,514	2,750	44,402	60.0	57.5	4.1
1957	112,265	66,929	64,071	5,947	58,123	2,859	45,336	59.6	57.1	4.3
1958	113,727	67,639	63,036	5,586	57,450	4,602	46,088	59.5	55.4	6.8
1959	115,329	68,369	64,630	5,565	59,065	3,740	46,960	59.3	56.0	5.5
1960	117,245	69,628	65,778	5,458	60,318	3,852	47,617	59.4	56.1	5.5
1961	118,771	70,459	65,746	5,200	60,546	4,714	48,312	59.3	55.4	6.7
1962	120,153	70,614	66,702	4,944	61,759	3,911	49,539	58.8	55.5	5.5
1963	122,416	71,833	67,762	4,687	63,076	4,070	50,583	58.7	55.4	5.7
1964	124,485	73,091	69,305	4,523	64,782	3,786	51,394	58.7	55.7	5.2
1965	126,513	74,455	71,088	4,361	66,726	3,366	52,058	58.9	56.2	4.5
1966	128,058	75,770	72,895	3,979	68,915	2,875	52,288	59.2	56.9	3.8
1967	129,874	77,347	74,372	3,844	70,527	2,975	52,527	59.6	57.3	3.8
1968	132,028	78,737	75,920	3,817	72,103	2,817	53,291	59.6	57.5	3.6
1969	134,335	80,734	77,902	3,606	74,296	2,832	53,602	60.1	58.0	3.5
1970	137,085	82,771	78,678	3,463	75,215	4,093	54,315	60.4	57.4	4.9
1971	140,216	84,382	79,367	3,394	75,972	5,016	55,834	60.2	56.6	5.9
1972	144,126	87,034	82,153	3,484	78,669	4,882	57,091	60.4	57.0	5.6
1973	147,096	89,429	85,064	3,470	81,594	4,365	57,667	60.8	57.8	4.9
1974	150,120	91,949	86,794	3,515	83,279	5,156	58,171	61.3	57.8	5.6
1975	153,153	93,775	85,846	3,408	82,438	7,929	59,377	61.2	56.1	8.5
1976	156,150	96,158	88,752	3,331	85,421	7,406	59,991	61.6	56.8	7.7
1977	159,033	99,009	92,017	3,283	88,734	6,991	60,025	62.3	57.9	7.1
1978	161,910	102,251	96,048	3,387	92,661	6,202	59,659	63.2	59.3	6.1
1979	164,863	104,962	98,824	3,347	95,477	6,137	59,900	63.7	59.9	5.8
1980	167,745	106,940	99,303	3,364	95,938	7,637	60,806	63.8	59.2	7.1
1981	170,130	108,670	100,397	3,368	97,030	8,273	61,460	63.9	59.0	7.6
1982	172,271	110,204	99,526	3,401	96,125	10,678	62,067	64.0	57.8	9.7
1983	174,215	111,550	100,834	3,383	97,450	10,717	62,665	64.0	57.9	9.6
1984	176,383	113,544	105,005	3,321	101,685	8,539	62,839	64.4	59.5	7.5
1985	178,206	115,461	107,150	3,179	103,971	8,312	62,744	64.8	60.1	7.2
1986	180,587	117,834	109,597	3,163	106,434	8,237	62,752	65.3	60.7	7.0
1987	182,753	119,865	112,440	3,208	109,232	7,425	62,888	65.6	61.5	6.2
1988	184,613	121,669	114,968	3,169	111,800	6,701	62,944	65.9	62.3	5.5
1989	186,393	123,869	117,342	3,199	114,142	6,528	62,523	66.5	63.0	5.3

[1] Not seasonally adjusted.
[2] Civilian labor force as percent of civilian noninstitutional population.
[3] Civilian employment as percent of civilian noninstitutional population.
[4] Unemployed as percent of civilian labor force.

See next page for continuation of table.

[Monthly data seasonally adjusted, except as noted]

Year or month	Civilian noninstitutional population [1]	Civilian labor force					Not in labor force	Civilian labor force participation rate [2]	Civilian employment/ population ratio [3]	Unemployment rate, civilian workers [4]
		Total	Employment			Unemployment				
			Total	Agricultural	Non-agricultural					
	Thousands of persons 16 years of age and over							Percent		
1990	189,164	125,840	118,793	3,223	115,570	7,047	63,324	66.5	62.8	5.6
1991	190,925	126,346	117,718	3,269	114,449	8,628	64,578	66.2	61.7	6.8
1992	192,805	128,105	118,492	3,247	115,245	9,613	64,700	66.4	61.5	7.5
1993	194,838	129,200	120,259	3,115	117,144	8,940	65,638	66.3	61.7	6.9
1994	196,814	131,056	123,060	3,409	119,651	7,996	65,758	66.6	62.5	6.1
1995	198,584	132,304	124,900	3,440	121,460	7,404	66,280	66.6	62.9	5.6
1996	200,591	133,943	126,708	3,443	123,264	7,236	66,647	66.8	63.2	5.4
1997	203,133	136,297	129,558	3,399	126,159	6,739	66,837	67.1	63.8	4.9
1998	205,220	137,673	131,463	3,378	128,085	6,210	67,547	67.1	64.1	4.5
1999	207,753	139,368	133,488	3,281	130,207	5,880	68,385	67.1	64.3	4.2
2000 [5]	212,577	142,583	136,891	2,464	134,427	5,692	69,994	67.1	64.4	4.0
2001	215,092	143,734	136,933	2,299	134,635	6,801	71,359	66.8	63.7	4.7
2002	217,570	144,863	136,485	2,311	134,174	8,378	72,707	66.6	62.7	5.8
2003	221,168	146,510	137,736	2,275	135,461	8,774	74,658	66.2	62.3	6.0
2004	223,357	147,401	139,252	2,232	137,020	8,149	75,956	66.0	62.3	5.5
2005	226,082	149,320	141,730	2,197	139,532	7,591	76,762	66.0	62.7	5.1
2006	228,815	151,428	144,427	2,206	142,221	7,001	77,387	66.2	63.1	4.6
2007	231,867	153,124	146,047	2,095	143,952	7,078	78,743	66.0	63.0	4.6
2008	233,788	154,287	145,362	2,168	143,194	8,924	79,501	66.0	62.2	5.8
2009	235,801	154,142	139,877	2,103	137,775	14,265	81,659	65.4	59.3	9.3
2010	237,830	153,889	139,064	2,206	136,858	14,825	83,941	64.7	58.5	9.6
2011	239,618	153,617	139,869	2,254	137,615	13,747	86,001	64.1	58.4	8.9
2012	243,284	154,975	142,469	2,186	140,283	12,506	88,310	63.7	58.6	8.1
2013	245,679	155,389	143,929	2,130	141,799	11,460	90,290	63.2	58.6	7.4
2014	247,947	155,922	146,305	2,237	144,068	9,617	92,025	62.9	59.0	6.2
2015	250,801	157,130	148,834	2,422	146,411	8,296	93,671	62.7	59.3	5.3
2016	253,538	159,187	151,436	2,460	148,976	7,751	94,351	62.8	59.7	4.9
2017	255,079	160,320	153,337	2,454	150,883	6,982	94,759	62.9	60.1	4.4
2018	257,791	162,075	155,761	2,425	153,336	6,314	95,716	62.9	60.4	3.9
2019	259,175	163,539	157,538	2,425	155,113	6,001	95,636	63.1	60.8	3.7
2020	260,329	160,742	147,795	2,349	145,446	12,947	99,587	61.7	56.8	8.1
2021	261,445	161,204	152,581	2,291	150,290	8,623	100,241	61.7	58.4	5.3
2022	263,973	164,287	158,291	2,290	156,001	5,996	99,686	62.2	60.0	3.6
2023	266,942	167,116	161,037	2,264	158,772	6,080	99,826	62.6	60.3	3.6
2022: Jan	263,202	163,615	157,066	2,329	154,477	6,549	99,587	62.2	59.7	4.0
Feb	263,324	163,807	157,528	2,357	154,974	6,279	99,517	62.2	59.8	3.8
Mar	263,444	164,212	158,219	2,379	155,564	5,993	99,232	62.3	60.1	3.6
Apr	263,559	163,922	157,888	2,332	155,514	6,034	99,637	62.2	59.9	3.7
May	263,679	164,280	158,314	2,335	156,048	5,966	99,399	62.3	60.0	3.6
June	263,835	164,100	158,116	2,288	156,037	5,984	99,735	62.2	59.9	3.6
July	264,012	164,065	158,282	2,413	156,028	5,783	99,946	62.1	60.0	3.5
Aug	264,184	164,741	158,758	2,163	156,741	5,983	99,443	62.4	60.1	3.6
Sept	264,356	164,649	158,894	2,165	156,811	5,755	99,707	62.3	60.1	3.5
Oct	264,535	164,679	158,729	2,214	156,626	5,950	99,856	62.3	60.0	3.6
Nov	264,708	164,441	158,485	2,219	156,258	5,956	100,267	62.1	59.9	3.6
Dec	264,844	164,998	159,300	2,317	156,970	5,698	99,846	62.3	60.1	3.5
2023: Jan	265,962	165,871	160,152	2,249	157,663	5,719	100,090	62.4	60.2	3.4
Feb	266,112	166,263	160,301	2,343	157,797	5,962	99,849	62.5	60.2	3.6
Mar	266,272	166,690	160,824	2,223	158,332	5,866	99,582	62.6	60.4	3.5
Apr	266,443	166,678	160,962	2,295	158,615	5,715	99,766	62.6	60.4	3.4
May	266,618	166,823	160,707	2,293	158,491	6,117	99,795	62.6	60.3	3.7
June	266,801	167,000	161,004	2,299	158,886	5,997	99,801	62.6	60.3	3.6
July	267,000	167,113	161,209	2,251	159,089	5,904	99,889	62.6	60.4	3.5
Aug	267,213	167,840	161,500	2,279	159,275	6,340	99,374	62.8	60.4	3.8
Sept	267,428	167,897	161,550	2,286	159,306	6,347	99,531	62.8	60.4	3.8
Oct	267,642	167,723	161,280	2,201	159,166	6,443	99,919	62.7	60.3	3.8
Nov	267,822	168,127	161,866	2,262	159,578	6,262	99,695	62.8	60.4	3.7
Dec	267,991	167,451	161,183	2,205	158,993	6,268	100,540	62.5	60.1	3.7

[5] Beginning in 2000, data for agricultural employment are for agricultural and related industries; data for this series and for nonagricultural employment are not strictly comparable with data for earlier years. Because of independent seasonal adjustment for these two series, monthly data will not add to total civilian employment.

Note: Labor force data in Tables B–22 through B–28 are based on household interviews and usually relate to the calendar week that includes the 12th of the month. Historical comparability is affected by revisions to population controls, changes in occupational and industry classification, and other changes to the survey. In recent years, updated population controls have been introduced annually with the release of January data, so data are not strictly comparable with earlier periods. Particularly notable changes were introduced for data in the years 1953, 1960, 1962, 1972, 1973, 1978, 1980, 1990, 1994, 1997, 1998, 2000, 2003, 2008 and 2012. For definitions of terms, area samples used, historical comparability of the data, comparability with other series, etc., see *Employment and Earnings* or concepts and methodology of the CPS at http://www.bls.gov/cps/documentation.htm#concepts.

Source: Department of Labor (Bureau of Labor Statistics).

TABLE B–23. Civilian employment by sex, age, and demographic characteristic, 1978–2023

[Thousands of persons 16 years of age and over, except as noted; monthly data seasonally adjusted]

Year or month	All civilian workers	Men 20 years and over	Women 20 years and over	Both sexes 16–19	White Total	White Men 20 years and over	White Women 20 years and over	Black or African American Total	Black or African American Men 20 years and over	Black or African American Women 20 years and over	Asian Total	Hispanic or Latino ethnicity Total	Hispanic Men 20 years and over	Hispanic Women 20 years and over
1978	96,048	52,143	35,836	8,070	84,936	46,594	30,975	9,102	4,483	4,047	....	4,527	2,568	1,537
1979	98,824	53,308	37,434	8,083	87,259	47,546	32,357	9,359	4,606	4,174	....	4,785	2,701	1,638
1980	99,303	53,101	38,492	7,710	87,715	47,419	33,275	9,313	4,498	4,267	....	5,527	3,142	1,886
1981	100,397	53,582	39,590	7,225	88,709	47,846	34,275	9,355	4,520	4,329	....	5,813	3,325	2,029
1982	99,526	52,891	40,086	6,549	87,903	47,209	34,710	9,189	4,414	4,347	....	5,805	3,354	2,040
1983	100,834	53,487	41,004	6,342	88,893	47,618	35,476	9,375	4,531	4,428	....	6,072	3,523	2,127
1984	105,005	55,769	42,793	6,444	92,120	49,461	36,823	10,119	4,871	4,773	....	6,651	3,825	2,357
1985	107,150	56,562	44,154	6,434	93,736	50,061	37,907	10,501	4,992	4,977	....	6,888	3,994	2,456
1986	109,597	57,569	45,556	6,472	95,660	50,818	39,050	10,814	5,150	5,128	....	7,219	4,174	2,615
1987	112,440	58,726	47,074	6,640	97,789	51,649	40,242	11,309	5,357	5,365	....	7,790	4,444	2,872
1988	114,968	59,781	48,383	6,805	99,812	52,466	41,316	11,658	5,509	5,548	....	8,250	4,680	3,047
1989	117,342	60,837	49,745	6,759	101,584	53,292	42,346	11,953	5,602	5,727	....	8,573	4,853	3,172
1990	118,793	61,678	50,535	6,581	102,261	53,685	42,796	12,175	5,692	5,884	....	9,845	5,609	3,567
1991	117,718	61,178	50,634	5,906	101,182	53,103	42,862	12,074	5,706	5,874	....	9,828	5,623	3,603
1992	118,492	61,496	51,328	5,669	101,669	53,357	43,327	12,151	5,681	5,978	....	10,027	5,757	3,693
1993	120,259	62,355	52,099	5,805	103,045	54,021	43,910	12,382	5,793	6,095	....	10,361	5,992	3,800
1994	123,060	63,294	53,606	6,161	105,190	54,676	45,116	12,835	5,964	6,320	....	10,788	6,189	3,989
1995	124,900	64,085	54,396	6,419	106,490	55,254	45,643	13,279	6,137	6,556	....	11,127	6,367	4,116
1996	126,708	64,897	55,311	6,500	107,808	55,977	46,164	13,542	6,167	6,762	....	11,642	6,655	4,341
1997	129,558	66,284	56,613	6,661	109,856	56,986	47,063	13,969	6,325	7,013	....	12,726	7,307	4,705
1998	131,463	67,135	57,278	7,051	110,931	57,500	47,342	14,556	6,530	7,290	....	13,291	7,570	4,928
1999	133,488	67,761	58,555	7,172	112,235	57,934	48,098	15,056	6,702	7,663	....	13,720	7,576	5,290
2000	136,891	69,634	60,067	7,189	114,424	59,119	49,145	15,156	6,741	7,703	6,043	15,735	8,859	5,903
2001	136,933	69,776	60,417	6,740	114,430	59,245	49,369	15,006	6,627	7,741	6,180	16,190	9,100	6,121
2002	136,485	69,734	60,420	6,332	114,013	59,124	49,448	14,872	6,652	7,610	6,215	16,590	9,341	6,367
2003	137,736	70,415	61,402	5,919	114,235	59,348	49,823	14,739	6,586	7,636	5,756	17,372	10,063	6,541
2004	139,252	71,572	61,773	5,907	115,239	60,159	50,040	14,909	6,681	7,707	5,994	17,930	10,385	6,752
2005	141,730	73,050	62,702	5,978	116,949	61,255	50,589	15,313	6,901	7,876	6,244	18,632	10,872	6,913
2006	144,427	74,431	63,834	6,162	118,833	62,259	51,359	15,765	7,079	8,068	6,522	19,613	11,391	7,321
2007	146,047	75,337	64,799	5,911	119,792	62,806	51,996	16,051	7,245	8,240	6,839	20,382	11,827	7,662
2008	145,362	74,750	65,039	5,573	119,126	62,304	52,124	15,953	7,151	8,260	6,917	20,346	11,769	7,707
2009	139,877	71,341	63,699	4,837	114,996	59,626	51,231	15,025	6,628	7,956	6,635	19,647	11,256	7,649
2010	139,064	71,230	63,456	4,378	114,168	59,438	50,997	15,010	6,680	7,944	6,705	19,906	11,438	7,788
2011	139,869	72,182	63,360	4,327	114,690	60,118	50,881	15,051	6,765	7,906	6,867	20,269	11,685	7,918
2012	142,469	73,403	64,640	4,426	114,769	60,193	50,911	15,856	7,104	8,313	7,705	21,878	12,212	8,858
2013	143,929	74,176	65,295	4,458	115,379	60,511	51,198	16,151	7,304	8,408	8,136	22,514	12,638	9,056
2014	146,305	75,471	66,287	4,548	116,788	61,289	51,798	16,732	7,613	8,663	8,325	23,492	13,202	9,431
2015	148,834	76,776	67,323	4,734	117,944	61,959	52,161	17,472	7,938	9,032	8,706	24,400	13,624	9,853
2016	151,436	78,084	68,387	4,965	119,313	62,575	52,771	17,982	8,228	9,219	9,213	25,249	14,055	10,217
2017	153,337	78,919	69,344	5,074	120,176	63,009	53,179	18,587	8,500	9,514	9,448	25,938	14,355	10,543
2018	155,761	80,211	70,424	5,126	121,461	63,719	53,682	19,091	8,745	9,751	9,832	27,012	14,873	11,045
2019	157,538	80,917	71,470	5,150	122,441	64,070	54,304	19,381	8,883	9,910	10,179	27,805	15,204	11,516
2020	147,795	76,227	66,873	4,695	115,341	60,570	51,048	17,873	8,150	9,176	9,437	25,952	14,333	10,593
2021	152,581	78,216	69,099	5,266	118,291	61,737	52,389	18,726	8,597	9,525	10,016	27,429	15,138	11,165
2022	158,291	81,409	71,283	5,600	121,908	63,743	53,767	19,937	9,294	10,034	10,615	29,299	15,997	12,049
2023	161,037	82,698	72,692	5,647	123,165	64,316	54,441	20,674	9,617	10,420	11,096	30,343	16,386	12,649
2022: Jan	157,066	80,640	70,887	5,539	121,438	63,526	53,489	19,564	9,030	9,948	10,479	28,908	15,880	11,770
Feb	157,528	81,220	70,835	5,473	121,878	63,878	53,609	19,686	9,277	9,881	10,244	29,174	16,096	11,831
Mar	158,219	81,262	71,321	5,637	122,276	63,920	53,881	19,729	9,199	9,951	10,448	29,185	15,977	11,922
Apr	157,888	81,186	71,126	5,576	121,593	63,522	53,663	19,896	9,324	9,990	10,487	29,112	15,986	11,852
May	158,314	81,356	71,383	5,574	121,682	63,591	53,724	20,099	9,405	10,073	10,622	29,219	16,125	11,838
June	158,116	81,212	71,316	5,588	121,601	63,490	53,759	19,996	9,359	10,032	10,584	29,335	16,130	11,945
July	158,282	81,197	71,607	5,478	121,818	63,485	54,057	19,948	9,236	10,124	10,655	29,144	15,844	12,110
Aug	158,758	81,332	71,650	5,775	122,116	63,589	54,049	19,838	9,162	10,037	10,791	29,549	15,971	12,272
Sept	158,894	81,874	71,425	5,594	122,268	64,022	53,840	20,069	9,349	10,082	10,852	29,494	15,965	12,315
Oct	158,729	81,927	71,208	5,593	122,062	64,059	53,670	20,043	9,307	10,098	10,815	29,465	16,012	12,213
Nov	158,485	81,691	71,074	5,720	121,688	63,678	53,532	20,166	9,430	10,091	10,732	29,392	15,923	12,194
Dec	159,300	82,051	71,570	5,680	122,549	64,171	53,935	20,199	9,449	10,104	10,677	29,642	16,055	12,328
2023: Jan	160,152	82,281	72,176	5,695	122,796	64,208	54,137	20,512	9,562	10,303	10,936	29,755	16,082	12,453
Feb	160,301	82,340	72,257	5,704	122,764	64,138	54,182	20,613	9,670	10,307	10,970	29,813	16,047	12,474
Mar	160,824	82,688	72,368	5,767	122,846	64,287	54,046	20,974	9,811	10,506	11,056	30,065	16,298	12,473
Apr	160,962	82,596	72,597	5,770	123,263	64,399	54,331	20,713	9,519	10,557	11,053	30,183	16,267	12,568
May	160,707	82,520	72,527	5,660	123,103	64,330	54,349	20,613	9,511	10,449	11,043	30,374	16,436	12,661
June	161,004	82,836	72,605	5,563	123,422	64,498	54,606	20,411	9,478	10,295	11,084	30,588	16,571	12,660
July	161,209	82,896	72,837	5,476	123,366	64,394	54,670	20,523	9,593	10,358	11,260	30,609	16,541	12,724
Aug	161,500	82,800	73,107	5,593	123,543	64,307	54,803	20,626	9,640	10,367	11,125	30,451	16,436	12,776
Sept	161,550	82,853	73,119	5,578	123,403	64,313	54,767	20,650	9,631	10,403	11,255	30,637	16,520	12,785
Oct	161,280	82,526	73,066	5,688	123,198	64,148	54,621	20,636	9,520	10,475	11,134	30,525	16,409	12,727
Nov	161,866	83,084	73,049	5,733	123,550	64,559	54,609	20,886	9,648	10,533	11,144	30,636	16,537	12,737
Dec	161,183	82,958	72,587	5,638	122,802	64,208	54,175	20,952	9,821	10,486	11,084	30,480	16,438	12,746

[1] Beginning in 2003, persons who selected this race group only. Persons whose ethnicity is identified as Hispanic or Latino may be of any race. Prior to 2003, persons who selected more than one race were included in the group they identified as the main race. Data for "black or African American" were for "black" prior to 2003. See *Employment and Earnings* or concepts and methodology of the Current Population Survey (CPS) at http://www.bls.gov/cps/documentation. htm#concepts for details.

Note: Detail will not sum to total because data for all race groups are not shown here.

See footnote 5 and Note, Table B–22.

Source: Department of Labor (Bureau of Labor Statistics).

TABLE B–24. Unemployment by sex, age, and demographic characteristic, 1978–2023

[Thousands of persons 16 years of age and over, except as noted; monthly data seasonally adjusted]

Year or month	All civilian workers	By sex and age			By race or ethnicity [1]									
		Men 20 years and over	Women 20 years and over	Both sexes 16–19	White			Black or African American			Asian	Hispanic or Latino ethnicity		
					Total	Men 20 years and over	Women 20 years and over	Total	Men 20 years and over	Women 20 years and over	Total	Total	Men 20 years and over	Women 20 years and over
1978	6,202	2,328	2,292	1,583	4,698	1,797	1,713	1,330	462	510	....	452	175	168
1979	6,137	2,308	2,276	1,555	4,664	1,773	1,699	1,319	473	513	....	434	168	160
1980	7,637	3,353	2,615	1,669	5,884	2,629	1,964	1,553	636	574	....	620	284	190
1981	8,273	3,615	2,895	1,763	6,343	2,825	2,143	1,731	703	671	....	678	321	212
1982	10,678	5,089	3,613	1,977	8,241	3,991	2,715	2,142	954	793	....	929	461	293
1983	10,717	5,257	3,632	1,829	8,128	4,098	2,643	2,272	1,002	878	....	961	491	302
1984	8,539	3,932	3,107	1,499	6,372	2,992	2,264	1,914	815	747	....	800	393	258
1985	8,312	3,715	3,129	1,468	6,191	2,834	2,283	1,864	757	750	....	811	401	269
1986	8,237	3,751	3,032	1,454	6,140	2,857	2,213	1,840	765	728	....	857	438	278
1987	7,425	3,369	2,709	1,347	5,501	2,584	1,922	1,684	666	706	....	751	374	241
1988	6,701	2,987	2,487	1,226	4,944	2,268	1,766	1,547	617	642	....	732	351	234
1989	6,528	2,867	2,467	1,194	4,770	2,149	1,758	1,544	619	625	....	750	342	276
1990	7,047	3,239	2,596	1,212	5,186	2,431	1,852	1,565	664	633	....	876	425	289
1991	8,628	4,195	3,074	1,359	6,560	3,284	2,248	1,723	745	698	....	1,092	575	339
1992	9,613	4,717	3,469	1,427	7,169	3,620	2,512	2,011	886	800	....	1,311	675	418
1993	8,940	4,287	3,288	1,365	6,655	3,263	2,400	1,844	801	729	....	1,248	629	418
1994	7,996	3,627	3,049	1,320	5,892	2,735	2,197	1,666	682	685	....	1,187	558	431
1995	7,404	3,239	2,819	1,346	5,459	2,465	2,042	1,538	593	620	....	1,140	530	404
1996	7,236	3,146	2,783	1,306	5,300	2,363	1,998	1,592	639	643	....	1,132	495	438
1997	6,739	2,882	2,585	1,271	4,836	2,140	1,784	1,560	585	673	....	1,069	471	401
1998	6,210	2,580	2,424	1,205	4,484	1,920	1,688	1,426	524	622	....	1,026	436	376
1999	5,880	2,433	2,285	1,162	4,273	1,813	1,616	1,309	480	561	....	945	374	376
2000	5,692	2,376	2,235	1,081	4,121	1,731	1,595	1,241	499	512	227	954	388	371
2001	6,801	3,040	2,599	1,162	4,969	2,275	1,849	1,416	573	582	288	1,138	495	436
2002	8,378	3,896	3,228	1,253	6,137	2,943	2,269	1,693	695	738	389	1,353	636	496
2003	8,774	4,209	3,314	1,251	6,311	3,125	2,276	1,787	760	772	366	1,441	693	555
2004	8,149	3,791	3,150	1,208	5,847	2,785	2,172	1,729	733	755	277	1,342	635	504
2005	7,591	3,392	3,013	1,186	5,350	2,450	2,054	1,700	699	734	259	1,191	536	464
2006	7,001	3,131	2,751	1,119	5,002	2,281	1,927	1,549	640	656	205	1,081	497	414
2007	7,078	3,259	2,718	1,101	5,143	2,408	1,930	1,445	622	588	229	1,220	576	446
2008	8,924	4,297	3,342	1,285	6,509	3,179	2,384	1,788	811	732	285	1,678	860	567
2009	14,265	7,555	5,157	1,552	10,648	5,746	3,745	2,606	1,286	1,032	522	2,706	1,474	911
2010	14,825	7,763	5,534	1,528	10,916	5,828	3,960	2,852	1,396	1,165	543	2,843	1,519	1,001
2011	13,747	6,898	5,450	1,400	9,889	5,046	3,818	2,831	1,360	1,204	518	2,629	1,345	984
2012	12,506	5,984	5,125	1,397	8,915	4,347	3,564	2,544	1,152	1,119	483	2,514	1,195	995
2013	11,460	5,568	4,565	1,327	8,033	3,994	3,102	2,429	1,082	1,069	448	2,257	1,090	855
2014	9,617	4,585	3,926	1,106	6,540	3,141	2,623	2,141	973	943	436	1,878	864	764
2015	8,296	3,959	3,371	966	5,662	2,751	2,249	1,846	835	811	347	1,726	820	686
2016	7,751	3,675	3,151	925	5,345	2,594	2,100	1,655	737	724	349	1,548	720	627
2017	6,982	3,287	2,868	827	4,765	2,288	1,923	1,501	663	657	333	1,401	632	585
2018	6,314	2,976	2,578	759	4,354	2,094	1,743	1,322	582	573	304	1,323	591	547
2019	6,001	2,819	2,435	746	4,159	1,967	1,664	1,251	571	527	280	1,248	553	497
2020	12,947	6,118	5,804	1,025	9,090	4,334	4,013	2,304	1,069	1,062	894	3,018	1,451	1,291
2021	8,623	4,302	3,625	696	5,854	2,957	2,411	1,756	845	791	529	1,995	986	812
2022	5,996	2,867	2,453	675	4,049	1,995	1,585	1,300	572	596	306	1,302	626	513
2023	6,080	2,985	2,382	713	4,162	2,091	1,580	1,212	542	538	344	1,475	730	557
2022: Jan	6,549	3,180	2,673	695	4,304	2,140	1,717	1,470	684	629	387	1,436	667	596
Feb	6,279	2,961	2,697	620	4,180	1,988	1,745	1,394	642	640	309	1,300	573	586
Mar	5,993	2,857	2,492	644	4,011	2,012	1,566	1,353	560	616	292	1,270	646	524
Apr	6,034	2,976	2,398	660	4,104	2,048	1,560	1,297	628	559	329	1,287	640	479
May	5,966	2,820	2,493	654	4,051	2,024	1,586	1,324	566	615	265	1,349	574	598
June	5,984	2,859	2,439	686	4,158	2,034	1,618	1,226	529	581	320	1,323	597	553
July	5,783	2,790	2,299	693	3,941	2,006	1,456	1,251	551	559	293	1,224	600	416
Aug	5,983	2,929	2,401	653	3,983	2,009	1,528	1,353	591	623	312	1,402	683	540
Sept	5,755	2,763	2,273	720	3,827	1,846	1,447	1,233	563	586	278	1,210	568	453
Oct	5,950	2,813	2,473	665	4,073	1,991	1,639	1,228	513	594	330	1,303	664	470
Nov	5,956	2,805	2,422	729	4,087	1,988	1,615	1,208	520	551	288	1,223	601	462
Dec	5,698	2,651	2,382	665	3,843	1,849	1,540	1,225	502	583	263	1,303	699	477
2023: Jan	5,719	2,759	2,295	665	3,933	1,916	1,547	1,173	537	508	325	1,455	760	578
Feb	5,962	2,805	2,446	711	4,036	1,968	1,603	1,252	524	563	387	1,703	894	624
Mar	5,866	2,877	2,355	635	4,110	2,022	1,660	1,138	547	477	318	1,459	688	588
Apr	5,715	2,797	2,324	595	3,978	1,962	1,573	1,050	458	495	321	1,403	695	534
May	6,117	2,962	2,503	652	4,179	2,100	1,629	1,243	570	587	338	1,283	682	456
June	5,997	2,941	2,358	698	3,936	2,008	1,462	1,294	596	585	360	1,354	627	545
July	5,904	2,874	2,330	699	3,986	2,033	1,503	1,248	537	564	269	1,410	673	536
Aug	6,340	3,151	2,407	781	4,387	2,228	1,619	1,155	516	513	362	1,558	736	587
Sept	6,347	3,271	2,333	743	4,352	2,302	1,583	1,251	570	487	332	1,478	736	570
Oct	6,443	3,161	2,421	861	4,414	2,215	1,588	1,266	528	590	356	1,531	719	537
Nov	6,262	3,172	2,350	739	4,223	2,136	1,521	1,285	651	534	404	1,465	729	523
Dec	6,268	3,050	2,460	758	4,424	2,197	1,669	1,143	473	528	353	1,602	824	601

[1] See footnote 1 and Note, Table B–23.

Note: See footnote 5 and Note, Table B–22.

Source: Department of Labor (Bureau of Labor Statistics).

TABLE B–25. Civilian labor force participation rate, 1978–2023

[Percent [1]; monthly data seasonally adjusted]

Year or month	All civilian workers	Men 20 years and over	Men 20–24 years	Men 25–54 years	Men 55 years and over	Women 20 years and over	Women 20–24 years	Women 25–54 years	Women 55 years and over	Both sexes 16–19 years	White	Black or African American	Asian	Hispanic or Latino ethnicity
1978	63.2	79.8	85.9	94.3	47.2	49.6	68.3	60.6	23.1	57.8	63.3	61.5	....	62.9
1979	63.7	79.8	86.4	94.4	46.6	50.6	69.0	62.3	23.2	57.9	63.9	61.4	....	63.6
1980	63.8	79.4	85.9	94.2	45.6	51.3	68.9	64.0	22.8	56.7	64.1	61.0	....	64.0
1981	63.9	79.0	85.5	94.1	44.5	52.1	69.6	65.3	22.7	55.4	64.3	60.8	....	64.1
1982	64.0	78.7	84.9	94.0	43.8	52.7	69.8	66.3	22.7	54.1	64.3	61.0	....	63.6
1983	64.0	78.5	84.8	93.8	43.0	53.1	69.9	67.1	22.4	53.5	64.3	61.5	....	63.8
1984	64.4	78.3	85.0	93.9	41.8	53.7	70.4	68.2	22.2	53.9	64.6	62.2	....	64.9
1985	64.8	78.1	85.0	93.9	41.0	54.7	71.8	69.6	22.0	54.5	65.0	62.9	....	64.6
1986	65.3	78.1	85.8	93.8	40.4	55.5	72.4	70.8	22.1	54.7	65.5	63.3	....	65.4
1987	65.6	78.0	85.2	93.7	40.4	56.2	73.0	71.9	22.0	54.7	65.8	63.8	....	66.4
1988	65.9	77.9	85.0	93.6	39.9	56.8	72.7	72.7	22.3	55.3	66.2	63.8	....	67.4
1989	66.5	78.1	85.3	93.7	39.6	57.7	72.4	73.6	23.0	55.9	66.7	64.2	....	67.6
1990	66.5	78.2	84.4	93.4	39.4	58.0	71.3	74.0	22.9	53.7	66.9	64.0	....	67.4
1991	66.2	77.7	83.5	93.1	38.5	57.9	70.1	74.1	22.6	51.6	66.6	63.3	....	66.5
1992	66.4	77.7	83.3	93.0	38.4	58.5	70.9	74.6	22.8	51.3	66.8	63.9	....	66.8
1993	66.3	77.3	83.2	92.6	37.7	58.5	70.9	74.6	22.8	51.5	66.8	63.2	....	66.2
1994	66.6	76.8	83.1	91.7	37.8	59.3	71.0	75.3	24.0	52.7	67.1	63.4	....	66.1
1995	66.6	76.7	83.1	91.6	37.9	59.4	70.3	75.6	23.9	53.5	67.1	63.7	....	65.8
1996	66.8	76.8	82.5	91.8	38.3	59.9	71.3	76.1	23.9	52.3	67.2	64.1	....	66.5
1997	67.1	77.0	82.5	91.8	38.9	60.5	72.7	76.7	24.6	51.6	67.5	64.7	....	67.9
1998	67.1	76.8	82.0	91.8	39.1	60.4	73.0	76.5	25.0	52.8	67.3	65.6	....	67.9
1999	67.1	76.7	81.9	91.7	39.6	60.7	73.2	76.8	25.6	52.0	67.3	65.8	....	67.7
2000	67.1	76.7	82.6	91.6	40.1	60.6	73.1	76.7	26.1	52.0	67.3	65.8	67.2	69.7
2001	66.8	76.5	81.6	91.3	40.9	60.6	72.7	76.4	27.0	49.6	67.0	65.3	67.2	69.5
2002	66.6	76.3	80.7	91.0	42.0	60.5	72.1	75.9	28.5	47.4	66.8	64.8	67.2	69.1
2003	66.2	75.9	80.0	90.6	42.6	60.6	70.8	75.6	30.0	44.5	66.5	64.3	66.4	68.3
2004	66.0	75.8	79.6	90.5	43.2	60.3	70.5	75.3	30.5	43.9	66.3	63.8	65.9	68.6
2005	66.0	75.8	79.1	90.5	44.2	60.4	70.1	75.3	31.4	43.7	66.3	64.2	66.1	68.0
2006	66.2	75.9	79.6	90.6	44.9	60.5	69.5	75.5	32.3	43.7	66.5	64.1	66.2	68.7
2007	66.0	75.9	78.7	90.9	45.2	60.6	70.1	75.4	33.2	41.3	66.4	63.7	66.5	68.8
2008	66.0	75.7	78.7	90.5	46.0	60.9	70.0	75.8	33.9	40.2	66.3	63.7	67.0	68.5
2009	65.4	74.8	76.2	89.7	46.3	60.8	69.6	75.6	34.7	37.5	65.8	62.4	66.0	68.0
2010	64.7	74.1	74.5	89.3	46.4	60.3	68.3	75.2	35.1	34.9	65.1	62.2	64.7	67.5
2011	64.1	73.4	74.7	88.7	46.3	59.8	67.8	74.7	35.1	34.1	64.5	61.4	64.6	66.5
2012	63.7	73.0	74.5	88.7	46.8	59.3	67.4	74.5	35.1	34.3	64.0	61.5	63.9	66.4
2013	63.2	72.5	73.9	88.4	46.5	58.8	67.5	73.9	35.1	34.5	63.5	61.2	64.6	66.0
2014	62.9	71.9	73.9	88.2	45.9	58.5	67.7	73.9	34.9	34.0	63.1	61.2	63.6	66.1
2015	62.7	71.7	73.0	88.3	45.9	58.2	68.3	73.7	34.7	34.3	62.8	61.5	62.8	65.9
2016	62.8	71.7	73.0	88.5	46.2	58.3	68.0	74.3	34.7	35.2	62.9	61.6	63.2	65.8
2017	62.9	71.6	74.1	88.6	46.1	58.5	68.5	75.0	34.7	35.2	62.8	62.3	63.6	66.1
2018	62.9	71.6	73.2	89.0	46.2	58.5	69.0	75.3	34.7	35.1	62.8	62.3	63.5	66.3
2019	63.1	71.6	74.0	89.1	46.3	58.9	70.4	76.0	35.0	35.3	63.0	62.5	64.0	66.8
2020	61.7	70.1	71.0	87.9	45.1	57.6	67.5	75.1	34.0	34.5	61.8	60.5	62.7	65.6
2021	61.7	69.8	73.0	88.0	44.2	57.3	68.6	75.3	33.3	36.2	61.5	60.9	63.8	65.5
2022	62.2	70.3	73.2	88.6	44.7	58.1	68.7	76.4	33.6	36.8	62.0	62.2	64.5	66.3
2023	62.6	70.4	72.5	89.1	44.2	58.6	70.1	77.4	33.6	36.9	62.3	63.1	65.0	66.9
2022: Jan	62.2	70.1	73.6	88.2	44.9	58.1	68.2	76.1	34.0	36.6	62.0	61.9	64.3	66.3
Feb	62.2	70.3	73.1	88.7	45.3	58.1	69.7	75.9	33.8	35.8	62.1	62.0	62.9	66.5
Mar	62.3	70.3	73.0	88.5	45.1	58.3	69.4	76.5	33.5	36.9	62.2	62.0	63.9	66.4
Apr	62.2	70.3	72.8	88.7	44.7	58.0	67.8	76.3	33.6	36.6	61.9	62.2	64.3	66.1
May	62.3	70.2	72.4	88.7	44.7	58.3	68.9	76.5	33.8	36.5	61.9	62.9	64.7	66.4
June	62.2	70.1	73.8	88.4	44.2	58.1	68.9	76.3	33.8	36.8	61.9	62.2	64.5	66.5
July	62.1	70.0	73.1	88.4	44.1	58.2	69.6	76.4	33.8	36.1	61.9	62.1	64.7	65.7
Aug	62.4	70.2	72.3	88.6	44.3	58.3	68.4	77.1	33.4	37.6	62.0	62.0	65.4	66.9
Sept	62.3	70.4	73.4	88.7	44.8	58.0	68.1	76.6	33.3	36.9	62.0	62.3	65.0	66.1
Oct	62.3	70.5	73.9	88.6	44.9	57.9	67.8	76.5	33.4	36.6	62.0	62.1	65.1	66.2
Nov	62.1	70.2	73.5	88.5	44.6	57.7	67.8	76.3	33.1	37.7	61.8	62.4	64.9	65.8
Dec	62.3	70.4	73.5	88.7	44.8	58.1	69.5	76.4	33.5	37.0	62.1	62.5	64.3	66.4
2023: Jan	62.4	70.1	72.0	88.5	44.8	58.4	71.0	76.9	33.3	37.1	62.1	62.9	64.2	66.4
Feb	62.5	70.2	73.3	89.0	44.2	58.5	70.6	77.2	33.3	37.4	62.1	63.3	65.1	66.9
Mar	62.6	70.5	74.4	89.1	44.3	58.5	69.5	77.2	33.5	37.3	62.2	64.0	64.8	66.8
Apr	62.6	70.3	71.9	89.1	44.1	58.6	69.8	77.5	33.5	37.0	62.3	62.9	64.8	66.8
May	62.6	70.3	72.9	89.1	44.0	58.7	69.9	77.6	33.5	36.7	62.3	63.1	65.0	66.8
June	62.6	70.5	73.0	89.2	44.2	58.6	68.9	77.8	33.4	36.4	62.3	62.7	65.4	67.3
July	62.6	70.5	72.3	89.4	44.0	58.7	68.9	77.5	33.9	35.8	62.3	62.8	65.5	67.3
Aug	62.8	70.5	72.6	89.3	44.0	58.9	69.7	77.7	34.1	37.0	62.5	62.7	65.6	67.1
Sept	62.8	70.6	72.0	89.6	44.2	58.8	70.7	77.4	33.9	36.6	62.4	63.0	65.7	67.2
Oct	62.7	70.2	71.1	89.0	44.0	58.8	70.5	77.6	33.8	37.9	62.3	63.0	65.3	67.0
Nov	62.8	70.6	72.4	89.3	44.6	58.7	70.9	77.3	33.7	37.5	62.3	63.7	65.0	66.9
Dec	62.5	70.4	71.7	89.2	44.3	58.4	70.9	77.1	33.2	37.0	62.1	63.4	63.9	66.7

[1] Civilian labor force as percent of civilian noninstitutional population in group specified.
[2] See footnote 1, Table B–23.

Note: Data relate to persons 16 years of age and over, except as noted.
See footnote 5 and Note, Table B–22.

Source: Department of Labor (Bureau of Labor Statistics).

TABLE B–26. Civilian employment/population ratio, 1978–2023

[Percent [1]; monthly data seasonally adjusted]

Year or month	All civilian workers	Men				Women				Both sexes 16–19 years	By race or ethnicity [2]			
		20 years and over	20–24 years	25–54 years	55 years and over	20 years and over	20–24 years	25–54 years	55 years and over		White	Black or African American	Asian	Hispanic or Latino ethnicity
1978	59.3	76.4	78.0	91.0	45.7	46.6	61.4	57.3	22.3	48.3	60.0	53.6	....	57.2
1979	59.9	76.5	78.9	91.1	45.2	47.7	62.4	59.0	22.5	48.5	60.6	53.8	....	58.3
1980	59.2	74.6	75.1	89.4	44.1	48.1	61.8	60.1	22.1	46.6	60.0	52.3	....	57.6
1981	59.0	74.0	74.2	89.0	42.9	48.6	61.8	61.2	21.9	44.6	60.0	51.3	....	57.4
1982	57.8	71.8	71.0	86.5	41.6	48.4	60.6	61.2	21.6	41.5	58.8	49.4	....	54.9
1983	57.9	71.4	71.3	86.1	40.6	48.8	60.9	62.0	21.4	41.5	58.9	49.5	....	55.1
1984	59.5	73.2	74.9	88.4	39.8	50.1	62.7	63.9	21.3	43.7	60.5	52.3	....	57.9
1985	60.1	73.3	75.3	88.7	39.3	51.0	64.1	65.3	21.1	44.4	61.0	53.4	....	57.8
1986	60.7	73.3	76.3	88.5	38.8	52.0	64.9	66.6	21.3	44.6	61.5	54.1	....	58.5
1987	61.5	73.8	76.8	89.0	39.0	53.1	66.1	68.2	21.3	45.5	62.3	55.6	....	60.5
1988	62.3	74.2	77.5	89.5	38.6	54.0	66.6	69.3	21.7	46.8	63.1	56.3	....	61.9
1989	63.0	74.5	77.8	89.9	38.3	54.9	66.4	70.4	22.4	47.5	63.8	56.9	....	62.2
1990	62.8	74.3	76.7	89.1	38.0	55.2	65.2	70.6	22.2	45.3	63.7	56.7	....	61.9
1991	61.7	72.7	73.8	87.5	36.8	54.6	63.2	70.1	21.9	42.0	62.6	55.4	....	59.8
1992	61.5	72.1	73.1	86.8	36.4	54.8	63.6	70.1	21.8	41.0	62.4	54.9	....	59.1
1993	61.7	72.3	73.8	87.0	35.9	55.0	64.0	70.4	22.0	41.7	62.7	55.0	....	59.1
1994	62.5	72.6	74.6	87.2	36.2	56.2	64.5	71.5	23.1	43.4	63.5	56.1	....	59.5
1995	62.9	73.0	75.4	87.6	36.5	56.5	64.0	72.2	23.0	44.2	63.8	57.1	....	59.7
1996	63.2	73.2	74.7	87.9	37.0	57.0	64.9	72.8	23.1	43.5	64.1	57.4	....	60.6
1997	63.8	73.7	75.2	88.4	37.7	57.8	66.8	73.5	23.8	43.4	64.6	58.2	....	62.6
1998	64.1	73.9	75.4	88.8	38.0	58.0	67.3	73.6	24.4	45.1	64.7	59.7	....	63.1
1999	64.3	74.0	75.6	89.0	38.5	58.5	68.0	74.1	24.9	44.7	64.8	60.6	....	63.4
2000	64.4	74.2	76.6	89.0	39.1	58.4	67.9	74.2	25.5	45.2	64.9	60.9	64.8	65.7
2001	63.7	73.3	74.2	87.9	39.6	58.1	67.3	73.4	26.3	42.3	64.2	59.7	64.2	64.9
2002	62.7	72.3	72.5	86.6	40.3	57.5	65.6	72.3	27.5	39.6	63.4	58.1	63.2	63.9
2003	62.3	71.7	71.5	85.9	40.7	57.5	64.2	72.0	28.9	36.8	63.0	57.4	62.4	63.1
2004	62.3	71.9	71.6	86.3	41.5	57.4	64.3	71.8	29.4	36.4	63.1	57.2	63.0	63.8
2005	62.7	72.4	71.5	86.9	42.7	57.6	64.5	72.0	30.4	36.5	63.4	57.7	63.4	64.0
2006	63.1	72.9	72.7	87.3	43.5	58.0	64.2	72.5	31.4	36.9	63.8	58.4	64.2	65.2
2007	63.0	72.8	71.7	87.5	43.7	58.2	65.0	72.5	32.2	34.8	63.6	58.4	64.3	64.9
2008	62.2	71.6	69.7	86.0	44.2	57.9	63.8	72.3	32.7	32.6	62.8	57.3	64.3	63.3
2009	59.3	67.6	63.3	81.5	43.0	56.2	61.1	70.2	32.6	28.4	60.2	53.2	61.2	59.7
2010	58.5	66.8	61.3	81.0	42.8	55.5	59.4	69.3	32.9	25.9	59.4	52.3	59.9	59.0
2011	58.4	67.0	63.0	81.4	43.1	55.0	58.7	69.0	32.9	25.8	59.4	51.7	60.0	58.9
2012	58.6	67.5	63.8	82.5	43.8	55.0	59.2	69.2	33.1	26.1	59.4	53.0	60.1	59.5
2013	58.6	67.4	63.5	82.8	43.8	54.9	59.8	69.3	33.3	26.6	59.4	53.2	61.2	60.0
2014	59.0	67.8	64.9	83.6	43.9	55.2	60.9	70.0	33.4	27.3	59.7	54.3	60.4	61.2
2015	59.3	68.1	65.1	84.4	44.1	55.4	62.5	70.3	33.5	28.5	59.9	55.7	60.4	61.6
2016	59.7	68.5	66.2	85.0	44.4	55.7	63.0	71.1	33.5	29.7	60.2	56.4	60.9	62.0
2017	60.1	68.8	67.9	85.4	44.6	56.1	64.2	72.1	33.6	30.3	60.4	57.6	61.5	62.7
2018	60.4	69.0	67.6	86.2	44.7	56.4	64.7	72.8	33.7	30.6	60.7	58.3	61.6	63.2
2019	60.8	69.2	68.3	86.4	45.1	56.9	66.4	73.7	34.0	30.9	61.0	58.7	62.3	63.9
2020	56.8	64.8	61.3	81.8	42.2	53.0	58.2	69.6	31.5	28.3	57.3	53.6	57.3	58.7
2021	58.4	66.2	65.9	83.6	42.3	54.5	63.0	71.7	31.9	32.0	58.6	55.7	60.6	61.1
2022	60.0	67.9	67.5	85.9	43.5	56.2	64.4	74.0	32.7	32.8	60.0	58.4	62.7	63.5
2023	60.3	67.9	67.2	86.3	43.0	56.8	66.0	75.1	32.8	32.8	60.2	59.6	63.1	63.8
2022: Jan	59.7	67.4	67.4	85.1	43.5	56.0	64.2	73.4	32.9	32.5	59.9	57.6	62.0	63.2
Feb	59.8	67.9	67.4	85.9	43.8	55.9	64.7	73.3	32.8	32.2	60.1	57.9	61.0	63.7
Mar	60.1	67.9	66.6	85.9	43.9	56.3	65.0	74.2	32.6	33.1	60.3	58.0	62.2	63.6
Apr	59.9	67.8	66.7	85.9	43.4	56.1	63.9	74.0	32.7	32.7	59.9	58.4	62.3	63.3
May	60.0	67.9	67.3	86.0	43.5	56.3	64.5	74.1	32.9	32.7	59.9	59.0	63.2	63.5
June	59.9	67.7	68.1	85.8	43.0	56.2	64.8	73.9	32.9	32.7	59.9	58.6	62.6	63.6
July	60.0	67.7	67.7	85.8	43.0	56.4	65.8	74.1	32.9	32.1	59.9	58.4	63.0	63.1
Aug	60.1	67.7	66.7	85.9	43.1	56.4	64.5	74.7	32.5	33.8	60.1	58.1	63.5	63.8
Sept	60.1	68.1	67.8	86.1	43.7	56.2	64.0	74.4	32.5	32.7	60.1	58.7	63.3	63.5
Oct	60.0	68.1	68.8	85.8	43.8	56.0	63.4	74.0	32.6	32.7	60.0	58.5	63.1	63.4
Nov	59.9	67.9	67.9	85.8	43.5	55.8	63.8	73.8	32.4	33.4	59.8	58.8	63.2	63.1
Dec	60.1	68.2	68.0	86.2	43.6	56.2	64.5	74.2	32.7	33.1	60.2	58.9	62.8	63.6
2023: Jan	60.2	67.8	66.4	85.8	43.7	56.6	66.5	74.7	32.5	33.2	60.2	59.5	62.3	63.3
Feb	60.2	67.9	67.5	86.2	43.1	56.6	66.4	74.9	32.4	33.3	60.1	59.7	62.9	63.3
Mar	60.4	68.1	69.2	86.4	43.1	56.7	65.3	75.0	32.7	33.6	60.2	60.7	63.0	63.7
Apr	60.4	68.0	67.5	86.3	43.0	56.8	66.5	75.1	32.7	33.6	60.3	59.9	63.0	63.8
May	60.3	67.9	67.7	86.3	42.8	56.7	66.1	75.1	32.6	32.9	60.2	59.6	63.1	64.1
June	60.3	68.1	68.0	86.5	42.8	56.8	65.2	75.2	32.7	32.3	60.4	58.9	63.4	64.4
July	60.4	68.1	67.1	86.6	43.0	56.9	64.6	75.3	33.1	31.8	60.3	59.2	64.0	64.3
Aug	60.4	68.0	66.5	86.4	42.8	57.1	65.6	75.3	33.2	32.4	60.4	59.4	63.5	63.9
Sept	60.4	68.0	66.0	86.4	43.1	57.0	66.8	75.3	33.0	32.3	60.3	59.4	63.8	64.1
Oct	60.3	67.6	65.5	85.9	42.8	56.9	66.1	75.3	32.9	32.9	60.1	59.3	63.3	63.8
Nov	60.4	68.0	67.2	86.2	43.1	56.9	66.5	75.1	32.8	33.2	60.3	60.0	62.7	63.9
Dec	60.1	67.9	67.1	86.1	43.0	56.5	66.4	74.8	32.3	32.6	59.9	60.1	61.9	63.4

[1] Civilian employment as percent of civilian noninstitutional population in group specified.
[2] See footnote 1, Table B–23.

Note: Data relate to persons 16 years of age and over, except as noted.
See footnote 5 and Note, Table B–22.

Source: Department of Labor (Bureau of Labor Statistics).

TABLE B–27. Civilian unemployment rate, 1978–2023

[Percent [1]; monthly data seasonally adjusted]

Year or month	All civilian workers	By sex and age			By race or ethnicity [2]				U-6 measure of labor underutilization [3]	By educational attainment (25 years & over)			
		Men 20 years and over	Women 20 years and over	Both sexes 16–19	White	Black or African American	Asian	Hispanic or Latino ethnicity		Less than a high school diploma	High school graduates, no college	Some college or associate degree	Bachelor's degree and higher [4]
1978	6.1	4.3	6.0	16.4	5.2	12.8	....	9.1	....	....	....	....	....
1979	5.8	4.2	5.7	16.1	5.1	12.3	....	8.3	....	....	....	....	....
1980	7.1	5.9	6.4	17.8	6.3	14.3		10.1					
1981	7.6	6.3	6.8	19.6	6.7	15.6		10.4					
1982	9.7	8.8	8.3	23.2	8.6	18.9		13.8					
1983	9.6	8.9	8.1	22.4	8.4	19.5		13.7					
1984	7.5	6.6	6.8	18.9	6.5	15.9		10.7					
1985	7.2	6.2	6.6	18.6	6.2	15.1		10.5					
1986	7.0	6.1	6.2	18.3	6.0	14.5		10.6					
1987	6.2	5.4	5.4	16.9	5.3	13.0		8.8					
1988	5.5	4.8	4.9	15.3	4.7	11.7		8.2					
1989	5.3	4.5	4.7	15.0	4.5	11.4		8.0					
1990	5.6	5.0	4.9	15.5	4.8	11.4		8.2					
1991	6.8	6.4	5.7	18.7	6.1	12.5		10.0					
1992	7.5	7.1	6.3	20.1	6.6	14.2		11.6		11.5	6.8	5.6	3.2
1993	6.9	6.4	5.9	19.0	6.1	13.0		10.8		10.8	6.3	5.2	2.9
1994	6.1	5.4	5.4	17.6	5.3	11.5		9.9	10.9	9.8	5.4	4.5	2.6
1995	5.6	4.8	4.9	17.3	4.9	10.4		9.3	10.1	9.0	4.8	4.0	2.4
1996	5.4	4.6	4.8	16.7	4.7	10.5		8.9	9.7	8.7	4.7	3.7	2.2
1997	4.9	4.2	4.4	16.0	4.2	10.0		7.7	8.9	8.1	4.3	3.3	2.0
1998	4.5	3.7	4.1	14.6	3.9	8.9		7.2	8.0	7.1	4.0	3.0	1.8
1999	4.2	3.5	3.8	13.9	3.7	8.0		6.4	7.4	6.7	3.5	2.8	1.8
2000	4.0	3.3	3.6	13.1	3.5	7.6	3.6	5.7	7.0	6.3	3.4	2.7	1.7
2001	4.7	4.2	4.1	14.7	4.2	8.6	4.5	6.6	8.1	7.2	4.2	3.3	2.3
2002	5.8	5.3	5.1	16.5	5.1	10.2	5.9	7.5	9.6	8.4	5.3	4.5	2.9
2003	6.0	5.6	5.1	17.5	5.2	10.8	6.0	7.7	10.1	8.8	5.5	4.8	3.1
2004	5.5	5.0	4.9	17.0	4.8	10.4	4.4	7.0	9.6	8.5	5.0	4.2	2.7
2005	5.1	4.4	4.6	16.6	4.4	10.0	4.0	6.0	8.9	7.6	4.7	3.9	2.3
2006	4.6	4.0	4.1	15.4	4.0	8.9	3.0	5.2	8.2	6.8	4.3	3.6	2.0
2007	4.6	4.1	4.0	15.7	4.1	8.3	3.2	5.6	8.3	7.1	4.4	3.6	2.0
2008	5.8	5.4	4.9	18.7	5.2	10.1	4.0	7.6	10.5	9.0	5.7	4.6	2.6
2009	9.3	9.6	7.5	24.3	8.5	14.8	7.3	12.1	16.2	14.6	9.7	8.0	4.6
2010	9.6	9.8	8.0	25.9	8.7	16.0	7.5	12.5	16.7	14.9	10.3	8.4	4.7
2011	8.9	8.7	7.9	24.4	7.9	15.8	7.0	11.5	15.9	14.1	9.4	8.0	4.3
2012	8.1	7.5	7.3	24.0	7.2	13.8	5.9	10.3	14.7	12.4	8.3	7.1	4.0
2013	7.4	7.0	6.5	22.9	6.5	13.1	5.2	9.1	13.8	11.0	7.5	6.4	3.7
2014	6.2	5.7	5.6	19.6	5.3	11.3	5.0	7.4	12.0	9.0	6.0	5.4	3.2
2015	5.3	4.9	4.8	16.9	4.6	9.6	3.8	6.6	10.4	8.0	5.4	4.5	2.6
2016	4.9	4.5	4.4	15.7	4.3	8.4	3.6	5.8	9.6	7.4	5.2	4.1	2.5
2017	4.4	4.0	4.0	14.0	3.8	7.5	3.4	5.1	8.5	6.5	4.6	3.8	2.3
2018	3.9	3.6	3.5	12.9	3.5	6.5	3.0	4.7	7.7	5.6	4.1	3.3	2.1
2019	3.7	3.4	3.3	12.7	3.3	6.1	2.7	4.3	7.2	5.4	3.7	3.0	2.1
2020	8.1	7.4	8.0	17.9	7.3	11.4	8.7	10.4	13.6	11.7	9.0	7.8	4.8
2021	5.3	5.2	5.0	11.7	4.7	8.6	5.0	6.8	9.4	8.3	6.2	5.1	3.1
2022	3.6	3.4	3.3	10.8	3.2	6.1	2.8	4.3	6.9	5.5	4.0	3.1	2.0
2023	3.6	3.5	3.2	11.2	3.3	5.5	3.0	4.6	6.9	5.6	3.9	3.0	2.1
2022: Jan	4.0	3.8	3.6	11.2	3.4	7.0	3.6	4.7	7.2	6.3	4.6	3.5	2.3
Feb	3.8	3.5	3.7	10.2	3.3	6.6	2.9	4.3	7.2	4.4	4.4	3.7	2.2
Mar	3.6	3.4	3.4	10.3	3.2	6.4	2.7	4.2	7.0	5.3	4.0	3.1	2.0
Apr	3.7	3.5	3.3	10.6	3.3	6.1	3.0	4.2	7.1	5.4	3.8	3.1	2.0
May	3.6	3.4	3.4	10.5	3.2	6.2	2.4	4.4	7.1	5.2	3.7	3.3	1.9
June	3.6	3.4	3.3	10.9	3.3	5.8	2.9	4.3	6.7	5.7	3.6	3.1	2.1
July	3.5	3.3	3.1	11.2	3.1	5.9	2.7	4.0	6.8	5.9	3.6	2.8	2.0
Aug	3.6	3.5	3.2	10.2	3.2	6.4	2.8	4.5	7.0	6.2	4.4	2.9	1.9
Sept	3.5	3.3	3.1	11.4	3.0	5.8	2.5	3.9	6.7	5.6	3.7	2.9	1.8
Oct	3.6	3.3	3.4	10.6	3.2	5.8	3.0	4.2	6.7	6.2	4.0	3.0	1.9
Nov	3.6	3.3	3.3	11.3	3.2	5.6	2.6	4.0	6.7	4.3	3.9	3.2	2.0
Dec	3.5	3.1	3.2	10.5	3.0	5.7	2.4	4.2	6.5	5.0	3.6	3.0	1.9
2023: Jan	3.4	3.2	3.1	10.5	3.1	5.4	2.9	4.7	6.7	4.5	3.8	2.9	2.0
Feb	3.6	3.3	3.3	11.1	3.2	5.7	3.4	5.4	6.8	5.8	3.6	3.3	2.1
Mar	3.5	3.4	3.2	9.9	3.2	5.1	2.8	4.6	6.7	4.8	4.0	3.0	2.0
Apr	3.4	3.3	3.1	9.3	3.1	4.8	2.8	4.4	6.6	5.4	3.9	2.9	1.9
May	3.7	3.5	3.3	10.3	3.3	5.7	3.0	4.1	6.8	5.7	3.9	3.2	2.0
June	3.6	3.4	3.1	11.2	3.1	6.0	3.1	4.2	6.9	6.0	3.9	3.0	2.0
July	3.5	3.4	3.1	11.3	3.1	5.7	2.3	4.4	6.7	5.3	3.3	3.1	2.0
Aug	3.8	3.7	3.2	12.3	3.4	5.3	3.2	4.9	7.1	5.4	3.9	3.1	2.2
Sept	3.8	3.8	3.1	11.8	3.4	5.7	2.9	4.6	7.0	5.5	4.1	3.0	2.2
Oct	3.8	3.7	3.2	13.1	3.5	5.8	3.1	4.8	7.2	5.8	4.0	3.1	2.1
Nov	3.7	3.7	3.1	11.4	3.3	5.8	3.5	4.6	7.0	6.3	4.1	2.8	2.1
Dec	3.7	3.5	3.3	11.9	3.5	5.2	3.1	5.0	7.1	6.0	4.2	3.1	2.1

[1] Unemployed as percent of civilian labor force in group specified.
[2] See footnote 1, Table B–23.
[3] Total unemployed, plus all persons marginally attached to the labor force, plus total employed part time for economic reasons, as a percent of the civilian labor force plus all persons marginally attached to the labor force.
[4] Includes persons with bachelor's, master's, professional, and doctoral degrees.

Note: Data relate to persons 16 years of age and over, except as noted.
See Note, Table B–22.

Source: Department of Labor (Bureau of Labor Statistics).

TABLE B–28. Unemployment by duration and reason, 1978–2023

[Thousands of persons, except as noted; monthly data seasonally adjusted [1]]

Year or month	Un-employ-ment	Duration of unemployment						Reason for unemployment					
		Less than 5 weeks	5–14 weeks	15–26 weeks	27 weeks and over	Average (mean) duration (weeks) [2]	Median duration (weeks)	Job losers [3]			Job leavers	Re-entrants	New entrants
								Total	On layoff	Other			
1978	6,202	2,865	1,923	766	648	11.9	5.9	2,585	712	1,873	874	1,857	885
1979	6,137	2,950	1,946	706	535	10.8	5.4	2,635	851	1,784	880	1,806	817
1980	7,637	3,295	2,470	1,052	820	11.9	6.5	3,947	1,488	2,459	891	1,927	872
1981	8,273	3,449	2,539	1,122	1,162	13.7	6.9	4,267	1,430	2,837	923	2,102	981
1982	10,678	3,883	3,311	1,708	1,776	15.6	8.7	6,268	2,127	4,141	840	2,384	1,185
1983	10,717	3,570	2,937	1,652	2,559	20.0	10.1	6,258	1,780	4,478	830	2,412	1,216
1984	8,539	3,350	2,451	1,104	1,634	18.2	7.9	4,421	1,171	3,250	823	2,184	1,110
1985	8,312	3,498	2,509	1,025	1,280	15.6	6.8	4,139	1,157	2,982	877	2,256	1,039
1986	8,237	3,448	2,557	1,045	1,187	15.0	6.9	4,033	1,090	2,943	1,015	2,160	1,029
1987	7,425	3,246	2,196	943	1,040	14.5	6.5	3,566	943	2,623	965	1,974	920
1988	6,701	3,084	2,007	801	809	13.5	5.9	3,092	851	2,241	983	1,809	816
1989	6,528	3,174	1,978	730	646	11.9	4.8	2,983	850	2,133	1,024	1,843	677
1990	7,047	3,265	2,257	822	703	12.0	5.3	3,387	1,028	2,359	1,041	1,930	688
1991	8,628	3,480	2,791	1,246	1,111	13.7	6.8	4,694	1,292	3,402	1,004	2,139	792
1992	9,613	3,376	2,830	1,453	1,954	17.7	8.7	5,389	1,260	4,129	1,002	2,285	937
1993	8,940	3,262	2,584	1,297	1,798	18.0	8.3	4,848	1,115	3,733	976	2,198	919
1994	7,996	2,728	2,408	1,237	1,623	18.8	9.2	3,815	977	2,838	791	2,786	604
1995	7,404	2,700	2,342	1,085	1,278	16.6	8.3	3,476	1,030	2,446	824	2,525	579
1996	7,236	2,633	2,287	1,053	1,262	16.7	8.3	3,370	1,021	2,349	774	2,512	580
1997	6,739	2,538	2,138	995	1,067	15.8	8.0	3,037	931	2,106	795	2,338	569
1998	6,210	2,622	1,950	763	875	14.5	6.7	2,822	866	1,957	734	2,132	520
1999	5,880	2,568	1,832	755	725	13.4	6.4	2,622	848	1,774	783	2,005	469
2000	5,692	2,558	1,815	669	649	12.6	5.9	2,517	852	1,664	780	1,961	434
2001	6,801	2,853	2,196	951	801	13.1	6.8	3,476	1,067	2,409	835	2,031	459
2002	8,378	2,893	2,580	1,369	1,535	16.6	9.1	4,607	1,124	3,483	866	2,368	536
2003	8,774	2,785	2,612	1,442	1,936	19.2	10.1	4,838	1,121	3,717	818	2,477	641
2004	8,149	2,696	2,382	1,293	1,779	19.6	9.8	4,197	998	3,199	858	2,408	686
2005	7,591	2,667	2,304	1,130	1,490	18.4	8.9	3,667	933	2,734	872	2,386	666
2006	7,001	2,614	2,121	1,031	1,235	16.8	8.3	3,321	921	2,400	827	2,237	616
2007	7,078	2,542	2,232	1,061	1,243	16.8	8.5	3,515	976	2,539	793	2,142	627
2008	8,924	2,932	2,804	1,427	1,761	17.9	9.4	4,789	1,176	3,614	896	2,472	766
2009	14,265	3,165	3,828	2,775	4,496	24.4	15.1	9,160	1,630	7,530	882	3,187	1,035
2010	14,825	2,771	3,267	2,371	6,415	33.0	21.4	9,250	1,431	7,819	889	3,466	1,220
2011	13,747	2,677	2,993	2,061	6,016	39.3	21.4	8,106	1,230	6,876	956	3,401	1,284
2012	12,506	2,644	2,866	1,859	5,136	39.4	19.3	6,877	1,183	5,694	967	3,345	1,316
2013	11,460	2,584	2,759	1,807	4,310	36.5	17.0	6,073	1,136	4,937	932	3,207	1,247
2014	9,617	2,471	2,432	1,497	3,218	33.7	14.0	4,878	1,007	3,871	824	2,829	1,086
2015	8,296	2,399	2,302	1,267	2,328	29.2	11.6	4,063	974	3,089	819	2,535	879
2016	7,751	2,362	2,226	1,158	2,005	27.5	10.6	3,740	966	2,774	858	2,330	823
2017	6,982	2,270	2,008	1,017	1,687	25.0	10.0	3,434	956	2,479	778	2,079	690
2018	6,314	2,170	1,876	917	1,350	22.7	9.3	2,990	852	2,138	794	1,928	602
2019	6,001	2,086	1,789	860	1,266	21.6	9.1	2,786	823	1,963	814	1,810	591
2020	12,947	3,708	4,728	2,516	1,995	16.5	9.7	9,770	6,371	3,399	683	1,969	526
2021	8,623	2,140	1,981	1,164	3,337	28.7	16.5	5,099	1,582	3,516	803	2,204	518
2022	5,996	2,216	1,711	756	1,314	22.6	8.7	2,767	830	1,936	857	1,891	482
2023	6,080	2,112	1,866	925	1,177	20.6	8.9	2,870	811	2,059	822	1,831	556
2022: Jan	6,549	2,472	1,611	786	1,715	24.5	10.0	3,267	993	2,274	950	1,961	438
Feb	6,279	2,145	1,768	803	1,615	26.3	10.0	2,994	857	2,136	959	1,951	428
Mar	5,993	2,305	1,723	567	1,422	24.2	8.8	2,725	710	2,015	786	2,035	481
Apr	6,034	2,277	1,608	647	1,354	24.8	8.5	2,932	921	2,011	793	1,856	502
May	5,966	2,030	1,757	696	1,333	22.4	8.9	2,713	822	1,891	768	1,960	531
June	5,984	2,240	1,536	816	1,296	22.3	8.1	2,570	743	1,827	836	2,020	472
July	5,783	2,097	1,849	656	1,166	22.1	8.3	2,668	879	1,789	843	1,821	477
Aug	5,983	2,214	1,828	864	1,181	22.3	8.5	2,763	808	1,956	902	1,817	447
Sept	5,755	2,156	1,619	822	1,164	20.2	8.1	2,519	796	1,723	905	1,795	454
Oct	5,950	2,189	1,803	775	1,216	20.8	8.0	2,718	862	1,855	863	1,863	492
Nov	5,956	2,247	1,665	815	1,229	21.5	8.4	2,730	778	1,952	829	1,799	556
Dec	5,698	2,218	1,645	792	1,106	19.5	8.3	2,596	788	1,808	824	1,786	502
2023: Jan	5,719	1,942	1,795	929	1,073	20.4	9.8	2,568	763	1,804	883	1,799	526
Feb	5,962	2,294	1,838	812	1,051	19.3	8.9	2,766	807	1,959	888	1,844	521
Mar	5,866	2,279	1,765	797	1,050	19.5	8.4	2,884	781	2,104	841	1,683	506
Apr	5,715	1,867	1,920	748	1,089	20.8	8.7	2,676	760	1,916	786	1,778	519
May	6,117	2,080	1,863	911	1,132	21.2	8.9	2,999	782	2,218	764	1,851	527
June	5,997	2,065	1,850	905	1,117	20.7	8.8	2,790	781	2,009	796	1,776	559
July	5,904	2,007	1,741	956	1,205	20.6	8.9	2,703	723	1,980	854	1,868	534
Aug	6,340	2,224	1,913	970	1,326	20.4	8.8	2,946	813	2,132	804	1,931	592
Sept	6,347	2,053	2,043	985	1,303	21.4	9.1	2,869	813	2,056	797	2,024	586
Oct	6,443	2,269	1,836	1,079	1,291	21.6	8.6	3,120	904	2,217	801	1,869	603
Nov	6,262	2,069	2,060	931	1,220	19.5	9.0	3,058	889	2,169	821	1,771	582
Dec	6,268	2,191	1,791	1,104	1,245	22.3	9.7	3,058	917	2,140	833	1,741	609

[1] Because of independent seasonal adjustment of the various series, detail will not sum to totals.
[2] Beginning with 2011, includes unemployment durations of up to 5 years; prior data are for up to 2 years.
[3] Beginning with 1994, job losers and persons who completed temporary jobs.

Note: Data relate to persons 16 years of age and over.
See Note, Table B–22.

Source: Department of Labor (Bureau of Labor Statistics).

TABLE B–29. Employees on nonagricultural payrolls, by major industry, 1978–2023

[Thousands of jobs; monthly data seasonally adjusted]

Year or month	Total non-agricultural employment	Total private	Goods-producing industries						Private service-providing industries		
			Total	Mining and logging	Construction	Manufacturing			Total	Trade, transportation, and utilities [1]	
						Total	Durable goods	Non-durable goods		Total	Retail trade
1978	86,826	71,014	24,156	902	4,322	18,932	11,770	7,162	46,858	17,633	9,882
1979	89,933	73,865	24,997	1,008	4,562	19,426	12,220	7,206	48,869	18,276	10,185
1980	90,533	74,158	24,263	1,077	4,454	18,733	11,679	7,054	49,895	18,387	10,249
1981	91,297	75,117	24,118	1,180	4,304	18,634	11,611	7,023	50,999	18,577	10,369
1982	89,689	73,706	22,550	1,163	4,024	17,363	10,610	6,753	51,156	18,430	10,377
1983	90,295	74,284	22,110	997	4,065	17,048	10,326	6,722	52,174	18,642	10,640
1984	94,548	78,389	23,435	1,014	4,501	17,920	11,050	6,870	54,954	19,624	11,227
1985	97,532	81,000	23,585	974	4,793	17,819	11,034	6,784	57,415	20,350	11,738
1986	99,500	82,661	23,318	829	4,937	17,552	10,795	6,757	59,343	20,765	12,082
1987	102,116	84,960	23,470	771	5,090	17,609	10,767	6,842	61,490	21,271	12,422
1988	105,378	87,838	23,909	770	5,233	17,906	10,969	6,938	63,929	21,942	12,812
1989	108,051	90,124	24,045	750	5,309	17,985	11,004	6,981	66,079	22,477	13,112
1990	109,527	91,112	23,723	765	5,263	17,695	10,737	6,958	67,389	22,632	13,185
1991	108,425	89,879	22,588	739	4,780	17,068	10,220	6,848	67,292	22,243	12,896
1992	108,799	90,012	22,095	689	4,608	16,799	9,946	6,853	67,917	22,085	12,826
1993	110,931	91,942	22,219	666	4,779	16,774	9,901	6,872	69,723	22,335	13,016
1994	114,393	95,118	22,774	659	5,095	17,020	10,132	6,889	72,344	23,081	13,485
1995	117,401	97,968	23,156	641	5,274	17,241	10,373	6,868	74,813	23,782	13,889
1996	119,828	100,289	23,409	637	5,536	17,237	10,486	6,751	76,880	24,183	14,133
1997	122,941	103,278	23,886	654	5,813	17,419	10,705	6,714	79,392	24,640	14,377
1998	126,146	106,237	24,354	645	6,149	17,560	10,911	6,649	81,883	25,122	14,596
1999	129,228	108,921	24,465	598	6,545	17,322	10,831	6,491	84,456	25,703	14,955
2000	132,011	111,222	24,649	599	6,787	17,263	10,877	6,386	86,573	26,153	15,262
2001	132,073	110,955	23,873	606	6,826	16,441	10,336	6,105	87,082	25,908	15,219
2002	130,634	109,121	22,557	583	6,716	15,259	9,485	5,774	86,564	25,417	15,003
2003	130,330	108,747	21,816	572	6,735	14,509	8,964	5,546	86,931	25,200	14,894
2004	131,769	110,148	21,882	591	6,976	14,315	8,925	5,390	88,266	25,440	15,033
2005	134,033	112,229	22,190	628	7,336	14,227	8,956	5,271	90,039	25,861	15,253
2006	136,435	114,462	22,530	684	7,691	14,155	8,981	5,174	91,931	26,172	15,325
2007	137,981	115,763	22,233	724	7,630	13,879	8,808	5,071	93,530	26,520	15,490
2008	137,224	114,714	21,334	766	7,162	13,406	8,463	4,943	93,380	26,181	15,251
2009	131,296	108,741	18,557	694	6,016	11,847	7,284	4,564	90,184	24,794	14,488
2010	130,345	107,854	17,751	705	5,518	11,528	7,064	4,464	90,104	24,523	14,404
2011	131,914	109,828	18,048	788	5,533	11,726	7,273	4,453	91,780	24,947	14,630
2012	134,157	112,237	18,420	848	5,646	11,927	7,470	4,457	93,817	25,353	14,801
2013	136,363	114,511	18,738	863	5,856	12,020	7,548	4,472	95,773	25,735	15,037
2014	138,939	117,058	19,226	891	6,151	12,185	7,674	4,512	97,831	26,253	15,313
2015	141,824	119,795	19,610	813	6,461	12,336	7,765	4,571	100,185	26,754	15,559
2016	144,335	122,111	19,749	668	6,728	12,354	7,714	4,640	102,362	27,124	15,777
2017	146,607	124,257	20,084	676	6,969	12,439	7,741	4,699	104,173	27,336	15,789
2018	148,908	126,454	20,704	727	7,288	12,688	7,946	4,742	105,750	27,549	15,728
2019	150,904	128,291	21,037	727	7,493	12,817	8,039	4,778	107,254	27,662	15,560
2020	142,186	120,200	20,023	600	7,257	12,167	7,573	4,594	100,177	26,624	14,809
2021	146,285	124,311	20,350	560	7,436	12,354	7,681	4,673	103,961	27,653	15,253
2022	152,520	130,329	21,179	605	7,763	12,812	7,968	4,844	109,150	28,632	15,489
2023 ᵖ	156,050	133,269	21,597	640	8,019	12,939	8,101	4,838	111,671	28,847	15,591
2022: Jan	150,014	127,958	20,764	575	7,587	12,602	7,838	4,764	107,194	28,283	15,395
Feb	150,876	128,823	20,903	582	7,672	12,649	7,858	4,791	107,920	28,554	15,554
Mar	151,370	129,318	21,011	590	7,704	12,717	7,907	4,810	108,307	28,600	15,543
Apr	151,642	129,557	21,069	597	7,704	12,768	7,937	4,831	108,488	28,606	15,493
May	151,928	129,815	21,129	599	7,743	12,787	7,946	4,841	108,686	28,602	15,436
June	152,348	130,233	21,182	608	7,757	12,817	7,955	4,862	109,051	28,686	15,492
July	153,038	130,773	21,252	614	7,786	12,852	7,981	4,871	109,521	28,728	15,512
Aug	153,281	131,017	21,291	611	7,798	12,882	8,010	4,872	109,726	28,758	15,536
Sept	153,536	131,265	21,340	615	7,826	12,899	8,021	4,878	109,925	28,730	15,519
Oct	153,897	131,596	21,387	618	7,839	12,930	8,045	4,885	110,209	28,739	15,510
Nov	154,155	131,791	21,420	625	7,860	12,935	8,055	4,880	110,371	28,714	15,488
Dec	154,291	131,924	21,448	630	7,884	12,934	8,075	4,859	110,476	28,706	15,485
2023: Jan	154,773	132,283	21,494	631	7,921	12,942	8,075	4,867	110,789	28,771	15,518
Feb	155,060	132,509	21,520	633	7,947	12,940	8,075	4,865	110,989	28,851	15,607
Mar	155,206	132,600	21,508	635	7,941	12,932	8,074	4,858	111,092	28,819	15,580
Apr	155,484	132,831	21,541	639	7,961	12,941	8,084	4,857	111,290	28,834	15,586
May	155,787	133,085	21,555	642	7,977	12,936	8,085	4,851	111,530	28,875	15,599
June	156,027	133,270	21,597	642	8,010	12,945	8,104	4,841	111,673	28,860	15,594
July	156,211	133,418	21,604	644	8,021	12,939	8,113	4,826	111,814	28,869	15,599
Aug	156,421	133,568	21,637	644	8,052	12,941	8,116	4,825	111,931	28,840	15,594
Sept	156,667	133,764	21,664	645	8,065	12,954	8,125	4,829	112,100	28,882	15,612
Oct	156,832	133,862	21,654	644	8,087	12,923	8,092	4,831	112,208	28,888	15,613
Nov	157,014	134,014	21,690	640	8,102	12,948	8,129	4,819	112,324	28,843	15,570
Dec ᵖ	157,347	134,292	21,723	641	8,126	12,956	8,142	4,814	112,569	28,901	15,614

[1] Includes wholesale trade, transportation and warehousing, and utilities, not shown separately.

Note: Data in Tables B–29 and B–30 are based on reports from employing establishments and relate to full- and part-time wage and salary workers in nonagricultural establishments who received pay for any part of the pay period that includes the 12th of the month. Not comparable with labor force data (Tables B–22 through B–28), which include proprietors, self-employed persons, unpaid family workers, and private household workers; which count persons as

See next page for continuation of table.

[Thousands of jobs; monthly data seasonally adjusted]

Year or month	Private industries—Continued						Government			
	Private service-providing industries—Continued									
	Information	Financial activities	Professional and business services	Education and health services	Leisure and hospitality	Other services	Total	Federal	State	Local
1978	2,287	4,599	6,997	6,427	6,411	2,505	15,812	2,893	3,474	9,446
1979	2,375	4,843	7,339	6,768	6,631	2,637	16,068	2,894	3,541	9,633
1980	2,361	5,025	7,571	7,077	6,721	2,755	16,375	3,000	3,610	9,765
1981	2,382	5,163	7,809	7,364	6,840	2,865	16,180	2,922	3,640	9,619
1982	2,317	5,209	7,875	7,526	6,874	2,924	15,982	2,884	3,640	9,458
1983	2,253	5,334	8,065	7,781	7,078	3,021	16,011	2,915	3,662	9,434
1984	2,398	5,553	8,493	8,211	7,489	3,186	16,159	2,943	3,734	9,482
1985	2,437	5,815	8,900	8,679	7,869	3,366	16,533	3,014	3,832	9,687
1986	2,445	6,128	9,241	9,086	8,156	3,523	16,838	3,044	3,893	9,901
1987	2,507	6,385	9,639	9,543	8,446	3,699	17,156	3,089	3,967	10,100
1988	2,585	6,500	10,121	10,096	8,778	3,907	17,540	3,124	4,076	10,339
1989	2,622	6,562	10,588	10,652	9,062	4,116	17,927	3,136	4,182	10,609
1990	2,688	6,614	10,882	11,024	9,288	4,261	18,415	3,196	4,305	10,914
1991	2,678	6,561	10,750	11,556	9,256	4,249	18,545	3,110	4,355	11,081
1992	2,641	6,559	11,007	11,948	9,437	4,240	18,787	3,111	4,408	11,267
1993	2,668	6,742	11,534	12,362	9,732	4,350	18,989	3,063	4,488	11,438
1994	2,738	6,910	12,216	12,872	10,100	4,428	19,275	3,018	4,576	11,682
1995	2,844	6,866	12,889	13,360	10,501	4,572	19,432	2,949	4,635	11,849
1996	2,940	7,018	13,510	13,761	10,777	4,690	19,539	2,877	4,606	12,056
1997	3,084	7,255	14,386	14,185	11,018	4,825	19,664	2,806	4,582	12,276
1998	3,218	7,566	15,200	14,570	11,232	4,976	19,909	2,772	4,612	12,525
1999	3,419	7,753	16,013	14,939	11,543	5,087	20,307	2,769	4,709	12,829
2000	3,630	7,783	16,725	15,252	11,862	5,168	20,790	2,865	4,786	13,139
2001	3,629	7,900	16,537	15,814	12,036	5,258	21,118	2,764	4,905	13,449
2002	3,395	7,956	16,041	16,398	11,986	5,372	21,513	2,766	5,029	13,718
2003	3,188	8,078	16,057	16,835	12,173	5,401	21,583	2,761	5,002	13,820
2004	3,118	8,105	16,470	17,230	12,493	5,409	21,621	2,730	4,982	13,909
2005	3,061	8,197	17,034	17,676	12,816	5,395	21,804	2,732	5,032	14,041
2006	3,038	8,367	17,652	18,154	13,110	5,438	21,974	2,732	5,075	14,167
2007	3,032	8,348	18,034	18,676	13,427	5,494	22,218	2,734	5,122	14,362
2008	2,984	8,206	17,830	19,228	13,436	5,515	22,509	2,762	5,177	14,571
2009	2,804	7,838	16,674	19,630	13,077	5,367	22,555	2,832	5,169	14,554
2010	2,707	7,695	16,824	19,975	13,049	5,330	22,490	2,977	5,137	14,376
2011	2,674	7,697	17,433	20,318	13,353	5,360	22,086	2,859	5,078	14,150
2012	2,676	7,783	18,037	20,769	13,768	5,430	21,920	2,820	5,055	14,045
2013	2,706	7,886	18,623	21,086	14,254	5,483	21,853	2,769	5,046	14,037
2014	2,726	7,977	19,174	21,439	14,696	5,567	21,882	2,733	5,050	14,098
2015	2,750	8,123	19,747	22,029	15,160	5,622	22,029	2,757	5,077	14,195
2016	2,794	8,287	20,168	22,639	15,660	5,691	22,224	2,795	5,110	14,319
2017	2,814	8,451	20,563	23,188	16,051	5,770	22,350	2,805	5,165	14,379
2018	2,839	8,590	21,008	23,638	16,295	5,831	22,455	2,800	5,173	14,481
2019	2,864	8,754	21,334	24,163	16,586	5,891	22,613	2,831	5,206	14,576
2020	2,721	8,704	20,376	23,275	13,148	5,329	21,986	2,930	5,135	13,921
2021	2,856	8,806	21,386	23,652	14,151	5,457	21,973	2,886	5,156	13,931
2022	3,063	9,062	22,537	24,336	15,827	5,694	22,191	2,867	5,111	14,213
2023 *p*	3,027	9,197	22,839	25,342	16,593	5,826	22,781	2,925	5,304	14,552
2022: Jan	2,987	8,935	22,176	23,883	15,328	5,602	22,056	2,878	5,094	14,084
Feb	2,991	8,983	22,303	23,996	15,444	5,649	22,053	2,871	5,083	14,099
Mar	3,022	9,002	22,450	24,053	15,523	5,657	22,052	2,869	5,065	14,118
Apr	3,034	9,038	22,425	24,107	15,611	5,667	22,085	2,865	5,080	14,140
May	3,060	9,051	22,454	24,179	15,670	5,670	22,113	2,864	5,096	14,153
June	3,083	9,058	22,522	24,265	15,760	5,677	22,115	2,851	5,103	14,161
July	3,089	9,073	22,614	24,400	15,910	5,707	22,265	2,864	5,129	14,272
Aug	3,089	9,089	22,637	24,469	15,973	5,711	22,264	2,859	5,139	14,266
Sept	3,098	9,095	22,678	24,542	16,055	5,727	22,271	2,863	5,148	14,260
Oct	3,095	9,123	22,726	24,637	16,150	5,739	22,301	2,871	5,143	14,287
Nov	3,108	9,134	22,726	24,726	16,205	5,758	22,364	2,875	5,161	14,328
Dec	3,095	9,145	22,733	24,773	16,255	5,769	22,367	2,876	5,131	14,360
2023: Jan	3,067	9,145	22,771	24,906	16,345	5,784	22,490	2,882	5,206	14,402
Feb	3,049	9,146	22,779	24,968	16,412	5,784	22,551	2,892	5,229	14,430
Mar	3,054	9,150	22,797	25,030	16,447	5,795	22,606	2,900	5,249	14,457
Apr	3,053	9,179	22,827	25,109	16,489	5,799	22,653	2,908	5,263	14,482
May	3,050	9,192	22,876	25,200	16,528	5,809	22,702	2,914	5,280	14,508
June	3,043	9,201	22,883	25,277	16,588	5,821	22,757	2,920	5,301	14,536
July	3,015	9,219	22,866	25,386	16,629	5,830	22,793	2,928	5,301	14,564
Aug	2,997	9,223	22,865	25,479	16,681	5,846	22,853	2,939	5,329	14,585
Sept	3,008	9,223	22,864	25,560	16,708	5,855	22,903	2,945	5,346	14,612
Oct	2,982	9,223	22,859	25,637	16,765	5,854	22,970	2,953	5,375	14,642
Nov	2,999	9,227	22,869	25,747	16,775	5,864	23,000	2,952	5,383	14,665
Dec *p*	3,017	9,240	22,904	25,831	16,813	5,863	23,055	2,957	5,398	14,700

Note (cont'd): employed when they are not at work because of industrial disputes, bad weather, etc., even if they are not paid for the time off; which are based on a sample of the working-age population; and which count persons only once—as employed, unemployed, or not in the labor force. In the data shown here, persons who work at more than one job are counted each time they appear on a payroll.

Establishment data for employment, hours, and earnings are classified based on the 2022 North American Industry Classification System (NAICS). For further description and details see *Employment and Earnings*.

Source: Department of Labor (Bureau of Labor Statistics).

TABLE B–30. Hours and earnings in private nonagricultural industries, 1978–2023

[Monthly data seasonally adjusted]

Year or month	All employees							Production and nonsupervisory employees[1]						
	Average weekly hours	Average hourly earnings		Average weekly earnings				Average weekly hours	Average hourly earnings		Average weekly earnings			
				Level		Percent change from year earlier					Level		Percent change from year earlier	
		Current dollars	1982–84 dollars[2]	Current dollars	1982–84 dollars[2]	Current dollars	1982–84 dollars[2]		Current dollars	1982–84 dollars[3]	Current dollars	1982–84 dollars[3]	Current dollars	1982–84 dollars[3]
1978								35.8	$5.88	$8.96	$210.17	$320.38	7.6	−0.1
1979								35.6	6.34	8.67	225.46	308.43	7.3	−3.7
1980								35.2	6.84	8.25	240.83	290.51	6.8	−5.8
1981								35.2	7.43	8.13	261.29	285.88	8.5	−1.6
1982								34.7	7.86	8.11	272.98	281.71	4.5	−1.5
1983								34.9	8.20	8.22	286.34	286.91	4.9	1.8
1984								35.1	8.49	8.22	298.08	288.56	4.1	.6
1985								34.9	8.73	8.17	304.37	284.72	2.1	−1.3
1986								34.7	8.92	8.21	309.69	285.17	1.7	.2
1987								34.7	9.14	8.12	317.33	282.07	2.5	−1.1
1988								34.6	9.44	8.07	326.50	279.06	2.9	−1.1
1989								34.5	9.81	8.00	338.42	276.04	3.7	−1.1
1990								34.3	10.20	7.91	349.63	271.03	3.3	−1.8
1991								34.1	10.51	7.83	358.46	266.91	2.5	−1.5
1992								34.2	10.77	7.79	368.17	266.40	2.7	−.2
1993								34.3	11.04	7.77	378.80	266.57	2.9	.1
1994								34.5	11.33	7.78	391.11	268.62	3.2	.8
1995								34.3	11.65	7.78	399.93	266.98	2.3	−.6
1996								34.3	12.04	7.81	413.17	268.12	3.3	.4
1997								34.5	12.51	7.94	431.67	273.90	4.5	2.2
1998								34.5	13.01	8.15	448.47	280.82	3.9	2.5
1999								34.3	13.48	8.26	463.07	283.74	3.3	1.0
2000								34.3	14.01	8.29	480.90	284.72	3.9	.3
2001								33.9	14.54	8.38	493.53	284.46	2.6	−.1
2002								33.9	14.96	8.50	506.48	287.94	2.6	1.2
2003								33.7	15.36	8.54	517.65	287.90	2.2	.0
2004								33.7	15.68	8.50	528.65	286.53	2.1	−.5
2005								33.8	16.11	8.43	543.91	284.77	2.9	−.6
2006								33.9	16.75	8.50	567.00	287.67	4.2	1.0
2007	34.4	$20.92	$10.09	$719.74	$347.13			33.8	17.41	8.59	589.09	290.53	3.9	1.0
2008	34.3	21.56	10.01	738.96	343.22	2.7	−1.1	33.6	18.06	8.56	607.10	287.65	3.1	−1.0
2009	33.8	22.17	10.33	749.92	349.55	1.5	1.8	33.1	18.60	8.87	615.82	293.77	1.4	2.1
2010	34.1	22.56	10.35	769.57	352.92	2.6	1.0	33.4	19.04	8.90	635.86	297.18	3.3	1.2
2011	34.3	23.03	10.24	790.79	351.56	2.8	−.4	33.6	19.43	8.77	652.75	294.60	2.7	−.9
2012	34.5	23.49	10.23	809.43	352.55	2.4	.3	33.7	19.73	8.72	665.56	294.20	2.0	−.1
2013	34.4	23.95	10.28	825.08	354.18	1.9	.5	33.7	20.13	8.78	677.62	295.49	1.8	.4
2014	34.5	24.46	10.33	844.77	356.84	2.4	.8	33.7	20.60	8.85	694.74	298.47	2.5	1.0
2015	34.5	25.02	10.56	864.10	364.57	2.3	2.2	33.7	21.03	9.07	708.73	305.74	2.0	2.4
2016	34.4	25.64	10.68	881.09	367.11	2.0	.7	33.6	21.53	9.20	723.20	308.96	2.0	1.1
2017	34.4	26.32	10.74	906.19	369.69	2.8	.7	33.7	22.05	9.22	742.42	310.57	2.7	.5
2018	34.5	27.11	10.80	936.37	372.90	3.3	.9	33.8	22.71	9.26	767.01	312.88	3.3	.7
2019	34.4	27.99	10.95	963.06	376.70	2.9	1.0	33.6	23.51	9.43	790.64	317.24	3.1	1.4
2020	34.6	29.35	11.34	1,014.38	391.94	5.3	4.0	33.9	24.68	9.78	837.39	331.97	5.9	4.6
2021	34.7	30.60	11.29	1,063.08	392.32	4.8	.1	34.2	25.90	9.75	886.54	333.90	5.9	.6
2022	34.5	32.26	11.02	1,114.30	380.76	4.8	−2.9	34.0	27.56	9.57	937.44	325.52	5.7	−2.5
2023 ᵖ	34.4	33.73	11.07	1,160.73	380.94	4.2	.0	33.9	28.94	9.68	980.00	327.77	4.5	.7
2022: Jan	34.5	31.63	11.19	1,091.24	386.14	4.5	−2.9	33.9	26.90	9.68	911.91	328.02	5.3	−2.8
Feb	34.7	31.65	11.12	1,098.26	385.88	5.6	−2.2	34.2	26.97	9.63	922.37	329.30	7.4	−1.2
Mar	34.7	31.84	11.08	1,104.85	384.33	5.0	−3.2	34.2	27.11	9.57	927.16	327.42	6.4	−2.7
Apr	34.7	31.95	11.07	1,108.67	384.14	4.9	−3.1	34.1	27.27	9.60	929.91	327.38	6.0	−2.7
May	34.6	32.08	11.01	1,109.97	381.08	4.7	−3.5	34.1	27.39	9.55	934.00	325.68	5.7	−3.1
June	34.6	32.20	10.93	1,114.12	378.02	4.8	−3.8	34.1	27.53	9.47	938.77	322.96	6.0	−3.3
July	34.6	32.33	10.97	1,118.62	379.67	4.6	−3.5	34.0	27.66	9.53	940.44	324.01	5.6	−3.1
Aug	34.5	32.44	10.98	1,119.18	378.97	4.8	−3.1	34.0	27.75	9.55	943.50	324.66	5.6	−2.8
Sept	34.6	32.54	10.97	1,125.88	379.67	4.5	−3.4	34.0	27.86	9.56	947.24	324.88	5.3	−2.9
Oct	34.6	32.70	10.97	1,131.42	379.69	4.7	−2.9	34.0	28.00	9.56	952.00	324.92	5.2	−2.5
Nov	34.5	32.83	10.99	1,132.64	379.32	4.2	−2.8	33.9	28.13	9.59	953.61	324.96	4.9	−2.1
Dec	34.4	32.94	11.02	1,133.14	378.99	3.7	−2.6	33.8	28.23	9.62	954.17	325.09	4.3	−1.9
2023: Jan	34.6	33.07	11.00	1,144.22	380.73	4.9	−1.4	34.0	28.31	9.59	962.54	326.16	5.6	−.6
Feb	34.5	33.15	10.99	1,143.68	379.14	4.1	−1.7	33.9	28.42	9.60	963.44	325.44	4.5	−1.2
Mar	34.4	33.31	11.04	1,145.86	379.67	3.7	−1.2	33.9	28.58	9.66	968.86	327.32	4.5	.0
Apr	34.3	33.44	11.04	1,146.99	378.65	3.5	−1.4	33.8	28.68	9.65	969.38	326.10	4.2	−.4
May	34.4	33.54	11.06	1,153.78	380.42	3.9	−.2	33.8	28.79	9.68	973.10	327.21	4.2	.5
June	34.4	33.70	11.09	1,159.28	381.54	4.1	.9	33.8	28.90	9.70	976.82	327.81	4.1	1.5
July	34.3	33.84	11.12	1,160.71	381.38	3.8	.5	33.8	29.03	9.73	981.21	328.80	4.3	1.5
Aug	34.4	33.91	11.07	1,166.50	380.87	4.2	.5	33.8	29.09	9.67	983.24	326.93	4.2	.7
Sept	34.4	34.01	11.06	1,169.94	380.49	3.9	.2	33.8	29.18	9.66	986.28	326.67	4.1	.6
Oct	34.3	34.10	11.07	1,169.63	380.22	3.4	.1	33.8	29.29	9.67	990.00	327.83	4.0	.9
Nov	34.4	34.23	11.12	1,177.51	382.41	4.0	.8	33.7	29.42	9.74	991.45	328.17	4.0	1.0
Dec ᵖ	34.3	34.36	11.13	1,178.55	381.59	4.0	.7	33.7	29.53	9.74	995.16	328.39	4.3	1.0

[1] Production employees in goods-producing industries and nonsupervisory employees in service-providing industries. These groups account for four-fifths of the total employment on private nonfarm payrolls.

[2] Current dollars divided by the consumer price index for all urban consumers (CPI-U) on a 1982–84=100 base.

[3] Current dollars divided by the consumer price index for urban wage earners and clerical workers (CPI-W) on a 1982–84=100 base.

Note: See Note, Table B–29.

Source: Department of Labor (Bureau of Labor Statistics).

TABLE B–31. Employment cost index, private industry, 2006–2023

Year and month	Total private			Goods-producing			Service-providing[1]			Manufacturing		
	Total compensation	Wages and salaries	Benefits[2]	Total compensation	Wages and salaries	Benefits[2]	Total compensation	Wages and salaries	Benefits[2]	Total compensation	Wages and salaries	Benefits[2]
Indexes on NAICS basis, December 2005=100; not seasonally adjusted												
December:												
2006	103.2	103.2	103.1	102.5	102.9	101.7	103.4	103.3	103.7	101.8	102.3	100.8
2007	106.3	106.6	105.6	105.0	106.0	103.2	106.7	106.8	106.6	103.8	104.9	101.7
2008	108.9	109.4	107.7	107.5	109.0	104.7	109.4	109.6	108.9	105.9	107.7	102.5
2009	110.2	110.8	108.7	108.6	110.0	105.8	110.8	111.1	109.9	107.0	108.9	103.6
2010	112.5	112.8	111.9	111.1	111.6	110.1	113.0	113.1	112.6	110.0	110.7	108.8
2011	115.0	114.6	115.9	113.8	113.5	114.4	115.3	114.9	116.4	113.1	112.7	113.9
2012	117.1	116.6	118.2	115.6	115.4	116.0	117.6	117.0	119.1	114.9	114.8	115.0
2013	119.4	119.0	120.5	117.7	117.6	118.0	120.0	119.4	121.5	117.0	117.2	116.6
2014	122.2	121.6	123.5	120.3	120.1	120.7	122.8	122.1	124.6	119.8	119.8	119.8
2015	124.5	124.2	125.1	123.2	123.2	123.1	124.9	124.5	125.9	122.8	123.0	122.5
2016	127.2	127.1	127.3	125.8	126.2	124.9	127.7	127.4	128.3	125.5	126.2	124.3
2017	130.5	130.6	130.2	128.9	129.3	128.0	131.0	131.0	131.2	128.9	129.3	128.0
2018	134.4	134.7	133.6	131.9	133.0	129.6	135.2	135.2	135.1	131.6	132.9	129.1
2019	138.0	138.7	136.2	135.8	137.5	132.5	138.7	139.1	137.6	135.3	137.1	131.9
2020	141.6	142.6	139.1	138.9	141.0	134.9	142.4	143.1	140.6	138.5	140.7	134.3
2021	147.8	149.7	143.2	144.0	146.6	138.7	148.9	150.5	144.8	143.5	146.4	138.2
2022	155.3	157.4	150.1	150.6	153.9	143.9	156.6	158.3	152.3	150.3	153.9	143.5
2023	161.6	164.1	155.5	156.3	160.2	148.6	163.1	165.2	157.9	155.8	159.7	148.3
2023: Mar	157.4	159.5	152.4	152.5	156.0	145.4	158.8	160.4	154.8	152.3	156.0	145.1
June	159.2	161.3	154.0	154.1	157.7	146.9	160.6	162.3	156.5	153.7	157.5	146.6
Sept	160.6	162.9	155.0	155.1	158.6	147.9	162.1	164.0	157.4	154.6	158.4	147.4
Dec	161.6	164.1	155.5	156.3	160.2	148.6	163.1	165.2	157.9	155.8	159.7	148.3
Indexes on NAICS basis, December 2005=100; seasonally adjusted												
2022: Mar	150.1	151.8	146.0	146.2	148.5	141.5	151.2	152.6	147.6	146.2	148.7	141.5
June	152.1	154.0	147.9	147.9	150.5	142.7	153.4	154.9	149.7	147.8	150.5	142.6
Sept	153.8	155.8	149.2	149.3	152.3	143.3	155.1	156.7	151.3	149.2	152.4	143.0
Dec	155.5	157.6	150.6	150.7	154.0	144.2	156.8	158.5	152.7	150.6	154.1	143.8
2023: Mar	157.3	159.5	152.3	152.6	156.3	145.2	158.7	160.3	154.6	152.2	156.0	144.9
June	158.9	161.1	153.7	153.7	157.3	146.5	160.3	162.1	156.2	153.6	157.4	146.3
Sept	160.5	162.8	155.0	155.0	158.6	147.9	161.9	163.8	157.4	154.6	158.4	147.5
Dec	161.9	164.3	156.0	156.5	160.3	149.0	163.3	165.4	158.4	156.1	160.0	148.6
Percent change from 12 months earlier, not seasonally adjusted												
December:												
2006	3.2	3.2	3.1	2.5	2.9	1.7	3.4	3.3	3.7	1.8	2.3	0.8
2007	3.0	3.3	2.4	2.4	3.0	1.5	3.2	3.4	2.8	2.0	2.5	.9
2008	2.4	2.6	2.0	2.4	2.8	1.5	2.5	2.6	2.2	2.0	2.7	.8
2009	1.2	1.3	.9	1.0	.9	1.1	1.3	1.4	.9	1.0	1.1	1.1
2010	2.1	1.8	2.9	2.3	1.5	4.1	2.0	1.8	2.5	2.8	1.7	5.0
2011	2.2	1.6	3.6	2.4	1.7	3.9	2.0	1.6	3.4	2.8	1.8	4.7
2012	1.8	1.7	2.0	1.6	1.7	1.4	2.0	1.8	2.3	1.6	1.9	1.0
2013	2.0	2.1	1.9	1.8	1.9	1.7	2.0	2.1	2.0	1.8	2.1	1.4
2014	2.3	2.2	2.5	2.2	2.1	2.3	2.3	2.3	2.6	2.4	2.2	2.7
2015	1.9	2.1	1.3	2.4	2.6	2.0	1.7	2.0	1.0	2.5	2.7	2.3
2016	2.2	2.3	1.8	2.1	2.4	1.5	2.2	2.3	1.9	2.2	2.6	1.5
2017	2.6	2.8	2.3	2.5	2.5	2.5	2.6	2.8	2.3	2.7	2.5	3.0
2018	3.0	3.1	2.6	2.3	2.9	1.3	3.2	3.2	3.0	2.1	2.8	.9
2019	2.7	3.0	1.9	3.0	3.4	2.2	2.6	2.9	1.9	2.8	3.2	2.2
2020	2.6	2.8	2.1	2.3	2.5	1.8	2.7	2.9	2.2	2.4	2.6	1.8
2021	4.4	5.0	2.9	3.7	4.0	2.8	4.6	5.2	3.0	3.6	4.1	2.9
2022	5.1	5.1	4.8	4.6	5.0	3.7	5.2	5.2	5.2	4.7	5.1	3.8
2023	4.1	4.3	3.6	3.8	4.1	3.3	4.2	4.4	3.7	3.7	3.8	3.3
2023: Mar	4.8	5.1	4.3	4.3	5.2	2.5	5.0	5.0	4.7	4.2	4.9	2.4
June	4.5	4.6	3.9	4.0	4.6	2.7	4.5	4.6	4.3	3.9	4.5	2.7
Sept	4.3	4.5	3.9	3.8	4.1	3.2	4.4	4.5	4.0	3.7	3.9	3.2
Dec	4.1	4.3	3.6	3.8	4.1	3.3	4.2	4.4	3.7	3.7	3.8	3.3
Percent change from 3 months earlier, seasonally adjusted												
2022: Mar	1.4	1.3	1.7	1.4	1.2	1.8	1.4	1.3	1.7	1.7	1.4	2.2
June	1.3	1.4	1.3	1.2	1.3	.8	1.5	1.5	1.4	1.1	1.2	.8
Sept	1.1	1.2	.9	.9	1.2	.4	1.1	1.2	1.1	.9	1.3	.3
Dec	1.1	1.2	.9	.9	1.1	.6	1.1	1.1	.9	.9	1.1	.6
2023: Mar	1.2	1.2	1.1	1.3	1.5	.7	1.2	1.1	1.2	1.1	1.2	.8
June	1.0	1.0	.9	.7	.6	.9	1.0	1.1	1.0	.9	.9	1.0
Sept	1.0	1.1	.8	.8	.8	1.0	1.0	1.0	.8	.7	.6	.8
Dec	.9	.9	.9	1.0	1.1	.7	.9	1.0	.6	1.0	1.0	.7

[1] On Standard Industrial Classification (SIC) basis, data are for service-producing industries.
[2] Employer costs for employee benefits.

Note: Changes effective with the release of March 2006 data (in April 2006) include changing industry classification to NAICS from SIC and rebasing data to December 2005=100. Historical SIC data are available through December 2005.

Data exclude farm and household workers.

Source: Department of Labor (Bureau of Labor Statistics).

TABLE B–32. Productivity and related data, business and nonfarm business sectors, 1973–2023

[Index numbers, 2017=100; quarterly data seasonally adjusted]

Year or quarter	Labor productivity (output per hour) Business sector	Nonfarm business sector	Output[1] Business sector	Nonfarm business sector	Hours of all persons[2] Business sector	Nonfarm business sector	Compensation per hour[3] Business sector	Nonfarm business sector	Real compensation per hour[4] Business sector	Nonfarm business sector	Unit labor costs Business sector	Nonfarm business sector	Value-added output price deflator[5] Business sector	Nonfarm business sector
1973	44.589	45.963	27.397	27.508	61.443	59.848	13.148	13.260	66.273	66.835	29.488	28.849	26.724	25.717
1974	43.817	45.198	26.979	27.097	61.572	59.952	14.372	14.509	65.241	65.862	32.800	32.101	29.341	28.384
1975	45.340	46.412	26.723	26.653	58.939	57.427	15.898	16.024	66.131	66.657	35.064	34.526	32.178	31.408
1976	46.849	48.027	28.529	28.560	60.896	59.466	17.167	17.271	67.522	67.930	36.644	35.961	33.857	33.120
1977	47.703	48.858	30.162	30.198	63.229	61.808	18.542	18.689	68.475	69.017	38.869	38.251	35.862	35.181
1978	48.272	49.556	32.086	32.225	66.469	65.028	20.101	20.289	69.372	70.022	41.641	40.943	38.342	37.471
1979	48.331	49.449	33.226	33.319	68.747	67.380	22.042	22.218	69.483	70.036	45.608	44.931	41.550	40.603
1980	48.311	49.427	32.925	33.038	68.153	66.842	24.400	24.601	69.169	69.738	50.507	49.772	45.243	44.461
1981	49.339	50.148	33.886	33.790	68.681	67.380	26.693	26.960	69.140	69.832	54.101	53.760	49.415	48.721
1982	49.059	49.736	32.913	32.756	67.088	65.860	28.668	28.924	70.029	70.654	58.437	58.156	52.231	51.728
1983	50.730	51.777	34.658	34.791	68.319	67.194	29.928	30.214	70.111	70.782	58.994	58.355	54.106	53.531
1984	52.178	52.933	37.732	37.731	72.315	71.281	31.252	31.516	70.287	70.882	59.895	59.540	55.636	55.011
1985	53.368	53.851	39.491	39.395	73.998	73.156	32.843	33.050	71.458	71.907	61.541	61.373	57.106	56.689
1986	54.870	55.451	40.926	40.882	74.587	73.726	34.697	34.953	74.237	74.783	63.235	63.033	57.878	57.494
1987	55.167	55.754	42.392	42.365	76.843	75.986	35.997	36.269	74.496	75.059	65.251	65.053	58.970	58.571
1988	55.998	56.671	44.208	44.292	78.946	78.157	37.907	38.131	75.666	76.115	67.693	67.286	60.847	60.365
1989	56.637	57.172	45.900	45.915	81.043	80.311	39.046	39.236	74.711	75.075	68.941	68.628	63.087	62.569
1990	57.760	58.141	46.635	46.606	80.739	80.161	41.481	41.584	75.636	75.823	71.816	71.522	65.182	64.706
1991	58.679	59.091	46.351	46.316	78.990	78.381	43.400	43.558	76.352	76.631	73.961	73.714	67.070	66.723
1992	61.404	61.732	48.313	48.196	78.681	78.074	46.067	46.265	79.075	79.415	75.023	74.945	68.158	67.845
1993	61.462	61.800	49.691	49.682	80.849	80.391	46.740	46.831	78.255	78.407	76.047	75.778	69.732	69.429
1994	61.814	62.227	52.087	51.970	84.264	83.517	47.080	47.288	77.209	77.551	76.164	75.993	70.974	70.714
1995	62.246	62.899	53.688	53.756	86.252	85.465	48.219	48.459	77.215	77.599	77.446	77.043	72.240	71.965
1996	63.763	64.215	56.181	56.171	88.109	87.473	49.937	50.128	77.888	78.187	78.316	78.063	73.376	72.963
1997	65.139	65.458	59.130	59.071	90.775	90.242	51.939	52.080	79.295	79.511	79.736	79.563	74.462	74.227
1998	67.365	67.651	62.383	62.381	92.604	92.211	55.002	55.093	82.849	82.984	81.648	81.437	74.660	74.496
1999	70.107	70.299	65.984	66.009	94.119	93.897	57.658	57.646	85.070	85.053	82.242	82.001	75.075	75.017
2000	72.282	72.398	68.945	68.896	95.383	95.163	61.653	61.689	87.975	88.027	85.295	85.209	76.453	76.473
2001	74.196	74.263	69.359	69.354	93.481	93.390	64.470	64.369	89.444	89.303	86.892	86.677	77.750	77.715
2002	77.331	77.442	70.545	70.524	91.225	91.067	65.902	65.846	90.009	89.932	85.221	85.026	78.325	78.364
2003	80.295	80.303	72.768	72.711	90.626	90.546	68.388	68.302	91.327	91.213	85.170	85.055	79.490	79.439
2004	82.800	82.688	75.964	75.850	91.744	91.730	71.573	71.412	93.096	92.887	86.440	86.363	81.489	81.299
2005	84.638	84.494	78.948	78.818	93.277	93.283	74.156	74.017	93.290	93.115	87.615	87.600	84.018	84.034
2006	85.509	85.337	81.535	81.446	95.352	95.440	77.013	76.864	93.838	93.656	90.064	90.071	86.390	86.479
2007	86.786	86.677	83.268	83.298	95.946	96.102	80.449	80.186	95.316	95.005	92.698	92.512	88.394	88.235
2008	88.080	88.034	82.533	82.557	93.702	93.779	82.941	82.749	94.628	94.410	94.165	93.997	89.700	89.543
2009	91.603	91.474	79.524	79.405	86.814	86.806	83.956	83.798	96.121	95.941	91.652	91.609	89.709	89.814
2010	94.635	94.559	82.078	82.004	86.731	86.722	85.434	85.347	96.253	96.155	90.277	90.257	90.818	90.787
2011	94.383	94.377	83.709	83.697	88.691	88.684	87.036	87.001	95.027	94.990	92.216	92.185	92.862	92.526
2012	95.002	95.071	86.413	86.490	90.959	90.974	89.177	89.046	95.371	95.231	93.868	93.662	94.538	94.117
2013	96.050	95.855	88.793	88.762	92.445	92.601	90.450	90.169	95.290	94.993	94.170	94.068	95.903	95.432
2014	96.718	96.671	91.754	91.783	94.867	94.943	92.676	92.542	96.035	95.895	95.821	95.728	97.307	96.958
2015	97.999	98.039	95.182	95.166	97.125	97.070	95.362	95.410	98.647	98.698	97.308	97.319	97.743	97.637
2016	98.712	98.722	97.148	97.089	98.415	98.346	96.638	96.688	98.692	98.743	97.898	97.940	98.394	98.471
2017	100.000	100.000	100.000	100.000	100.000	100.000	100.000	100.000	100.000	100.000	100.000	100.000	100.000	100.000
2018	101.479	101.375	103.445	103.441	101.937	102.038	103.387	103.364	100.922	100.900	101.880	101.962	102.071	102.138
2019	103.674	103.679	106.386	106.495	102.616	102.716	107.402	107.398	102.973	102.969	103.596	103.587	103.485	103.584
2020	108.918	109.036	103.435	103.518	94.966	94.939	116.064	116.167	109.815	109.914	106.560	106.540	103.833	103.959
2021	110.885	110.857	110.928	111.009	100.039	100.137	121.802	121.803	109.933	109.934	109.845	109.874	109.135	108.976
2022 ᵖ	108.843	108.805	113.069	113.287	103.882	104.119	126.425	126.255	105.564	105.422	116.154	116.038	117.642	117.183
2023 ᵖ	110.304	110.151	116.024	116.205	105.186	105.496	131.787	131.545	105.700	105.506	119.476	119.423	121.415	121.172
2020: I	104.691	104.716	105.862	105.959	101.119	101.187	111.463	111.521	105.546	105.600	106.469	106.499	103.980	104.040
II	109.456	109.758	95.825	95.922	87.546	87.394	117.700	117.932	112.447	112.668	107.531	107.447	102.733	102.968
III	111.273	111.277	105.325	105.399	94.655	94.718	116.153	116.110	109.689	109.649	104.386	104.344	103.908	104.074
IV	110.169	110.326	106.729	106.792	96.878	96.796	118.865	119.027	111.491	111.652	107.885	107.886	104.602	104.655
2021: I	110.700	110.770	108.466	108.499	97.982	97.950	118.759	118.897	110.224	110.352	107.280	107.337	106.292	106.306
II	110.993	111.003	110.358	110.428	99.428	99.482	120.873	120.938	110.059	110.119	108.900	108.170	107.944	107.944
III	110.432	110.345	111.257	111.358	100.747	100.918	122.685	122.610	109.931	109.864	111.095	111.115	109.904	109.642
IV	111.205	111.100	113.630	113.749	102.181	102.385	124.529	124.396	109.265	109.148	111.982	111.968	112.033	111.875
2022: I	109.286	109.299	112.760	112.930	103.179	103.322	124.815	124.750	107.099	107.043	114.209	114.136	114.631	114.306
II	108.359	108.304	112.399	112.614	103.728	103.980	125.397	125.205	105.120	104.959	115.724	115.606	117.522	117.033
III	108.420	108.416	113.157	113.402	104.369	104.599	127.514	127.365	105.455	105.332	117.610	117.478	118.676	118.169
IV	108.947	108.834	113.961	114.201	104.603	104.932	127.487	127.205	104.355	104.124	117.018	116.880	119.713	119.200
2023: I	108.793	108.617	114.553	114.711	105.294	105.611	129.520	129.233	105.044	104.811	119.051	118.981	120.691	120.345
II	109.705	109.570	115.116	115.270	104.932	105.202	131.372	131.194	105.837	105.694	119.750	119.736	121.007	120.761
III	111.010	110.877	116.703	116.893	105.128	105.426	132.620	132.408	105.906	105.737	119.467	119.420	121.855	121.645
IV ᵖ	111.920	111.758	117.724	117.947	105.186	105.537	133.913	133.623	106.211	105.981	119.650	119.564	122.081	121.908

[1] Output refers to real gross domestic product in the sector.
[2] Hours at work of all persons engaged in sector, including hours of employees, proprietors, and unpaid family workers. Estimates based primarily on establishment data.
[3] Wages and salaries of employees plus employers' contributions for social insurance and private benefit plans. Also includes an estimate of wages, salaries, and supplemental payments for the self-employed.
[4] Hourly compensation divided by consumer price series. The trend for 1978-2022 is based on the consumer price index retroactive series (CPI-U-RS). The change for prior years and recent quarters is based on the consumer price index for all urban consumers (CPI-U).
[5] Current dollar output divided by the output index.

Source: Department of Labor (Bureau of Labor Statistics).

[Percent change from preceding period; quarterly data at seasonally adjusted annual rates]

Year or quarter	Labor productivity (output per hour) Business sector	Nonfarm business sector	Output[1] Business sector	Nonfarm business sector	Hours of all persons[2] Business sector	Nonfarm business sector	Compensation per hour[3] Business sector	Nonfarm business sector	Real compensation per hour[4] Business sector	Nonfarm business sector	Unit labor costs Business sector	Nonfarm business sector	Value-added output price deflator[5] Business sector	Nonfarm business sector
1973	3.0	3.1	6.9	7.2	3.8	4.1	7.9	7.6	1.6	1.3	4.8	4.4	5.2	3.6
1974	-1.7	-1.7	-1.5	-1.5	.2	.2	9.3	9.4	-1.6	-1.5	11.2	11.3	9.8	10.4
1975	3.5	2.7	-.9	-1.6	-4.3	-4.2	10.6	10.4	1.4	1.2	6.9	7.6	9.7	10.7
1976	3.3	3.5	6.8	7.2	3.3	3.6	8.0	7.8	2.1	1.9	4.5	4.2	5.2	5.5
1977	1.8	1.7	5.7	5.7	3.8	3.9	8.0	8.2	1.4	1.6	6.1	6.4	5.9	6.2
1978	1.2	1.4	6.4	6.7	5.1	5.2	8.4	8.6	1.3	1.5	7.1	7.0	6.9	6.5
1979	.1	-.2	3.6	3.4	3.4	3.6	9.7	9.5	.2	.0	9.5	9.7	8.4	8.4
1980	.0	.0	-.9	-.8	-.9	-.8	10.7	10.7	-.5	-.4	10.7	10.8	8.9	9.5
1981	2.1	1.5	2.9	2.3	.8	.8	9.4	9.6	.0	.1	7.1	8.0	9.2	9.6
1982	-.6	-.8	-2.9	-3.1	-2.3	-2.3	7.4	7.3	1.3	1.2	8.0	8.2	5.7	6.2
1983	3.4	4.1	5.3	6.2	1.8	2.0	4.4	4.5	.1	.2	1.0	.3	3.6	3.5
1984	2.9	2.2	8.9	8.5	5.8	6.1	4.4	4.3	.3	.1	1.5	2.0	2.8	2.8
1985	2.3	1.7	4.7	4.4	2.3	2.6	5.1	4.9	1.7	1.4	2.7	3.1	2.6	3.1
1986	2.8	3.0	3.6	3.8	.8	.8	5.6	5.8	3.9	4.0	2.8	2.7	1.4	1.4
1987	.5	.5	3.6	3.6	3.0	3.1	3.7	3.8	.3	.4	3.2	3.2	1.9	1.9
1988	1.5	1.6	4.3	4.5	2.7	2.9	5.3	5.1	1.6	1.4	3.7	3.4	3.2	3.1
1989	1.1	.9	3.8	3.7	2.7	2.8	3.0	2.9	-1.3	-1.4	1.8	2.0	3.7	3.7
1990	2.0	1.7	1.6	1.5	-.4	-.2	6.2	6.0	1.2	1.0	4.2	4.2	3.3	3.4
1991	1.6	1.6	-.6	-.6	-2.2	-2.2	4.6	4.7	.9	1.1	3.0	3.1	2.9	3.1
1992	4.6	4.5	4.2	4.1	-.4	-.4	6.1	6.2	3.6	3.6	1.4	1.7	1.6	1.7
1993	.1	.1	2.9	3.1	2.8	3.0	1.5	1.2	-1.0	-1.3	1.4	1.1	2.3	2.3
1994	.6	.7	4.8	4.6	4.2	3.9	.7	1.0	-1.3	-1.1	.2	.3	1.8	1.9
1995	.7	1.1	3.1	3.4	2.4	2.3	2.4	2.5	.0	.1	1.7	1.4	1.8	1.8
1996	2.4	2.1	4.6	4.5	2.2	2.3	3.6	3.4	.9	.8	1.1	1.3	1.6	1.4
1997	2.2	1.9	5.2	5.2	3.0	3.2	4.0	3.9	1.8	1.7	1.8	1.9	1.5	1.7
1998	3.4	3.4	5.5	5.6	2.0	2.2	5.9	5.8	4.5	4.4	2.4	2.4	.3	.4
1999	4.1	3.9	5.8	5.8	1.6	1.8	4.8	4.6	2.7	2.5	.7	.7	.6	.7
2000	3.1	3.0	4.5	4.4	1.3	1.3	6.9	7.0	3.4	3.5	3.7	3.9	1.8	1.9
2001	2.6	2.6	.6	.7	-2.0	-1.9	4.6	4.3	1.7	1.4	1.9	1.7	1.7	1.6
2002	4.2	4.3	1.7	1.7	-2.4	-2.5	2.2	2.3	.6	.7	-1.9	-1.9	.7	.8
2003	3.8	3.7	3.2	3.1	-.7	-.6	3.8	3.7	1.5	1.4	-.1	.0	1.5	1.4
2004	3.1	3.0	4.4	4.3	1.2	1.3	4.7	4.6	1.9	1.8	1.5	1.5	2.5	2.3
2005	2.2	2.2	3.9	3.9	1.7	1.7	3.6	3.6	.2	.2	1.4	1.4	3.1	3.4
2006	1.0	1.0	3.3	3.3	2.2	2.3	3.9	3.8	.6	.6	2.8	2.8	2.8	2.9
2007	1.5	1.6	2.1	2.3	.6	.7	4.5	4.3	1.6	1.4	2.9	2.7	2.3	2.0
2008	1.5	1.6	-.9	-.9	-2.3	-2.4	3.1	3.2	-.7	-.6	1.6	1.6	1.5	1.5
2009	4.0	3.9	-3.6	-3.8	-7.4	-7.4	1.2	1.3	1.6	1.6	-2.7	-2.5	.0	.3
2010	3.3	3.4	3.2	3.3	-.1	-.1	1.8	1.8	.1	.2	-1.5	-1.5	1.2	1.1
2011	-.3	-.2	2.0	2.1	2.3	2.3	1.9	1.9	-1.3	-1.2	2.1	2.1	2.3	1.9
2012	.7	.7	3.2	3.3	2.6	2.6	2.5	2.4	.4	.3	1.8	1.6	1.8	1.8
2013	1.1	.8	2.8	2.6	1.6	1.8	1.4	1.3	-.1	-.2	.3	.4	1.4	1.3
2014	.7	.9	3.3	3.4	2.6	2.5	2.5	2.6	.8	.9	1.8	1.8	1.5	1.6
2015	1.3	1.4	3.7	3.7	2.4	2.2	2.9	3.1	2.7	2.9	1.6	1.7	.4	.7
2016	.7	.7	2.1	2.0	1.3	1.3	1.3	1.3	.0	.0	.6	.6	.7	.9
2017	1.3	1.3	2.9	3.0	1.6	1.7	3.5	3.4	1.3	1.3	2.1	2.1	1.6	1.6
2018	1.5	1.4	3.4	3.4	1.9	2.0	3.4	3.4	.9	.9	1.9	2.0	2.1	2.1
2019	2.2	2.3	2.8	3.0	.7	.7	3.9	3.9	2.0	2.1	1.7	1.6	1.4	1.4
2020	5.1	5.2	-2.8	-2.8	-7.5	-7.6	8.1	8.2	6.6	6.7	2.9	2.9	.3	.4
2021	1.8	1.7	7.2	7.2	5.3	5.5	4.9	4.9	.1	.0	3.1	3.1	5.1	4.8
2022 ᴾ	-1.8	-1.9	1.9	2.1	3.8	4.0	3.8	3.7	-4.0	-4.1	5.7	5.6	7.8	7.5
2023 ᴾ	1.3	1.2	2.6	2.6	1.3	1.3	4.2	4.2	.1	.1	2.9	2.9	3.2	3.4
2020: I	-1.1	-1.2	-7.2	-7.3	-6.2	-6.2	10.1	10.3	8.6	8.7	11.3	11.6	.6	.5
II	19.5	20.7	-32.9	-32.8	-43.8	-44.4	24.3	25.1	28.8	29.6	4.0	3.6	-4.7	-4.1
III	6.8	5.7	46.0	45.8	36.7	38.0	-5.2	-6.0	-9.5	-10.3	-11.2	-11.1	4.7	4.4
IV	-3.9	-3.4	5.4	5.4	9.7	9.1	9.6	10.4	6.7	7.5	14.1	14.3	2.7	2.3
2021: I	1.9	1.6	6.7	6.5	4.6	4.9	-.3	-.4	-4.5	-4.6	-2.2	-2.0	6.6	6.5
II	1.1	.8	7.2	7.3	6.0	6.4	7.3	7.0	-.6	-.8	6.2	6.1	7.3	6.3
III	-2.0	-2.4	3.3	3.4	5.4	5.9	6.1	5.6	-.5	-.9	8.3	8.2	6.6	6.4
IV	2.8	2.8	8.8	8.9	5.8	5.9	6.1	6.0	-2.4	-2.6	3.2	3.1	8.0	8.4
2022: I	-6.7	-6.3	-3.0	-2.8	4.0	3.7	.9	1.1	-7.7	-7.5	8.2	8.0	9.6	9.0
II	-3.4	-3.6	-1.3	-1.1	2.1	2.6	1.9	1.5	-7.2	-7.6	5.4	5.3	10.5	9.9
III	.2	.4	2.7	2.8	2.5	2.4	6.9	7.1	1.3	1.4	6.7	6.6	4.0	3.9
IV	2.0	1.6	2.9	2.8	.9	1.3	-.1	-.5	-4.1	-4.5	-2.0	-2.0	3.5	3.5
2023: I	-.6	-.8	2.1	1.8	2.7	2.6	6.5	6.5	2.7	2.7	7.1	7.4	3.3	3.9
II	3.4	3.6	2.0	2.0	-1.4	-1.5	5.8	6.2	3.1	3.4	2.4	2.6	1.1	1.4
III	4.8	4.9	5.6	5.8	.7	.9	3.9	3.8	.3	.2	-.9	-1.1	2.8	3.0
IV ᴾ	3.3	3.2	3.5	3.7	.2	.4	4.0	3.7	1.2	.9	.6	.5	.7	.9

[1] Output refers to real gross domestic product in the sector.
[2] Hours at work of all persons engaged in the sector. See footnote 2, Table B–32.
[3] Wages and salaries of employees plus employers' contributions for social insurance and private benefit plans. Also includes an estimate of wages, salaries, and supplemental payments for the self-employed.
[4] Hourly compensation divided by a consumer price index. See footnote 4, Table B–32.
[5] Current dollar output divided by the output index.

Note: Percent changes are calculated using index numbers to three decimal places and may differ slightly from percent changes based on indexes in Table B–32, which are rounded to one decimal place.

Source: Department of Labor (Bureau of Labor Statistics).

TABLE B–34. Industrial production indexes, major industry divisions, 1978–2023

[2017=100, except as noted; monthly data seasonally adjusted]

Year or month	Total industrial production [1]		Manufacturing					Mining	Utilities
	Index, 2017=100	Percent change from year earlier [2]	Total [1]	Percent change from year earlier [2]	Durable	Nondurable	Other (non-NAICS) [1]		
1978	50.1	5.5	48.5	6.1	30.9	75.6	159.7	89.0	55.7
1979	51.6	3.0	50.0	3.1	32.4	76.1	163.0	91.8	56.9
1980	50.3	−2.6	48.2	−3.6	31.0	73.8	168.6	93.5	57.3
1981	51.0	1.3	48.7	1.0	31.3	74.4	172.7	96.1	58.1
1982	48.3	−5.2	46.0	−5.5	28.6	73.3	174.7	91.4	56.1
1983	49.6	2.7	48.2	4.8	30.0	76.8	179.7	86.5	56.5
1984	54.1	8.9	52.9	9.8	34.3	80.3	188.0	92.1	59.9
1985	54.7	1.2	53.8	1.6	35.0	80.7	195.4	90.4	61.4
1986	55.3	1.0	55.0	2.2	35.6	83.0	199.4	83.8	61.9
1987	58.2	5.2	58.1	5.7	37.7	87.5	210.8	84.7	64.9
1988	61.2	5.2	61.2	5.3	40.5	90.4	209.8	86.9	68.9
1989	61.7	.9	61.7	.8	41.0	91.0	206.9	86.0	71.0
1990	62.3	1.0	62.2	.8	41.1	92.5	204.4	87.1	72.4
1991	61.4	−1.5	61.0	−1.9	39.9	92.1	196.1	85.3	74.2
1992	63.2	2.9	63.3	3.7	41.9	94.6	192.1	83.7	74.2
1993	65.3	3.3	65.5	3.5	44.3	95.9	193.4	83.5	76.7
1994	68.7	5.3	69.4	5.9	48.1	99.2	191.7	85.0	78.3
1995	71.9	4.6	72.9	5.1	52.1	101.0	191.7	84.9	81.1
1996	75.2	4.5	76.5	4.9	56.8	101.3	189.9	86.5	83.4
1997	80.6	7.2	82.9	8.4	63.6	105.1	205.9	88.1	83.2
1998	85.3	5.9	88.5	6.7	70.3	106.7	218.2	86.5	85.5
1999	89.0	4.4	93.0	5.1	76.3	107.4	224.5	82.1	88.1
2000	92.5	3.9	96.8	4.1	81.8	107.9	223.9	83.9	90.7
2001	89.7	−3.0	93.3	−3.6	78.6	104.8	209.3	84.1	90.3
2002	90.0	.3	93.7	.5	78.9	106.0	202.3	80.2	93.0
2003	91.1	1.3	95.0	1.3	81.0	106.2	196.5	80.3	94.5
2004	93.6	2.7	97.9	3.1	84.9	107.9	197.4	80.3	95.9
2005	96.7	3.4	101.9	4.1	89.9	110.6	196.8	79.3	98.0
2006	98.9	2.3	104.6	2.6	94.2	111.2	194.5	81.2	97.7
2007	101.5	2.6	107.5	2.8	98.9	112.5	183.4	81.9	100.8
2008	97.9	−3.5	102.3	−4.8	95.5	105.8	167.4	83.0	100.4
2009	86.8	−11.4	88.3	−13.8	77.7	97.7	140.0	78.7	97.5
2010	91.6	5.5	93.5	5.9	86.2	99.8	129.4	82.5	101.2
2011	94.5	3.1	96.2	2.9	91.5	100.0	123.4	87.7	100.8
2012	97.4	3.1	98.7	2.6	96.6	100.0	116.3	94.7	98.5
2013	99.3	2.0	99.6	.9	98.7	100.0	110.6	100.6	100.7
2014	102.3	3.0	100.8	1.1	101.5	99.3	109.2	111.3	102.0
2015	100.9	−1.4	100.2	−.5	100.4	99.7	105.2	104.6	101.2
2016	98.7	−2.2	99.4	−.8	98.4	100.5	102.5	91.5	100.8
2017	100.0	1.3	100.0	.6	100.0	100.0	100.0	100.0	100.0
2018	103.2	3.2	101.3	1.3	103.1	99.6	96.7	113.3	104.9
2019	102.4	−.7	99.3	−2.0	100.2	98.7	92.5	120.8	104.0
2020	95.1	−7.2	92.8	−6.6	91.2	94.9	85.3	102.9	101.0
2021	99.2	4.4	97.4	5.0	96.8	98.5	87.4	106.1	103.0
2022	102.6	3.4	100.0	2.7	101.0	100.0	83.8	113.4	106.2
2023 p	102.8	.2	99.4	−.6	101.2	98.7	81.2	119.0	104.3
2022: Jan	101.0	2.3	98.7	1.5	98.8	99.4	85.5	108.3	108.5
Feb	101.7	6.6	99.8	6.9	100.0	100.5	86.0	107.9	106.8
Mar	102.5	4.4	100.6	4.6	100.9	101.2	87.8	110.6	104.6
Apr	102.8	4.6	100.8	4.6	101.6	100.8	86.1	111.1	106.1
May	102.8	3.7	100.4	3.1	101.2	100.5	83.7	112.3	107.0
June	102.7	3.2	100.0	2.7	100.8	100.2	82.1	113.9	106.7
July	103.1	3.0	100.2	1.9	101.5	100.0	80.7	115.5	106.9
Aug	103.2	3.1	100.4	2.4	101.6	100.3	80.3	115.8	106.0
Sept	103.5	4.5	100.6	3.6	102.0	100.3	82.3	117.2	104.9
Oct	103.4	3.1	100.8	2.4	102.2	100.3	84.0	117.4	102.4
Nov	103.1	1.9	100.0	.7	101.1	99.9	83.5	116.6	105.8
Dec	101.5	.6	97.9	−1.3	99.8	96.9	83.9	114.3	109.2
2023: Jan	102.5	1.5	99.5	.9	100.8	99.1	86.2	118.7	101.3
Feb	102.6	.9	99.9	.1	101.0	99.6	86.6	117.5	100.5
Mar	102.7	.2	99.1	−1.6	100.0	99.1	83.9	118.0	106.8
Apr	103.2	.3	99.9	−.8	101.6	99.4	79.3	118.7	104.3
May	102.9	.1	99.8	−.6	101.8	98.9	78.9	118.4	103.7
June	102.3	−.4	99.1	−.9	101.2	98.1	79.3	119.1	102.0
July	103.2	.1	99.5	−.7	102.0	98.0	79.7	120.0	107.0
Aug	103.2	.0	99.5	−.9	101.7	98.5	79.1	119.3	107.7
Sept p	103.3	−.2	99.6	−1.0	101.9	98.6	79.0	120.3	106.7
Oct p	102.5	−.9	98.8	−1.9	100.2	98.4	80.8	119.2	105.7
Nov p	102.4	−.6	99.0	−1.0	101.3	97.9	80.4	118.1	105.0
Dec p	102.5	.2	99.1	1.2	100.8	98.5	79.5	119.2	103.9

[1] Total industry and total manufacturing series include manufacturing as defined in the North American Industry Classification System (NAICS) plus those industries—logging and newspaper, periodical, book, and directory publishing—that have traditionally been considered to be manufacturing and included in the industrial sector.
[2] Percent changes based on unrounded indexes.

Note: Data based on NAICS; see footnote 1.

Source: Board of Governors of the Federal Reserve System.

TABLE B–35. Capacity utilization rates, 1978–2023

[Percent [1]; monthly data seasonally adjusted]

Year or month	Total industry [2]	Manufacturing				Mining	Utilities	Stage-of-process		
		Total [2]	Durable goods	Nondurable goods	Other (non-NAICS) [2]			Crude	Primary and semi-finished	Finished
1978	85.1	84.4	83.8	85.3	85.1	89.6	87.2	88.6	86.2	82.3
1979	85.0	84.0	83.9	83.9	85.6	91.1	87.2	89.9	85.9	81.6
1980	80.7	78.7	77.5	79.7	86.8	91.3	85.5	89.3	78.9	79.2
1981	79.6	77.0	75.3	78.9	87.5	90.9	84.4	89.3	77.4	77.5
1982	73.6	70.9	66.5	76.4	87.4	84.1	80.0	82.3	70.6	73.1
1983	75.0	73.5	68.9	79.4	87.9	79.9	79.3	80.0	74.6	73.0
1984	80.5	79.4	77.0	82.1	89.5	86.0	81.9	85.9	81.2	77.2
1985	79.3	78.1	75.8	80.5	90.3	84.7	81.8	84.1	79.8	76.6
1986	78.6	78.4	75.4	81.8	88.7	76.6	80.9	78.5	79.7	77.1
1987	81.2	81.0	77.6	84.8	90.5	80.3	83.5	82.9	82.8	78.7
1988	84.3	84.0	81.9	86.2	88.5	84.1	86.8	86.4	85.8	81.7
1989	83.7	83.2	81.7	85.0	85.5	85.1	86.8	86.8	84.6	81.7
1990	82.4	81.5	79.2	84.2	83.7	86.9	86.6	88.0	82.5	80.6
1991	80.0	78.6	75.5	82.3	80.8	85.4	87.8	85.6	79.9	78.5
1992	80.7	79.7	77.3	82.7	80.2	85.3	86.4	86.0	81.4	78.5
1993	81.6	80.5	78.8	82.7	81.4	85.8	88.2	85.9	83.2	78.6
1994	83.5	82.8	81.6	84.6	81.4	86.8	88.3	87.9	86.2	79.3
1995	83.9	83.1	82.1	84.5	82.3	87.7	89.4	89.0	86.3	79.7
1996	83.3	82.1	81.4	83.1	80.6	90.5	90.8	89.1	85.4	79.3
1997	84.1	83.0	82.3	83.7	85.5	91.8	90.1	90.4	85.9	80.4
1998	82.9	81.7	80.9	82.2	86.8	89.3	92.6	87.0	84.2	80.4
1999	81.9	80.6	80.5	80.0	87.1	86.2	94.2	86.1	84.4	78.1
2000	81.6	79.9	80.0	78.9	87.5	90.5	94.3	88.6	84.1	77.0
2001	76.2	73.9	71.8	75.6	82.9	89.8	90.1	85.5	77.5	72.6
2002	75.0	73.1	70.2	76.0	81.5	85.9	87.6	83.2	77.6	70.5
2003	76.1	74.1	71.3	76.9	81.5	87.7	85.7	85.0	78.4	71.4
2004	78.2	76.6	74.2	78.9	82.4	88.2	84.4	86.6	80.4	73.4
2005	80.2	78.6	76.6	80.6	82.1	88.5	85.0	86.7	82.0	75.8
2006	80.6	78.9	77.7	80.2	79.5	90.1	83.6	88.2	81.5	76.4
2007	80.8	79.0	78.5	79.8	76.9	89.4	85.8	88.7	81.1	77.3
2008	77.8	74.7	74.6	74.4	78.4	90.0	84.2	87.7	76.9	73.8
2009	68.4	65.2	61.3	69.7	66.5	80.8	80.5	78.4	65.5	67.8
2010	73.3	70.2	68.6	72.9	62.3	84.2	82.9	83.6	71.4	70.9
2011	76.0	73.1	72.6	74.6	63.2	86.4	81.4	85.1	74.1	73.2
2012	76.8	74.3	75.2	74.3	62.1	87.8	78.4	85.9	74.5	74.4
2013	77.1	74.4	75.3	74.5	62.4	86.8	80.0	85.8	75.7	73.5
2014	78.7	75.7	77.1	75.0	65.1	89.4	80.8	87.6	77.3	74.8
2015	77.1	76.1	76.6	76.4	66.5	80.7	80.0	79.6	77.4	75.7
2016	75.4	75.4	74.9	76.5	68.2	71.5	78.9	74.1	76.7	74.4
2017	76.6	76.3	76.1	77.1	70.3	77.9	77.3	78.4	77.3	75.1
2018	79.7	78.3	78.6	78.3	71.3	87.4	80.6	85.9	80.0	76.5
2019	78.6	77.1	76.7	77.9	72.1	87.4	79.1	85.7	78.7	75.5
2020	72.8	72.6	69.6	76.2	70.4	71.9	75.1	73.7	73.4	71.8
2021	77.6	77.1	74.1	80.5	75.9	82.5	74.9	82.8	77.4	75.4
2022	80.3	79.2	76.8	81.7	77.1	89.7	75.2	88.5	79.0	77.5
2023 [p]	79.3	77.8	75.7	79.9	78.7	93.2	71.5	91.0	76.8	76.4
2022: Jan	79.4	78.4	75.7	81.3	76.6	86.6	77.8	86.5	79.0	76.4
Feb	79.9	79.3	76.6	82.2	77.4	86.2	76.5	86.5	79.7	76.9
Mar	80.5	79.9	77.2	82.8	79.4	88.2	74.7	88.1	79.7	77.6
Apr	80.7	79.9	77.6	82.5	78.3	88.4	75.5	88.1	79.8	77.9
May	80.6	79.6	77.2	82.2	76.4	89.1	76.0	88.5	79.7	77.5
June	80.5	79.2	76.8	81.9	75.3	90.1	75.6	89.3	79.0	77.5
July	80.7	79.3	77.2	81.7	74.4	91.2	75.5	89.9	79.2	77.6
Aug	80.7	79.4	77.2	81.9	74.4	91.2	74.7	89.7	78.9	78.0
Sept	80.8	79.5	77.3	81.9	76.6	92.1	73.7	90.2	79.0	77.9
Oct	80.6	79.5	77.4	81.8	78.5	92.1	71.8	89.9	78.4	78.2
Nov	80.3	78.9	76.4	81.5	78.5	91.3	74.0	89.1	78.6	77.4
Dec	78.9	77.1	75.3	79.0	79.1	89.4	76.1	86.5	77.4	76.5
2023: Jan	79.6	78.3	75.9	80.7	81.7	92.8	70.4	89.8	76.8	77.7
Feb	79.5	78.5	75.9	81.0	82.4	91.9	69.6	90.1	76.8	77.3
Mar	79.5	77.8	75.1	80.5	80.2	92.3	73.8	90.4	77.3	76.4
Apr	79.8	78.4	76.2	80.8	76.1	92.8	71.8	90.3	77.1	77.6
May	79.5	78.2	76.3	80.3	76.1	92.6	71.2	90.5	76.9	77.1
June	78.9	77.6	75.7	79.5	76.9	93.3	69.9	90.9	76.3	76.1
July	79.5	77.8	76.2	79.3	77.5	94.0	73.1	91.4	77.1	76.6
Aug	79.5	77.7	75.9	79.6	77.3	93.6	73.4	91.3	77.2	76.4
Sept [p]	79.5	77.7	75.9	79.6	77.5	94.4	72.5	92.1	77.2	76.0
Oct [p]	78.7	77.0	74.6	79.4	79.6	93.7	71.6	91.5	76.6	75.1
Nov [p]	78.6	77.1	75.3	78.9	79.5	92.9	70.9	91.1	76.4	75.2
Dec [p]	78.6	77.1	74.8	79.3	79.0	93.8	70.0	91.9	76.0	75.2

[1] Output as percent of capacity.
[2] See footnote 1 and Note, Table B–34.

Source: Board of Governors of the Federal Reserve System.

TABLE B–36. New private housing units started, authorized, and completed and houses sold, 1978–2023

[Thousands; monthly data at seasonally adjusted annual rates]

Year or month	New housing units started				New housing units authorized [1]				New housing units completed	New houses sold
	Total	Type of structure			Total	Type of structure				
		1 unit	2 to 4 units [2]	5 units or more		1 unit	2 to 4 units	5 units or more		
1978	2,020.3	1,433.3	125.1	462.0	1,800.5	1,182.6	130.6	487.3	1,867.5	817
1979	1,745.1	1,194.1	122.0	429.0	1,551.8	981.5	125.4	444.8	1,870.8	709
1980	1,292.2	852.2	109.5	330.5	1,190.6	710.4	114.5	365.7	1,501.6	545
1981	1,084.2	705.4	91.2	287.7	985.5	564.3	101.8	319.4	1,265.7	436
1982	1,062.2	662.6	80.1	319.6	1,000.5	546.4	88.3	365.8	1,005.5	412
1983	1,703.0	1,067.6	113.5	522.0	1,605.2	901.5	133.7	570.1	1,390.3	623
1984	1,749.5	1,084.2	121.4	543.9	1,681.8	922.4	142.6	616.8	1,652.2	639
1985	1,741.8	1,072.4	93.5	576.0	1,733.3	956.6	120.1	656.6	1,703.3	688
1986	1,805.4	1,179.4	84.0	542.0	1,769.4	1,077.6	108.4	583.5	1,756.4	750
1987	1,620.5	1,146.4	65.1	408.7	1,534.8	1,024.4	89.3	421.1	1,668.8	671
1988	1,488.1	1,081.3	58.7	348.0	1,455.6	993.8	75.7	386.1	1,529.8	676
1989	1,376.1	1,003.3	55.3	317.6	1,338.4	931.7	66.9	339.8	1,422.8	650
1990	1,192.7	894.8	37.6	260.4	1,110.8	793.9	54.3	262.6	1,308.0	534
1991	1,013.9	840.4	35.6	137.9	948.8	753.5	43.1	152.1	1,090.8	509
1992	1,199.7	1,029.9	30.9	139.0	1,094.9	910.7	45.8	138.4	1,157.5	610
1993	1,287.6	1,125.7	29.4	132.6	1,199.1	986.5	52.4	160.2	1,192.7	666
1994	1,457.0	1,198.4	35.2	223.5	1,371.6	1,068.5	62.2	241.0	1,346.9	670
1995	1,354.1	1,076.2	33.8	244.1	1,332.5	997.3	63.8	271.5	1,312.6	667
1996	1,476.8	1,160.9	45.3	270.8	1,425.6	1,069.5	65.8	290.3	1,412.9	757
1997	1,474.0	1,133.7	44.5	295.8	1,441.1	1,062.4	68.4	310.3	1,400.5	804
1998	1,616.9	1,271.4	42.6	302.9	1,612.3	1,187.6	69.2	355.5	1,474.2	886
1999	1,640.9	1,302.4	31.9	306.6	1,663.5	1,246.7	65.8	351.1	1,604.9	880
2000	1,568.7	1,230.9	38.7	299.1	1,592.3	1,198.1	64.9	329.3	1,573.7	877
2001	1,602.7	1,273.3	36.6	292.8	1,636.7	1,235.6	66.0	335.2	1,570.8	908
2002	1,704.9	1,358.6	38.5	307.9	1,747.7	1,332.6	73.7	341.4	1,648.4	973
2003	1,847.7	1,499.0	33.5	315.2	1,889.2	1,460.9	82.5	345.8	1,678.7	1,086
2004	1,955.8	1,610.5	42.3	303.0	2,070.1	1,613.4	90.4	366.2	1,841.9	1,203
2005	2,068.3	1,715.8	41.1	311.4	2,155.3	1,682.0	84.0	389.3	1,931.4	1,283
2006	1,800.9	1,465.4	42.7	292.8	1,838.9	1,378.2	76.6	384.1	1,979.4	1,051
2007	1,355.0	1,046.0	31.7	277.3	1,398.4	979.9	59.6	359.0	1,502.8	776
2008	905.5	622.0	17.5	266.0	905.4	575.6	34.4	295.4	1,119.7	485
2009	554.0	445.1	11.6	97.3	583.0	441.1	20.7	121.1	794.4	375
2010	586.9	471.2	11.4	104.3	604.6	447.3	22.0	135.3	651.7	323
2011	608.8	430.6	10.9	167.3	624.1	418.5	21.6	184.0	584.9	306
2012	780.6	535.3	11.4	233.9	829.7	518.7	25.9	285.1	649.2	368
2013	924.9	617.6	13.6	293.7	990.8	620.8	29.0	341.1	764.4	429
2014	1,003.3	647.9	13.7	341.7	1,052.1	640.3	29.9	382.0	883.8	437
2015	1,111.8	714.5	11.5	385.8	1,182.6	696.0	32.1	454.5	968.2	501
2016	1,173.8	781.5	11.5	380.8	1,206.6	750.8	34.8	421.1	1,059.7	561
2017	1,203.0	848.9	11.4	342.7	1,282.0	820.0	37.2	424.8	1,152.9	613
2018	1,249.9	875.8	13.9	360.3	1,328.8	855.3	39.7	433.8	1,184.9	617
2019	1,290.0	887.7	13.4	388.9	1,386.0	862.1	42.6	481.4	1,255.1	683
2020	1,379.6	990.5	12.3	376.8	1,471.1	979.4	47.2	444.5	1,286.9	822
2021	1,601.0	1,127.2	11.7	462.1	1,737.0	1,115.4	52.9	568.8	1,341.0	771
2022	1,552.6	1,005.2	16.4	531.0	1,665.1	975.6	54.8	634.7	1,390.5	641
2023 [p]	1,413.1	944.5	13.1	455.5	1,470.6	909.2	52.8	508.6	1,452.5	668
2022: Jan	1,669	1,157		502	1,898	1,242	57	599	1,256	810
Feb	1,771	1,211		528	1,817	1,199	55	563	1,371	773
Mar	1,713	1,179		519	1,877	1,135	57	685	1,356	707
Apr	1,803	1,176		614	1,795	1,085	58	652	1,361	611
May	1,543	1,067		447	1,708	1,033	60	615	1,446	636
June	1,561	1,010		543	1,701	948	55	698	1,392	563
July	1,371	898		458	1,658	918	56	684	1,396	543
Aug	1,505	919		566	1,586	885	51	650	1,355	638
Sept	1,463	887		559	1,588	865	52	671	1,438	567
Oct	1,432	858		560	1,555	850	55	650	1,348	577
Nov	1,427	804		609	1,402	795	54	553	1,543	582
Dec	1,357	887		461	1,409	748	49	612	1,390	636
2023: Jan	1,340	823		506	1,354	748	54	552	1,377	649
Feb	1,436	835		588	1,482	796	48	638	1,577	625
Mar	1,380	843		515	1,437	829	52	556	1,528	640
Apr	1,348	847		489	1,417	856	58	503	1,416	679
May	1,583	1,012		563	1,496	902	54	540	1,534	710
June	1,418	930		473	1,441	924	52	465	1,492	683
July	1,451	988		454	1,443	930	47	466	1,334	728
Aug	1,305	948		350	1,541	948	59	534	1,370	654
Sept	1,356	966		376	1,471	963	49	459	1,459	698
Oct	1,376	974		384	1,498	969	48	481	1,375	676
Nov [p]	1,525	1,124		388	1,467	977	47	443	1,448	615
Dec [p]	1,460	1,027		417	1,493	999	49	445	1,574	664

[1] Authorized by issuance of local and building permits in permit-issuing places: beginning with 2023, annually updated universe of approximately 20,000 places; 20,100 for 2014–2022; 19,300 for 2004–2013; 19,000 for 1994–2003; 17,000 for 1984–93; and 16,000 for 1978–83.

[2] Monthly data do not meet publication standards because tests for identifiable and stable seasonality do not meet reliability standards.

Note: One-unit estimates prior to 1999, for new housing units started and completed and for new houses sold, include an upward adjustment of 3.3 percent to account for structures in permit-issuing areas that did not have permit authorization.

Source: Department of Commerce (Bureau of the Census).

TABLE B–37. Manufacturing and trade sales and inventories, 1981–2023

[Amounts in millions of dollars; monthly data seasonally adjusted]

Year or month	Total manufacturing and trade			Manufacturing			Merchant wholesalers [1]			Retail trade			Retail and food services sales
	Sales [2]	Inventories [3]	Ratio [4]	Sales [2]	Inventories [3]	Ratio [4]	Sales [2]	Inventories [3]	Ratio [4]	Sales [2,5]	Inventories [3]	Ratio [4]	
SIC: [6]													
1981	355,822	545,786	1.53	168,129	283,413	1.69	101,180	129,654	1.28	86,514	132,719	1.53	
1982	347,625	573,908	1.67	163,351	311,852	1.95	95,211	127,428	1.36	89,062	134,628	1.49	
1983	369,286	590,287	1.56	172,547	312,379	1.78	99,225	130,075	1.28	97,514	147,833	1.44	
1984	410,124	649,780	1.53	190,682	339,516	1.73	112,199	142,452	1.23	107,243	167,812	1.49	
1985	422,583	664,039	1.56	194,538	334,749	1.73	113,459	147,409	1.28	114,586	181,881	1.52	
1986	430,419	662,738	1.55	194,657	322,654	1.68	114,960	153,574	1.32	120,803	186,510	1.56	
1987	457,735	709,848	1.50	206,326	338,109	1.59	122,968	163,903	1.29	128,442	207,836	1.55	
1988	497,157	767,222	1.49	224,619	369,374	1.57	134,521	178,801	1.30	138,017	219,047	1.54	
1989	527,039	815,455	1.52	236,698	391,212	1.63	143,760	187,009	1.28	146,581	237,234	1.58	
1990	545,909	840,594	1.52	242,686	405,073	1.65	149,506	195,833	1.29	153,718	239,688	1.56	
1991	542,815	834,609	1.53	239,847	390,950	1.65	148,306	200,448	1.33	154,661	243,211	1.54	
1992	567,176	842,809	1.48	250,394	382,510	1.54	154,150	208,302	1.32	162,632	251,997	1.52	
NAICS: [6]													
1992	540,199	835,800	1.53	242,002	378,609	1.57	147,261	196,914	1.31	150,936	260,277	1.67	167,842
1993	567,195	863,125	1.50	251,708	379,806	1.50	154,018	204,842	1.30	161,469	278,477	1.68	179,425
1994	609,854	926,395	1.46	269,843	399,934	1.44	164,575	221,978	1.29	175,436	304,483	1.66	194,186
1995	654,689	985,385	1.48	289,973	424,802	1.44	179,915	238,392	1.29	184,801	322,191	1.72	204,219
1996	686,923	1,004,646	1.45	299,766	430,366	1.44	190,362	241,058	1.27	196,796	333,222	1.67	216,983
1997	723,443	1,045,495	1.42	319,558	443,227	1.37	198,154	258,454	1.26	205,731	343,814	1.64	227,178
1998	742,391	1,077,183	1.44	324,984	448,373	1.39	202,260	272,297	1.32	215,147	356,513	1.62	237,746
1999	786,178	1,137,260	1.40	335,991	463,004	1.35	216,597	290,182	1.30	233,591	384,074	1.59	257,249
2000	833,868	1,195,894	1.41	350,715	480,748	1.35	234,546	309,191	1.29	248,606	405,955	1.59	273,961
2001	818,160	1,118,552	1.42	330,875	427,353	1.38	232,096	297,536	1.32	255,189	393,663	1.58	281,576
2002	823,234	1,139,523	1.36	326,227	423,028	1.29	236,294	301,310	1.26	260,713	415,185	1.55	288,256
2003	854,700	1,147,795	1.34	334,616	408,302	1.25	248,190	308,274	1.22	271,894	431,219	1.56	301,038
2004	926,002	1,241,744	1.30	359,081	441,222	1.19	277,501	340,128	1.17	289,421	460,394	1.56	320,550
2005	1,005,821	1,314,197	1.27	395,173	474,639	1.17	303,208	367,858	1.17	307,440	471,700	1.51	340,479
2006	1,069,032	1,408,670	1.28	417,963	523,476	1.20	328,438	398,782	1.17	322,631	486,412	1.49	357,863
2007	1,128,176	1,488,235	1.28	443,288	563,043	1.22	351,956	424,614	1.17	332,932	500,578	1.49	369,978
2008	1,160,778	1,465,826	1.31	455,750	543,273	1.26	377,085	445,828	1.20	327,943	476,725	1.52	365,965
2009	988,905	1,331,656	1.38	368,648	505,025	1.39	319,217	398,149	1.29	301,039	428,482	1.47	338,706
2010	1,089,044	1,450,634	1.27	409,273	553,726	1.28	361,600	443,424	1.15	318,171	453,484	1.39	357,081
2011	1,206,873	1,567,399	1.26	457,658	607,035	1.29	407,302	489,090	1.15	341,913	471,274	1.35	383,192
2012	1,267,540	1,658,383	1.28	474,727	625,223	1.30	434,294	525,851	1.18	358,519	507,309	1.38	402,199
2013	1,306,286	1,727,487	1.29	484,511	631,970	1.30	450,177	550,651	1.19	371,599	544,866	1.41	416,910
2014	1,346,243	1,790,144	1.32	490,751	642,904	1.31	448,779	585,989	1.22	386,713	561,251	1.43	434,807
2015	1,303,366	1,823,618	1.39	461,086	638,382	1.40	448,448	597,488	1.33	393,832	587,748	1.46	445,910
2016	1,295,793	1,858,223	1.42	446,966	636,017	1.42	444,791	612,169	1.36	404,035	610,037	1.50	458,848
2017	1,357,498	1,918,490	1.39	462,400	659,143	1.39	475,081	633,488	1.31	420,018	625,859	1.48	477,739
2018	1,437,077	2,003,231	1.36	490,889	677,778	1.37	508,551	671,552	1.28	437,637	653,901	1.46	498,594
2019	1,434,243	2,044,039	1.42	477,871	707,875	1.45	506,655	680,098	1.35	449,716	656,066	1.47	514,094
2020	1,381,767	1,992,749	1.44	433,655	702,549	1.62	483,776	666,591	1.37	464,336	623,609	1.34	518,608
2021	1,633,167	2,261,369	1.29	506,634	808,730	1.49	582,982	787,304	1.24	543,551	665,335	1.15	613,851
2022	1,837,375	2,544,325	1.34	576,843	859,340	1.47	669,280	922,363	1.32	591,252	762,622	1.24	672,579
2023 ᵖ	1,840,179	2,558,186	1.38	577,724	857,691	1.48	658,607	897,214	1.37	603,848	803,281	1.30	694,403
2022: Jan	1,773,910	2,298,300	1.30	548,615	815,755	1.49	652,880	798,466	1.22	572,415	684,079	1.20	644,750
Feb	1,795,138	2,340,280	1.30	556,083	824,080	1.48	661,122	820,640	1.24	577,933	695,560	1.20	653,552
Mar	1,836,218	2,391,911	1.30	571,908	835,879	1.46	675,072	842,273	1.25	589,238	713,759	1.21	667,050
Apr	1,846,445	2,417,279	1.31	574,944	839,163	1.46	676,130	861,124	1.27	595,371	716,992	1.20	675,899
May	1,854,827	2,458,607	1.33	584,273	849,775	1.46	677,277	880,699	1.30	593,733	728,133	1.23	674,915
June	1,877,083	2,491,271	1.33	589,257	854,146	1.45	689,421	893,648	1.30	598,405	743,477	1.24	680,515
July	1,850,912	2,503,621	1.35	580,514	854,794	1.47	676,134	898,136	1.33	594,264	750,691	1.26	675,822
Aug	1,853,265	2,523,653	1.36	583,139	854,458	1.47	673,526	909,675	1.35	596,600	759,520	1.27	680,252
Sept	1,850,231	2,527,512	1.37	584,299	856,494	1.47	671,790	912,421	1.36	594,142	758,597	1.28	678,202
Oct	1,860,550	2,533,813	1.36	587,385	859,672	1.46	670,584	918,419	1.37	602,581	755,722	1.25	688,352
Nov	1,840,786	2,538,986	1.38	583,301	858,983	1.47	663,558	924,177	1.39	593,927	755,826	1.27	679,045
Dec	1,825,183	2,544,325	1.39	577,671	859,340	1.49	660,305	922,363	1.40	587,257	762,622	1.30	672,336
2023: Jan	1,851,731	2,544,079	1.37	581,720	860,359	1.48	666,800	918,368	1.38	603,211	765,352	1.27	692,501
Feb	1,848,051	2,545,762	1.38	578,124	859,843	1.49	669,258	918,818	1.37	600,669	767,101	1.28	687,942
Mar	1,820,425	2,539,799	1.40	574,737	852,572	1.48	651,407	916,687	1.41	594,281	770,540	1.30	681,673
Apr	1,819,130	2,541,956	1.40	571,029	855,448	1.50	651,292	913,713	1.40	596,809	772,795	1.29	684,636
May	1,821,163	2,540,827	1.40	573,181	853,314	1.49	648,024	909,919	1.40	599,958	777,594	1.30	689,158
June	1,817,784	2,537,207	1.40	574,298	851,905	1.48	642,750	903,730	1.41	600,736	781,572	1.30	690,518
July	1,832,603	2,539,181	1.39	578,270	852,634	1.47	650,541	901,379	1.39	603,792	785,168	1.30	694,415
Aug	1,858,079	2,548,843	1.37	585,976	855,320	1.46	663,717	900,267	1.36	608,386	793,256	1.30	699,540
Sept	1,875,441	2,553,086	1.36	585,918	856,463	1.46	676,890	900,294	1.33	612,633	796,329	1.30	705,304
Oct	1,855,380	2,550,320	1.37	585,038	856,465	1.48	666,780	897,858	1.35	610,561	795,997	1.30	703,528
Nov	1,858,288	2,547,514	1.37	580,730	856,730	1.48	666,104	894,024	1.34	611,454	796,760	1.30	705,981
Dec ᵖ	1,867,206	2,558,186	1.37	580,992	857,691	1.48	670,883	897,214	1.34	615,331	803,281	1.31	709,890

[1] Excludes manufacturers' sales branches and offices.
[2] Annual data are averages of monthly not seasonally adjusted figures.
[3] Seasonally adjusted, end of period. Inventories beginning with January 1982 for manufacturing are not comparable with earlier periods.
[4] Inventory/sales ratio. Monthly inventories are inventories at the end of the month to sales for the month. Annual data beginning with 1982 are the average of monthly ratios for the year. Annual data for 1981 are the ratio of December inventories to monthly average sales for the year.
[5] Food services included on Standard Industrial Classification (SIC) basis and excluded on North American Industry Classification System (NAICS) basis. See last column for retail and food services sales.
[6] Effective in 2001, data classified based on NAICS. Data on NAICS basis available beginning with 1992. Earlier data based on SIC. Data on both NAICS and SIC basis include semiconductors.

Source: Department of Commerce (Bureau of the Census).

Prices

TABLE B–38. Changes in consumer price indexes, 1981–2023

[For all urban consumers; percent change]

Year or month	All items	All items less food and energy					Food			Energy[4]		C-CPI-U[5]
		Total[1]	Shelter[2]	Medical care[3]	Apparel	New vehicles	Total[1]	At home	Away from home	Total[1,3]	Gasoline	
						December to December, NSA						
1981	8.9	9.5	9.9	12.5	3.5	6.8	4.3	2.9	7.1	11.9	9.4	
1982	3.8	4.5	2.4	11.0	1.6	1.4	3.1	2.3	5.1	1.3	−6.7	
1983	3.8	4.8	4.7	6.4	2.9	3.3	2.7	1.8	4.1	−.5	−1.6	
1984	3.9	4.7	5.2	6.1	2.0	2.5	3.8	3.6	4.2	.2	−2.5	
1985	3.8	4.3	6.0	6.8	2.8	3.6	2.6	2.0	3.8	1.8	3.0	
1986	1.1	3.8	4.6	7.7	.9	5.6	3.8	3.7	4.3	−19.7	−30.7	
1987	4.4	4.2	4.8	5.8	4.8	1.8	3.5	3.5	3.7	8.2	18.6	
1988	4.4	4.7	4.5	6.9	4.7	2.2	5.2	5.6	4.4	.5	−1.8	
1989	4.6	4.4	4.9	8.5	1.0	2.4	5.6	6.2	4.6	5.1	6.5	
1990	6.1	5.2	5.2	9.6	5.1	2.0	5.3	5.8	4.5	18.1	36.8	
1991	3.1	4.4	3.9	7.9	3.4	3.2	1.9	1.3	2.9	−7.4	−16.2	
1992	2.9	3.3	2.9	6.6	1.4	2.3	1.5	1.5	1.4	2.0	2.0	
1993	2.7	3.2	3.0	5.4	.9	3.3	2.9	3.5	1.9	−1.4	−5.9	
1994	2.7	2.6	3.0	4.9	−1.6	3.3	2.9	3.5	1.9	2.2	6.4	
1995	2.5	3.0	3.5	3.9	.1	1.9	2.1	2.0	2.2	−1.3	−4.2	
1996	3.3	2.6	2.9	3.0	−.2	1.8	4.3	4.9	3.1	8.6	12.4	
1997	1.7	2.2	3.4	2.8	1.0	−.9	1.5	1.0	2.6	−3.4	−6.1	
1998	1.6	2.4	3.3	3.4	−.7	.0	2.3	2.1	2.5	−8.8	−15.4	
1999	2.7	1.9	2.5	3.7	−.5	−.3	1.9	1.7	2.3	13.4	30.1	
2000	3.4	2.6	3.4	4.2	−1.8	.0	2.8	2.9	2.4	14.2	13.9	2.6
2001	1.6	2.7	4.2	4.7	−3.2	−.1	2.8	2.6	3.0	−13.0	−24.9	1.3
2002	2.4	1.9	3.1	5.0	−1.8	−2.0	1.5	.8	2.3	10.7	24.8	2.0
2003	1.9	1.1	2.2	3.7	−2.1	−1.8	3.6	4.5	2.3	6.9	6.8	1.7
2004	3.3	2.2	2.7	4.2	−.2	.6	2.7	2.4	3.0	16.6	26.1	3.2
2005	3.4	2.2	2.6	4.3	−1.1	−.4	2.3	1.7	3.2	17.1	16.1	2.9
2006	2.5	2.6	4.2	3.6	.9	−.9	2.1	1.4	3.2	2.9	6.4	2.3
2007	4.1	2.4	3.1	5.2	−.3	−.3	4.9	5.6	4.0	17.4	29.6	3.7
2008	.1	1.8	1.9	2.6	−1.0	−3.2	5.9	6.6	5.0	−21.3	−43.1	.2
2009	2.7	1.8	.3	3.4	1.9	4.9	−.5	−2.4	1.9	18.2	53.5	2.5
2010	1.5	.8	.4	3.3	−1.1	−.2	1.5	1.7	1.3	7.7	13.8	1.3
2011	3.0	2.2	1.9	3.5	4.6	3.2	4.7	6.0	2.9	6.6	9.9	2.9
2012	1.7	1.9	2.2	3.2	1.8	1.6	1.8	1.3	2.5	.5	1.7	1.5
2013	1.5	1.7	2.5	2.0	.6	.4	1.1	.4	2.1	.5	−1.0	1.3
2014	.8	1.6	2.9	3.0	−2.0	.5	3.4	3.7	3.0	−10.6	−21.0	.5
2015	.7	2.1	3.2	2.6	−.9	.2	.8	−.4	2.6	−12.6	−19.7	.4
2016	2.1	2.2	3.6	4.1	−.1	.3	−.2	−2.0	2.3	5.4	9.1	1.8
2017	2.1	1.8	3.2	1.8	−1.6	−.5	1.6	.9	2.5	6.9	10.7	1.7
2018	1.9	2.2	3.2	2.0	−.1	−.3	1.6	.6	2.8	−.3	−2.1	1.5
2019	2.3	2.3	3.2	4.6	−1.2	.1	1.8	.7	3.1	3.4	7.9	1.8
2020	1.4	1.6	1.8	1.8	−3.9	2.0	3.9	3.9	3.9	−7.0	−15.2	1.5
2021	7.0	5.5	4.1	2.2	5.8	11.8	6.3	6.5	6.0	29.3	49.6	6.5
2022	6.5	5.7	7.5	4.0	2.9	5.9	10.4	11.8	8.3	7.3	−1.5	6.4
2023	3.4	3.9	6.2	.5	1.0	1.0	2.7	1.3	5.2	−2.0	−1.9	3.0
						Change from year earlier, NSA						
2022: Jan	7.5	6.0	4.4	2.5	5.3	12.2	7.0	7.4	6.4	27.0	40.0	6.8
Feb	7.9	6.4	4.7	2.4	6.6	12.4	7.9	8.6	6.8	25.6	38.0	7.3
Mar	8.5	6.5	5.0	2.9	6.8	12.5	8.8	10.0	6.9	32.0	48.0	8.1
Apr	8.3	6.2	5.1	3.2	5.4	13.2	9.4	10.8	7.2	30.3	43.6	7.9
May	8.6	6.0	5.5	3.7	5.0	12.6	10.1	11.9	7.4	34.6	48.7	8.3
June	9.1	5.9	5.6	4.5	5.2	11.4	10.4	12.2	7.7	41.6	59.9	8.7
July	8.5	5.9	5.7	4.8	5.1	10.4	10.9	13.1	7.6	32.9	44.0	8.1
Aug	8.3	6.3	6.2	5.4	5.1	10.1	11.4	13.5	8.0	23.8	25.6	7.9
Sept	8.2	6.6	6.6	6.0	5.5	9.4	11.2	13.0	8.5	19.8	18.2	7.9
Oct	7.7	6.3	6.9	5.0	4.1	8.4	10.9	12.4	8.6	17.6	17.5	7.6
Nov	7.1	6.0	7.1	4.2	3.6	7.2	10.6	12.0	8.5	13.1	10.1	7.0
Dec	6.5	5.7	7.5	4.0	2.9	5.9	10.4	11.8	8.3	7.3	−1.5	6.4
2023: Jan	6.4	5.6	7.9	3.1	3.1	5.8	10.1	11.3	8.2	8.7	1.5	6.4
Feb	6.0	5.5	8.1	2.3	3.3	5.8	9.5	10.2	8.4	5.2	−2.0	6.0
Mar	5.0	5.6	8.2	1.5	3.3	6.1	8.5	8.4	8.8	−6.4	−17.4	4.8
Apr	4.9	5.5	8.1	1.1	3.6	5.4	7.7	7.1	8.6	−5.1	−12.2	4.7
May	4.0	5.3	8.0	.7	3.5	4.7	6.7	5.8	8.3	−11.7	−19.7	3.7
June	3.0	4.8	7.8	.1	3.1	4.1	5.7	4.7	7.7	−16.7	−26.5	2.9
July	3.2	4.7	7.7	−.5	3.2	3.5	4.9	3.6	7.1	−12.5	−19.9	3.0
Aug	3.7	4.3	7.3	−1.0	3.1	2.9	4.3	3.0	6.5	−3.6	−3.3	3.6
Sept	3.7	4.1	7.2	−1.4	2.3	2.5	3.7	2.4	6.0	−.5	3.0	3.5
Oct	3.2	4.0	6.7	−.8	2.6	1.9	3.3	2.1	5.4	−4.5	−5.3	3.0
Nov	3.1	4.0	6.5	.2	1.1	1.3	2.9	1.7	5.3	−5.4	−8.9	2.8
Dec	3.4	3.9	6.2	.5	1.0	1.0	2.7	1.3	5.2	−2.0	−1.9	3.0

[1] Includes other items not shown separately.
[2] Data beginning with 1983 incorporate a rental equivalence measure for homeowners' costs.
[3] Commodities and services.
[4] Household energy--electricity, utility (piped) gas service, fuel oil, etc.--and motor fuel.
[5] Chained consumer price index (C-CPI-U) introduced in 2002. Reflects the effect of substitution that consumers make across item categories in response to changes in relative prices. Data for 2023 are subject to revision.

Source: Department of Labor (Bureau of Labor Statistics).

TABLE B–39. Price indexes for personal consumption expenditures, and percent changes, 1973–2023

[Chain-type price index numbers, 2017=100; monthly data seasonally adjusted]

Year or month	Personal consumption expenditures (PCE)						Percent change from year earlier					
	Total	Goods	Services	Food¹	Energy goods and services²	PCE less food and energy	Total	Goods	Services	Food¹	Energy goods and services²	PCE less food and energy
1973	22.455	37.970	16.389	24.492	14.317	23.003	5.4	6.0	4.8	12.7	8.6	3.8
1974	24.793	42.709	17.778	28.217	18.667	24.825	10.4	12.5	8.5	15.2	30.4	7.9
1975	26.860	46.159	19.302	30.338	20.507	26.899	8.3	8.1	8.6	7.5	9.9	8.4
1976	28.333	47.966	20.641	30.902	21.883	28.534	5.5	3.9	6.9	1.9	6.7	6.1
1977	30.176	50.526	22.203	32.722	23.732	30.369	6.5	5.3	7.6	5.9	8.4	6.4
1978	32.276	53.626	23.910	35.853	25.068	32.382	7.0	6.1	7.7	9.6	5.6	6.6
1979	35.143	58.698	25.915	39.374	31.260	34.743	8.9	9.5	8.4	9.8	24.7	7.3
1980	38.928	65.271	28.610	42.685	40.840	37.936	10.8	11.2	10.4	8.4	30.6	9.2
1981	42.415	70.120	31.541	45.726	46.332	41.260	9.0	7.4	10.2	7.1	13.4	8.8
1982	44.771	72.031	34.017	46.929	47.141	43.942	5.6	2.7	7.9	2.6	1.7	6.5
1983	46.676	73.331	36.106	47.468	47.582	46.191	4.3	1.8	6.1	1.1	.9	5.1
1984	48.439	74.718	37.985	48.894	48.182	48.106	3.8	1.9	5.2	3.0	1.3	4.1
1985	50.128	75.917	39.843	49.426	48.690	50.060	3.5	1.6	4.9	1.1	1.1	4.1
1986	51.219	75.562	41.480	50.589	42.663	51.788	2.2	−.5	4.1	2.4	−12.4	3.5
1987	52.802	77.992	42.726	52.186	43.135	53.460	3.1	3.2	3.0	3.2	1.1	3.2
1988	54.865	80.048	44.769	53.742	43.465	55.732	3.9	2.6	4.8	3.0	.8	4.2
1989	57.261	83.128	46.880	56.576	46.033	58.045	4.4	3.8	4.7	5.3	5.9	4.2
1990	59.775	86.532	49.029	59.340	49.925	60.397	4.4	4.1	4.6	4.9	8.5	4.1
1991	61.774	88.647	50.946	61.203	50.146	62.554	3.3	2.4	3.9	3.1	.4	3.6
1992	63.420	89.717	52.758	61.673	50.380	64.456	2.7	1.2	3.6	.8	.5	3.0
1993	65.000	90.496	54.582	62.535	50.838	66.206	2.5	.9	3.5	1.4	.9	2.7
1994	66.356	91.417	56.066	63.582	51.036	67.688	2.1	1.0	2.7	1.7	.4	2.2
1995	67.754	92.271	57.632	64.960	51.438	69.163	2.1	.9	2.8	2.2	.8	2.2
1996	69.203	93.285	59.214	66.942	53.846	70.474	2.1	1.1	2.7	3.1	4.7	1.9
1997	70.407	93.177	60.883	68.218	54.411	71.718	1.7	−.1	2.8	1.9	1.0	1.8
1998	70.967	91.777	62.172	69.075	49.818	72.630	.8	−1.5	2.1	1.3	−8.4	1.3
1999	72.001	92.258	63.409	70.206	51.836	73.583	1.5	.5	2.0	1.6	4.1	1.3
2000	73.822	94.089	65.210	71.850	61.307	74.898	2.5	2.0	2.8	2.3	18.3	1.8
2001	75.302	94.018	67.292	73.946	62.839	76.317	2.0	−.1	3.2	2.9	2.5	1.9
2002	76.291	93.122	69.033	75.063	59.176	77.593	1.3	−1.0	2.6	1.5	−5.8	1.7
2003	77.894	93.003	71.336	76.484	66.654	78.845	2.1	−.1	3.3	1.9	12.6	1.6
2004	79.827	94.311	73.528	78.870	74.217	80.396	2.5	1.4	3.1	3.1	11.3	2.0
2005	82.127	96.203	75.998	80.248	87.026	82.158	2.9	2.0	3.4	1.7	17.3	2.2
2006	84.440	97.494	78.750	81.597	96.940	84.126	2.8	1.3	3.6	1.7	11.4	2.4
2007	86.607	98.576	81.388	84.781	102.776	86.001	2.6	1.1	3.3	3.9	6.0	2.2
2008	89.170	101.524	83.783	89.944	117.422	87.688	3.0	3.0	2.9	6.1	14.3	2.0
2009	88.921	99.084	84.432	91.013	95.195	88.503	−.3	−2.4	.8	1.2	−18.9	.9
2010	90.514	100.533	86.077	91.285	104.698	89.785	1.8	1.5	1.9	.3	10.0	1.4
2011	92.804	104.325	87.742	94.930	121.281	91.209	2.5	3.8	1.9	4.0	15.8	1.6
2012	94.534	105.620	89.648	97.183	123.001	92.897	1.9	1.2	2.2	2.4	1.4	1.9
2013	95.781	105.049	91.659	98.140	121.900	94.285	1.3	−.5	2.2	1.0	−.9	1.5
2014	97.121	104.542	93.795	100.016	120.890	95.697	1.4	−.5	2.3	1.9	−.8	1.5
2015	97.299	101.350	95.462	101.141	99.190	96.874	.2	−3.1	1.8	1.1	−18.0	1.2
2016	98.284	99.710	97.629	100.130	91.982	98.426	1.0	−1.6	2.3	−1.0	−7.3	1.6
2017	100.000	100.000	100.000	100.000	100.000	100.000	1.7	.3	2.4	−.1	8.7	1.6
2018	102.047	100.811	102.626	100.517	108.054	101.899	2.0	.8	2.6	.5	8.1	1.9
2019	103.513	100.427	104.972	101.528	105.750	103.577	1.4	−.4	2.3	1.0	−2.1	1.6
2020	104.635	99.646	107.054	104.891	96.798	104.942	1.1	−.8	2.0	3.3	−8.5	1.3
2021	109.001	104.572	111.103	108.162	116.904	108.736	4.2	4.9	3.8	3.1	20.8	3.6
2022	116.043	113.548	117.066	119.330	146.893	114.437	6.5	8.6	5.4	10.3	25.7	5.2
2023ᵖ	120.370	114.877	122.982	125.259	139.009	119.121	3.7	1.2	5.1	5.0	−5.4	4.1
2022: Jan	112.829	109.914	114.094	112.730	133.090	111.972	6.3	8.8	5.0	6.5	28.1	5.4
Feb	113.496	111.014	114.523	114.163	136.946	112.436	6.5	9.6	5.0	7.7	26.7	5.6
Mar	114.446	112.521	115.169	115.564	148.893	112.880	6.9	10.5	5.0	8.9	33.1	5.5
Apr	114.789	112.592	115.658	116.434	147.106	113.248	6.6	9.6	5.1	9.6	31.5	5.3
May	115.446	113.552	116.148	118.010	152.110	113.656	6.7	9.7	5.1	10.6	35.6	5.1
June	116.495	115.239	116.853	119.168	162.677	114.297	7.1	10.5	5.4	11.0	42.8	5.2
July	116.511	114.713	117.161	120.647	154.423	114.534	6.6	9.5	5.1	11.8	33.4	5.0
Aug	116.890	114.586	117.810	121.618	147.713	115.158	6.5	8.6	5.4	12.2	24.1	5.2
Sept	117.314	114.539	118.484	122.438	144.819	115.686	6.6	8.1	5.7	11.8	20.0	5.5
Oct	117.842	114.988	119.053	123.100	148.124	116.087	6.3	7.3	5.8	11.5	18.2	5.3
Nov	118.104	114.748	119.581	123.701	146.023	116.417	5.9	6.2	5.8	11.2	13.5	5.1
Dec	118.348	114.176	120.258	124.190	140.792	116.868	5.4	4.8	5.8	11.1	6.9	4.9
2023: Jan	119.011	114.792	120.945	124.698	143.475	117.461	5.5	4.4	6.0	10.6	7.8	4.9
Feb	119.386	114.994	121.413	124.986	142.819	117.883	5.2	3.6	6.0	9.5	4.3	4.8
Mar	119.530	114.730	121.774	124.742	137.598	118.279	4.4	2.0	5.7	7.9	−7.6	4.8
Apr	119.893	115.038	122.165	124.723	138.727	118.642	4.4	2.2	5.6	6.9	−5.7	4.8
May	120.020	114.882	122.441	124.919	133.395	118.984	4.0	1.2	5.4	5.9	−12.3	4.7
June	120.221	114.794	122.797	124.790	134.192	119.189	3.2	−.4	5.1	4.7	−17.5	4.3
July	120.373	114.492	123.192	125.082	134.319	119.332	3.3	−.2	5.1	3.7	−13.0	4.2
Aug	120.803	115.390	123.370	125.395	142.555	119.449	3.3	.7	4.7	3.1	−3.5	3.7
Sept	121.267	115.588	123.976	125.770	144.958	119.642	3.4	.9	4.6	2.7	.1	3.6
Octᵖ	121.299	115.235	124.214	126.079	141.100	120.010	2.9	.2	4.3	2.4	−4.7	3.4
Novᵖ	121.218	114.401	124.539	125.928	137.282	120.088	2.6	−.3	4.1	1.8	−6.0	3.2
Decᵖ	121.421	114.192	124.963	125.998	137.688	120.294	2.6	.0	3.9	1.5	−2.2	2.9

¹ Food consists of food and beverages purchased for off-premises consumption; food services, which include purchased meals and beverages, are not classified as food.
² Consists of gasoline and other energy goods and of electricity and gas services.

Source: Department of Commerce (Bureau of Economic Analysis).

TABLE B–40. Money stock and debt measures, 1986–2023

[Averages of daily figures, except debt end-of-period basis; billions of dollars, seasonally adjusted]

Year and month	M1 Sum of currency, demand deposits, travelers checks, and other checkable deposits; includes savings deposits beginning May 2020 [1]	M2 M1 plus savings deposits, retail MMMF balances, and small time deposits [2]	Debt Debt of domestic nonfinancial sectors [3]	Percent change — From year or 6 months earlier [4] M1	Percent change — From year or 6 months earlier [4] M2	From previous period [5] Debt
December:						
1986	724.7	2,728.0	8,227.1	16.9	9.5	12.0
1987	750.2	2,826.4	8,974.8	3.5	3.6	9.0
1988	786.7	2,988.2	9,797.4	4.9	5.7	9.2
1989	792.9	3,152.5	10,549.7	.8	5.5	7.5
1990	824.7	3,271.8	11,268.6	4.0	3.8	6.6
1991	897.0	3,372.2	11,799.2	8.8	3.1	4.7
1992	1,024.9	3,424.7	12,351.8	14.3	1.6	4.7
1993	1,129.6	3,474.5	13,080.3	10.2	1.5	5.8
1994	1,150.7	3,486.4	13,775.8	1.9	.3	5.3
1995	1,127.5	3,629.5	14,469.2	−2.0	4.1	4.9
1996	1,081.3	3,818.6	15,237.6	−4.1	5.2	5.3
1997	1,072.3	4,032.9	16,117.6	−.8	5.6	5.8
1998	1,095.0	4,375.2	17,256.3	2.1	8.5	7.1
1999	1,122.2	4,638.0	18,437.0	2.5	6.0	6.7
2000	1,088.6	4,925.0	19,295.6	−3.0	6.2	4.7
2001	1,183.2	5,433.8	20,402.8	8.7	10.3	5.8
2002	1,220.2	5,772.0	21,780.5	3.1	6.2	6.8
2003	1,306.2	6,067.3	23,516.0	7.0	5.1	7.8
2004	1,376.0	6,418.3	26,446.1	5.3	5.8	9.1
2005	1,374.3	6,681.9	28,770.7	−.1	4.1	8.8
2006	1,366.6	7,071.6	31,227.7	−.6	5.8	8.5
2007	1,373.4	7,471.6	33,733.9	.5	5.7	8.1
2008	1,601.7	8,192.1	35,568.7	16.6	9.6	5.8
2009	1,692.8	8,496.0	36,542.8	5.7	3.7	3.6
2010	1,836.7	8,801.8	37,920.5	8.5	3.6	4.2
2011	2,165.7	9,660.1	39,184.5	17.9	9.8	3.7
2012	2,460.7	10,459.7	40,834.7	13.6	8.3	4.7
2013	2,674.2	11,035.0	42,481.6	8.7	5.5	4.3
2014	2,947.3	11,684.9	44,074.0	10.2	5.9	3.8
2015	3,100.0	12,346.8	45,892.0	5.2	5.7	4.5
2016	3,345.6	13,213.4	47,857.5	7.9	7.0	4.4
2017	3,618.8	13,857.9	50,020.0	8.2	4.9	4.3
2018	3,773.0	14,362.7	52,698.7	4.3	3.6	4.7
2019	4,021.2	15,320.7	55,148.2	6.6	6.7	4.7
2020	17,827.5	19,114.6	61,948.1	....	24.8	12.3
2021	20,494.7	21,549.3	66,426.4	15.0	12.7	6.3
2022	19,820.9	21,358.3	70,235.4	−3.3	−.9	5.7
2023 p	18,101.4	20,865.2		−8.7	−2.3	
2022: Jan	20,506.3	21,562.3		10.0	8.7	
Feb	20,533.7	21,570.7		8.1	6.9	
Mar	20,664.5	21,697.8	67,806.1	8.0	7.0	8.3
Apr	20,650.7	21,677.2		6.1	5.3	
May	20,638.8	21,665.5		3.8	3.3	
June	20,607.5	21,666.1	68,873.3	1.1	1.1	6.2
July	20,588.5	21,703.5		.8	1.3	
Aug	20,479.7	21,659.6		−.5	.8	
Sept	20,280.9	21,525.1	69,653.3	−3.7	−1.6	4.5
Oct	20,099.2	21,433.2		−5.3	−2.3	
Nov	19,964.9	21,399.3		−6.5	−2.5	
Dec	19,820.9	21,358.3	70,235.4	−7.6	−2.8	3.2
2023: Jan	19,555.0	21,221.7		−10.0	−4.4	
Feb	19,312.3	21,099.8		−11.4	−5.2	
Mar	18,938.4	20,876.0	70,897.9	−13.2	−6.0	3.8
Apr	18,591.7	20,705.4		−15.0	−6.8	
May	18,560.1	20,820.8		−14.1	−5.4	
June	18,490.3	20,854.5	72,008.4	−13.4	−4.7	6.3
July	18,428.1	20,863.8		−11.5	−3.4	
Aug	18,303.5	20,825.6		−10.4	−2.6	
Sept	18,171.7	20,755.4	72,950.3	−8.1	−1.2	5.2
Oct	18,080.9	20,725.7		−5.5	.2	
Nov	18,045.9	20,767.5		−5.5	−.5	
Dec p	18,101.4	20,865.2		−4.2	.1	

[1] Beginning May 2020, M1 includes savings deposits. Prior to May 2020, savings deposits were not included in M1. See the H.6 statistical release for additional details.
[2] Money market mutual fund (MMMF). Savings deposits include money market deposit accounts.
[3] Consists of outstanding debt securities and loans of the U.S. Government, State and local governments, and private nonfinancial sectors. Quarterly data shown in last month of quarter. End-of-year data are for fourth quarter.
[4] Annual changes are from December to December; monthly changes are from six months earlier at an annual rate.
[5] Debt growth of domestic nonfinancial sectors is the seasonally adjusted borrowing flow divided by the seasonally adjusted level of debt outstanding in the previous period. Annual changes are from fourth quarter to fourth quarter; quarterly changes are from previous quarter at an annual rate.

Note: For further information on the composition of M1 and M2, see the H.6 release.

For further information on the debt of domestic nonfinancial sectors and the derivation of debt growth, see the Z.1 release.

Source: Board of Governors of the Federal Reserve System.

TABLE B–41. Consumer credit outstanding, 1973–2023

[Amount outstanding (end of month); millions of dollars, seasonally adjusted]

Year and month	Total consumer credit [1]	Revolving	Nonrevolving [2]
December:			
1973	190,086.31	11,342.22	178,744.09
1974	198,917.84	13,241.26	185,676.58
1975	204,002.00	14,495.27	189,506.73
1976	225,721.59	16,489.05	209,232.54
1977	260,562.70	37,414.82	223,147.88
1978	306,100.39	45,690.95	260,409.43
1979	348,589.11	53,596.43	294,992.67
1980	351,920.05	54,970.05	296,950.00
1981	371,301.44	60,928.00	310,373.44
1982	389,848.74	66,348.30	323,500.44
1983	437,068.86	79,027.25	358,041.61
1984	517,278.98	100,385.63	416,893.35
1985	599,711.23	124,465.80	475,245.43
1986	654,750.24	141,068.15	513,682.08
1987	686,318.77	160,853.91	525,464.86
1988 [3]	731,917.76	184,593.12	547,324.64
1989	794,612.18	211,229.83	583,382.34
1990	808,230.57	238,642.62	569,587.95
1991	798,028.97	263,768.55	534,260.42
1992	806,118.69	278,449.67	527,669.02
1993	865,650.58	309,908.02	555,742.56
1994	997,301.74	365,569.56	631,732.19
1995	1,140,744.36	443,920.09	696,824.27
1996	1,253,437.09	507,516.57	745,920.52
1997	1,324,757.33	540,005.56	784,751.77
1998	1,420,996.44	581,414.78	839,581.66
1999	1,531,105.96	610,696.47	920,409.49
2000	1,716,969.72	682,646.37	1,034,323.35
2001	1,867,852.87	714,840.73	1,153,012.14
2002	1,972,112.21	750,947.45	1,221,164.76
2003	2,077,360.69	768,258.31	1,309,102.38
2004 [3]	2,192,246.17	799,552.18	1,392,693.99
2005 [3]	2,290,928.13	829,518.36	1,461,409.78
2006	2,456,715.70	923,876.78	1,532,838.92
2007	2,609,476.53	1,001,625.30	1,607,851.24
2008	2,643,788.96	1,003,997.04	1,639,791.92
2009	2,555,016.64	916,076.63	1,638,940.01
2010 [3]	2,646,811.26	839,102.67	1,807,708.59
2011	2,756,224.86	840,164.23	1,916,060.63
2012	2,912,905.02	839,980.84	2,072,924.18
2013	3,090,467.78	854,138.80	2,236,328.97
2014	3,309,539.85	887,381.64	2,422,158.21
2015 [3]	3,400,223.22	898,082.65	2,502,140.57
2016	3,636,435.66	960,095.49	2,676,340.17
2017	3,830,751.67	1,016,806.67	2,813,944.99
2018	4,007,041.89	1,053,847.41	2,953,194.48
2019	4,192,191.46	1,091,988.96	3,100,202.51
2020	4,184,852.57	974,594.50	3,210,258.07
2021	4,548,536.16	1,053,530.37	3,495,005.79
2022	4,894,041.43	1,212,609.01	3,681,432.42
2023 [p]	5,010,283.93	1,314,257.94	3,696,025.99
2022: Jan	4,566,065.30	1,062,787.67	3,503,277.63
Feb	4,597,746.03	1,073,831.20	3,523,914.83
Mar	4,636,412.84	1,096,869.15	3,539,543.69
Apr	4,664,763.21	1,110,667.40	3,554,095.81
May	4,691,513.61	1,120,280.55	3,571,233.07
June	4,724,939.85	1,134,712.94	3,590,226.91
July	4,751,620.76	1,146,992.41	3,604,628.35
Aug	4,779,192.82	1,161,976.38	3,617,216.45
Sept	4,806,780.51	1,171,508.15	3,635,272.36
Oct	4,842,165.47	1,185,503.87	3,656,661.60
Nov	4,875,038.31	1,201,084.07	3,673,954.24
Dec	4,894,041.43	1,212,609.01	3,681,432.42
2023: Jan	4,916,136.59	1,223,019.11	3,693,117.48
Feb	4,927,157.05	1,226,382.86	3,700,774.19
Mar	4,945,936.43	1,240,096.61	3,705,839.82
Apr	4,960,313.58	1,253,588.47	3,706,725.11
May	4,959,445.40	1,261,508.31	3,697,937.09
June	4,971,610.20	1,260,463.51	3,711,146.69
July	4,983,110.63	1,271,047.38	3,712,063.25
Aug	4,967,955.59	1,287,912.61	3,680,042.98
Sept	4,978,098.20	1,292,228.39	3,685,869.81
Oct	4,985,242.91	1,295,284.52	3,689,958.39
Nov	5,008,723.24	1,313,216.67	3,695,506.57
Dec [p]	5,010,283.93	1,314,257.94	3,696,025.99

[1] Covers most short- and intermediate-term credit extended to individuals. Credit secured by real estate is excluded.
[2] Includes automobile loans and all other loans not included in revolving credit, such as loans for mobile homes, education, boats, trailers, or vacations. These loans may be secured or unsecured. Beginning with 1977, includes student loans extended by the Federal Government and by SLM Holding Corporation.
[3] Data newly available result in breaks in these series between the prior period and subsequent months.

Source: Board of Governors of the Federal Reserve System.

TABLE B–42. Bond yields and interest rates, 1953–2023

[Percent per annum]

Year	Bills (at auction)[1] 3-month	6-month	Constant maturities[2] 3-year	10-year	30-year	Corporate bonds (Moody's) Aaa[3]	Baa	High-grade municipal bonds (Standard & Poor's)	Home mortgage yields[4]	Prime rate charged by banks[5]	Discount window (Federal Reserve Bank of New York)[5,6] Primary credit	Adjustment credit	Federal funds rate[7]
1953	1.931	....	2.47	2.85	....	3.20	3.74	2.72	....	3.17	....	1.99	....
1954	.953	....	1.63	2.40	....	2.90	3.51	2.37	....	3.05	....	1.60	....
1955	1.753	....	2.47	2.82	....	3.06	3.53	2.53	....	3.16	....	1.89	1.79
1956	2.658	....	3.19	3.18	....	3.36	3.88	2.93	....	3.77	....	2.77	2.73
1957	3.267	....	3.98	3.65	....	3.89	4.71	3.60	....	4.20	....	3.12	3.11
1958	1.839	....	2.84	3.32	....	3.79	4.73	3.56	....	3.83	....	2.15	1.57
1959	3.405	3.832	4.46	4.33	....	4.38	5.05	3.95	....	4.48	....	3.36	3.31
1960	2.93	3.25	3.98	4.12	....	4.41	5.19	3.73	....	4.82	....	3.53	3.21
1961	2.38	2.61	3.54	3.88	....	4.35	5.08	3.46	....	4.50	....	3.00	1.95
1962	2.78	2.91	3.47	3.95	....	4.33	5.02	3.18	....	4.50	....	3.00	2.71
1963	3.16	3.25	3.67	4.00	....	4.26	4.86	3.23	....	4.50	....	3.23	3.18
1964	3.56	3.69	4.03	4.19	....	4.40	4.83	3.22	....	4.50	....	3.55	3.50
1965	3.95	4.05	4.22	4.28	....	4.49	4.87	3.27	....	4.54	....	4.04	4.07
1966	4.88	5.08	5.23	4.93	....	5.13	5.67	3.82	....	5.63	....	4.50	5.11
1967	4.32	4.63	5.03	5.07	....	5.51	6.23	3.98	....	5.63	....	4.19	4.22
1968	5.34	5.47	5.68	5.64	....	6.18	6.94	4.51	....	6.31	....	5.17	5.66
1969	6.68	6.85	7.02	6.67	....	7.03	7.81	5.81	....	7.96	....	5.87	8.21
1970	6.43	6.53	7.29	7.35	....	8.04	9.11	6.51	....	7.91	....	5.95	7.17
1971	4.35	4.51	5.66	6.16	....	7.39	8.56	5.70	7.54	5.73	....	4.88	4.67
1972	4.07	4.47	5.72	6.21	....	7.21	8.16	5.27	7.38	5.25	....	4.50	4.44
1973	7.04	7.18	6.96	6.85	....	7.44	8.24	5.18	8.04	8.03	....	6.45	8.74
1974	7.89	7.93	7.84	7.56	....	8.57	9.50	6.09	9.19	10.81	....	7.83	10.51
1975	5.84	6.12	7.50	7.99	....	8.83	10.61	6.89	9.05	7.86	....	6.25	5.82
1976	4.99	5.27	6.77	7.61	....	8.43	9.75	6.49	8.87	6.84	....	5.50	5.05
1977	5.27	5.52	6.68	7.42	7.75	8.02	8.97	5.56	8.85	6.83	....	5.46	5.54
1978	7.22	7.58	8.29	8.41	8.49	8.73	9.49	5.90	9.64	9.06	....	7.46	7.94
1979	10.05	10.02	9.70	9.43	9.28	9.63	10.69	6.39	11.20	12.67	....	10.29	11.20
1980	11.51	11.37	11.51	11.43	11.27	11.94	13.67	8.51	13.74	15.26	....	11.77	13.35
1981	14.03	13.78	14.46	13.92	13.45	14.17	16.04	11.23	16.63	18.87	....	13.42	16.39
1982	10.69	11.08	12.93	13.01	12.76	13.79	16.11	11.57	16.04	14.85	....	11.01	12.24
1983	8.63	8.75	10.45	11.10	11.18	12.04	13.55	9.47	13.24	10.79	....	8.50	9.09
1984	9.53	9.77	11.92	12.46	12.41	12.71	14.19	10.15	13.88	12.04	....	8.80	10.23
1985	7.47	7.64	9.64	10.62	10.79	11.37	12.72	9.18	12.43	9.93	....	7.69	8.10
1986	5.98	6.03	7.06	7.67	7.78	9.02	10.39	7.38	10.19	8.33	....	6.32	6.80
1987	5.82	6.05	7.68	8.39	8.59	9.38	10.58	7.73	10.21	8.21	....	5.66	6.66
1988	6.69	6.92	8.26	8.85	8.96	9.71	10.83	7.76	10.34	9.32	....	6.20	7.57
1989	8.12	8.04	8.55	8.49	8.45	9.26	10.18	7.24	10.32	10.87	....	6.93	9.21
1990	7.51	7.47	8.26	8.55	8.61	9.32	10.36	7.25	10.13	10.01	....	6.98	8.10
1991	5.42	5.49	6.82	7.86	8.14	8.77	9.80	6.89	9.25	8.46	....	5.45	5.69
1992	3.45	3.57	5.30	7.01	7.67	8.14	8.98	6.41	8.39	6.25	....	3.25	3.52
1993	3.02	3.14	4.44	5.87	6.59	7.22	7.93	5.63	7.31	6.00	....	3.00	3.02
1994	4.29	4.66	6.27	7.09	7.37	7.96	8.62	6.19	8.38	7.15	....	3.60	4.21
1995	5.51	5.59	6.25	6.57	6.88	7.59	8.20	5.95	7.93	8.83	....	5.21	5.83
1996	5.02	5.09	5.99	6.44	6.71	7.37	8.05	5.75	7.81	8.27	....	5.02	5.30
1997	5.07	5.18	6.10	6.35	6.61	7.26	7.86	5.55	7.60	8.44	....	5.00	5.46
1998	4.81	4.85	5.14	5.26	5.58	6.53	7.22	5.12	6.94	8.35	....	4.92	5.35
1999	4.66	4.76	5.49	5.65	5.87	7.04	7.87	5.43	7.44	8.00	....	4.62	4.97
2000	5.85	5.92	6.22	6.03	5.94	7.62	8.36	5.77	8.05	9.23	....	5.73	6.24
2001	3.44	3.39	4.09	5.02	5.49	7.08	7.95	5.19	6.97	6.91	....	3.40	3.88
2002	1.62	1.69	3.10	4.61	5.43	6.49	7.80	5.05	6.54	4.67	....	1.17	1.67
2003	1.01	1.06	2.10	4.01	....	5.67	6.77	4.73	5.83	4.12	2.12	....	1.13
2004	1.38	1.57	2.78	4.27	....	5.63	6.39	4.63	5.84	4.34	2.34	....	1.35
2005	3.16	3.40	3.93	4.29	....	5.24	6.06	4.29	5.87	6.19	4.19	....	3.22
2006	4.73	4.80	4.77	4.80	4.91	5.59	6.48	4.42	6.41	7.96	5.96	....	4.97
2007	4.41	4.48	4.35	4.63	4.84	5.56	6.48	4.42	6.34	8.05	5.86	....	5.02
2008	1.48	1.71	2.24	3.66	4.28	5.63	7.45	4.80	6.03	5.09	2.39	....	1.92
2009	.16	.29	1.43	3.26	4.08	5.31	7.30	4.64	5.04	3.25	.50	....	.16
2010	.14	.20	1.11	3.22	4.25	4.94	6.04	4.16	4.69	3.25	.72	....	.18
2011	.06	.10	.75	2.78	3.91	4.64	5.66	4.29	4.45	3.25	.75	....	.10
2012	.09	.13	.38	1.80	2.92	3.67	4.94	3.14	3.66	3.25	.75	....	.14
2013	.06	.09	.54	2.35	3.45	4.24	5.10	3.96	3.98	3.25	.75	....	.11
2014	.03	.06	.90	2.54	3.34	4.16	4.85	3.78	4.17	3.25	.75	....	.09
2015	.06	.17	1.02	2.14	2.84	3.89	5.00	3.48	3.85	3.26	.76	....	.13
2016	.33	.46	1.00	1.84	2.59	3.67	4.72	3.07	3.65	3.51	1.01	....	.39
2017	.94	1.05	1.58	2.33	2.89	3.74	4.44	3.36	3.99	4.10	1.60	....	1.00
2018	1.94	2.10	2.63	2.91	3.11	3.93	4.80	3.53	4.54	4.91	2.41	....	1.83
2019	2.08	2.07	1.94	2.14	2.58	3.39	4.38	3.38	3.94	5.28	2.78	....	2.16
2020	.38	.39	.42	.89	1.56	2.48	3.60	2.41	3.11	3.54	.64	....	.37
2021	.04	.06	.46	1.45	2.06	2.70	3.39	2.00	2.96	3.25	.25	....	.08
2022	2.04	2.44	3.05	2.95	3.11	4.07	5.07	3.85	5.34	4.86	1.86	....	1.69
2023	5.08	5.08	4.30	3.96	4.09	4.81	5.86	4.31	6.81	8.20	5.20	....	5.03

[1] High bill rate at auction, issue date within period, bank-discount basis. On or after October 28, 1998, data are stop yields from uniform-price auctions. Before that date, they are weighted average yields from multiple-price auctions.

See next page for continuation of table.

Year and month	U.S. Treasury securities					Corporate bonds (Moody's)		High-grade municipal bonds (Standard & Poor's)	Home mortgage yields [4]	Prime rate charged by banks [5]	Discount window (Federal Reserve Bank of New York) [5,6]		Federal funds rate [7]
	Bills (at auction) [1]		Constant maturities [2]										
	3-month	6-month	3-year	10-year	30-year	Aaa [3]	Baa				Primary credit	Adjustment credit	
										High-low	High-low	High-low	
2019: Jan	2.41	2.47	2.52	2.71	3.04	3.93	5.12	3.61	4.46	5.50–5.50	3.00–3.00	....	2.40
Feb	2.40	2.45	2.48	2.68	3.02	3.79	4.95	3.57	4.37	5.50–5.50	3.00–3.00	....	2.40
Mar	2.41	2.45	2.37	2.57	2.98	3.77	4.84	3.43	4.27	5.50–5.50	3.00–3.00	....	2.41
Apr	2.38	2.39	2.31	2.53	2.94	3.69	4.70	3.27	4.14	5.50–5.50	3.00–3.00	....	2.42
May	2.35	2.36	2.16	2.40	2.82	3.67	4.63	3.11	4.07	5.50–5.50	3.00–3.00	....	2.39
June	2.20	2.14	1.78	2.07	2.57	3.42	4.46	2.87	3.80	5.50–5.50	3.00–3.00	....	2.38
July	2.13	2.03	1.80	2.06	2.57	3.29	4.28	3.32	3.77	5.50–5.50	3.00–3.00	....	2.40
Aug	1.97	1.91	1.51	1.63	2.12	2.98	3.87	3.61	3.62	5.25–5.25	2.75–2.75	....	2.13
Sept	1.93	1.85	1.59	1.70	2.16	3.03	3.91	3.57	3.61	5.25–5.00	2.75–2.50	....	2.04
Oct	1.68	1.66	1.53	1.71	2.19	3.01	3.93	3.67	3.69	5.00–4.75	2.50–2.25	....	1.83
Nov	1.55	1.55	1.61	1.81	2.28	3.06	3.94	3.26	3.70	4.75–4.75	2.25–2.25	....	1.55
Dec	1.54	1.55	1.63	1.86	2.30	3.01	3.88	3.26	3.72	4.75–4.75	2.25–2.25	....	1.55
2020: Jan	1.53	1.53	1.52	1.76	2.22	2.94	3.77	3.00	3.62	4.75–4.75	2.25–2.25	....	1.55
Feb	1.54	1.50	1.31	1.50	1.97	2.78	3.61	2.66	3.47	4.75–4.75	2.25–2.25	....	1.58
Mar	.46	.45	.50	.87	1.46	3.02	4.29	3.07	3.45	4.75–3.25	2.25–0.25	....	.65
Apr	.15	.17	.28	.66	1.27	2.43	4.13	2.86	3.31	3.25–3.25	0.25–0.25	....	.05
May	.12	.15	.22	.67	1.38	2.49	3.95	2.69	3.23	3.25–3.25	0.25–0.25	....	.05
June	.16	.18	.22	.73	1.49	2.41	3.65	2.69	3.16	3.25–3.25	0.25–0.25	....	.08
July	.13	.15	.17	.62	1.31	2.14	3.31	1.75	3.02	3.25–3.25	0.25–0.25	....	.09
Aug	.10	.12	.16	.65	1.36	2.25	3.27	1.88	2.94	3.25–3.25	0.25–0.25	....	.10
Sept	.11	.12	.16	.68	1.42	2.31	3.36	2.10	2.89	3.25–3.25	0.25–0.25	....	.09
Oct	.10	.11	.19	.79	1.57	2.35	3.44	2.15	2.83	3.25–3.25	0.25–0.25	....	.09
Nov	.09	.10	.22	.87	1.62	2.30	3.30	2.10	2.77	3.25–3.25	0.25–0.25	....	.09
Dec	.09	.09	.19	.93	1.67	2.26	3.16	1.97	2.68	3.25–3.25	0.25–0.25	....	.09
2021: Jan	.09	.09	.20	1.08	1.82	2.45	3.24	1.61	2.74	3.25–3.25	0.25–0.25	....	.09
Feb	.04	.06	.21	1.26	2.04	2.70	3.42	1.13	2.81	3.25–3.25	0.25–0.25	....	.08
Mar	.03	.05	.32	1.61	2.34	3.04	3.74	1.74	3.08	3.25–3.25	0.25–0.25	....	.07
Apr	.02	.04	.35	1.64	2.30	2.90	3.60	1.84	3.06	3.25–3.25	0.25–0.25	....	.07
May	.02	.03	.32	1.62	2.32	2.96	3.62	1.63	2.96	3.25–3.25	0.25–0.25	....	.06
June	.03	.04	.39	1.52	2.16	2.79	3.44	2.16	2.98	3.25–3.25	0.25–0.25	....	.08
July	.05	.05	.40	1.32	1.94	2.57	3.24	2.22	2.87	3.25–3.25	0.25–0.25	....	.10
Aug	.06	.05	.42	1.28	1.92	2.55	3.24	2.38	2.84	3.25–3.25	0.25–0.25	....	.09
Sept	.04	.05	.47	1.37	1.94	2.53	3.23	2.30	2.90	3.25–3.25	0.25–0.25	....	.08
Oct	.05	.06	.67	1.58	2.06	2.68	3.35	2.43	3.07	3.25–3.25	0.25–0.25	....	.08
Nov	.05	.07	.82	1.56	1.94	2.62	3.28	2.30	3.07	3.25–3.25	0.25–0.25	....	.08
Dec	.06	.14	.95	1.47	1.85	2.65	3.30	2.24	3.10	3.25–3.25	0.25–0.25	....	.08
2022: Jan	.14	.31	1.25	1.76	2.10	2.93	3.58	2.47	3.45	3.25–3.25	0.25–0.25	....	.08
Feb	.34	.64	1.65	1.93	2.25	3.25	3.97	2.78	3.76	3.25–3.25	0.25–0.25	....	.08
Mar	.46	.82	2.09	2.13	2.41	3.43	4.29	3.22	4.17	3.50–3.25	0.50–0.25	....	.20
Apr	.80	1.24	2.72	2.75	2.81	3.76	4.66	3.74	4.98	3.50–3.50	0.50–0.50	....	.33
May	.98	1.46	2.79	2.90	3.07	4.13	5.12	4.06	5.23	4.00–3.50	1.00–0.50	....	.77
June	1.48	2.07	3.15	3.14	3.25	4.24	5.27	4.01	5.52	4.75–4.00	1.75–1.00	....	1.21
July	2.24	2.75	3.03	2.90	3.10	4.06	5.21	3.96	5.41	5.50–4.75	2.50–1.75	....	1.68
Aug	2.61	3.01	3.23	2.90	3.13	4.07	5.15	3.99	5.22	5.50–5.50	2.50–2.50	....	2.33
Sept	3.09	3.53	3.88	3.52	3.56	4.59	5.69	4.53	6.11	6.25–5.50	3.25–2.50	....	2.56
Oct	3.67	4.13	4.38	3.98	4.04	5.10	6.26	4.70	6.90	6.25–6.25	3.25–3.25	....	3.08
Nov	4.14	4.47	4.34	3.89	4.00	4.90	6.07	4.52	6.81	7.00–6.25	4.00–3.25	....	3.78
Dec	4.29	4.58	4.05	3.62	3.66	4.43	5.59	4.19	6.36	7.50–7.00	4.50–4.00	....	4.10
2023: Jan	4.53	4.68	3.91	3.53	3.66	4.40	5.50	4.03	6.27	7.50–7.50	4.50–4.50	....	4.33
Feb	4.65	4.80	4.23	3.75	3.80	4.56	5.59	4.18	6.26	7.75–7.50	4.75–4.50	....	4.57
Mar	4.72	4.78	4.09	3.66	3.77	4.60	5.71	4.19	6.54	8.00–7.75	5.00–4.75	....	4.65
Apr	4.98	4.80	3.76	3.46	3.68	4.47	5.53	4.06	6.34	8.00–8.00	5.00–5.00	....	4.83
May	5.14	4.99	3.82	3.57	3.86	4.67	5.77	4.20	6.43	8.25–8.00	5.25–5.00	....	5.06
June	5.20	5.22	4.27	3.75	3.87	4.65	5.75	4.14	6.71	8.25–8.25	5.25–5.25	....	5.08
July	5.25	5.26	4.47	3.90	3.96	4.66	5.74	4.19	6.84	8.50–8.25	5.50–5.25	....	5.12
Aug	5.30	5.29	4.59	4.17	4.28	4.95	6.02	4.43	7.07	8.50–8.50	5.50–5.50	....	5.33
Sept	5.32	5.30	4.74	4.38	4.47	5.13	6.16	4.58	7.20	8.50–8.50	5.50–5.50	....	5.33
Oct	5.33	5.33	4.89	4.80	4.95	5.61	6.63	4.99	7.62	8.50–8.50	5.50–5.50	....	5.33
Nov	5.29	5.26	4.64	4.50	4.66	5.28	6.29	4.62	7.44	8.50–8.50	5.50–5.50	....	5.33
Dec	5.26	5.15	4.19	4.02	4.14	4.74	5.64	4.09	6.82	8.50–8.50	5.50–5.50	....	5.33

[2] Yields on the more actively traded issues adjusted to constant maturities by the Department of the Treasury. The 30-year Treasury constant maturity series was discontinued on February 18, 2002, and reintroduced on February 9, 2006.
[3] Beginning with December 7, 2001, data for corporate Aaa series are industrial bonds only.
[4] Contract interest rate on commitments for 30-year first-lien prime conventional conforming home purchase mortgage with a loan-to-value of 80 percent.
[5] For monthly data, high and low for the period.
[6] Primary credit replaced adjustment credit as the Federal Reserve's principal discount window lending program effective January 9, 2003.
[7] Beginning March 1, 2016, the daily effective federal funds rate is a volume-weighted median of transaction-level data collected from depository institutions in the Report of Selected Money Market Rates (FR 2420). Between July 21, 1975 and February 29, 2016, the daily effective rate was a volume-weighted mean of rates on brokered trades. Prior to that, the daily effective rate was the rate considered most representative of the day's transactions, usually the one at which most transactions occurred.

Sources: Department of the Treasury, Board of Governors of the Federal Reserve System, Federal Home Loan Mortgage Corporation, Moody's Investors Service, Bloomberg, and Standard & Poor's.

TABLE B–43. Mortgage debt outstanding by type of property and of financing, 1963–2023

[Billions of dollars]

End of year or quarter	All proper-ties	Farm proper-ties	Nonfarm properties Total	Nonfarm properties 1- to 4-family houses	Nonfarm properties Multi-family proper-ties	Nonfarm properties Com-mercial proper-ties	Government underwritten Total [1]	Government underwritten 1- to 4-family houses Total	Government underwritten 1- to 4-family houses FHA-insured	Government underwritten 1- to 4-family houses VA-guaran-teed	Conventional [2] Total	Conventional [2] 1- to 4-family houses
1963	279.3	16.8	262.4	185.1	30.0	47.3	73.4	65.9	35.0	30.9	189.0	119.2
1964	307.0	18.9	288.1	202.3	34.6	51.2	77.2	69.2	38.3	30.9	210.9	133.1
1965	334.5	21.2	313.3	219.4	38.2	55.7	81.2	73.1	42.0	31.1	232.2	146.3
1966	358.5	23.1	335.5	232.7	41.3	61.5	84.1	76.1	44.8	31.3	251.4	156.7
1967	382.1	25.0	357.0	246.0	44.8	66.2	88.2	79.9	47.4	32.5	268.9	166.0
1968	411.4	27.2	384.2	262.9	48.3	73.0	93.4	84.4	50.6	33.8	290.8	178.5
1969	439.9	29.0	410.9	278.7	53.2	79.1	100.2	90.2	54.5	35.7	310.7	188.5
1970	469.4	30.5	438.9	292.2	60.1	86.5	109.2	97.3	59.9	37.3	329.6	195.0
1971	517.9	32.4	485.5	318.4	70.1	97.0	120.7	105.2	65.7	39.5	364.8	213.2
1972	589.8	35.4	554.4	357.4	82.9	114.2	131.1	113.0	68.2	44.7	423.3	244.4
1973	666.5	39.8	626.7	399.8	93.2	133.7	135.0	116.2	66.2	50.0	491.7	283.6
1974	728.4	44.9	683.5	435.2	100.0	148.3	140.2	121.3	65.1	56.2	543.3	313.9
1975	785.6	49.9	735.7	474.0	100.7	161.0	147.0	127.7	66.1	61.6	588.7	346.3
1976	870.5	55.4	815.1	535.0	105.9	174.2	154.0	133.5	66.5	67.0	661.1	401.5
1977	999.2	63.9	935.3	627.7	114.3	193.3	161.7	141.6	68.0	73.6	773.5	486.1
1978	1,150.7	72.8	1,077.9	738.3	125.2	214.5	176.4	153.4	71.4	82.0	901.5	584.9
1979	1,317.0	86.8	1,230.3	855.8	135.0	239.4	199.0	172.9	81.0	92.0	1,031.3	682.8
1980	1,457.8	97.5	1,360.3	957.9	142.5	259.9	225.1	195.2	93.6	101.6	1,135.3	762.7
1981	1,579.5	107.2	1,472.3	1,030.2	142.4	299.7	238.9	207.6	101.3	106.2	1,233.4	822.6
1982	1,661.3	111.3	1,550.0	1,070.2	146.1	333.7	248.9	217.9	108.0	109.9	1,301.1	852.3
1983	1,850.6	113.7	1,736.9	1,186.3	161.2	389.4	279.8	248.8	127.4	121.4	1,457.1	937.4
1984	2,092.0	112.4	1,979.6	1,321.5	186.1	471.9	294.8	265.9	136.7	129.1	1,684.7	1,055.7
1985	2,368.5	94.1	2,274.5	1,526.9	205.9	541.7	328.3	288.6	153.0	135.8	1,946.1	1,238.1
1986	2,655.6	84.1	2,571.5	1,730.1	239.4	602.0	370.5	328.6	185.5	143.1	2,201.0	1,401.5
1987	2,954.3	75.8	2,878.5	1,928.5	258.4	691.6	431.4	387.9	235.5	152.4	2,447.0	1,540.6
1988	3,271.9	70.8	3,201.1	2,162.8	274.5	763.7	459.7	414.2	258.8	155.4	2,741.4	1,748.6
1989	3,523.6	68.8	3,454.8	2,369.6	287.0	798.2	486.8	440.1	282.8	157.3	2,967.9	1,929.5
1990	3,779.5	67.6	3,711.8	2,606.8	287.4	817.6	517.9	470.9	310.9	160.0	3,193.9	2,135.9
1991	3,930.7	67.5	3,863.2	2,774.7	284.1	804.4	537.2	493.3	330.6	162.7	3,326.0	2,281.4
1992	4,040.8	67.9	3,972.9	2,942.1	270.9	759.9	533.3	489.8	326.0	163.8	3,439.6	2,452.3
1993	4,171.5	68.4	4,103.1	3,101.1	267.8	734.2	513.4	469.5	303.2	166.2	3,589.7	2,631.7
1994	4,336.3	69.9	4,266.3	3,278.6	268.5	719.2	559.3	514.2	336.8	177.3	3,707.0	2,764.4
1995	4,522.1	71.7	4,450.3	3,446.4	274.4	729.5	584.3	537.1	352.3	184.7	3,866.1	2,909.4
1996	4,802.8	74.4	4,728.4	3,682.8	286.7	758.9	620.3	571.2	379.2	192.0	4,108.1	3,111.6
1997	5,115.9	78.5	5,037.4	3,917.6	298.8	821.1	656.7	605.7	405.7	200.0	4,380.8	3,311.8
1998	5,603.2	83.1	5,520.1	4,275.8	334.5	909.8	674.0	623.8	417.9	205.9	4,846.1	3,652.0
1999	6,209.6	87.2	6,122.4	4,701.2	375.2	1,046.0	731.5	678.8	462.3	216.5	5,390.9	4,022.4
2000	6,766.6	84.7	6,681.9	5,125.0	404.5	1,152.5	773.1	719.9	499.9	220.1	5,908.8	4,405.0
2001	7,450.1	88.5	7,361.6	5,678.0	446.1	1,237.4	772.7	718.5	497.4	221.2	6,588.9	4,959.5
2002	8,358.7	95.4	8,263.3	6,434.4	486.3	1,342.6	759.3	704.0	486.2	217.7	7,504.0	5,730.4
2003	9,364.8	83.2	9,281.6	7,260.3	559.7	1,461.6	709.2	653.3	438.7	214.6	8,572.4	6,607.1
2004	10,646.7	95.7	10,551.0	8,292.1	609.3	1,649.6	660.2	604.1	398.1	206.0	9,890.8	7,688.0
2005	12,112.9	104.8	12,008.1	9,448.5	674.3	1,885.3	606.6	550.4	348.4	202.0	11,401.5	8,898.1
2006	13,525.5	108.0	13,417.5	10,530.8	717.5	2,169.2	600.2	543.5	336.9	206.6	12,817.3	9,987.3
2007	14,609.6	112.7	14,497.0	11,252.3	810.5	2,434.1	609.2	552.6	342.6	210.0	13,887.8	10,699.7
2008	14,690.0	134.7	14,555.3	11,150.9	852.9	2,551.5	807.2	750.7	534.0	216.7	13,748.1	10,400.2
2009	14,445.4	146.0	14,299.4	10,961.0	862.9	2,475.5	1,005.0	944.3	752.6	191.7	13,294.4	10,016.7
2010	13,893.0	154.1	13,738.9	10,523.4	863.0	2,352.5	1,227.6	1,156.1	934.4	221.7	12,511.2	9,367.4
2011	13,567.7	167.2	13,400.5	10,281.3	863.3	2,255.9	1,368.6	1,291.3	1,036.0	255.3	12,031.9	8,990.0
2012	13,331.3	173.4	13,157.9	10,047.7	891.2	2,219.0	1,544.8	1,459.7	1,165.4	294.2	11,613.1	8,588.1
2013	13,344.5	185.2	13,159.3	9,959.6	940.9	2,258.8	3,927.2	3,832.6	3,480.8	351.8	9,232.1	6,127.1
2014	13,486.8	196.8	13,290.0	9,936.6	1,009.1	2,344.3	4,130.9	4,028.1	3,615.3	412.8	9,159.1	5,908.5
2015	13,883.3	208.8	13,674.5	10,076.4	1,118.8	2,479.3	4,432.7	4,326.7	3,851.3	475.4	9,241.8	5,749.6
2016	14,333.6	226.0	14,107.6	10,278.8	1,236.3	2,592.4	4,764.8	4,654.9	4,106.9	548.1	9,342.8	5,623.9
2017	14,911.6	236.2	14,675.4	10,595.9	1,363.2	2,716.3	5,079.1	4,958.2	4,344.3	613.9	9,596.4	5,637.8
2018	15,463.8	245.8	15,218.0	10,897.8	1,488.4	2,831.8	5,380.0	5,246.5	4,562.3	684.2	9,838.0	5,651.2
2019	16,034.7	267.9	15,766.8	11,180.3	1,622.1	2,964.4	5,664.1	5,522.9	4,788.6	734.3	10,102.7	5,657.4
2020	16,788.2	288.6	16,499.6	11,650.9	1,755.3	3,093.4	6,053.8	5,908.0	5,108.2	799.7	10,445.8	5,743.0
2021	18,312.2	324.4	17,987.8	12,784.1	1,910.4	3,293.3	6,480.3	6,325.5	5,442.1	883.4	11,507.5	6,458.6
2022	19,585.3	334.8	19,250.5	13,614.9	2,075.0	3,560.6	6,784.7	6,626.5	5,670.9	955.5	12,465.9	6,988.4
2022: I	18,577.5	327.0	18,250.5	12,941.0	1,952.1	3,357.5	6,562.9	6,408.4	5,504.0	904.5	11,687.6	6,532.6
II	18,995.3	329.6	18,665.7	13,220.0	1,995.8	3,450.0	6,640.8	6,485.4	5,562.4	923.0	12,024.9	6,734.5
III	19,319.7	332.2	18,987.5	13,448.9	2,034.9	3,503.8	6,719.7	6,562.8	5,621.9	940.9	12,267.8	6,886.1
IV	19,585.3	334.8	19,250.5	13,614.9	2,075.0	3,560.6	6,784.7	6,626.5	5,670.9	955.5	12,465.9	6,988.4
2023: I	19,727.1	339.8	19,387.3	13,676.5	2,107.4	3,603.5	6,839.1	6,679.1	5,711.7	967.4	12,548.2	6,997.3
II	19,884.7	344.8	19,539.9	13,774.1	2,135.8	3,630.0	6,909.2	6,747.5	5,767.8	979.7	12,630.7	7,026.6
III [p]	20,033.5	349.9	19,683.6	13,863.5	2,163.5	3,656.5	6,687.8	6,525.2	5,530.5	994.7	12,995.8	7,338.3

[1] Includes Federal Housing Administration (FHA)–insured multi-family properties, not shown separately.
[2] Derived figures. Total includes multi-family and commercial properties with conventional mortgages, not shown separately.

Source: Board of Governors of the Federal Reserve System, based on data from various Government and private organizations.

TABLE B–44. Mortgage debt outstanding by holder, 1963–2023

[Billions of dollars]

End of year or quarter	Total	Major financial institutions			Other holders		
		Total	Depository Institutions [1], [2]	Life insurance companies	Federal and related agencies [3]	Mortgage pools or trusts [4]	Individuals and others
1963	279.3	214.6	164.1	50.5	11.3	0.5	52.9
1964	307.0	238.8	183.6	55.2	11.6	.6	56.0
1965	334.5	262.4	202.4	60.0	12.7	.9	58.6
1966	358.5	279.5	214.8	64.6	16.2	1.3	61.5
1967	382.1	296.4	228.9	67.5	18.9	2.0	64.7
1968	411.4	317.3	247.3	70.0	22.6	2.5	69.0
1969	439.9	336.6	264.6	72.0	27.9	3.2	72.2
1970	469.4	352.9	278.5	74.4	33.6	4.8	78.2
1971	517.9	389.2	313.7	75.5	36.8	9.5	82.3
1972	589.8	443.8	366.8	76.9	40.1	14.4	91.5
1973	666.5	500.7	419.4	81.4	46.6	18.0	101.1
1974	728.4	539.3	453.1	86.2	60.7	21.5	106.9
1975	785.6	576.1	486.9	89.2	72.6	28.5	108.4
1976	870.5	640.7	549.1	91.6	76.0	40.7	113.2
1977	999.2	735.3	638.4	96.8	83.7	56.8	123.4
1978	1,150.7	837.5	731.3	106.2	100.2	70.4	142.7
1979	1,317.0	928.6	810.2	118.4	121.2	94.8	172.4
1980	1,457.8	988.0	857.0	131.1	142.9	114.0	213.0
1981	1,579.5	1,034.1	896.4	137.7	160.4	129.0	256.0
1982	1,661.3	1,019.6	877.6	142.0	176.9	178.5	286.3
1983	1,850.6	1,108.4	957.4	151.0	188.5	244.8	309.0
1984	2,092.0	1,248.2	1,091.5	156.7	201.6	300.0	342.2
1985	2,368.5	1,368.7	1,196.9	171.8	213.0	392.4	394.4
1986	2,655.6	1,483.3	1,289.5	193.8	202.1	549.5	420.6
1987	2,954.3	1,631.5	1,419.1	212.4	188.5	700.8	433.4
1988	3,271.9	1,797.8	1,564.9	232.9	192.5	785.7	495.9
1989	3,523.6	1,897.4	1,643.2	254.2	197.8	922.2	506.1
1990	3,779.5	1,918.8	1,651.0	267.9	239.0	1,085.9	535.7
1991	3,930.7	1,846.2	1,586.7	259.5	266.0	1,269.6	549.0
1992	4,040.8	1,770.5	1,528.5	242.0	286.1	1,440.0	544.3
1993	4,171.5	1,784.2	1,560.4	223.9	311.9	1,561.1	514.2
1994	4,336.3	1,832.5	1,616.7	215.8	307.8	1,696.9	499.1
1995	4,522.1	1,904.1	1,691.0	213.1	303.9	1,812.0	502.0
1996	4,802.8	1,984.6	1,776.2	208.5	291.9	1,989.1	537.1
1997	5,115.9	2,084.9	1,877.9	207.0	284.4	2,166.5	580.1
1998	5,603.2	2,195.1	1,981.3	213.8	291.5	2,487.1	629.5
1999	6,209.6	2,394.6	2,163.6	231.0	319.6	2,832.3	663.1
2000	6,766.6	2,619.2	2,383.1	236.2	339.9	3,097.5	710.1
2001	7,450.1	2,791.0	2,547.9	243.1	372.0	3,532.4	754.7
2002	8,358.7	3,089.5	2,839.3	250.1	432.3	3,978.4	858.6
2003	9,364.8	3,387.5	3,126.4	261.2	694.1	4,330.3	952.9
2004	10,646.7	3,926.5	3,653.0	273.5	703.2	4,834.5	1,182.5
2005	12,112.9	4,396.5	4,110.8	285.7	665.4	5,710.0	1,341.1
2006	13,525.5	4,784.0	4,479.8	304.1	687.5	6,629.5	1,424.7
2007	14,609.6	5,065.7	4,738.6	327.1	725.2	7,434.4	1,384.3
2008	14,690.0	5,055.6	4,711.8	343.8	791.3	7,592.7	1,250.4
2009	14,445.4	4,795.0	4,467.6	327.4	800.5	7,649.8	1,200.1
2010	13,893.0	4,590.9	4,271.8	319.2	5,121.9	3,108.4	1,071.8
2011	13,567.7	4,452.5	4,117.9	334.6	5,031.7	3,034.3	1,049.2
2012	13,331.3	4,439.4	4,092.5	346.9	4,933.7	2,947.6	1,010.5
2013	13,344.5	4,413.3	4,047.0	366.3	4,992.3	2,773.5	1,165.5
2014	13,486.8	4,547.4	4,159.2	388.2	4,987.0	2,742.7	1,209.8
2015	13,883.3	4,804.4	4,373.7	430.7	5,036.4	2,793.6	1,248.9
2016	14,333.6	5,096.2	4,631.3	465.5	5,146.8	2,826.6	1,263.4
2017	14,911.6	5,308.1	4,801.5	506.7	5,313.4	2,971.5	1,318.5
2018	15,463.8	5,487.6	4,919.5	568.1	5,456.9	3,143.7	1,375.6
2019	16,034.7	5,709.5	5,090.4	619.2	5,634.5	3,255.3	1,435.4
2020	16,788.2	5,775.7	5,131.0	644.7	6,269.6	3,261.6	1,481.3
2021	18,312.2	5,975.9	5,285.0	690.9	7,057.2	3,391.0	1,888.1
2022	19,585.3	6,575.6	5,818.5	757.1	7,491.5	3,587.9	1,929.7
2022: I	18,577.5	6,066.9	5,354.6	712.3	7,245.1	3,437.9	1,827.5
II	18,995.3	6,272.6	5,541.4	731.2	7,344.2	3,497.2	1,881.3
III	19,319.7	6,444.0	5,700.7	743.3	7,417.3	3,553.6	1,904.8
IV	19,585.3	6,575.6	5,818.5	757.1	7,491.5	3,587.9	1,929.7
2023: I	19,727.1	6,655.7	5,887.0	768.7	7,491.6	3,630.2	1,949.5
II	19,884.7	6,720.5	5,938.5	782.0	7,526.9	3,677.6	1,959.6
III [p]	20,033.5	6,776.2	5,982.2	793.9	7,574.4	3,708.8	1,602.5

[1] Includes savings banks and savings and loan associations. Data reported by Federal Savings and Loan Insurance Corporation–insured institutions include loans in process for 1987 and exclude loans in process beginning with 1988.
[2] Includes loans held by nondeposit trust companies but not loans held by bank trust departments.
[3] Includes Government National Mortgage Association (GNMA or Ginnie Mae), Federal Housing Administration, Veterans Administration, Farmers Home Administration (FmHA), Federal Deposit Insurance Corporation, Resolution Trust Corporation (through 1995), and in earlier years Reconstruction Finance Corporation, Homeowners Loan Corporation, Federal Farm Mortgage Corporation, and Public Housing Administration. Also includes U.S.-sponsored agencies such as Federal National Mortgage Association (FNMA or Fannie Mae), Federal Land Banks, Federal Home Loan Mortgage Corporation (FHLMC or Freddie Mac), Federal Agricultural Mortgage Corporation (Farmer Mac, beginning 1994), Federal Home Loan Banks (beginning 1997), and mortgage pass-through securities issued or guaranteed by GNMA, FHLMC, FNMA, FmHA, or Farmer Mac. Other U.S. agencies (amounts small or current separate data not readily available) included with "individuals and others."
[4] Includes private mortgage pools.

Source: Board of Governors of the Federal Reserve System, based on data from various Government and private organizations.

TABLE B–45. Federal receipts, outlays, surplus or deficit, and debt, fiscal years 1959–2025

[Billions of dollars; fiscal years]

Fiscal year or period	Total			On-budget			Off-budget			Federal debt (end of period)		Addendum: Gross domestic product
	Receipts	Outlays	Surplus or deficit (−)	Receipts	Outlays	Surplus or deficit (−)	Receipts	Outlays	Surplus or deficit (−)	Gross Federal	Held by the public	
1959	79.2	92.1	−12.8	71.0	83.1	−12.1	8.3	9.0	−0.7	287.5	234.7	504.6
1960	92.5	92.2	.3	81.9	81.3	.5	10.6	10.9	−.2	290.5	236.8	534.3
1961	94.4	97.7	−3.3	82.3	86.0	−3.8	12.1	11.7	.4	292.6	238.4	546.6
1962	99.7	106.8	−7.1	87.4	93.3	−5.9	12.3	13.5	−1.3	302.9	248.0	585.7
1963	106.6	111.3	−4.8	92.4	96.4	−4.0	14.2	15.0	−.8	310.3	254.0	618.2
1964	112.6	118.5	−5.9	96.2	102.8	−6.5	16.4	15.7	.6	316.1	256.8	661.7
1965	116.8	118.2	−1.4	100.1	101.7	−1.6	16.7	16.5	.2	322.3	260.8	709.3
1966	130.8	134.5	−3.7	111.7	114.8	−3.1	19.1	19.7	−.6	328.5	263.7	780.5
1967	148.8	157.5	−8.6	124.4	137.0	−12.6	24.4	20.4	4.0	340.4	266.6	836.5
1968	153.0	178.1	−25.2	128.1	155.8	−27.7	24.9	22.3	2.6	368.7	289.5	897.6
1969	186.9	183.6	3.2	157.9	158.4	−.5	29.0	25.2	3.7	365.8	278.1	980.3
1970	192.8	195.6	−2.8	159.3	168.0	−8.7	33.5	27.6	5.9	380.9	283.2	1,046.7
1971	187.1	210.2	−23.0	151.3	177.3	−26.1	35.8	32.8	3.0	408.2	303.0	1,116.6
1972	207.3	230.7	−23.4	167.4	193.5	−26.1	39.9	37.2	2.7	435.9	322.4	1,216.3
1973	230.8	245.7	−14.9	184.7	200.0	−15.2	46.1	45.7	.3	466.3	340.9	1,352.7
1974	263.2	269.4	−6.1	209.3	216.5	−7.2	53.9	52.9	1.1	483.9	343.7	1,482.9
1975	279.1	332.3	−53.2	216.6	270.8	−54.1	62.5	61.6	.9	541.9	394.7	1,606.9
1976	298.1	371.8	−73.7	231.7	301.1	−69.4	66.4	70.7	−4.3	629.0	477.4	1,786.1
Transition quarter	81.2	96.0	−14.7	63.2	77.3	−14.1	18.0	18.7	−.7	643.6	495.5	471.7
1977	355.6	409.2	−53.7	278.7	328.7	−49.9	76.8	80.5	−3.7	706.4	549.1	2,024.3
1978	399.6	458.7	−59.2	314.2	369.6	−55.4	85.4	89.2	−3.8	776.6	607.1	2,273.5
1979	463.3	504.0	−40.7	365.3	404.9	−39.6	98.0	99.1	−1.1	829.5	640.3	2,565.6
1980	517.1	590.9	−73.8	403.9	477.0	−73.1	113.2	113.9	−.7	909.0	711.9	2,791.9
1981	599.3	678.2	−79.0	469.1	543.0	−73.9	130.2	135.3	−5.1	994.8	789.4	3,133.2
1982	617.8	745.7	−128.0	474.3	594.9	−120.6	143.5	150.9	−7.4	1,137.3	924.6	3,313.4
1983	600.6	808.4	−207.8	453.2	660.9	−207.7	147.3	147.4	−.1	1,371.7	1,137.3	3,536.0
1984	666.4	851.8	−185.4	500.4	685.6	−185.3	166.1	166.2	−.1	1,564.6	1,307.0	3,949.2
1985	734.0	946.3	−212.3	547.9	769.4	−221.5	186.2	176.9	9.2	1,817.4	1,507.3	4,265.1
1986	769.2	990.4	−221.2	568.9	806.8	−237.9	200.2	183.5	16.7	2,120.5	1,740.6	4,526.3
1987	854.3	1,004.0	−149.7	640.9	809.2	−168.4	213.4	194.8	18.6	2,346.0	1,889.8	4,767.7
1988	909.2	1,064.4	−155.2	667.7	860.0	−192.3	241.5	204.4	37.1	2,601.1	2,051.6	5,138.6
1989	991.1	1,143.7	−152.6	727.4	932.8	−205.4	263.7	210.9	52.8	2,867.8	2,190.7	5,554.7
1990	1,032.0	1,253.0	−221.0	750.3	1,027.9	−277.6	281.7	225.1	56.6	3,206.3	2,411.6	5,898.8
1991	1,055.0	1,324.2	−269.2	761.1	1,082.5	−321.4	293.9	241.7	52.2	3,598.2	2,689.0	6,093.2
1992	1,091.2	1,381.5	−290.3	788.8	1,129.2	−340.4	302.4	252.3	50.1	4,001.8	2,999.7	6,416.3
1993	1,154.3	1,409.4	−255.1	842.4	1,142.8	−300.4	311.9	266.6	45.3	4,351.0	3,248.4	6,775.3
1994	1,258.6	1,461.8	−203.2	923.5	1,182.4	−258.8	335.0	279.4	55.7	4,643.3	3,433.1	7,176.9
1995	1,351.8	1,515.7	−164.0	1,000.7	1,227.1	−226.4	351.1	288.7	62.4	4,920.6	3,604.4	7,560.4
1996	1,453.1	1,560.5	−107.4	1,085.6	1,259.6	−174.0	367.5	300.9	66.6	5,181.5	3,734.1	7,951.3
1997	1,579.2	1,601.1	−21.9	1,187.2	1,290.5	−103.2	392.0	310.6	81.4	5,369.2	3,772.3	8,451.0
1998	1,721.7	1,652.5	69.3	1,305.9	1,335.9	−29.9	415.8	316.6	99.2	5,478.2	3,721.1	8,930.8
1999	1,827.5	1,701.8	125.6	1,383.0	1,381.1	1.9	444.5	320.8	123.7	5,605.5	3,632.4	9,479.6
2000	2,025.2	1,789.0	236.2	1,544.6	1,458.2	86.4	480.6	330.8	149.8	5,628.7	3,409.8	10,117.1
2001	1,991.1	1,862.8	128.2	1,483.6	1,516.0	−32.4	507.5	346.8	160.7	5,769.9	3,319.6	10,525.7
2002	1,853.1	2,010.9	−157.8	1,337.8	1,655.2	−317.4	515.3	355.7	159.7	6,198.4	3,540.4	10,828.9
2003	1,782.3	2,159.9	−377.6	1,258.5	1,796.9	−538.4	523.8	363.0	160.8	6,760.0	3,913.4	11,278.8
2004	1,880.1	2,292.8	−412.7	1,345.4	1,913.3	−568.0	534.7	379.5	155.2	7,354.7	4,295.5	12,028.4
2005	2,153.6	2,472.0	−318.3	1,576.1	2,069.7	−493.6	577.5	402.2	175.3	7,905.3	4,592.2	12,840.0
2006	2,406.9	2,655.1	−248.2	1,798.5	2,233.0	−434.5	608.4	422.1	186.3	8,451.4	4,829.0	13,636.8
2007	2,568.0	2,728.7	−160.7	1,932.9	2,275.0	−342.2	635.1	453.6	181.5	8,950.7	5,035.1	14,305.4
2008	2,524.0	2,982.5	−458.6	1,865.9	2,507.8	−641.8	658.0	474.8	183.3	9,986.1	5,803.1	14,796.6
2009	2,105.0	3,517.7	−1,412.7	1,451.0	3,000.7	−1,549.7	654.0	517.0	137.0	11,875.9	7,544.7	14,467.3
2010	2,162.7	3,457.1	−1,294.4	1,531.0	2,902.4	−1,371.4	631.7	554.7	77.0	13,528.8	9,018.9	14,884.4
2011	2,303.5	3,603.1	−1,299.6	1,737.7	3,104.5	−1,366.8	565.8	498.6	67.2	14,764.2	10,128.2	15,466.5
2012	2,450.0	3,526.6	−1,076.6	1,880.5	3,019.0	−1,138.5	569.5	507.6	61.9	16,050.9	11,281.1	16,109.4
2013	2,775.1	3,454.9	−679.8	2,101.8	2,821.1	−719.2	673.3	633.8	39.5	16,719.4	11,982.7	16,687.8
2014	3,021.5	3,506.3	−484.8	2,285.9	2,800.2	−514.3	735.6	706.1	29.5	17,794.5	12,779.9	17,428.1
2015	3,249.9	3,691.9	−442.0	2,479.5	2,948.8	−469.3	770.4	743.1	27.3	18,120.1	13,116.7	18,164.3
2016	3,268.0	3,852.6	−584.7	2,457.8	3,077.9	−620.2	810.2	774.7	35.5	19,539.5	14,167.6	18,641.3
2017	3,316.2	3,981.6	−665.5	2,465.6	3,180.4	−714.9	850.6	801.2	49.4	20,205.7	14,665.4	19,375.2
2018	3,329.9	4,109.0	−779.1	2,475.2	3,260.4	−785.2	854.7	848.6	6.2	21,462.3	15,749.6	20,436.3
2019	3,463.4	4,447.0	−983.6	2,549.1	3,540.3	−991.3	914.3	906.6	7.7	22,669.5	16,800.7	21,275.3
2020	3,421.2	6,553.6	−3,132.5	2,455.7	5,598.0	−3,142.3	965.4	955.6	9.8	26,902.5	21,016.7	21,292.4
2021	4,047.1	6,822.5	−2,775.4	3,094.8	5,818.6	−2,723.8	952.3	1,003.8	−51.5	28,385.6	22,284.0	22,936.5
2022	4,897.3	6,273.3	−1,375.9	3,831.4	5,192.1	−1,360.7	1,066.0	1,081.2	−15.2	30,838.6	24,253.4	25,305.7
2023	4,440.9	6,134.7	−1,693.7	3,247.2	4,913.6	−1,666.4	1,193.8	1,221.1	−27.3	32,999.0	26,235.6	26,982.4
2024 (estimates)	5,081.5	6,940.9	−1,859.4	3,841.5	5,629.0	−1,787.5	1,240.0	1,311.9	−71.8	35,107.9	28,156.2	28,255.4
2025 (estimates)	5,484.9	7,266.0	−1,781.0	4,200.6	5,870.0	−1,669.4	1,284.4	1,396.0	−111.6	37,096.4	29,983.8	29,340.3

Note: Fiscal years through 1976 were on a July 1–June 30 basis; beginning with October 1976 (fiscal year 1977), the fiscal year is on an October 1–September 30 basis. The transition quarter is the three-month period from July 1, 1976 through September 30, 1976.

See Budget of the United States Government, Fiscal Year 2025, for additional information.

Sources: Department of Commerce (Bureau of Economic Analysis), Department of the Treasury, and Office of Management and Budget.

TABLE B–46. Federal receipts, outlays, surplus or deficit, and debt, as percent of gross domestic product, fiscal years 1954–2025

[Percent; fiscal years]

Fiscal year or period	Receipts	Outlays		Surplus or deficit (−)	Federal debt (end of period)	
		Total	National defense		Gross Federal	Held by public
1954	18.0	18.3	12.7	−0.3	70.0	58.0
1955	16.1	16.8	10.5	−.7	67.5	55.8
1956	17.0	16.1	9.7	.9	62.2	50.7
1957	17.3	16.5	9.8	.7	58.8	47.3
1958	16.8	17.4	9.9	−.6	59.1	47.8
1959	15.7	18.3	9.7	−2.5	57.0	46.5
1960	17.3	17.3	9.0	.1	54.4	44.3
1961	17.3	17.9	9.1	−.6	53.5	43.6
1962	17.0	18.2	8.9	−1.2	51.7	42.3
1963	17.2	18.0	8.6	−.8	50.2	41.1
1964	17.0	17.9	8.3	−.9	47.8	38.8
1965	16.5	16.7	7.1	−.2	45.4	36.8
1966	16.8	17.2	7.4	−.5	42.1	33.8
1967	17.8	18.8	8.5	−1.0	40.7	31.9
1968	17.0	19.8	9.1	−2.8	41.1	32.3
1969	19.1	18.7	8.4	.3	37.3	28.4
1970	18.4	18.7	7.8	−.3	36.4	27.1
1971	16.8	18.8	7.1	−2.1	36.6	27.1
1972	17.0	19.0	6.5	−1.9	35.8	26.5
1973	17.1	18.2	5.7	−1.1	34.5	25.2
1974	17.8	18.2	5.4	−.4	32.6	23.2
1975	17.4	20.7	5.4	−3.3	33.7	24.6
1976	16.7	20.8	5.0	−4.1	35.2	26.7
Transition quarter	17.2	20.3	4.7	−3.1	34.1	26.3
1977	17.6	20.2	4.8	−2.7	34.9	27.1
1978	17.6	20.2	4.6	−2.6	34.2	26.7
1979	18.1	19.6	4.5	−1.6	32.3	25.0
1980	18.5	21.2	4.8	−2.6	32.6	25.5
1981	19.1	21.6	5.0	−2.5	31.8	25.2
1982	18.6	22.5	5.6	−3.9	34.3	27.9
1983	17.0	22.9	5.9	−5.9	38.8	32.2
1984	16.9	21.6	5.8	−4.7	39.6	33.1
1985	17.2	22.2	5.9	−5.0	42.6	35.3
1986	17.0	21.9	6.0	−4.9	46.8	38.5
1987	17.9	21.1	5.9	−3.1	49.2	39.6
1988	17.7	20.7	5.7	−3.0	50.6	39.9
1989	17.8	20.6	5.5	−2.7	51.6	39.4
1990	17.5	21.2	5.1	−3.7	54.4	40.9
1991	17.3	21.7	4.5	−4.4	59.1	44.1
1992	17.0	21.5	4.6	−4.5	62.4	46.8
1993	17.0	20.8	4.3	−3.8	64.2	47.9
1994	17.5	20.4	3.9	−2.8	64.7	47.8
1995	17.9	20.0	3.6	−2.2	65.1	47.7
1996	18.3	19.6	3.3	−1.4	65.2	47.0
1997	18.7	18.9	3.2	−.3	63.5	44.6
1998	19.3	18.5	3.0	.8	61.3	41.7
1999	19.3	18.0	2.9	1.3	59.1	38.3
2000	20.0	17.7	2.9	2.3	55.6	33.7
2001	18.9	17.7	2.9	1.2	54.8	31.5
2002	17.1	18.6	3.2	−1.5	57.2	32.7
2003	15.8	19.2	3.6	−3.3	59.9	34.7
2004	15.6	19.1	3.8	−3.4	61.1	35.7
2005	16.8	19.3	3.9	−2.5	61.6	35.8
2006	17.6	19.5	3.8	−1.8	62.0	35.4
2007	18.0	19.1	3.9	−1.1	62.6	35.2
2008	17.1	20.2	4.2	−3.1	67.5	39.2
2009	14.5	24.3	4.6	−9.8	82.1	52.2
2010	14.5	23.2	4.7	−8.7	90.9	60.6
2011	14.9	23.3	4.6	−8.4	95.5	65.5
2012	15.2	21.9	4.2	−6.7	99.6	70.0
2013	16.6	20.7	3.8	−4.1	100.2	71.8
2014	17.3	20.1	3.5	−2.8	102.1	73.3
2015	17.9	20.3	3.2	−2.4	99.8	72.2
2016	17.5	20.7	3.2	−3.1	104.8	76.0
2017	17.1	20.6	3.1	−3.4	104.3	75.7
2018	16.3	20.1	3.1	−3.8	105.0	77.1
2019	16.3	20.9	3.2	−4.6	106.6	79.0
2020	16.1	30.8	3.4	−14.7	126.3	98.7
2021	17.6	29.7	3.3	−12.1	123.8	97.2
2022	19.4	24.8	3.0	−5.4	121.9	95.8
2023	16.5	22.7	3.0	−6.3	122.3	97.2
2024 (estimates)	18.0	24.6	3.2	−6.6	124.3	99.6
2025 (estimates)	18.7	24.8	3.2	−6.1	126.4	102.2

Note: See Note, Table B–45.

Sources: Department of the Treasury and Office of Management and Budget.

TABLE B–47. Federal receipts and outlays, by major category, and surplus or deficit, fiscal years 1959–2025

[Billions of dollars; fiscal years]

Fiscal year or period	Receipts (on-budget and off-budget)					Outlays (on-budget and off-budget)										Surplus or deficit (−) (on-budget and off-budget)
	Total	Individual income taxes	Corporation income taxes	Social insurance and retirement receipts	Other	Total	National defense		International affairs	Health	Medicare	Income security	Social security	Net interest	Other	
							Total	Department of Defense, military								
1959	79.2	36.7	17.3	11.7	13.5	92.1	49.0	....	3.1	0.7	....	8.2	9.7	5.8	15.5	−12.8
1960	92.5	40.7	21.5	14.7	15.6	92.2	48.1	....	3.0	.8	....	7.4	11.6	6.9	14.4	.3
1961	94.4	41.3	21.0	16.4	15.7	97.7	49.6	....	3.2	.9	....	9.7	12.5	6.7	15.2	−3.3
1962	99.7	45.6	20.5	17.0	16.5	106.8	52.3	50.1	5.6	1.2	....	9.2	14.4	6.9	17.2	−7.1
1963	106.6	47.6	21.6	19.8	17.6	111.3	53.4	51.1	5.3	1.5	....	9.3	15.8	7.7	18.3	−4.8
1964	112.6	48.7	23.5	22.0	18.5	118.5	54.8	52.6	4.9	1.8	....	9.7	16.6	8.2	22.6	−5.9
1965	116.8	48.8	25.5	22.2	20.3	118.2	50.6	48.8	5.3	1.8	....	9.5	17.5	8.6	25.0	−1.4
1966	130.8	55.4	30.1	25.5	19.8	134.5	58.1	56.6	5.6	2.5	0.1	9.7	20.7	9.4	28.5	−3.7
1967	148.8	61.5	34.0	32.6	20.7	157.5	71.4	70.1	5.6	3.4	2.7	10.3	21.7	10.3	32.1	−8.6
1968	153.0	68.7	28.7	33.9	21.7	178.1	81.9	80.4	5.3	4.4	4.6	11.8	23.9	11.1	35.1	−25.2
1969	186.9	87.2	36.7	39.0	23.9	183.6	82.5	80.8	4.6	5.2	5.7	13.1	27.3	12.7	32.6	3.2
1970	192.8	90.4	32.8	44.4	25.2	195.6	81.7	80.1	4.3	5.9	6.2	15.6	30.3	14.4	37.2	−2.8
1971	187.1	86.2	26.8	47.3	26.8	210.2	78.9	77.5	4.2	6.8	6.6	22.9	35.9	14.8	40.0	−23.0
1972	207.3	94.7	32.2	52.6	27.8	230.7	79.2	77.6	4.8	8.7	7.5	27.6	40.2	15.5	47.3	−23.4
1973	230.8	103.2	36.2	63.1	28.3	245.7	76.7	75.0	4.1	9.4	8.1	28.3	49.1	17.3	52.8	−14.9
1974	263.2	119.0	38.6	75.1	30.6	269.4	79.3	77.9	5.7	10.7	9.6	33.7	55.9	21.4	52.9	−6.1
1975	279.1	122.4	40.6	84.5	31.5	332.3	86.5	84.9	7.1	12.9	12.9	50.2	64.7	23.2	74.9	−53.2
1976	298.1	131.6	41.4	90.8	34.3	371.8	89.6	87.9	6.4	15.7	15.8	60.8	73.9	26.7	82.8	−73.7
Transition quarter	81.2	38.8	8.5	25.2	8.8	96.0	22.3	21.8	2.5	3.9	4.3	15.0	19.8	6.9	21.4	−14.7
1977	355.6	157.6	54.9	106.5	36.6	409.2	97.2	95.1	6.4	17.3	19.3	61.0	85.1	29.9	93.0	−53.7
1978	399.6	181.0	60.0	121.0	37.7	458.7	104.5	102.3	7.5	18.5	22.8	61.5	93.9	35.5	114.7	−59.2
1979	463.3	217.8	65.7	138.9	40.8	504.0	116.3	113.6	7.5	20.5	26.5	66.4	104.1	42.6	120.2	−40.7
1980	517.1	244.1	64.6	157.8	50.6	590.9	134.0	130.9	12.7	23.2	32.1	86.5	118.5	52.5	131.3	−73.8
1981	599.3	285.9	61.1	182.7	69.5	678.2	157.5	153.9	13.1	26.9	39.1	100.3	139.6	68.8	133.0	−79.0
1982	617.8	297.7	49.2	201.5	69.3	745.7	185.3	180.7	12.3	27.4	46.6	108.1	156.0	85.0	125.0	−128.0
1983	600.6	288.9	37.0	209.0	65.6	808.4	209.9	204.4	11.8	28.6	52.6	123.0	170.7	89.8	121.8	−207.8
1984	666.4	298.4	56.9	239.4	71.8	851.8	227.4	220.9	15.9	30.4	57.5	113.4	178.2	111.1	117.9	−185.4
1985	734.0	334.5	61.3	265.2	73.0	946.3	252.7	245.1	16.2	33.5	65.8	129.0	188.6	129.5	131.0	−212.3
1986	769.2	349.0	63.1	283.9	73.2	990.4	273.4	265.4	14.1	35.9	70.2	120.7	198.8	136.0	141.3	−221.2
1987	854.3	392.6	83.9	303.3	74.5	1,004.0	282.0	273.9	11.6	40.0	75.1	124.1	207.4	138.6	125.2	−149.7
1988	909.2	401.2	94.5	334.3	79.2	1,064.4	290.4	281.9	10.5	44.5	78.9	130.4	219.3	151.8	138.7	−155.2
1989	991.1	445.7	103.3	359.4	82.7	1,143.7	303.6	294.8	9.6	48.4	85.0	137.6	232.5	169.0	158.2	−152.6
1990	1,032.0	466.9	93.5	380.0	91.5	1,253.0	299.3	289.7	13.8	57.7	98.1	148.8	248.6	184.3	202.4	−221.0
1991	1,055.0	467.8	98.1	396.0	93.1	1,324.2	273.3	262.3	15.8	71.1	104.5	172.6	269.0	194.4	223.4	−269.2
1992	1,091.2	476.0	100.3	413.7	101.3	1,381.5	298.3	286.8	16.1	89.4	119.0	199.7	287.6	199.3	172.1	−290.3
1993	1,154.3	509.7	117.5	428.3	98.8	1,409.4	291.1	278.5	17.2	99.3	130.6	210.1	304.6	198.7	157.8	−255.1
1994	1,258.6	543.1	140.4	461.5	113.7	1,461.8	281.6	268.6	17.1	107.1	144.7	217.2	319.6	202.9	171.5	−203.2
1995	1,351.8	590.2	157.0	484.5	120.1	1,515.7	272.1	259.4	16.4	115.4	159.9	223.8	335.8	232.1	160.3	−164.0
1996	1,453.1	656.4	171.8	509.4	115.4	1,560.5	265.7	253.1	13.5	119.3	174.2	229.7	349.7	241.1	167.3	−107.4
1997	1,579.2	737.5	182.3	539.4	120.1	1,601.1	270.5	258.3	15.2	123.8	190.0	235.0	365.3	244.0	157.4	−21.9
1998	1,721.7	828.6	188.7	571.8	132.6	1,652.5	268.2	255.8	13.1	131.4	192.8	237.7	379.2	241.1	189.0	69.3
1999	1,827.5	879.5	184.7	611.8	151.5	1,701.8	274.8	261.2	15.2	141.0	190.4	242.4	390.0	229.8	218.1	125.6
2000	2,025.2	1,004.5	207.3	652.9	160.6	1,789.0	294.4	281.0	17.2	154.5	197.1	253.7	409.4	222.9	239.7	236.2
2001	1,991.1	994.3	151.1	694.0	151.7	1,862.8	304.7	290.2	16.5	172.2	217.4	269.7	433.0	206.2	243.2	128.2
2002	1,853.1	858.3	148.0	700.8	146.0	2,010.9	348.5	331.8	22.3	196.5	230.9	312.7	456.0	170.9	273.2	−157.8
2003	1,782.3	793.7	131.8	713.0	143.9	2,159.9	404.7	387.1	21.2	219.6	249.4	334.6	474.7	153.1	302.6	−377.6
2004	1,880.1	809.0	189.4	733.4	148.4	2,292.8	455.8	436.4	26.9	240.1	269.4	333.0	495.5	160.2	311.8	−412.7
2005	2,153.6	927.2	278.3	794.1	154.0	2,472.0	495.3	474.1	34.6	250.6	298.6	345.8	523.3	184.0	339.8	−318.3
2006	2,406.9	1,043.9	353.9	837.8	171.2	2,655.1	521.8	499.3	29.5	252.8	329.9	352.4	548.5	226.6	393.5	−248.2
2007	2,568.0	1,163.5	370.2	869.6	164.7	2,728.7	551.3	528.5	28.5	266.4	375.4	365.9	586.2	237.1	317.9	−160.7
2008	2,524.0	1,145.7	304.3	900.2	173.7	2,982.5	616.1	594.6	28.9	280.6	390.8	431.2	617.0	252.8	365.2	−458.6
2009	2,105.0	915.3	138.2	890.9	160.5	3,517.7	661.0	636.7	37.5	334.4	430.1	533.1	683.0	186.9	651.7	−1,412.7
2010	2,162.7	898.5	191.4	864.8	207.9	3,457.1	693.5	666.7	45.2	369.1	451.6	622.1	706.7	196.2	372.6	−1,294.4
2011	2,303.5	1,091.5	181.1	818.8	212.1	3,603.1	705.6	678.1	45.7	372.5	485.7	597.3	730.8	230.0	435.7	−1,299.6
2012	2,450.0	1,132.2	242.3	845.3	230.2	3,526.6	677.9	650.9	36.8	346.8	471.8	541.2	773.3	220.4	458.4	−1,076.6
2013	2,775.1	1,316.4	273.5	947.8	237.4	3,454.9	633.4	607.8	46.5	358.3	497.8	536.4	813.6	220.9	348.0	−679.8
2014	3,021.5	1,394.6	320.7	1,023.5	282.7	3,506.3	603.5	577.9	46.9	409.5	511.7	513.6	850.5	229.0	341.7	−484.8
2015	3,249.9	1,540.8	343.8	1,065.3	300.0	3,691.9	589.7	562.5	52.0	482.3	546.2	508.8	887.8	223.2	402.0	−442.0
2016	3,268.0	1,546.1	299.6	1,115.1	307.3	3,852.6	593.4	565.4	45.3	511.3	594.5	514.1	916.1	240.0	437.9	−584.7
2017	3,316.2	1,587.1	297.0	1,161.9	270.1	3,981.6	598.7	568.9	46.3	533.2	597.3	503.4	944.9	262.6	495.3	−665.5
2018	3,329.9	1,683.5	204.7	1,170.7	270.9	4,109.0	631.3	600.8	48.9	551.2	588.7	495.3	987.8	325.0	480.9	−779.1
2019	3,463.4	1,717.9	230.2	1,243.1	272.1	4,447.0	685.7	653.7	53.0	584.8	651.0	514.8	1,044.4	375.2	538.0	−983.6
2020	3,421.2	1,608.7	211.8	1,310.0	290.7	6,553.6	724.6	690.4	67.7	747.6	776.2	1,263.6	1,095.8	345.5	1,532.6	−3,132.5
2021	4,047.1	2,044.4	371.8	1,314.1	316.8	6,822.5	753.9	717.6	47.0	796.5	696.5	1,647.7	1,134.6	352.3	1,394.1	−2,775.4
2022	4,897.3	2,632.1	424.9	1,483.5	356.8	6,273.3	765.6	726.5	71.9	914.1	755.1	866.1	1,218.7	475.9	1,205.9	−1,375.9
2023	4,440.9	2,176.5	419.6	1,614.5	230.4	6,134.7	820.3	775.9	69.3	888.6	847.5	774.7	1,354.3	658.3	721.8	−1,693.7
2024 (estimates)	5,081.5	2,503.4	612.8	1,720.5	244.9	6,940.9	907.7	859.5	69.8	858.0	847.4	760.5	1,458.0	888.6	1,150.8	−1,859.4
2025 (estimates)	5,484.9	2,679.2	668.1	1,896.8	240.8	7,266.0	926.8	878.5	66.5	888.9	946.0	936.8	1,549.7	965.5	985.7	−1,781.0

Note: See Note, Table B–45.

Sources: Department of the Treasury and Office of Management and Budget.

TABLE B–48. Federal receipts, outlays, surplus or deficit, and debt, fiscal years 2020–2025

[Millions of dollars; fiscal years]

Description	Actual				Estimates	
	2020	2021	2022	2023	2024	2025
RECEIPTS, OUTLAYS, AND SURPLUS OR DEFICIT						
Total:						
Receipts	3,421,164	4,047,111	4,897,339	4,440,947	5,081,546	5,484,948
Outlays	6,553,620	6,822,461	6,273,259	6,134,672	6,940,904	7,265,963
Surplus or deficit (–)	–3,132,456	–2,775,350	–1,375,920	–1,693,725	–1,859,358	–1,781,015
On-budget:						
Receipts	2,455,736	3,094,788	3,831,364	3,247,192	3,841,506	4,200,568
Outlays	5,598,038	5,818,614	5,192,104	4,913,572	5,629,034	5,869,973
Surplus or deficit (–)	–3,142,302	–2,723,826	–1,360,740	–1,666,380	–1,787,528	–1,669,405
Off-budget:						
Receipts	965,428	952,323	1,065,975	1,193,755	1,240,040	1,284,380
Outlays	955,582	1,003,847	1,081,155	1,221,100	1,311,870	1,395,990
Surplus or deficit (–)	9,846	–51,524	–15,180	–27,345	–71,830	–111,610
OUTSTANDING DEBT, END OF PERIOD						
Gross Federal debt	26,902,455	28,385,562	30,838,586	32,988,990	35,107,906	37,096,435
Held by Federal Government accounts	5,885,786	6,101,522	6,585,141	6,753,388	6,951,721	7,112,662
Held by the public	21,016,669	22,284,040	24,253,445	26,235,602	28,156,185	29,983,773
Federal Reserve System	4,445,477	5,433,156	5,634,940	4,952,914	....	....
Other	16,571,192	16,850,884	18,618,505	21,282,688	....	....
RECEIPTS BY SOURCE						
Total: On-budget and off-budget	3,421,164	4,047,111	4,897,339	4,440,947	5,081,546	5,484,948
Individual income taxes	1,608,663	2,044,377	2,632,146	2,176,481	2,503,366	2,679,224
Corporation income taxes	211,845	371,831	424,865	419,584	612,781	668,080
Social insurance and retirement receipts	1,309,955	1,314,088	1,483,527	1,614,456	1,720,543	1,896,817
On-budget	344,527	361,765	417,552	420,701	480,503	612,437
Off-budget	965,428	952,323	1,065,975	1,193,755	1,240,040	1,284,380
Excise taxes	86,780	75,274	87,728	75,802	99,715	109,896
Estate and gift taxes	17,624	27,140	32,550	33,668	29,035	32,623
Customs duties and fees	68,551	79,985	99,908	80,338	81,384	60,671
Miscellaneous receipts	117,746	134,416	136,615	40,618	34,722	37,637
Deposits of earnings by Federal Reserve System	81,880	100,054	106,674	581	....	....
All other	35,866	34,362	29,941	40,037	34,722	37,637
OUTLAYS BY FUNCTION						
Total: On-budget and off-budget	6,553,620	6,822,461	6,273,259	6,134,672	6,940,904	7,265,963
National defense	724,588	753,897	765,649	820,263	907,728	926,763
International affairs	67,722	46,951	71,873	69,313	69,830	66,484
General science, space, and technology	34,022	35,534	37,404	41,276	43,784	43,831
Energy	7,083	5,977	–9,132	–406	27,109	39,136
Natural resources and environment	42,450	44,151	41,384	47,387	93,980	73,192
Agriculture	47,298	47,398	33,065	33,651	39,460	33,713
Commerce and housing credit	572,071	307,847	–19,075	100,765	57,993	13,485
On-budget	574,474	310,581	–18,658	94,996	56,850	13,061
Off-budget	–2,403	–2,734	–417	5,769	1,143	424
Transportation	145,623	154,291	131,024	126,417	144,683	150,180
Community and regional development	81,878	44,655	69,963	86,553	124,845	60,795
Education, training, employment, and social services	237,754	298,406	677,305	–2,189	292,207	187,707
Health	747,582	796,450	914,081	888,555	858,013	888,926
Medicare	776,225	696,458	755,094	847,544	847,442	946,011
Income security	1,263,639	1,647,729	866,097	774,655	760,507	936,628
Social security	1,095,816	1,134,586	1,218,663	1,354,317	1,457,998	1,549,737
On-budget	39,893	34,862	48,524	50,800	55,931	60,883
Off-budget	1,055,923	1,099,724	1,170,139	1,303,517	1,402,067	1,488,854
Veterans benefits and services	218,655	234,282	274,404	301,600	346,332	370,124
Administration of justice	71,997	71,430	71,323	80,432	89,905	87,352
General government	180,109	273,941	133,214	38,199	42,673	51,027
Net interest	345,470	352,338	475,887	658,267	888,597	965,470
On-budget	424,274	425,591	543,625	724,774	956,824	1,034,525
Off-budget	–78,804	–73,253	–67,738	–66,507	–68,227	–69,055
Allowances					–7,328	24,513
Undistributed offsetting receipts	–106,362	–123,860	–234,964	–131,927	–144,854	–149,311
On-budget	–87,228	–103,970	–214,135	–110,248	–121,741	–125,078
Off-budget	–19,134	–19,890	–20,829	–21,679	–23,113	–24,233

Note: See Note, Table B–45.

Sources: Department of the Treasury and Office of Management and Budget.

TABLE B–49. Federal and State and local government current receipts and expenditures, national income and product accounts (NIPA) basis, 1973–2023

[Billions of dollars; quarterly data at seasonally adjusted annual rates]

Year or quarter	Total government			Federal Government			State and local government			Addendum: Net Grants-in-aid to State and local governments
	Current receipts	Current expenditures	Net government saving (NIPA)	Current receipts	Current expenditures	Net Federal Government saving (NIPA)	Current receipts	Current expenditures	Net State and local government saving (NIPA)	
1973	388.8	421.5	−32.7	249.2	287.6	−38.3	173.0	167.4	5.6	33.5
1974	430.2	473.9	−43.7	278.5	319.8	−41.3	186.6	189.0	−2.3	34.9
1975	441.2	549.9	−108.6	276.8	374.8	−97.9	208.0	218.7	−10.7	43.6
1976	505.7	591.0	−85.3	322.6	403.5	−80.9	232.2	236.6	−4.4	49.1
1977	567.4	640.3	−72.9	363.9	437.3	−73.4	258.3	257.8	.5	54.8
1978	646.1	703.3	−57.2	423.8	485.9	−62.0	285.8	280.9	4.9	63.5
1979	729.3	777.9	−48.6	487.0	534.4	−47.4	306.3	307.5	−1.2	64.0
1980	799.9	894.6	−94.7	533.7	622.5	−88.8	335.9	341.8	−5.9	69.7
1981	919.1	1,017.4	−98.2	621.1	709.1	−88.1	367.5	377.6	−10.2	69.4
1982	940.9	1,131.0	−190.1	618.7	786.0	−167.4	388.5	411.3	−22.8	66.3
1983	1,002.1	1,227.7	−225.6	644.8	851.9	−207.2	425.3	443.7	−18.4	67.9
1984	1,115.0	1,311.7	−196.7	711.2	907.7	−196.5	476.1	476.3	−.2	72.3
1985	1,217.0	1,418.7	−201.7	775.7	975.0	−199.2	517.5	519.9	−2.4	76.2
1986	1,292.9	1,512.8	−219.9	817.9	1,033.8	−215.9	557.4	561.3	−4.0	82.4
1987	1,406.6	1,586.7	−180.1	899.5	1,065.2	−165.7	585.5	599.9	−14.4	78.4
1988	1,507.1	1,678.3	−171.3	962.4	1,122.4	−160.0	630.4	641.7	−11.3	85.7
1989	1,632.0	1,810.7	−178.7	1,042.5	1,201.8	−159.4	681.4	700.7	−19.3	91.8
1990	1,713.3	1,952.9	−239.5	1,087.6	1,290.9	−203.3	730.0	766.3	−36.3	104.4
1991	1,763.6	2,072.2	−308.5	1,107.8	1,356.2	−248.4	779.8	840.0	−60.1	124.0
1992	1,848.6	2,254.2	−405.6	1,154.4	1,488.9	−334.5	836.0	907.0	−71.1	141.7
1993	1,953.1	2,339.3	−386.2	1,231.0	1,544.6	−313.5	877.8	950.4	−72.6	155.7
1994	2,097.3	2,417.2	−319.9	1,329.3	1,585.0	−255.6	934.8	999.1	−64.2	166.8
1995	2,223.5	2,536.5	−312.9	1,417.4	1,659.5	−242.1	980.6	1,051.4	−70.8	174.5
1996	2,388.2	2,621.8	−233.6	1,536.3	1,715.7	−179.4	1,033.3	1,087.5	−54.2	181.5
1997	2,565.5	2,699.9	−134.4	1,667.4	1,759.4	−92.0	1,086.2	1,128.7	−42.4	188.1
1998	2,738.0	2,767.4	−29.3	1,789.8	1,788.4	1.4	1,149.0	1,179.7	−30.7	200.8
1999	2,908.9	2,879.5	29.5	1,906.0	1,836.8	69.1	1,222.1	1,261.8	−39.7	219.2
2000	3,138.2	3,019.9	118.2	2,067.8	1,908.1	159.7	1,303.5	1,345.0	−41.5	233.1
2001	3,124.4	3,229.2	−104.7	2,032.4	2,017.3	15.0	1,353.3	1,473.1	−119.8	261.3
2002	2,968.3	3,419.8	−451.4	1,870.9	2,138.7	−267.8	1,386.2	1,569.8	−183.6	288.7
2003	3,044.6	3,624.0	−579.4	1,896.1	2,293.5	−397.4	1,470.2	1,652.2	−182.0	321.7
2004	3,274.1	3,817.4	−543.3	2,028.1	2,421.6	−393.5	1,578.4	1,728.2	−149.8	332.3
2005	3,677.8	4,075.3	−397.4	2,304.7	2,598.5	−293.8	1,716.6	1,820.3	−103.7	343.5
2006	4,012.2	4,320.1	−307.9	2,538.8	2,760.7	−221.9	1,814.4	1,900.4	−86.0	341.0
2007	4,209.6	4,599.6	−390.0	2,668.3	2,928.0	−259.7	1,900.4	2,030.7	−130.4	359.1
2008	4,125.0	4,972.0	−847.0	2,582.1	3,207.0	−624.9	1,914.1	2,136.2	−222.1	371.2
2009	3,698.5	5,284.0	−1,585.5	2,242.1	3,485.2	−1,243.2	1,914.6	2,256.9	−342.3	458.1
2010	3,932.7	5,560.0	−1,627.3	2,446.3	3,764.6	−1,318.4	1,991.7	2,300.6	−309.0	505.2
2011	4,128.3	5,639.5	−1,511.2	2,573.6	3,807.8	−1,234.1	2,027.2	2,304.2	−277.0	472.5
2012	4,309.6	5,667.1	−1,357.5	2,700.8	3,773.5	−1,072.7	2,053.3	2,338.1	−284.8	444.4
2013	4,829.6	5,729.5	−899.9	3,136.3	3,770.3	−633.9	2,143.4	2,409.4	−266.0	450.1
2014	5,054.1	5,885.7	−831.6	3,294.4	3,888.4	−594.0	2,254.7	2,492.3	−237.6	495.0
2015	5,285.5	6,059.5	−774.0	3,448.4	4,005.8	−557.4	2,370.2	2,586.8	−216.6	533.1
2016	5,329.2	6,238.7	−909.5	3,460.7	4,128.0	−667.3	2,425.3	2,667.4	−242.2	556.7
2017	5,456.9	6,418.5	−961.6	3,503.7	4,240.5	−736.8	2,513.5	2,738.4	−224.8	560.4
2018	5,643.7	6,749.9	−1,106.2	3,583.1	4,489.5	−906.4	2,643.2	2,843.0	−199.9	582.6
2019	5,884.0	7,134.3	−1,250.3	3,704.2	4,748.6	−1,044.4	2,788.8	2,994.7	−205.9	609.0
2020	5,974.5	8,920.8	−2,946.3	3,775.2	6,669.6	−2,894.4	3,078.0	3,129.9	−51.9	878.8
2021	6,856.3	9,352.9	−2,496.6	4,388.6	7,128.6	−2,739.9	3,577.9	3,334.6	243.4	1,110.3
2022	7,689.8	8,691.7	−1,001.9	4,976.3	6,038.5	−1,062.2	3,662.4	3,602.1	60.4	948.9
2023 ᴾ		9,207.5			6,375.8			3,776.3		944.5
2020: I	5,991.0	7,317.8	−1,326.8	3,799.8	4,870.1	−1,070.4	2,829.4	3,085.8	−256.5	638.2
II	5,636.3	10,551.1	−4,914.8	3,543.7	8,830.0	−5,286.3	3,481.2	3,109.8	371.5	1,388.6
III	6,032.6	9,541.5	−3,508.9	3,798.0	7,114.8	−3,316.9	2,971.6	3,163.7	−192.1	737.0
IV	6,238.0	8,272.6	−2,034.7	3,959.3	5,863.6	−1,904.3	3,029.9	3,160.3	−130.4	751.3
2021: I	6,457.8	10,628.0	−4,170.2	4,123.3	8,171.3	−4,048.0	3,116.3	3,238.5	−122.2	781.8
II	6,770.8	9,283.2	−2,512.4	4,333.0	7,603.7	−3,270.7	4,083.7	3,325.4	758.3	1,645.9
III	6,946.3	8,952.8	−2,006.5	4,470.7	6,660.1	−2,189.4	3,560.1	3,377.2	182.9	1,084.4
IV	7,250.2	8,547.4	−1,297.2	4,627.6	6,079.1	−1,451.6	3,551.6	3,397.2	154.4	929.0
2022: I	7,671.7	8,468.7	−797.0	4,954.1	5,928.4	−974.4	3,655.1	3,477.7	177.4	937.5
II	7,743.0	8,609.6	−866.5	5,025.0	5,985.5	−960.5	3,679.8	3,585.8	93.9	961.8
III	7,685.4	8,737.7	−1,052.3	4,991.7	6,064.4	−1,072.7	3,643.9	3,623.5	20.4	950.2
IV	7,659.2	8,950.8	−1,291.6	4,934.5	6,175.7	−1,241.2	3,670.9	3,721.3	−50.4	946.2
2023: I	7,346.8	9,083.9	−1,737.1	4,651.1	6,324.8	−1,673.7	3,670.3	3,733.7	−63.4	974.6
II	7,290.8	9,141.3	−1,850.4	4,680.6	6,346.3	−1,665.7	3,584.3	3,769.0	−184.7	974.1
III	7,393.5	9,282.8	−1,889.2	4,724.4	6,400.4	−1,676.0	3,587.6	3,800.8	−213.2	918.5
IV ᴾ		9,322.2			6,431.7			3,801.5		911.0

Note: Federal grants-in-aid to State and local governments are reflected in Federal current expenditures and State and local current receipts. Total government current receipts and expenditures have been adjusted to eliminate this duplication.

Source: Department of Commerce (Bureau of Economic Analysis).

Table B–50. State and local government revenues and expenditures, fiscal years 1958–2021

[Millions of dollars]

Fiscal year [1]	General revenues by source [2]							General expenditures by function [2]				
	Total	Property taxes	Sales and gross receipts taxes	Individual income taxes	Corporation net income taxes	Revenue from Federal Government	All other [3]	Total [4]	Education	Highways	Public welfare [4]	All other [4,5]
1958	41,219	14,047	9,829	1,759	1,018	4,865	9,701	44,851	15,919	8,567	3,818	16,547
1959	45,306	14,983	10,437	1,994	1,001	6,377	10,514	48,887	17,283	9,592	4,136	17,876
1960	50,505	16,405	11,849	2,463	1,180	6,974	11,634	51,876	18,719	9,428	4,404	19,325
1961	54,037	18,002	12,463	2,613	1,266	7,131	12,562	56,201	20,574	9,844	4,720	21,063
1962	58,252	19,054	13,494	3,037	1,308	7,871	13,488	60,206	22,216	10,357	5,084	22,549
1963	62,891	20,089	14,456	3,269	1,505	8,722	14,850	64,815	23,776	11,135	5,481	24,423
1963–64	68,443	21,241	15,762	3,791	1,695	10,002	15,952	69,302	26,286	11,664	5,766	25,586
1964–65	74,000	22,583	17,118	4,090	1,929	11,029	17,251	74,678	28,563	12,221	6,315	27,579
1965–66	83,036	24,670	19,085	4,760	2,038	13,214	19,269	82,843	33,287	12,770	6,757	30,029
1966–67	91,197	26,047	20,530	5,825	2,227	15,370	21,198	93,350	37,919	13,932	8,218	33,281
1967–68	101,264	27,747	22,911	7,308	2,518	17,181	23,599	102,411	41,158	14,481	9,857	36,915
1968–69	114,550	30,673	26,519	8,908	3,180	19,153	26,117	116,728	47,238	15,417	12,110	41,963
1969–70	130,756	34,054	30,322	10,812	3,738	21,857	29,973	131,332	52,718	16,427	14,679	47,508
1970–71	144,927	37,852	33,233	11,900	3,424	26,146	32,372	150,674	59,413	18,095	18,226	54,940
1971–72	167,535	42,877	37,518	15,227	4,416	31,342	36,156	168,549	65,813	19,021	21,117	62,598
1972–73	190,222	45,283	42,047	17,994	5,425	39,264	40,210	181,357	69,713	18,615	23,582	69,447
1973–74	207,670	47,705	46,098	19,491	6,015	41,820	46,542	199,222	75,833	19,946	25,085	78,358
1974–75	228,171	51,491	49,815	21,454	6,642	47,034	51,735	230,722	87,858	22,528	28,156	92,180
1975–76	256,176	57,001	54,547	24,575	7,273	55,589	57,191	256,731	97,216	23,907	32,604	103,004
1976–77	285,157	62,527	60,641	29,246	9,174	62,444	61,125	274,215	102,780	23,058	35,906	112,472
1977–78	315,960	66,422	67,596	33,176	10,738	69,592	68,435	296,984	110,758	24,609	39,140	122,478
1978–79	343,236	64,944	74,247	36,932	12,128	75,164	79,822	327,517	119,448	28,440	41,898	137,731
1979–80	382,322	68,499	79,927	42,080	13,321	83,029	95,467	369,086	133,211	33,311	47,288	155,276
1980–81	423,404	74,969	85,971	46,426	14,143	90,294	111,599	407,449	145,784	34,603	54,105	172,957
1981–82	457,654	82,067	93,613	50,738	15,028	87,282	128,925	436,733	154,282	34,520	57,996	189,935
1982–83	486,753	89,105	100,247	55,129	14,258	90,007	138,008	466,516	163,876	36,655	60,906	205,080
1983–84	542,730	96,457	114,097	64,871	16,798	96,935	153,571	505,008	176,108	39,419	66,414	223,068
1984–85	598,121	103,757	126,376	70,361	19,152	106,158	172,317	553,899	192,686	44,989	71,479	244,745
1985–86	641,486	111,709	135,005	74,365	19,994	113,099	187,314	605,623	210,819	49,368	75,868	269,568
1986–87	686,860	121,203	144,091	83,935	22,425	114,857	200,350	657,134	226,619	52,355	82,650	295,510
1987–88	726,762	132,212	156,452	88,350	23,663	117,602	208,482	704,921	242,683	55,621	89,090	317,527
1988–89	786,129	142,400	166,336	97,806	25,926	125,824	227,838	762,360	263,898	58,105	97,879	342,479
1989–90	849,502	155,613	177,885	105,640	23,566	136,802	249,996	834,818	288,148	61,057	110,518	375,094
1990–91	902,207	167,999	185,570	109,341	22,242	154,099	262,955	908,108	309,302	64,937	130,402	403,467
1991–92	979,137	180,337	197,731	115,638	23,880	179,174	282,376	981,253	324,652	67,351	158,723	430,526
1992–93	1,041,643	189,744	209,649	123,235	26,417	198,663	293,935	1,030,434	342,287	68,370	170,705	449,072
1993–94	1,100,490	197,141	223,628	128,810	28,320	215,492	307,099	1,077,665	353,287	72,067	183,394	468,916
1994–95	1,169,505	203,451	237,268	137,931	31,406	228,771	330,677	1,149,863	378,273	77,109	196,703	497,779
1995–96	1,222,821	209,440	248,993	146,844	32,009	234,891	350,645	1,193,276	398,859	79,092	197,354	517,971
1996–97	1,289,237	218,877	261,418	159,042	33,820	244,847	371,233	1,249,984	418,416	82,062	203,779	545,727
1997–98	1,365,762	230,150	274,883	175,630	34,412	255,048	395,639	1,318,042	450,365	87,214	208,120	572,343
1998–99	1,434,029	239,672	290,993	189,309	33,922	270,628	409,505	1,402,369	483,259	93,018	218,957	607,134
1999–2000	1,541,322	249,178	309,290	211,661	36,059	291,950	443,186	1,506,797	521,612	101,336	237,336	646,512
2000–01	1,647,161	263,689	320,217	226,334	35,296	324,033	477,592	1,626,063	563,572	107,235	261,622	693,634
2001–02	1,684,879	279,191	324,123	202,832	28,152	360,546	490,035	1,736,866	594,694	115,295	285,464	741,413
2002–03	1,763,212	296,683	337,787	199,407	31,369	389,264	508,702	1,821,917	621,335	117,696	310,783	772,102
2003–04	1,887,397	317,941	361,027	215,215	33,716	423,112	536,386	1,908,543	655,182	117,215	340,523	795,622
2004–05	2,026,034	335,779	384,266	242,273	43,256	438,558	581,902	2,012,110	688,314	126,350	365,295	832,151
2005–06	2,197,475	364,559	417,735	268,667	53,081	452,791	640,458	2,123,663	728,917	136,502	373,846	884,398
2006–07	2,330,611	388,905	440,470	290,278	60,955	464,914	685,089	2,264,035	774,170	145,011	389,259	955,595
2007–08	2,421,977	409,540	449,945	304,902	57,231	477,441	722,919	2,406,183	826,061	153,831	408,920	1,017,372
2008–09	2,429,672	434,818	434,128	270,942	46,280	537,949	705,555	2,500,796	851,689	154,338	437,184	1,057,586
2009–10	2,510,846	443,947	435,571	261,510	44,108	623,801	701,909	2,542,231	860,118	155,912	460,230	1,065,971
2010–11	2,618,037	445,771	463,979	285,293	48,422	648,750	726,966	2,583,805	862,271	153,895	494,682	1,072,957
2011–12	2,598,745	445,854	482,172	307,897	48,877	580,604	733,341	2,595,947	870,321	159,498	491,158	1,074,971
2012–13	2,687,495	453,458	503,298	339,666	52,853	583,294	754,672	2,631,945	878,957	160,260	518,035	1,074,693
2013–14	2,768,260	465,100	522,014	343,001	54,558	602,175	781,412	2,723,022	906,016	165,051	547,889	1,104,066
2014–15	2,920,320	484,251	544,359	368,862	57,130	658,012	807,707	2,844,289	934,353	171,084	616,515	1,122,338
2015–16	3,018,372	504,593	559,625	375,310	53,581	693,989	831,274	2,964,238	973,025	177,982	655,532	1,157,699
2016–17	3,119,577	524,566	581,275	384,689	52,805	711,477	864,764	3,082,543	1,015,892	181,112	679,963	1,205,576
2017–18	3,303,125	547,387	618,251	429,820	56,871	741,067	909,729	3,213,322	1,048,329	194,538	709,690	1,260,766
2018–19	3,464,411	576,888	644,354	446,770	67,841	762,035	966,522	3,359,786	1,093,843	202,752	748,636	1,314,555
2019–20	3,626,857	601,106	652,466	424,764	60,791	911,026	976,704	3,511,375	1,132,137	205,697	794,272	1,379,269
2020–21	4,076,400	630,208	689,885	545,142	98,713	1,120,201	992,251	3,684,674	1,143,137	206,436	865,128	1,469,973

[1] Fiscal years not the same for all governments. See Note.
[2] Excludes revenues or expenditures of publicly owned utilities and liquor stores and of insurance-trust activities. Intergovernmental receipts and payments between State and local governments are also excluded.
[3] Includes motor vehicle license taxes, other taxes, and charges and miscellaneous revenues.
[4] Includes intergovernmental payments to the Federal Government.
[5] Includes expenditures for libraries, hospitals, health, employment security administration, veterans' services, air transportation, sea and inland port facilities, parking facilities, police protection, fire protection, correction, protective inspection and regulation, sewerage, natural resources, parks and recreation, housing and community development, solid waste management, financial administration, judicial and legal, general public buildings, other government administration, interest on general debt, and other general expenditures, not elsewhere classified.

Note: Except for States listed, data for fiscal years listed from 1963–64 to 2020–21 are the aggregation of data for government fiscal years that ended in the 12-month period from July 1 to June 30 of those years; Texas used August and Alabama and Michigan used September as end dates. Data for 1963 and earlier years include data for government fiscal years ending during that particular calendar year.

Source: Department of Commerce (Bureau of the Census).

TABLE B–51. U.S. Treasury securities outstanding by kind of obligation, 1983–2023

[Billions of dollars]

End of fiscal year or month	Total Treasury securities outstanding [1]	Marketable							Nonmarketable				
		Total [2]	Treasury bills	Treasury notes	Treasury bonds	Treasury inflation-protected securities			Total	U.S. savings securities [3]	Foreign series [4]	Government account series	Other [5]
						Total	Notes	Bonds					
1983	1,376.3	1,024.0	340.7	557.5	125.7				352.3	70.6	11.5	234.7	35.6
1984	1,560.4	1,176.6	356.8	661.7	158.1				383.8	73.7	8.8	259.5	41.8
1985	1,822.3	1,360.2	384.2	776.4	199.5				462.1	78.2	6.6	313.9	63.3
1986	2,124.9	1,564.3	410.7	896.9	241.7				560.5	87.8	4.1	365.9	102.8
1987	2,349.4	1,676.0	378.3	1,005.1	277.6				673.4	98.5	4.4	440.7	129.8
1988	2,601.4	1,802.9	398.5	1,089.6	299.9				798.5	107.8	6.3	536.5	148.0
1989	2,837.9	1,892.8	406.6	1,133.2	338.0				945.2	115.7	6.8	663.7	159.0
1990	3,212.7	2,092.8	482.5	1,218.1	377.2				1,119.9	123.9	36.0	779.4	180.6
1991	3,664.5	2,390.7	564.6	1,387.7	423.4				1,273.9	135.4	41.6	908.4	188.5
1992	4,063.8	2,677.5	634.3	1,566.3	461.8				1,386.3	150.3	37.0	1,011.0	188.0
1993	4,410.7	2,904.9	658.4	1,734.2	497.4				1,505.8	169.1	42.5	1,114.3	179.9
1994	4,691.7	3,091.6	697.3	1,867.5	511.8				1,600.1	178.6	42.0	1,211.7	167.8
1995	4,953.0	3,260.4	742.5	1,980.3	522.6				1,692.6	183.5	41.0	1,324.3	143.8
1996	5,220.8	3,418.4	761.2	2,098.7	543.5				1,802.4	184.1	37.5	1,454.7	126.1
1997	5,407.6	3,439.6	701.9	2,122.2	576.2	24.4	24.4		1,968.0	182.7	34.9	1,608.5	141.9
1998	5,518.7	3,331.0	637.6	2,009.1	610.4	58.8	41.9	17.0	2,187.6	180.8	35.1	1,777.3	194.4
1999	5,647.3	3,233.0	653.2	1,828.8	643.7	92.4	67.6	24.8	2,414.3	180.0	31.0	2,005.2	198.1
2000	5,622.1	2,992.8	616.2	1,611.3	635.3	115.0	81.6	33.4	2,629.4	177.7	25.4	2,242.9	183.3
2001 [1]	5,807.5	2,930.7	734.9	1,433.0	613.0	134.9	95.1	39.7	2,876.7	186.5	18.3	2,492.1	179.9
2002	6,228.2	3,136.7	868.3	1,521.6	593.0	138.9	93.7	45.1	3,091.5	193.3	12.5	2,707.3	178.4
2003	6,783.2	3,460.7	918.2	1,799.5	576.9	166.1	120.0	46.1	3,322.5	201.6	11.0	2,912.2	197.7
2004	7,379.1	3,846.1	961.5	2,109.6	552.0	223.0	164.5	58.5	3,533.0	204.2	5.9	3,130.0	192.9
2005	7,932.7	4,084.9	914.3	2,328.8	520.7	307.1	229.1	78.0	3,847.8	203.6	3.1	3,380.6	260.5
2006	8,507.0	4,303.0	911.5	2,447.2	534.7	395.6	293.9	101.7	4,203.9	203.7	3.0	3,722.7	274.5
2007	9,007.7	4,448.1	958.1	2,458.0	561.1	456.9	335.7	121.2	4,559.5	197.1	3.0	4,026.8	332.6
2008	10,024.7	5,236.0	1,489.8	2,624.8	582.9	524.5	380.2	144.3	4,788.7	194.3	3.0	4,297.7	293.8
2009	11,909.8	7,009.7	1,992.5	3,773.8	679.8	551.7	396.2	155.5	4,900.1	192.5	4.9	4,454.3	248.4
2010	13,561.6	8,498.3	1,788.5	5,255.9	849.9	593.8	421.1	172.7	5,063.3	188.7	4.2	4,645.3	225.1
2011	14,790.3	9,624.5	1,477.5	6,412.5	1,020.4	705.7	509.4	196.3	5,165.8	185.1	3.0	4,793.9	183.8
2012	16,066.2	10,749.7	1,616.0	7,120.7	1,198.2	807.7	584.7	223.0	5,316.5	183.8	3.0	4,939.3	190.4
2013	16,738.2	11,596.2	1,530.0	7,758.0	1,366.2	936.4	685.5	250.8	5,142.0	180.0	3.0	4,803.1	156.0
2014	17,824.1	12,294.2	1,411.0	8,167.8	1,534.1	1,044.7	765.2	279.5	5,529.9	176.7	3.0	5,212.5	137.7
2015	18,150.6	12,853.8	1,358.0	8,372.7	1,688.3	1,135.4	832.1	303.3	5,296.9	172.8	.3	5,013.5	110.3
2016	19,573.4	13,660.6	1,647.0	8,631.0	1,825.5	1,210.0	881.6	328.3	5,912.8	167.5	.3	5,604.1	141.0
2017	20,244.9	14,199.8	1,801.9	8,805.5	1,951.7	1,286.5	933.3	353.2	6,045.1	161.7	.3	5,771.1	112.0
2018	21,516.1	15,278.0	2,239.9	9,154.4	2,127.8	1,376.4	993.4	383.0	6,238.0	156.8	.3	5,977.6	103.4
2019	22,719.4	16,347.3	2,377.0	9,762.8	2,319.1	1,455.7	1,044.9	410.8	6,372.1	152.3	.3	6,133.7	85.8
2020	26,945.4	20,374.9	5,028.9	10,663.8	2,673.5	1,523.2	1,092.7	430.5	6,570.5	148.6	.3	6,196.3	225.3
2021	28,428.9	21,878.7	3,714.1	12,578.9	3,347.6	1,652.7	1,180.2	472.5	6,550.2	143.6	.3	6,243.3	163.0
2022	30,928.9	23,694.1	3,644.6	13,703.8	3,874.4	1,840.5	1,306.8	533.7	7,234.8	166.2	.3	6,929.8	138.5
2023	33,167.4	25,753.8	5,260.4	13,729.5	4,246.9	1,935.9	1,364.9	571.1	7,413.7	175.7	.0	7,117.3	120.7
2022: Jan	30,012.4	22,918.9	3,961.1	13,141.6	3,530.0	1,705.0	1,224.0	481.1	7,093.5	148.8	.3	6,804.3	140.2
Feb	30,290.4	23,196.0	4,055.0	13,227.6	3,589.2	1,720.9	1,227.8	493.1	7,094.4	149.3	.3	6,800.3	144.5
Mar	30,401.0	23,286.1	3,929.0	13,348.5	3,631.5	1,751.9	1,254.8	497.2	7,114.8	149.7	.3	6,814.7	150.2
Apr	30,374.7	23,255.1	3,827.9	13,409.5	3,656.3	1,736.2	1,234.4	501.7	7,119.5	153.1	.3	6,815.3	150.9
May	30,499.6	23,307.2	3,672.9	13,516.3	3,731.4	1,775.8	1,267.5	508.3	7,192.5	157.7	.3	6,891.3	143.3
June	30,568.6	23,311.6	3,523.9	13,583.6	3,766.6	1,806.0	1,294.7	511.3	7,257.0	160.4	.3	6,959.1	137.3
July	30,595.7	23,355.4	3,514.9	13,631.0	3,788.0	1,790.0	1,273.3	516.7	7,240.4	162.5	.3	6,944.6	133.0
Aug	30,936.1	23,675.0	3,725.0	13,672.1	3,844.4	1,824.7	1,291.1	533.5	7,261.1	164.3	.3	6,968.3	128.2
Sept	30,928.9	23,694.1	3,644.6	13,703.8	3,874.4	1,840.5	1,306.8	533.7	7,234.8	166.2	.3	6,929.8	138.5
Oct	31,238.3	23,743.5	3,666.0	13,734.2	3,904.3	1,860.9	1,327.4	533.5	7,494.8	172.5	.3	7,188.2	133.9
Nov	31,413.3	23,953.5	3,811.9	13,717.9	3,941.9	1,881.7	1,347.1	534.6	7,459.8	173.2	.3	7,157.4	129.0
Dec	31,419.9	23,939.5	3,697.4	13,751.9	3,959.9	1,908.3	1,371.6	536.8	7,480.4	173.5	.3	7,179.3	127.3
2023: Jan	31,455.0	24,127.6	3,938.9	13,753.8	4,001.9	1,870.8	1,334.5	536.3	7,327.4	176.4	.3	7,024.1	126.6
Feb	31,459.3	24,282.6	4,057.8	13,730.5	4,033.7	1,876.3	1,330.6	545.7	7,176.7	177.1	.3	6,872.1	127.3
Mar	31,458.4	24,382.2	4,068.8	13,737.9	4,063.7	1,905.6	1,355.7	549.9	7,076.2	177.8	.0	6,772.6	125.8
Apr	31,458.2	24,286.2	3,942.6	13,774.3	4,082.8	1,880.1	1,327.2	552.9	7,172.0	178.8	.0	6,863.2	130.0
May	31,464.5	24,328.2	3,993.4	13,718.3	4,140.5	1,904.9	1,350.0	554.9	7,136.3	178.5	.0	6,835.3	122.4
June	32,332.3	24,886.6	4,466.7	13,724.0	4,170.5	1,933.6	1,376.0	557.6	7,445.6	178.2	.0	7,150.7	116.7
July	32,608.6	25,138.0	4,770.5	13,732.1	4,200.4	1,902.0	1,342.9	559.1	7,470.6	177.7	.0	7,178.6	114.3
Aug	32,914.1	25,477.6	5,073.9	13,702.5	4,226.9	1,917.1	1,347.2	569.9	7,436.6	176.6	.0	7,148.9	111.0
Sept	33,167.4	25,753.8	5,260.4	13,729.5	4,246.9	1,935.9	1,364.9	571.1	7,413.7	175.7	.0	7,117.3	120.7
Oct	33,699.6	26,003.5	5,457.0	13,762.3	4,292.9	1,966.3	1,392.8	573.5	7,696.1	174.1	.0	7,402.4	119.6
Nov	33,878.7	26,271.9	5,671.1	13,729.6	4,333.6	1,986.7	1,411.7	575.0	7,606.8	172.9	.0	7,315.1	118.7
Dec	34,001.5	26,371.7	5,675.8	13,758.2	4,354.6	2,006.2	1,431.4	574.8	7,629.8	171.9	.0	7,344.7	113.1

[1] Data beginning with January 2001 are interest-bearing and non-interest-bearing securities; prior data are interest-bearing securities only.
[2] Data from 1986 to 2002 and 2005 forward include Federal Financing Bank securities, not shown separately. Beginning with data for January 2014, includes Floating Rate Notes, not shown separately.
[3] Through 1996, series is U.S. savings bonds. Beginning 1997, includes U.S. retirement plan bonds, U.S. individual retirement bonds, and U.S. savings notes previously included in "other" nonmarketable securities.
[4] Nonmarketable certificates of indebtedness, notes, bonds, and bills in the Treasury foreign series of dollar-denominated and foreign-currency-denominated issues.
[5] Includes depository bonds; retirement plan bonds through 1996; Rural Electrification Administration bonds; State and local bonds; special issues held only by U.S. Government agencies and trust funds and the Federal home loan banks; for the period July 2003 through February 2004, depositary compensation securities; and for the period August 2008 through April 2016, Hope bonds for the HOPE For Homeowners Program.

Note: The fiscal year is on an October 1–September 30 basis.

Source: Department of the Treasury.

TABLE B–52. Estimated ownership of U.S. Treasury securities, 2009–2023

[Billions of dollars]

End of month	Total public debt [1]	Federal Reserve and Intra-governmental holdings [2]	Held by private investors									
			Total privately held	Depository institutions [3]	U.S. savings bonds [4]	Pension funds		Insurance companies	Mutual funds [6]	State and local governments	Foreign and international [7]	Other investors [8]
						Private [5]	State and local governments					
2009: Mar	11,126.9	4,785.2	6,341.7	125.7	194.0	155.4	137.0	191.0	721.1	588.2	3,265.7	963.7
June	11,545.3	5,026.8	6,518.5	140.8	193.6	164.1	144.6	200.0	711.8	588.5	3,460.8	914.2
Sept	11,909.8	5,127.1	6,782.7	198.2	192.5	167.2	145.6	210.2	668.5	583.6	3,570.6	1,046.3
Dec	12,311.3	5,276.9	7,034.4	202.5	191.3	175.6	151.4	222.0	668.8	585.6	3,685.1	1,152.1
2010: Mar	12,773.1	5,259.8	7,513.3	269.3	190.2	183.0	153.6	225.7	678.5	585.0	3,877.9	1,350.1
June	13,201.8	5,345.1	7,856.7	266.1	189.6	190.8	150.1	231.8	676.8	584.4	4,070.0	1,497.1
Sept	13,561.6	5,350.5	8,211.1	322.8	188.7	198.2	145.2	240.6	671.0	586.0	4,324.2	1,534.4
Dec	14,025.2	5,656.2	8,368.9	319.3	187.9	206.8	153.7	248.4	721.7	595.7	4,435.6	1,499.9
2011: Mar	14,270.0	5,958.9	8,311.1	321.0	186.7	215.8	157.9	253.5	749.4	585.3	4,481.4	1,360.1
June	14,343.1	6,220.4	8,122.7	279.4	186.0	251.8	158.0	254.8	753.7	572.2	4,690.6	976.1
Sept	14,790.3	6,328.0	8,462.4	293.8	185.1	373.6	155.7	259.6	788.7	557.9	4,912.1	935.8
Dec	15,222.8	6,439.6	8,783.3	279.7	185.2	391.9	160.7	297.3	927.9	562.2	5,006.9	971.4
2012: Mar	15,582.3	6,397.2	9,185.1	317.0	184.8	406.6	169.4	298.1	1,015.4	567.4	5,145.1	1,081.2
June	15,855.5	6,475.8	9,379.7	303.2	184.7	427.4	171.2	293.6	997.8	585.4	5,310.9	1,105.4
Sept	16,066.2	6,446.8	9,619.4	338.2	183.8	453.9	181.7	292.6	1,080.7	596.9	5,476.1	1,015.4
Dec	16,432.7	6,523.7	9,909.1	347.7	182.5	468.0	183.6	292.7	1,031.8	599.6	5,573.8	1,229.4
2013: Mar	16,771.6	6,656.8	10,114.8	338.9	181.7	463.4	193.4	284.3	1,066.7	615.6	5,725.0	1,245.7
June	16,738.2	6,773.3	9,964.9	300.2	180.9	444.5	187.7	281.3	1,000.1	612.6	5,595.0	1,362.6
Sept	16,738.2	6,834.2	9,904.0	293.2	180.0	347.8	187.5	276.6	986.1	624.3	5,652.8	1,355.7
Dec	17,352.0	7,205.3	10,146.6	321.1	179.2	464.9	181.3	274.5	983.3	633.6	5,792.6	1,316.2
2014: Mar	17,601.2	7,301.5	10,299.7	368.4	178.3	474.3	184.3	280.1	1,060.4	632.0	5,948.3	1,173.7
June	17,632.6	7,461.0	10,171.6	409.5	177.6	482.6	198.3	291.0	986.2	638.8	6,018.7	968.8
Sept	17,824.1	7,490.8	10,333.2	471.1	176.7	490.7	198.7	301.4	1,075.8	628.7	6,069.2	920.8
Dec	18,141.4	7,578.9	10,562.6	516.8	175.9	507.1	199.2	310.5	1,121.8	654.5	6,157.7	919.0
2015: Mar	18,152.1	7,521.3	10,630.8	518.1	174.9	447.8	176.7	308.5	1,170.4	663.3	6,172.6	998.4
June	18,152.0	7,536.5	10,615.5	518.5	173.9	373.8	185.7	307.7	1,139.8	652.8	6,163.1	1,100.1
Sept	18,150.6	7,488.7	10,661.9	519.1	172.8	305.3	171.0	310.0	1,195.1	646.0	6,105.9	1,236.8
Dec	18,922.2	7,711.2	11,211.0	547.4	171.6	504.7	174.5	310.1	1,318.3	680.9	6,146.2	1,357.1
2016: Mar	19,264.9	7,801.4	11,463.6	562.9	170.3	524.4	170.4	319.1	1,404.1	694.9	6,284.4	1,333.0
June	19,381.6	7,911.2	11,470.4	580.6	169.0	537.9	185.0	333.7	1,434.2	712.6	6,279.1	1,238.3
Sept	19,573.4	7,863.5	11,709.9	626.8	167.5	545.6	203.8	345.2	1,600.4	710.9	6,155.9	1,353.8
Dec	19,976.9	8,005.6	11,971.3	663.1	165.8	538.0	218.8	334.2	1,705.4	717.3	6,006.3	1,622.4
2017: Mar	19,846.4	7,941.1	11,905.3	657.4	164.2	444.2	239.5	342.6	1,715.2	724.6	6,075.3	1,542.3
June	19,844.6	7,943.4	11,901.1	620.5	162.8	425.9	262.8	352.8	1,645.8	710.1	6,151.9	1,568.5
Sept	20,244.9	8,036.9	12,208.0	610.5	161.7	570.8	266.5	364.3	1,739.6	704.0	6,301.9	1,488.7
Dec	20,492.7	8,132.1	12,360.6	636.7	160.4	432.1	289.4	377.9	1,850.8	735.0	6,211.3	1,667.1
2018: Mar	21,089.9	8,086.6	13,003.3	637.8	159.0	589.7	300.1	366.9	2,048.2	715.8	6,223.4	1,962.5
June	21,195.3	8,106.9	13,088.5	663.1	157.8	605.0	307.3	360.2	1,902.9	726.8	6,225.0	2,140.4
Sept	21,516.1	8,068.1	13,447.9	682.0	156.8	615.3	301.7	361.3	1,957.2	730.7	6,225.9	2,417.0
Dec	21,974.1	8,095.0	13,879.1	769.7	155.7	637.3	367.9	360.5	2,094.9	713.2	6,270.1	2,509.9
2019: Mar	22,028.0	7,999.1	14,028.9	769.5	154.5	443.6	357.6	361.1	2,189.2	752.7	6,474.0	2,526.7
June	22,023.5	7,945.2	14,078.4	808.2	153.4	470.4	386.5	363.6	2,037.0	751.4	6,625.9	2,482.0
Sept	22,719.4	8,023.6	14,695.8	909.4	152.3	691.1	343.3	366.8	2,319.7	766.8	6,923.5	2,222.8
Dec	23,201.4	8,359.9	14,841.5	935.1	151.3	705.3	333.4	368.7	2,412.8	793.1	6,844.2	2,297.6
2020: Mar	23,686.9	9,279.7	14,407.2	947.6	150.0	758.9	330.4	396.8	2,501.7	862.1	6,949.5	1,510.2
June	26,477.4	10,157.7	16,319.6	1,157.9	149.8	766.9	290.1	403.2	3,695.4	1,034.8	7,052.1	1,769.4
Sept	26,945.4	10,371.9	16,573.5	1,241.1	148.6	772.6	318.0	414.3	3,724.9	1,059.7	7,069.2	1,825.1
Dec	27,747.8	10,809.2	16,938.6	1,265.2	147.1	770.6	354.4	398.2	3,784.6	1,111.9	7,070.7	2,035.9
2021: Mar	28,132.6	11,095.5	17,037.1	1,347.9	145.7	761.2	345.8	391.9	3,951.4	1,099.6	7,038.3	1,955.2
June	28,529.4	11,382.9	17,146.5	1,433.1	144.6	787.5	395.5	421.2	3,778.5	1,313.7	7,518.9	1,353.4
Sept	28,428.9	11,579.1	16,849.8	1,540.3	143.6	622.7	390.7	423.8	3,238.0	1,394.2	7,570.9	1,525.6
Dec	29,617.2	12,125.9	17,491.3	1,734.0	142.6	809.6	411.3	419.3	3,411.7	1,440.7	7,740.4	1,378.2
2022: Mar	30,401.0	12,281.3	18,119.7	1,754.1	149.7	810.3	379.9	374.5	3,290.7	1,420.0	7,604.2	2,336.4
June	30,568.6	12,399.7	18,168.9	1,807.7	160.4	807.4	352.2	366.1	2,890.3	1,555.5	7,416.9	2,812.5
Sept	30,928.9	12,264.7	18,664.2	1,736.8	166.2	807.8	315.8	366.8	2,604.3	1,529.4	7,251.5	3,885.5
Dec	31,419.9	12,401.4	19,018.5	1,713.6	173.5	818.0	323.4	391.3	2,416.2	1,563.3	7,290.1	4,329.2
2023: Mar	31,458.4	12,044.6	19,413.8	1,615.6	177.8	601.9	361.7	405.9	2,413.9	1,648.9	7,556.9	4,631.2
June	32,332.3	11,976.9	20,355.4	1,556.0	178.2	899.5	383.1	411.9	2,595.7	1,645.8	7,607.0	5,078.3
Sept	33,167.4	11,790.1	21,377.4	1,559.7	175.7	882.4	379.7	434.6	3,075.4	1,617.3	7,604.1	5,648.5
Dec	34,001.5	11,848.1	22,153.4	....	171.9	....	....	....	....	....	....	....

[1] Face value.
[2] Federal Reserve holdings exclude Treasury securities held under repurchase agreements.
[3] Includes U.S. chartered depository institutions, foreign banking offices in U.S., banks in U.S. affiliated areas, credit unions, and bank holding companies.
[4] Current accrual value includes myRA.
[5] Includes Treasury securities held by the Federal Employees Retirement System Thrift Savings Plan "G Fund."
[6] Includes money market mutual funds, mutual funds, and closed-end investment companies.
[7] Includes nonmarketable foreign series, Treasury securities, and Treasury deposit funds. Excludes Treasury securities held under repurchase agreements in custody accounts at the Federal Reserve Bank of New York. Estimates reflect benchmarks to this series at differing intervals; for further detail, see *Treasury Bulletin* and http://www.treasury.gov/resource-center/data-chart-center/tic/pages/index.aspx.
[8] Includes individuals, Government-sponsored enterprises, brokers and dealers, bank personal trusts and estates, corporate and noncorporate businesses, and other investors.

Source: Department of the Treasury.

TABLE B–53. Corporate profits with inventory valuation and capital consumption adjustments, 1973–2023

[Billions of dollars; quarterly data at seasonally adjusted annual rates]

Year or quarter	Corporate profits with inventory valuation and capital consumption adjustments	Taxes on corporate income	Corporate profits after tax with inventory valuation and capital consumption adjustments		
			Total	Net dividends	Undistributed profits with inventory valuation and capital consumption adjustments
1973	133.4	45.6	87.8	34.2	53.5
1974	125.7	47.2	78.5	38.8	39.7
1975	138.9	46.3	92.6	38.3	54.3
1976	174.3	59.4	114.9	44.9	70.0
1977	205.8	68.5	137.3	50.7	86.6
1978	238.6	77.9	160.7	57.8	102.9
1979	249.2	80.7	168.5	67.0	101.5
1980	223.1	75.5	147.6	76.0	71.6
1981	245.9	70.3	175.6	83.9	91.7
1982	227.8	51.3	176.5	88.5	88.0
1983	277.9	66.4	211.5	96.4	115.1
1984	337.3	81.5	255.8	102.0	153.8
1985	353.1	81.6	271.5	111.7	159.7
1986	323.6	91.9	231.7	121.1	110.6
1987	370.8	112.7	258.1	119.9	138.2
1988	416.2	124.3	292.0	145.5	146.5
1989	418.7	124.4	294.3	179.3	115.0
1990	419.3	121.8	297.5	193.6	104.0
1991	448.7	117.8	330.9	202.1	128.8
1992	481.3	131.9	349.4	206.5	142.9
1993	530.7	155.0	375.7	221.7	154.0
1994	634.1	172.7	461.4	258.6	202.9
1995	716.7	194.4	522.2	283.5	238.7
1996	803.6	211.4	592.2	323.9	268.3
1997	889.9	224.8	665.1	359.9	305.2
1998	835.2	221.8	613.4	386.6	226.7
1999	866.8	227.4	639.4	375.4	264.0
2000	826.4	233.4	593.0	413.1	179.9
2001	787.2	170.1	617.0	402.9	214.1
2002	930.4	160.7	769.7	427.5	342.2
2003	1,077.1	213.8	863.3	455.0	408.3
2004	1,320.5	278.5	1,042.0	579.8	462.2
2005	1,530.0	379.7	1,150.3	579.3	571.0
2006	1,696.1	430.1	1,266.0	715.8	550.1
2007	1,595.8	391.8	1,204.0	818.3	385.7
2008	1,345.6	255.9	1,089.7	841.4	248.3
2009	1,425.7	203.9	1,221.7	634.7	587.0
2010	1,774.5	272.3	1,502.2	636.0	866.2
2011	1,862.4	280.8	1,581.7	788.0	793.7
2012	2,057.7	334.6	1,723.1	945.3	777.8
2013	2,081.1	362.4	1,718.7	997.3	721.4
2014	2,212.8	406.9	1,805.9	1,059.9	746.0
2015	2,173.1	396.1	1,777.0	1,128.7	648.3
2016	2,144.3	376.0	1,768.3	1,139.4	628.9
2017	2,225.2	297.2	1,928.1	1,253.9	674.2
2018	2,365.2	297.4	2,067.7	1,319.9	747.8
2019	2,470.3	297.4	2,172.9	1,416.8	756.1
2020	2,383.3	307.5	2,075.8	1,496.7	579.1
2021	2,922.8	404.6	2,518.1	1,814.7	703.4
2022	3,208.7	542.4	2,666.3	1,887.3	779.0
2023 *p*				1,849.2	
2020: I	2,262.4	268.6	1,993.8	1,460.1	533.7
II	2,061.1	276.2	1,785.0	1,453.4	331.6
III	2,725.8	339.0	2,386.8	1,479.6	907.3
IV	2,483.7	346.2	2,137.6	1,593.9	543.7
2021: I	2,752.8	351.8	2,401.0	1,658.8	742.2
II	2,988.5	392.2	2,596.3	1,789.6	806.7
III	2,959.0	405.7	2,553.3	1,878.6	674.7
IV	2,990.6	468.7	2,521.9	1,931.9	590.0
2022: I	3,027.1	529.1	2,497.9	1,932.9	565.1
II	3,260.0	547.4	2,712.6	1,920.7	791.9
III	3,299.3	544.7	2,754.6	1,855.6	899.0
IV	3,248.4	548.3	2,700.1	1,839.8	860.2
2023: I	3,165.1	576.5	2,588.6	1,840.2	748.4
II	3,172.1	570.3	2,601.8	1,855.8	746.0
III	3,280.7	582.8	2,697.9	1,837.6	860.3
IV *p*				1,863.1	

Source: Department of Commerce (Bureau of Economic Analysis).

TABLE B–54. Corporate profits by industry, 1973–2023

[Billions of dollars; quarterly data at seasonally adjusted annual rates]

Year or quarter	Total	Corporate profits with inventory valuation adjustment and without capital consumption adjustment												Rest of the world
		Domestic industries												
		Total	Financial			Nonfinancial								
			Total	Federal Reserve banks	Other	Total	Manu-factur-ing	Trans-porta-tion [1]	Utilities	Whole-sale trade	Retail trade	Infor-mation	Other	
SIC: [2]														
1973	126.6	111.7	21.1	4.5	16.6	90.6	55.0	10.2		8.8	7.0		9.6	14.9
1974	123.3	105.8	20.8	5.7	15.1	85.1	51.0	9.1		12.2	2.8		10.0	17.5
1975	144.2	129.6	20.4	5.6	14.8	109.2	63.0	11.7		14.3	8.4		11.8	14.6
1976	182.1	165.6	25.6	5.9	19.7	140.0	82.5	17.5		13.7	10.9		15.3	16.5
1977	212.8	193.7	32.6	6.1	26.5	161.1	91.5	21.2		16.4	12.8		19.2	19.1
1978	246.7	223.8	40.8	7.6	33.1	183.1	105.8	25.5		16.7	13.1		22.0	22.9
1979	261.2	226.6	42.0	9.4	32.6	184.6	107.1	21.6		20.0	10.7		25.2	34.6
1980	240.2	204.7	34.8	11.8	23.0	169.9	97.6	22.2		18.5	7.0		24.6	35.5
1981	250.4	220.7	28.7	14.4	14.3	192.0	112.5	25.1		23.7	10.7		20.1	29.7
1982	222.7	190.1	25.1	15.2	9.9	165.0	89.6	28.1		20.7	14.3		12.3	32.6
1983	254.6	219.5	34.3	14.6	19.7	185.2	97.3	34.3		21.9	19.3		12.3	35.1
1984	293.6	257.1	34.1	16.4	17.7	223.0	114.2	44.7		30.4	21.5		12.1	36.6
1985	288.3	250.2	45.1	16.3	28.8	205.1	107.1	39.1		24.6	22.8		11.4	38.1
1986	272.4	233.0	55.5	15.5	40.0	177.4	75.6	39.3		24.4	23.4		14.7	39.5
1987	319.4	271.4	65.1	16.2	48.9	206.2	101.8	42.0		18.9	23.3		20.3	48.0
1988	368.0	311.0	68.7	18.1	50.6	242.3	132.8	46.8		20.4	19.8		22.5	57.0
1989	377.5	310.3	82.7	20.6	62.1	227.6	122.3	41.9		22.0	20.9		20.5	67.1
1990	392.8	316.7	91.2	21.8	69.4	225.5	120.9	43.5		19.4	20.3		21.3	76.1
1991	430.4	353.9	116.6	20.7	95.9	237.3	109.3	54.5		22.3	26.9		24.3	76.5
1992	463.9	390.8	136.5	18.3	118.2	254.2	109.8	57.7		25.3	28.1		33.4	73.1
1993	508.1	431.1	126.1	16.7	109.4	305.1	122.9	70.1		26.5	39.7		45.8	76.9
1994	598.6	520.6	135.2	18.5	116.7	385.4	162.6	83.9		31.4	46.3		61.2	78.0
1995	677.4	584.5	150.8	22.9	127.8	433.7	199.8	89.0		28.0	43.9		73.1	92.9
1996	755.9	653.9	161.9	22.5	139.4	492.0	220.4	91.2		39.9	52.0		88.5	102.0
1997	831.1	723.6	182.4	24.3	158.1	541.2	248.5	81.0		48.1	63.4		100.3	107.6
1998	770.5	667.8	165.6	25.6	140.0	502.1	220.4	72.6		50.6	72.3		86.3	102.8
1999	793.8	672.0	186.4	26.7	159.8	485.6	219.4	49.3		46.8	72.5		97.6	121.7
2000	769.6	624.0	189.6	31.2	158.3	434.4	205.9	33.8		50.4	68.9		75.4	145.7
NAICS: [2]														
1998	770.5	667.8	165.6	25.6	140.0	502.1	193.4	12.7	33.3	57.3	62.6	33.0	109.7	102.8
1999	793.8	672.0	186.4	26.7	159.8	485.6	188.0	7.2	34.4	55.5	48.4	28.5	123.5	121.7
2000	769.6	624.0	189.6	31.2	158.3	434.4	175.5	9.5	24.3	59.5	51.5	-11.9	126.1	145.7
2001	725.6	556.8	223.7	28.9	194.8	333.1	75.1	-.7	22.5	51.1	71.3	-26.4	140.1	168.8
2002	815.7	659.0	280.4	23.5	256.9	378.6	78.2	-6.5	10.5	53.5	83.3	5.0	154.6	156.8
2003	976.1	817.2	317.9	20.0	297.8	499.3	123.8	4.4	13.2	56.6	87.9	28.1	185.4	158.9
2004	1,248.3	1,053.2	368.3	20.0	348.3	684.9	186.1	11.9	21.1	72.7	94.0	61.6	237.5	195.1
2005	1,670.2	1,444.5	436.1	26.5	409.6	1,008.4	279.7	28.4	32.4	96.0	123.3	100.7	347.9	225.7
2006	1,861.7	1,622.0	443.3	33.8	409.5	1,178.6	352.9	40.8	55.2	105.0	133.6	115.2	376.0	239.7
2007	1,770.5	1,432.8	345.8	36.0	309.8	1,087.0	321.1	23.3	49.6	102.8	119.4	120.5	350.3	337.8
2008	1,403.9	1,013.7	138.3	35.1	103.2	875.4	240.0	29.3	30.4	92.7	82.2	98.8	302.1	390.2
2009	1,508.3	1,159.5	389.5	47.3	342.2	770.0	164.7	21.7	23.4	88.9	107.9	87.0	276.4	348.8
2010	1,831.1	1,445.3	437.5	71.6	365.9	1,007.8	281.8	44.6	30.6	99.3	115.9	102.3	333.4	385.8
2011	1,802.2	1,389.6	414.3	76.0	338.3	975.4	296.0	30.6	10.2	97.2	115.1	95.7	330.6	412.6
2012	2,203.9	1,798.6	519.0	71.8	447.2	1,279.6	403.0	54.4	13.8	137.9	155.7	112.0	402.8	405.4
2013	2,234.1	1,835.2	480.7	79.7	401.0	1,354.5	440.0	45.0	27.8	146.3	153.3	138.6	403.5	398.8
2014	2,356.1	1,951.2	536.1	103.5	432.7	1,415.1	453.1	55.7	32.4	151.2	157.8	131.0	433.9	404.9
2015	2,295.5	1,900.3	512.4	100.7	411.7	1,387.9	421.5	61.1	19.9	153.9	170.4	134.8	426.3	395.2
2016	2,245.2	1,825.3	511.8	92.0	419.8	1,313.5	327.9	64.7	9.4	130.0	176.6	163.3	441.6	419.9
2017	2,247.5	1,748.6	491.6	78.3	413.4	1,257.0	299.9	59.6	13.8	127.4	151.7	143.0	461.5	498.9
2018	2,266.6	1,746.0	478.9	68.1	410.8	1,267.1	361.7	45.1	16.5	108.2	145.6	115.2	474.6	520.6
2019	2,376.7	1,843.7	575.2	59.2	515.9	1,268.5	353.2	34.5	11.9	125.9	150.3	134.3	458.4	533.0
2020	2,478.2	2,029.9	535.9	85.4	450.5	1,493.9	328.1	38.4	27.4	157.8	243.3	119.6	579.4	448.3
2021	2,992.1	2,558.4	581.5	108.4	473.1	1,977.0	464.1	94.6	33.6	171.6	276.3	156.5	780.2	433.6
2022	3,426.7	2,953.9	598.6	55.3	543.3	2,355.3	708.7	103.0	42.6	226.1	285.1	167.7	822.1	472.8
2021: I	2,798.5	2,326.0	529.3	78.2	451.2	1,796.7	406.2	78.1	33.4	142.6	278.1	140.0	718.4	472.5
II	3,040.1	2,631.6	573.2	109.3	463.9	2,058.4	462.6	112.5	29.8	168.3	314.5	162.0	808.7	408.5
III	3,033.1	2,615.2	603.2	123.5	479.6	2,012.0	458.8	93.8	35.6	185.8	261.1	159.9	817.0	417.9
IV	3,096.5	2,660.9	620.1	122.6	497.5	2,040.8	528.8	94.2	35.8	189.6	251.5	164.1	776.8	435.6
2022: I	3,198.2	2,775.5	615.9	135.3	480.6	2,159.6	647.7	80.1	38.4	173.7	260.9	163.9	794.8	422.7
II	3,468.5	2,990.0	602.7	122.2	480.5	2,387.3	709.8	116.1	41.0	196.7	291.5	164.5	867.7	478.5
III	3,541.4	3,051.1	610.8	33.4	577.5	2,440.2	719.6	112.5	49.7	268.5	286.6	167.1	836.3	490.3
IV	3,498.8	2,998.9	564.8	-69.7	634.5	2,434.1	757.6	103.1	41.2	265.5	301.6	175.3	789.7	499.9
2023: I	3,502.8	3,010.8	591.7	-125.0	716.7	2,419.2	739.0	111.2	42.7	233.4	315.1	172.4	805.4	492.0
II	3,513.6	2,999.5	537.0	-159.8	696.7	2,462.5	711.4	126.8	49.7	227.8	353.3	187.7	805.9	514.1
III	3,620.1	3,097.2	546.1	-164.4	710.5	2,551.1	743.9	116.5	45.0	233.5	374.3	193.3	844.6	522.9

[1] Data on Standard Industrial Classification (SIC) basis include transportation and public utilities. Those on North American Industry Classification System (NAICS) basis include transporation and warehousing. Utilities classified separately in NAICS (as shown beginning 1998).

[2] SIC-based industry data use the 1987 SIC for data beginning in 1987 and the 1972 SIC for prior data. NAICS-based data use 2017 NAICS.

Note: Industry data on SIC basis and NAICS basis are not necessarily the same and are not strictly comparable.

Source: Department of Commerce (Bureau of Economic Analysis).

TABLE B–55. Historical stock prices and yields, 1949–2003

End of year	Common stock prices (end of period)[1]									Common stock yields (Standard & Poor's) (percent)[5]	
	New York Stock Exchange (NYSE) indexes[2]						Dow Jones industrial average[2]	Standard & Poor's composite index (1941–43=10)[2]	Nasdaq composite index (Feb. 5, 1971=100)[2]	Dividend-price ratio[6]	Earnings-price ratio[7]
	Composite (Dec. 31, 2002= 5,000)[3]	December 31, 1965=50									
		Composite	Industrial	Transportation	Utility[4]	Finance					
1949							200.52	16.76		6.59	15.48
1950							235.42	20.41		6.57	13.99
1951							269.23	23.77		6.13	11.82
1952							291.90	26.57		5.80	9.47
1953		13.60					280.90	24.81		5.80	10.26
1954		19.40					404.39	35.98		4.95	8.57
1955		23.71					488.40	45.48		4.08	7.95
1956		24.35					499.47	46.67		4.09	7.55
1957		21.11					435.69	39.99		4.35	7.89
1958		28.85					583.65	55.21		3.97	6.23
1959		32.15					679.36	59.89		3.23	5.78
1960		30.94					615.89	58.11		3.47	5.90
1961		38.93					731.14	71.55		2.98	4.62
1962		33.81					652.10	63.10		3.37	5.82
1963		39.92					762.95	75.02		3.17	5.50
1964		45.65					874.13	84.75		3.01	5.32
1965	528.69	50.00	50.00	50.00	50.00	50.00	969.26	92.43		3.00	5.59
1966	462.28	43.72	43.13	47.56	90.38	44.91	785.69	80.33		3.40	6.63
1967	569.18	53.83	56.59	49.66	86.76	53.80	905.11	96.47		3.20	5.73
1968	622.79	58.90	61.69	56.27	91.64	76.48	943.75	103.86		3.07	5.67
1969	544.86	51.53	54.74	37.85	77.54	67.87	800.36	92.06		3.24	6.08
1970	531.12	50.23	52.91	35.70	81.64	64.34	838.92	92.15		3.83	6.45
1971	596.68	56.43	60.53	49.56	78.78	73.83	890.20	102.09	114.12	3.14	5.41
1972	681.79	64.48	70.33	47.69	84.34	83.34	1,020.02	118.05	133.73	2.84	5.50
1973	547.93	51.82	56.60	37.53	68.66	64.51	850.86	97.55	92.19	3.06	7.12
1974	382.03	36.13	39.15	26.36	53.30	39.84	616.24	68.56	59.82	4.47	11.59
1975	503.73	47.64	52.73	32.98	66.94	45.20	852.41	90.19	77.62	4.31	9.15
1976	612.01	57.88	63.36	42.57	82.54	59.23	1,004.65	107.46	97.88	3.77	8.90
1977	555.12	52.50	56.43	40.50	81.08	53.85	831.17	95.10	105.05	4.62	10.79
1978	566.96	53.62	58.87	41.58	75.38	55.01	805.01	96.11	117.98	5.28	12.03
1979	655.04	61.95	70.24	50.64	73.80	63.45	838.74	107.94	151.14	5.47	13.46
1980	823.27	77.86	91.52	76.19	76.90	70.83	963.99	135.76	202.34	5.26	12.66
1981	751.90	71.11	80.89	66.85	80.10	73.68	875.00	122.55	195.84	5.20	11.96
1982	856.79	81.03	93.02	73.63	86.94	85.00	1,046.54	140.64	232.41	5.81	11.60
1983	1,006.41	95.18	111.35	98.09	92.48	94.32	1,258.64	164.93	278.60	4.40	8.03
1984	1,013.91	96.38	110.58	90.61	103.14	97.63	1,211.57	167.24	247.35	4.64	10.02
1985	1,285.66	121.59	139.27	113.97	126.38	131.29	1,546.67	211.28	324.93	4.25	8.12
1986	1,465.31	138.59	160.11	117.65	147.54	140.05	1,895.95	242.17	348.83	3.49	6.09
1987	1,461.61	138.23	167.04	118.57	134.62	114.57	1,938.83	247.08	330.47	3.08	5.48
1988	1,652.25	156.26	189.42	146.60	149.38	128.19	2,168.57	277.72	381.38	3.64	8.01
1989	2,062.30	195.04	232.76	178.33	204.00	156.15	2,753.20	353.40	454.82	3.45	7.42
1990	1,908.45	180.49	223.60	141.49	182.60	122.06	2,633.66	330.22	373.84	3.61	6.47
1991	2,426.04	229.44	285.82	201.87	204.26	172.68	3,168.83	417.09	586.34	3.24	4.79
1992	2,539.92	240.21	294.39	214.72	209.66	200.83	3,301.11	435.71	676.95	2.99	4.22
1993	2,739.44	259.08	315.26	270.48	229.92	216.82	3,754.09	466.45	776.80	2.78	4.46
1994	2,653.37	250.94	318.10	222.46	198.41	195.80	3,834.44	459.27	751.96	2.82	5.83
1995	3,484.15	329.51	413.29	301.96	252.90	274.25	5,117.12	615.93	1,052.13	2.56	6.09
1996	4,148.07	392.30	494.38	352.30	259.91	351.17	6,448.27	740.74	1,291.03	2.19	5.24
1997	5,405.19	511.19	630.38	466.25	335.19	495.96	7,908.25	970.43	1,570.35	1.77	4.57
1998	6,299.94	595.81	743.65	482.38	445.94	521.42	9,181.43	1,229.23	2,192.69	1.49	3.46
1999	6,876.10	650.30	828.21	466.70	511.15	516.61	11,497.12	1,469.25	4,069.31	1.25	3.17
2000	6,945.57	656.87	803.29	462.76	440.54	646.95	10,786.85	1,320.28	2,470.52	1.15	3.63
2001	6,236.39	589.80	735.71	438.81	329.84	593.69	10,021.50	1,148.08	1,950.40	1.32	2.95
2002	5,000.00	472.87	583.95	395.81	233.08	510.46	8,341.63	879.82	1,335.51	1.61	2.92
2003[3]	6,440.30	572.56	735.50	519.58	265.58	655.12	10,453.92	1,111.92	2,003.37	1.77	3.84

[1] End of period.

[2] Includes stocks as follows: for NYSE, all stocks listed; for Dow Jones industrial average, 30 stocks; for Standard & Poor's (S&P) composite index, 500 stocks; and for Nasdaq composite index, over 5,000.

[3] The NYSE relaunched the composite index on January 9, 2003, incorporating new definitions, methodology, and base value. (The composite index based on December 31, 1965=50 was discontinued.) Subset indexes on financial, energy, and health care were released by the NYSE on January 8, 2004 (see Table B–56). NYSE indexes shown in this table for industrials, utilities, transportation, and finance were discontinued.

[4] Effective April 1993, the NYSE doubled the value of the utility index to facilitate trading of options and futures on the index. Indexes prior to 1993 reflect the doubling.

[5] Based on 500 stocks in the S&P composite index.

[6] Aggregate cash dividends (based on latest known annual rate) divided by aggregate market value based on Wednesday closing prices. Monthly data are averages of weekly figures; annual data are averages of monthly figures.

[7] Quarterly data are ratio of earnings (after taxes) for four quarters ending with particular quarter-to-price index for last day of that quarter. Annual data are averages of quarterly ratios.

Sources: New York Stock Exchange, Dow Jones & Co., Inc., Standard & Poor's, and Nasdaq Stock Market.

TABLE B–56. Common stock prices and yields, 2000–2023

| End of year or month | Common stock prices (end of period) [1] | | | | | | | Common stock yields (Standard & Poor's) (percent) [4] | |
| | New York Stock Exchange (NYSE) indexes (December 31, 2002=5,000) [2,3] | | | | Dow Jones industrial average [2] | Standard & Poor's composite index (1941–43=10) [2] | Nasdaq composite index (Feb. 5, 1971=100) [2] | Dividend-price ratio [5] | Earnings-price ratio [6] |
	Composite	Financial	Energy	Health care					
2000	6,945.57				10,786.85	1,320.28	2,470.52	1.15	3.63
2001	6,236.39				10,021.50	1,148.08	1,950.40	1.32	2.95
2002	5,000.00	5,000.00	5,000.00	5,000.00	8,341.63	879.82	1,335.51	1.61	2.92
2003	6,440.30	6,676.42	6,321.05	5,925.97	10,453.92	1,111.92	2,003.37	1.77	3.84
2004	7,250.06	7,493.92	7,934.49	6,119.07	10,783.01	1,211.92	2,175.44	1.72	4.89
2005	7,753.95	7,996.94	10,109.61	6,458.20	10,717.50	1,248.29	2,205.32	1.83	5.36
2006	9,139.02	9,552.22	11,967.88	6,958.64	12,463.15	1,418.30	2,415.29	1.87	5.78
2007	9,740.32	8,300.68	15,283.81	7,170.42	13,264.82	1,468.36	2,652.28	1.86	5.29
2008	5,757.05	3,848.42	9,434.01	5,340.73	8,776.39	903.25	1,577.03	2.37	3.54
2009	7,184.96	4,721.02	11,415.03	6,427.27	10,428.05	1,115.10	2,269.15	2.40	1.86
2010	7,964.02	4,958.62	12,520.29	6,501.53	11,577.51	1,257.64	2,652.87	1.98	6.04
2011	7,477.03	4,062.88	12,409.61	7,045.61	12,217.56	1,257.60	2,605.15	2.05	6.77
2012	8,443.51	5,114.54	12,606.06	7,904.06	13,104.14	1,426.19	3,019.51	2.24	6.20
2013	10,400.33	6,353.68	14,557.54	10,245.31	16,576.66	1,848.36	4,176.59	2.14	5.57
2014	10,839.24	6,707.16	12,533.54	11,967.04	17,823.07	2,058.90	4,736.05	2.04	5.25
2015	10,143.42	6,305.68	9,343.81	12,385.19	17,425.03	2,043.94	5,007.41	2.10	4.59
2016	11,056.89	6,961.56	11,503.76	11,907.20	19,762.60	2,238.83	5,383.12	2.19	4.17
2017	12,808.84	8,235.89	11,470.58	14,220.58	24,719.22	2,673.61	6,903.39	1.97	4.22
2018	11,374.39	6,969.48	9,341.44	15,158.38	23,327.46	2,506.85	6,635.28	1.90	4.66
2019	13,913.03	8,700.11	10,037.30	18,070.10	28,538.44	3,230.78	8,972.60	1.93	4.53
2020	14,524.80	8,292.85	6,502.78	20,045.67	30,606.48	3,756.07	12,888.28	1.89	3.28
2021	17,164.13	10,175.36	9,146.18	24,345.65	36,338.30	4,766.18	15,644.97	1.38	3.79
2022	15,184.31	8,668.77	13,051.89	23,439.84	33,147.25	3,839.50	10,466.48	1.57	4.79
2023	16,852.89	9,881.78	13,259.54	24,167.14	37,689.54	4,769.83	15,011.35	1.62	
2021: Jan	14,397.20	8,072.62	6,733.84	20,208.09	29,982.62	3,714.24	13,070.69	1.55	
Feb	15,010.47	8,853.18	7,774.59	19,760.30	30,932.37	3,811.15	13,192.35	1.49	
Mar	15,601.74	9,240.02	7,995.97	20,388.89	32,981.55	3,972.89	13,246.87	1.48	3.23
Apr	16,219.33	9,773.10	8,005.80	21,141.32	33,874.85	4,181.17	13,962.68	1.39	
May	16,555.66	10,112.15	8,440.17	21,494.66	34,529.45	4,204.11	13,748.74	1.38	
June	16,555.35	9,889.35	8,787.30	21,796.88	34,502.51	4,297.50	14,503.95	1.37	3.69
July	16,602.29	9,923.19	8,163.13	22,679.73	34,935.47	4,395.26	14,672.68	1.34	
Aug	16,806.44	10,162.18	8,052.76	23,180.04	35,360.73	4,522.68	15,259.24	1.32	
Sept	16,144.92	9,934.02	8,784.79	21,846.16	33,843.92	4,307.54	14,448.58	1.33	4.07
Oct	17,016.41	10,455.70	9,460.44	23,131.46	35,819.56	4,605.38	15,498.39	1.33	
Nov	16,318.97	9,756.72	8,829.04	22,267.26	34,483.72	4,567.00	15,537.69	1.29	
Dec	17,164.13	10,175.36	9,146.18	24,345.65	36,338.30	4,766.18	15,644.97	1.29	4.15
2022: Jan	16,659.78	10,200.96	10,648.50	22,894.30	35,131.86	4,515.55	14,239.88	1.33	
Feb	16,313.89	9,875.64	11,142.11	22,757.28	33,892.60	4,373.94	13,751.40	1.38	
Mar	16,670.91	9,971.24	12,065.19	23,828.90	34,678.35	4,530.41	14,220.52	1.41	4.37
Apr	15,615.25	9,139.65	11,791.27	22,944.86	32,977.21	4,131.93	12,334.64	1.42	
May	15,827.05	9,297.74	13,336.34	23,217.06	32,990.12	4,132.15	12,081.39	1.55	
June	14,487.64	8,313.35	11,252.27	22,640.69	30,775.43	3,785.38	11,028.74	1.64	5.08
July	15,327.71	8,901.55	12,171.38	23,258.76	32,845.13	4,130.29	12,390.69	1.64	
Aug	14,801.25	8,563.40	12,304.08	21,713.32	31,510.43	3,955.00	11,816.20	1.56	
Sept	13,472.18	7,747.27	11,004.62	20,936.54	28,725.51	3,585.62	10,575.62	1.71	5.22
Oct	14,747.03	8,481.92	13,240.72	22,560.24	32,732.95	3,871.98	10,988.15	1.78	
Nov	15,780.02	9,083.61	13,551.07	23,695.65	34,589.77	4,080.11	11,468.00	1.70	
Dec	15,184.31	8,668.77	13,051.89	23,439.84	33,147.25	3,839.50	10,466.48	1.72	4.50
2023: Jan	16,036.39	9,432.80	13,434.64	23,027.98	34,086.04	4,076.60	11,584.55	1.71	
Feb	15,428.97	9,139.29	12,724.58	22,041.91	32,656.70	3,970.15	11,455.54	1.67	
Mar	15,374.91	8,494.23	12,455.61	22,550.28	33,274.15	4,109.31	12,221.91	1.73	4.26
Apr	15,545.88	8,699.82	12,895.29	23,395.71	34,098.16	4,169.48	12,226.58	1.67	
May	14,887.14	8,346.55	11,635.80	22,397.48	32,908.27	4,179.83	12,935.29	1.67	
June	15,875.91	8,907.96	12,504.78	23,378.02	34,407.60	4,450.38	13,787.92	1.59	4.07
July	16,427.29	9,305.43	13,328.62	23,604.11	35,559.53	4,588.96	14,346.02	1.54	
Aug	16,000.37	8,988.61	13,467.87	23,602.11	34,721.91	4,507.66	14,034.97	1.55	
Sept	15,398.21	8,668.91	13,852.13	22,951.48	33,507.50	4,288.05	13,219.32	1.57	4.30
Oct	14,919.20	8,332.44	13,275.28	22,337.96	33,052.87	4,193.80	12,851.24	1.62	
Nov	16,088.84	9,258.87	13,250.97	23,464.37	35,950.89	4,567.80	14,226.22	1.56	
Dec	16,852.89	9,881.78	13,259.54	24,167.14	37,689.54	4,769.83	15,011.35	1.50	

[1] End of year or month.
[2] Includes stocks as follows: for NYSE, all stocks listed (in 2023, over 2,270); for Dow Jones industrial average, 30 stocks; for Standard & Poor's (S&P) composite index, 500 stocks; and for Nasdaq composite index, in 2023, about 3,400.
[3] The NYSE relaunched the composite index on January 9, 2003, incorporating new definitions, methodology, and base value. Subset indexes on financial, energy, and health care were released by the NYSE on January 8, 2004.
[4] Based on 500 stocks in the S&P composite index.
[5] Aggregate cash dividends (based on latest known annual rate) divided by aggregate market value based on Wednesday closing prices. Monthly data are averages of weekly figures, annual data are averages of monthly figures.
[6] Quarterly data are ratio of earnings (after taxes) for four quarters ending with particular quarter-to-price index for last day of that quarter. Annual data are averages of quarterly ratios.

Sources: New York Stock Exchange, Dow Jones & Co., Inc., Standard & Poor's, and Nasdaq Stock Market.

TABLE B–57. U.S. international transactions, 1973–2023

[Millions of dollars; quarterly data seasonally adjusted]

Year or quarter	Goods [2]			Services			Balance on goods and services	Primary income receipts and payments			Balance on secondary Income [3]	Balance on current account	Current account balance as a percentage of GDP
	Exports	Imports	Balance on goods	Exports	Imports	Balance on services		Receipts	Payments	Balance on primary income			
1973	71,410	70,499	911	19,832	18,843	989	1,900	21,809	9,656	12,153	-6,914	7,140	0.5
1974	98,306	103,811	-5,505	22,591	21,378	1,212	-4,293	27,587	12,084	15,503	-9,248	1,961	.1
1975	107,088	98,185	8,903	25,497	21,996	3,500	12,403	25,351	12,565	12,786	-7,076	18,117	1.1
1976	114,745	124,228	-9,483	27,971	24,570	3,402	-6,082	29,374	13,312	16,062	-5,686	4,296	.2
1977	120,816	151,907	-31,091	31,486	27,640	3,845	-27,247	32,355	14,218	18,137	-5,227	-14,336	-.7
1978	142,075	176,002	-33,927	36,353	32,189	4,164	-29,763	42,087	21,680	20,407	-5,788	-15,143	-.6
1979	184,439	212,007	-27,568	39,693	36,689	3,003	-24,566	63,835	32,961	30,874	-6,593	-285	.0
1980	224,250	249,750	-25,500	47,585	41,492	6,093	-19,407	72,605	42,533	30,072	-8,349	2,318	.1
1981	237,044	265,067	-28,023	57,355	45,503	11,851	-16,172	86,529	53,626	32,903	-11,702	5,029	.2
1982	211,157	247,642	-36,485	64,078	51,750	12,330	-24,156	96,522	61,359	35,163	-16,545	-5,537	-.2
1983	201,799	268,901	-67,102	64,307	54,973	9,335	-57,767	96,031	59,643	36,388	-17,311	-38,691	-1.1
1984	219,926	332,418	-112,492	71,168	67,748	3,418	-109,074	115,639	80,574	35,065	-20,334	-94,344	-2.3
1985	215,915	338,088	-122,173	73,156	72,863	294	-121,879	105,046	79,324	25,722	-21,999	-118,155	-2.7
1986	223,344	368,425	-145,081	86,690	80,147	6,543	-138,539	102,798	87,304	15,494	-24,131	-147,176	-3.2
1987	250,208	409,765	-159,557	98,661	90,788	7,874	-151,683	113,603	99,309	14,294	-23,265	-160,655	-3.3
1988	320,230	447,189	-126,959	110,920	98,525	12,394	-114,566	141,666	122,981	18,685	-25,274	-121,153	-2.3
1989	359,916	477,665	-117,749	127,087	102,480	24,607	-93,142	166,384	146,560	19,824	-26,169	-99,487	-1.8
1990	387,401	498,438	-111,037	147,833	117,660	30,173	-80,865	176,894	148,345	28,549	-26,654	-78,969	-1.3
1991	414,083	491,020	-76,937	164,260	118,459	45,802	-31,136	155,327	131,198	24,129	9,904	2,897	.0
1992	439,631	536,528	-96,897	177,251	119,566	57,685	-39,212	139,082	114,845	24,237	-36,635	-51,613	-.8
1993	456,943	589,394	-132,451	185,920	123,780	62,141	-70,311	141,606	116,287	25,319	-39,811	-84,805	-1.2
1994	502,859	668,690	-165,831	200,395	133,057	67,338	-98,493	169,447	152,302	17,145	-40,265	-121,612	-1.7
1995	575,204	749,374	-174,170	219,183	141,397	77,786	-96,384	213,661	192,771	20,890	-38,074	-113,567	-1.5
1996	612,113	803,113	-191,000	239,489	152,554	86,935	-104,065	229,530	207,212	22,318	-43,017	-124,764	-1.5
1997	678,366	876,794	-198,428	256,087	165,932	90,155	-108,273	261,357	248,750	12,607	-45,062	-140,726	-1.6
1998	670,416	918,637	-248,221	262,758	180,677	82,081	-166,140	266,244	261,978	4,266	-53,187	-215,062	-2.4
1999	698,524	1,035,592	-337,068	278,001	196,742	81,258	-255,809	302,540	292,566	9,974	-40,777	-286,612	-3.0
2000	784,940	1,231,722	-446,783	298,023	220,927	77,096	-369,686	365,612	350,980	14,632	-46,863	-401,918	-3.9
2001	731,331	1,153,701	-422,370	284,035	222,039	61,997	-360,373	311,364	288,120	23,244	-56,953	-394,082	-3.7
2002	698,036	1,173,281	-475,245	288,059	233,480	54,579	-420,666	306,391	288,886	17,506	-52,949	-456,110	-4.2
2003	730,446	1,272,089	-541,643	297,740	252,340	45,401	-496,243	346,931	317,677	29,254	-55,300	-522,289	-4.6
2004	823,584	1,488,349	-664,766	344,536	290,609	53,927	-610,838	432,839	386,256	46,583	-71,634	-635,890	-5.2
2005	913,016	1,695,820	-782,804	378,487	312,225	66,262	-716,542	536,294	492,108	44,186	-76,876	-749,232	-5.7
2006	1,040,905	1,878,194	-837,289	423,086	349,329	73,756	-763,533	669,919	653,945	15,974	-69,088	-816,646	-5.9
2007	1,165,151	1,986,347	-821,196	495,664	385,464	110,199	-710,997	816,938	752,582	64,356	-89,910	-736,550	-5.1
2008	1,308,795	2,141,287	-832,492	540,791	420,650	120,142	-712,350	820,244	708,225	112,019	-96,192	-696,523	-4.7
2009	1,070,331	1,580,025	-509,694	522,461	407,538	114,923	-394,771	653,222	537,684	115,539	-100,496	-379,729	-2.6
2010	1,290,279	1,938,950	-648,671	582,041	436,456	145,584	-503,087	723,223	553,311	169,911	-98,834	-432,009	-2.9
2011	1,498,887	2,239,886	-740,999	644,665	458,188	186,477	-554,522	791,469	589,038	202,431	-103,211	-455,302	-2.9
2012	1,562,630	2,303,749	-741,119	684,823	469,610	215,213	-525,906	791,613	593,754	197,859	-90,134	-418,181	-2.6
2013	1,593,708	2,294,247	-700,539	719,413	465,736	253,678	-446,861	811,501	616,041	195,460	-88,115	-339,516	-2.0
2014	1,635,563	2,385,480	-749,917	757,051	491,086	265,965	-483,952	845,858	645,623	200,235	-86,339	-370,056	-2.1
2015	1,511,381	2,273,249	-761,868	769,397	498,305	271,092	-490,776	824,929	639,724	185,205	-102,882	-408,453	-2.2
2016	1,457,393	2,207,195	-749,802	783,431	513,088	270,343	-479,458	857,240	660,798	196,442	-113,199	-396,216	-2.1
2017	1,557,003	2,356,345	-799,343	837,474	555,070	282,404	-516,939	995,442	737,501	257,942	-108,618	-367,616	-1.9
2018	1,676,913	2,555,662	-878,749	865,549	565,395	300,155	-578,594	1,102,964	847,689	255,275	-116,530	-439,849	-2.1
2019	1,655,098	2,512,358	-857,260	891,177	593,313	297,865	-559,395	1,139,310	891,911	247,400	-129,756	-441,751	-2.1
2020	1,433,852	2,346,727	-912,875	726,296	466,301	259,995	-652,881	957,891	776,923	180,968	-125,227	-597,140	-2.8
2021	1,765,884	2,849,395	-1,083,511	801,143	559,205	241,938	-841,573	1,077,227	927,297	149,930	-139,802	-831,445	-3.5
2022	2,089,925	3,272,935	-1,183,010	928,530	696,707	231,823	-951,188	1,217,853	1,069,300	148,552	-120,660	-923,296	-3.8
2020: I	401,250	596,416	-195,166	203,585	136,948	66,637	-128,529	259,840	200,292	59,547	-31,465	-100,447	-1.9
II	287,952	510,734	-222,782	167,719	101,739	65,980	-156,802	212,454	175,910	36,543	-28,969	-149,227	-3.0
III	357,754	601,018	-243,265	171,996	108,602	63,394	-179,871	239,163	193,652	45,511	-32,902	-167,262	-3.1
IV	386,896	638,559	-251,663	182,997	119,013	63,984	-187,679	246,435	207,069	39,366	-31,891	-180,203	-3.3
2021: I	412,953	673,259	-260,306	188,791	121,628	67,163	-193,144	264,323	215,123	49,199	-31,605	-175,550	-3.1
II	433,608	700,001	-266,393	195,434	132,150	63,285	-203,109	264,149	229,940	34,209	-31,319	-200,219	-3.4
III	441,989	713,752	-271,763	202,751	148,914	53,837	-217,926	272,509	240,627	31,882	-40,682	-226,725	-3.8
IV	477,335	762,383	-285,048	214,166	156,513	57,653	-227,395	276,246	241,607	34,639	-36,195	-228,951	-3.7
2022: I	490,438	823,225	-332,786	220,887	164,101	56,787	-276,000	280,000	251,196	28,804	-36,704	-283,899	-4.5
II	534,973	843,880	-308,907	231,489	173,524	57,965	-250,942	298,649	256,486	42,163	-40,005	-248,784	-3.9
III	546,789	813,966	-267,176	235,318	178,855	56,463	-210,713	312,696	273,204	39,492	-51,536	-222,757	-3.4
IV	517,725	791,865	-274,140	240,836	180,228	60,608	-213,532	326,508	288,414	38,094	-40,716	-216,154	-3.3
2023: I	526,548	789,815	-263,268	242,671	181,201	61,470	-201,798	339,004	307,558	31,446	-44,120	-214,472	-3.2
II	497,270	772,770	-275,500	249,525	177,824	71,701	-203,799	350,315	318,070	32,245	-45,251	-216,805	-3.2
III p	516,414	777,367	-260,953	252,187	175,971	76,216	-184,737	362,114	332,107	30,007	-45,574	-200,304	-2.9

[1] Current and capital account statistics in the international transactions accounts differ slightly from statistics in the National Income and Product Accounts (NIPAs) because of adjustments made to convert the international statistics to national accounting concepts. A reconciliation can be found in NIPA table 4.3B.

[2] Adjusted from Census data to align with concepts and definitions used to prepare the international and national economic accounts. The adjustments are necessary to supplement coverage of Census data, to eliminate duplication of transactions recorded elsewhere in the international accounts, to value transactions according to a standard definition, and for earlier years, to record transactions in the appropriate period.

See next page for continuation of table.

[Millions of dollars; quarterly data seasonally adjusted]

Year or quarter	Balance on capital account [1]	Net U.S. acquisition of financial assets excluding financial derivatives [net increase in assets / financial outflow (+)]					Net U.S. incurrence of liabilities excluding financial derivatives [net increase in liabilities / financial inflow (+)]				Financial derivatives other than reserves, net transactions	Net lending (+) or net borrowing (–) from financial account transactions [5]	Statistical discrepancy
		Total	Direct investment assets	Portfolio investment assets	Other investment assets	Reserve assets [4]	Total	Direct investment liabilities	Portfolio investment liabilities	Other investment liabilities			
1973		22,874	11,353	672	11,007	−158	18,388	2,800	4,790	10,798		4,486	−2,654
1974		34,745	9,052	1,853	22,373	1,467	35,228	4,761	5,500	24,967		−483	−2,444
1975		39,703	14,244	6,247	18,363	849	16,870	2,603	12,761	1,506		22,833	4,717
1976		51,269	11,949	8,885	27,877	2,558	37,840	4,347	16,165	17,328		13,429	9,134
1977		34,785	11,891	5,459	17,060	375	52,770	3,728	37,615	11,427		−17,985	−3,651
1978		61,130	16,057	3,626	42,179	−732	66,275	7,896	30,083	28,296		−5,145	9,997
1979		66,053	25,223	12,430	27,267	1,133	40,693	11,876	−13,502	42,319		25,360	25,647
1980		86,968	19,222	6,042	53,550	8,154	62,036	16,918	23,825	21,293		24,932	22,614
1981		114,147	9,624	15,650	83,697	5,176	85,684	25,196	17,509	42,979		28,463	23,433
1982		142,722	19,397	12,395	105,965	4,965	109,897	27,475	19,695	62,727		32,825	38,362
1983		74,690	20,844	2,063	50,588	1,195	95,715	18,688	18,382	58,645		−21,025	17,666
1984		50,740	26,770	3,498	17,340	3,132	126,413	34,832	38,695	52,886		−75,673	18,673
1985		47,064	21,241	3,008	18,957	3,858	146,544	22,057	68,004	56,483		−99,480	18,677
1986		107,252	19,524	8,984	79,057	−313	223,854	30,946	104,497	88,411		−116,602	30,570
1987		84,058	39,795	7,903	45,508	−9,148	251,863	63,232	79,631	109,000		−167,805	−7,149
1988		105,747	21,701	4,589	75,544	3,913	244,008	56,910	86,786	100,312		−138,261	−17,108
1989	−207	182,908	50,973	31,166	75,476	25,293	230,302	75,801	74,852	79,649		−47,394	52,299
1990	−7,221	103,985	59,934	30,557	11,336	2,158	162,109	71,247	25,767	65,095		−58,124	28,066
1991	−5,129	75,753	49,253	32,053	210	−5,763	119,586	34,535	72,562	12,489		−43,833	−41,601
1992	1,449	84,899	58,755	50,684	−20,639	−3,901	178,842	30,315	92,199	56,328		−93,943	−43,776
1993	−714	199,399	82,799	137,917	−22,696	1,379	278,607	50,211	174,387	54,009		−79,208	6,313
1994	−1,112	188,758	89,988	54,088	50,028	−5,346	312,995	55,942	131,849	125,204		−124,237	−1,514
1995	−221	363,555	110,041	143,506	100,266	9,742	446,393	69,067	254,431	122,895		−82,838	30,951
1996	−8	424,548	103,024	160,179	168,013	−6,668	559,027	97,644	392,107	69,276		−134,479	−9,706
1997	−256	502,024	121,352	121,036	258,626	1,010	720,999	122,150	311,105	287,744		−218,975	−77,995
1998	−7	385,936	174,751	132,186	72,216	6,783	452,901	211,152	225,878	15,871		−66,965	148,106
1999	−6,428	526,612	247,484	141,007	146,868	−8,747	765,215	312,449	278,697	174,069		−238,603	54,437
2000	−4,217	587,682	186,371	159,713	241,308	290	1,066,074	349,124	441,966	274,984		−478,392	−72,257
2001	12,170	386,331	146,041	106,919	128,442	4,911	788,345	172,496	431,492	184,357		−402,032	−20,120
2002	−3,825	319,175	178,984	79,532	56,978	3,681	821,844	111,056	504,155	206,634		−502,668	−42,734
2003	−8,499	371,104	195,218	133,059	44,351	−1,524	911,660	117,107	550,163	244,390		−540,556	−9,768
2004	−4,344	1,058,661	374,006	191,956	495,505	−2,806	1,600,881	213,642	867,340	519,899		−542,220	98,014
2005	950	562,996	52,591	267,290	257,210	−14,094	1,277,056	142,345	832,037	302,673		−714,059	34,223
2006	−7,439	1,324,623	283,800	493,366	549,830	−2,373	2,120,480	298,464	1,126,735	695,280	−29,710	−825,567	−1,482
2007	−6,057	1,563,467	523,889	380,807	658,649	122	2,190,087	346,615	1,156,612	686,860	−6,222	−632,841	109,765
2008	−172	−317,590	343,584	−284,269	−381,754	4,848	462,408	341,091	523,683	−402,367	32,947	−747,053	−50,358
2009	−5,877	131,082	312,597	375,883	−609,654	52,256	325,644	161,082	357,352	−192,789	−44,816	−239,379	146,227
2010	−6,891	958,737	349,829	199,620	407,454	1,835	1,391,042	264,039	820,434	306,569	−14,076	−446,381	−7,481
2011	−9,020	492,556	436,615	85,365	−45,301	15,877	983,522	263,499	311,626	408,397	−35,006	−525,972	−61,650
2012	931	171,359	377,239	243,182	−453,522	4,460	632,034	250,343	747,017	−365,327	7,064	−453,611	−36,361
2013	−6,559	626,189	392,796	457,734	−221,242	−3,099	1,052,068	288,131	511,987	251,949	2,222	−423,657	−77,582
2014	−6,535	865,694	387,528	581,668	−99,920	−3,583	1,109,443	251,857	697,607	159,979	−54,335	−298,084	78,506
2015	−7,940	144,104	302,072	107,154	−258,831	−6,292	503,468	511,434	213,910	−221,876	−27,035	−386,400	29,993
2016	−6,606	336,438	299,814	37,489	−2,955	2,090	706,693	474,388	231,265	1,040	7,827	−362,427	40,394
2017	12,394	1,161,984	409,413	540,728	213,533	−1,690	1,559,219	380,823	790,810	387,586	23,998	−373,237	−18,016
2018	−4,261	429,710	−130,720	381,863	173,578	4,989	712,178	214,716	303,075	194,387	−20,404	−302,872	141,238
2019	−6,456	315,580	114,924	−11,453	207,450	4,659	832,266	315,983	233,469	282,814	−41,670	−558,356	−110,149
2020	−5,610	959,138	286,663	406,368	257,133	8,974	1,622,963	138,364	946,560	538,038	−5,107	−668,932	−66,182
2021	−2,511	1,242,954	394,069	711,511	23,381	113,993	1,992,760	493,086	614,250	885,424	−39,028	−788,834	45,122
2022	−4,603	840,582	426,251	372,494	36,023	5,814	1,564,676	388,078	810,154	366,445	−80,698	−804,792	171,406
2020: I	−2,907	849,195	23,611	104,828	721,001	−245	983,919	36,134	29,069	918,715	−25,136	−159,859	−56,505
II	−987	−203,699	78,651	35,819	−323,129	4,960	−143,767	−54,238	324,300	−413,829	−11,702	−71,634	58,581
III	−592	67,273	146,512	137,091	−218,150	1,820	264,286	119,191	170,786	−25,691	28,425	−168,589	−734
IV	−1,123	246,369	37,889	128,630	77,411	2,438	518,524	37,276	422,405	58,844	3,306	−268,850	−87,523
2021: I	−2,729	455,994	85,464	337,324	35,307	−2,100	632,398	59,130	393,559	179,710	−2,216	−178,620	−341
II	−869	252,456	133,861	175,898	−57,781	477	465,779	133,256	160,388	172,136	−7,319	−220,643	−19,555
III	3,001	473,479	95,865	303,444	−38,432	112,603	679,479	174,252	191,447	313,780	−6,796	−212,796	10,928
IV	−1,914	61,024	78,879	−105,155	84,287	3,013	215,103	126,448	−131,143	219,798	−22,697	−176,776	54,089
2022: I	−2,048	397,478	146,201	191,963	58,381	932	672,370	126,531	264,362	281,476	6,102	−268,790	17,158
II	−3,292	367,359	99,520	239,508	27,150	1,181	454,494	73,273	384,377	−3,155	−45,911	−13,081	119,030
III	4,158	336,063	74,788	271,824	−11,346	797	518,520	121,427	262,475	134,618	−33,940	−216,396	2,203
IV	−3,421	−260,318	105,743	−330,819	−38,162	2,903	−80,707	66,847	−101,060	−46,494	−6,949	−186,560	33,015
2023: I	−5,913	208,346	108,734	8,109	90,725	778	556,677	112,094	299,510	145,073	−1,727	−350,058	−129,673
II	−2,737	201,852	86,516	38,966	76,098	272	337,499	111,530	402,487	−176,518	−4,741	−140,388	79,154
III [p]	−2,106	323,357	101,614	47,181	174,163	400	463,018	80,841	193,074	189,102	1,068	−138,592	63,818

[3] Includes U.S. government and private transfers, such as U.S. government grants and pensions, fines and penalties, withholding taxes, personal transfers, insurance-related transfers, and other current transfers.
[4] Consists of monetary gold, special drawing rights (SDRs), the U.S. reserve position in the International Monetary Fund (IMF), and other reserve assets, including foreign currencies.
[5] Net lending means that U.S. residents are net suppliers of funds to foreign residents, and net borrowing means the opposite.

Source: Department of Commerce (Bureau of Economic Analysis).

TABLE B–58. U.S. international trade in goods on balance of payments (BOP) and Census basis, and trade in services on BOP basis, 1994–2023

[Billions of dollars; monthly data seasonally adjusted]

Year or month	Goods: Exports (f.a.s. value)[1,2]							Goods: Imports (customs value)[6]							Services (BOP basis)	
	Total, BOP basis[3,4]	Census basis (by end-use category)						Total, BOP basis[4]	Census basis (by end-use category)						Exports[4]	Imports[4]
		Total, Census basis[3,5]	Foods, feeds, and beverages	Industrial supplies and materials	Capital goods except automotive	Automotive vehicles, parts, and engines	Consumer goods (nonfood) except automotive		Total, Census basis[5]	Foods, feeds, and beverages	Industrial supplies and materials	Capital goods except automotive	Automotive vehicles, parts, and engines	Consumer goods (nonfood) except automotive		
1994	502.9	512.6	42.0	121.4	205.0	57.8	60.0	668.7	663.3	31.0	162.1	184.4	118.3	146.3	200.4	133.1
1995	575.2	584.7	50.5	146.2	233.0	61.8	64.4	749.4	743.5	33.2	181.8	221.4	123.8	159.9	219.2	141.4
1996	612.1	625.1	55.5	147.7	253.0	65.0	70.1	803.1	795.3	35.7	204.5	228.1	128.9	172.0	239.5	152.6
1997	678.4	689.2	51.5	158.2	294.5	74.0	77.4	876.8	869.7	39.7	213.8	253.3	139.8	193.8	256.1	165.9
1998	670.4	682.1	46.4	148.3	299.4	72.4	80.3	918.6	911.9	41.2	200.1	269.5	148.7	217.0	262.8	180.7
1999	698.5	695.8	46.0	147.5	310.8	75.3	80.9	1,035.6	1,024.6	43.6	221.4	295.7	179.0	241.9	278.0	196.7
2000	784.9	781.9	47.9	172.6	356.9	80.4	89.4	1,231.7	1,218.0	46.0	299.0	347.0	195.9	281.8	298.0	220.9
2001	731.3	729.1	49.4	160.1	321.7	75.4	88.3	1,153.7	1,141.0	46.6	273.9	298.0	189.8	284.3	284.0	222.0
2002	698.0	693.1	49.6	156.8	290.4	78.9	84.4	1,173.3	1,161.4	49.7	267.7	283.3	203.7	307.8	288.1	233.5
2003	730.4	724.8	55.0	173.0	293.7	80.6	89.9	1,272.1	1,257.1	55.8	313.8	295.9	210.1	333.9	297.7	252.3
2004	823.6	814.9	56.6	203.9	327.5	89.2	103.2	1,488.3	1,469.7	62.1	412.8	343.6	228.2	372.9	344.5	290.6
2005	913.0	901.1	59.0	233.0	358.4	98.4	115.3	1,695.8	1,673.5	68.1	523.8	379.3	239.4	407.2	378.5	312.2
2006	1,040.9	1,026.0	66.0	276.0	404.0	107.3	129.1	1,878.2	1,853.9	74.9	602.0	418.3	256.6	442.6	423.1	349.3
2007	1,165.2	1,148.2	84.3	316.4	433.0	121.3	146.0	1,986.3	1,957.0	81.7	634.7	444.5	256.7	474.6	495.7	385.5
2008	1,308.8	1,287.4	108.3	388.0	457.7	121.5	161.3	2,141.3	2,103.6	89.0	779.5	453.7	231.2	481.6	540.8	420.7
2009	1,070.3	1,056.0	93.9	296.5	391.2	81.7	149.5	1,580.0	1,559.6	81.6	462.4	370.5	157.7	427.3	522.5	407.5
2010	1,290.3	1,278.5	107.7	391.7	447.5	112.0	165.2	1,939.0	1,913.9	91.7	603.1	449.4	225.1	483.2	582.0	436.5
2011	1,498.9	1,482.5	126.2	501.1	494.0	133.0	175.3	2,239.9	2,208.0	107.5	755.8	510.8	254.6	514.1	644.7	458.2
2012	1,562.6	1,545.8	133.0	501.2	527.2	146.2	181.7	2,303.7	2,276.3	110.3	730.6	548.7	297.8	516.9	684.8	469.6
2013	1,593.7	1,578.5	136.2	508.2	534.4	152.7	188.8	2,294.2	2,268.0	115.1	681.5	555.7	308.8	531.7	719.4	465.7
2014	1,635.6	1,621.9	143.7	505.8	551.5	159.8	199.0	2,385.5	2,356.4	125.9	667.0	594.1	328.6	557.1	757.1	491.1
2015	1,511.4	1,503.3	127.7	427.0	539.5	151.9	197.7	2,273.2	2,248.8	127.8	486.0	602.5	349.2	594.2	769.4	498.3
2016	1,457.4	1,451.5	130.5	397.3	519.7	150.4	193.7	2,207.2	2,186.8	130.0	443.3	589.7	349.9	583.1	783.4	513.1
2017	1,557.0	1,547.2	132.8	465.2	533.4	157.9	197.7	2,356.3	2,339.6	137.8	507.0	639.8	358.2	601.4	837.5	555.1
2018	1,676.9	1,665.8	133.1	541.2	563.2	158.8	206.0	2,555.7	2,536.1	147.3	574.6	690.9	371.1	645.4	865.5	565.4
2019	1,655.1	1,645.9	131.0	529.5	550.5	163.1	205.6	2,512.4	2,491.7	150.5	520.6	674.8	374.5	653.0	891.2	593.3
2020	1,433.9	1,430.0	139.3	466.5	463.2	129.4	175.0	2,346.7	2,331.5	154.3	478.7	643.4	309.2	639.6	726.3	466.3
2021	1,765.9	1,757.8	164.5	637.6	521.2	146.4	222.3	2,849.4	2,828.9	182.1	649.1	760.0	345.7	767.4	801.1	559.2
2022	2,089.9	2,065.2	179.9	830.8	572.7	159.7	245.7	3,272.9	3,242.5	208.3	808.7	863.7	398.9	841.6	928.5	696.7
2023 p	2,050.7	2,019.5	162.5	728.0	601.2	179.0	260.4	3,112.4	3,084.1	200.3	677.8	857.2	458.4	760.9	1,002.8	714.5
2022: Jan	158.3	157.3	14.2	59.8	46.0	12.3	19.2	264.7	262.6	16.9	62.3	68.9	32.2	71.9	72.4	52.6
Feb	161.4	160.1	14.9	60.7	46.1	12.2	20.5	266.4	264.2	16.9	65.4	69.7	30.5	71.1	73.5	55.4
Mar	170.7	168.4	15.0	67.6	46.4	12.8	20.4	292.1	289.6	17.5	75.6	73.1	32.3	80.2	75.0	56.1
Apr	175.8	173.6	17.2	69.9	47.2	13.0	20.4	282.0	279.4	17.9	70.6	71.4	33.7	75.2	77.0	56.8
May	177.9	176.0	15.6	72.8	47.3	13.3	21.1	281.4	278.6	17.9	71.9	71.4	33.6	73.7	77.2	57.8
June	181.3	179.1	16.2	76.5	46.7	13.0	20.8	280.5	277.8	17.8	72.8	71.9	31.5	73.7	77.3	58.9
July	182.9	180.8	15.3	76.2	48.2	14.2	20.4	273.1	270.4	17.0	70.7	72.8	33.1	67.2	77.8	59.2
Aug	183.1	179.5	15.4	74.0	48.6	13.3	21.3	269.6	266.9	17.3	66.7	71.5	33.9	67.8	78.4	59.3
Sept	180.8	178.0	14.1	72.4	49.6	13.6	21.5	271.3	268.6	17.2	64.5	74.5	34.6	68.5	79.1	60.3
Oct	175.6	173.6	14.2	69.7	49.5	13.7	19.4	273.8	271.4	17.6	65.1	74.5	35.4	68.3	79.9	60.0
Nov	172.5	170.8	13.6	67.2	48.5	13.9	21.0	256.5	254.0	17.1	62.5	71.9	32.7	60.0	80.3	60.1
Dec	169.6	168.0	14.3	64.1	48.7	14.3	19.7	261.5	259.1	17.0	60.6	72.0	35.3	64.1	80.7	60.2
2023: Jan	177.8	175.6	14.9	64.8	49.8	15.6	23.5	268.0	265.5	17.4	60.3	72.4	37.9	66.8	80.5	60.5
Feb	171.8	169.0	15.1	61.7	49.1	13.6	22.4	262.2	259.7	17.0	59.6	72.8	36.2	62.9	80.9	60.6
Mar	176.2	172.8	14.3	64.7	49.5	14.2	22.5	257.3	254.7	16.8	57.5	70.5	35.1	64.2	81.3	60.1
Apr	167.0	163.3	14.3	58.4	49.1	14.1	20.8	262.6	260.2	16.3	59.5	70.7	37.1	66.0	82.6	59.3
May	164.9	162.3	12.4	57.0	49.0	15.2	21.6	255.5	253.4	15.8	56.2	71.5	37.3	61.2	83.5	59.2
June	164.7	162.3	12.4	56.3	49.8	15.1	21.2	252.3	250.3	16.2	53.8	69.3	38.6	61.7	83.5	59.3
July	168.2	165.1	12.3	57.6	49.9	16.8	21.3	257.5	255.4	16.8	52.3	71.5	39.4	64.2	83.3	58.4
Aug	171.1	168.7	12.3	60.3	50.9	15.4	22.3	255.3	252.9	16.7	55.0	69.7	38.6	62.3	84.2	58.1
Sept	176.5	173.6	13.8	61.9	51.0	16.0	22.9	262.2	259.9	16.6	56.2	71.3	40.5	64.3	84.7	59.5
Oct	173.2	171.0	13.5	63.0	51.1	15.0	20.8	262.6	260.1	16.8	56.0	73.1	39.5	64.1	85.2	59.7
Nov	168.1	165.8	13.3	59.5	51.2	14.2	20.3	256.5	254.2	16.9	55.1	72.3	39.3	59.9	86.2	59.7
Dec p	171.2	170.0	13.9	62.8	50.9	13.7	21.0	260.3	257.9	16.9	56.3	71.9	38.9	63.3	87.0	60.1

[1] Department of Defense shipments of grant-aid military supplies and equipment under the Military Assistance Program are excluded from total exports through 1985 and included beginning 1986.

[2] F.a.s. (free alongside ship) value basis at U.S. port of exportation for exports.

[3] Beginning with data for 1989, exports have been adjusted for undocumented exports to Canada and are included in the appropriate end-use categories. For prior years, only total exports include this adjustment.

[4] Beginning with data for 1999, exports of goods under the U.S. Foreign Military Sales program and fuel purchases by foreign air and ocean carriers in U.S. ports are included in goods exports (BOP basis) and excluded from services exports. Beginning with data for 1999, imports of petroleum abroad by U.S. military agencies and fuel purchases by U.S. air and ocean carriers in foreign ports are included in goods imports (BOP basis) and excluded from services imports.

[5] Total includes "other" exports or imports, not shown separately.

[6] Total arrivals of imported goods other than in-transit shipments.

[7] Total includes revisions not reflected in detail.

[8] Total exports are on a revised statistical month basis; end-use categories are on a statistical month basis.

Note: Goods on a Census basis are adjusted to a BOP basis by the Bureau of Economic Analysis, in line with concepts and definitions used to prepare international and national accounts. The adjustments are necessary to supplement coverage of Census data, to eliminate duplication of transactions recorded elsewhere in international accounts, to value transactions according to a standard definition, and for earlier years, to record transactions in the appropriate period. Data include international trade of the U.S. Virgin Islands, Puerto Rico, and U.S. Foreign Trade Zones.

Source: Department of Commerce (Bureau of the Census and Bureau of Economic Analysis).

TABLE B–59. U.S. international trade in goods and services by area and country, 2000–2022

[Millions of dollars]

Item	2000	2005	2010	2015	2018	2019	2020	2021	2022
EXPORTS									
Total, all countries	1,082,963	1,291,503	1,872,320	2,280,778	2,542,462	2,546,276	2,160,147	2,567,027	3,018,455
Europe	298,654	366,823	510,936	608,049	705,063	735,529	633,089	723,624	905,721
Euro area [1]	174,591	214,207	292,815	350,143	403,641	433,677	377,779	430,361	536,122
France	30,821	35,241	45,279	50,074	58,237	60,012	42,890	46,996	68,638
Germany	45,379	55,246	75,023	81,184	93,262	96,758	87,700	97,587	113,715
Italy	16,665	18,556	22,787	24,628	32,506	33,279	25,767	28,184	37,079
United Kingdom	73,995	83,456	104,891	126,762	145,472	147,130	120,202	130,030	158,939
Canada	204,237	246,291	307,571	341,365	368,991	362,297	309,637	367,303	428,569
Latin America and Other Western Hemisphere	228,633	259,832	416,623	551,389	594,182	584,967	476,315	611,067	723,404
Brazil	22,112	21,574	53,767	58,667	65,834	66,965	49,381	61,910	75,436
Mexico	127,581	141,856	187,487	267,794	299,176	289,849	236,067	308,267	362,485
Venezuela	9,476	9,395	15,918	14,212	9,160	3,623	2,264	3,108	3,788
Asia and Pacific	301,451	342,228	523,350	633,923	731,554	716,470	628,631	739,670	816,983
China	21,862	50,685	113,576	163,329	180,596	167,475	166,311	191,988	197,279
India	6,731	13,294	29,243	38,838	55,830	58,012	43,335	58,299	73,067
Japan	101,554	93,383	104,991	106,619	122,537	124,628	102,244	112,016	119,883
Korea, Republic of	35,106	37,867	56,700	66,254	80,779	80,967	69,150	85,981	95,963
Singapore	24,557	26,657	39,743	43,049	57,043	54,105	53,098	67,090	80,525
Taiwan	30,603	29,104	36,896	39,016	41,921	42,910	39,821	47,285	55,317
Middle East	28,617	48,702	70,477	102,159	98,238	102,183	76,038	82,334	94,212
Africa	17,203	22,891	40,278	41,229	41,534	41,748	33,066	38,706	45,165
IMPORTS									
Total, all countries	1,452,650	2,008,045	2,375,407	2,771,554	3,121,057	3,105,670	2,813,028	3,408,600	3,969,643
Europe	359,220	493,562	566,372	704,961	808,185	854,846	775,372	907,414	1,024,237
Euro area [1]	216,802	304,574	341,235	444,164	506,179	537,759	464,254	550,986	641,690
France	41,344	47,725	56,562	66,202	72,413	78,324	57,237	69,154	85,198
Germany	75,710	110,075	114,861	158,863	160,095	163,947	146,272	169,612	190,569
Italy	31,593	39,767	37,778	53,782	66,247	69,467	53,980	67,039	80,250
United Kingdom	70,962	84,200	96,034	115,152	124,396	128,550	105,137	119,218	138,868
Canada	253,312	319,543	310,341	334,249	362,898	363,420	308,904	401,731	490,672
Latin America and Other Western Hemisphere	255,760	362,652	468,190	528,383	588,303	597,459	509,551	625,700	756,420
Brazil	15,340	26,401	30,094	35,155	36,620	37,469	27,936	36,484	45,421
Mexico	148,493	188,385	248,694	327,768	378,266	393,822	346,420	417,046	501,545
Venezuela	19,192	34,662	33,394	16,215	13,475	2,144	317	435	555
Asia and Pacific	507,527	682,521	841,359	1,091,819	1,226,094	1,180,349	1,140,484	1,358,107	1,545,480
China	103,340	251,791	377,619	499,697	558,324	469,514	448,654	526,133	563,635
India	12,480	23,426	44,940	69,771	83,990	87,528	77,484	102,422	118,844
Japan	164,972	162,613	147,993	164,737	178,614	181,022	152,768	167,355	190,067
Korea, Republic of	45,726	51,175	59,293	82,529	85,328	89,204	86,516	108,853	131,527
Singapore	21,837	19,241	23,668	25,232	35,798	37,219	39,925	38,891	41,811
Taiwan	44,272	40,690	41,740	47,629	53,221	61,676	66,764	86,983	105,517
Middle East	44,500	81,361	95,038	79,353	88,661	70,169	49,502	69,191	98,675
Africa	31,076	69,516	93,001	32,713	45,382	39,343	29,159	44,984	52,378
BALANCE (excess of exports +)									
Total, all countries	−369,686	−716,542	−503,087	−490,776	−578,594	−559,395	−652,881	−841,573	−951,188
Europe	−60,566	−126,739	−55,436	−96,911	−103,121	−119,317	−142,284	−183,790	−118,516
Euro area [1]	−42,211	−90,367	−48,420	−94,021	−102,538	−104,082	−86,475	−120,625	−105,567
France	−10,523	−12,484	−11,284	−16,128	−14,175	−18,312	−14,347	−22,159	−16,560
Germany	−30,330	−54,830	−39,838	−77,679	−66,832	−67,188	−58,572	−72,025	−76,854
Italy	−14,927	−21,211	−14,991	−29,154	−33,742	−36,188	−28,214	−38,855	−43,171
United Kingdom	3,033	−744	8,856	11,611	21,077	18,580	15,065	10,812	20,071
Canada	−49,075	−73,252	−2,770	7,116	6,094	−1,123	733	−34,428	−62,102
Latin America and Other Western Hemisphere	−27,127	−102,820	−51,567	23,005	5,879	−12,492	−33,236	−14,633	−33,015
Brazil	6,772	−4,827	23,672	23,512	29,214	29,496	21,445	25,426	30,016
Mexico	−20,912	−46,528	−61,207	−59,974	−79,090	−103,973	−110,353	−108,779	−139,060
Venezuela	−9,716	−25,266	−17,476	−2,003	−4,315	1,479	1,948	2,673	3,234
Asia and Pacific	−206,076	−340,293	−318,009	−457,897	−494,541	−463,879	−511,853	−618,438	−728,497
China	−81,478	−201,106	−264,042	−336,368	−377,728	−302,039	−282,343	−334,145	−366,356
India	−5,749	−10,132	−15,697	−30,933	−28,160	−29,516	−34,149	−44,124	−45,776
Japan	−63,418	−69,230	−43,002	−58,118	−56,077	−56,395	−50,525	−55,339	−70,183
Korea, Republic of	−10,620	−13,308	−2,593	−16,275	−4,549	−8,238	−17,366	−22,871	−35,564
Singapore	2,720	7,415	16,075	17,817	21,245	16,887	13,174	28,198	38,714
Taiwan	−13,668	−11,586	−4,843	−8,612	−11,300	−18,766	−26,943	−39,698	−50,200
Middle East	−15,883	−32,659	−24,561	22,806	9,577	32,014	26,536	13,143	−4,464
Africa	−13,872	−46,625	−52,723	8,516	−3,848	2,405	3,907	−6,278	−7,214

[1] Euro area consists of Austria, Belgium, Finland, France, Germany, Ireland, Italy, Luxembourg, Netherlands, Portugal, Spain and Greece (beginning in 2001), Slovenia (2007), Cyprus and Malta (2008), Slovakia (2009), Estonia (2011), Latvia (2014), and Lithuania (2015).

Note: Data are on a balance of payments basis. For further details, and additional data by country, see Survey of Current Business, October 2023.

Source: Department of Commerce (Bureau of Economic Analysis).

TABLE B–60. Foreign exchange rates, 2003–2023

[Foreign currency units per U.S. dollar, except as noted; certified noon buying rates in New York]

Period	Australia (dollar)[1]	Brazil (real)	Canada (dollar)	China, P.R. (yuan)	EMU Members (euro)[1,2]	India (rupee)	Japan (yen)	Mexico (peso)	South Korea (won)	Sweden (krona)	Switzerland (franc)	United Kingdom (pound)[1]
March 1973	1.4129	....	0.9967	2.2401	....	7.55	261.90	0.013	398.85	4.4294	3.2171	2.4724
2003	.6524	3.0750	1.4008	8.2772	1.1321	46.59	115.94	10.793	1,192.08	8.0787	1.3450	1.6347
2004	.7365	2.9262	1.3017	8.2768	1.2438	45.26	108.15	11.290	1,145.24	7.3480	1.2428	1.8330
2005	.7627	2.4352	1.2115	8.1936	1.2449	44.00	110.11	10.894	1,023.75	7.4710	1.2459	1.8204
2006	.7535	2.1738	1.1340	7.9723	1.2563	45.19	116.31	10.906	954.32	7.3718	1.2532	1.8434
2007	.8391	1.9461	1.0734	7.6058	1.3711	41.18	117.76	10.928	928.97	6.7550	1.1999	2.0020
2008	.8537	1.8326	1.0660	6.9477	1.4726	43.39	103.39	11.143	1,098.71	6.5846	1.0816	1.8545
2009	.7927	1.9976	1.1412	6.8307	1.3935	48.33	93.68	13.498	1,274.63	7.6539	1.0860	1.5661
2010	.9200	1.7600	1.0298	6.7696	1.3261	45.65	87.78	12.624	1,155.74	7.2053	1.0432	1.5452
2011	1.0332	1.6723	.9887	6.4630	1.3931	46.58	79.70	12.427	1,106.94	6.4878	.8862	1.6043
2012	1.0359	1.9535	.9995	6.3093	1.2859	53.37	79.82	13.154	1,126.16	6.7721	.9377	1.5853
2013	.9683	2.1570	1.0300	6.1478	1.3281	58.51	97.60	12.758	1,094.67	6.5124	.9269	1.5642
2014	.9034	2.3512	1.1043	6.1620	1.3297	61.00	105.74	13.302	1,052.29	6.8576	.9147	1.6484
2015	.7522	3.3360	1.2791	6.2827	1.1096	64.11	121.05	15.874	1,130.96	8.4350	.9628	1.5284
2016	.7445	3.4839	1.3243	6.6400	1.1072	67.16	108.66	18.667	1,159.34	8.5541	.9848	1.3555
2017	.7671	3.1910	1.2984	6.7569	1.1301	65.07	112.10	18.884	1,129.04	8.5430	.9842	1.2890
2018	.7481	3.6513	1.2957	6.6090	1.1817	68.37	110.40	19.218	1,099.29	8.6945	.9784	1.3363
2019	.6952	3.9440	1.3269	6.9081	1.1194	70.38	109.02	19.247	1,165.80	9.4604	.9937	1.2768
2020	.6899	5.1587	1.3422	6.9042	1.1410	74.14	106.78	21.546	1,180.56	9.2167	.9389	1.2829
2021	.7515	5.3958	1.2533	6.4508	1.1830	73.94	109.84	20.284	1,144.89	8.5812	.9144	1.3764
2022	.6951	5.1605	1.3014	6.7290	1.0534	78.58	131.46	20.121	1,291.78	10.1177	.9550	1.2371
2023	.6644	4.9946	1.3494	7.0809	1.0817	82.57	140.50	17.733	1,306.76	10.6089	.8984	1.2440
2022: I	.7249	5.2230	1.2664	6.3478	1.1216	75.24	116.36	20.506	1,206.18	9.3467	.9241	1.3407
II	.7144	4.9213	1.2764	6.6084	1.0646	77.19	129.73	20.053	1,260.46	9.8436	.9652	1.2564
III	.6833	5.2455	1.3062	6.8520	1.0066	79.78	138.35	20.234	1,341.11	10.5552	.9666	1.1767
IV	.6574	5.2550	1.3577	7.1120	1.0218	82.15	141.36	19.681	1,359.38	10.7252	.9636	1.1754
2023: I	.6833	5.1948	1.3529	6.8423	1.0730	82.20	132.44	18.653	1,276.34	10.4426	.9251	1.2153
II	.6681	4.9515	1.3430	7.0130	1.0888	82.17	137.35	17.689	1,315.68	10.5291	.8988	1.2519
III	.6548	4.8811	1.3410	7.2445	1.0884	82.69	144.53	17.055	1,313.19	10.8059	.8832	1.2663
IV	.6513	4.9529	1.3613	7.2247	1.0761	83.24	147.78	17.546	1,321.85	10.6571	.8864	1.2419

Trade-weighted value of the U.S. dollar

	Nominal			Real[6]		
	Broad index (January 2006=100)[3]	Advanced foreign economies index (January 2006=100)[4]	Emerging market economies index (January 2006=100)[5]	Broad index (January 2006=100)[3]	Advanced foreign economies index (January 2006=100)[4]	Emerging market economies index (January 2006=100)[5]
2003	....	....	....	....	....	....
2004	....	....	....	....	....	....
2005	....	....	....	....	....	....
2006	98.6005	97.6833	99.8103	98.9338	98.3159	99.7478
2007	93.8100	92.0715	96.1170	94.2683	93.6198	95.1198
2008	90.8801	88.4517	94.1271	90.9823	90.8430	91.2054
2009	96.7509	92.8232	101.9953	95.3395	94.7210	96.1151
2010	93.0541	90.1336	97.1416	90.8030	92.0390	89.6131
2011	88.7767	84.8522	93.9916	86.3053	87.3412	85.2971
2012	91.6361	88.0233	96.5231	88.5160	90.8670	86.1915
2013	92.7611	90.6492	96.0312	88.7300	93.8602	83.8223
2014	95.5876	93.4349	98.9391	90.7209	97.0250	84.7803
2015	108.1696	108.1483	109.5239	101.1900	111.8303	91.5824
2016	113.0665	109.3636	118.1858	105.4089	114.0184	97.3945
2017	112.8101	108.9520	118.0903	104.8580	114.1623	96.2857
2018	112.0032	106.4902	119.0076	104.0881	112.2297	96.4624
2019	115.7334	110.2673	122.7186	107.1969	116.7231	98.3728
2020	117.7809	109.0631	128.3959	108.7706	116.4080	101.4856
2021	113.1162	104.5205	123.5588	106.2920	114.1761	98.8303
2022	120.7044	115.0954	128.0962	115.0710	126.9564	104.3963
2023	120.4892	115.4193	127.3109	114.4805	126.5345	103.6775
2022: I	115.4998	108.3814	124.4032	110.2394	119.8544	101.3795
II	118.9632	113.4850	126.1849	113.6720	125.6333	102.9509
III	123.5362	118.7559	130.1054	117.7619	131.0839	105.9519
IV	124.8215	119.7419	131.7159	118.6105	131.2541	107.3028
2023: I	120.3423	115.5038	126.9249	114.5533	126.7079	103.6723
II	119.5897	114.5662	126.3512	113.7468	125.5258	103.1637
III	120.2048	115.0455	127.1142	114.0425	125.9395	103.3658
IV	121.8611	116.6005	128.8976	115.5794	127.9649	104.5082

[1] U.S. dollars per foreign currency unit.
[2] European Economic and Monetary Union (EMU) members consists of Austria, Belgium, Finland, France, Germany, Ireland, Italy, Luxembourg, Netherlands, Portugal, Spain and Greece (beginning in 2001), Slovenia (2007), Cyprus and Malta (2008), Slovakia (2009), Estonia (2011), Latvia (2014), Lithuania (2015), and Croatia (2023).
[3] Weighted average of the foreign exchange value of the U.S. dollar against the currencies of a broad group of major U.S. trading partners.
[4] Subset of the broad index. Consists of currencies of the Euro area, Australia, Canada, Japan, Sweden, Switzerland, and the United Kingdom.
[5] Subset of the broad index currencies that are emerging market economies. For details, see *Revisions to the Federal Reserve Dollar Indexes*, January 2019.
[6] Adjusted for changes in consumer price indexes for the United States and other countries.

Source: Board of Governors of the Federal Reserve System.

TABLE B–61. Growth rates in real gross domestic product by area and country, 2005–2024

[Percent change]

Area and country	2005–2014 annual average	2015	2016	2017	2018	2019	2020	2021	2022	2023 [1]	2024 [1]
World	3.9	3.4	3.2	3.8	3.6	2.8	−2.8	6.3	3.5	3.1	3.1
Advanced economies	1.5	2.3	1.8	2.5	2.3	1.7	−4.2	5.6	2.6	1.6	1.5
Of which:											
United States	1.6	2.7	1.7	2.2	2.9	2.3	−2.8	5.9	1.9	2.5	2.1
Euro area [2]	0.8	2.0	1.9	2.6	1.8	1.6	−6.1	5.6	3.4	.5	.9
Germany	1.4	1.5	2.2	2.7	1.0	1.1	−3.8	3.2	1.8	−.3	.5
France	1.0	1.0	1.0	2.5	1.8	1.9	−7.7	6.4	2.5	.8	1.0
Italy	−0.5	.8	1.3	1.7	.9	.5	−9.0	7.0	3.7	.7	.7
Spain	0.5	3.8	3.0	3.0	2.3	2.0	−11.2	6.4	5.8	2.4	1.5
Japan	0.5	1.6	.8	1.7	.6	−.4	−4.2	2.2	1.0	1.9	.9
United Kingdom	1.3	2.4	2.2	2.4	1.7	1.6	−11.0	7.6	4.3	.5	.6
Canada	1.9	.7	1.0	3.0	2.8	1.9	−5.1	5.0	3.8	1.1	1.4
Other advanced economies	3.2	2.3	2.6	3.1	2.8	2.0	−1.6	5.7	2.7	1.7	2.1
Emerging market and developing economies	6.0	4.3	4.4	4.8	4.6	3.6	−1.8	6.9	4.1	4.1	4.1
Regional groups:											
Emerging and Developing Asia	8.3	6.8	6.8	6.6	6.4	5.2	−.5	7.5	4.5	5.4	5.2
China	10.0	7.0	6.9	6.9	6.8	6.0	2.2	8.4	3.0	5.2	4.6
India [3]	7.7	8.0	8.3	6.8	6.5	3.9	−5.8	9.1	7.2	6.7	6.5
ASEAN-5 [4]	5.2	4.6	4.8	5.2	5.0	4.3	−4.4	4.0	5.5	4.2	4.7
Emerging and Developing Europe	3.7	1.0	1.8	4.2	3.6	2.5	−1.6	7.3	1.2	2.7	2.8
Russia	3.4	−2.0	.2	1.8	2.8	2.2	−2.7	5.6	−1.2	3.0	2.6
Latin America and the Caribbean	3.4	.3	−.8	1.3	1.1	.2	−7.0	7.3	4.2	2.5	1.9
Brazil	3.5	−3.5	−3.3	1.3	1.8	1.2	−3.3	5.0	3.0	3.1	1.7
Mexico	1.8	2.7	1.8	1.9	2.0	−.3	−8.7	5.8	3.9	3.4	2.7
Middle East and Central Asia	4.5	3.0	4.3	2.5	2.8	1.6	−2.6	4.3	5.5	2.0	2.9
Saudi Arabia	4.2	4.7	2.4	−.1	2.8	.8	−4.3	3.9	8.7	−1.1	2.7
Sub-Saharan Africa	5.5	3.2	1.5	3.0	3.3	3.2	−1.6	4.7	4.0	3.3	3.8
Nigeria	6.9	2.7	−1.6	.8	1.9	2.2	−1.8	3.6	3.3	2.8	3.0
South Africa	3.0	1.3	.7	1.2	1.6	.3	−6.0	4.7	1.9	.6	1.0

[1] All figures are forecasts as published by the International Monetary Fund. For the United States, advance estimates by the Department of Commerce show that real GDP rose 2.5 percent in 2023.
[2] Euro area consists of Austria, Belgium, Finland, France, Germany, Ireland, Italy, Luxembourg, Netherlands, Portugal, Spain and Greece (beginning in 2001), Slovenia (2007), Cyprus and Malta (2008), Slovakia (2009), Estonia (2011), Latvia (2014), Lithuania (2015), and Croatia (2023).
[3] Data and forecasts are presented on a fiscal year basis and output growth is based on GDP at market prices.
[4] Consists of Indonesia, Malaysia, Philippines, Thailand, and Vietnam.

Note: For details on data shown in this table, see *World Economic Outlook*, October 2023, and *World Economic Outlook Update*, January 2024, published by the International Monetary Fund.

Sources: International Monetary Fund and Department of Commerce (Bureau of Economic Analysis).

www.ingramcontent.com/pod-product-compliance
Lightning Source LLC
Chambersburg PA
CBHW071825270326
41929CB00013B/1899